Date Due			
MY 19 70			
Jo 2 '70			

THE
DRAMATIC WORKS OF
THOMAS DEKKER

THE
DRAMATIC WORKS OF
THOMAS DEKKER

EDITED BY
FREDSON BOWERS
Professor of English Literature
University of Virginia

VOLUME II

THE HONEST WHORE, PART I
(WITH THOMAS MIDDLETON)
THE HONEST WHORE, PART II
THE MAGNIFICENT ENTERTAINMENT
GIVEN TO KING JAMES
WESTWARD HO
(WITH JOHN WEBSTER)
NORTHWARD HO
(WITH JOHN WEBSTER)
THE WHORE OF BABYLON

CAMBRIDGE
AT THE UNIVERSITY PRESS
1955

PUBLISHED BY
THE SYNDICS OF THE CAMBRIDGE UNIVERSITY PRESS
London Office: Bentley House, N.W.1
American Branch: New York
Agents for Canada, India, and Pakistan: Macmillan

Printed in Great Britain at the University Press, Cambridge
(Brooke Crutchley, University Printer)

CONTENTS

Foreword — *page* vii

THE HONEST WHORE, PART 1
    (WITH THOMAS MIDDLETON) — 1

THE HONEST WHORE, PART 2 — 131

THE MAGNIFICENT ENTERTAINMENT GIVEN TO
    KING JAMES — 229

WESTWARD HO
    (WITH JOHN WEBSTER) — 311

NORTHWARD HO
    (WITH JOHN WEBSTER) — 405

THE WHORE OF BABYLON — 491

FOREWORD

THE procedures and conventions adopted in editing these texts are described in the introduction 'The Text of this Edition' in Volume I.

In the present volume only one extension in editorial method requires mention. Several plays contain formes which were unlocked more than once for press-correction, and it is necessary not only to record the details of this successive alteration to the type but also to specify the copies which exhibit the correction in its various stages as well as those providing the earliest or uncorrected state of the type. The convention adopted is the following. When more than one round of press-variation is found, the copies which exhibit only this first stage of alteration, and no other, are listed with the identification, 1*st stage corrected*. In the line below, under *Uncorrected*, are listed as usual those copies containing the earliest known state of the typesetting for the forme. The next notation, 2*nd stage corrected*, lists the copies containing the text of the forme in a subsequent state of additional correction to that of the first stage. Copies under 3*rd stage corrected* would contain a third round of alterations.

In the interests of precision I isolate copies according as their formes are uncorrected or in various stages of correction. But it should be clear that copies listed under the 1*st stage* do not contain any of the alterations indicated as occurring in the 2*nd stage*, nor do copies in the first and second stages contain alterations made exclusively in the copies listed under 3*rd stage*. Correspondingly, any copy with a forme in the 2*nd stage* must be taken as also exhibiting the first-stage alterations; and any forme in the 3*rd stage* contains, of course, all the alterations made in the type in the first and second rounds of correction, as well as the additional variants which identify its particular later state of proof-reading.

F. B.

THE
Honest Whore,

With,

The Humours of the Patient Man, and the Longing Wife.

Tho: Dekker.

LONDON
Printed by V. S. for Iohn Hodgets, and are to
be solde at his shop in Paules
church-yard 1604.

TEXTUAL INTRODUCTION

THE first part of *The Honest Whore* by Dekker and Thomas Middleton (Greg, *Bibliography*, no. 204) was entered in the Stationers' Register on 9 November 1604 by Thomas Man the younger: 'Entred for his copye vnder the hand of mʳ Pasfeild A Booke called. The humors of the patient man. The longinge wyfe and the honest whore.' Greg remarks, 'In spite of the entrance of the copy to Man, Hodgets here [on the title-page] appears as publisher, but in view of the imprint of (c)[1] it seems doubtful whether he really acted as anything but bookseller.' The date of composition is fairly well established by the payment of £5 from Henslowe to Dekker and Middleton for 'the pasyent man & the onest hore' between 1 January and 14 March 1604 on account of the Prince's men.[2] Although this payment was only in earnest of the play, we may presume that copy was delivered to the company before mid-1604. On the evidence of the Register entry, the first quarto, collating A–K⁴, must have been published in late November of the same year.

There is every reason to suppose that the printing was authorized and that a good manuscript was sent to the press. Indeed, the descriptive stage-directions which for all their detail are usually permissive, the lack of uniformity in the speech-prefixes for Candido's wife,[3] and also the preserved fragment of continuous scene numbering,[4] lead to the view that the printer's copy was the

---

[1] *I.e.* Q3, for which the imprint reads, 'Printed by V.S. and are to be sold by Iohn Hodgets at his shoppe in Paules church-yard 1605.' The title-page is printed substantially from the standing type of Q1, in the imprint of which the phrase was 'Printed by V.S. for Iohn Hodgets and are to be solde....'

[2] The actor Towne, for whom the part of the sweeper in V.ii was especially written, was a member of this company.

[3] Since she is given the prefix *Viola*, the name also provided in the stage-direction, only in I.ii but is invariably *Wife* in prefix and direction thereafter, the evidence is perhaps less significant than if there had been random variation. The change from one form to the other takes place between two scenes both present in sheet B; hence the alteration to *Wife* is not compositorial but instead a reflection of the manuscript.

[4] The first scene to be numbered is III.i, given as 'SCENA 7', and thereafter the scenes are numbered in order, except for the unnumbered scene 12 (IV.iii), to '13. SCE.' or IV.iv. Whether the scene number precedes or follows SCENA is a distinguishing mark of the two compositors who typeset this section.

foul papers or a transcript from them. There are no certain signs of prompt-book origin, and the only two possible hints are both suspect.[1]

The first quarto of 1604 was set up in three sections comprising sheets A–B, C–D, and E–K. Sheets A–B, containing the title-page with its imprint listing V[alentine] S[immes] as the printer, distinguish themselves from the rest by the use of medial v and j (a practice silently altered in the present text in the interest of uniformity). Lower-case roman running-titles with heading capitals are employed, two skeletons to the sheet, and the printer's measure is 90 mm. With sheet C the type slightly changes, the measure shrinks to 87 mm., and the running-titles (again two skeletons to the sheet) are composed of italic full capitals. With sheet E there comes another slight change in the fount accompanied by different settings of the running-titles though still in italic capitals. This final section of the play, E–K, appears to have been machined on two presses, one of which printed sheets E, F, H; and the other, sheets G, I, K. Sheets E and F, both formes, are imposed and printed by one and the same skeleton, and this skeleton also imposes both formes of H. A different single skeleton is used for both formes of sheet G. This skeleton thereupon imposes the inner forme of I and both formes of K, while the skeleton of H imposes the outer forme of I. The interlocking of the skeleton-formes shows that the E–K section was printed in one shop, a fact buttressed by the invariable signing of the four leaves in this section as against only the first three leaves in each gathering in sections A–B and C–D. The pattern of the skeleton-formes suggests the use of two presses, and this hypothesis is strengthened by the evidence of the printer's measure. The usual

---

[1] In II.i.45 early editors conjectured that *Sing* before *prety wantons* was not part of Bellafront's song but instead a stage-direction crept into the text; but this theory has not found universal favour. In Q1 *Sing* begins a line at the left margin. Hence if it is a misplaced direction, for which there is no actual evidence, it would presumably be a prompt notation. In V.ii.335 *Bow a little*, which in Q1 hypermetrically prefixes line 335, might also be taken as an intrusive direction. Its meaning in the text is admittedly obscure, but it is not quite the kind of direction one would imagine a prompter adding in the left margin of a manuscript, and hence is doubtful—like *Sing*—even as an indication of a book-keeper marking foul papers for later transcription of prompt. If *Bow a little* is an author's certainly very minute direction confused as text, its position to the left is perhaps odd.

measure throughout sheets E and F is 86–87 mm. On G3 recto, however, this measure expands to 88–89 and continues so for two pages to G4 recto. Again, on H2^v–4^v the normal measure expands to 89 mm., and once more on I2^v–4^v. It would appear, therefore, that the original plan in this shop was to print with one compositor and one press. The use of only one skeleton for both formes in contrast to the two of A–B and C–D suggests that this workman was a rather slow typesetter. With the second half of sheet G the second compositor began to alternate. This introduction of a second workman under the circumstances would be matched by the appearance of a second press. Some interest inheres to the fact that it is only in this shop that the continuous scene numbers appear, though dropping out towards the end, perhaps as in copy.[1]

Although the paper does not differ by sections as does the printing,[2] no reason exists to believe that Valentine Simmes printed any more than the first two sheets. The other printers are unidentified. The division among three printing houses is evidence of some haste in production. For example, earlier in the year Thomas Man the younger had allocated the first edition of Dekker's *Magnificent Entertainment* among five printers to rush it into print at the earliest possible moment.

Thomas Man's editions of *The Honest Whore* and *The Magnificent Entertainment* share another characteristic in that part of the type in each was kept standing and used in a second edition; moreover, apparently authoritative corrections appear in both books in the second edition. The circumstances of the publication of the second edition of *The Honest Whore*, with a change of title to *The Converted Courtesan*, are obscure since this second edition is known in only two copies, both imperfect and lacking the title-leaf as well as the

---

[1] There seems to be a mechanical reason, not a literary significance, for the appearance of these scene numbers. That they came from the manuscript is evident, since the shop that printed sheets E–K would not be likely to have information about the number of preceding scenes. That they are present only in what we now assign as the third and fourth acts, therefore, cannot be used as evidence of authorship, since it seems almost certain that the compositors of A–B and C–D must simply have omitted to set the continuous numbering presumably present in the manuscript and also made no other numerical division into acts or scenes.

[2] If, as frequently, the publisher provided the paper, uniformity is no argument against sectional printing in different shops.

final leaves of text. In the Bodleian copy the last two leaves, K3 and K4, are wanting as well as A1, but in the Folger Shakespeare Library copy the last leaf of I and all four leaves of K are missing. The loss of leaves at front and back in the only two known copies would ordinarily not be accepted as fortuitous. But it is difficult to see why the final two leaves should have been torn out deliberately, whatever might have been the reasons for cancelling the title without substitution; and hence it is probable that rough handling has accidentally affected both.

The use of standing type to print more than the legally allowed edition-sheet was prohibited by the rules of the Stationers' Company. Presumably a publisher conscious that he could sell an extra quota of copies but not necessarily enough to cover the cost of duplicate typesetting might in isolated cases make private arrangements by which his printers compounded with their compositors to forestall protests. That Man would be tempted in April of 1604 to circumvent the rules in order to produce large quantities of a coronation souvenir is understandable. Yet it may seem to be more than a coincidence that sometime after July of the same year William Aspley should combine with his printer Valentine Simmes to put out a second edition of Marston's *Malcontent* partly from standing type, and revised by the author; and later still that Man should employ Simmes for *The Honest Whore*, in which precisely the same procedure was followed. Finally, in early 1606 William Cotton published Marston's *Parasitaster*, printed by Thomas Pafort in a similar revised second edition in part from standing type. It may well be conjectured that at this time an attempt was being made with dramatic quartos to circumvent the Stationers' make-work rules. There are no records preserved that the Company took measures, but on the other hand no further such quartos were printed after *Parasitaster*.[1] That in each second edition the author—either Dekker or Marston—was available to correct and even to revise copy is one of the more suspicious circumstances. There are

---

[1] These cases are surveyed in my 'Notes on Standing Type in Elizabethan Printing', *Papers of the Bibliographical Society of America*, XL (1946), 205–224, but without reaching very satisfactory conclusions. See also the introduction in the present volume to *The Magnificent Entertainment*.

TEXTUAL INTRODUCTION

very likely peculiar and perhaps even related matters concerning these publications which we have as yet failed to grasp.

The running-titles of the second edition of *The Honest Whore* throughout label it 'The Converted Courtesan'.[1] By their typesettings these separate the quarto into four sections: A–B The converted Curtezan;[2] C–D *THE CONVERTED | CVRTIZAN*;[3] E–F *The conuerted Courtizan*; and G–K *THE CONVERTED | CVRTIZAN*. In these sheets, A–B are printed from the same two skeleton-formes, C–D also from two skeletons, E and F each from two but the typesetting of the running-titles differing in F from E (perhaps indicating only the use of two presses). Sheet G was imposed from two skeleton-formes, and sheet H irregularly from one skeleton in a different setting. The skeleton imposing the inner forme of G thereupon was used to print both inner and outer I; that imposing outer G printed both inner and outer K. The settings differ from those of sheets C–D. On the evidence of the skeleton formes in G–K, two presses doubtless machined these four sheets.

If the unique typography of their running-titles can be trusted, sheets E and F were printed in a different shop from G–K, the

---

[1] That it was also 'The Converted Courtesan' on the title-page is indicated by the fact that whereas Q3, in which sheet A is imposed from the second-edition typesetting, prints its *Honest Whore* title-page in the same typesetting found in Q1, yet the title itself, 'THE Honest Whore' has been reset. It follows that the Q3 change in setting was necessitated by the substitution in the lost Q2 title-page of 'The Converted Courtesan' for the original Q1 title, and its return in Q3. See *The Library*, 4th series XIII (1938), 340–341. Greg's speculations that Dekker instituted the change in title are not necessarily proved by the Register entry in 1608 of Part 2 as 'the second parte of the conu'ted Courtisan or honest Whore'. References in the text of Part 1 as at II.i.456, III.iii.100, and IV.i.196 seem to indicate the author's original intention to entitle it 'The Honest Whore', and similar references appear in Part 2. If he changed his mind, it must have been done within a relatively brief interval; and if so, it is odd that Q3 should restore the rejected title and the Part 2 title (and text) confirm it. That Dekker made corrections and revisions in the Q2 text does not demonstrate that the change in title was submitted to him or that he ever knew it was forthcoming. We simply do not know the reasons for the alteration, and it would be sheer speculation, though plausible, to connect it with the publisher's plan to conceal the illicit nature of the Q2 printing.

[2] In both the first and second editions the running-titles in sheets A–B are in roman type as against the italic of the other sheets.

[3] In the second edition, as in the first, the typography of the C–D running-titles resembles that of later sheets although the actual typesetting differs. Thus it is barely possible that in Q2 sheets C–D were printed in the same shop as sheets G–K.

reassignment from the division of Q1 being made, perhaps, to speed up production. A peculiarity exists, however. When earlier in the year *The Magnificent Entertainment* had been reprinted in a similar manner and with some reassignment of sections, if a sheet was reassigned it was reset by the new printer. On the contrary, although E(o) is reset in *The Converted Courtesan*, E(i) remains standing, as does F(i) and most of F(o). It would appear that standing type was transferred on this occasion from one shop to another.

Of the 74 type-pages of text preserved in Q2, 39 are reimpressed from the standing type of Q1, and 35 are reset. This proportion of about one-half the typesetting kept standing is what we find in the other similar books. Also conventional, and especially significant, is the fact that when only one forme of a sheet is reset, the outer forme is chosen and the inner left standing. The proportion of standing pages is somewhat unequal in the sections printed by different shops, in so far as the sections may stand for separate houses. Thus in Q2 sheets A–B, both formes of sheet A (6 pages) are standing, and both formes of sheet B (8 pages) reset. In the C–D section, the outer forme of C and sig. C1^v of inner C (5 pages) are reset; the remaining pages of inner C and both formes of D (11 pages) are standing. Sheets E and F contain reset outer E and reset sig. F1 of outer F (5 pages); otherwise, E(i), F(i), and the remaining pages of F(o) are standing (11 pages). In the G–K section the resetting for the first time outbalances the standing type, for here we have both formes of G, outer H, outer I, and sig. K2^v of outer K reset (17 pages), and only inner H, inner I, sigs. K1^v, 2 of inner K, and sig. K1 of outer K standing (11 pages). On the other hand, if on the evidence of similar typography though not identical typesetting in the running-titles we associate sections C–D and G–K, we find that precisely twenty-two pages of type are standing and twenty-two reset, in so far as sheet K is preserved in Q2. This may be significant and a slight added reason to assign the two sections as coming from the same shop, although the difference in the skeleton-formes is troublesome to explain and hence it may be safer to conjecture that the shops differed.

The resetting only of C1^v of inner C, the first sheet of the C–D section, may indicate that when this forme was machined in Q1 the printer had not been instructed to hold the type for a second edition. The resetting of F1, the first seven lines of F2^v, and the first sixteen of F3 in outer F is perhaps more likely to represent repair of pied type, since sheet E began this section in Q1 and apparently also in Q2.[1] If the G–K section be viewed as a self-contained unit, what we can recover of the resetting in sheet K is inexplicable. Clearly the resetting was not by formes, since K1 of the outer forme is standing, versus K2^v reset. Whether there was a plan to the resetting which the last two leaves of the sheet would have revealed, or whether this page merely pied, cannot be determined. If C–D and G–K are estimated as one unit, however, it may have been that, to preserve exactly one-half of the type-pages of the whole standing, two further pages in sheet K were also reset.

The formes of standing type comprise A(i, o), C(i) substantially, D(i, o), E(i), F(i, o) substantially, H(i), I(i), and three pages of K(i, o). In most of these formes textual corrections and revisions appear in Q2 both in the substantives and in the accidentals. Some of these changes, as the two slight ones in A(i, o) at I.i.58, 137, the only alterations in the formes of A (besides the change on the lost title-page), could readily have been made by any publisher's or printing-house editor; but with the exception of sheet F(i, o) no printing section of Q2 but contains variants that go well beyond the province of an editor or of a printing-house. Enough copies of Q1 are not preserved to guarantee that when a forme of Q2 shows only minor variants these were actually made in standing type between impressions and do not represent the type in a press-corrected Q1 state, the uncorrected state alone being known from the four extant Q1 copies. But the odds strongly favour the working hypothesis that the invariant formes in known copies of Q1 (supplemented by some sheets of Q3) represent the corrected state of the type if variance ever existed; and hence we are bound to assume that the observed Q2 variants in standing type were in fact made subsequent to Q1 impression.

---

[1] It may somehow be significant that only in sheet F does the standing type in Q2 seem to contain no authoritative changes. This is one of the two sheets apparently transferred from one printing shop to another for the second edition. But authoritative variants appear in E.

The source of these corrections and revisions is not so clear as one would wish. Many of the corrections are of minor matters not beyond the competence of an editor to alter; but some are certainly more scrupulous and would seem to require authority, such as the alteration of Q1 *Malauella* to *Malauolta* at II.i.91, and the rewriting of II.i.223 but especially of 300–302. Such a small but interesting matter as the correction of Bellafront's Q1 *What* to *Whaat* at II.i.38 speaks for a considerable intimacy with the text (see her *shaall* at line 219), and there may be significance in the extremely minor change of Q1 *dost* at I.v.228 to the spelling *doest*, which is that of Dekker's addition to *Sir Thomas More* though scarcely unique with him. The occasional relining of prose as verse argues for authorial care, and there would seem to be little question that the alterations stem from some authority, which was presumably Dekker.[1] This being so, an editor is bound to accept them in all cases unless, in specific lines, there is some strong presumption that another agency was operating as well.

[1] Of course the printer on some few occasions may have added various of his own corrections if he observed what he considered to be errors. What I take to be a printer's variant in standing type occurs in sheet F at III.iii.106; and if this is so then the only other variant in standing type in this sheet, the minor alteration in the stage-direction at line 19, is the printer's work as well. Moreover, the compositor may not always have made the corrections in the precise form marked for him. Very likely at I.v.129, for example, he set a comma for what had been marked as an apostrophe, and perhaps at II.i.27 the preservation of the comma after *arise* was an error if it was not merely the result of the corrector's own carelessness. So, *accurs'd* at II.i.130 in Q2 does not necessarily represent the actual spelling of the marked correction for Q1 *a curst*. Yet there are only a few places where variants which seem to be non-compositorial are suspect. At first sight Q2 *We are* for Q1 *Were* at I.v.121 (instead of expected *We're*) seems like a sophistication; but the fact that the line is slightly indented in Q1 argues for the loss of a type, which could have been a space plus *a* as well as a simple apostrophe. Moreover, if an author is correcting errors like this at a later date, he cannot always remember the precise form originally written. (If this could be strongly inferred, an editor would correct the original reading in preference to the author's inadvertent variant.) At II.i.204 the substitution of *melancholy* for what seems to have been the fashionable pronunciation *malancholy* might seem to be a sophistication, and the dropping of the first-person pronoun *I* at line 215 is difficult to understand; yet these take place in an authoritatively corrected page and, without stronger evidence against them, must be credited. Perhaps the clearest case may be the repointing of I.v.222 in Q2 where in my opinion the strong stop after *groundes* is incorrect and the Q1 error lay rather in the light stop after *shame* in line 221. On the other hand, occasional failure to correct errors is, of course, no proof that the corrector did not have authority.

TEXTUAL INTRODUCTION

The problem is more difficult, naturally, when variants are encountered in the reset formes. Here, in the nature of the case, the minor authoritative improvement in an accidental cannot be differentiated from a normal non-authoritative compositorial variant; and since compositor's variants are sure to predominate there is no possible way, usually, in which an editor can be certain that he is recovering authority. With substantive variants, of course, he is in a stronger position. For example, little difficulty is encountered in assessing the authoritative nature of the substantive corrections and revisions in reset sheet B of Q2 (I.ii.58–I.v.35), and hence in accepting such a change as *hurts* for Q1 *haunts* at I.iii.71 as more likely to be authoritative than compositorial, even though a modern critic with somewhat different values might normally consider *haunts* to be the superior because the more vivid reading.[1]

The precise manner in which the authority corrected copy for Q2 is of particular interest to an editor, because such a determination may fix bounds to the extent of acceptable alterations. It is a very odd fact that though no question obtains that reset sheet B was considerably revised and corrected in an authoritative manner, nevertheless no substantive variants which are indubitably authoritative occur in reset outer C, or sig. C1ᵛ, or outer E. Moreover, in the final section G–K those variants in reset type that might qualify as authoritative are so few as to lead one to query their true nature. There are only six in these seventeen reset pages which may have any claim. Among these is included the alteration on sig. G3 of Q1 *Benedict* to *Benedect* at IV.i.184 and the addition on the same page of *vp* at IV.ii.3. The first is of possible significance only because of the alterations in reset sheet B of Q1 *Benedicke* to *Benedict*; but the case is quite different here and a compositor could easily have normalized the name on G3. Correspondingly, the addition of *vp* on this page is obviously called for and requires no authority for its insertion. Also on G3 comes the correction in the

---

[1] Nevertheless, *haunts* is doubtless just such a compositorial misreading in Q1 as *Softly ₐ sweete Doctor*: for *Softly, see Doctor ₐ*. This last, incidentally, is an excellent example of the manner in which this Q1 compositor punctuated a phrase to suit his preconceptions of its meaning. Q1 has this curious feature that whereas both sheets A and B were set by the same workman, sheet A is very correct and required only two trifling changes in Q2, but sheet B was corrupt and required considerable correction.

stage-direction to the opening of IV.ii, *Poli* to *Poh*, repeated at IV.iii.51 S.D. and 66, both on G4^v. Since the correct *Poh* form was found in G(i) on sig. G3^v, it is not impossible that the fact of error was detected in the outer forme from the inner, where it had been press-corrected in Q1 very likely in the same shop. However, this slight clustering of minor variants on sig. G3 may just possibly be indicative of some attention. The next case comes in the tempting substitution on sig. H3 of *far* to replace *for* at IV.iv.35; but plausible as the change is, it may well be suspect as the only one in the forme that can have any pretensions and as occurring in a section where authorial revision has not been clearly demonstrated. Finally, the relining of prose as verse on sig. I.2^v (V.ii.59–61) is the most definite instance in this whole section that editorial attention has been given to a reset page. With this exception, and the minor clustering of variants on G3, there is no certain sign of authority in the correction of the copy for reset pages in section G–K; and when these are compared with the substantive correction and revision made in pages of standing type throughout Q2, and in reset sheet B, the suspicion seems justified that the variants in G–K may have been due merely to printing-house initiative. Hence the odds seem to favour the curious fact that on the whole, except for reset sheet B, the authoritative variants in Q2 are confined to the pages of standing type,[1] this being true for all the different printers' sections except the first.

Such an odd state of affairs may possibly align *The Converted Courtesan* variants with the Q2 variants in *The Magnificent Entertainment* as due to some other process than the distribution for copy of leaves of Q1 which Dekker had systematically marked for correction. Since there is no literary reason why authorial variants should not appear in the reset as well as the standing pages, the explanation must be sought mechanically.

The fact to be faced is that authoritative alterations appear in standing-type pages but not (except for a few very doubtful cases) in pages subsequently reset. It would appear, therefore, that the

[1] One excepts F(i, o) standing, in which no clearly authoritative variants appear. Whether this fact is somehow due to the transfer of the Q2 printing of the sheet from one shop to another cannot be determined.

corrections and revisions were made in this standing type in the brief interval before the distributed pages were reset. There are difficulties in the hypothesis, but it may have been that Dekker submitted to the publisher a marked copy of Q1 and the publisher in turn sent it to the printers, beginning with the shop that had printed sheets G–K and was to print the same sheets again. This printer passed the marked copy on to the shop that had taken over sheets E–F, and so to the shop printing C–D and finally to Simmes printing A–B. At this time, however, the distributed pages had not been reset; and hence the printers, instead of abstracting the sheets which they were to print again, merely made the necessary alterations in the standing type in their shops[1] and sent on the quarto to the next man. Finally it came to rest with Simmes, who was thus the only printer able to reset his pages, in sheet B, according to the marked copy.[2]

It would be well to have a more certain explanation, but in fact the general propositions which must guide an editor are sufficiently clear on the evidence as it stands. Certain of the alterations made

---

[1] Possibly the shop that had printed Q1 sheets E–K made the corrections in E(?) and F at this time if the type-pages had not been passed on to the new printer for Q2.

[2] The prime difficulty in this hypothesis is that the consistency of operation in two, and perhaps three, shops forces us to conjecture that the printers either had destroyed or returned their manuscript copy and had not been provided with copies of Q1 to use for resetting their parts of Q2 at the time the marked copy was sent to them. On the other hand, why the marked quarto was not itself broken up and used for copy is quite inexplicable. Moreover, we must take it that the printers made no attempt, once resetting was ordered, to secure the corrected quarto again. The case would be somewhat simplified if the printer of G–K made the changes in E–F, so that the Q2 printer of E–F may never have known of the corrected copy, and if this G–K printer also printed Q2 C–D, but this last is very doubtful. However, the enquiry may be too scrupulous; and a simple misunderstanding may have led to the crucial quarto being passed around without its sheets being detached to serve as copy for Q2. Other possibilities are not encouraging. It is difficult to believe that Dekker went to the different houses (as he went to Lownes for the *Entertainment*) which pulled proof for him from the type that was standing and accepted his on-the-spot alterations or that the printers submitted to the publisher proofs of their standing type and that this was transmitted to Dekker. In either case, he could have marked a copy of Q1 for each house and thus assured himself of alterations in the reset pages. A single marked copy sent by the author to the publisher and by him to the printers, without a clear understanding that sheets were to be removed to serve as printer's copy for Q2, seems to come as close to the facts as we can guess.

in standing type appear to be of such a revisory nature as to surpass the competence of a printing-house editor, and in this case there is no need to conjecture the presence of a publisher's editor other than the author. Although the case for Dekker as the source of the corrections and revisions cannot be demonstrated, he is the most logical candidate, since Middleton's part in the play seems to have been relatively minor. There is nothing to suggest that the alterations in the standing type are not all of a piece, with one or two minor exceptions which may be laid to the printing house. As a general rule, therefore, these alterations from Q2 must be incorporated in the text. This applies as well to the authoritative substantive alterations in reset sheet B, although here—according to current textual theory—Q1 must remain the copy-text since it contains that typesetting which stands in nearest relation to the author's manuscript in its accidentals. Since no authority can be demonstrated for the variants found in the reset formes of any sheet after B, an editor is bound to reject any variants as revisions and to accept only those Q2 variants in reset pages which appear to him to be necessary or desirable alterations, even though unauthoritative in their origin. Thus whereas Q2 has superior authority in its pages re-impressed from standing type, the authority of Q1 is paramount for substantives as for accidentals in all pages which were reset in Q2 save for the substantive variants in sheet B. Finally, the incidence of error in the text is likely to be higher when Q1 is the only authority; and emendation may be made in such pages the more freely. Emendation is not barred when Q2 becomes one's substantive authority, since various errors were overlooked by the corrector; nevertheless, freedom to emend is more restricted in these pages than elsewhere.

Since it is desirable for a reader to have before him an accurate table of the relationship between Q1 and Q2 in terms of the present edition, I give the following abstract:

I.i.1–I.ii.58 (hee haz |) A2–4^v *standing*
I.ii.58–I.v.35 B1–4^v *reset*

I.v.36–112 C1–1^v *reset*
I.v.113–115 C2 *reset (these two lines were transferred to the foot of reset*

C1ᵛ *in* Q2 *in order to make room for the relining of prose as verse in ll. 142–147*)
I.v.116–153 C2 *standing*
I.v.154–217 C2ᵛ–3 *reset*
I.v.218–II.i.10 (looke) |) C3ᵛ *chiefly standing* (*the type seems to have been slightly disturbed and a word or two here and there reset, but substantially it is the standing type of* Q1)
II.i.10–46 (to day |) C4 *standing*
II.i.46–81 C4ᵛ *reset*
II.i.82–262 D1–3 *standing*
II.i.263–295 D3ᵛ *chiefly standing* (*beginning with line 315 the type-page pied irregularly on the left side and was reset as necessary. Spelling variants in this resetting are not listed in the present edition*)
II.i.296–367 D4–4ᵛ *standing*

II.i.368–405 E1 *reset*
II.i.406–III.i.20 E1ᵛ–2 *standing*
III.i.21–96 E2ᵛ–3 *reset*
III.i.97–171 E3ᵛ–4 *standing*
III.i.172–208 E4ᵛ *reset*
III.i.209–248 F1 *reset*
III.i.249–IV.i.35 F1ᵛ–4ᵛ *standing*
IV.i.36–IV.iii.66 G1–4ᵛ *reset*
IV.iii.67–104 H1 *reset*
IV.iii.105–176 H1ᵛ–2 *standing*
IV.iii.177–IV.iv.63 (friend |) H2ᵛ–3 *reset*
IV.iv.63–V.i.6 H3ᵛ–4 *standing*
V.i.7–44 H4ᵛ *reset*
V.i.45–79 I1 *reset*
V.i.80–V.ii.35 (none |) I1ᵛ–2 *standing*
V.ii.35–114 I2ᵛ–3 *reset*
V.ii.115–189 (ime |) I3ᵛ–4 *standing*
V.ii.189–230 I4ᵛ *reset*
V.ii.231–339 K1–2 *standing*
V.ii.340–374 K2ᵛ *reset*
V.ii.375–518 K3–4ᵛ (*leaves wanting in extant copies*)

The third quarto, which by courtesy we may call an edition, Q3, appeared with the date 1605: 'London Printed by V.S. and are to be solde by Iohn Hodgets at his shoppe in Paules church-yard 1605.' In this edition, sheets A, B, and H are reimpressed from the standing type of the corresponding type-pages in Q2 but with a reset title and head-title on A1 and A2, respectively, returning to the form

The Honest Whore;[1] and with reset running-titles also returning to the original title: 'The Honest Whore.' in A–B and '*THE HONEST WHORE.*' in sheet H, in each case the typography corresponding to that in the appropriate sheets in Q1. The following sheets are of the same impression as those in Q1: C–D, F–G, I–K. Sheet E is of the same impression as that in Q2 and therefore preserves its running-title *The conuerted Courtizan*.

This Q3, known only from the unique copy in the Dyce Collection, seems to have been constructed to use up odd quantities of remainder sheets from Q1 pieced out by Q2; and possibly if further copies were discovered they might vary slightly in the assortment of sheets. Since sheets C–D, F–G, and I–K are the same sheets as in Q1, they have no independent textual value distinct from Q1. As it turns out, however, the two known variant formes in Q1 (inner G and outer K) are represented in the uncorrected state in this copy of Q3; and the uncorrected state of outer C is preserved only in the sheet in the Dyce Q3. There is some reason, then, to assign these Q3 sheets of the Q1 impression as partly segregated less perfect copies later utilized as remainders. Collation for press-variants of these Q1 sheets bound in Q3 reveals no other variant states than have been mentioned. It would be too much, merely on the strength of these three formes, to expect that all of the Q1 sheets found in the Dyce Q3 were necessarily in an uncorrected state whenever variant states were printed, and hence that we possess in the three uncorrected formes of Q3 all the evidence obtainable about the proof-reading of Q1. Yet the odds perhaps favour the hypothesis that the collation of the Q1 sheets in Q3 against the four extant copies of Q1 has established as many variant formes as might have been discovered in many more copies. Collation of Q3 sheet E from Q2 against the two extant copies of Q2 has disclosed no variants. Finally, collation of reimpressed Q2 sheets A–B and H against the corresponding sheets in Q2 reveals that no alterations whatever were made in the type between these impressions. Hence, except for the question of press-variants

[1] The imprint differs in its form and setting in the Q3 title-page from that in Q1, but whether the change occurred in the lost Q2 title or between Q2 and Q3 we have no means of knowing.

TEXTUAL INTRODUCTION

in the Q1 sheets, Q3 has no independent textual authority, and its agreement with the readings of Q1 or of Q2 has no bearing whatever on the relative authority of these readings. For this reason, Q3 has not been listed as an independent authority in the footnotes.

The two remaining early editions of *The Honest Whore* are mere reprints, Q4 of Q1, and Q5 of Q4. They have no authority. Q4 was printed by Nicholas Okes for Robert Basse, probably in late 1615, since the title-page by press-alteration may be dated 1615 or 1616. The last edition in the seventeenth century was Q5, printed in 1635 by Okes to be sold by Richard Collins.

The text of *The Honest Whore*, Part I was reprinted in Vol. I of *A Select Collection of Old Plays* (1744), edited by Robert Dodsley; it is referred to here as D1. The copy-text for this edition is not quite certain, since there is a considerable mixture of readings, but was very likely Q4 with collation of Q1 and Q5. In 1780 the D1 text was reprinted in D2, the second edition of Dodsley with notes by Isaac Reed. D2 was the source of an unaltered reprint in *Ancient British Drama*, vol. I (1810), edited by Sir Walter Scott. In 1825 D2 was re-edited in D3, *A Select Collection of Old Plays, a New Edition*, in which J. P. Collier built on the work of Reed and the additional notes of Alexander Gilchrist. The copy-text was stated to be the 1604 edition (Q1), collated with Q4 and Q5, and there is evidence that a fresh collation was in fact made. In 1840 Alexander Dyce re-edited the play in *The Works of Thomas Middleton*, vol. III, utilizing the copy of Q3 in his possession though not taking full advantage of its variant readings from sheets A–B, E, and H of Q2 type. This is the first edition to employ, though indirectly, any of the Q2 revisions. The 1873 Pearson reprint was based on Q3. In 1887 Ernest Rhys included the play in his Mermaid volume of Dekker, his text being based principally on Dyce. W. A. Neilson's *Chief Elizabethan Dramatists* (1911) seems to have gone back independently to Q1, though largely based on Dyce and Rhys. Finally, in 1933 Hazelton Spencer in *Elizabethan Plays* came upon the Folger Shakespeare Library copy of Q2 when his text was in proof, and was able to incorporate various of its readings, although unsystematically and without bibliographical logic.

The present text uses Q1 as copy-text as determined by collation of the only four extant copies at the British Museum (C.34.c.24), the Folger Shakespeare Library, the Henry E. Huntington Library, and the New York Public Library, together with the Q1 sheets bound in the Dyce Q3, the only extant copy, preserved at the Victoria and Albert Museum. Since an analysis of the curious bibliographical evidence seems to dictate the view that with only a few possible exceptions the alterations made in standing type in Q2 are authoritative but the variants found in reset formes (sheet B excepted) are unauthoritative, the former are incorporated in the text and the latter rejected except in so far as some few appear to be necessary or desirable alterations even though unauthoritative. The two extant copies of Q2, the Bodleian copy (imperfect, wanting A1, K3–4) and the Folger copy (imperfect, wanting A1, I4, K1–4) have been collated without discovery of any variation. Copies of Q4 of 1615–16 from the British Museum (644.b.19) and Folger Shakespeare Library, and of Q5 from the British Museum (644.b.21[1]) and Folger have been collated, though independently, against the copy-text, their substantive and semi-substantive variants recorded, and some few emendations accepted even though unauthoritative.

Because of the complex textual situation, the apparatus differs slightly in its procedure from that ordinarily adopted in these volumes. The footnotes, as usual, are concerned with the substantive emendations made in the copy-text and the recording of their immediate sources. Since the state of the type in Q2, whether standing or reset, is of major importance for the authority of the Q2 variants, this information is always provided by adding (r) *reset* or (s) *standing* to the Q2 siglum. However, because the variable authority of Q2 assumed in this edition rests only on a working hypothesis, not only are all rejected readings from Q2 standing type listed in the footnotes—whether substantive or accidental—but also all rejected *substantive* readings from the reset portions of Q2. This means that no attempt has been made (except for the conventionally recorded semi-substantives of emphasis and modification found in the Historical Collation) to list rejected accidental readings from the reset pages of Q2. In the List of Emendations of Accidentals and in the Historical Collation the recording of the facts about the state of the Q2 type has not been thought sufficiently necessary to enforce a more complex system of sigla; but whether the type was standing or reset can always be recovered from the table of the typesetting given above. In the footnotes Q3 has not been recorded as an independent authority since in no case does the text of the only extant copy differ from Q1 or Q2 save, as remarked, for preserving the original state of the typesetting before press-correction in the outer forme of C, a sheet from the Q1 impression.

[PERSONS

GASPARO TREBATZI, Duke of Milan
HIPPOLITO, in love with Infelice
MATHEO, his friend
CASTRUCHIO ⎫
PIORATTO   ⎬ Courtiers
FLUELLO   ⎪
SINEZI   ⎭
CANDIDO, a linen-draper
FUSTIGO, brother to Candido's wife
GEORGE, journeyman to Candido
DOCTOR BENEDICT
FRIAR ANSELMO
ROGER, servant to Bellafront
CRAMBO ⎫ bravos
POH   ⎭
Sweeper, acted by Towne
Servant to Hippolito
Servant to Doctor Benedict
1. and 2. Apprentices to Candido
INFELICE, daughter to the Duke
BELLAFRONT, the honest whore
VIOLA, wife to Candido
MISTRESS FINGERLOCK, a bawd
　　Officers, Madmen, Servants]

The Honest Whore

ACTVS PRIMVS. SCÆNA PRIMA.

Enter at one doore a Funerall, a Coronet lying on the Hearse, Scutchins and Garlands hanging on the sides, attended by Gasparo Trebatzi, *Duke of* Millan, Castruchio, Sinezi. Pioratto, Fluello, *and others at an other doore. Enter* Hipolito *in discontented apparance:* Matheo *a Gentleman his friend, labouring to hold him backe.*

Duke. Behold, yon Commet shewes his head againe;
Twice hath he thus at crosse-turnes throwne on vs
Prodigious lookes: Twice hath he troubled
The waters of our eyes. See, hee's turnde wilde;
Go on in Gods name.
All. On afore there ho.
Duke. Kinsmen and friends, take from your manly sides
Your weapons to keepe backe the desprate boy
From doing violence to the innocent dead.
Hip. I pry thee deere *Matheo.*
Math. Come, y'are mad.
Hip. I do arest thee murderer: set downe, 10
Villaines set downe that sorrow, tis all mine.
Duke. I do beseech you all, for my bloods sake
Send hence your milder spirits, and let wrath
Ioine in confederacie with your weapons points;
If he proceede to vexe vs, let your swordes
Seeke out his bowells: funerall griefe loathes words.
All. Set on.
Hip. Set downe the body.
Math. O my Lord?
Y'are wrong: i'th open streete? you see shees dead.
Hip. I know shee is not dead.
Duke. Franticke yong man,
Wilt thou beleeue these gentlemen? pray speake: 20

21

Thou doost abuse my childe, and mockst the teares
That heere are shed for her: If to behold
Those roses withered, that set out her cheekes:
That paire of starres that gaue her body light,
Darkned and dim for euer: All those riuers
That fed her veines with warme and crimson streames,
Froxen and dried vp: If these be signes of death,
Then is she dead. Thou vnreligious youth,
Art not ashamde to emptie all these eyes
Of funerall teares, (a debt due to the dead, 30
As mirth is to the liuing:) Sham'st thou not
To haue them stare on thee? harke, thou art curst
Euen to thy face, by those that scarce can speake.
Hip. My Lord.
Duke. What wouldst thou haue? is she not dead?
Hip. Oh, you ha killd her by your crueltie.
Duke. Admit I had, thou killst her now againe;
And art more sauage then a barbarous Moore.
Hip. Let me but kisse her pale and bloodlesse lip.
Duke. O fie, fie, fie.
Hip. Or if not touch her, let me looke on her. 40
Math. As you regard your honour —
Hip. Honour! smoake.
Math. Or if you lou'de hir liuing, spare her now.
Duke. I, well done sir, you play the gentleman:
Steale hence: tis nobly done: away: Ile ioyne
My force to yours, to stop this violent torment:
Passe on. *Exeunt [attendants] with funerall.*
Hip. *Matheo*, thou doost wound me more.
Math. I giue you phisicke noble friend, not wounds.
Duke. Oh well said, well done, a true gentleman:
Alacke, I know the sea of louers rage
Comes rushing with so strong a tide: it beates 50
And beares downe all respects of life, of honour,
Of friends, of foes: forget her, gallant youth.
Hip. Forget her?

*45 torment] *stet* Q 1–2 (s)

22

Duke. Na, na, be but patient:
For why deaths hand hath sued a strict diuorse
Twixt her and thee: whats beautie but a coarse?
What but faire sand-dust are earths purest formes:
Queenes bodies are but trunckes to put in wormes.
Math. Speake no more sentences, my good lord, but slip hence; you see they are but fits, ile rule him I warrant ye. I, so, treade gingerly, your Grace is heere somewhat too long already. [*Exit Duke.*] Sbloud the ieast were now, if hauing tane some knockes o'th pate already, he should get loose againe, and like a madde Oxe, tosse my new blacke cloakes into the kennell. I must humour his lordship: my lord *Hipolito*, is it in your stomacke to goe to dinner?
Hip. Where is the body?
Math. The body, as the Duke spake very wisely, is gone to be wormd.
Hip. I cannot rest, ile meete it at next turne,
Ile see how my loue lookes.
                    Mathæo *holds him ins armes.*
Math. How your loue lookes? worse than a scarre-crowe, wrastle not with me: the great felow giues the fall for a duckat.
Hip. I shall forget my selfe.
Math. Pray do so, leaue your selfe behinde your selfe, and go whither you will. Sfoote, doe you long to haue base roags that maintaine a saint *Anthonies* fire in their noses (by nothing but two peny Ale) make ballads of you? if the Duke had but so much mettle in him, as is in a coblers awle, he woud ha beene a vext thing: he and his traine had blowne you vp, but that their powlder haz taken the wet of cowards: youle bleed three pottles of Aligant, by this light, if you follow em, and then wee shall haue a hole made in a wrong place, to haue Surgeons roll thee vp like a babie in swadling clowts.
Hip. What day is to day, *Mathæo*?
Math. Yea mary, this is an easie question: why to day is, let me see, thurseday.
Hip. Oh, thurseday.

*54 For why] *stet* Q1–2(s)   58 *Math.*] *Matheo* Q2(s); *Mathew* Q1

Math. Heeres a coile for a dead commoditie, sfoote women when they are aliue are but dead commodities, for you shall haue one woman lie vpon many mens hands. 90
Hip. Shee died on monday then.
Math. And thats the most villainous day of all the weeke to die in: and she was wel, and eate a messe of water-grewel on monday morning.
Hip. I, it cannot be,
Such a bright taper should burne out so soone.
Math. O yes my Lord, so soone: why I ha knowne them, that at dinner haue bin aswell, and had so much health, that they were glad to pledge it, yet before three a clocke haue bin found dead drunke. 100
Hip. On thursday buried! and on monday died,
Quicke haste birlady: sure her winding sheete
Was laide out fore her bodie, and the wormes
That now must feast with her, were euen bespoke,
And solemnely inuited like strange guests.
Math. Strange feeders they are indeede my lord, and like your ieaster or yong Courtier, will enter vpon any mans trencher without bidding.
Hip. Curst be that day for euer that robd her
Of breath, and me of blisse, henceforth let it stand 110
Within the Wizardes booke (the kalendar)
Markt with a marginall finger, to be chosen
By theeues, by villaines, and blacke murderers,
As the best day for them to labour in.
If henceforth this adulterous bawdy world
Be got with childe with treason, sacrilege,
Atheisme, rapes, treacherous friendship, periurie,
Slaunder, (the beggars sinne) lies, (sinne of fooles)
Or anie other damnd impieties,
On *Monday* let em be deliuered: 120
I sweare to thee *Mathæo*, by my soule,
Heereafter weekely on that day ile glew
Mine eie-lids downe, because they shall not gaze

*100 drunke.] *stet* Q 1–2 (s)

24

On any female cheeke. And being lockt vp
In my close chamber, there ile meditate
On nothing but my *Infælices* end,
Or on a dead mans scull drawe out mine owne.
Math. Youle doe all these good workes now euery monday, because it is so bad: but I hope vppon tuesday morning I shall take you with a wench. 130
Hip. If euer whilst fraile bloud through my veins runne,
On womans beames I throw affection,
Saue her thats dead: or that I loosely flie
To'th shoare of any other wafting eie,
Let me not prosper heauen. I will be true,
Euen to her dust and ashes: could her tombe
Stand whilst I liude, so long that it might rot,
That should fall downe, but she be ne're forgot.
Math. If you haue this strange monster, Honestie, in your belly, why so, Iig-makers and chroniclers shall picke somthing out of you: 140 but and I smell not you and a bawdy house out within these tenne daies, let my nose be as bigge as an English bag-pudding: Ile followe your lordship, though it be to the place aforenamed.
Exeunt.

[ACT I, SCENE ii]

Enter Fustigo *in some fantastike Sea-suite at one doore, a Porter meets him at another.*

Fust. How now porter, will she come?
Port. If I may trust a woman sir, she will come.
Fust. Theres for thy paines, godamercy, if euer I stand in neede of a wench that will come with a wet finger, Porter, thou shalt earne my mony before anie *Clarissimo* in *Millane*; yet so god sa mee shees mine owne sister body and soule, as I am a christian Gentleman; farewell, ile ponder till shee come: thou hast bin no bawde in fetching this woman, I assure thee.

137 liude, so long▲] Q2(s); ~▲~~, Q1
*5 *Clarissimo*] stet Q1–2(s)

25

Port. No matter if I had sir, better men than Porters are bawdes.
Fust. O God sir, manie that haue borne offices. But Porter, art sure thou wentst into a true house?
Port. I thinke so, for I met with no thieues.
Fust. Nay but arte sure it was my sister *Viola*.
Port. I am sure by all superscriptions it was the partie you ciphered.
Fust. Not very tall.
Port. Nor very lowe, a midling woman.
Fust. Twas she faith, twas she, a prettie plumpe cheeke like mine.
Port. At a blush, alittle very much like you.
Fust. Gods so, I woud not for a duckat she had kickt vp hir heeles, for I ha spent an abomination this voyage, marie I did it amongst sailers and gentlemen: theres alittle modicum more porter for making thee stay, farewell honest porter.
Port. I am in your debt sir, God preserue you.   *Exit.*

Enter Viola [*wife to* Candido].

Fust. Not so neither, good porter, gods lid, yonder she coms. Sister *Viola*, I am glad to see you stirring: its newes to haue mee heere, ist not sister?
Wife. Yes trust me: I wondred who should be so bolde to send for me, you are welcome to *Millan* brother.
Fust. Troth sister I heard you were married to a verie rich chuffe, and I was very sorie for it, that I had no better clothes, and that made me send: for you knowe wee Millaners loue to strut vpon Spanish leather. And how does all our friends?
Wife. Very well; you ha trauelled enough now, I trowe, to sowe your wilde oates.
Fust. A pox on em; wilde oates, I ha not an oate to throw at a horse, troth sister I ha sowde my oates, and reapt two hundred duckats if I had em, heere, mary I must intreate you to lend me some thirty or forty till the ship come, by this hand ile discharge at my day, by this hand.
Wife. These are your olde oaths.

28 *Wife.*] *throughout this scene in* Q1 *the speech-prefix is* Viola. Q2 *agrees* (r, s) *up to* I.ii.94 (*start of sig.* B1ᵛ *reset*), *at which point the form* Wife., *subsequently invariable with only one exception, begins.*

Fust. Why sister, doe you thinke ile forsweare my hand?
Wife. Well, well, you shall haue them: put your selfe into better fashion, because I must imploy you in a serious matter.
Fust. Ile sweate like a horse if I like the matter.
Wife. You ha cast off all your olde swaggering humours.
Fust. I had not sailde a league in that great fish-pond (the sea) but I cast vp my very gall.
Wife. I am the more sory, for I must imploy a true swaggerer.
Fust. Nay by this yron sister, they shall finde I am powlder and touch-box, if they put fire once into me.
Wife. Then lend me your eares.
Fust. Mine eares are yours deere sister.
Wife. I am married to a man that haz wealth enough, and wit enough.
Fust. A linnen Draper I was tolde sister.
Wife. Very true, a graue Cittizen; I want nothing that a wife can wish from a husband: but heeres the spite, hee haz not all things belonging to a man.
Fust. Gods my life, hee's a verie mandrake, or else (God blesse vs) one a these whiblins, and thats woorse, and then all the children that he gets lawfully of your body sister, are bastards by a statute.
Wife. O you runne ouer me too fast brother, I haue heard it often said, that hee who cannot be angry, is no man. I am sure my husband is a man in print, for all things else, saue onely in this, no tempest can moue him.
Fust. Slid, would he had beene at sea with vs, hee should ha beene moude and moude agen, for Ile be sworne la, our drunken ship reelde like a Dutchman.
Wife. No losse of goods can increase in him a wrinckle, no crabbed language make his countenance sowre, the stubburnnes of no seruant shake him, he haz no more gall in him than a Doue, no more sting than an Ant: Musitian will he neuer bee, (yet I finde much musicke in him,) but he loues no frets, and is so free from anger, that many times I am ready to bite off my tongue, because it wants that vertue which all womens tongues haue (to anger their husbands:) Brother, mine can by no thunder turne him into a sharpenes.

Fust. Belike his blood sister, is well brewd then.
Wife. I protest to thee *Fustigo*, I loue him most affectionately, but I know not — I ha such a tickling within mee — such a strange longing; nay, verily I doo long.
Fust. Then y'are with childe sister, by all signes and tokens; nay, I am partly a Phisitian, and partly something else. I ha read *Albertus Magnus*, and *Aristotles* emblemes.
Wife. Y'are wide ath bow hand still brother: my longings are not wanton, but wayward: I long to haue my patient husband eate vp a whole Porcupine, to the intent, the bristling quills may sticke about his lippes like a flemmish mustacho, and be shot at me: I shall be leaner then the new Moone, vnlesse I can make him horne mad.
Fust. Sfoote halfe a quarter of an houre does that: make him a cuckold.
Wife. Puh, he would count such a cut no vnkindenes.
Fust. The honester Cittizen he, then make him drunke and cut off his beard.
Wife. Fie, fie, idle, idle, hee's no French-man, to fret at the losse of a little scalde haire. No brother, thus it shall be, you must be secret.
Fust. As your Mid-wife I protest sister, or a Barber-surgeon.
Wife. Repaire to the *Tortoys* heere in Saint *Christophers* streete, I will send you mony, turne your selfe into a braue man: insteed of the armes of your mistris, let your sword and your militarie scarfe hang about your necke.
Fust. I must haue a great Horse-mans French feather too sister.
Wife. O, by any meanes, to shew your light head, else your hat will sit like a coxcombe: to be briefe, you must bee in all points a most terrible wide-mouth'd swaggerer.
Fust. Nay, for swaggering points let me alone.
Wife. Resort then to our shop, and (in my husbands presence) kisse me, snatch rings, iewells, or any thing; so you giue it backe agen brother in secret.
Fust. By this hand sister.
Wife. Sweare as if you came but new from knighting.

*85 emblemes] *stet* Q1–2(r)

Fust. Nay, Ile sweare after four hundred a yeare.
Wife. Swagger worse then a Lieuetenant among fresh-water souldiers, call me your loue, your yngle, your coosen, or so; but sister at no hand.
Fust. No, no, It shall be coosen, or rather cuz, thats the gulling word betweene the Cittizens wiues and their mad-caps, that man em to the garden; to call you one a my naunts, sister, were as good as call you arrant whoore: no, no, let me alone to cosen you rarely.
Wife. H'az heard I haue a brother, but neuer saw him, therefore put on a good face.
Fust. The best in *Millan* I warrant.
Wife. Take vp wares, but pay nothing, rifle my bosome, my pocket, my purse, the boxes for mony to dice with all; but brother, you must giue all backe agen in secret.
Fust. By this welkin that heere roares? I will, or else let me neuer know what a secret is: why sister do you thinke Ile cunni-catch you, when you are my coosen? Gods my life, then I were a starke Asse; if I fret not his guts, beg me for a foole.
Wife. Be circumspect, and do so then, farewell.
Fust. The *Tortoys* sister? Ile stay there; forty duckats.   *Exit.*
Wife. Thither Ile send: this law can none deny,
Women must haue their longings, or they die.
                                                              Exit.

[ACT I, Scene iii]

Gasparo *the Duke,* Doctor *Benedict, two seruants.*

Duke. Giue charge that none do enter, locke the doores;
And fellowes, what your eyes and eares receaue,
Vpon your liues trust not the gadding aire
To carry the least part of it: the glasse,
The houre-glasse.
Doct.   Heere my Lord.
Duke.   Ah, tis neere spent.

    120 mad-caps] Q2(r); olde dames Q1
    121 my naunts,] Q2(r) [naunts$_\Lambda$]; mine aunts, Q1
  *129 roares?] Q1; ~$_\Lambda$ Q2(r)   *5 neere] D1; meere Q1-2(r)-5

But Doctor *Benedict*, does your Art speake truth?
Art sure the soporiferous streame will ebbe,
And leaue the Christall banks of her white body
(Pure as they were at first) iust at the houre?
Doct. Iust at the houre my Lord.
                    [*Draw curtains*. Infælice *on a bed.*]
Duke.   Vncurtaine her.   10
Softly, see Doctor what a coldish heate
Spreads ouer all her bodie.
Doct.   Now it workes:
The vitall spirits that by a sleepie charme
Were bound vp fast, and threw an icie crust
On her exterior parts, now gin to breake:
Trouble her not my Lord.
Duke.   Some stooles, you calld
For musicke, did you not? Oh ho, it speakes,
It speakes, watch sirs her waking, note those sands,
Doctor sit downe: A Dukedome that should wey
Mine owne downe twice, being put into one scale,   20
And that fond desperate boy *Hipolito*,
Making the weight vp, should not (at my hands)
Buy her i'th tother, were her state more light
Than hers, who makes a dowrie vp with almes.
Doctor Ile starue her on the Appenine
Ere he shall marrie her: I must confesse,
Hipolito is nobly borne; a man,
Did not mine enemies blood boile in his veines,
Whom I would court to be my sonne in law?
But Princes whose high spleenes for empery swell, 30
Are not with easie arte made paralell.
2. Seru. She wakes my Lord.
Duke.   Looke Doctor *Benedict*.
I charge you on your liues maintaine for truth
What ere the Doctor or my selfe auerre,
For you shall beare her hence to *Bergamo*.

11 Softly, see Doctor˄] Q2(r); Softly ˄ sweete Doctor: Q1
*14 crust] Dyce *suggestion*; rust Q1–2(r)–5   35 Bergamo] Q2(r); *Bergaine* Q1

30

Infæ. Oh God, what fearefull dreames?
Doct. Lady.
Infæ. Ha.
Duke. Girle.
Why *Infælice*, how ist now, ha, speake?
Infæ. I'me well, what makes this Doctor heere? I'me well.
Duke. Thou wert not so euen now, sicknes pale hand
Laid hold on thee euen in the midst of feasting;   40
And when a cup crownde with thy louers health
Had toucht thy lips, a sencible cold dew
Stood on thy cheekes, as if that death had wept
To see such beautie alter.
Infæ. I remember
I sate at banquet, but felt no such change.
Duke. Thou hast forgot then how a messenger
Came wildely in with this vnsauorie newes
That he was dead.
Infæ. What messenger? whoes dead?
Duke. *Hipolito*, alacke, wring not thy hands.
Infæ. I saw no messenger, heard no such newes.   50
Doct. Trust me you did sweete Lady.
Duke. La you now.
2 Seruants. Yes indeede Madam.
Duke. La you now, tis well, good knaues.
Infæ. You ha slaine him, and now you'le murder mee.
Duke. Good *Infælice* vexe not thus thy selfe,
Of this the bad report before did strike
So coldly to thy heart, that the swift currents
Of life were all frozen vp.
Infæ. It is vntrue,
Tis most vntrue, O most vnnaturall father!
Duke. And we had much to do by Arts best cunning,
To fetch life backe againe.

---

40 midst] Q2(r); deadst Q1   41 cup] Q2(r); cap Q1
44 alter] Q2(r); alterd Q1   52 *2 Seruants.*] Q1; *2 Ser.* Q2(r)
52 well, good knaues] Q2(r); well ⌃ God knowes Q1
56 thy] Q2(r); the Q1

Doct.   Most certaine Lady.   60
Duke. Why la you now, you'le not beleeue mee, friends,
Sweate we not all? had we not much to do?
2 Seruants. Yes indeede my Lord, much.
Duke. Death drew such fearefull pictures in thy face,
That were *Hipolito* aliue agen,
I'de kneele and woo the noble gentleman
To be thy husband: now I sore repent
My sharpenes to him, and his family;
Nay, do not weepe for him, we all must die:
Doctor, this place where she so oft hath seene   70
His liuely presence, hurts her, does it not?
Doct. Doubtlesse my Lord it does.
Duke.   It does, it does.
Therefore sweete girle thou shalt to *Bergamo*.
Infæ. Euen where you will, in any place theres woe.
Duke. A Coach is ready, *Bergamo* doth stand
In a most wholesome aire, sweete walkes, theres diere,
I, thou shalt hunt and send vs venison,
Which like some goddesse in the *Ciprian* groues,
Thine owne faire hand shall strike; sirs, you shall teach her
To stand, and how to shoote, I, she shall hunt: 80
Cast off this sorrow. In girle, and prepare
This night to ride away to *Bergamo*.
Infæ. O most vnhappie maid.   *Exit.*
Duke.   Follow her close.
No words that she was buried on your liues,
Or that her ghost walkes now after shees dead;
Ile hang you if you name a funerall.
1. Ser. Ile speake Greeke my Lord, ere I speake that deadly word.
2. Ser. And Ile speake Welch, which is harder then Greek.
                                                       Exeunt.
Duke. Away, looke to her; Doctor *Benedict*,

      63 2 *Seruants.*] Dyce (*see line* 52 *above*); 2 *Ser.* Q1–2(r)–5
      66 I'de] Q2(r); Ile Q1   71 hurts Q2(r) [hnrts]; haunts Q1
      78 goddesse] Q2(r); gods Q1   78 *Ciprian*] Q2(r); *Coprian* Q1
      83 her] Q2(r); it Q1

  Did you obserue how her complexion altred   90
  Vpon his name and death, O would t'were true.
Doct. It may my Lord.
Duke.   May? how? I wish his death.
Doct. And you may haue your wish; say but the word,
  And tis a strong Spell to rip vp his graue:
  I haue good knowledge with *Hipolito*;
  He calls me friend, Ile creepe into his bosome,
  And sting him there to death; poison can doo't.
Duke. Performe it; Ile create thee halfe mine heire.
Doct. It shall be done, although the fact be fowle.
Duke. Greatnes hides sin, the guilt vpon my soule.   100
                 Exeunt.

[ACT I, Scene iv]

    Enter Castruchio, Pioratto, *and* Fluello.

Cast. Signior *Pioratto*, signior *Fluello*, shalls be merry? shalls play the wags now?
Flu. I, any thing that may beget the childe of laughter.
Cast. Truth I haue a pretty sportiue conceit new crept into my braine, will mooue excellent mirth.
Pio. Lets ha't, lets ha't, and where shall the sceane of mirth lie?
Cast. At signior *Candidoes* house, the patient man, nay the monstrous patient man; they say his bloud is immoueable, that he haz taken all patience from a man, and all constancie from a woman.
Flu. That makes so many whoores nowadayes.   10
Cast. I, and so many knaues too.
Pio. Well sir.
Cast. To conclude, the reporte goes, hees so milde, so affable, so suffering, that nothing indeede can mooue him: now do but thinke what sport it will be to make this fellow (the mirror of patience) as angry, as vext, and as madde as an English cuckolde.
Flu. O, twere admirable mirth, that: but how wilt be done signior?
Cast. Let me alone, I haue a tricke, a conceit, a thing, a deuice will

sting him yfaith, if he haue but a thimble full of blood ins belly, or
a spleene not so bigge as a tauerne token. 20
Pio. Thou stirre him? thou mooue him? thou anger him? alas, I
know his approoued temper: thou vex him? why hee haz a patience
aboue mans iniuries: thou maiest sooner raise a spleene in an
Angell, than rough humour in him: why ile giue you instance for
it. This wonderfully temperd signior *Candido* vppon a time inuited
home to his house certaine Neapolitane lordes of curious taste,
and no meane pallats, coniuring his wife, of all loues, to prepare
cheere fitting for such honourable trencher-men. Shee (iust of a
womans nature, couetous to trie the vttermost of vexation, and
thinking at last to gette the starte of his humour) willingly neglected 30
the preparation, and became vnfurnisht, not onely of dainty, but
of ordinary dishes. He (according to the mildenesse of his breast)
entertained the lordes, and with courtly discourse beguiled the time
(as much as a Cittizen might doe:) to conclude, they were hungry
lordes, for there came no meate in; their stomackes were plainely
gulld, and their teeth deluded, and (if anger could haue seizd a man)
there was matter enough yfaith to vex any citizen in the world, if
hee were not too much made a foole by his wife.
Flu. I, Ile sweare for't: sfoote, had it beene my case, I should ha
playde mad trickes with my wife and family: first I woulde ha 40
spitted the men, stewd the maides, and bak't the mistresse, and so
serued them in.
Pio. Why twould ha tempted any bloud but his,
And thou to vex him? thou to anger him
With some poore shallow ieast?
Cast. Sbloud signior *Pioratto*, (you that disparage my conceit) ile
wage a hundred duckats vppon the head on't, that it mooues him,
fretts him, and galles him.
Pio. Done, tis a lay, ioyne golls on't: witnes signior *Fluello.*
Cast. Witnes: tis done: 50
Come, follow mee: the house is not farre off,
Ile thrust him from his humour, vex his breast,
And winne a hundred duckats by one ieast.
Exeunt.

*43 tempted] Q 2 (r); tempred Q 1

34

[ACT I, Scene v]

Enter Candidoes Wife, George, *and two prentices in the shoppe.*

Wife. Come, you put vp your wares in good order heere, do you not thinke you, one peece cast this way, another that way? you had neede haue a patient maister indeede.

Geo. I, ile be sworne, for we haue a curst mistris.

Wife. You mumble, do you mumble? I would your maister or I could be a note more angry: for two patient folkes in a house spoyle all the seruants that euer shall come vnder them.

1. *Prent.* You patient! I, so is the diuell when he is horne madde.

Enter Castruchio, Fluello, *and* Pioratto.

All three. Gentlemen, what do you lacke? what ist you buy? See fine hollands, fine cambrickes, fine lawnes.

Geo. What ist you lacke?

2. *Prent.* What ist you buy?

Cast. Wheres signior *Candido* thy maister?

Geo. Faith signior, hees alittle negotiated, hee'le appeare presently.

Cast. Fellow, lets see a lawne, a choice one sirra.

Geo. The best in all *Millan*, Gentlemen, and this is the peece. I can fit you Gentlemen with fine callicoes too for dublets, the onely sweete fashion now, most delicate and courtlie, a meeke gentle calico, cut vpon two double affable taffataes, ah, most neate, feate, and vnmatchable.

Flu. A notable voluble-tongde villaine.

Pio. I warrant this fellow was neuer begot without much prating.

Cast. What, and is this shee saist thou?

Geo. I, and the purest shee that euer you fingerd since you were a gentleman: looke how euen she is, look how cleane she is, ha, as euen as the browe of *Cinthia*, and as cleane as your sonnes and heires when they ha spent all.

Cast. Puh, thou talkst, pox on't tis rough.

Geo. How? is she rough? but if you bid pox on't sir, twill take away the roughnesse presently.

Flu. Ha signior; haz he fitted your French curse?

Geo. Looke you Gentleman, heeres an other, compare them I pray, *compara Virgilium cum Homero,* compare virgins with harlots.

Cast. Puh, I ha seene better, and as you terme them, euener and cleaner.

Geo. You may see further for your mind, but trust me you shall not find better for your body.

Enter Candido.

Cast. O here he comes, lets make as tho we passe,
Come, come, weele try in some other shop.

Cand. How now? what's the matter?

Geo. The gentlemen find fault with this lawne, fall out with it, and without a cause too.

Cand. Without a cause!
And that makes you to let 'em passe away,
Ah, may I craue a word with you gentlemen?

Flu. He calls vs.

Cast. Makes the better for the iest.

Cand. I pray come neare, — y'are very welcome gallants,
Pray pardon my mans rudenesse, for I feare me
Ha's talkt aboue a prentice with you, — Lawnes!
Looke you kind gentlemen — this! no: — I this:
Take this vpon my honest-dealing faith,
To be a true weaue, not too hard, nor slack,
But eene as farre from falshood, as from black.

Cast. Well, how doe you rate it?

Cand. Very conscionably, eighteen shillings a yard.

Cast. That's too deare: how many yards does the whole piece containe thinke you?

Cand. Why, some seuenteen yardes I thinke, or there abouts,
How much would serue your turne, I pray?

Cast. Why let me see — would it were better too.

Cand. Truth, tis the best in *Millan* at fewe words.

56 conscionably] Q1; conscionable Q2(r)
56 eighteen shillings] 18.*s* Q1; 18. Q2(r)

Cast.   Well: let me haue then — a whole penny-worth.
Cand.   Ha, ha: y'are a merry gentleman.
Cast.   A pennorth I say.
Cand.   Of lawne!
Cast.   Of lawne? I of lawne, a pennorth, sblood dost not heare? a whole pennorth, are you deaffe?
Cand.   Deaffe? no Syr: but I must tell you,
Our wares doe seldome meete such customers.   70
Cast.   Nay, and you and your lawnes be so squemish, fare you well.
Cand.   Pray stay, a word, pray Signior: for what purpose is it I beseech you?
Cast.   Sblood, whats that to you: Ile haue a penny-worth.
Cand.   A penny-worth! why you shall: Ile serue you presently.
2. *Prent.*   Sfoot, a penny-worth mistris!
Wife.   A penny-worth! call you these Gentlemen?
Cast.   No, no: not there.
Cand.   What then kinde Gentle-man? what at this corner here?
Cast.   No nor there neither.   80
Ile haue it iust in the middle, or els not.
Cand.   Iust in the middle: — ha — you shall too: what?
Haue you a single penny?
Cast.   Yes, heeres one.
Cand.   Lend it me I pray.
Flu.   An exlent followed iest.
Wife.   What will he spoile the Lawne now?
Cand.   Patience, good wife.
Wife.   I, that patience makes a foole of you: Gentlemen, you might ha found some other Citizen to haue made a kind gull on, besides my husband.   90
Cand.   Pray Gentlemen take her to be a woman,
Do not regard her language. — O kinde soule:
Such words will driue away my customers.
Wife.   Customers with a murren: call you these customers?
Cand.   Patience, good wife.
Wife.   Pax, a your patience.

77 *Wife.*] *Mist.* Q1–2(r)–5
*79 Gentle-man?] Q1; gentleemen Q2(r)

THE HONEST WHORE, PART I [I. v

Geo. Sfoot mistris, I warrant these are some cheating companions.
Cand. Looke you Gentleman, theres your ware, I thank you,
   I haue your mony heare; pray know my shop, 100
   Pray let me haue your custome.
Wife. Custome quoth a.
Cand. Let me take more of your money.
Wife. You had need so.
Pio. Harke in thine eare, thast lost an hundred duckets.
Cast. Well, well, I knowt: ist possible that *Homo*,
   Should be nor man, nor woman: not once mooud;
   No not at such an iniurie, not at all!
   Sure hees a pigeon, for he has no gall.
Flu. Come, come, y'are angry tho you smother it: 110
   Yare vext ifaith, — confesse.
Cand.   Why Gentle-men
   Should you conceit me to be vext or moou'd?
   He has my ware, I haue his money fort,
   And thats no Argument I am angry: no,
   The best Logitian can not proue me so.
Flu. Oh, but the hatefull name of a pennyworth of lawne,
   And then cut out ith middle of the peece:
   Pah, I guesse it by my selfe, twould moue a Lambe
   Were he a Lynnen-draper — twould ifaith.
Cand. Well, giue me leaue to answer you for that, 120
   We are set heere to please all customers,
   Their humours and their fancies: — offend none:
   We get by many, if we leese by one.
   May be his minde stood to no more then that,
   A penworth serues him, and mongst trades tis found,
   Deny a pennorth, it may crosse a pound.
   Oh, he that meanes to thriue, with patient eye
   Must please the diuell, if he come to buy.

99 Gentleman] Q1; Gentlemen Q2(r) (*see line 79 above and note*)
100 mony heare;] Q2(r); ~ ; ~ , Q1   101 Pray let] Q1; *om.* Pray Q2(r)
105 an] Q1; a Q2(r)   116 of lawne] Q2(s); oflawne Q1
117 out‸] Q2(s); ~ , Q1   118 twould] Q2(s); would Q1
121 We are] Q2(s); Were Q1

38

I. v]   THE HONEST WHORE, PART I

Flu.   O wondrous man, patient 'boue wrong or woe,
   How blest were men, if women could be so.   130
Cand.   And to expresse how well my brest is pleasde,
   And satisfied in all: — *George*, fill a beaker.   *Exit* George.
   Ile drinke vnto that Gentleman, who lately
   Bestowed his mony with me.
Wife.   Gods my life,
   We shall haue all our gaines drunke out in beakers,
   To make amends for pennyworths of lawne.   *Enter* George.
Cand.   Here wife, begin you to the Gentleman.
Wife.   I begin to him?   [*Casts down the drink.*]
Cand.   *George*, filt vp againe:
   Twas my fault, my hand shooke.   *Exit* George.
Pio.   How strangely this doth showe?   140
   A patient man linkt with a waspish shrowe.
Flu.   A siluer and gilt beaker: I haue a tricke
   To worke vpon that beaker, sure twil fret him,
   It cannot choose but vexe him. Signior *Castruchio*,
   In pittie to thee, I haue a conceit,
   Wil saue thy hundred Duckets yet, twil doot,
   And work him to impatience.
Cast.   Sweet *Fluello*,
   I should be bountiful to that conceit.
Flu.   Well tis enough.   *Enter* George.
Cand.   Here Gentleman to you,   150
   I wish your custome, yare exceeding welcome.
Cast.   I pledge you Signior *Candido*, —
   Heere to you, that must receiue a hundred Duccats.
Pio.   Ile pledge them deepe yfaith *Castruchio*,
   Signior *Fluello*?
Flu.   Come: play't off: to me,
   I am your last man.

*129 patient 'boue] patient, boue Q2(s); patient ∧ boue Q1
129 woe] Q1; wo Q2(s) [*probably for line justification*]
132 *George*,] Q2(s); ~ . Q1
142–147 Fluello's *speech lined as verse in* Q2(s); *as prose in* Q1
153 to] Q2(s); *om.* Q1   155–156 Come:...man.] Q1; Q2(r) *prints as one line*
*155 off: to me,] stet Q1–2(r)

39

Cand.   *George*, supply the cup.
Flu.   So, so, good honest *George*,
Here Signior *Candido*, all this to you.
Cand.   Oh you must pardon me, I vse it not.
Flu.   Will you not pledge me then?
Cand.   Yes, but not that:
Great loue is showne in little.
Flu.   Blurt on your sentences, —
Sfoot you shall pledge mee all.
Cand.   Indeed I shall not.
Flu.   Not pledge me? Sblood, Ile cary away the beaker then.
Cand.   The beaker! Oh! that at your pleasure sir.
Flu.   Now by this drinke I will.
Cast.   Pledge him, heele do't else.
Flu.   So: I ha done you right, on my thumbe naile,
What will you pledge me now?
Cand.   You know me syr,
I am not of that sin.
Flu.   Why then farewell:
Ile beare away the beaker by this light.
Cand.   Thats as you please, tis very good.
Flu.   Nay it doth please me, and as you say, tis a very good one:
Farewell Signior *Candido*.
Pio.   Farewell *Candido*.
Cand.   Y'are welcome gentlemen.
Cast.   Heart not mou'd yet?
I thinke his patience is aboue our wit.   *Exeunt.*
Geo.   I told you before mistresse, they were all cheaters.
Wife.   Why foole, why husband, why madman, I hope you will
not let 'em sneake away so with a siluer and gilt beaker, the best in
the house too: goe fellowes make hue and cry after them.
Cand.   Pray let your tongue lye still, all wil be well:
Come hither *George*, hye to the Constable,
And in calme order wish him to attach them,
Make no great stirre, because they're gentlemen,
And a thing partly done in meriment,

    181 lye] Q1; be Q2(r)   183 in calme] Q1; in all calme Q2(r)

  Tis but a size aboue a iest thou knowst.
Therefore pursue it mildly, goe be gone,
The Constabl's hard by, bring him along, —
Make hast againe.   *Exit* George.
Wife. O y'are a goodly patient Woodcocke, are you not now? See what your patience comes too: euery one sadles you, and rydes you, youle be shortly the common stone-horse of *Myllan*: a womans well holp't vp with such a meacocke, I had rather haue a husband that would swaddle me thrice a day, then such a one, that will be guld twice in halfe an hower, Oh I could burne all the wares in my shop for anger.
Cand. Pray weare a peacefull temper, be my wife,
That is, be patient: for a wife and husband
Share but one soule between them: this being knowne,
Why should not one soule then agree in one?
Wife. Hang your agreements: But if my beaker be gone —
                 Exit.

    Enter Castruchio, Fluello, Pioratto, *and* George.

Cand. Oh, heare they come.
Geo. The Constable syr, let 'em come along with me, because there should be no wondring: he staies at dore.
Cast. Constable goodman *Abram*.
Flu. Now Signior *Candido*, Sblood why doe you attach vs?
Cast. Sheart! attach vs!
Cand. Nay sweare not gallants,
Your oathes may moue your soules, but not moue me,
You haue a siluer beaker of my wiues.
Flu. You say not true: tis gilt.
Cand.   Then you say true.
And being gilt, the guilt lyes more on you.
Cast. I hope y'are not angry syr.
Cand.   Then you hope right,
For I am not angry.
Pio.   No, but a little mou'de.
Cand. I mou'd! twas you were mou'd, you were brought hither.

    204 wondring:] Q4; ~ , Q1–2(r)–3

Cast. But you (out of your anger and impatience,)
Caus'd vs to be attacht.
Cand.   Nay you misplace it.
Out of my quiet sufferance I did that,
And not of any wrath, had I showne anger,
I should haue then pursude you with the lawe,   220
And hunted you to shame; as many worldlings
Doe build their anger vpon feebler groundes,
The mores the pitty, many loose their liues
For scarce so much coyne as will hide their palme,
Which is most cruell: those haue vexed spirits
That pursue liues: in this opinion rest,
The losse of Millions could not moue my brest.
Flu. Thou art a blest man, and with peace doest deale,
Such a meeke spirit can blesse a common weale.
Cand. Gentlemen, now tis vpon eating time,   230
Pray part not hence, but dyne with me to day.
Cast. I neuer heard a courtier yet say nay
To such a motion. Ile not be the first.
Pio. Nor I.
Flu. Nor I.
Cand. The constable shall beare you company,
George call him in, let the world say what it can,
Nothing can driue me from a patient man.
                                                            Exeunt.

    218 sufferance] Q2(s); sufferaence Q1
   *221 shame;] D1; ~ , Q1–2(s)–5
    222 groundes,] Q1; grounds; Q2(s)
    224 palme,] Q2(s); ~ : Q1
    225 cruell:] ~ , Q1–2(s)–5 (eds. *choose semi-colon or full stop*)
    226 liues:] Q2(s); ~ , Q1
    228 doest] Q2(s); dost Q1
    232 courtier] Q2(s); carter Q1

[ACT II, Scene i]

Enter Roger with a stoole, cushin, looking-glasse, and chafing-dish. Those being set downe, he pulls out of his pocket, a violl with white cullor in it, and two boxes, one with white, another red painting. He places all things in order and a candle by them, singing with the ends of old Ballads as he does it. At last Bellafront (as he rubs his cheeke with the cullors) whistles within.

Rog. A non forsooth.
Bell. What are you playing the roague about?
Rog. About you forsooth: I'me drawing vp a hole in your white silke stocking.
Bell. Is my glasse there? and my boxes of complexion?
Rog. Yes forsooth: your boxes of complexion are here I thinke: yes tis here: her's your two complexions, and if I had all the foure complexions, I should nere set a good face vpont, some men I see are borne vnder hard-fauourd plannets as well as women: zounds I looke worse now then I did before, and it makes her face glister 10 most damnably, theres knauery in dawbing I hold my life, or else this is onely female *Pomatum*.

Enter Bellafronte not full ready, without a gowne, shee sits downe, with her bodkin curles her haire, cullers her lips.

Bell. Wheres my ruffe and poker you block-head?
Rog. Your ruffe, and your poker, are ingendring together vpon the cup-bord of the Court, or the Court-cup-bord.
Bell. Fetch 'em: Is the poxe in your hammes, you can goe no faster?
Rog. Wood the pox were in your fingers, vnlesse you could leaue flinging; catch. *Exit.*

7 two] Q2(s); twe Q1
*8 I] Q2(s); *I* Q1
14 ruffe, and your poker] Q2(s); ruffe, your pocker Q1
16 hammes] Q2(s); hames Q1

43

Bell. Ile catch you, you dog, by and by: do you grumble?   20
            Cupid *is a God,*   *She sings.*
            As naked as my naile,
            Ile whip him with a rod,
            If he my true loue faile.   [*Enter* Roger.]
Rog. Thers your ruffe, shall I poke it?
Bell. Yes honest *Roger*, no stay: pry thee good boy, hold here,
Downe, downe, downe, downe, I fall downe, and arise I neuer shall.
Rog. Troth Mistris then leaue the trade if you shall neuer rise.
Bell. What trade? good-man *Abram.*
Rog. Why that, of down and arise, or the falling trade.   30
Bell. Ile fall with you by and by.
Rog. If you doe, I know who shall smart fort:
Troth Mistris, what do I looke like now?
Bell. Like as you are: a panderly Sixpenny Rascall.
Rog. I may thanke you for that: no faith, I looke like an old Prouerbe, *Hold the Candle before the diuell.*
Bell. Vds life, Ile sticke my knife in your Guts and you prate to me so: Whaat?
     Well met, pug, the pearle of beautie: vmh, vmh.   *She sings.*
     How now sir knaue, you forget your dutie, vmh, vmh.   40
     Marry muffe Sir, are you growne so daintie; fa, la, la, &c.
     Is it you Sir? the worst of twentie, fa la, la, leera la.
Pox on you, how doest thou hold my glasse?
Rog. Why, as I hold your doore: with my fingers.
Bell. Nay pray thee sweet hony *Roger* hold vp handsomely. (*Sing.*)
Prety Wantons warble, &c. We shall ha guests to day, I lay my little meadenhead, my nose itches, so.
Rog. I said so too last night, when our Fleas twing'd me.
Bell. So, Poke my ruffe now, my gowne, my gown, haue I my fall? Wher's my fall *Roger*?   *One knocks.* 50
Rog. Your fall forsooth is behind.

     27 downe, *I*] Q2(s); down, *I* Q1
     27 arise *I* neuer shall.] Q2(s) [arise,]; arise, downe, *I* neuer shall arise. Q1
     30 of] Q2(s); if Q1   30 arise,] Q2(s); ~ ∧ Q1
     32 doe,] Q2(s); ~ ∧ Q1   35 no faith,] Q2(s); infaith ∧ Q1
     38 Whaat] Q2(s); What Q1   45 *Bell.*] Q2(s); *Hell.* Q1
    *45–6 (*Sing.*) *Prety*] *Sing prety* Q1–2(s)–5

II. i] THE HONEST WHORE, PART I

Bell. Gods my pittikins, some foole or other knocks.
Rog. Shall I open to the foole mistresse?
Bell. And all these bables lying thus? away with it quickly, I, I, knock and be dambde, whosoeuer you be. So: giue the fresh Salmon lyne now: let him come a shoare, hee shall serue for my breakefast, tho he goe against my stomack.

   Roger *fetch in* Fluello, Castruchio, *and* Pioratto.

Flu. Morrow coz.
Cast. How does my sweete acquaintance?
Pio. Saue thee little Marmoset: how doest thou good pretty roague? 60
Bell. Well, Godamercy good pretty rascall.
Flu. Roger some light I pry thee.
Rog. You shall Signior, for we that liue here in this vale of misery, are as darke as hell.   *Exit for a candle.*
Cast. Good Tabacco, *Fluello*?
Flu. Smell?
Pio. It may be tickling geere: for it plaies with my nose already.
             Enter Roger.
Rog. Her's another light Angell, Signior.
Bell. What? you pyed curtal, whats that you are neighing?
Rog. I say God send vs the light of heauen, or some more Angels. 70
Bell. Goe fetch some wyne, and drinke halfe of it.
Rog. I must fetch some wyne gentlemen and drinke halfe of it.
Flu. Here *Roger*.
Cast. No let me send pry thee.
Flu. Hold you canker worme.
Rog. You shall send both, if you please Signiors.
Pio. Stay, whats best to drinke a mornings?
Rog. Hypocras sir, for my mistres, if I fetch it, is most deare to her.
Flu. Hypocras! ther then, her's a teston for you, you snake.
Rog. Right syr, her's three shillings sixpence for a pottle and a 80 manchet—   *Exit.*
Cast. Her's most *Herculian Tobacco*, ha-some acquaintance?
Bell. Fah, not I, makes your breath stinke, like the pisse of a Foxe. Acquaintance, where supt you last night?

  57 S.D. *fetch*] Fetch Q1; *fetches* Q2(r)   69 you] Q2(r); yon Q1
  82 *Herculian*] Q2(s) [Herculian]; *herculaniã* Q1

45

Cast. At a place sweete acquaintance where your health danc'de the Canaries y'faith: you should ha ben there.
Bell. I there among your Punkes, marry fah, hang-em: scorn't: will you neuer leaue sucking of egs in other folkes hens neasts.
Cast. Why in good troth, if youle trust me acquaintance, there was not one hen at the board, aske *Fluello*.
Flu. No faith Coz; none but Cocks, signior *Malauolta* drunke to thee.
Bell. O, a pure beagle; that horse-leach there?
Flu. And the knight, Sir *Oliuer Lollio*, swore he wold bestow a taffata petticoate on thee, but to breake his fast with thee.
Bell. With me! Ile choake him then, hang him Mole-catcher, its the dreamingst snotty-nose.
Pio. Well, many tooke that *Lollio* for a foole, but he's a subtile foole.
Bell. I, and he has fellowes: of all filthy dry-fisted knights, I cannot abide that he should touch me.
Cast. Why wench, is he scabbed?
Bell. Hang him, heele not liue to bee so honest, nor to the credite to haue scabbes about him, his betters haue em: but I hate to weare out any of his course knight-hood, because hee's made like an Aldermans night-gowne, fac'st all with conny before, and within nothing but Foxe: this sweete *Oliuer*, will eate Mutton till he be ready to burst, but the leane-iawde slaue wil not pay for the scraping of his trencher.
Pio. Plague him, set him beneath the salt, and let him not touch a bit, till euery one has had his full cut.
Flu. *Sordello*, the Gentleman-Vsher, came into vs too, marry twas in our cheese, for he had beene to borrow mony for his Lord, of a Citizen.
Cast. What an asse is that Lord, to borrow money of a Citizen.
Bell. Nay, Gods my pitty, what an asse is that Citizen to lend mony to a Lord.

---

*87 I there] stet Q1–2(s)   91 *Malauolta*] Q2(s); *Malauella* Q1
94 *Lollio*] Q2(s); *Lollilo* Q1   110 salt] Q2(s); sault Q1
112 *Sordello*] Q2(s); *Lord Ello* Q1   114 Citizen] Q1; itizen Q2(s)
117 to] Q2(s); of Q1

Enter Matheo *and* Hypolito, *who saluting the Company as a stranger, walkes off.* Roger *comes in sadly behind them, with a potle-pot, and stands aloofe off.*

Math. Saue you Gallants, signior *Fluello,* exceedingly well met, as I may say.
Flu. Signior *Matheo,* exceedingly well met too, as I may say. 120
Math. And how fares my little prettie Mistris?
Bell. Eene as my little pretie seruant; sees three court dishes before her, and not one good bit in them: how now? why the diuell standst thou so? Art in a trance?
Rog. Yes forsooth.
Bell. Why dost not fil out their wine?
Rog. Forsooth tis fild out already: all the wine that the signior has bestowde vpon you is cast away, a Porter ranne a tilt at me, and so fac'st me downe that I had not a drop.
Bell. Ime accurs'd to let such a withered Artichocke-faced Rascall 130 grow vnder my nose: now you looke like an old he cat, going to the gallowes: Ile be hangde if he ha not put vp the mony to cony-catch vs all.
Rog. No truely forsooth, tis not put vp yet.
Bell. How many Gentlemen hast thou serued thus?
Rog. None but fiue hundred, besides prentices and seruingmen.
Bell. Doest thinke Ile pocket it vp at thy hands?
Rog. Yes forsooth, I feare you will pocket it vp.
Bell. Fye, fye, cut my lace good seruant, I shall ha the mother presently, Im'e so vext at this horse-plumme. 140
Flu. Plague, not for a scald pottle of wine.
Math. Nay, sweete *Bellafronte,* for a little Pigs wash.
Cast. Here *Roger,* fetch more, a mischance. Yfaith Acquaintance.
Bell. Out of my sight, thou vngodly puritanical creature.
Rog. For the tother pottle? yes forsooth. *Exit.*
Bell. Spill that too: what Gentleman is that, seruant? your Friend?

128 tilt] Dyce *suggestion;* litle Q 1–2(s)–5
130 accurs'd] Q 2(s); a curst Q 1
140 presently,] Q 2(s); ~ ∧ Q 1
146 that,] Q 4; ~ ∧ Q 1–2(s)–3   146 seruant?] Q 1; ~ ∧ Q 2(s)

Math. Gods so a stoole, a stoole, if you loue me Mistris entertaine this Gentleman respectiuely, and bid him welcome.
Bell. Hees very welcome, pray Sir sit.
Hip. Thankes Lady.
Flu. Count *Hypolito*, ist not? cry you mercie signior, you walke here all this while, and we not heed you? let me bestow a stoole vpon you beseech you, you are a stranger here, we know the fashions ath house.
Cast. Please you be heere my Lord.   *Tabacco.*
Hip. No good *Castruchio*.
Flu. You haue abandoned the Court I see my lord since the death of your mistresse, well she was a delicate piece — beseech you sweete—, come let vs serue vnder the cullors of your acquaintance stil, for all that: please you to meete here at the lodging of my cuz, I shall bestow a banquet vpon you.
Hip. I neuer can deserue this kindnesse syr.
    What may this lady be, whom you call cuz?
Flu. Faith syr a poore gentlewoman, of passing good cariage, one that has some sutes in law, and lyes here in an Atturnies house.
Hip. Is she married?
Flu. Hah, as all your punks are, a captens wife, or so? neuer saw her before, my Lord?
Hip. Neuer, trust me a goodly creature.
Flu. By gad when you know her as we do, youle swear she is the prettiest, kindest, sweetest, most bewitching honest ape vnder the pole. A skin, your satten is not more soft, nor lawne whiter.
Hip. Belike then shees some sale curtizan.
Flu. Troth as all your best faces are, a good wench.
Hip. Great pitty that shees a good wench.
Math. Thou shalt haue it ifaith mistresse: how now signiors? what? whispering? did not I lay a wager I should take you within seuen daies in a house of vanity.
Hip. You did, and I beshrew your heart, you haue won.
Math. How do you like my mistresse?

Hip. Well, for such a mistresse: better, if your mistresse be not your master.
I must breake manners gentlemen, fare you well.
Math. Sfoote you shall not leaue vs.
Bell. The gentleman likes not the tast of our company.
Omn. Beseech you stay.
Hip. Trust me my affaires becken for me, pardon me.
Math. Will you call for me halfe an houre hence here?
Hip. Perhaps I shall.
Math. Perhaps? fah! I know you can, sweare to me you wil. 190
Hip. Since you will presse me, on my word I will. *Exit.*
Bell. What sullen picture is this, seruant?
Math. Its Count *Hipolito*, the braue Count.
Pio. As gallant a spirit, as any in *Millan* you sweete Iewe.
Flu. Oh hees a most essentiall gentleman, coz.
Cast. Did you neuer heare of Count *Hipolito*, acquaintance?
Bell. Marymuffe a your counts, and be no more life in 'em.
Math. Hees so malcontent! sirra *Bellafronte*, and you be honest gallants, lets sup together, and haue the count with vs: thou shalt sit at the vpper end puncke. 200
Bell. Puncke, you sowcde gurnet?
Math. Kings truce: come, ile bestow the supper to haue him but laugh.
Cast. He betraies his youth too grosly to that tyrant melancholy.
Math. All this is for a woman.
Bell. A woman! some whore! what sweet Iewell ist?
Pio. Wod she heard you.
Flu. Troth so wud I.
Cast. And I by heauen.
Bell. Nay good seruant, what woman? 210
Math. Pah.
Bell. Pry thee tell me, a busse and tell me: I warrant hees an honest fellowe, if hee take on thus for a wench: good roague who?

182 your] Q2(s); you Q1
190 can,] Q2(s); ~ ₐ Q1
196 *Hipolito*,] Dyce; *Hipolitos* ₐ Q1–2(s)–5
198 *Bellafronte*] Q2(s); *Bellafronta* Q1
204 melancholy] Q2(s); malancholy Q1

Math. Byth Lord I will not, must not, faith mistresse: ist a match sirs? this night, at *Th'antilop*: for thers best wine, and good boyes.
Omn. Its done, at *Th'antilop*.
Bell. I cannot be there to night.
Math. Cannot? bith lord you shall.
Bell. By the Lady I will not: shaall!
Flu. Why then put it off till fryday: wut come then cuz?   220
Bell. Well.   *Enter* Roger.
Math. Y'are the waspishest Ape. *Roger*, put your mistresse in mind, your scuruy mistris heere, to sup with vs on friday next: y'are best come like a madwoman without a band, in your wast-coate, and the lynings of your kirtle outward, like euery common hackney that steales out at the back gate of her sweet knights lodging.
Bell. Goe, goe, hang your selfe.
Cast. Its dinner time *Matheo*, shalls hence?
Omn. Yes, yes, farewell wench.   *Exeunt.* 230
Bell. Farewell boyes: *Roger* what wine sent they for?
Rog. Bastard wine, for if it had bin truly begotten, it wud not ha bin ashamde to come in, her's six shillings to pay for nursing the bastard.
Bell. A company of rookes! O good sweete *Roger*, run to the Poulters and buy me some fine Larkes.
Rog. No woodcocks?
Bell. Yes faith a couple, if they be not deare.
Rog. Ile buy but one, theres one already here.   *Exit.*

Enter Hipolito

Hip. Is the gentleman (my friend) departed mistresse?   240
Bell. His backe is but new-turnd syr.
Hip.   Fare you well.
Bell. I can direct you to him.
Hip.   Can you? pray.

   215 antilop: for] Q2(s) [antilop:,]; antilop: I, for Q.1
   216 line printed in italic Q1-2(s)-5
   223 mind, your scuruy mistris heere, to] Q2(s) [scurny]; mind to Q1 (Q2 has minor spelling variants not listed here since they probably arise from the new line-justification)

II. i] THE HONEST WHORE, PART I

Bell. If you please stay, heele not be absent long.
Hip. I care not much.
Bell.   Pray sit forsooth.
Hip.   I'me hot.
  If I may vse your roome, ile rather walke.
Bell. At your best pleasure — whew — some rubbers there.
Hip. Indeed ile non: — Indeed I will not: thanks.
  Pretty-fine-lodging. I perceiue my friend
  Is old in your acquaintance.
Bell.   Troth syr, he comes
  As other gentlemen, to spend spare howers;   250
  If your selfe like our roofe (such as it is)
  Your owne acquaintance may be as old as his.
Hip. Say I did like; what welcome should I find?
Bell. Such as my present fortunes can afford.
Hip. But would you let me play *Mathæos* part?
Bell. What part?
Hip.   Why imbrace you: dally with you, kisse:
  Faith tell me, will you leaue him, and loue me?
Bell. I am in bondes to no man syr.
Hip.   Why then,
  Y'are free for any man: if any, me.
  But I must tell you Lady, were you mine,   260
  You should be all mine: I could brooke no sharers,
  I should be couetous, and sweepe vp all.
  I should be pleasures vsurer: faith I should.
Bell. O fate!
Hip.   Why sigh you Lady? may I knowe?
Bell. T'has neuer bin my fortune yet to single
  Out that one man, whose loue could fellow mine,
  As I haue euer wisht it: ô my Stars!
  Had I but met with one kind gentleman,
  That would haue purchacde sin alone, to himselfe,
  For his owne priuate vse, although scarce proper: 270

  243 please stay, heele] Q1; pleasey   heele Q2(s) [*type dropped out*]
  245 If I may] Q2(s); *Hipo.* If may Q1
  *263 I should be] Q1–2(s); I would *catchword*

51   4-2

Indifferent hansome: meetly legd and thyed:
And my allowance reasonable — yfaith,
According to my body — by my troth,
I would haue bin as true vnto his pleasures,
Yea, and as loyall to his afternoones,
As euer a poore gentlewoman could be.
Hip. This were well now, to one but newly fledg'd,
And scarce a day old in this suttle world:
Twere prettie Art, good bird-lime: cunning net:
But come, come, faith — confesse: how many men   280
Haue drunke this selfe-same protestation,
From that red tycing lip?
Bell.   Indeed not any.
Hip. Indeed? and blush not!
Bell.   No, in truth not any.
Hip. Indeed! in truth! — how warily you sweare?
Tis well: if ill it be not: yet had I
The ruffian in me, and were drawne before you
But in light cullors, I doe know indeed,
You would not sweare indeede, But thunder oathes
That should shake heauen, drowne the harmonious sphers,
And pierce a soule (that lou'd her makers honour)   290
With horror and amazement.
Bell.   Shall I sweare?
Will you beleeue me then?
Hip.   Worst then of all,
Our sins by custome, seeme (at last) but small.
Were I but o're your threshold, a next man,
And after him a next, and then a fourth,
Should haue this golden hooke, and lasciuious baite,
Throwne out to the full length, why let me tell you:
I ha seene letters sent from that white hand,
Tuning such musicke to *Matheos* eare.
Bell. Mathæo! thats true, but if youle beleeue   300

288 would] Q2(r); could Q1
300–302 but if youle...heart.] Q2(s) [yonr]; but beleeue it, I | No sooner had laid hold vpon your presence, | But straight mine eye conueid you to my heart. Q1

My honest tongue, mine eyes no sooner met you,
But they conueid and lead you to my heart.
Hip. Oh, you cannot faine with me, why, I know Lady,
This is the common fashion of you all,
To hooke in a kind gentleman, and then
Abuse his coyne, conueying it to your louer,
And in the end you shew him a french trick,
And so you leaue him, that a coach may run
Betweene his legs for bredth.
Bell.   O by my soule!   310
Not I: therein ile proue an honest whore,
In being true to one, and to no more.
Hip. If any be disposde to trust your oath,
Let him: ile not be he. I know you feine
All that you speake, I: for a mingled harlot,
Is true in nothing but in being false.
What! shall I teach you how to loath your selfe?
And mildly too: not without sense or reason.
Bell. I am content, I would faine loath my selfe,
If you not loue me.
Hip.   Then if your gratious blood
Be not all wasted, I shall assay to doo't.   320
Lend me your silence, and attention, —
You haue no soule,
That makes you wey so light: heauens treasure bought it,
And halfe a crowne hath sold it: for your body,
Its like the common shoare, that still receiues
All the townes filth. The sin of many men
Is within you, and thus much I suppose,
That if all your committers stood in ranke,
Theide make a lane, (in which your shame might dwell)
And with their spaces reach from hence to hell.   330
Nay, shall I vrge it more, there has bene knowne,

    301 mine] Q1; my Q2(s?)   304 fashion] Q2(s); passion Q1
    314 I] *i.e.* aye (*see* III.i.22 *for similar pointing*)
    *319–327 Then if…much I suppose,] *see textual note*
    325 Its] Q2(s); Is Q1 (*see textual note to ll.* 319–327)
    327 Is] Q1; Tis Q2(s) (*see textual note to ll.* 319–327)

53

As many by one harlot, maym'd and dismembred,
As would ha stuft an Hospitall: this I might
Apply to you, and perhaps doe you right:
O y'are as base as any beast that beares,
Your body is ee'ne hirde, and so are theirs.
For gold and sparkling iewels, (if he can)
Youle let a Iewe get you with christian:
Be he a Moore, a Tartar, tho his face
Looke vglier then a dead mans scull,   340
Could the diuel put on a humane shape,
If his purse shake out crownes, vp then he gets,
Whores will be rid to hell with golden bits:
So that y'are crueller then Turkes, for they
Sell Christians onely, you sell your selues away.
Why those that loue you, hate you: and will terme you
Lickerish damnation: wish themselues halfe sunke
After the sin is laid out, and ee'ne curse
Their fruitlesse riot, (for what one begets
Another poisons) lust and murder hit,   350
A tree being often shooke, what fruit can knit?
Bell. O me vnhappy!
Hip.   I can vexe you more;
A harlot is like *Dunkirke*, true to none,
Swallowes both English, Spanish, fulsome Dutch,
Blacke-beard Italian, last of all the French,
And he sticks to you faith: giues you your diet,
Brings you acquainted, first with monsier Doctor,
And then you know what followes.
Bell.   Misery.
Ranke, stinking, and most loathsome misery.
Hip. Me thinks a toad is happier then a whore,   360
That with one poison swells, with thousands more
The other stocks her veines: harlot? fie! fie,
You are the miserablest Creatures breathing,
The very slaues of nature: marke me else,
You put on rich attires, others eyes weare them,

  *355 Blacke-beard] Blacke-doord Q 1–2(s)–5

54

You eat, but to supply your blood with sin,
And this strange curse ee'ne haunts you to your graues.
From fooles you get, and spend it vpon slaues:
Like Beares and Apes, y'are bayted and shew tricks
For money; but your Bawd the sweetnesse licks. 370
Indeed you are their Iourney-women, and doe
All base and damnd workes they list set you to:
So that you n'ere are rich; for doe but shew me,
In present memory, or in ages past,
The fayrest and most famous Courtezan,
Whose flesh was dear'st; that raisd the price of sin,
And held it vp; to whose intemperate bosome,
Princes, Earles, Lords, the worst has bin a knight,
The mean'st a Gentleman, haue offred vp
Whole Hecatombs of sighs, and raind in showres 380
Handfuls of gold, yet for all this, at last
Diseases suckt her marrow, then grew so poore,
That she has begd, e'ene at a beggers doore.
And (wherin heau'n has a finger) when this Idoll,
From coast to coast, has leapt on forrayne shores,
And had more worship, then th'outlandish whores:
When seuerall Nations haue gone ouer her,
When for eache seuerall City she has seene,
Her Maydenhead has bin new, and bin sold deare:
Did liue wel there, and might haue dyde vnknown, 390
And vndefam'd; back comes she to her owne,
And there both miserably liues and dyes,
Scornd euen of those, that once ador'd her eyes,
As if her fatall-circled life, thus ranne,
Her pride should end there, where it first began.
What do you weepe to heare your Story read?
Nay, if you spoyle your cheeks, Ile read no more.
Bell. O yes, I pray proceed:
Indeed 'twill do me good to weepe indeed.
Hip. To giue those teares a rellish, this I adde, 400
Y'are like the Iewes, scatterd, in no place certain,
Your daies are tedious, your houres burdensome:

And wer't not for full suppers, midnight Reuels,
Dauncing, wine, ryotous meetings, which doe drowne,
And bury quite in you all vertuous thoughts,
And on your eye-lids hang so heauily,
They haue no power to looke so high as heauen,
Youde sit and muse on nothing but despayre,
Curse that deuil *Lust*, that so burnes vp your blood,
And in ten thousand shiuers breake your glasse 410
For his temptation. Say you taste delight,
To haue a golden Gull from rize to Set,
To meat you in his hote luxurious armes,
Yet your nights pay for all: I know you dreame
Of warrants, whips, and Beadles, and then start
At a dores windy creake: thinke euery Weezle
To be a Constable: and euery Rat
A long tayld Officer: Are you now not slaues?
Oh you haue damnation without pleasure for it!
Such is the state of Harlots. To conclude, 420
When you are old, and can well paynt no more,
You turne Bawd, and are then worse then before:
Make vse of this: farewell.
Bell.   Oh, I pray stay.
Hip. I see *Matheo* comes not: time hath bard me,
Would all the Harlots in the towne had heard me.   *Exit.*
Bell. Stay yet a little longer. No: quite gone!
Curst be that minute (for it was no more,
So soone a mayd is chang'd into a Whore)
Wherein I first fell, be it for euer blacke;
Yet why should sweet *Hipolito* shun mine eyes; 430
For whose true loue I would becom pure-honest,
Hate the worlds mixtures, and the smiles of gold:
Am I not fayre? Why should he flye me then?
Faire creatures are desir'd, not scornd of men.
How many Gallants haue drunk healthes to me,
Out of their daggerd armes, and thought them blest,
Enioying but mine eyes at prodigall feasts!

        424 I see] Q2(s); See Q1

And does *Hipolito* detest my loue?
Oh, sure their heedlesse lusts, but flattred me,
I am not pleasing, beautifull nor young.   440
Hipolito hath spyed some vgly blemish,
Eclipsing all my beauties: I am foule:
Harlot! I, that's the spot that taynts my soule:
His weapon left heere? O fit instrument,
To let forth all the poyson of my flesh!
Thy Maister hates me, cause my bloud hath rang'd:
But when tis forth, then heele beleeue Ime chang'd.

     Enter Hipolito.

Hip. Mad woman, what art doing?
Bell.   Eyther loue me,
Or cleaue my bosome on thy Rapiers poynt:
Yet doe not neyther; for thou then destroyst   450
That which I loue thee for (thy vertues) here, here,
Th'art crueller, and kilst me with disdayne:
To die so, sheds no bloud, yet tis worse payne. *Exit* Hipolito.
Not speake to me! not looke! not bid farewell!
Hated! this must not be, some meanes Ile try.
Would all Whores were as honest now, as I.
               Exit.

[ACT III, Scene i]

Enter Candido, *his* Wife, George, *and two Prentices in the shop*: Fustigo *enters, walking by.*

Geo. See Gentlemen, what you lack? a fine Holland, a fine Cambrick, see what you buy.

1. *Prent.* Holland for shirts, Cambrick for bands, what ist you lack?

  444 His weapon...instrument,] Q2(s); What! has he left his weapon heere behind him, | And gone forgetfull? O fit instrument ₐ Q1
  449 Or cleaue...on] Q2(s); Or split my heart vpon Q1
  454 not looke...farewell!] Q2(s); not bid farewell! a scorne! Q1
  456 S.D. *Exit.*] D¹; *Exeunt.* Q1–2(s)–5
  S.H. ACT III, Scene i] Dyce; SCENA 7. Q1–2(s)–5

Fust. Sfoot, I lack em all, nay more, I lack money to buy em: let me see, let me looke agen: masse this is the shop; What Coz! sweet Coz! how dost ifayth, since last night after candlelight? we had good sport ifayth, had we not? and when shals laugh agen?
Wife. When you will, Cozen.
Fust. Spoke like a kind Lacedemonian: I see yonders thy husband.
Wife. I, ther's the sweet youth, God blesse him.
Fust. And how ist Cozen? and how? how ist thou squall?
Wife. Well, Cozen, how fare you?
Fust. How fare I? troth, for sixpence a meale, wench, as wel as heart can wish, with Calues chaldrons and chitterlings, besides I haue a *Punck* after supper, as good as a rosted Apple.
Cand. Are you my wiues Cozen?
Fust. I am, sir, what hast thou to do with that?
Cand. O, nothing but y'are welcome.
Fust. The Deuils dung in thy teeth: Ile be welcom whether thou wilt or no, I: What Ring's this Coz? very pretty and fantasticall ifayth, lets see it.
Wife. Puh! nay you wrench my finger.
Fust. I ha sworne Ile ha't, and I hope you wil not let my othes be crackt in the ring, wil you? I hope, sir, you are not mallicolly at this for all your great lookes: are you angry?
Cand. Angry? not I sir, nay, if she can part
So easily with her Ring, tis with my heart.
Geo. Suffer this, sir, and suffer all, a whoreson Gull, to —
Cand. Peace, *George*, when she has reapt what I haue sown,
Sheele say, one grayne tastes better of her owne,
Then whole sheaues gatherd from anothers land:
Wit's neuer good, till bought at a deare hand.
Geo. But in the meane time she makes an Asse of some body.
2. *Prent.* See, see, see, sir, as you turne your backe, they doe nothing but kisse.
Cand. No matter, let 'em: when I touch her lip,
I shall not feele his kisses, no nor misse

19 I] Q2(s); A Q1

Any of her lip: no harme in kissing is. 40
Looke to your businesse, pray, make vp your wares.
Fust. Troth Coz, and well remembred, I would thou wouldst giue mee fiue yards of Lawne, to make my *Punke* some falling bands a the fashion, three falling one vpon another: for that's the new edition now: she's out of linnen horribly too, troth, sha's neuer a good smock to her back neyther, but one that has a great many patches in't, and that I'm faine to weare my selfe for want of shift to: prithee put me into holesom napery, and bestow some cleane commodities vpon vs.
Wife. Reach me those Cambricks, and the Lawnes hither. 50
Cand. What to doe wife? to lauish out my goods vpon a foole?
Fust. Foole! Sneales, eate the foole, or Ile so batter your crowne, that it shall scarce go for fiue shillings.
2. *Prent.* Do you heare sir? y'are best be quiet, and say a foole tels you so.
Fust. Nailes, I think so, for thou telst me.
Cand. Are you angry sir, because I namde the foole?
Trust me, you are not wise, in mine owne house;
And to my face to play the Anticke thus:
If youle needs play the madman, choose a stage 60
Of lesser compasse, where few eyes may note
Your actions errour; but if still you misse,
As heere you doe, for one clap, ten will hisse.
Fust. Zwounds Cozen, he talks to me, as if I were a scuruy Tragedian.
2. *Prent.* Sirra *George*, I ha thought vpon a deuice, how to breake his pate, beat him soundly, and ship him away.
Geo. Doo't.
2. *Prent.* Ile go in, passe thorow the house, giue some of our fellow Prentices the watch-word when they shal enter, then come 70
and fetch my master in by a wile, and place one in the hall to hold him in conference, whilst we cudgell the Gull out of his coxcombe.
Geo. Doo't: away, doo't.
Wife. Must I call twice for these Cambricks and lawnes?
Cand. Nay see, you anger her, *George*, prithee dispatch.

*40 lip] Q1; lips Q2(r) 57 the] *i.e.*, thee

THE HONEST WHORE, PART I   [III. i

2. *Prent.*   Two of the choisest pieces are in the warehouse sir.
Cand.   Go fetch them presently.   *Exit* 2. *Prentice.*
Fust.   I, do, make haste, sirra.
Cand.   Why were you such a stranger all this while, being my
wiues Cozen?   80
Fust.   Stranger? no sir, Ime a natural Millaner borne.
Cand.   I perceyue still it is your naturall guize to mistake me, but
you are welcom sir, I much wish your acquaintance.
Fust.   My acquaintance? I scorne that ifayth; I hope my acquaint-
ance goes in chaines of gold three and fifty times double: you
know who I meane, Coz, the posts of his gate are a paynting to.

Enter the 2. *Prentice.*

2. *Prent.*   Signior *Pandulfo* the Marchant desires conference with
you.
Cand.   Signior *Pandulfo*? Ile be with him straight.
Attend your mistris and the Gentleman.   *Exit.* 90
Wife.   When do you shew those pieces?
Fust.   I, when doe you shew those pieces?
Omn.   Presently sir, presently, we are but charging them.
Fust.   Come sirra, you Flat-cap, where be these whites?
Geo.   Flat-cap? heark in your eare sir, yare a flat foole, an Asse,
a gull, and Ile thrum you: do you see this cambrick sir?
Fust.   Sfoot, Coz, a good iest, did you heare him? he told me in
my eare, I was a flat foole, an Asse, a Gull, and Ile thrum you: doe
you see this Cambrick sir?
Wife.   What, not my men, I hope?   100
Fust.   No, not your men, but one of your men ifayth.
1. *Prent.*   I pray sir, come hither, what say you to this? heres an
excellent good one.
Fust.   I marry, this likes me well, cut me off some halfe score yards.
2. *Prent.*   Let your whores cut, yare an impudent coxcomb, you
get none, and yet Ile thrum you. — A very good Cambrick sir.

*77 S.D. 2. *Prentice.*] 1. *Prentice.* Q1–2(r)–5
92 *Fust.* I, when...pieces?] Q1; *om.* Q2(r)
98 thrum] Q2(s); thrumb Q1
102 heres Q2(s); here Q1

60

III. i] THE HONEST WHORE, PART I

Fust. Agen, agen, as God iudge me: Sfoot, Coz, they stand thrumming here with me all day, and yet I get nothing.
1. *Prent.* A word I pray sir, you must not be angry, prentices haue hote blouds, young fellowes, — What say you to this piece? looke you, tis so delicate, so soft, so euen, so fine a thrid, that a Lady may weare it.
Fust. Sfoot I thinke so, if a Knight marry my Punck, a Lady shall weare it: cut me off twenty yards: th'art an honest lad.
1. *Prent.* Not without mony, gull, and ile thrum you to.
Omn. Gull, weele thrum you.
Fust. O Lord, sister, did you not heare something cry thump? zounds your men here make a plaine Asse of me.
Wife. What, to my face so impudent?
Geo. I, in a cause so honest, weele not suffer
Our masters goods to vanish monylesse.
Wife. You will not suffer them.
2. *Prent.*   No, and you may blush,
In going about to vex so mild a brest,
As is our masters.
Wife.   Take away those pieces.
Cozen, I giue them freely.
Fust. Masse, and Ile take em as freely.
Omn. Weele make you lay em down agen more freely.
                              [*Beat* Fustigo.]
Wife. Help, help, my brother wilbe murdered.

           Enter Candido.

Cand. How now, what coyle is here? forbeare, I say.
Geo. He cals vs Flatcaps, and abuses vs.
Cand. Why, sirs? do such examples flow from me?
Wife. They are of your keeping sir, alas poore brother.
Fust. I fayth they ha pepperd me, sister: looke, doost not spin? call you these Prentices? Ile nere play at cards more when clubs is trump: I haue a goodly coxcomb, sister, haue I not?

117 thump] Q2(s); thrum Q1
133 doost] *i.e.* doos't *or* does it (the head) spin

Cand. Sister and brother, brother to my wife.
Fust. If you haue any skill in Heraldry, you may soone know that, breake but her pate, and you shal see her blood and mine is all one.
Cand. A Surgeon, run, a Surgeon: [*Exit* 1. *Prent.*]
Why then wore you that forged name of Cozen?
Fust. Because its a common thing to call Coz, and Ningle now adayes all the world ouer.
Cand. Cozen! A name of much deceyt, folly and sin,
For vnder that common abused word,
Many an honest tempred Cityzen
Is made a monster, and his wife traynd out
To foule adulterous action, full of fraud.
I may well call that word, A Cities Bawd.
Fust. Troth, brother, my sister would needs ha me take vpon me to gull your patience a little: but it has made double Gules on my coxcomb.
Wife. What, playing the woman? blabbing now you foole?
Cand. O, my wife did but exercise a iest vpon your wit.
Fust. Sfoot, my wit bleeds for't, me thinks.
Cand. Then let this warning more of sence afford.
The name of Cozen is a bloudy word.
Fust. Ile nere call Coz agen whilst I liue, to haue such a coyle about it: this should be a Coronation day; for my head runnes Claret lustily. *Exit.*

Enter an Officer.

Cand. Go wish the Surgeon to haue great respect.
[*Exit* 2. *Prent.*]
How now, my friend, what, do they sit to day?
Off. Yes sir, they expect you at the Senate-house.
Cand. I thank your paines, Ile not be last man there.
Exit Officer.
My gowne, *George*, goe, my gowne. A happy land,
Where graue men meet each cause to vnderstand,
Whose consciences are not cut out in brybes,
To gull the poore mans right: but in euen scales,

141 Ningle] Q2(s); mingle Q1

Peize rich and poore, without corruptions veyles.
Come, wheres the gowne?
Geo. I cannot find the key sir. 170
Cand. Request it of your mistris.
Wife. Come not to me for any key.
Ile not be troubled to deliuer it.
Cand. Good wife, kind wife, it is a needfull trouble,
But for my gowne.
Wife. Mothes swallow downe your gowne:
You set my teeth an edge with talking on't.
Cand. Nay prythee, sweet, I cannot meet without it,
I should haue a great fine set on my head.
Wife. Set on your coxcomb: tush, fine me no fines.
Cand. Beleeue me (sweet) none greets the Senate-house, 180
Without his Robe of reuerence, that's his Gowne.
Wife. Wel, then y'are like to crosse that custome once,
You get nor key, nor gowne, and so depart:
This tricke will vexe him sure, and fret his heart. *Exit.*
Cand. Stay, let me see, I must haue some deuice,
My cloke's too short: fy, fy, no cloke will doo't:
It must be something fashioned like a gowne,
With my armes out: oh *George*, come hither *George*,
I prythee lend me thine aduice.
Geo. Troth sir, were it any but you, they would break open chest. 190
Cand. O no, breake open chest! thats a Theeues office:
Therein you counsell me against my bloud:
'Twould shew impatience that, any meeke meanes
I would be glad to imbrace. Masse I haue got it:
Go, step vp, fetch me downe one of the Carpets,
The saddest colourd Carpet, honest *George*,
Cut thou a hole ith middle for my necke,
Two for mine armes, nay prithee looke not strange.
Geo. I hope you doe not thinke sir, as you meane.
Cand. Prithee about it quickly, the houre chides me: 200
Warily *George*, softly, take heed of eyes. *Exit* George.
Out of two euils hee's accounted wise,
That can picke out the least; the Fine imposde

For an vn-gowned Senator, is about
Forty Cruzadoes, the Carpet not 'boue foure.
Thus haue I chosen the lesser euill yet,
Preseru'd my patience, foyld her desperate wit.

Enter George.

Geo. Here, sir, heer's the Carpet.
Cand. O well done, *George*, weele cut it iust ith midst:
Tis very well I thanke thee, helpe it on.
Geo. It must come ouer your head, sir, like a wenches peticoate.
Cand. Th'art in the right, good *George*, it must indeed.
Fetch me a nightcap: for Ile gyrd it close,
As if my health were queazy: 'twill show well
For a rude carelesse night-gowne, wil't not thinkst?
Geo. Indifferent wel, sir, for a night-gowne, being girt and pleated.
Cand. I, and a night-cap on my head.
Geo. Thats true sir, Ile run and fetch one, and a staffe.
Exit George.
Cand. For thus they cannot chuse but conster it,
One that is out of health, takes no delight,
Weares his apparell without appetite,
And puts on heedles rayment without forme. *Enter* George.
So so, kind *George*, be secret now: and prithee
Do not laugh at me till Ime out of sight.
Geo. I laugh? not I sir.
Cand. Now to the Senate-house:
Me thinks, Ide rather weare, without a frowne,
A patient Carpet, then an angry Gowne. *Exit.*
Geo. Now looks my Master iust like one of our carpet knights,
only hee's somwhat the honester of the two.

Enter Candidoes Wife.

Wife. What, is your master gone?
Geo. Yes forsooth, his backe is but new turnd.
Wife. And in his cloke? did he not vexe and sweare?
Geo. No, but heele make you sweare anon: no indeed, hee went away like a lambe.

Wife. Key sinke to hell: still patient, patient still!
I am with child to vexe him: prythee *George*,
If ere thou lookst for fauour at my hands,
Vphold one Iest for me.
Geo. Against my master? 240
Wife. Tis a meere iest in fayth: say, wilt thou doo't?
Geo. Well, what ist?
Wife. Heere, take this key, thou knowst where all things lie,
Put on thy masters best apparell, Gowne,
Chayne, Cap, Ruffe, euery thing, be like himselfe,
And 'gainst his comming home, walke in the shop,
Fayne the same cariage, and his patient looke,
'Twill breed but a iest thou knowst, speake, wilt thou?
Geo. 'Twill wrong my masters patience.
Wife. Prythee *George*. 250
Geo. Well, if youle saue me harmlesse, and put me vnder couert barne, I am content to please you, prouided it may breed no wrong against him.
Wife. No wrong at all: here take the Key, be gone:
If any vex him, this: if not this, none.
                                                    Exeunt.

[ACT III, SCENE ii]

Enter a Bawd *and* Roger.

Bawd. O *Roger*, *Roger*, where's your mistris, wher's your mistris? there's the finest, neatest Gentleman at my house, but newly come ouer: O where is she, where is she, where is she?
Rog. My mistris is abroad, but not amongst em: my mistris is not the whore now that you take her for.
Bawd. How? is she not a whore? do you go about to take away her good name, *Roger*? you are a fine Pandar indeed.
Rog. I tell you, *Madona Finger-locke*, I am not sad for nothing, I ha not eaten one good meale this three and thirty dayes: I had wont to get sixteene pence by fetching a pottle of Hypocras: but 10

S.H. ACT III, Scene ii] Dyce; SCENA. 8. Q1–2(s)–5

now those dayes are past: we had as good doings, *Madona Finger-locke*, she within dores and I without, as any poore yong couple in *Millain*.

Bawd. Gods my life, and is she chang'd now?

Rog. I ha lost by her squeamishnesse, more then would haue builded twelue bawdy houses.

Bawd. And had she no time to turn honest but now? what a vile woman is this? twenty pound a night, Ile be sworne, *Roger*, in good gold and no siluer: why here was a time, if she should ha pickt out a time, it could not be better! gold ynough stirring; choyce of men, choyce of haire, choyce of beards, choyce of legs, and choyce of euery, euery, euery thing: it cannot sink into my head, that she should be such an Asse. *Roger*, I neuer beleeue it.

Rog. Here she comes now.

Enter Bellafronte.

Bawd. O sweet *Madona*, on with your loose gowne, your felt and your feather, there's the sweetest, propest, gallantest Gentleman at my house, he smells all of Muske and Amber greece, his pocket full of Crownes, flame-colour'd dublet, red satin hose, Carnation silk stockins, and a leg and a body, oh!

Bell. Hence, thou our sexes monster, poysonous Bawd,
Lusts Factor, and damnations Orator,
Gossip of hell, were all the Harlots sinnes
Which the whole world conteynes, numbred together,
Thine farre exceeds them all; of all the creatures
That euer were created, thou art basest:
What serpent would beguile thee of thy Office?
It is detestable: for thou liu'st
Vpon the dregs of Harlots, guard'st the dore,
Whilst couples goe to dauncing: O course deuill!
Thou art the bastards curse, thou brandst his birth,
The lechers French disease; for thou dry-suckst him:
The Harlots poyson, and thine owne confusion.

Bawd. Mary come vp with a pox, haue you no body to raile against, but your Bawd now?

17 *Bawd.*] Q 4; *om.* Q 1–2(s)–3

Bell. And you, Knaue Pandar, kinsman to a Bawd.
Rog. You and I, *Madona*, are Cozens.
Bell. Of the same bloud and making, neere allyed,
Thou, that slaue to sixpence, base-mettald villayne.
Rog. Sixpence? nay that's not so; I neuer took vnder two shillings foure pence, I hope I know my fee.
Bell. I know not against which most to inueigh:
For both of you are damnd so equally.
Thou neuer spar'st for oathes: swearst any thing,
As if thy soule were made of shoe-leather.
God dam me, Gentleman, if she be within,
When in the next roome she's found dallying.
Rog. If it be my vocation to sweare, euery man in his vocation: I hope my betters sweare and dam themselues, and why should not I?
Bell. *Roger*, you cheat kind gentlemen?
Rog. The more gulls they.
Bell. Slaue, I casheere thee.
Bawd. And you do casheere him, he shalbe entertaynd.
Rog. Shall I? then blurt a your seruice.
Bell. As hell would haue it, entertaynd by you!
I dare the deuill himselfe to match those two. *Exit.*
Bawd. Mary gup, are you growne so holy, so pure, so honest with a pox?
Rog. Scuruy honest Punck! But stay *Madona*, how must our agreement be now? for you know I am to haue all the commings in at the hall dore, and you at the chamber dore.
Bawd. True *Roger* except my vailes.
Rog. Vailes, what vailes?
Bawd. Why as thus, if a couple come in a Coach, and light to lie down a little, then *Roger*, thats my fee, and you may walk abroad; for the Coach-man himselfe is their Pandar.
Rog. Is a so? in truth I haue almost forgot, for want of exercise: But how if I fetch this Citizens wife to that Gull, and that *Madona* to that Gallant, how then?

*48 that slaue] *stet* Q 1–2 (s)

Bawd. Why then, *Roger*, you are to haue sixpence a lane, so many 80
lanes, so many sixpences.
Rog. Ist so? then I see we two shall agree and liue together.
Bawd. I *Roger*, so long as there be any Tauernes and bawdy
houses in *Millain*.

Exeunt.

[ACT III, Scene iii]

Enter Bellafronte *with a Lute, pen, inke and paper being placde before her.*

Song.

The Courtiers flattring Iewels,
(Temptations onely fewels)
The Lawyers ill-got monyes,
That sucke vp poore Bees Honyes:
The Citizens sonne's ryot,
The gallants costly dyet:
Silks and Veluets, Pearles and Ambers,
Shall not draw me to their Chambers.
Silks and Veluets, &c.   Shee writes.

Oh, tis in vayne to write: it will not please,   10
Inke on this paper would ha but presented
The foule blacke spots that sticke vpon my soule,
And rather make me lothsomer, then wrought
My loues impression in *Hipolitoes* thought.
No, I must turne the chaste leaues of my brest,
And pick out some sweet meanes to breed my rest.
Hipolito, beleeue me I will be
As true vnto thy heart, as thy heart to thee,
And hate all men, their gifts and company.

S.H. ACT III, Scene iii] Dyce; SCENA 9. Q1–2(s)–5
6 *gallants*] D¹; *gallant* Q1–2(s)–5

Enter Matheo, Castruchio, Fluello, Pioratto.

Math. You, goody Punck, *subaudi* Cockatrice, O yare a sweet whore of your promise, are you not think you? how wel you came to supper to vs last night: mew, a whore and breake her word! nay you may blush, and hold downe your head at it wel ynough: Sfoot, aske these gallants if we staid not till we were as hungry as Seriants.

Flu. I, and their Yeoman too.

Cast. Nay fayth *Acquaintance*, let me tell you, you forgat your selfe too much: we had excellent cheere, rare vintage, and were drunke after supper.

Pio. And when wee were in our Woodcocks (sweete Rogue) a brace of Gulles, dwelling here in the City, came in and payd all the shot.

Math. Pox on her, let her alone.

Bell. O, I pray doe, if you be Gentlemen:
I pray depart the house; beshrew the dore
For being so easily entreated: fayth,
I lent but little eare vnto your talke,
My mind was busied otherwise in troth,
And so your words did vnregarded passe:
Let this suffice, I am not as I was.

Flu. I am not what I was! no Ile be sworne thou art not: for thou wert honest at fiue, and now th'art a Puncke at fifteene: thou wert yesterday a simple whore, and now th'art a cunning Conny-catching Baggage to day.

Bell. Ile say Ime worse, I pray forsake me then,
I doe desire you leaue me, Gentlemen,
And leaue your selues: O be not what you are,
(Spendthrifts of soule and body)
Let me perswade you to forsake all Harlots,
Worse then the deadliest poysons, they are worse:
For o're their soules hangs an eternall curse,
In being slaues to slaues, their labours perish,

19 S.D. *Fluello,*] Q1; *Fluello, and* Q2(s)
52 being slaues] Q1; being slaue Q2(r)

Th'are seldome blest with fruit; for ere it blossoms,
Many a worme confounds it.
They haue no issue but foule vgly ones,
That run along with them, e'ene to their graues:
For stead of children, they breed ranke diseases,
And all, you Gallants, can bestow on them,
Is that French Infant, which n'ere acts but speaks:
What shallow sonne and heire then, foolish gallant, 60
Would waste all his inheritance, to purchase
A filthy loathd disease? and pawne his body
To a dry euill: that vsurie's worst of all,
When th'interest will eate out the principall.

Math. Sfoot, she guls em the best: this is alwaies her fashion, when she would be rid of any company that she cares not for, to inioy mine alone.

Flu. Whats here? instructions, Admonitions, and Caueats? come out, you scabberd of vengeance.

Math. *Fluello,* spurne your hounds when they fyste, you shall 70 not spurne my Punk, I can tell you my bloud is vext.

Flu. Pox a your bloud: make it a quarrell.

Math. Y'are a Slaue, will that serue turne?

Omn. Sbloud, hold, hold.

Cast. *Matheo, Fluello,* for shame put vp.

Math. Spurne my sweet Varlet!

Bell. O how many thus
Mou'd with a little folly, haue let out
Their soules in Brothell houses, fell downe and dyed
Iust at their Harlots foot, as 'twere in pride. 80

Flu. *Matheo,* we shall meet.

Math. I, I, any where, sauing at Church: pray take heed we meet not there.

Flu. Adue, Damnation.

Cast. Cockatrice, farewell.

Pio. There's more deceit in women, then in hel. *Exeunt.*

Math. Ha, ha, thou doest gull em so rarely, so naturally: if I did

---

53 blossoms] Q 1; blossom Q 2 (r)

not think thou hadst bin in earnest: thou art a sweet Rogue for't
ifayth.
Bell. Why are not you gone to, Signior *Matheo*?
I pray depart my house: you may beleeue me,
In troth I haue no part of Harlot in me.
Math. How's this?
Bell. Indeed I loue you not: but hate you worse
Then any man, because you were the first
Gaue money for my soule; you brake the Ice,
Which after turnd a puddle: I was led
By your temptation to be miserable:
I pray seeke out some other that will fall,
Or rather (I pray) seeke out none at all.
Math. Ist possible, to be impossible, an honest whore! I haue
heard many honest wenches turne strumpets with a wet finger;
but for a Harlot to turne honest, is one of *Hercules* labours: It was
more easie for him in one night to make fifty queanes, then to make
one of them honest agen in fifty yeeres: come, I hope thou doost
but iest.
Bell. Tis time to leaue off iesting, I had almost
Iested away Saluation: I shall loue you,
If you will soone forsake me.
Math. God buy thee.
Bell. Oh, tempt no more women: shun their weighty curse,
Women (at best) are bad, make them not worse,
You gladly seeke our sexes ouerthrow,
But not to rayse our states: for all your wrongs,
Will you vouchsafe me but due recompence,
To marry with me?
Math. How, marry with a Punck, a Cockatrice, a Harlot? mary
foh, Ile be burnt thorow the nose first.
Bell. Why la? these are your othes: you loue to vndo vs,
To put heauen from vs, whilst our best houres waste:
You loue to make vs lewd, but neuer chaste.
Math. Ile heare no more of this: this ground vpon,
Th'art damn'd for altring thy Religion.   *Exit.*

106 *Bell.*] Q2(s); ~, Q1

Bell. Thy lust and sin speake so much: go thou my ruine,
The first fall my soule tooke; by my example
I hope few maydens now will put their heads
Vnder mens girdels: who least trusts, is most wise:
Mens othes do cast a mist before our eyes.
My best of wit be ready: now I goe,
By some deuice to greet *Hipolito*.

[*Exit.*]

[ACT IV, SCENE i]

*Enter a seruant setting out a Table, on which he places
a scull, a picture, a booke and a Taper.*

Seru. So, this is Monday morning, and now must I to my huswifry: would I had bin created a Shoomaker; for all the gentle craft are gentlemen euery Monday by their Copy, and scorne (then) to worke one true stitch. My master meanes sure to turne me into a student; for here's my booke, here my deske, here my light; this my close chamber, and heere my Punck: so that this dull drowzy first day of the weeke, makes me halfe a Priest, halfe a Chandler, halfe a paynter, halfe a Sexton, I and halfe a Bawd: for (all this day) my office is to do nothing but keep the dore. To proue it, looke you, this good-face and yonder gentleman (so soone as euer my back's turnd) wilbe naught together.

Enter Hipolito.

Hip. Are all the windowes shut?
Seru. Close sir, as the fist of a Courtier that hath stood in three raignes.
Hip. Thou art a faythfull seruant, and obseru'st
The Calender, both of my solemne vowes,
And ceremonious sorrow: Get thee gone,
I charge thee on thy life, let not the sound
Of any womans voyce pierce through that dore.

S.H. ACT IV, Scene i] Dyce; SCENA 10. Q1–2(s)–5

Seru. If they do, my Lord, Ile pearce some of them. What will your Lordship haue to breakfast?
Hip. Sighs.
Seru. What to dinner?
Hip. Teares.
Seru. The one of them, my Lord, will fill you too full of wind, the other wet you too much. What to supper?
Hip. That which (now) thou canst not get me, the constancy of a woman.
Seru. Indeed thats harder to come by then euer was *Ostend*.
Hip. Prythee away.
Seru. Ile make away my selfe presently, which few Seruants will doe for their Lords; but rather helpe to make them away: Now to my dore-keeping, I hope to picke something out of it. *Exit.*
Hip. My *Infelices* face: her brow, her eye,
The dimple on her cheeke: and such sweet skill,
Hath from the cunning workemans pencill flowne,
These lippes looke fresh and liuely as her owne,
Seeming to mooue and speake. Las! now I see,
The reason why fond women loue to buy
Adulterate complexion: here 'tis read,
False coulours last after the true be dead.
Of all the Roses grafted on her cheekes,
Of all the graces dauncing in her eyes,
Of all the Musick set vpon her tongue,
Of all that was past womans excellence,
In her white bosome, looke! a painted board,
Circumscribes all: Earth can no blisse affoord.
Nothing of her, but this? this cannot speake,
It has no lap for me to rest vpon,
No lip worth tasting: here the wormes will feed,
As in her coffin: hence then idle Art,
True loue's best picturde in a true-loues heart.
Here art thou drawne sweet maid, till this be dead,
So that thou liu'st twice, twice art buried.
Thou figure of my friend, lye there. Whats here?
Perhaps this shrewd pate was mine enimies:

Las! say it were: I need not feare him now:
For all his braues, his contumelious breath,
His frownes (tho dagger-pointed) all his plot,
(Tho 'nere so mischieuous) his Italian pilles,
His quarrels, and (that common fence) his law,
See, see, they're all eaten out; here's not left one;
How cleane they're pickt away! to the bare bone!
How mad are mortals then to reare great names
On tops of swelling houses? or to weare out
Their fingers ends (in durt,) to scrape vp gould!
Not caring so (that Sumpter-horse) the back
Be hung with gawdy trappings, with what course,
Yea rags most beggerly, they cloath the soule:
Yet (after all) their *Gay-nes* lookes thus foule.
What fooles are men to build a garish tombe,
Onely to saue the carcasse whilst it rots,
To maintein't long in stincking, make good carion,
But leaue no good deeds to preserue them sound,
For good deedes keepe men sweet, long aboue ground.
And must all come to this; fooles, wise, all hether;
Must all heads thus at last be laid together:
Draw me my picture then, thou graue neate workeman,
After this fashion, not like this; these coulours
In time kissing but ayre, will be kist off,
But heres a fellow; that which he layes on,
Till doomes day, alters not complexion.
Death's the best Painter then: They that draw shapes,
And liue by wicked faces, are but Gods Apes,
They come but neere the life, and there they stay.
This fellow drawes life to: his Art is fuller,
The pictures which he makes are without coulour.

Enter his seruant.

Seru. Heres a person would speake with you Sir.
Hip. Hah!
Seru. A parson sir would speake with you.

59 plot] Q1; plots Q2(r)   *84 wicked] *stet* Q1–2(r)

Hip. Vicar?
Seru. Vicar? no sir, has too good a face to be a Vicar yet, a youth, a very youth.
Hip. What youth? of man or woman? lock the dores.
Seru. If it be a woman, mary-bones and Potato pies keepe me for medling with her, for the thing has got the breeches, tis a male-varlet sure my Lord, for a womans tayler nere measurd him.
Hip. Let him giue thee his message and be gone.
Seru. He sayes hees signior *Mathæos* man, but I know he lyes.
Hip. How doest thou know it? 100
Seru. Cause has nere a beard: tis his boy I thinke sir, whosoere paide for his nursing.
Hip. Send him and keepe the doore. [*Exit seruant.*]
 Fata si liceat mihi,   *Reades.*
 Fingere arbitrio meo,
 Temperem Zephyro leui.
 Vela.
Ide saile were I to choose, not in the Ocean,
Cedars are shaken, when shrubs doe feele no bruize,

    Enter Bellafronte *like a Page.*

How? from *Mathæo.*
Bell.   Yes my Lord.
Hip.   Art sick? 110
Bell. Not all in health my Lord.
Hip.   Keepe off.
Bell.   I do:
Hard fate when women are compeld to wooe. [*Aside.*]
Hip. This paper does speake nothing.
Bell.   Yes my Lord,
Matter of life it speakes, and therefore writ
In hidden Caracter; to me instruction
My maister giues, And (lesse you please to stay
Till you both meet) I can the text display.
Hip. Doe so: read out.
Bell.   I am already out:
Looke on my face, and read the strangest story!

Hip. What villaine, ho? *Enter his seruant.* 120
Seru. Call you my Lord?
Hip. Thou slaue, thou hast let in the diuell.
Seru. Lord blesse vs, where? hees not clouen my Lord that I can
see: besides the diuell goes more like a Gentleman than a Page:
good my Lord *Boon couragio.*
Hip. Thou hast let in a woman, in mans shape.
And thou art dambd for't.
Seru. Not dambd I hope for putting in a woman to a Lord.
Hip. Fetch me my Rapier, — do not: I shall kill thee.
Purge this infected chamber of that plague, 130
That runnes vpon me thus: Slaue, thrust her hence.
Seru. Alas my Lord, I shall neuer be able to thrust her hence
without helpe: come Mermaid you must to Sea agen.
Bell. Here me but speake, my words shall be all Musick:
Here me but speake.
Hip. Another beates the dore,
T'other Shee-diuell, looke.
Seru. Why then hell's broke loose.
Hip. Hence, guard the chamber: let no more come on,
Exit [seruant].
One woman serues for mans damnation.
Beshrew thee, thou doost make me violate, 140
The chastest and most sanctimonious vow,
That ere was entred in the court of heauen:
I was on meditations spottles wings,
Vpon my iorney thether; like a storme
Thou beats my ripened cogitations,
Flat to the ground: and like a theife doost stand,
To steale deuotion from the holy land.
Bell. If woman were thy mother; if thy hart,
Bee not all Marble, (or ift Marble be)
Let my teares soften it, to pitty me, 150
I doe beseech thee doe not thus with scorne,
Destroy a woman.
Hip. Woman I beseech thee,
Get thee some other suite, this fits thee not,

I would not grant it to a kneeling Queene,
I cannot loue thee, nor I must not: See,
The copy of that obligation,
Where my soule's bound in heauy penalties.
Bell. She's dead you told me, shele let fal her suite.
Hip. My vowes to her, fled after her to heauen,
  Were thine eyes cleere as mine, thou mightst behold her, 160
Watching vpon yon battlements of starres,
How I obserue them: should I breake my bond,
This bord would riue in twaine, these wooden lippes
Call me most periurde villaine, let it suffice,
I ha set thee in the path; Ist not a signe,
I loue thee, when with one so most most deare,
Ile haue thee fellowes? All are fellowes there.
Bell. Be greater then a king, saue not a body,
But from eternall shipwracke keepe a soule,
If not, and that againe, sinnes path I tread, 170
The griefe be mine, the guilt fall on thy head.
Hip. Stay and take Phisicke for it, read this booke,
Aske counsell of this head whats to be done,
Hele strike it dead that tis damnation,
If you turne turke againe, oh doe it not,
Tho heauen cannot allure you to doe well,
From doing ill let hell fright you: and learne this,
The soule whose bosome lust did neuer touch,
Is Gods faire bride, and maidens soules are such:
The soule that leauing chastities white shore, 180
Swims in hot sensuall streames, is the diuels whore.
How now: who comes. *Enter his seruant.*
Seru. No more knaues my Lord that weare smocks: heres a letter
from doctor *Benedict*; I would not enter his man, tho he had haires
at his mouth, for feare he should be a woman, for some women
haue beardes, mary they are halfe witches. Slid you are a sweete
youth to weare a codpeece, and haue no pinnes to sticke vpont.
Hip. Ile meete the doctor, tell him, yet to night

176 Tho] Q4; The Q1–2(r)–3
184 *Benedict*] Q2(r); *Benedect* Q1

I cannot: but at morrow rising Sunne
I will not faile: go: woman fare thee well.   *Exeunt.* 190
Bell. The lowest fall can be but into hell,
It does not moue him. I must therefore fly,
From this vndoing Cittie, and with teares,
Wash off all anger from my fathers brow,
He cannot sure but ioy seeing me new borne,
A woman honest first and then turne whore,
Is (as with me) common to thousands more,
But from a strumpet to turne chast: that sound,
Has oft bin heard, that woman hardly found.
   Exit.

[ACT IV, Scene ii]

Enter Fustigo, Crambo *and* Poh.

Fust. Hold vp your hands gentlemen: heres one, two, three, (nay I warrant they are sound pistols, and without flawes, I had them of my sister, and I know she vses to put vp nothing thats crackt,) three, foure, fiue, sixe, seuen, eight and nine, by this hand bring me but a piece of his bloud, and you shall haue nine more. Ile lurke in a tauerne not far off, and prouide supper to close vp the end of the Tragedy, the linnen drapers remember — stand toot I beseech you, and play your partes perfectly.

Cram. Looke you Signior, tis not your golde that we way.

Fust. Nay, nay, way it and spare not; if it lacke one graine of 10 corne, Ile giue you a bushell of wheate to make it vp.

Cram. But by your fauour Signior, which of the seruants is it, because wele punish iustly.

Fust. Mary tis the head man; you shall tast him by his tongue, a pretty tall prating felow, with a *Tuscalonian* beard.

Poh. Tuscalonian: very good.

Fust. Cods life I was neere so thrumd since I was a gentleman: my coxcombe was dry beaten as if my haire had beene hemp.

*190 go:] Q1; ~ ∧ Q2(r)
S.H. ACT IV, Scene ii] Dyce; 11. SCE. Q1–2(r)–5
S.D. Poh] Q2(r); Poli Q1   3 vp] Q2(r); *om.* Q1

IV. ii, IV. iii]   THE HONEST WHORE, PART I

Cram. Wele dry beate some of them.
Fust. Nay it grew so high, that my sister cryed murder out very 20
manfully: I haue her consent in a manner to haue him pepperd,
els ide not doot to win more then ten cheaters do at a rifling: breake
but his pate or so, onely his mazer, because ile haue his head in a
cloath aswell as mine, hees a linnen draper and may take enough.
I could enter mine action of battery against him, but we may haps
be both dead and rotten before the lawyers would end it.
Cram. No more to doe, but insconce your selfe i'th tauerne;
prouide no great cheare, couple of Capons, some Phesants, Plouers,
an Oringeado-pie or so: but how bloudy so ere the day be, sally
you not forth. 30
Fust. No, no, nay if I stir, some body shal stinke: ile not budge:
ile lie like a dog in a manger.
Cram. Well, well, to the tauerne, let not our supper be raw, for
you shall haue blood enough — your belly full.
Fust. Thats all so god sa me, I thirst after, bloud for bloud, bump
for bump, nose for nose, head for head, plaster for plaster, and so
farewell: what shal I call your names because ile leaue word, if any
such come to the barre.
Cram. My name is Corporall *Crambo*.
Poh. And mine Lieutenant *Poh*.   *Exit.* 40
Cram. *Poh* is as tall a man as euer opened Oyster: I would not be
the diuell to meete *Poh*, farewell.
Fust. Nor I by this light, if *Poh* be such a *Poh*.
                                                            Exeunt.

[ACT IV, SCENE iii]

Enter Candidoes Wife, *in her shop, and the two Prentises.*

Wife. Whats a clocke now.
2. *Prent.*   Tis almost twelue.
Wife.   Thats well.
The Senate will leaue wording presently:
But is *George* ready?

22 ide] ile Q1–2(r)–5 (*see* I.iii.66)   40 S.D. *Exit.*] *Exeunt.* Q1–2(r)–5

79

2. *Prent.*   Yes forsooth, hees furbisht.
Wife. Now as you euer hope to win my fauour,
Throw both your duties and respects on him,
With the like awe as if he were your maister,
Let not your lookes betray it with a smile,
Or ieering glaunce to any customer,
Keepe a true Setled countenance, and beware,
You laugh not whatsoeuer you heare or see.   10
2. *Prent.* I warrant you mistris, let vs alone for keeping our countenance: for if I list, theres neuer a foole in all *Myllan* shal make me laugh, let him play the foole neuer so like an Asse, whether it be the fat Court foole, or the leane Cittie foole.
Wife. Enough then, call downe *George*.
2. *Prent.*   I heare him comming.

Enter George.

Wife. Be redy with your legs then, let me see
How curtzy would become him: gallantly!
Beshrew my bloud a proper seemely man,
Of a choice carriage, walkes with a good port.
Geo. I thanke you mistris, my back's broad enough, now my   20
Maisters gown's on.
Wife. Sure I should thinke it were the least of sin,
To mistake the maister, and to let him in.
Geo. Twere a good Comedy of errors that yfaith.
2. *Prent.* Whist, whist, my maister.

Enter Candido, *and Exit presently.*

Wife. You all know your taskes: gods my life, whats that hee has got vpon's backe? who can tell?
Geo. That can I, but I will not.
Wife. Girt about him like a mad-man: what: has he lost his cloake too: this is the maddest fashion that ere I saw.   30
What said he *George* when he passde by thee?
Geo. Troth Mistris nothing: not so much as a Bee, he did not hum: not so much as a bawd he did not hem: not so much as a Cuckold he did not ha: neither hum, hem, nor ha, onely starde me in the

face, past along, and made hast in, as if my lookes had workt with
him, to giue him a stoole.
Wife. Sure hees vext now, this trick has mou'd his Spleene,
Hees angred now, because he vttred nothing,
And wordlesse wrath breakes out more violent:
May be heele striue for place, when he comes downe, 40
But if thou lou'st me *George*, affoord him none.
Geo. Nay let me alone to play my maisters prize, as long as my
Mistrisse warrants me: Ime sure I haue his best clothes on, and I
scorne to giue place to any that is inferiour in apparell to me, thats
an Axiom, a principle, and is obseru'd as much as the fashion; let
that perswade you then, that Ile shoulder with him for the vpper
hand in the shop, as long as this chaine will mainteine it.
Wife. Spoke with the spirit of a Maister, tho with the tongue of a
Prentise.

Enter Candido *like a Prentise.*

Why how now mad-man? what in your tricksicoates! 50
Cand. O peace good Mistrisse:

Enter Crambo *and* Poh.

See what you lack, what ist you buy? pure Callicoes, fine Hollands,
choise Cambrickes, neate Lawnes: see what you buy? pray come
neere, my Maister will vse you well, hee can affoord you a penny-
worth.
Wife. I that he can, out of a whole peece of Lawne yfaith.
Cand. Pray see your choise here Gentlemen.
Wife. O fine foole? what, a mad-man? a patient mad-man? who
euer heard of the like? well sir Ile fit you and your humour
presently: what? crosse-points, Ile vntie em all in a trice, Ile vex 60
you faith: Boy take your cloake, quick, come.
Exit [*with* 1. *Prentise*].
Cand. Be couered *George*, this chaine, and welted gowne,
Bare to this coate: then the worlds vpside downe.
Geo. Vmh, vmh, hum.
Cram. Thats the shop, and theres the fellow.

51 S.D. Poh] Q2(r); Poli Q1

Poh.   I but the Maister is walking in there.
Cram.   No matter, weele in.
Poh.   Sbloud doest long to lye in Limbo?
Cram.   And Limbo be in hell, I care not.
Cand.   Looke you Gentlemen, your choise: Cambricks? 70
Cram.   No sir, some shirting.
Cand.   You shall.
Cram.   Haue you none of this strip'd Canuas for doublets.
Cand.   None strip'd sir, but plaine.
2. *Prent.*   I thinke there be one peece strip'd within.
Geo.   Step sirra and fetch it, hum, hum hum.
            [*Exit 2. Prentise and return presently.*]
Cand.   Looke you Gentlemen, Ile make but one spredding, heres a peece of cloth, fine, yet shall weare like Yron, tis without fault, take this vpon my word, tis without fault.
Cram.   Then tis better than you sirra. 80
Cand.   I, and a number more, ô that each soule
  Were but as spotlesse as this Innocent white,
  And had as few brakes in it.
Cram.   Twould haue some then: there was a fray here last day in this shop.
Cand.   There was indeed a little flea-biting.
Poh.   A Gentleman had his pate broake, call you that but a flea-biting.
Cand.   He had so.
Cram.   Zownes doe you stand in't?   *He strikes him.* 90
Geo.   Sfoot clubs, clubs, prentices, downe with em, ah you roagues, strike a Cittizen in's shop.   [*Beat them.*]
Cand.   None of you stir I pray, forbeare good *George*.
Cram.   I beseech you sir, we mistooke our markes, deliuer vs our weapons.
Geo.   Your head bleeds sir, cry clubs.
Cand.   I say you shall not, pray be patient,
  Giue them their weapons, sirs you're best be gone,
  I tell you here are boyes more tough then Beares:
  Hence, least more fists do walke about your eares. 100

66 *Poh.*] Q2(r); *Poli.* Q1

Both. We thanke you sir. *Exeunt.*
Cand. You shall not follow them.
Let them alone pray, this did me no harme,
Troth I was cold, and the blow made me warme,
I thanke em for't: besides I had decreed
To haue a vaine prickt, I did meane to bleede,
So that theres mony sau'd: they are honest men,
Pray vse em well, when they appeare agen.
Geo. Yes sir, weele vse em like honest men.
Cand. I well said *George*, like honest men, tho they be arrant 110
knaues, for thats the phrase of the citty; helpe to lay vp these
wares.
    Enter Candido's Wife, *with Officers.*
Wife. Yonder he stands.
Off. What in a Prentise-coate?
Wife. I, I, mad, mad, pray take heed.
Cand. How now? what newes with them? what make they with
my wife? officers? is she attachd? looke to your wares.
Wife. He talkes to himselfe, oh hees much gone indeed.
Off. Pray pluck vp a good heart, be not so fearfull,
Sirs hearke, weele gather to him by degrees.
Wife. I, I, by degrees I pray: oh me! what makes he with the 120
Lawne in his hand, heele teare all the ware in my shop.
Off. Feare not, weele catch him on a sudden.
Wife. O you had need do so, pray take heed of your warrant.
Off. I warrant mistris. — Now Signior *Candido?*
Cand. Now sir, what newes with you sir?
Wife. What newes with you he sayes: oh hees far gon.
Off. I pray feare nothing, lets alone with him,
Signior, you looke not like your selfe me thinkes,
(Steale you a tother side) y'are changde, y'are altred.
Cand. Changde sir, why true sir, is change strange, tis not the 130
fashion vnlesse it alter: Monarkes turne to beggers; beggers creepe
into the nests of Princes, Maisters serue their prentises: Ladies
their Seruingmen, men turne to women.

111 phrase] Q2(s); praise Q1   112 S.D. Candido's] Q2(s); *his* Q1
117 officers?] Q2(s); ~ ₐ Q1

Off. And women turne to men.
Cand. I, and women turne to men, you say true, ha ha, a mad world, a mad world.
Off. Haue we caught you sir?
Cand. Caught me: well, well: you haue caught me.
Wife. Hee laughes in your faces. 140
Geo. A rescue Prentises, my maister's catch-pold.
Off. I charge you keepe the peace, or haue your legs gartered with Yrons, we haue from the Duke a warrant strong enough for what we doe.
Cand. I pray rest quiet, I desire no rescue.
Wife. La: he desires no rescue, las poore heart,
He talkes against himselfe.
Cand. Well, whats the matter?
Off. Looke to that arme,
Pray make sure worke, double the cord.
Cand. Why, why? 150
Wife. Looke how his head goes! should he get but loose,
Oh twere as much as all our liues were worth.
Off. Feare not, weele make all sure for our owne safetie.
Cand. Are you at leisure now? well, whats the matter?
Why do I enter into bonds thus? ha?
Off. Because y'are mad, put feare vpon your wife.
Wife. Oh I, I went in danger of my life, euery minute.
Cand. What? am I mad say you, and I not know it?
Off. That proues you mad, because you know it not.
Wife. Pray talke as little to him as you can, 160
You see hees too farre spent.
Cand. Bound with strong corde!
A Sisters thred yfaith had beene enough,
To lead me any where: Wife do you long?
You are mad too, or els you do me wrong.
Geo. But are you mad indeed Maister?
Cand. My Wife sayes so,
And what she sayes, *George,* is all trueth you know:

161 corde!] Q2(s); ~, Q1
162 Sisters] Q2(s); Cisters Q1

And whether now? to *Bethlem Monastery?* —
Ha! whether?
Off.   Faith eene to the mad-mens pound.   170
Cand.   A Gods name, still I feele my patience sound.   *Exeunt.*
Geo.   Come weele see whether he goes, if the maister be mad,
we are his seruants, and must follow his steps, weele be mad caps
too; Farewell mistrisse, you shall haue vs all in Bedlam.   *Exeunt.*
Wife.   I thinke, I ha fitted now, you and your clothes,
If this moue not his patience, nothing can,
Ile sweare then I haue a saint, and not a man.
                                                            Exit.

[ACT IV, Scene iv]

Enter Duke: Doctor: Fluello, Castruchio, Pioratto
[*who exeunt presently*].

Duke.   Giue vs a little leaue. Doctor your newes.
Doct.   I sent for him my Lord: at last he came,
And did receiue all speech that went from me,
As gilded pilles made to prolong his health:
My credit with him wrought it: for, some men,
Swallow euen empty hookes, like fooles, that feare
No drowning where tis deepest, cause tis cleare:
In th'end we sat and eate: a health I dranke
To *Infœlices* sweete departed soule,
(This traine I knew would take.)
Duke.   Twas excellent.   10
Doct.   He fell with such deuotion on his knees,
To pledge the same —
Duke.   Fond superstitious foole?
Doct.   That had he beene inflam'd with zeale of prayer,
He could not power't out with more reuerence.
About my necke he hung, wept on my cheeke,
Kist it, and swore, he would adore my lippes,
Because they brought forth *Infœlices* name.

S.H. ACT IV, Scene iv] Dyce; 13. SCE. Q1–2(r)–5

85

Duke. Ha, ha, alacke, alacke.
Doct. The cup he lifts vp high, and thus he said,
Here noble maid: drinkes, and was poisoned.   20
Duke. And died?
Doct.   And died my Lord.
Duke.   Thou in that word,
Hast peicd mine aged houres out with more yeares,
Than thou hast taken from *Hipolito,*
A noble youth he was, but lesser branches
Hindring the greaters growth, must be lopt off,
And feede the fire: Doctor w'are now all thine,
And vse vs so: be bold.
Doct.   Thankes gracious Lord:
My honoured Lord —
Duke. Hmh.
Doct. I doe beseech your grace to bury deepe,   30
This bloudy act of mine.
Duke.   Nay, nay, for that,
Doctor looke you toot: me it shall not moue,
Thei'r curst that ill doe, not that ill do loue.
Doct. You throw an angry forehead on my face,
But be you pleas'd, backward thus for to looke,
That for your good, this euill I vndertooke —
Duke. I, I, we conster so.
Doct. And onely for your loue.
Duke.   Confest: tis true.
Doct. Nor let it stand against me as a bar,
To thrust me from your presence: nor beleeue   40
(As Princes haue quicke thoughts,) that now my finger
Being deept in blood, I will not spare the hand,
But that for gold (as what can golde not doe?)
I may be hi'rde to worke the like on you.
Duke. Which to preuent —
Doct.   Tis from my hart as far —
Duke. No matter Doctor, cause ile feareles sleepe,
And that you shall stand cleare of that suspition

35 for *stet* Q1; far Q2(r)

86

I banish thee for euer from my court.
This principle is olde but true as fate,
Kings may loue treason, but the traitor hate. *Exit.* 50
Doct. Ist so: nay then Duke, your stale principle
With one as stale, the Doctor thus shall quit,
He fals himselfe that digs anothers pit,
How now: where is he? will he meete me?
                    Enter the Doctors man.
Doct. man. Meete you sir, he might haue met with three fencers
in this time and haue receiued lesse hurt then by meeting one
Doctor of Phisicke: why sir has walkt vnder the olde Abbey wall
yonder this houre, till hees more colde then a Cittizens country
house in Ianiuere, you may smell him behinde sir; la you: yonder
he comes.   60
Doct. Leaue me.
              Enter Hipolito.
Doct. man. Ith lurch if you will.   *Exit.*
Doct. O my most noble friend.
Hip.   Few but your selfe,
Could haue inticd me thus, to trust the Aire,
With my close sighes, you send for me: what newes?
Doct. Come you must doff this blacke: die that pale cheeke,
Into his owne colour; goe: Attire your selfe
Fresh as a bridegroome, when he meetes his bride,
The Duke has done much treason to thy loue,
Tis now reuealed, tis now to be reuengde,   70
Be mery honord friend, thy Lady liues.
Hip. What Lady?
Doct.   *Infælice*, Shees reuiude;
Reuiude: alacke! death neuer had the hart,
To take breath from her.
Hip.   Vmh: I thanke you sir,
Phisicke prolongs life, when it cannot saue,
This helpes not my hopes, mine are in their graue:
You doe some wrong to mocke me.

53 digs] Q1; dig Q2(r)   62 Ith] Q2(r); Itch Q1

Doct.   By that loue,
Which I haue euer borne you, what I speake
Is trueth: the maiden liues: that funerall,
Dukes teares, the mourning, was all counterfet,   80
A sleepy draught cozend the world and you,
I was his minister and then chambred vp,
To stop discouery.
Hip.   O trecherous Duke!
Doct.   He cannot hope so certainely for blisse,
As he beleeues that I haue poysond you:
He woode me toot, I yeelded, and confirm'd him,
In his most bloudy thoughts.
Hip.   A very deuill!
Doct.   Her did he closely coach to *Bergamo*,
And thither —
Hip.   Will I ride, stood *Bergamo*,
In the low countries of blacke hell, ile to her.   90
Doct.   You shall to her, but not to *Bergamo*,
How passion makes you fly beyond your selfe.
Much of that weary iourney I ha' cut off,
For she by letters hath intelligence,
Of your supposed death, her owne interment,
And all those plots, which that false Duke, (her father)
Has wrought against you: And sheele meete you.
Hip.   O when?
Doct.   Nay see: how couetous are your desires,
Earely to morrow morne.
Hip.   O where good father.
Doct.   At *Bethlem* monasterie: are you pleasd now?   100
Hip.   At *Bethlem* monasterie: the place well fits,
It is the scoole where those that loose their wits,
Practise againe to get them: I am sicke
Of that disease, all loue is lunaticke.
Doct.   Weele steale away (this night) in some disguise,

         80 mourning] Q2(s); morning Q1
         86 woode] Q2(s); wode Q1   89 thither—] Q2(s) ~? Q1
         105 away (this night)] Q2(s); ~, ~ ~ ~ Q1

   Father *Anselmo*, a most reuerend Frier,
Expects our comming, before whom weele lay,
Reasons so strong, that he shall yeeld, in bands,
Of holy wedlocke, to tie both your hands.
Hip. This is such happinesse: 110
That to beleeue it, tis impossible.
Doct. Let all your ioyes then die in misbeliefe,
I will reueale no more.
Hip.   O yes good father,
I am so well acquainted with despaire,
I know not how to hope: I beleeue all.
Doct. Weele hence this night, much must be done, much said:
But if the Doctor faile not in his charmes,
Your Lady shall ere morning fill these armes.
Hip. Heauenly Phisition: far thy fame shall spred,
That mak'st two louers speake when they be dead. 120
            Exeunt.

[ACT V, SCENE i]

   Candido's Wife, *and* George: Pioratto *meetes them.*

Wife. O watch good *George*, watch which way the Duke comes.
Geo. Here comes one of the butter flies, aske him.
Wife. Pray sir, comes the duke this way.
Pio. He's vpon comming mistris.   *Exit.*
Wife. I thanke you sir: *George* are there many madfolkes, where thy Maister lies.
Geo. O yes, of all countries some, but especially mad greekes, they swarme: troth mistris, the world is altered with you, you had not wont to stand thus with a paper humblie complaining: but you're well enough seru'd: prouander prickt you, as it does many of our 10 Cittie-wiues besides.
Wife. Doest thinke *George* we shall get him forth.
Geo. Truly mistris I cannot tel, I thinke youle hardly get him

  108 bands] Q2(s); bonds Q1 119 spred] Q2(s); sprede Q1

forth: why tis strange! Sfoot I haue known many women that haue had mad rascals to their husbands, whom they would belabour by all meanes possible to keepe em in their right wits, but of a woman to long to turne a tame man into a madman, why the diuell himselfe was neuer vsde so by his dam.

Wife. How does he talke *George*! ha! good *George* tell me.

Geo. Why youre best go see.

Wife. Alas I am afraid.

Geo. Afraid! you had more need be ashamd: he may rather be afraid of you.

Wife. But *George* hees not starke mad, is hee? hee does not raue, hees not horne-mad *George* is he?

Geo. Nay I know not that, but he talkes like a Iustice of peace, of a thousand matters and to no purpose.

Wife. Ile to the monastery: I shall be mad till I inioy him, I shalbe sick till I see him, yet when I doe see him, I shall weepe out mine eyes.

Geo. I, ide faine see a woman weepe out her eyes; thats as true, as to say, a mans cloake burnes; when it hangs in the water: I know youle weepe mistrisse, but what saies the painted cloth.

> *Trust not a woman when she cryes,*
> *For sheele pump water from her eyes,*
> *With a wet finger, and in faster showers,*
> *Then Aprill when he raines downe flowers.*

Wife. I but *George*, that painted cloath is worthy to be hangd vp for lying, all women haue not teares at will, vnlesse they haue good cause.

Geo. I but mistrisse how easily will they find a cause, and as one of our Cheese-trenchers sayes very learnedly:

> *As out of Wormwood Bees suck Hony,*
> *As from poore clients Lawyers firke mony,*
> *As Parsley from a roasted cunny.*
> *So tho the day be nere so sunny,*
> *If wiues will haue it raine, downe then it driues,*
> *The calmest husbands make the stormest wiues.*

Wife. True *George*, but I ha don storming now.

*49 True] Dyce; Tame Q 1–2 (r)–5

Geo. Why thats well done, good mistris throw aside this fashion 50
of your humor, be not so phantasticall in wearing it, storme no
more, long no more. — This longing has made you come short of
many a good thing that you might haue had from my Maister:
Here comes the Duke.

Enter Duke, Fluello, Pioratto, Sinezi.

Wife. Oh I beseech you pardon my offence,
In that I durst abuse your Graces warrant,
Deliuer foorth my husband good my Lord.
Duke. Who is her husband?
Flu.   *Candido* my Lord.
Duke. Where is he?
Wife.   Hees among the lunaticks,
He was a man made vp without a gall,   60
Nothing could moue him, nothing could conuert
His meeke bloud into fury, yet like a monster,
I often beate at the most constant rock
Of his vnshaken patience, and did long
To vex him.
Duke.   Did you so?
Wife.   And for that purpose,
Had warrant from your Grace, to cary him
To *Bethlem Monastery*, whence they will not free him,
Without your Graces hand that sent him in.
Duke. You haue longd fayre; tis you are mad I feare,
Its fit to fetch him thence, and keepe you there: 70
If he be mad, why would you haue him forth?
Geo. And please your grace, hees not starke mad, but onely talkes
like a young Gentleman, somewhat phantastically, thats all: theres
a thousand about your court, citty and countrie madder then he.
Duke. Prouide a warrant, you shall haue our hand.
Geo. Heres a warrant ready drawne my Lord.
Duke. Get pen and Inck, get pen and inck.

54 S.D. Sinezi] Q4; Sinere Q1–2(r)–3
77 *Duke.*] Q4; *Cast.* Q1–2(r)–3

Enter Castruchio.

Cast. Where is my Lord the Duke?
Duke. How now? more mad men.
Cast. I haue strange newes my Lord.
Duke. Of what? of whom?
Cast. Of *Infælice*, and a mariage. 80
Duke. Ha! where? with whom.
Cast. *Hipolito.*
Geo. Here my Lord.
Duke. Hence with that woman, voyd the roome.
Flu. Away, the Duke's vext.
Geo. Whoop, come mistris the Duke's mad too.

Exeunt [*Wife and* George].

Duke. Who told me that *Hipolito* was dead?
Cast. He that can make any man dead, the Doctor: but my Lord, hees as full of life as wilde-fire, and as quick: *Hipolito*, the Doctor, and one more rid hence this euening; the Inne at which they light is *Bethlem Monasterie*: *Infæliche* comes from *Bergamo*, and meetes 90 them there: *Hipolito* is mad, for he meanes this day to be maryed, the after-noone is the houre, and Frier *Anselmo* is the knitter.
Duke. From *Bergamo*? ist possible? it cannot be,
  It cannot be.
Cast.   I will not sweare my Lord,
  But this intelligence I tooke from one,
  Whose braines workes in the plot.
Duke. Whats he?
Cast. *Mathæo.*
Flu. *Mathæo* knowes all.
Pio. Hees *Hipolitoes* bosome.
Duke. How farre stands *Bethlem* hence?
Omn. Six or seauen miles.
Duke. Ist euen so,
  Not maried till the afternoone you say? 100
  Stay, stay, lets worke out some preuention: how:
  This is most strange, can none but mad-men serue

90 *Monasterie*] Q2(s); *Monastarie* Q1

To dresse their wedding dinner? All of you,
Get presently to horse; disguise your selues
Like Countrie-Gentlemen,
Or riding cittizens, or so: and take
Each man a seuerall path, but let vs meete,
At *Bethlem Monasterie*, some space of time
Being spent betweene the arriuall each of other,
As if we came to see the Lunaticks.   110
To horse, away, be secret on your liues,
Loue must be punisht that vniustly thriues.   *Exeunt.*
Flu. Be secret on your liues! *Castruchio*
Y'are but a scuruy Spaniell; honest Lord,
Good Lady: Zounds their loue is iust, tis good,
And Ile preuent you, tho I swim in bloud.
                                                                                      Exit.

[ACT V, SCENE ii]

 Enter Frier Anselmo, Hipolito, Mathæo, Infæliche.

Hip. Nay, nay, resolue good father, or deny.
Ans. You presse me to an act, both full of danger,
And full of happinesse, for I behold
Your fathers frownes, his threats, nay perhaps death,
To him that dare doe this, yet noble Lord,
Such comfortable beames breake through these clowdes,
By this blest mariage, that (your honord word
Being pawnd in my defence) I will tie fast,
The holy wedding Knot.
Hip.   Tush feare not the Duke.
Ans. O sonne,   10
Wisely to feare: Is to be free from feare.
Hip. You haue our words, and you shall haue our liues,
To guard you safe from all ensuing danger.
Math. I, I, chop em vp and away.
Ans. Stay, when ist fit for me, safest for you,
To entertaine this busines.
Hip.   Not till the euening.

Ans. Be't so, there is a chappell stands hard by,
Vpon the West end of the Abbey wall,
Thether conuay your selues, and when the sunne
Hath turnd his back vpon this vpper world, 20
Ile mary you, that done, no thundring voice,
Can breake the sacred bond, yet Lady here
You are most safe.
Infæ. Father your lou's most deere.
Math. I well said, locke vs into some little roome by our selues that we may be mad for an houre or two.
Hip. O good *Mathæo* no, lets make no noise.
Math. How! no noise! do you know where you are: sfoot amongst all the mad-caps in *Millan:* so that to throw the house out at window will be the better, and no man will suspect that we lurke here to steale mutton: the more sober we are, the more scuruy tis. And 30 tho the Frier tell vs, that heere we are safest, i'me not of his minde, for if those lay here that had lost there mony, none would euer looke after them, but heare are none but those that haue lost their wits, so that if hue and cry be made, hether theile come, and my reason is, because none goes to be married till he be starke mad.
Hip. Muffle your selues, yonders *Fluello.*

Enter Fluello.

Math. Zounds!
Flu. O my Lord these cloakes are not for this raine, the tempest is too great: I come sweating to tell you of it, that you may get out of it. 40
Math. Why whats the matter.
Flu. Whats the matter! you haue matterd it faire: the Duke's at hand.
Omn. The Duke?
Flu. The very Duke.
Hip. Then all our plots
Are turnd vpon our heads; and we are blown vp
With our own vnderminings. Sfoot how comes he,
What villaine durst betray our being here.

34 so] Q4; o Q1–2(s)–3

Flu. *Castruchio, Castruchio* tolde the Duke, and *Mathæo* here told 50
Castruchio.
Hip. Would you betray me to *Castruchio*?
Math. Sfoot he dambd himselfe to the pit of hell if he spake ont
agen.
Hip. So did you sweare to me, so were you dambd.
Math. Pox on em, and there be no faith in men, if a man shall not
beleeue oathes: he tooke bread and salt by this light, that he would
neuer open his lips.
Hip. Oh God, oh God.
Ans. Sonne be not desperate,
Haue patience, you shal trip your enemy downe, 60
By his owne slights, how far is the Duke hence.
Flu. Hees but new set out: *Castruchio, Pioratto* and *Sineʒi* come
along with him: you haue time enough yet to preuent them if you
haue but courage.
Ans. You shall steale secretly into the Chappell,
And presently be maried; if the duke
Abide here still, spite of ten thousand eyes,
You shall scape hence like Friers.
Hip. O blest disguise: O happy man.
Ans. Talke not of happinesse till your closde hand, 70
Haue her bith' forhead, like the lock of time,
Bee not too slow, nor hasty, now you clime,
Vp to the towre of blisse, onely be wary
And patient, thats all, if you like my plot
Build and dispatch, if not, farewell, then not.
Hip. O Yes, we doe applaud it, weele dispute,
No longer, but will hence and execute.
Fluello youle stay here, let vs be gon,
The ground that fraighted louers tread vpon,
Is stucke with thornes.
Ans. Come then, away: tis meete, 80
To escape those thornes, to put on winged feete. *Exeunt.*

69 disguise] Q2(r); disguisde Q1
72 not] Q2(r); nor Q1
79 fraighted] *stet* Q1; *i.e.*, frighted *as in* Q2(r)

95

Math. No words I pray *Fluello*, for it stands vs vpon.
Flu. Oh sir, let that be your lesson. [*Exit* Matheo.]
 Alas poore louers, on what hopes and feares,
 Men tosse themselues for women. When shees got,
 The best has in her that which pleaseth not.

Enter to Fluello, *the* Duke, Castruchio, Pioratto *and*
Sinezi *from seuerall dores muffled.*

Duke. Whose there!
Cast. My Lord.
Duke. Peace, send that Lord away,
 A Lordship will spoile all, lets be all fellowes.
 Whats he.
Cast. *Fluello*, or els *Sinezi* by his little legs.
Omn. All friends, all friends.
Duke. What! met vpon the very point of time,
 Is this the place.
Pio. This is the place my Lord.
Duke. Dreame you on Lordships! come, no more Lordes pray:
 You haue not seene these louers yet.
Omn. Not yet.
Duke. *Castruchio* art thou sure this wedding feate,
 Is not till afternoone?
Cast. So tis giuen out my Lord.
Duke. Nay, nay, tis like, theeues must obserue their houres,
 Louers watch minuts like Astronomers,
 How shall the *Interim* houres by vs be spent.
Flu. Lets all goe see the madmen.
Omn. Mas content.

Enter Towne *like a sweeper.*

Duke. Oh here comes one, question him, question him.
Flu. How now honest fellow dost thou belong to the house.
Sweep. Yes forsooth, I am one of the implements; I swepe the
 madmens roomes, and fetch straw for em, and buy chaines to tie
 em, and rods to whip em, I was a mad wag my selfe here once, but
 I thanke father *Anselm* he lasht me into my right minde agen.

109 Sweep.] *throughout this scene speech-prefixes in* Qq *are* Tow.

Duke.   *Anselmo* is the Frier must marry them,
Question him where he is.
Cast.   And where is father *Anselmo* now?
Sweep.   Mary hees gon but eene now.
Duke.   I, well done, tell me, whether is he gone?
Sweep.   Why to God a mighty.
Flu.   Ha, ha, this fellow is a foole, talkes idlelie.
Pio.   Sirra are all the mad folkes in *Millan* brought hither?   120
Sweep.   How all, theres a wise question indeede: why if al the mad folkes in *Millan* should come hither, there would not be left ten men in the Citty.
Duke.   Few gentlemen or Courtiers here, ha.
Sweep.   Oh yes? abundance, aboundance, lands no sooner fall into their hands, but straight they runne out a their wits: Citizens sons and heires are free of the house by their fathers copy: Farmers sons come hither like geese (in flocks) and when they ha sould all their corne fields, here they sit and picke the straws.
Sin.   Me thinks you should haue women here aswel as men.   130
Sweep.   Oh, I: a plague on em, theres no ho with them, they are madder then march haires.
Flu.   Are there no lawyers here amongst you?
Sweep.   Oh no, not one: neuer any lawyer, we dare not let a lawyer come in, for heele make em mad faster than we can recouer em.
Duke.   And how long ist er'e you recouer any of these.
Sweep.   Why according to the quantitie of the Moone thats got into em, an Aldermans sonne will be mad a great while a very great   140 while, especially if his friends left him well, a whore will hardly come to her wits agen: a puritane ther's no hope of him, vnlesse he may pull downe the steeple and hang himselfe it'h bell-ropes.
Flu.   I perceiue all sorts of fish come to your net.
Sweep.   Yes intruth, we haue blockes for all heads, we haue good store of wilde oates here: for the Courtier is mad at the Cittizen, the Cittizen is madde at the Country man, the shoomaker is mad at the cobler, the cobler at the carman, the punke is mad that the Marchants wife is no whore, the Marchants wife is mad that the

146 man] Q2(s); men Q1

puncke is so common a whore: gods so, heres father *Anselm*, pray
say nothing that I tel tales out of the schoole.   *Exit.* 150

           Enter Anselmo.

Omn.   God blesse you father.
Ans.   Thanke you gentlemen.
Cast.   Pray may we see some of those wretched Soules,
That here are in your keeping?
Ans.   Yes: you shall,
But gentlemen I must disarme you then,
There are of mad men, as there are of tame,
All humourd not alike: we haue here some,
So apish and phantastike, play with a fether,
And tho twould greeue a soule, to see Gods image,
So blemisht and defac'd, yet do they act
Such anticke and such pretty lunacies,   160
That spite of sorrow they will make you smile:
Others agen we haue like hungry Lions,
Fierce as wilde Buls, vntameable as flies,
And these haue oftentimes from strangers sides
Snatcht rapiers suddenly, and done much harme,
Whom if youle see, you must be weaponlesse.
Omn.   With all our harts.
Ans.   Here: take these weapons in,
Stand of a little pray, so, so, tis well:
Ile shew you here a man that was sometimes,
A very graue and wealthy Cittizen,   170
Has serud a prentiship to this misfortune,
Bin here seuen yeares, and dwelt in *Bergamo*.
Duke.   How fell he from himselfe?
Ans.   By losse at Sea:
Ile stand aside, question him you alone,
For if he spy me, heele not speake a word,
Vnlesse hees throughly vext.
           Discouers an old man, wrapt in a Net.

     149 *Anselm*,] Q2(s); *Anselmo.* Q1
     173 himselfe] Q2(s); his wits Q1

Flu. Alas poore soule.
Cast. A very old man.
Duke. God speed father.
1. *Mad.* God speed the plough: thou shalt not speed me. 180
Pio. We see you old man, for all you daunce in a net.
1. *Mad.* True, but thou wilt daunce in a halter, and I shal not see thee.
Ans. O, doe not vex him pray.
Cast. Are you a Fisherman father?
1. *Mad.* No, i'me neither fish nor flesh.
Flu. What do you with that net then?
1. *Mad.* Doest not see foole! theres a fresh Salmon in't: if you step one foot furder, youle be ouer shoes, for you see ime ouer head and ear in the salt-water: and if you fal into this whirlpoole 190 where I am, y'are drownd: y'are a drownd rat. — I am fishing here for fiue ships, but I cannot haue a good draught, for my net breakes still, and breakes, but Ile breake some of your necks and I catch you in my clutches. Stay, stay, stay, stay, stay — wheres the wind, wheres the wind, wheres the winde: wheres the winde: out you guls, you goose-caps, you gudgeon-eaters! do you looke for the wind in the heauens? ha ha ha ha, no no, looke there, looke there, looke there, the winde is always at that doore: hearke how it blowes, pooff, pooff, pooff.
Omn. Ha ha ha. 200
1. *Mad.* Do you laugh at Gods creatures? do you mock old age you roagues? is this gray beard and head counterfet, that you cry ha ha ha? — Sirra, art not thou my eldest sonne?
Pio. Yes indeed father.
1. *Mad.* Then th'art a foole, for my eldest sonne had a polt foote, crooked legs, a vergis face, and a peare-coullourd beard; I made him a scholler, and he made himselfe a foole. — Sirra! thou there? hould out thy hand.
Duke. My hand, wel, here tis.
1. *Mad.* Looke, looke, looke, looke: has he not long nailes, and 210 short haire?
Flu. Yes monstrous short haire, and abhominable long nailes.
1. *Mad.* Ten-peny nailes are they not?

Flu. Yes ten-peny nailes.

1. *Mad.* Such nailes had my second boy: kneele downe thou varlet, and aske thy father blessing. — Such nailes had my midlemost sonne and I made him a Promoter: and he scrapt, and scrapt, and scrapt, till he got the diuell and all: but he scrapt thus and thus, and thus, and it went vnder his legs, till at length a company of Kites taking him for carion, swept vp all, all, all, all, all, all. — If you loue your liues, looke to your selues, see, see, see, see, the Turkes gallies are fighting with my ships, Bownce goes the guns — oooh! cry the men: romble romble goe the waters — Alas! there! tis sunke — tis sunck: I am vndon, I am vndon, you are the dambd Pirates haue vndone me, — you are bith Lord, you are, you are, stop em, you are.

Ans. Why how now Syrra, must I fall to tame you?

1. *Mad.* Tame me? no: ile be madder than a roasted Cat: see, see, I am burnt with gunpowder, these are our close fights.

Ans. Ile whip you, if you grow vnruly thus.

1. *Mad.* Whip me? out you toad: — whip me? what iustice is this, to whip me because Ime a begger? — Alas? I am a poore man: a very poore man: I am starud, and haue had no meate by this light, euer since the great floud, I am a poore man.

Ans. Well, well, be quiet and you shall haue meate.

1. *Mad.* I, I, pray do, for looke you, here be my guts: these are my ribs, — you may looke through my ribs, — see how my guts come out — these are my red guttes, my very guts, oh, oh!

Ans. Take him in there. [*Exit* 1. *Madman.*]

Omn. A very pitious sight.

Cast. Father I see you haue a busie charge.

Ans. They must be vsde like children, pleasd with toyes,
And anon whipt for their vnrulinesse:
Ile shew you now a paire quite different
From him thats gon; he was all words: and these
Vnlesse you vrge em, seldome spend their speech,
          [*Enter* 2. *and* 3. *Madmen.*]
But saue their tongues — la you — this hithermost
Fell from the happy quietnesse of mind,

222 goes] Q 1; goe Q 2 (r)   247 saue] Q 1 (c)–Q 2 (s); haue Q 1 (u)

About a maiden that he loude, and dyed:
He followed her to church, being full of teares, 250
And as her body went into the ground,
He fell starke mad. That is a maryed man,
Was iealous of a faire, but (as some say)
A very vertuous wife, and that spoild him.
2. *Mad.* All these are whoremongers, and lay with my wife: whore, whore, whore, whore, whore.
Flu. Obserue him.
2. *Mad.* Gaffer shoomaker, you puld on my wiues pumps, and then crept into her pantofles: lye there, lye there, — this was her Tailer, — you cut out her loose-bodied gowne, and put in a yard 260 more then I allowed her, lye there by the shomaker: ô, maister Doctor! are you here: you gaue me a purgation, and then crept into my wiues chamber, to feele her pulses, and you said, and she sayd, and her mayd said, that they went pit a pat — pit a pat — pit a pat, — Doctor Ile put you anon into my wiues vrinall: — heigh, come a loft Iack? this was her schoolmaister, and taught her to play vpon the Virginals, and still his Iacks leapt vp, vp: you prickt her out nothing but bawdy lessons, but Ile prick you all, — Fidler — Doctor — Tayler — Shoomaker, — Shoomaker — Fidler — Doctor — Tayler — so! lye with my wife agen now. 270
Cast. See how he notes the other now he feedes.
2. *Mad.* Giue me some porridge.
3. *Mad.* Ile giue thee none.
2. *Mad.* Giue me some porridge.
3. *Mad.* Ile not giue thee a bit.
2. *Mad.* Giue me that flap-dragon.
3. *Mad.* Ile not giue thee a spoonefull: thou liest, its no Dragon; tis a Parrat, that I bought for my sweete heart, and ile keepe it.
2. *Mad.* Heres an Almond for Parrat.
3. *Mad.* Hang thy selfe. 280
2. *Mad.* Heres a roape for Parrat.
3. *Mad.* Eate it, for ile eate this.
2. *Mad.* Ile shoote at thee and thow't giue me none.
3. *Mad.* Wut thou?
2. *Mad.* Ile run a tilt at thee and thow't giue me none.

3. *Mad.* Wut thou? doe and thou dar'st.
2. *Mad.* Bownce.
3. *Mad.* Ooh! I am slaine — murder, murder, murder, I am slaine, my braines are beaten out.
Ans. How now you villaines, bring me whips: ile whip you. 290
3. *Mad.* I am dead, I am slaine, ring out the bel, for I am dead.
Duke. How will you do now sirra? you ha kild him.
2. *Mad.* Ile answer't at Sessions: he was eating of Almond Butter, and I longd for't: the child had neuer bin deliuered out of my belly, if I had not kild him, Ile answer't at sessions, so my wife may be burnt ith hand too.
Ans. Take em in both: bury him, for hees dead.
3. *Mad.* I indeed, I am dead, put me I pray into a good pit hole.
2. *Mad.* Ile answer't at Sessions. *Exeunt.*

Enter Bellafronte *mad.*

Ans. How now huswife, whether gad you? 300
Bell. A nutting forsooth: how doe you gaffer? how doe you gaffer? theres a French cursie for you too.
Flu. Tis *Bellafronte.*
Pio. Tis the puncke bith Lord.
Duke. Father whats she I pray?
Ans.   As yet I know not,
She came but in this day, talkes little idlely
And therefore has the freedome of the house.
Bell. Doe not you know me? nor you? nor you, nor you?
Omn. No indeede.
Bell. Then you are an Asse, and you are an Asse, and you are an 310 Asse, for I know you.
Ans. Why, what are they? come: tell me, what are they?
Bell. Three fishwiues: will you buy any gudgeons! gods santy yonder come Friers, I know them too, how doe you Frier?

313 Three] Q2(s); The're Q1
313 gudgeons!] Q2(s); ~, Q1

v. ii] THE HONEST WHORE, PART I

Enter Hipolito, Mathæo, *and* Infæliche *disguisde
in the Habets of Friers.*

Ans. Nay, nay, away, you must not trouble Friers.
  The duke is here, speake nothing.   [*Aside to them.*]
Bell. Nay indeed you shall not goe: weele run at barlibreak first,
  and you shalbe in hell.
Math. My puncke turnd mad whore, as all her fellowes are?
Hip. Speake nothing, but steale hence, when you spie time. 320
Ans. Ile locke you vp if y'are vnruly, fie.
Bell. Fie! mary fo: they shall not goe indeed till I ha tolde em
  their fortunes.
Duke. Good Father giue her leaue.
Bell. I pray, good father, and Ile giue you my blessing.
Ans. Wel then be briefe, but if you are thus vnruly,
  Ile haue you lockt vp fast.
Pio. Come, to their fortunes.
Bell. Let me see: one, two, three, and four, ile begin with the little
  Frier first, heres a fine hand indeed, I neuer saw Frier haue such 330
  a dainty hand: heres a hand for a Lady, you ha good fortune now,
  O see, see what a thred heres spun,
  You loue a Frier better then a Nun,
  Yet long youle loue no Frier, nor no Friers sonne.
                                           Bow a little.
  The line of life is out, yet i'me afraid,
  For all your holy, youle not die a maide,
  God giue you ioy.
  Now to you Frier *Tucke.*
Math. God send me good lucke.
Bell. You loue one, and one loues you. 340
  You are a false knaue, and shees a Iew,
  Here is a Diall that false euer goes.
Math. O your wit drops.

---

316 here,] Q2(s); ~ ₐ Q1
331–332 you ha...spun,] Q2(s); heres your fortune, Q1
*334 *Bow a little.*] Bow a little, Q1–2(s)–5 (*as text prefixed to line* 335)
343 wit] Q1(c)–Q2(r); wet Q1(u)

103

Bell. Troth so does your nose,
Nay lets shake hands with you too: [*To* Hipolito.]
Pray open, heres a fine hand,
Ho Fryer ho, God be here,
So he had need: youle keepe good cheere,
Heres a free table, but a frozen breast,
For youle starue those that loue you best.   350
Yet you haue good fortune, for if I am no lyar,
Then you are no Frier, nor you, nor you no Frier.
Haha haha.   *Discouers them.*
Duke. Are holy habits cloakes for villanie?
Draw all your weapons.
Hip.   Doe, draw all your weapons.
Duke. Where are your weapons, draw.
Omn. The Frier has guld vs of em.
Math.   O rare tricke:
You ha learnt one mad point of Arithmaticke.
Hip. Why swels your spleene so hie? against what bosome,
Would you your weapons draw? hers! tis your daughters: 360
Mine! tis your sonnes.
Duke.   Sonne?
Math.   Sonne, by yonder Sunne.
Hip. You cannot shed bloud here, but tis your owne,
To spill your owne bloud were damnation,
Lay smooth that wrinckled brow, and I will throw
My selfe beneath your feete,
Let it be rugged still and flinted o're,
What can come forth but sparkles, that will burne,
Your selfe and vs? Shees mine; my claymes most good,
Shees mine by marriage, tho shees yours by bloud.
Ans. I haue a hand deare Lord, deepe in this act,   370
For I foresaw this storme, yet willingly
Put fourth to meete it? Oft haue I seene a father
Washing the wounds of his deare sonne in teares,
A sonne to curse the sword that strucke his father,

369 Shees] Q1; *Ans.* Shees Q2(r)
370 *Ans.*] D¹; *om.* Q1, 3–5; *misplaced before* 369 *in* Q2(r)

104

Both slaine ith quarrell of your families,
Those scars are now tane off: And I beseech you,
To seale our pardon, all was to this end
To turne the ancient hates of your two houses
To fresh greene friendship: that your Loues might looke, 380
Like the springs forehead, comfortably sweete,
And your vext soules in peacefull vnion meete,
Their bloud will now be yours, yours will be theirs,
And happinesse shall crowne your siluer haires.
Flu. You see my Lord theres now no remedy
Omn. Beseech your Lordship.
Duke. You beseech faire, you haue me in place fit
To bridle me, rise Frier, you may be glad
You can make madmen tame, and tame men mad,
Since fate hath conquered, I must rest content,
To striue now would but ad new punishment: 390
I yeeld vnto your happinesse, be blest,
Our families shall henceforth breath in rest.
Omn. O happy change.
Duke.   Yours now is my consent,
I throw vpon your ioyes my full content.
Bell. Am not I a good girle, for finding the Frier in the wel? gods
so you are a braue man: will not you buy me some Suger plums
because I am so good a fortune teller.
Duke. Would thou hadst wit thou pretty soule to aske,
As I haue will to giue.
Bell. Pretty soule, a prety soule is better than a prety body: do 400
not you know my prety soule? I know you: Is not your name
Mathæo.
Math. Yes lamb.
Bell. Baa, lamb! there you lie for I am mutton; looke fine man, he
was mad for me once, and I was mad for him once, and he was
madde for her once, and were you neuer mad? yes I warrant. I had
a fine iewell once, a very fine iewell and that naughty man stoale
it away from me, a very fine iewell.

375 *The Bodleian copy of* Q2 *is imperfect and wanting from this line, the first on sig.* K3.   *394 content] Q4; consent Q1

Duke. What iewell pretty maide.
Bell. Maide nay thats a lie, O twas a very rich iewell, calde a
    Maidenhead, and had not you it leerer.
Math. Out you mad Asse away.
Duke. Had he thy Maiden-head?
    He shall make thee amends, and marry thee.
Bell. Shall he? ô braue Arthur of Bradly then?
Duke. And if he beare the minde of a Gentleman,
    I know he will.
Math. I thinke I rifled her of some such paltry Iewell.
Duke. Did you? then mary her, you see the wrong
    Has led her spirits into a lunacie.
Math. How, marry her my Lord? sfoot marry a mad-woman: let
    a man get the tamest wife he can come by, sheele be mad enough
    afterward, doe what he can.
Duke. Nay then, father *Anselmo* here shall do his best,
    To bring her to her wits, and will you then?
Math. I cannot tell, I may choose.
Duke. Nay then law shall compell: I tell you sir,
    So much her hard fate moues me: you should not breath
    Vnder this ayre, vnlesse you marryed her.
Math. Well then, when her wits stand in their right place, ile
    mary her.
Bell. I thanke your grace, *Mathæo* thou art mine,
    I am not mad, but put on this disguise,
    Onely for you my Lord, for you can tell   [*To* Hipolito.]
    Much wonder of me, but you are gon: farewell.
    Mathæo thou didst first turne my soule black,
    Now make it white agen, I doe protest,
    Ime pure as fire now, chaste as *Cynthias* brest.
Hip. I durst be sworne *Mathæo* she's indeed.
Math. Cony-catcht, guld, must I saile in your flie-boate,
    Because I helpt to reare your maine-mast first:
    Plague found you fort, — tis well.
    The Cuckolds stampe goes currant in all Nations,
    Some men haue hornes giuen them at their creations,
    If I be one of those, why so: its better

To take a common wench, and make her good,
Than one that simpers, and at first, will scarse
Be tempted forth ouer the threshold dore,
Yet in one sennight, zounds, turnes arrant whore,
Come wench, thou shalt be mine, giue me thy gols, 450
Weele talke of legges hereafter: see my Lord.
God giue vs ioy.
Omn. God giue you ioy.

Enter Candidoes Wife *and* George.

Geo. Come mistris we are in Bedlam now, mas and see, we come in pudding-time, for heres the Duke.
Wife. My husband good my Lord.
Duke. Haue I thy husband?
Cast. Its *Candido* my Lord, he's here among the lunaticks: father *Anselmo*, pray fetch him forth: [*Exit* Anselmo] this mad-woman is his wife, and tho shee were not with child, yet did she long most 460 spitefully to haue her husband mad, and because shee would be sure, he should turne Iew, she placde him here in *Bethlem*, yonder he comes.

Enter Candido *with* Anselmo.

Duke. Come hither Signior — Are you mad.
Cand. You are not mad.
Duke. Why I know that.
Cand. Then may you know, I am not mad, that know
You are not mad, and that you are the duke:
None is mad here but one — How do you wife:
What do you long for now? — pardon my Lord, 470
Shee had lost her childes nose els: I did cut out
Penniworths of Lawne, the Lawne was yet mine owne:
A carpet was my gowne, yet twas mine owne,
I wore my mans coate, yet the cloath mine owne,
Had a crackt crowne, the crowne was yet mine owne,
She sayes for this Ime mad, were her words true,

473 was my] Q4; was yet my Q1, 3

I should be mad indeed — ô foolish skill,
Is patience madnesse? Ile be a mad-man still.
Wife. Forgiue me, and ile vex your spirit no more.
Duke. Come, come, weele haue you friends, ioyne hearts, ioyne hands. 480
Cand. See my Lord, we are euen,
Nay rise, for ill-deeds kneele vnto none but heauen.
Duke. Signior, me thinkes, patience has laid on you
Such heauy waight, that you should loath it.
Cand. Loath it?
Duke. For he whose brest is tender, bloud so coole,
That no wrongs heate it, is a patient foole,
What comfort do you finde in being so calme.
Cand. That which greene wounds receiue from soueraigne balme.
Patience my Lord; why tis the soule of peace:
Of all the vertues tis neerst kin to heauen. 490
It makes men looke like Gods; the best of men
That ere wore earth about him, was a sufferer,
A soft, meeke, patient, humble, tranquill spirit,
The first true Gentleman that euer breathd;
The stock of *Patience* then cannot be poore,
All it desires, it has; what Monarch more?
It is the greatest enemy to law
That can be, for it doth embrace all wrongs,
And so chaines vp, lawyers and womens tongues.
Tis the perpetuall prisoners liberty: 500
His walkes and Orchards: 'tis the bond-slaues freedome,
And makes him seeme prowd of each yron chaine:
As tho he wore it more for state then paine.
It is the beggers Musick, and thus sings,
Although their bodies beg, their soules are kings:
O my dread liege! It is the sap of blisse,
Reares vs aloft; makes men and Angels kisse,
And (last of all) to end a houshould strife,
It is the hunny gainst a waspish wife.
Duke. Thou giu'st it liuely coulours: who dare say 510
He's mad, whose words march in so good aray?

Twere sinne all women should such husbands haue.
For euery man must then be his wiues slaue.
Come therefore you shall teach our court to shine,
So calme a spirit is worth a golden Mine,
Wiues (with meeke husbands) that to vex them long,
In Bedlam must they dwell, els dwell they wrong.
Exeunt.

FINIS.

TEXTUAL NOTES

I.i

45 torment]   Although adopted by no editor, Dyce's suggestion *torrent* is attractive, especially since in line 49 the Duke shortly employs a flood image, and several water images are found in his speeches in I.iii. It is possible that an error was overlooked by the corrector of the standing type in this forme; nevertheless, *torment* is a quite satisfactory enough reading not to require emendation.

54 For why]   The lack of Qq punctuation after these words—if accurate—would make them a conjunction meaning *because*; this is the interpretation given by Dyce and all following editors. On the other hand, the colon after *patient* ending the line above is rather a heavy mark if a conjunction is to follow. Hence it is possible to query whether D$^{1-3}$ were not perhaps correct to take the phrase adverbially and to place after it a comma or question mark. The adverbial meaning, equally common in the period, would be roughly, *for what reason?*

100 drunke.]   Neilson and Spencer, perhaps correctly, prefix a dash to this word in order to emphasize the jest.

I.ii

5 *Clarissimo*]   Dyce provides the emendation *Clarissimo*['s] which reflects the sense intended but is not required by the construction.

85 emblemes]   Editors between D^1 and Rhys emend to *Problems*, a book containing some medical directions published in 1595. Neilson and Spencer retain the Qq reading and thus do not destroy a manifestation of Fustigo's ignorance.

129 roares?]   The query standing for an exclamation in Q1 has been retained, despite its absence in Q2(r), on the chance that it was intended to represent a sample of Fustigo's acted swaggering.

I.iii

5 neere]   Simple minim error seems to explain this overlooked error. That it is an error, and that the glass has not *merely* (i.e. completely) run out, is clear from the context.

14 crust]   Although Q1 *rust* is unaltered in Q2(r), Dyce's emendation *crust* seems necessary. The image is of a stream in winter (*bound up fast*), confirmed by lines 56–57: *So coldly to thy heart, that the swift currents | Of life were all frozen up.*

I.iv

43 tempted] This is the Q2(r) alteration of Q1 *tempred*. The confusion of *r* and *t* is so common that the error could reside in either quarto. However, *temper* has been used in its normal sense of evenly balanced temperament in lines 22 and 25 immediately above, and the only possible sense that could be made of it here in line 43 is an obscurely ironic one. All editors from D3 (which independently emended Q1) have chosen *tempted*.

I.v

79 Gentle-man?] The reset Q2 reading *gentlemen* is certainly wrong here, since Candido is addressing only Castruchio. It is worthy of note that Q1 has used the singular vocative form earlier in line 32, Q2 concurring; and in general, except perhaps in line 51 where the plural form may be in error, Q1's distinction between plural and singular seems to be conscious and sound. The Q2 alteration to the plural here, and again in line 99, comes in a reset portion where simple compositorial sophistication is to be expected. As an analogy, see the similar unauthoritative change made by Q5 at line 150.

129 patient 'boue] Q2(s) altered Q1 *patient boue* to *patient, boue*. Since the need for a pause here is very dubious, it seems likely that the compositor misread as a comma the marking for an apostrophe.

155 off: to me,] Dyce, Rhys, and Neilson alter to 'off to me;' but Spencer keeps the original stronger stop after *off*. Since the meaning is largely indifferent, there is no positive need to infer Q transposition of punctuation; moreover, for a parallel see 2 *Honest Whore*, IV.iii.111.

221 shame;] The syntax of this passage has caused difficulty, especially since only commas appear in Q1 to mark the major divisions. Certain changes intended to clarify the syntax were made in Q2(s). The Q2 substitution of a comma for Q1 colon after *palme* in line 224 is obviously required, and a similar alteration after *liues* in line 226 is clearly an improvement. That Q2 failed to make the pointing heavier after *cruell* (line 225) is of no particular consequence. However, the lack of any change in the comma after *shame* (line 221) and the Q2 substitution in the next line of a semicolon for the Q1 comma after *groundes* indicates clearly what modification the corrector intended. At first sight it is a plausible one, the intended sense being, 'Even as many worldlings do build their anger upon feebler grounds, I [with a more serious grievance] should have made you suffer the full rigours of the law had I been angry.' But then the next statement begins very abruptly. When the lines are carefully scrutinized, four points become clear. (1) The *many* who *lose their lives* are the victims of the worldlings. (2) Candido is not associating himself with the worldlings, but using their example as a contrast to his actions. (3) In the Q2 reading, the use of the

comparative *feebler* is difficult to understand in a complete statement. (4) The essential contrast being developed is that some victims of revengeful worldlings have lost their lives for stealing a very small sum, whereas the gallants—who have made away with a very valuable object—have been well treated in comparison by Candido. This last would appear to represent the real sense of the passage, but it can be clarified in the Q only if a second complex sentence with introductory dependent clause begins with *As many worldlings*. The Q2 corrector would appear to have been in error here in analysing the syntax. All editors, the earliest independently, have joined in placing a heavy stop after *grounds* and a lighter stop beforehand after *shame*, except Dyce who punctuates both with semicolons, and Spencer who uses commas. This treatment begs the issue.

II.i

8 I] The alteration of Q1 italic *I* to roman in Q2(s) has no significance for meaning. Italic capital *I* is sprinkled through the page owing to the exhaustion of the printer's case. However, this is the only place that Q2 substituted a roman sort.

45 *Sing*] D[1-2] print this word in roman, and a note in D[3] argues it is a stage-direction, a view also held by Dyce and Rhys. Neilson and Spencer print it as the first word of the song, although Spencer notes the possibility that it is a direction. Even though positive indentification of the song is wanting, and Q2(s) supports Q1, the metre and lining as well as the analogy of line 21 above encourage the belief that *Sing* is an author's direction mistaken for text.

87 I there...scorn't:] Elizabethan orthography being what it is, this line may read as an exclamation, *I* being a pronoun (as all editors take it), or else the sense may be, 'Aye, there among your punks', as in line 100. Either is possible, and the lack of a comma does not disqualify the second, although the first is perhaps just slightly preferable. All editors except Dyce have inserted a pronoun *I* before *scorn't*. However, in what seems to be a reproduction of fashionable speech in Part 2 of this play, such pronouns are often missing.

159 —beseech you sweete,—] Dyce and all succeeding editors place a dash after *for all that* in line 160 in the belief that this marks the end of a parenthetic apology to Bellafront for Fluello's praise of Infelice and the assertion that this praise does not affect their admiration for Bellafront. But the clear sense is that Fluello is urging Hippolito not to withdraw from their fellowship because of his mistress' death (*i.e.* 'for all that') and is therefore inviting him to join them in Bellafront's circle. *Beseech you sweet*, therefore, probably reflects some stage business involving Bellafront, or is addressed to her as an anticipatory request for permission to make the invitation that follows. Although *sweet* is permissible addressed to Hippolito, it does not

seem that the gallants are on sufficient terms of familiarity with him for this to be natural. The point is a fine one, but it would seem, also, that the common compositorial error of transposition has affected the punctuation and that Q 'stil: for all that,' requires emendation to 'stil, for all that:'.

169 Neuer, trust me] The lack of any punctuation in all quartos leaves the modification in doubt. All editors have associated *trust me* with *Never* by placing a heavy stop after *me*. Despite a parallel for this at I.ii.28, the more idiomatic emendation is suggested by line 187 below.

263 I should be] Difficult as it often is to ignore the evidence of a catchword, which in theory is set with the compositor's eye fresh from the manuscript, yet the variant catchword *would* for the following words *I should* does not recommend itself here.

319 ff. Then if your gratious blood....] Not only is the lineation of Q 1–2 (s) in error in this speech but there are two curious Q 2 alterations in the readings. The two quartos line as follows: 'Then...wasted, | I...doo't. | Lend...soule, | That...it, | And...body | *Is* [Q 2 *Its*]...receiues | All...men | *Is* [Q 2 *Tis*]...suppose,'. It is obvious that one or more short lines have thrown the compositor off. Whether Hippolito's speech opens with the regular Q pentameter 'Then if your gratious blood be not all wasted,' followed by the short line 'I shall assay to doo't.', or whether as lined here in conformity with all editors, his opening words complete Bellafront's last line is not to be determined perhaps, except that the editorial relining necessitates only one short line in the speech, not two, and therefore seems preferable. At any rate, this matter does not affect the corruption that follows. Editors thereupon have followed Dyce in assigning the short line as 'Heauens treasure bought it,'. If one wanted maximum balance, one would certainly line, 'You haue no soule, that makes you wey so light: | Heauens treasure bought it, and halfe a crowne hath solde it:' and assign the following, 'For your body' as the next necessary short line. However, when one enquires how the compositor came to misline the passage in the first place, one decides that certainly failure to complete Bellafront's speech with the first short line 'Then if your gratious blood' threw off the lineation originally, but it was the inclusion of the short line 'You haue no soule,' which seems to have ended the mislineation. This passage causes further difficulty in evaluating the correctness of the changes in standing type in Q 2, the substitution of *Its* for Q 1 *Is* in line 325, and of *Tis* in line 327 for Q 1 *Is*. In Q 1 the compositor's case had run short of roman 'I' and 'T' so that lines begin in Q 1: '*T*hat makes... | And halfe... | *I*s like... | All the... | *I*s within... | *T*hat if...' and so on, with corresponding internal italic sorts. There would seem to be no grounds for conjecturing that the alterations to the two '*I*s' readings resulted from a faulty attempt in Q 2 to substitute roman for italic type or wilfully to justify loose lines. The first '*I*s' (line 325) is changed to '*I*ts'

with the same partially broken italic *I* retained; moreover, no other italic letters are touched, and no signs exist of dislocation in the typesetting. We must take it, therefore, that the compositor was making corrections and that there was a distinct intention to alter one or both of the Q1 readings to accord with the markings in his copy. As a consequence, the question resolves itself into a consideration whether both alterations are correct, both faulty, or whether one is correct and the other an error and, if so, which. The words being so similar, it is obvious that the Q2 readings are not revisions but attempted corrections. My own view is that only one 'Is' was marked for correction and that the compositor as a part either of one operation or of two altered one of the readings correctly, and the other wrongly in confusion. Of the two Q2 variants, the first is more acceptable than the second, and I have adopted it, since *Is* for *Its* could have arisen quite readily from Q1 compositorial misunderstanding of the sense of the manuscript. If the 'For' in the phrase 'For your body' were to be taken by the compositor as meaning *because*, the 'improvement' of manuscript *Its* to *Is* follows almost inevitably. On the other hand, in my view this 'For' means *As for*. The scheme of the passage demands a consideration of Bellafront's plight divided into the two parts of soul and body. Hippolito first takes up the condition of her soul, and then re-enforces his conclusions by examining, in parallel, the state of her body. The first part is introduced by the statement 'You haue no soule'; he then turns to the second with the introduction 'For [*i.e.* As for] your body'. The Q2 correction of *Is* to *Its* is accepted, therefore. The second Q2 variant is more difficult. But since it is simpler to conjecture single rather than double error in Q1, my own view is that the copy for Q2 was marked only to correct line 325, that this correction was made, and that the second alteration may well have resulted when the same or another workman surveyed the page, and by an eye-skip looking at the wrong *Is* in Q2 type, repaired what he thought had been a failure to correct. This hypothesis offers a mechanical reason to account for the second error as resulting from the accident that two similar words began lines with only a single-line separation. If it be accepted, one further question remains: given the identification of the Q1 error as the *Is* of line 325, was the alteration to *Its* correct in that line, or was the mistaken correction *Tis* in line 327 the right one for line 325. Demonstration is impossible, but there may be grounds for conjecturing that *Its* was the correct alteration. If the corrector had written *Tis* in his copy, it is more than a little strange that the compositor in altering line 325 *Is* inserted a lower-case *t* between the standing types *I* and *s*. However, it is more likely —on the evidence of preserved Elizabethan proof-sheets—that only a *t* would have been indicated for insertion. In such a case, the reading at line 325 has every reason to be correct; but *Its* at line 327 is rough, and *Tis* would seem to be a compositor's rationalization. We have, then, single error in Q1 corrected as double error, by mischance, in Q2.

[II. i, III. ii]   TEXTUAL NOTES

355 Blacke-beard] Since D¹ the conventional emendation for Qq *Blacke-doord* has been *Back-door'd*; but no use of the adjectival form is recorded in *O.E.D.*, and hence the supposition that *back-door'd* can mean *sly* or *devious* (from the noun) is rather suspect. I believe that the corruption rests in the second element and not in the first. But one can only guess at what the word might be. Although *-browd*, *-pard*, *-biled*, and even *-heart* and *-burnt* are all possibilities, I select *blacke-beard* as the most plausible orthographically and as supported by *Westward Ho*, II.iii.129–130, 'I hold my life the blacke-beard her husband whissels for her.' It would seem that *blacke-beard* in this passage is associated with jealousy and possibly—through some conventional idea of virility—with amorousness. If so, the analogy with the present emendation in *The Honest Whore* would be a good one. For a further parallel, see *Blurt Master Constable* (1602), sig. C4: 'this Flaxen hayr'd men are such pu-lers, and such midlers, and such Chicken-heartes (and yet great quarrellers) that when they Court a Ladye, they are for the better part bound to the peace: no, no, no, no, your blacke hayred man (so hee bee fayre) is your onely sweet man, & in any seruice, the most actiue'.

III.i

40 lip] Reset Q2's variant reading *lips* is almost certainly a compositorial error. No other example of a possibly authoritative change comes in the reset type of this outer forme of sheet E.

77 S.D. *Exit 2. Prentice.*] All editors have retained the Qq direction *Exit 1. Prentice*; moreover, Dyce and his successors give the 2. Prentice an exit at line 73, and alter Qq speech-prefix from 2. *Prent.* to 1. *Prent.* at line 76, thus assuming three errors, in all, instead of one. But 2. Prentice needs an excuse to leave the shop, which he finds in the statement that two of the choicest pieces are in the warehouse. We need not suppose that he ever bothers to bring the pieces in. Moreover, since the chief dramatic reason to take him off the stage is to give him the chance to return with the invented call of Pandulfo, a device for removing Candido from the ensuing action, we are under no obligation to assume that the other apprentices ever came on the stage to beat Fustigo (the watchword is never given) or that lines 93, 116 are delivered within by these apprentices as marked by most editors. The speech-prefix *Omnes*, as shown probably by line 127, represents only George and the two apprentices already on the stage. After all, a dramatic company had some limits to the number of actors it employed.

III.ii

48 that slaue] This may well be corrupt although not so certainly in error as to enforce emendation. *Thou* is presumably addressed to Roger, and *that slaue* is placed in apposition. There is little question that *slaue* is a noun here and not a verb. Hence if there is error, only *that* can come in question.

Possibly it is a misreading for a repeated *thou* (y^u) or manuscript ye could have been misread as y^t. But the Qq reading is not impossible as it stands, and the alternatives have no great appeal.

IV.i

84 wicked faces] This phrase has previously appeared in *The Shoemakers' Holiday*: see textual note for III.ii.45. In view of the direct association made between painters and wrinkled faces in *The Whore of Babylon*, II.i.125, if it were not for the second use here, which would force us to assume identical double error, the tempting emendation in either place would certainly have been *wrinkld faces*. Although double error is not unknown within single plays, one always hesitates to invoke it in support of emendation, especially if it must arise from two different manuscripts. Sense of some sort may possibly be made in both passages. The *wicks* are the lips. If *wicked* be taken as Dekker's private pun, the allusion is doubtless to faces made ugly by prominent lips or over-large mouths.

190 go: woman fare thee well.] In spite of the fact that all editors from D^1 place the heavy stop after *woman*, taking it that *go* is addressed to Bellafront, it seems fairly obvious that *go* is an order to the servant (who doubtless departs by one door as Hippolito is moving towards the other).

V.i

49 True] For *Tame*, the Qq reading, Dyce suggested *True*, an emendation which Spencer adopted. It is more probable that we have a misreading here than that the Wife is objecting to the last line of George's posy, and is saying that it is not *calm* but *tame* husbands who make their wives stormy; nevertheless, she has learned her lesson and will storm no longer.

V.ii

334 Bow a little.] Though prefixed in roman to line 335, and appearing on a standing-type page, these words cannot be text. No editor has fancied them as a confused stage-direction, but it is difficult to conceive what else they can be.

394 content] Unfortunately, at this point imperfect Q2 has deserted us. Editors have customarily preferred 'Yours now is my content, | I throw... full consent.' No serious change in meaning is involved whichever Q1 *consent* is emended to *content*; but it may seem more natural for the first to have contaminated the second, as is usual in such repetitions, even though the reverse is not impossible. There is some interest in the fact that Q4 independently so read it on the sense alone.

PRESS-VARIANTS IN Q1 (1604)

[Copies collated: BM (British Museum C.34.c.24), DFo (Folger Shakespeare Library), CSmH (Henry E. Huntington Library), NN (New York Public Library). To these are added the Q1 sheets C–D, F–G, I–K present in the unique copy of Q3 in the Dyce Collection at the Victoria and Albert Museum.]

SHEET C (*outer forme*)

Corrected: BM, CSmH, DFo, NN
Uncorrected: Q3

Sig. C2ᵛ.
 I.v.175 cheaters] chraters
Sig. C4ᵛ.
 II.i.55 dambde] dambe
   65 *Fluello?*] *Fluello.*

SHEET G (*inner forme*)

Corrected: DFo.
Uncorrected: BM, CSmH, NN, Q3.

Sig. G2.
 IV.i.111 wooe·] wooe.
Sig. G3ᵛ.
 IV.ii.41 *Cram. Poh* is] *Cram. Poli.* Is

SHEET K (*outer forme*)

1st stage corrected: Q3
Uncorrected: CSmH, DFo

Sig. K1.
 V.ii.247 faue] haue

2nd stage corrected: NN

Sig. K1.
 V.ii.343 wit] wet

3rd stage corrected: BM

Sig. K4ᵛ.
 V.ii.504 fings,] fings

EMENDATIONS OF ACCIDENTALS

[When the emendation is taken from one of the quarto editions, the earliest source is given, and the readings of the earlier quartos but not of the later. When the alteration differs from the reading of any quarto, all the quarto readings are provided, but—as in similar lists for other plays—save in exceptional circumstances no source is indicated. Emendations taken from the standing type of Q2 are listed in the footnotes to the text.]

I.i

S.D. Pioratto,] ~ ₍ₐ₎ Q1–5
10 downe,] ~ . Q1–5
30 dead,] ~ ,) Q1–3; ~ ₍ₐ₎) Q4–5
31 liuing:)] ~ : ₍ₐ₎ Q1–5

41 honour —] ~ . Q1–5
52 foes:...her,] ~ ,... ~ ₍ₐ₎ Q1–5
140 so,] ~ ₍ₐ₎ Q1–5

I.ii

77 thunder₍ₐ₎] Q2; ~ : Q1
132 Asse; if] Q2; Asse, if Q1
123 H'az] Q2; Haz Q1

I.iii

S.D. Benedict] Q2; Benedicke Q1
5 The houre-glasse.] *run-on with line 4 in* Q1–5
6, 32 Benedict] Q2; Benedicke Q1
19–20 wey | Mine owne] Q2; Q1 *lines* wey mine | Owne
20 scale,] Q2; ~ : Q1
27 borne;] ~ , Q1–5
27 man,] Q2; ~ ; Q1
33 truth₍ₐ₎] Q2; ~ , Q1

34 auerre,] Q2; ~ ₍ₐ₎ Q1
37 *Infælice*] *Infælisha* Q1, 4–5; *Infælica* Q2–3
40 feasting;] Q2; ~ , Q1
54 *Infælice*] *Infælishæ* Q1, 4–5; *Infelica* Q2–3
58 father!] Q4; ~ ? Q1–3
62 all?] Q2; ~ , Q1
89 Benedict] Q2; *Benedick* Q1

I.iv

19 of blood] Q2; ofblood Q1
22 patience] Q2; patieuce Q1
27 wife,] ~ ₍ₐ₎ Q1–5

I.v

21 notable voluble-tongde] notable-voluble tongde Q1–5
60 turne, I pray?] Q2 [tutne]; ~ ? ... ~ . Q1

71 squemish, fare] *lined in* Q1–5 squemish, | Fare
99–101 Looke...custome.] *prose in* Q1–5

118

[I. v, III. iii]   EMENDATIONS OF ACCIDENTALS

127 thriue, ... eye₀] Q4; ~₀ ... ~, Q1–3
138 him?] ~ . Q1–3; ~ ! Q4–5
147–148 Sweet...conceit.] *prose in* Q1–5
152–153 I pledge...Duccats.] *prose in* Q1–5
161–162 Blurt...all.] *one line in* Q1–5

168–169 You...sin.] *one line in* Q1–5
185 meriment,] ~ . Q1–5
186 knowst.] ~ , Q1–5
189 Make hast againe.] *run-on with line* 188 *in* Q1–5
201 gone—] ~. Q1–3; ~ .—Q4–5
203 let 'em] Q2; let'em Q1
213–214 Then...angry.] *one line in* Q1–5

II.i

S.D. *it, and...painting. He*] *it. And...painting, he* Q1–5
S.D. *cullors*)] Q4; ~ , Q1–3
16 'em] Q4; e'm Q1–3
20 dog,] ~ ₀ Q1–5
21–24 *Cupid...faile.*] *couplet in* Q1–5
27 *downe, and*] ~ ₀ ~ Q1–5
45 handsomely.] ~ ₀ Q1–5
46 day,] ~ . Q1–5
49 So,] Q4; ~ ₀ Q1–3
106 fac'st] facst Q1–3; fac'd Q4–5
108 leane-iawde slaue] leane iawde-slaue Q1–5
112 -Vsher,] ~ , Q1–5
117 S.D. *Company*₀...*stranger,*] Dᵢ; ~ , ... ~ ₀ Q1–5

130 Artichocke-faced Rascall] Artichocke faced-Rascall Q1–5
132 cony-|catch] cony-catch Q1
160 stil, ...that:] ~ : ... ~, Q1–5
168 Lord?] ~ . Q1–4; ~ , Q5
170 she is] Q4; sheis Q1–3
191 me, ...word₀] ~ ₀ ... ~ , Q1–5
192 this,] ~ ₀ Q1–5
213 who?] Q4; ~ : Q1–3
216 done,] ~ ₀ Q1–5
224 band,] Q4; ~ ₀ Q1–3
224 wast-|coate] wastcoate Q1
266 mine,] ~ . Q1–5
313 he.] ~ , Q1–5
324 body,] ~ ₀ Q1–5
427 more,] Q4; ~ . Q1–3

III.i

52 Sneales,] Dyce; ~ ₀ Q1–5
97 Sfoot,] Q1–3 *cw*; ~ ₀ Q1–5 *text*
139–140 A Surgeon...Cozen?] Rhys; *prose in* Q1–5

175 But] but Q1–5
176 You] Q2; you Q1
181 Without] Q2; without Q1
201 eyes.] ~ , Q1–5
223–224 So...sight.] *prose in* Q1–5

III.ii

11–12 *Finger-locke*] Q4; *Finger-loeke* Q1–3

III.iii

43–44 Conny-|catching] Conny-catching Q1
112 ouerthrow,] ~ : Q1–5

113 states:] ~ ₀ Q1–5
113 wrongs,] ~ . Q1–5 ±

119

IV.i

62 one;] ~? [turned] Q1, 3; ~?
 Q2; ~ : Q4–5
74 sound,] Q4; ~ . Q1–3
75 ground.] ~ , Q1–5
76 fooles,] Q4; ~ ; Q1–3
76 hether;] ~ , Q1–5
83 Death's] Q4; Deaths' Q1–3

85 stay.] ~ , Q1–5
107 *Vela.*] Dyce; *run-on with line* 106 *in* Q1–5
115 instruction] Q2; insttuction Q1
176 well,] Q4; ~ ₐ Q1–3
181 whore.] Q4; ~ , Q1–3
186 witches.] Q4; ~ , Q1–3

IV.ii

3 of] Q4; (~ Q1–3
5 bloud,] Q4; ~ . Q1–3
10 not;] ~ , Q1–5
11 corne,] Q4; ~ ; Q1–3

14 tongue,] Q4; ~ ₐ Q1–3
17 thrumd] thrumbd Q1–5
27 tauerne] Q2 [tauern]; taueren Q1

IV.iii

S.D. Candidoes] Q2; Condidoes Q1
3 ready?] Q4; ~ , Q1–3 ±
16 then,] Q2; ~ ₐ Q1
16 see ₐ] Q4; ~ , Q1–3
19 carriage,] Q4; ~ ₐ Q1–3
38 nothing,] ~ : Q1–5
39 violent:] ~ , Q1–5

54–55 penny-|worth] pennyworth Q1
58 what,] Q4; ~ ₐ Q1–3
121 I, I,] Q4; ~ , ~ . Q1–3
123 not,] Q4; ~ ₐ Q1–3
139 caught ₐ] Q4; ~ : Q1–3
169 Ha! whether?] *run-on with line* 168 *in* Q1–5

IV.iv

6 fooles,] Q2; ~ . Q1
7 cause] Q2; Cause Q1
12 same —] ~ . Q1–5
19 lifts] Q2; lifs Q1
28 Lord —] ~ : Q1–5
36 vndertooke —] ~ , Q1–5 ±
45 preuent —] Q2; ~ . Q1
45 far —] ~ . Q1–5
54 me?] Q4; ~ : Q1–3

62 lurch] Q2; lnrch Q1
76 hopes,] Q4; ~ . Q1–3
83 Duke!] Q4; ~ : Q1–3
84 blisse,] Q4; ~ : Q1–3
85 you:] Q4; ~ , Q1–3
93 I ha'] I'ha Q1–3; I ha Q4–5
97 when?] ~ : Q1–3; ~ ! Q4–5
116 said:] Q4; ~ ₐ Q1–3

V.i

5 *George*] Q4; *Geroge* Q1–3
7 greekes,] ~ ₐ Q1–5
84 the] Q4; rhe Q1–3

99 Ist euen so,] *prefixed to line* 100 *in* Q1–5
100 afternoone] Q4; afternoonc Q1–3

120

V.ii

3 behold₍ₐ₎] Q4; ~ . Q1–3
7 (your)] ₍ₐ₎ ~ Q1–5
10 O sonne,] *prefixed to line* 11 *in* Q1–5
21 thundring] Q4; thnndring Q1–3
23 You are most safe.] *run-on with line* 22 *in* Q1–5
24 said,] Q4; ~ ₍ₐ₎ Q1–3
27 amongst] mongst Q4–5; amonst Q1–3
36 selues,] Q4; ~ ₍ₐ₎ Q1–3
42 Duke's] Duk's Q1–5
46–49 Then...here.] Q2; *prose in* Q1
52 *Castruchio?*] Q2 [~ ,]; *Chastruchio*, Q1
59–61 Sonne...hence] Q2; *prose in* Q1
59 desperate,] Q2; ~ ₍ₐ₎ Q1
75 not,] Q2; ~ ₍ₐ₎ Q1
80 stucke] Q2; stuke Q1
85 When] when Q1–5
85 got,] ~ ₍ₐ₎ Q1–5
97 come,] ~ ₍ₐ₎ Q1–5
97 Lordes₍ₐ₎] Q4; ~ : Q1–3
97 pray:] Q4; ~ ₍ₐ₎ Q1, 3; ~ , Q2
199 blowes, pooff,] Q4; ~ , ~ ₍ₐ₎ Q1–3

220 vp all, all, all,] Q4; ... ~ ₍ₐ₎ Q1–3
277 Dragon;] ~ ₍ₐ₎ Q1–4; ~ , Q5
321 vnruly,] Q4; ~ ₍ₐ₎ Q1–3
329 see:] ~ ₍ₐ₎ Q1–3; ~ , Q4–5
331 now,] Q4; ~ ₍ₐ₎ Q2
337 God...ioy.] *run-on with line* 336 *in* Q1–5
345 Nay...too:] Q4; *run-on with line* 344 *in* Q1–3
352 Frier.] ~ ₍ₐ₎ Q1–5
362 bloud] Q2; blould Q1
379 friendship: ...looke,] ~ , ... ~ : Q1, 3–5 ±
387 Frier,] Q4; ~ . Q1, 3
406 warrant.] Q4; ~ ₍ₐ₎ Q1, 3
411 Maidenhead] Q1, 3 *text*; mai- Q1, 3 *cw*
413–414 Had he...thee.] Q4; *one line in* Q1, 3
462 yonder] Q4; youder Q1, 3
474 coate,] Q4; ~ . Q1, 3
484 it?] ~ , Q1, 3; ~ ! Q4–5
485 tender,] Q4; ~ ₍ₐ₎ Q1, 3
488 balme.] Q4; ~ , Q1, 3
502 chaine:] ~ . Q1, 3; ~ , Q4–5
503 paine.] ~ : Q1, 3–5

HISTORICAL COLLATION OF EARLY EDITIONS

[The five quartos to 1635 are here collated against the present text, only substantive and semi-substantive variants being given. The lemmata are those of the present text; variants with their sigla appear after the square bracket. Omission of a siglum indicates that the quarto concerned agrees with the text.]

I.i

S.D. *Hearse*] *Heare* Q 4–5
7 desprate] desperate Q 4–5
9 pry] pray Q 4–5
17 Lord?] ~ ! Q 4–5
41 regard] regarded Q 5
45 yours] your Q 4–5

78 is] *om.* Q 5
82 roll] role Q 4–5
89 one woman] many women Q 5
103 fore] for Q 5
137 liude, so long] ~ ˌ ~ ~, Q 1, 4–5

I.ii

5 anie] an Q 4; *om.* Q 5
17 Nor] Not Q 4–5
29 you are] your Q 4–5
32 made] maste Q 5
32 vpon] vp Q 5
34, 46 ha] haue Q 4–5
44 you] yon Q 4

95 and] and and Q 5
120 mad-caps] olde dames Q 1, 4–5
121 my naunts] mine aunts Q 1, 4–5
129 roares?] ~ ˌ Q 2–5 ±
131 coosen?] ~ , Q 2–3
132 Asse; if] Asse, if Q 1, 4–5
134 sister?] ~ ! Q 2–3

I.iii

5 neere] meere Q 1–5
11 see] sweete Q 1, 4–5
14 crust] rust Q 1–5
35 *Bergamo*] *Bergaine* Q 1, 4–5
40 midst] deadst Q 1, 4–5
41 cup] cap Q 1, 4–5
43 had] *om.* Q 4–5
44 alter] alterd Q 1, 4–5
46 forgot] forgotten Q 5
52, 63 2 *Seruants.*] 2 *Ser.* Q 2–3
52 good knaues] God knowes Q 1, 4, 5
56 thy] the Q 1, 4–5

58 father?] ~ ! Q 4–5
62 all?] ~ , Q 1, 4–5
66 I'de] Ile Q 1, 4–5
71 hurts] hnrts Q 2–3; haunts Q 1, 4–5
77 venison] some venison Q 5
78 goddesse] gods Q 1, 4–5
78 *Cyprian*] *Coprian* Q 1, 4–5
83 her] it Q 1, 4–5
90 you] *om.* Q 4–5
90 altred] altered Q 4–5
93 may] way Q 2–3

122

I.iv, II.i]   HISTORICAL COLLATION OF EARLY EDITIONS

I.iv

25 wonderfully] wonderfull Q 4–5
31 vnfurnisht] vnfurnish Q 5
36 anger] auger Q 2–3
39 I,] om. Q 5
43 ha] haue Q 5
43 tempted] tempred Q 1

I.v

2 you, . . . way?] ~ ? . . . , Q 2–3
8 is] om. Q 4–5
27 ha] om. Q 4–5
40 now?] ~ ; Q 4–5
47 the better] om. the Q 4–5
48 neare, —] ~ , ∧ Q 5
54 eene] euen Q 2
56 conscionably] conscionable Q 2
56 shillings] om. Q 2
60 turne, I pray?] ~ ? . . . ~ . Q 1, 3–5
63 then —] ~ ∧ Q 4–5
72 is] s Q 5
74 you:] ~ ? Q 2
79 Gentle-man?] gentle*e*men, Q 2; Gentleman, Q 4–5
80 nor] not Q 4–5
90 found] found found Q 2
94 away my] away all my Q 4–5
97 Pax] Pox Q 5
99 Gentleman] Gentlemen Q 2
100 mony ∧ heare;] ~ ; ~ , Q 1, 3–5
101 Pray let] om. Pray Q 2
102 quoth] puoth Q 2
105 an] a Q 2
118 twould] would Q 1, 3–5
121 We are] Were Q 1, 3; We're Q 4–5
125 penworth] penyworth Q 4–5
136 pennyworths] a pennyworth Q 5
138 him?] ~ . Q 1–3; ~ ! Q 4–5
150 Gentleman] Gentlemen Q 5
153 to] om. Q 1, 3–5
155 *Fluello?*] ~ . Q 4–5
170 the] this Q 4–5
181 lye] be Q 2
183 in calme] in all calme Q 2
201 gone —] ~ . Q 1–3
223 pitty,] ~ ; Q 4–5
232 courtier] carter Q 1, 3–5

II.i

7 two twe Q 1, 3
14 and] om. Q 1, 3–5
20 by and] om. by Q 5
27 arise, I neuer shall.] arise, downe, I neuer shall arise. Q 1, 3–5
29 trade?] ~ ∧ Q 5
29 *Abram.*] ~ ? Q 5
30 of] if Q 1, 3–5
35 no faith] infaith Q 1, 3–5
38 Whaat?] What? Q 1, 3; what, Q 4–5
42 *Sir?*] ~ , Q 4–5
43 glasse?] ~ . Q 4–5
45–6 (*Sing.*) Prety] *Sing prety* Q 1–5
57 S.D. fetch] *fetches* Q 2
60 thee] me Q 5
62 pry] pray Q 4–5
66 Smell?] ~ . Q 5
69 What?] ~ ∧ Q 2, 5
69 you] yon Q 1, 3–4
69 neighing?] ~ . Q 4–5
70 Angels] Anhels Q 2
77 mornings] morning Q 5
82 *Herculian*] *herculanian* Q 1, 3
87 scorn't] I scorn't Q 4–5
88 neasts.] ~ ? Q 4–5
91 *Malauolta*] *Malauella* Q 1, 3–5
94 *Lollio*] *Lollilo* Q 1, 3
112 *Sordello*] *Lord Ello* Q 1, 3–5
115 Citizen.] ~ ! Q 4–5

123

THE HONEST WHORE, PART I   [II. i, III. i

117 to] of Q 1, 3
122 little pretie] pretie little Q 5
127 signior] signiors Q 4–5
128 tilt] litle Q 1–5
130 accurs'd] a curst Q 1, 3–5
142 wash.] ~ ! Q 4–5
146 seruant?] ~ ,~ Q 2
152 heed] heard Q 1, 3–5
160 the] my Q 1, 3–5
165 has] hath Q 4–5
165 some] soms Q 5
167 so?] ~ : Q 4–5
168 Lord?] ~ . Q 1–5 ±
170 she is] sheis Q 1–3
176 haue it] ha Q 1, 3–5
176 signiors? what?] ~ , ~ , Q 4–5
182 your] you Q 1, 3
190 can,] ~ ,~ Q 1, 3–5
196 *Hipolito,*] *Hipolitos* ,~ Q 1–5
198 malcontent] mal content Q 5
201 gurnet?] ~ . Q 4–5
206 sweet] *om.* Q 5
212 Pry thee] I pry thee Q 4; I prithee Q 5
213 who?] ~ : Q 1–3
215 for] I, for Q 1, 3–5
219 shaall!] shall? Q 4–5
223 your scuruy mistris heere] *om.* Q 1, 3–5
243 stay] sta Q 2
245 If I may] *Hipo.* If may Q 1, 3
264 Lady?] ~ , Q 4–5
283 Indeed?] ~ : Q 4–5
283 not!] not I. Q 4–5
284 sweare?] ~ . Q 4–5
288 would] could Q 1, 3–5
291 sweare?] ~ , Q 4–5

300–302 but if youle...heart.] but beleeue it, I | No sooner had laid hold vpon your presence, | But straight mine eye conueid you to my heart. Q 1, 3–5
301 mine] my Q 2
304 fashion] passion Q 1, 3–5
306 it] *om.* Q 4–5
309 O ,~ ...soule!] ~ ! ... ~ ,~ Q 4–5
310 ile] I Q 5
316 selfe?] ~ . Q 4–5 ±
325 Its] Is Q 1, 3–5
327 Is] Tis Q 2
328 your] *om.* Q 4–5
342 out] our Q 5
355 Blacke-beard] Blacke-doord Q 1–5
361 one] on Q 4
362 harlot?] ~ : Q 4–5 ±
366 supply] supple Q 4–5
386 th'] the Q 4–5
414 you] your Q 5
416 creake] cracke Q 5
418 now] *om.* Q 4–5
424 I] *om.* Q 1, 4–5
433 fayre?] ~ : Q 4–5 ±
444 His weapon...instrument,] What! has he left his weapon heere behind him, | And gone forgetfull? O fit instrument ,~ Q 1, 4–5
449 Or...on] Or split my heart vpon Q 1, 4–5
454 not looke...farewell!] not bid farewell! a scorne! Q 1, 4–5
456 S.D. *Exit.*] *Exeunt.* Q 1–5

III.i

13 Cozen?...how?] ~ , ... ~, Q 4–5
19 I] A Q 1
33 land] hand Q 5

40 lip] lips Q 2–3
45 sha's] she'as Q 4–5
51 wife?] ~ , Q 4–5
52 batter] butter Q 5

124

[III. i, III. iii] HISTORICAL COLLATION OF EARLY EDITIONS

62 you] yon Q5
77 S.D. 2. Prentice.] 1. Prentice. Q1–5
86 who] what Q5
92 *Fust.* I, ...pieces] *om.* Q2–3
94 whites] whits Q5
95 Flat-cap?] ~ : Q4–5
101 your men] your man Q5
102 this?] ~ : Q4–5
102 heres] here Q1, 4–5
110 piece?] ~ : Q4–5
111 so delicate, so soft] so soft, so delicate Q4–5
114 me] *om.* Q5

117 thump] thrum Q1, 4–5
122 You will] You'le Q4–5
131 sirs?] ~ : Q4–5
141 Ningle] mingle Q1, 4–5
149 ha] haue Q5
150 Gules] Gulles Q4–5
152 foole?] ~ . Q4–5
176 an] on Q5
182 then y'are like] y'are like then Q5
233 in his] in's Q4–5
233 cloke?] ~ , Q4–5
241 in fayth] *om.* Q4–5

III.ii

2 mistris?] ~ : Q4–5
6 How?] ~ , Q4–5
17 *Bawd.*] *om.* Q1–3
27 Amber] Ambler Q5

32 the] *om.* Q4–5
49 shillings] shilling Q5
60 gentlemen?] ~ . Q4–5
66 those] these Q5

III.iii

6 gallants] gallant Q1–5
10 in] *om.* Q5
19 S.D. Fluello,] Fluello, *and* Q2
20 goody] goodly Q5
26 Yeoman] Yeomen Q4–5
52 being slaues] ... slaue Q2
53 blossoms] blossom Q2
63 a] *om.* Q5
70 fyste] foiste Q4–5
76 *Math.* Spurne...Varlet!] *om.* Q4–5
77–80 O how...pride.] *prose in* Q4–5
78 a little] *om.* Q4–5
82–83 I, I...there.] *lined in* Q4–5 Church: | Pray
92 How's] How is Q4–5
100 impossible,] ~ ! Q4–5
104 come, I hope...] *begins new line* Q4–5

106–108 Tis time...me] *lined in* Q4–5 Tis...iesting, | I... Saluation: | I...me.
107 away] away my Q4–5
109 buy] b with Q4; be with Q5
110 Oh...curse] *lined in* Q4–5 women: | Shun
111 them] em Q4–5
116 How,] ~ ! Q4–5
118 Why...vs,] *lined in* Q4–5 la? | These
119 whilst] while Q4–5
123–126 Thy lust...wise:] *lined in* Q4–5 Thy...much: | Go... tooke; | By...now | Will... girdels: | Who...wise:
123 much:] ~ ! Q4–5
124 my example] mine... Q4–5

IV.i

11 back's] backe is Q4–5
49 lap] lip Q4–5
54 art] are Q5
59 plot] plots Q2
61 fence] sense Q4–5
77 last] length Q5
77 laid] brought Q5
85 but] hut Q4
87 The...coulour.] *om.* Q5
101 whosoere] whoe're Q4–5
105 *meo*] *mea* Q4–5
138 on] in Q4–5

145 beats] beatst Q4–5
161 battlements] battlement Q4–5
165 the] thy Q4–5
166 most most] most Q4–5
176 Tho] The Q1–3
182 comes.] ~ ? Q4–5
187 vpont] vpon it Q4–5
188–190 Ile...well.] *lined in* Q4–5
    Ile...cannot: | But...faile: |
    Go...well.
190 go: woman‸] ~ ‸ ~ ‸ Q2;
    ~ ‸ ~, Q4–5

IV.ii

S.D. Poh] Poli Q1, 3–5
2 them] em Q4–5
3 of...and] (~ ... ‸ ~ Q1–3;
    ‸ ~ ... (~ Q4–5
3 vp] *om.* Q1, 3–5
4 three] *om.* Q4–5
15 beard] beasd Q2
16 Poh.] Poli. Q4–5
16 Tuscalonian:] ~ ? Q2; ~ !
    Q4–5
17 Cods] Gods Q5

20 murder out] out murder Q4–5
21 her] here Q5
25 haps] perhaps Q4–5
28 couple] a couple Q4–5
38 barre.] ~ ? Q4–5
40 Poh....Poh.] Poli....Poli.]
    Q4–5
41 Poh] Poli Q1(u), 4–5
42, 43 Poh] Poli Q4–5
43 S.D. Exit.] Exeunt. Q1–5

IV.iii

1 now.] ~ ? Q2, 4–5
3 ready?] ~ , Q1–3 ±
10 whatsoeuer] whatsoe'r Q4–5
12 neuer] not Q4–5
13 neuer] ne'r Q4–5
20–21 I...on.] *lined in* Q4–5
    mistris, | My
22 it were] twere Q4–5
23 to] *om.* Q4–5
24 that] *om.* Q4–5
26–27 You...tell?] *lined in* Q4–5
    life! | Whats
26 life,] ~ ! Q4–5
27 vpon's] on's Q4–5

29–31 Girt...saw.] *lined in* Q4–5
    Girt...man, | What...too? |
    This...saw.
30 too:] ~ ? Q4–5
35 workt] wrought Q4–5
37 Spleene] speene Q2
50 -man?] ~ , Q4–5
50 tricksicoates!] ~ ? Q4–5
51 S.D. Poh] Poli Q1, 3–5
53 buy?] ~ : Q4–5
58 foole? ... -man? ...man?]
    ~ ! ~ ! ~ ! Q4–5
60 what?] ~ , Q4–5
60 -points,] ~ ! Q4–5

IV. iii, IV. iv] HISTORICAL COLLATION OF EARLY EDITIONS

61 faith] ifaith Q4–5
66 *Poh.*] *Poli.* Q1, 3–5
68 *Poh.*] *Poli.* Q4–5
70 you Gentlemen...Cambricks?] you, heere's choice Cambricks. Q4–5
73 doubtlets.] ~ ? Q4–5
83 brakes] brackes Q4–5
84–85 Twould...shop.] *lined in* Q4–5 then: | There
87 *Poh.*] *Poli.* Q4–5
87–88 A...biting.] *lined in* Q4–5 broake, | Call
88 biting.] ~ ? Q4–5
90 in't?] ~ ⋀ Q2–3; to it? Q4–5
91–92 Sfoot...shop.] *lined in* Q4–5 em, | Ah
92 shop.] ~ ? Q4–5
98 you're] y'are Q4–5
111 phrase] praise Q1, 4–5
112 S.D. Candido's] *his* Q1, 4–5
114 Prentise-] Prentises Q4–5
116–117 How...wares.] *lined in* Q4–5 How...them? | What... wife? | Officers...wares.

116 now?] ~ ! Q4–5
117 officers?] ~ ⋀ Q1; ~ , Q4–5
121–122 I...shop.] *lined in* Q4–5 I...me! | What...hand, | Heele...shop.
122 hand,] ~ ? Q4–5
125 *Candido?*] ~ . Q4–5
126 you sir?] you? Q4–5
127 you⋀ ...sayes:] ~ ? ... ~ ! Q4–5
130 y'are changde] y're ~ Q5
151 Looke how his] See how's Q4–5
151 goes!] ~ , Q4–5
151 but] *om.* Q4–5
152 Oh] *om.* Q4–5
155 ha?] ~ ! Q4–5
158 What?] ~ , Q4–5
160 as little to him] to him as little Q4–5
161 corde!] ~ , Q1, 4–5
168 now?] ~ , Q4–5
175 ha] haue Q4–5
175 fitted] fitted you Q4–5

IV.iv

11 on his] on's Q4–5
12 foole?] ~ ! Q4–5
21–22 Thou...yeares,] *lined in* Q4–5 Thou...peicd | Mine... yeares,
26 w'are] we'are Q5
29 Hmh] hum Q4–5
35 for] far Q2–3
41 haue] ha Q4–5
51 so:] ~ ? Q2–3
53 digs] dig Q2–3
54 now:] ~ ! Q4–5
54 meete] not meete Q5
54 me?] ~ : Q1–3
55 sir,] ~ ? Q2–3
57 has] he has Q4–5

62 Ith] Itch Q1, 4–5
63 friend.] ~ ! Q4–5
65 send] sent Q4–5
70 reuealed] reueal'd Q4–5
80 mourning] morning Q1
83 Duke!] ~ : Q1–3
85 you] her Q4–5
88 Her] Here Q5
89 thither —] ~ ? Q1; ~ ⋀ Q4–5
97 when?] ~ : Q1–3; ~ ! Q4–5
99 father.] ~ ? Q4–5
100 monasterie:] ~ ! Q5
101 monasterie:] ~ ! Q4–5
108 bands] bonds Q1, 4–5
119 Phisition:] ~ ! Q4–5

V.i

S.D. Pioratto] Piratto Q5
1 comes] commeth Q4-5
3 way.] ~ ? Q4-5
6 lies.] ~ ? Q4-5
7 especially] specially Q4-5
9 you're] y'are Q4-5
12 forth.] ~ ? Q4-5
14 haue...haue] ha...ha Q4-5
20 youre] y'are Q4-5
29 till] vntill Q4-5
33 cloth.] ~ ? Q4-5
45 *cunny*] *cunuy* Q2
49 True] Tame Q1-5
54 S.D. Sinezi] Sinere Q1-3
66-67 Had...him,] *lined in* Q4-5 to | *Bethlem*
67 they will] the'l Q4-5

69 haue] ha Q4-5
75 Prouide] Prouides Q5
77 *Duke*.] *Cast.* Q1-3
77 get pen and inck.] *om.* Q5
78 now?...men.] ~ !... ~ ? Q4-5
79 haue] ha Q4-5
81 whom.] ~ ? Q4-5
86 *Duke*.] *Geo.* Q4
90 *Infæliche*] *Infelices* Q4-5
94 It cannot be.] *om.* Q4-5
96 workes] worke Q4-5
99 euen] *om.* Q4-5
100 you say?] *om.* Q4-5
101 how:] ~ ! Q4-5
113 liues!] ~ : Q4-5

V.ii

S.D. Infæliche] Infelices Q4-5
2-9 You presse...Knot.] *prose in* Q4-5
10 sonne,] ~ ! Q4-5
15-16 Stay...busines.] *prose in* Q4-5
15 safest] and safest Q4-5
16 busines.] ~ ? Q4-5
17 Be't] Be it Q4-5
17 is a chappell stands] stands a chappell Q4-5
21-23 Ile...safe.] *prose in* Q4-5
27 are:] ~ ? Q4-5
27 amongst] amonst Q1-3; mongst Q4-5
31 i'me] I am Q4-5
34 so] o Q1-3
41 matter.] ~ ? Q4-5
42 matter!] ~ ? Q4-5
44 Duke?] ~ ! Q4-5
48 he,] ~ ? Q4-5
49 here.] ~ ? Q4-5
50 *Castruchio*,] *om.* Q4-5
52 *Castruchio*?] ~ , Q1, 3

53 the pit of] *om.* Q4-5
59 Oh God,] *om.* Q4-5
59 God.] ~ ! Q4-5
60 Haue] ha Q4-5
61 hence.] ~ ? Q4-5
65 You] Ye Q4-5
69 disguise:] disguisde: Q1, 3; disguise! Q4-5
69 man.] ~ ! Q4-5
72 not] nor Q1, 3
81 escape] scape Q4-5
82 I] *om.* Q4-5
82 vpon] on Q4-5
84 louers,] ~ ! Q4-5
87 there!] ~ ? Q4-5
91 he.] ~ ? Q4-5
94 What!...time,] ~,... ~ ? Q4-5
94 met] meet Q5
95 place.] ~ ? Q4-5
97 pray] I pray Q5
98 yet.] ~ ! Q4-5
100-101 *Castruchio*...afternoone?] *prose in* Q4-5

v. ii] HISTORICAL COLLATION OF EARLY EDITIONS

105 spent.] ~ ? Q4–5
108 How now] Now Q4–5
108 thou] om. Q4–5
108 house.] ~ ? Q4–5
112 right mind] wits Q4–5
113 *Anselmo*] *Anselme* Q4–5
116 eene] euen Q4–5
119 fellow is] fellow's Q4–5
119 idlelie] idelie Q4–5
120 Sirra] om. Q4–5
121 all,] ~ ! Q4–5
121 wise] om. Q4–5
125 yes?] ~ , Q4–5
126 a] of Q4–5
131 them, they are] 'em, they're Q4–5
133 here] om. Q4–5
137 these.] ~ ? Q4–5
146 man] men Q1, 3
149 gods] god Q4–5
149 *Anselm*] *Anselmo* Q1, 3–5
151 Thanke] I thanke Q4–5
159 do they] they do Q5
161 they will] they'l Q4–5
161 you] yon Q5
173 himselfe] his wits Q1, 3–5
177 soule.] ~ ! Q4–5
186 i'me] I am Q4–5
188 foole!] ~ ? Q4–5
189 ime] I am Q4–5
190 ear] eares Q5
190 the] om. Q4–5
190 and] om. Q4–5
194 stay, stay —] om. Q4–5
194–195 wind, ...wind,] ~ ? ... ~ ? Q4–5
195 wheres the winde:] om. Q4–5
198 looke there,] om. Q4–5
199 pooff, pooff, pooff] puffe, puffe, puffe Q4–5
201 laugh] laught Q2
206 vergis] veriuice Q4–5
207 Sirra! ...there?] ~ , ... ~ : Q4–5

210 looke:] om. Q4–5
219 and thus,] om. Q4–5
220 all, all, all,] om. Q4–5
221 see,] om. Q4–5
222 goes] goe Q2
224 Alas! there!] ~ , ~ ; Q4–5
225 bith] by the Q4–5
227 Syrra,] ~ ! Q4–5
228 me?] ~ ! Q4–5
228 no] na Q4–5
231 me?] ~ ! Q4–5
232 Ime] I am Q4–5
232 Alas?] ~ ! Q4–5
234 euer] neuer Q4–5
236 I, I,] ~ , ~ ˄ Q4–5
238 oh!] ~ . Q4–5
242 pleasd] pleased Q4–5
247 saue] haue Q1(u), Q3–5
252 That] This Q4–5
256 whore, whore,] om. Q4–5
262 here:] ~ ? Q4–5
266 Iack?] ~ : Q4–5
270 so!] ~ , Q4–5
283 and thow't] if thou'lt Q4–5
285 and thow't] if thou Q4; if thou't Q5
288 Ooh!] O ˄ Q4–5
288–289 Ooh...out.] *lined in* Q4–5 murder, | I
288 slaine —] ~ ! Q4–5
290 villaines,] ~ ! Q4–5
291 I am slaine] om. I am Q4–5
298 into] in Q4–5
306 but in] in but Q4–5
308 nor you? nor you, nor you?] nor you, nor you. Q4–5
313 Three] The're Q1, 3; They are Q4–5
313 gudgeons!] ~ , Q1, 3; ~ ? Q4–5
320 Speake] Say Q4–5
322 fo] so Q4–5
331–332 you ha...spun,] heres your fortune, Q1, 3–5

335 i'me] I am Q 4–5
336 your] y'are Q 4–5
343 wit] wet Q 1(u), 3–5
353 Haha haha.] Ha, ha, ha. Q 4–5
356 weapons,] ~ ? Q 4–5
357 tricke:] ~ ! Q 4–5
359–361 Why...sonnes.] *lined in* Q 4–5 Why...hie? | Gainst... draw? | Hers...sonnes.
359 against] Gainst Q 4–5
360 you] ye Q 4–5
360 draw? hers!] ~ ₐ ~, Q 4–5
361 Mine!] ~ , Q 4–5
361 sonnes.] ~ ? Q 2
361 Sonne?] ~ ₐ Q 2; ~ ! Q 4–5
364 I will] I'le Q 4–5
367 sparkles] sparkes Q 4–5
368 most] *om.* Q 4–5
369 Shees] *Ans.* Shees Q 2
370 *Ans.*] *om.* Q 1–5
379 To...looke,] *lined in* Q 4–5 friendship, | That
389 conquered] conquerd Q 4–5
393 change.] ~ ! Q 4–5
394 content] consent Q 1, 3
408 fine iewell.] fine and a rich iewell. Q 4–5
409 maide.] ~ ? Q 4–5
412 Asse ₐ] ~ ! Q 4–5

415 then?] ~ ! Q 4–5
418 such] *om.* Q 5
427 law] the law Q 5
428–429 So...her.] *prose in* Q 4–5
430 their] the Q 5
441 first:] ~ ? Q 4–5
444 haue] ha Q 4–5
444 giuen] giu'n Q 4–5
445 its] tis Q 5
449 zounds] *om.* Q 4–5
454 mas and] *om.* Q 4–5, *which start new line with* See
464 mad.] ~ ? Q 4–5
467 Then...know] *lined in* Q 4–5 that | Know
468 You are...you are] y'are... y'are Q 4–5
469 wife:] ~ ? Q 4–5
472 yet] *om.* Q 4–5
473 was my] was yet my Q 1, 3
475 yet] *om.* Q 4–5
476 Ime] I am Q 4–5
477 skill,] ~ ! Q 4–5
480 Come...hands.] *lined in* Q 4–5: friends, | Ioyne
484 it?] ~ . Q 1, 3; ~ ! Q 4–5
487 calme.] ~ ? Q 4–5
506 sap of] same Q 4–5
517 S.D. *Exeunt.*] *om.* Q 4–5

THE
SECOND
PART OF THE
HONEST VVHORE,

VVITH THE HVMORS
of the Patient Man, the Impatient
Wife: the Honeſt Whore, perſwaded by
ſtrong Arguments to turne Curtizan
againe: her braue refuting thoſe
Arguments.

And laſtly, the Comicall Paſſages of an Italian
Bridewell, where the Scæne ends.

Written by THOMAS DEKKER.

LONDON,
Printed by *Elizabeth All-de,* for *Nathaniel Butter.*
An. Dom. 1 6 3 0.

TEXTUAL INTRODUCTION

So far as we have evidence, *The Second Part of The Honest Whore*, first and only quarto printed in 1630 by Elizabeth Allde for Nathaniel Butter (Greg, *Bibliography*, no. 435), was Dekker's unassisted work. It is generally supposed that composition followed shortly after Part 1. The earliest known reference is the entry in the Stationers' Register (but without fee) on 29 April 1608 to Thomas Man the younger, publisher of Part I: 'Entred for his copie vnder thand*es* of Sr Geo. Bucke knight and m^r Seton Warden A booke called the second p*ar*te of the conu'ted Courtisan or honest Whore'. This entry seems to have produced no edition, and perhaps not even copyright, for on 29 June 1630 Nathaniel Butter entered for his copy: 'vnder the handes of Sr Hen: Herbert and mr Purfoote, The second part of the Honest Hoore by Th. Dekker'. On 21 May 1639 'The second part of the honest whore' was one of twenty-five books transferred by Butter to M. Flesher, confirming the order of the Court of 11 May. Part 2 is so frequently found bound with the 1635 reprint of Part 1 (printed by Okes and sold by R. Collins) that it may be reasonable to conjecture that the stationers owning the respective copyrights made an agreement for sale of a collected edition.

What copy Man used for his entry, whether it was returned to the author or the theatrical company, lost, or passed on as property until it finally reached Butter's hands, is unknown and perhaps unknowable. However, the characteristics of the 1630 quarto are not inconsonant with those of foul papers; although an edited transcript from a prompt-book is not impossible, especially if that book had retained various of Dekker's descriptive directions. But on the whole, especially when we consider the fairly numerous appearances of Dekker's spelling and punctuation habits, foul papers (or a transcript of them) seems the more probable copy. In this connexion, the difficulty about the name of Beraldo in I.i, ii, and the errors in the stage-direction and speech-prefixes in I.iii involving the 1. Guest, perhaps identified in the manuscript as *Long-hat*, should not be overlooked as appropriate for foul-papers copy. On

TEXTUAL INTRODUCTION

the whole, the text has been transmitted without abnormal error save for the compositor's frequent habit of setting verse as prose. Each sheet was imposed with the same two skeleton-formes, and there is every reason to believe that only one compositor and press were employed.

Part 2 has been reprinted by the same editors listed for Part 1.

The present edition is based on a collation of the following seventeen copies, which represent the majority of those recorded: British Museum copy 1 (644.b.21[2]) and copy 2 (C.12.f.4[3]); Bodleian copy 1 (Mal. 235[4]), copy 2 (Mal.788[2]), and copy 3 (Mal. 192[6], imperfect, wanting L 2–4); Dyce Collection in the Victoria and Albert Museum; Worcester College, Oxford; University of Chicago; Library of Congress; Folger Shakespeare Library copy 1 (cs 47) and copy 2 (cs 224); Harvard University; Henry E. Huntington Library; Newberry Library; New York Public Library; University of Texas; and Yale University. The Bodleian copy 3 has been in part marked for production, almost certainly not a contemporary one, with some cuts and text alterations.

[PERSONS

DUKE OF MILAN
HIPPOLITO, husband to Infelice
MATHEO, husband to Bellafront
LODOVICO SFORZA a knight,
BERALDO
CAROLO
FONTINELL
ASTOLFO } Courtiers

ORLANDO FRISCOBALDO, father to Bellafront
CANDIDO, a linen-draper
ANTONIO GEORGIO, a poor scholar
BRYAN, an Irish footman
BOTS, a pander
CONSTABLE
MASTERS OF BRIDEWELL

INFELICE, wife to Hippolito and daughter to the Duke
BELLAFRONT, wife to Matheo
BRIDE, wife to Candido
MISTRESS HORSELEECH, a bawd
DOROTHEA TARGET
PENELOPE WHORE-HOUND
CATHERINA BOUNTINALL } Whores

Citizens, Prentices, Servants, Pages, Vintners,
Billmen, Beadles.]

The Honest Whore

ACTUS PRIMUS, Scæna Prima

Enter at one doore Beraldo, Carolo, Fontinell, Astolfo, *with Seruingmen, or Pages attending on them; at another doore enter* Lodouico, *meeting them.*

Lod. Good day, Gallants.
Omn. Good morrow, sweet *Lodouico*.
Lod. How doest thou *Carolo*.
Caro. Faith, as Physicions doe in a Plague, see the World sicke, and am well my selfe.
Font. Here's a sweet morning, Gentlemen.
Lod. Oh, a morning to tempt *Ioue* from his Ningle *Ganimed*, which is but to giue Dary Wenches greene gownes as they are going a milking; what, is thy Lord stirring yet?
Asto. Yes, he will not be horst this houre, sure.   10
Ber. My Lady sweares he shall, for she longs to bee at Court.
Caro. Oh, wee shall ride switch and spurre, would we were there once.

Enter Bryan *the Footeman.*

Lod. How now, is thy Lord ready?
Bryan. No so crees sa mee, my Lady will haue some little Tyng in her pelly first.
Caro. Oh, then they'le to breakefast.
Lod. Footman, does my Lord ride y'th Coach with my Lady, or on horsebacke?
Bryan. No foot la, my Lady will haue me Lord sheet wid her, my 20
Lord will sheet in de one side, and my Lady sheet in de toder side.
                                                                Exit.
Lod. My Lady sheet in de toder side: did you euer here a Rascall talke so like a Pagan? Is't not strange that a fellow of his starre, should bee seene here so long in *Italy*, yet speake so from a Christian?

21 S.D. *Exit.*] D²; *Exeunt* Q

Enter Anthonio Georgio, *a poore Scholler.*

Asto. An Irishman in *Italy*! that so strange! why, the nation haue running heads.   *Exchange Walke.*

Lod. Nay *Carolo*, this is more strange, I ha bin in *France*, theres few of them: Mary, *England* they count a warme chimny corner, and there they swarme like Crickets to the creuice of a Brew-house; but Sir, in *England* I haue noted one thing.   30

Omn. What's that, what's that of *England?*

Lod. Mary this Sir, what's he yonder?

Ber. A poore fellow would speake with my Lord.

Lod. In *England*, Sir, troth I euer laugh when I thinke on't: to see a whole Nation should be mark't i'th forehead, as a man may say, with one Iron: why Sir, there all Costermongers are Irishmen.

Caro. Oh, that's to show their Antiquity, as comming from *Eue*, who was an Apple-wife, and they take after the Mother.

Omn. Good, good, ha, ha.

Lod. Why then, should all your Chimny-sweepers likewise be 40 Irishmen? answer that now, come, your wit.

Caro. Faith, that's soone answered, for Saint *Patricke* you know keepes Purgatory, hee makes the fire, and his Country-men could doe nothing, if they cannot sweepe the Chimnies.

Omn. Good agen.

Lod. Then, Sir, haue you many of them (like this fellow) (especially those of his haire) Footmen to Noblemen and others, and the Knaues are very faithfull where they loue, by my faith very proper men many of them, and as actiue as the cloudes, whirre, hah.

Omn. Are they so?   50

Lod. And stout! exceeding stout; Why, I warrant, this precious wild Villaine, if hee were put to't, would fight more desperately then sixteene Dunkerkes.

Asto. The women they say are very faire.

Lod. No, no, our Country Bona Robaes, oh! are the sugrest delicious Rogues.

Asto. Oh, looke, he has a feeling of them.

Lod. Not I, I protest, there's a saying when they commend

Nations: It goes, the Irishman for his hand, Welshman for a leg, the Englishman for a face, the Dutchman for beard. 60
Font. I faith, they may make swabbers of them.
Lod. The Spaniard, let me see, for a little foot (I take it) the Frenchman, what a pox hath he? and so of the rest. Are they at breakfast yet? come walke.
Asto. This *Lodouico,* is a notable tounged fellow.
Font. Discourses well.
Ber. And a very honest Gentleman.
Asto. Oh! hee's well valued by my Lord.

Enter Bellafront *with a Petition.*

Font. How now, how now, what's she?
Ber. Let's make towards her. 70
Bell. Will it be long, sir, ere my Lord come forth?
Asto. Would you speake with my Lord?
Lod. How now, what's this, a Nurses Bill? hath any here got thee with child, and now will not keepe it?
Bell. No sir, my businesse is vnto my Lord.
Lod. Hee's about his owne wifes now, hee'le hardly dispatch two causes in a morning.
Asto. No matter what he saies, faire Lady, hee's a Knight, there's no hold to be taken at his words.
Font. My Lord will passe this way presently. 80
Ber. A pretty plumpe Rogue.
Asto. A good lusty bouncing baggage.
Ber. Doe you know her?
Lod. A pox on her, I was sure her name was in my Table-booke once, I know not of what cut her dye is now, but she has beene more common then Tobacco: this is she that had the name of the Honest Whore.
Omn. Is this she?
Lod. This is the Blackamore that by washing was turned white: this is the Birding Peece new scowred: this is shee that (if any of 90 her religion can be saued) was saued by my Lord *Hipolito.*
Asto. She has beene a goodly creature.

76 wifes] Dyce; wife Q

Lod. She has bin! that's the Epitaph of all Whores, I'm well acquainted with the poore Gentleman her Husband. Lord! what fortunes that man has ouerreached? She knowes not me, yet I haue beene in her company, I scarce know her, for the beauty of her cheeke hath (like the Moone) suffred strange Eclipses since I beheld it: but women are like Medlars (no sooner ripe but rotten.) A woman last was made, but is spent first,
Yet man is oft proued, in performance worst. 100
Omn. My Lord is come.

Enter Hypolito, Infæliche, *and two waiting women.*

Hip. We ha wasted halfe this morning: morrow *Lodouico.*
Lod. Morrow Madam.
Hip. Let's away, to Horse.
Omn. I, I to Horse, to Horse.
Bell. I doe beseech your Lordship, let your eye Read o're this wretched paper.
Hip. I'm in hast, Pray the good woman take some apter time.
Infæ. Good Woman doe.
Bell. Oh las! it does concerne A poore mans life.
Hip. Life! sweet heart? Seat your selfe, Il'e but read this and come. 110
Lod. What stockings haue you put on this morning, Madam? if they be not yellow, change them; that paper is a Letter from some Wench to your Husband.
Infæ. Oh sir, that cannot make me iealous. *Exeunt.*
Hip. Your busines, sir, to me?
Ant. Yes my good Lord.
Hip. Presently sir; are you *Mathæos* wife.
Bell. That most vnfortunate woman.
Hip. I'm sorry These stormes are fallen on him, I loue *Mathæo.* And any good shall doe him, hee and I Haue sealed two bonds of friendship, which are strong 120

107 the] *i.e.* thee

140

In me, how euer Fortune does him wrong;
He speakes here hee's condemned. Is't so?
Bell.   Too true.
Hip. What was he whom he killed? Oh, his name's here;
Iacomo, sonne to the Florentine
Old *Iacomo*, a dog, that to meet profit,
Would to the very eyelids wade in blood
Of his owne children.
Tell *Mathæo*, the Duke my father hardly shall
Deny his signed pardon, 'twas faire fight, yes,
If rumors tongue goe true, so writes he here.   130
To morrow morning I returne from Court,
Pray be you here then. Ile haue done sir straight:
But in troth say, are you *Mathæos* wife?
You haue forgot me.
Bell.   No, my Lord.
Hip.   Your Turner,
That made you smooth to run an euen byas,
You know I loued you when your very soule
Was full of discord: art not a good wench still?
Bell. Vmph, when I had lost my way to heauen, you shewed it:
I was new borne that day.

Enter Lodouico.

Lod. S'foot, my Lord, your Lady askes if you haue not left your 140
     Wench yet? When you get in once, you neuer haue done: come,
     come, come, pay your old score, and send her packing, come.
Hip. Ride softly on before, Ile oretake you.
Lod. Your Lady sweares she'll haue no riding on before, without
     ye.
Hip. Prethee good *Lodouico*.
Lod. My Lord pray hasten.
Hip. I come:
To morrow let me see you, fare you well:

                    *124 *Iacomo*] Spencer; old *Iacomo* Q
                    125 Old *Iacomo*] Spencer; *Iacomo* Q

Commend me to *Mathæo*: pray one word more: 150
Does not your father liue about the Court?
Bell. I thinke he does, but such rude spots of shame
Stick on my cheeke, that he scarce knowes my name.
Hip. *Orlando Friscabaldo*, Is't not?
Bell.   Yes my Lord.
Hip. What does he for you?
Bell.   All he should: when Children
From duty start, Parents from loue may swarue.
He nothing does: for nothing I deserue.
Hip. Shall I ioyne him vnto you, and restore you
To wonted grace?
Bell.   It is impossible.   *Exit* Bellafront
Hip. It shall be put to tryall: fare you well: 160
The face I would not looke on! sure then 'twas rare,
When in despight of griefe, 'tis still thus faire.
Now, sir, your businesse with me.
Ant.   I am bold
To expresse my loue and duty to your Lordship
In these few leaues.
Hip.   A Booke!
Ant.   Yes my good Lord.
Hip. Are you a Scholler?
Ant.   Yes, my Lord, a poore one.
Hip. Sir, you honor me.
Kings may be Schollers Patrons, but faith tell me,
To how many hands besides hath this bird flowne,
How many partners share with me?
Ant.   Not one 170
In troth, not one: your name I held more deare,
I'm not (my Lord) of that low Character.
Hip. Your name I pray?
Ant.   Antonio Georgio.
Hip. Of *Millan*?
Ant.   Yes my Lord.
Hip.   Ile borrow leaue
To read you o're and then we'll talke: till then

Drinke vp this gold, good wits should loue good wine,
This of your loues, the earnest that of mine.
How now, sir, where's your Lady, not gone yet?

Enter Bryan.

Bryan. I fart di Lady is runne away from dee, a mighty deale of
ground, she sent me backe for dine owne sweet face, I pray dee 180
come my Lord away, wut tow goe now?
Hip. Is the Coach gone? Saddle my Horse the sorrell.
Bryan. A pox a de Horses nose, he is a lowsy rascally fellow, when
I came to gird his belly, his scuruy guts rumbled, di Horse farted
in my face, and dow knowest, an Irishman cannot abide a fart, but
I haue saddled de Hobby-horse, di fine Hobby is ready, I pray dee
my good sweet Lord, wut tow goe now, and I will runne to de
Deuill before dee?
Hip. Well, sir, I pray lets see you Master Scholler.
Bry. Come I pray dee, wut come sweet face? Goe. 190
Exeunt.

[ACT I, SCENE ii]

Enter Lodouico, Carolo, Astolpho, Beraldo.

Lod. Gods so, Gentlemen, what doe we forget?
Omn. What?
Lod. Are not we all enioyned as this day, Thursday is't not? I as
that day to be at the Linnen-drapers house at dinner?
Caro. *Signior Candido*, the patient man.
Asto. Afore *Ioue*, true, vpon this day hee's married.
Ber. I wonder, that being so stung with a Waspe before, he dares
venture againe to come about the eaues amongst Bees.
Lod. Oh 'tis rare sucking a sweet Hony-combe; pray Heauen his
old wife be buried deepe enough, that she rise not vp to call for 10
her daunce, the poore Fidlers Instruments would cracke for it,
shee'd tickle them: at any hand lets try what mettle is in his new
Bride, if there be none, we'll put in some; troth it's a very noble

Citizen, I pitty he should marry againe, Ile walke along, for it is a good old fellow.

Caro. I warrant, the Wiues of *Millan* would giue any fellow twenty thousand Duckets, that could but haue the face to beg of the Duke, that all the Citizens in *Millan* might be bound to the peace of patience, as the Linnen-draper is.

Lod. Oh fy vpon't, 'twould vndoe all vs that are Courtiers, we should haue no whoe with the wenches then. 20

Enter Hipollito.

Omn. My Lord's come.
Hip. How now, what newes?
Omn. None.
Lod. Your Lady is with the Duke her Father.
Hip. And we'll to them both presently, whoe's that?

Enter Orlando Friscobaldo.

Omn. Signior Friscabaldo.
Hip. *Friscabaldo*, oh! pray call him, and leaue me, wee two haue businesse.
Caro. Ho *Signior*! *Signior Friscabaldo*. 30
The Lord *Hipollito*. *Exeunt.*
Orl. My Noble Lord: my Lord *Hipollito*! the Dukes Sonne! his braue Daughters braue Husband! how does your honord Lordship! does your Nobility remember so poore a Gentleman as *Signior Orlando Friscabaldo*! old mad *Orlando*!
Hip. Oh sir, our friends! they ought to be vnto vs as our Iewels, as dearely valued, being locked vp, and vnseene, as when we weare them in our hands. I see, *Friscabaldo*, age hath not command of your blood, for all Times sickle has gone ouer you, you are *Orlando* still. 40
Orl. Why my Lord, are not the fields mowen and cut downe, and stript bare, and yet weare they not pide coates againe? tho my head be like a Leeke, white: may not my heart be like the blade, greene?
Hip. Scarce can I read the Stories on your brow,
Which age hath writ there, you looke youthfull still.

Orl. I eate Snakes, my Lord, I eate Snakes. My heart shall neuer haue a wrinkle in it, so long as I can cry hem with a cleare voice.
Hip. You are the happier man, sir.
Orl. Happy man! Ile giue you (my Lord) the true picture of a happy man; I was turning leaues ouer this morning, and found it, 50 an excellent Italian Painter drew it. If I haue it in the right colours, Ile bestow it on your Lordship.
Hip. I stay for it.
Orl. He that makes gold his wife, but not his whore,
He that at noone-day walkes by a prison doore,
He that 'ith Sunne is neither beame nor moate,
He that's not mad after a Petticoate,
He for whom poore mens curses dig no graue,
He that is neither Lords nor Lawyers slaue,
He that makes This his Sea, and That his Shore, 60
He that in's Coffin is richer then before,
He that counts Youth his Sword, and Age his Staffe,
He whose right hand carues his owne Epitaph,
He that vpon his death-bed is a Swan,
And Dead, no Crow, he is a happy man.
Hip. It's very well, I thanke you for this Picture.
Orl. After this Picture (my Lord) doe I striue to haue my face drawne: For I am not couetous, am not in debt, sit neither at the Dukes side, nor lie at his feete. Wenching and I haue done, no man I wrong, no man I feare, no man I fee; I take heed how farre I 70 walke, because I know yonders my home. I would not die like a rich man, to carry nothing away saue a winding sheete: but like a good man, to leaue *Orlando* behind me. I sowed leaues in my Youth, and I reape now Bookes in my Age. I fill this hand, and empty this, and when the bell shall toll for me, if I proue a Swan, and go singing to my nest, why so? If a Crow! throw me out for carrion, and pick out mine eyes. May not old *Friscabaldo* (my Lord) be merry now! ha?
Hip. You may, would I were partner in your mirth.
Orl. I haue a little, haue all things; I haue nothing; I haue no wife, 80 I haue no child, haue no chick, and why should not I be in my *Iocundare*?

Hip. Is your wife then departed?
Orl. She's an old dweller in those high Countries, yet not from me, here, she's there but before me: when a Knaue and a Queane are married, they commonly walke like Serieants together: but a good couple are seldome parted.
Hip. You had a Daughter too sir, had you not?
Orl. Oh my Lord! this old Tree had one Branch, (and but one Branch growing out of it) It was young, it was faire, it was straight; 90 I pruinde it daily, drest it carefully, kept it from the winde, help'd it to the Sunne, yet for all my skill in planting, it grew crooked, it bore Crabs; I hewed it downe.
What's become of it, I neither know, nor care.
Hip. Then can I tell you whats become of it;
That Branch is witherd.
Orl. So 'twas long agoe.
Hip. Her name I thinke was *Bellafront*, she's dead.
Orl. Ha? dead?
Hip. Yes, what of her was left, not worth the keeping, 100 Euen in my sight was throwne into a Graue.
Orl. Dead! my last and best peace goe with her, I see deaths a good trencherman, he can eat course homely meat, as well as the daintiest.
Hip. Why, *Friscabaldo*, was she homely?
Orl. O my Lord! a Strumpet is one of the Deuils Vines; al the sinnes like so many Poles are stucke vpright out of hell, to be her props, that she may spread vpon them. And when she's ripe, euery Slaue has a pull at her, then must she be prest. The yong beautifull Grape sets the teeth of Lust on edge, yet to taste that lickrish Wine, 110 is to drinke a mans owne damnation. Is she dead?
Hip. Shee's turned to earth.
Orl. Wod she were turn'd to heauen; Vmh, is she dead! I am glad the world has lost one of his Idols; no Whoremonger will at midnight beat at the doores; In her graue sleepe all my shame, and her owne; and all my sorrowes, and all her sinnes.
Hip. I'm glad you are wax, not marble; you are made
Of mans best temper, there are now good hopes

*84–85 there...me:] here: ...me, Q

146

That all those heapes of ice about your heart,
By which a fathers loue was frozen vp,
Are thawed in these sweet showres fetcht from your eyes,
We are ne'r like Angels till our passion dyes,
She is not dead, but liues vnder worse fate,
I thinke she's poore, and more to clip her wings,
Her Husband at this houre lies in the Iayle,
For killing of a man: to saue his blood,
Ioyne all your force with mine: mine shall be showne:
The getting of his life preserues your owne.
Orl. In my daughter you will say! does she liue then?
I am sorry I wasted teares vpon a Harlot, but the best is I haue a
handkercher to drinke them vp, sope can wash them all out agen.
Is she poore?
Hip. Trust me, I thinke she is.
Orl. Then she's a right Strumpet; I ne'r knew any of their trade
rich two yeeres together; Siues can hold no water, nor Harlots
hoord vp money; they haue many vents, too many sluces to let it
out; Tauernes, Taylors, Bawds, Panders, Fidlers, Swaggerers,
Fooles and Knaues, doe all waite vpon a common Harlots trencher:
she is the Gally-pot to which these Drones flye: not for loue to the
pot, but for the sweet sucket within it, her money, her money.
Hip. I almost dare pawne my word, her bosome
Giues warmth to no such Snakes; when did you see her?
Orl. Not seuenteene Summers.
Hip. Is your hate so old?
Orl. Older; it has a white head, and shall neuer dye. Till she be
buried, her wrongs shall be my bedfellow.
Hip. Worke yet his life, since in it liues her fame.
Orl. No, let him hang, and halfe her infamy departs out of the
world: I hate him for her; he taught her first to taste poyson; I hate
her for her selfe, because she refused my Physicke.
Hip. Nay but *Friscabaldo.*
Orl. I detest her, I defie both, she's not mine, she's —
Hip. Heare her but speake.

119 those] Dyce; these Q
145–146 dye. Till] dye ⌀ till ⌀ (D² + *place full stop after* buried)

Orl. I loue no Maremaides, Ile not be caught with a quaill pipe.
Hip. Y'are now beyond all reason.
Orl. I am then a Beast. Sir, I had rather be a beast, and not dishonor my creation, then be a doting father, and like Time, be the destruction of mine owne broode.
Hip. Is't dotage to relieue your child being poore?
Orl. Is't fit for an old man to keepe a whore? 160
Hip. 'Tis charity too.
Orl. 'Tis foolery; releeue her! Were her cold limbes stretcht out vpon a Beere, I would not sell this durt vnder my nailes to buy her an houres breath, nor giue this haire, vnlesse it were to choke her.
Hip. Fare you well, for Ile trouble you no more. *Exit.*
Orl. And fare you well sir, goe thy waies, we haue few Lords of thy making, that loue wenches for their honesty; Las my Girle! art thou poore? pouerty dwells next doore to despaire, there's but a wall betweene them; despaire is one of hells Catch-poles; and 170 lest that Deuill arrest her, Ile to her, yet she shall not know me; she shall drinke of my wealth, as beggers doe of running water, freely, yet neuer know from what Fountaines head it flowes. Shall a silly bird picke her owne brest to nourish her yong ones, and can a father see his child starue? That were hard; The Pelican does it, and shall not I. Yes, I will victuall the Campe for her, but it shall be by some stratagem; that knaue there her husband will be hanged I feare, Ile keepe his necke out of the nooze if I can, he shall not know how.

Enter two Seruing-men.

Orl. How now knaues, whither wander you? 180
1. *Seru.* To seeke your Worship.
Orl. Stay, which of you has my purse, what money haue you about you?
2. *Seru.* Some fifteene or sixteene pounds, sir.
Orl. Giue it me, I thinke I haue some gold about me; yes, it's well; leaue my Lodging at Court, and get you home. Come sir, tho I neuer turned any man out of doores, yet Ile be so bold as to pull your Coate ouer your eares.

1. *Seru.* What doe you meane to doe sir?
Orl. Hold thy tongue knaue, take thou my Cloake, I hope I play not the paltry Merchant in this bartring; bid the Steward of my house, sleepe with open eyes in my absence, and to looke to all things, whatsoeuer I command by Letters to be done by you, see it done. So, does it sit well?
2. *Seru.* As if it were made for your Worship.
Orl. You proud Varlets, you need not bee ashamed to weare blue, when your Master is one of your fellowes; away, doe not see me.
Both. This is excellent. *Exeunt.*
Orl. I should put on a worse suite too; perhaps I will. My Vizard is on, now to this maske. Say I should shaue off this Honor of an old man, or tye it vp shorter; Well, I will spoyle a good face for once.
My beard being off, how should I looke? euen like
A Winter Cuckoo, or vnfeatherd Owle;
Yet better lose this haire, then lose her soule.
Exit.

[ACT I, Scene iii]

Enter Candido, Lodouico, [Astolfo,] *and* Carolo. 1. Guest *wearing a long hat, other Guests, and* Bride *with Prentises.*

Cand. O Gentlemen, so late, y'are very welcome, pray sit downe.
Lod. *Carolo*, did'st ere see such a nest of Caps?
Asto. Me thinkes it's a most ciuill and most comely sight.
Lod. What does he 'ith middle looke like?
Asto. Troth like a spire steeple in a Country Village ouerpeering so many thatcht houses.
Lod. It's rather a long pike staffe against so many bucklers without pikes; they sit for all the world like a paire of Organs, and hee's the tall great roaring pipe 'ith middest.
Asto. Ha, ha, ha, ha.
Cand. What's that you laugh at, *Signiors*?
Lod. Troth shall I tell you, and aloude Ile tell it,

*S.D. 1. Guest *wearing a long hat,*] Lodouico ₐ Q

We laugh to see (yet laugh we not in scorne)
Amongst so many Caps that long Hat worne.
1. *Guest.* Mine is as tall a felt as any is this day in *Millan*, and therefore I loue it, for the blocke was cleft out for my head, and fits me to a haire.
Cand. Indeed you are good obseruers, it shewes strange.
But Gentlemen, I pray neither contemne,
Nor yet deride a ciuill ornament;
I could build so much in the round Caps praise,
That 'boue this hye roofe, I this flat would raise.
Lod. Prethee sweet Bridegrome doo't.
Cand. So all these guests will pardon me, Ile doo't.
Omn. With all our hearts.
Cand. Thus then in the Caps honor,
To euery Sex and state, both Nature, Time,
The Countries lawes, yea and the very Clime
Doe allot distinct habits, the spruce Courtier
Iets vp and downe in silke: the Warrier
Marches in buffe, the Clowne plods on in gray:
But for these vpper garments thus I say,
The Sea-man has his Cap, par'd without brim,
The Gallants head is featherd, that fits him;
The Soldier has his Murren, women ha Tires;
Beasts haue their head-peeces, and men ha theirs.
Lod. Proceed.
Cand. Each degree has his fashion, it's fit then,
One should be laid by for the Citizen,
And that's the Cap which you see swels not hye,
For Caps are Emblems of humility;
It is a Citizens badge, and first was worne
By'th Romanes; for when any Bondmans turne
Came to be made a Freeman: thus 'twas said,
He to the Cap was call'd; that is, was made
Of *Rome* a Freeman, but was first close shorne,
And so a Citizens haire is still short worne.

15 1. *Guest.*] Dyce; *Lodo.* Q
22 'boue] Dyce; loue Q

Lod. That close shauing made Barbers a Company, and now euery
   Citizen vses it.
Cand. Of Geometricke figures the most rare,
   And perfect'st are the Circle and the square,
   The Citty and the Schoole much build vpon
   These figures, for both loue proportion.
   The City Cap is round, the Schollers square,
   To shew that Gouernment and learning are
   The perfect'st limbes i'th body of a State:
   For without them, all's disproportionate.
   If the Cap had no honor, this might reare it,
   The Reuerend Fathers of the Law doe weare it.
   It's light for Summer, and in cold it sits
   Close to the scull, a warme house for the wits;
   It shewes the whole face boldly, 'tis not made
   As if a man to looke out were afraide,
   Nor like a Drapers shop with broad darke shed,
   For hee's no Citizen that hides his head.
   Flat Caps as proper are to Citty Gownes,
   As to Armors Helmets, or to Kings their Crownes.
   Let then the City Cap by none be scornd,
   Since with it Princes heads haue beene adornd.
   If more the round Caps honor you would know,
   How would this long Gowne with this steeple show?
Omn. Ha, ha, ha: most vile, most vgly.
Cand. Pray *Signior* pardon me, 'twas done in iest.
Bride. A cup of claret wine there.
1. *Prent.* Wine: yes forsooth, wine for the Bride.
Caro. You ha well set out the Cap, sir.
Lod. Nay, that's flat.
1. *Guest.* A health.
Lod. Since his Cap's round, that shall goe round. Be bare,
   For in the Caps praise all of you haue share.

                The Bride *hits the Prentice on the lips.*
Lod. The Bride's at cuffes.

        63 out] Dyce; on't Q
        78 1. *Guest.*] *Long.* Q

Cand. Oh, peace I pray thee, thus far off I stand,
I spied the error of my seruants,
She call'd for Claret, and you fill'd out Sacke;
That cup giue me, 'tis for an old mans backe,
And not for hers. Indeed 'twas but mistaken,
Aske all these else.
Omn. No faith, 'twas but mistaken.
1. *Prent.* Nay, she tooke it right enough.
Cand. Good *Luke* reach her that glasse of Claret.
Here, Mistris Bride, pledge me there.
Bride. Now Ile none. *Exit* Bride.
Cand. How now?
Lod. Looke what your Mistris ayles.
1. *Prent.* Nothing, sir, but about filling a wrong glasse, a scuruy tricke.
Cand. I pray you hold your tongue,
My seruant there tells me she is not well.
Omn. Step to her, step to her.
Lod. A word with you: doe ye heare? This wench (your new wife) will take you downe in your wedding shooes, vnlesse you hang her vp in her wedding garters.
Cand. How, hang her in her garters?
Lod. Will you be a tame Pidgeon still? shall your backe be like a Tortoys shell, to let Carts goe ouer it, yet not to breake? This Shee-cat will haue more liues then your last Pusse had, and will scratch worse, and mouze you worse: looke toot.
Cand. What would you haue me doe, sir?
Lod. What would I haue you doe? Sweare, swagger, brawle, fling; for fighting it's no matter, we ha had knocking Pusses enow already; you know, that a woman was made of the rib of a man, and that rib was crooked. The Morall of which is, that a man must from his beginning be crooked to his wife; be you like an Orange to her, let her cut you neuer so faire, be you sowre as vineger; will you be ruled by me?
Cand. In any thing that's ciuill, honest, and iust.
Lod. Haue you euer a Prentices suite will fit me?
Cand. I haue the very same which my selfe wore.

Lod. Ile send my man for't within this halfe houre, and within this two houres Ile be your Prentice: the Hen shall not ouercrow the Cocke, Ile sharpen your spurres
Cand. It will be but some iest, sir?
Lod. Onely a iest: farewell, come *Carolo*. *Exeunt.*
Omn. Wee'll take our leaues, Sir, too.
Cand. Pray conceite not ill of my wiues sodaine rising. This young Knight, Sir *Lodouico*, is deepe seene in Phisicke, and he tells me, the disease call'd the Mother, hangs on my wife, it is a vehement heauing and beating of the Stomacke, and that swelling did with the paine thereof crampe vp her arme, that hit his lips, and brake the glasse: no harme, it was no harme.
Omn. No, *Signior*, none at all.
Cand. The straightest arrow may flye wide by chance.
But come, we'll cloze this brawle vp in some dance.
Exeunt.

[ACT II, SCENE i]

Enter Bellafront *and* Matheo.

Bell. Oh my sweet Husband, wert thou in thy graue,
And art aliue agen? O welcome, welcome.
Mat. Doest know me? my cloake prethee lay't vp. Yes faith, my winding sheete was taken out of Lauender, to be stucke with Rosemary, I lackt but the knot here, or here; yet if I had had it, I should ha made a wry mouth at the world like a Playse: but sweetest villaine, I am here now, and I will talke with thee soone.
Bell. And glad am I th'art here.
Math. Did these heeles caper in shackles? I my little plumpe rogue, Ile beare vp for all this, and flye hye. *Cat∫o Cat∫o.*
Bell. Matheo?
Math. What sayest, what sayest? Oh braue fresh ayre, a pox on these Grates and gingling of Keyes, and rattling of Iron. Ile beare vp, Ile flye hye wench, hang? Tosse.

9 I] A Q   *14 hang? Tosse] ~ ˌ ~ Q

Bell. *Matheo,* prethee make thy prison thy glasse,
And in it view the wrinkles, and the scarres,
By which thou wert disfigured, viewing them, mend them.
Math. Ile goe visit all the mad rogues now, and the good roaring
boyes.
Bell. Thou doest not heare me? 20
Math. Yes faith doe I.
Bell. Thou hast beene in the hands of misery,
And tane strong Physicke, prethee now be sound.
Math. Yes. S'foot, I wonder how the inside of a Tauerne lookes
now. Oh when shall I bizle, bizle?
Bell. Nay see, th'art thirsty still for poyson, come,
I will not haue thee swagger.
Math. Honest Apes face.
Bell. 'Tis that sharpned an axe to cut thy throate.
Good Loue, I would not haue thee sell thy substance 30
And time (worth all) in those damned shops of Hell;
Those Dycing houses, that stand neuer well,
But when they stand most ill, that foure-squared sinne
Has almost lodg'd vs in the beggers Inne.
Besides (to speake which euen my soule does grieue)
A sort of Rauens haue hung vpon thy sleeue,
And fed vpon thee: good *Mat.* (if you please)
Scorne to spread wing amongst so base as these;
By them thy fame is speckled, yet it showes
Cleare amongst them; so Crowes are faire with Crowes. 40
Custome in sinne, giues sinne a louely dye.
Blacknesse in Mores is no deformity.
Math. *Bellafront, Bellafront,* I protest to thee, I sweare, as I hope
for my soule, I will turne ouer a new leafe, the prison I confesse
has bit me, the best man that sayles in such a Ship, may be lowsy.
Bell. One knockes at doore.
Math. Ile be the Porter: they shall see, a Iayle cannot hold a braue
spirit, Ile flye hye. *Exit.*

37–38 good *Mat*...these;] D3 *query*; good *Mat.* (if you please) so base as | Scorne
to spread wing amongst these; Q
44 for] Dyce; *om.* Q

154

Bell. How wilde is his behauiour! oh, I feare
He's spoyld by prison, he's halfe damned comes there,
But I must sit all stormes: when a full sayle
His fortunes spred, he loued me: being now poore,
Ile beg for him, and no wife can doe more.

Enter Matheo, *and* Orlando *like a Seruingman.*

Math. Come in pray, would you speake with me, sir?
Orl. Is your name *Signior Matheo*?
Math. My name is *Signior Matheo.*
Orl. Is this Gentlewoman your wife, sir?
Math. This Gentlewoman is my wife, sir.
Orl. The Destinies spin a strong and euen thread of both your loues: the Mothers owne face, I ha not forgot that, I'm an old man, sir, and am troubled with a whoreson salt rhewme, that I cannot hold my water. Gentlewoman, the last man I serued was your Father.
Bell. My Father? any tongue that sounds his name,
Speakes Musicke to me: welcome good old man.
How does my father? liues he? has he health?
How does my father? I so much doe shame him,
So much doe wound him, that I scarce dare name him.
Orl. I can speake no more.
Math. How now old Lad, what doest cry?
Orl. The rhewme still, sir, nothing else; I should be well seasond, for mine eyes lye in brine: looke you, sir, I haue a suite to you.
Math. What is't, my little white pate?
Orl. Troth, sir, I haue a mind to serue your Worship.
Math. To serue me? Troth, my friend, my fortunes are, as a man may say —
Orl. Nay looke you, sir, I know when all sinnes are old in vs, and goe vpon Crutches, that Couetousnesse does but then lie in her Cradle; 'Tis not so with me. Letchery loues to dwell in the fairest lodging, and Couetousnesse in the oldest buildings, that are ready to fall: but my white head, sir, is no Inne for such a gossip. If a Seruingman at my yeeres be not stored with bisket enough, that has sayled about the world, to serue him the voyage out, of his life, and

to bring him East-home; Ill pitty but all his daies should be fasting daies: I care not so much for wages, for I haue scraped a handfull of gold together; I haue a little money, sir, which I would put into your Worships hands, not so much to make it more —
Math. No, no, you say well, thou sayest well; but I must tell you: How much is the money, sayest thou?
Orl. About twenty pound, Sir.
Math. Twenty pound? Let me see: that shall bring thee in, after ten *per centum, per annum.*
Orl. No, no, no, sir, no; I cannot abide to haue money ingender: fye vpon this siluer Lechery, fye; if I may haue meat to my mouth, and rags to my backe, and a flock-bed to snort vpon, when I die, the longer liuer take all.
Math. A good old Boy, yfaith, if thou seruest me, thou shalt eat as I eat, drinke as I drinke, lye as I lye, and ride as I ride.
Orl. That's if you haue money to hire horses.   [*Aside.*]
Math. *Front.* What doest thou thinke on't? This good old Lad here shall serue me.
Bell. Alas, *Matheo,* wilt thou load a backe
That is already broake?
Math. Peace, pox on you, peace, there's a tricke in't, I flye hye, it shall be so, *Front.* as I tell you: giue me thy hand, thou shalt serue me yfaith: welcome: as for your money —
Orl. Nay, looke you sir, I haue it here.
Math. Pesh, keepe it thy selfe, man, and then th'art sure 'tis safe.
Orl. Safe! and 'twere ten thousand Duckets, your Worship should be my cash-keeper; I haue heard what your Worship is — [*aside*] an excellent dunghill Cocke, to scatter all abroad: but Ile venture twenty pounds on's head.
Math. And did'st thou serue my Worshipfull Father-in-law, *Signior Orlando Friscabaldo,* that mad man once?
Orl. I serued him so long, till he turned me out of doores.
Math. It's a notable Chuffe, I ha not seene him many a day.
Orl. No matter and you ne'r see him: it's an arrant Grandy, a Churle, and as damnd a cut-throat.

*98 as I drinke...ride.] D²; as *I* drinke, lye as *I* lye, and ride as *I* ride. Q

Bell. Thou villaine, curb thy tongue, thou art a Iudas,
To sell thy Masters name to slander thus.
Math. Away Asse, he speakes but truth, thy father is a —
Bell. Gentleman.
Math. And an old knaue, there's more deceit in him then in six-
teene Poticaries: it's a Deuill, thou maist beg, starue, hang, damne;
does he send thee so much as a cheese?
Orl. Or so much as a Gammon of Bacon, hee'll giue it his Dogs
first.
Math. A Iayle, a Iayle.
Orl. A Iew, a Iew, sir.
Math. A Dog.
Orl. An English Mastiffe, sir.
Math. Pox rot out his old stinking garbage.
Bell. Art not ashamed to strike an absent man thus?
Art not ashamed to let this vild Dog barke,
And bite my Father thus? Ile not indure it;
Out of my doores, base slaue.
Math. Your dores! a vengeance? I shall liue to cut that old
rogues throat, for all you take his part thus.
Orl. He shall liue to see thee hangd first. [*Aside.*]

Enter Hipollito.

Math. Gods so my Lord, your Lordship is most welcome,
I'm proud of this, my Lord.
Hip.   Was bold to see you.
 Is that your wife?
Math.   Yes sir.
Hip.   Ile borrow her lip.
Math. With all my heart, my Lord.
Orl. Who's this, I pray sir?
Math. My Lord *Hipollito*: what's thy name?
Orl. Pacheco.
Math. *Pacheco*, fine name; Thou seest, *Pacheco*, I keepe company
with no Scondrels, nor base fellowes.
Hip. Came not my Footman to you?

Bell.   Yes my Lord.
Hip.   I sent by him a Diamond and a Letter,   150
Did you receiue them?
Bell.   Yes my Lord, I did.
Hip.   Read you the letter?
Bell.   O're and o're 'tis read.
Hip.   And faith your answer?
Bell.   Now the time's not fit,
You see, my Husbands here.
Hip.   Ile now then leaue you,
And choose mine houre; but ere I part away,
Harke you, remember I must haue no nay.
Matheo, I will leaue you.
Math.   A glasse of wine.
Hip.   Not now, Ile visit you at other times.
Y'are come off well then?
Math.   Excellent well, I thanke your Lordship: I owe you my life, 160
my Lord; and will pay my best blood in any seruice of yours.
Hip.   Ile take no such deare payment, harke you *Matheo*,
I know, the prison is a gulfe, if money
Runne low with you, my purse is yours: call for it.
Math.   Faith my Lord, I thanke my starres, they send me downe
some; I cannot sinke, so long as these bladders hold.
Hip.   I will not see your fortunes ebbe, pray try.
To starue in full barnes were fond modesty.
Math.   Open the doore, sirra.
Hip.   Drinke this,   170
And anon I pray thee giue thy Mistris this.   *Exit.*
Orl.   O Noble Spirit, if no worse guests here dwell,
My blue coate sits on my old shoulders well.
Math.   The onely royall fellow, he's bounteous as the Indies,
what's that he said to thee, *Bellafront*?
Bell.   Nothing.
Math.   I prethee good Girle?
Bell.   Why I tell you nothing.
Math.   Nothing? it's well: trickes, that I must be beholden to a
scald hot-liuerd gotish Gallant, to stand with my cap in my hand, 180

and vaile bonnet, when I ha spred as lofty sayles as himselfe, wud
I had beene hanged. Nothing? *Pacheco,* brush my cloake.
Orl. Where is't, sir?
Math. Come, wee'll flye hye.
Nothing? there is a whore still in thine eye. *Exit.*
Orl. My twenty pounds flyes high, O wretched woman,
This varlet's able to make *Lucrece* common.
How now Mistris? has my Master dyed you into this sad colour?
Bell. Fellow, be gone I pray thee, if thy tongue
Itch after talke so much, seeke out thy Master,   190
Th'art a fit instrument for him.
Orl. Zownes, I hope he will not play vpon me?
Bell. Play on thee? no, you two will flye together,
Because you are rouing arrowes of one feather.
Would thou wouldst leaue my house, thou ne'r shalt please me,
Weaue thy nets ne'r so hye,
Thou shalt be but a spider in mine eye.
Th'art ranke with poyson, poyson temperd well,
Is food for health; but thy blacke tongue doth swell
With venome, to hurt him that gaue thee bread,   200
To wrong men absent, is to spurne the dead.
And so did'st thou thy Master, and my Father.
Orl. You haue small reason to take his part; for I haue heard him
say fiue hundred times, you were as arrant a whore as euer stiffned
tiffany neckcloathes in water-starch vpon a Saturday 'ith afternoone.
Bell. Let him say worse, when for the earths offence
Hot vengeance through the marble cloudes is driuen,
Is't fit earth shoot agen those darts at heauen?
Orl. And so if your Father call you whore, you'll not call him old
knaue: *Friscabaldo,* she carries thy mind vp and downe; she's   210
thine owne flesh, blood, and bone; troth Mistris, to tell you true,
the fireworkes that ran from me vpon lines against my good old
Master, your father, were but to try how my young Master, your
Husband loued such squibs: but it's well knowne, I loue your
father as my selfe; Ile ride for him at mid-night, runne for you by
Owle-light; Ile dye for him, drudge for you; Ile flye low, and Ile
flye hye (as my Master saies) to doe you good, if you'll forgiue me.

Bell. I am not made of marble: I forgiue thee.
Orl. Nay, if you were made of marble, a good Stone-cutter might cut you: I hope the twenty pound I deliuered to my Master, is in a sure hand.
Bell. In a sure hand I warrant thee for spending.
Orl. I see my yong Master is a madcap, and a *bonus socius*, I loue him well, Mistris: yet as well as I loue him, Ile not play the knaue with you; looke you, I could cheat you of this purse full of money; but I am an old Lad, and I scorne to cunny-catch: yet I ha beene Dog at a Cony in my time.
Bell. A purse, where hadst it?
Orl. The Gentleman that went away, whisperd in mine eare, and charged me to giue it you.
Bell. The Lord *Hipollito*?
Orla. Yes, if he be a Lord, he gaue it me.
Bell. 'Tis all gold.
Orl. 'Tis like so: it may be, he thinkes you want money, and therefore bestowes his almes brauely, like a Lord.
Bell. He thinkes a siluer net can catch the poore,
Here's baite to choake a Nun, and turne her whore.
Wilt thou be honest to me?
Orl. As your nailes to your fingers, which I thinke neuer deceiued you.
Bell. Thou to this Lord shalt goe, commend me to him,
And tell him this, the Towne has held out long,
Because (within) 'twas rather true, then strong.
To sell it now were base; Say 'tis no hold
Built of weake stuffe, to be blowne vp with gold.
He shall beleeue thee by this token, or this;
If not, by this.   [*Gives purse, ring, letters.*]
Orl. Is this all?
Bell. This is all.
Orl. Mine owne Girle still.   [*Aside.*]
Bell. A Starre may shoote, not fall.   *Exit* Bellafront.
Orl. A Starre? nay, thou art more then the moone, for thou hast neither changing quarters, nor a man standing in thy circle with a bush of thornes. Is't possible the Lord *Hipollito*, whose face is

as ciuill as the outside of a Dedicatory Booke, should be a Mutton-munger? A poore man has but one Ewe, and this Grandy Sheepe-biter leaues whole Flockes of fat Weathers (whom he may knocke downe) to deuoure this. Ile trust neither Lord nor Butcher with quicke flesh for this tricke; the Cuckoo I see now sings all the yeere, though euery man cannot heare him, but Ile spoyle his notes; can neither Loue-letters nor the Deuils common Pick-lockes (Gold) nor Precious Stones make my Girle draw vp her Percullis: hold out still, wench.
All are not Bawds (I see now) that keepe doores,
Nor all good wenches that are markt for Whores.

260

Exit.

[ACT II, Scene ii]

Enter Candido, Lodouico *like a Prentice.*

Lod. Come, come, come, what doe yee lacke, sir? what doe ye lacke, sir? what is't ye lacke, sir? is not my Worship well suited? did you euer see a Gentleman better disguised?
Cand. Neuer, beleeue me, *Signior*.
Lod. Yes, but when he has bin drunke: there be Prentices would make mad Gallants, for they would spend all, and drinke, and whore, and so forth; and I see we Gallants could make mad Prentices. How does thy wife like me? Nay, I must not be so sawcy, then I spoyle all: pray you how does my Mistris like me?
Cand. Well: for she takes you for a very simple fellow. *10*
Lod. And they that are taken for such, are commonly the arrantest knaues: but to our Comedy, come.
Cand. I shall not act it, chide you say, and fret,
And grow impatient: I shall neuer doo't.
Lod. S'blood, cannot you doe as all the world does? counterfet.
Cand. Were I a Painter, that should liue by drawing
Nothing but Pictures of an angry man,
I should not earne my colours; I cannot doo't.
Lod. Remember y'are a Linnen Draper, and that if you giue your

wife a yard, she'll take an ell: giue her not therefore a quarter of 20
your yard, not a nayle.
Cand. Say I should turne to Ice, and nip her loue
Now 'tis but in the bud.
Lod. Well, say she's nipt.
Cand. It will so ouercharge her heart with griefe,
That like a Cannon, when her sighes goe off,
She in her duty either will recoyle,
Or breake in pieces, and so dye: her death,
By my vnkindnesse might be counted murther.
Lod. Dye? neuer, neuer; I doe not bid you beat her, nor giue her 30
blacke eyes, nor pinch her sides: but crosse her humours. Are not
Bakers armes the skales of Iustice? yet is not their bread light? and
may not you I pray bridle her with a sharpe bit, yet ride her gently?
Cand. Well, I will try your pills,
Doe you your faithfull seruice, and bee ready
Still at a pinch to helpe me in this part,
Or else I shall be out cleane.
Lod. Come, come, Ile prompt you.
Cand. Ile call her forth now, shall I?
Lod. Doe, doe, brauely. 40
Cand. *Luke*, I pray bid your Mistris to come hither.
Lod. *Luke*, I pray bid your Mistris to come hither.
Cand. Sirra, bid my wife come to me: why, when?
Luke. Presently, sir, she comes. —   *Within.*
Lod. La you, there's the eccho, she comes.

Enter Bride.

Bride. What is your pleasure with me?
Cand.   Mary wife,
I haue intent, and (you see) this stripling here,
He beares good will and liking to my trade,
And meanes to deale in Linnen.
Lod. Yes indeed, sir, I would deale in Linnen, if my Mistris like 50
me so well as I like her?

23 bud] D³ *query*; blood Q   25 ouercharge] D²; ouerchange Q
45 S.D. *Enter*] D²; *Exit* Q

162

Cand. I hope to finde him honest, pray good wife
Looke that his bed and chamber be made ready.
Bride. Y'are best to let him hire mee for his maide?
I looke to his bed? looke too't your selfe.
Cand. Euen so?
I sweare to you a great oath —
Lod. Sweare, cry Zoundes.
Cand. I will not, goe to wife, I will not —
Lod. That your great oath?
Cand. Swallow these gudgeons. 60
Lod. Well said.
Bride. Then fast then, you may choose.
Cand. You know at Table
What trickes you played, swaggerd, broke glasses! Fie,
Fie, fie, fie: and now before my Prentice here
You make an asse of me; thou, (what shall I call thee?)
Bride. Euen what you will.
Lod. Call her arrant whore.
Cand. Oh fie, by no meanes, then she'll call me Cuckold,
Sirrah, goe looke to'th shop: how does this show?
Lod. Excellent well, Ile goe looke to the shop, sir. Fine Cambricks, 70
Lawnes, what doe you lacke. *Exit* Lodouico [*into the shop*].
Cand. A curst Cowes milke I ha drunke once before,
And 'twas so ranke in taste, Ile drinke no more.
Wife, Ile tame you.
Bride. You may, sir, if you can,
But at a wrastling I haue seene a fellow
Limbd like an Oxe, throwne by a little man.
Cand. And so you'll throw me. Reach me (Knaues) a yard.
Lod. A Yard for my Master.
1. Prent. My Master is growne valiant.
Cand. Ile teach you fencing trickes. 80
Omn. Rare, rare; a prize.
Lod. What will you doe, sir?
Cand. Mary, my good Prentice, nothing but breathe my wife.

55 so?] Dyce; ~ ∧ Q   62 *Bride.*] Dyce; *Cand.* Q
62 *Cand.*] Dyce; *om.* Q

Bride. Breathe me with your yard?
Lod. No, he'll but measure you out, forsooth.
Bride. Since you'll needes fence, handle your weapon well,
For if you take a yard, Ile take an ell.
Reach me an ell.
Lod. An ell for my Mistris.
Keep the lawes of the Noble Science, sir, and measure weapons
with her; your yard is a plaine Heathenish weapon; 'tis too short,
she may giue you a handfull, and yet you'l not reach her.
Cand. Yet I ha the longer arme, come fall too't roundly,
And spare not me (wife) for Ile lay't on soundly.
If o're husbands their wiues will needes be Masters,
We men will haue a law to win't at wasters.
Lod. 'Tis for the breeches, is't not?
Cand. For the breeches.
Bride. Husband I am for you, Ile not strike in iest.
Cand. Nor I.
Bride. But will you signe to one request?
Cand. What's that?
Bride. Let me giue the first blow.
Cand. The first blow, wife, shall I? *Prompt?*
Lod. Let her ha'te.
If she strike hard, in to her, and breake her pate.
Cand. A bargaine. Strike.
Bride. Then guard you from this blow,
For I play all at legges, but 'tis thus low. *She kneeles.*
Behold, I am such a cunning Fencer growne,
I keepe my ground, yet downe I will be throwne
With the least blow you giue me, I disdaine
The wife that is her husbands Soueraigne.
She that vpon your pillow first did rest,
They say, the breeches wore, which I detest:
The taxe which she imposed vpon you, I abate you,
If me you make your Master, I shall hate you.
The world shall iudge who offers fairest play;
You win the breeches, but I win the day.
Cand. Thou winst the day indeed, giue me thy hand,

Ile challenge thee no more: my patient brest
Plaid thus the Rebell, onely for a iest:
Here's the rancke rider that breakes Colts, 'tis he
Can tame the mad folkes, and curst wiues.
Bride.   Who, your man? 120
Cand. My man? my Master, tho his head be bare,
But he's so courteous, he'll put off his haire.
Lod. Nay, if your seruice be so hot, a man cannot keepe his haire
on, Ile serue you no longer.
Bride. Is this your Schoolemaster?
Lod. Yes faith, wench, I taught him to take thee downe: I hope
thou canst take him downe without teaching;
You ha got the conquest, and you both are friends.
Cand. Beare witnes else.
Lod.   My Prentiship then ends.
Cand. For the good seruice you to me haue done, 130
I giue you all your yeeres.
Lod.   I thanke you Master.
Ile kisse my Mistris now, that she may say,
My man was bound, and free all in one day.
                                        Exeunt.

[ACT III, Scene i]

Enter Orlando, *and* Infælice.

Infæ. From whom saiest thou?
Orl. From a poore Gentlewoman, Madam, whom I serue.
Infæ. And whats your businesse?
Orl. This, Madam: my poore Mistris has a waste piece of ground,
which is her owne by inheritance, and left to her by her mother;
There's a Lord now that goes about, not to take it cleane from her,
but to inclose it to himselfe, and to ioyne it to a piece of his
Lordships.
Infæ. What would she haue me doe in this?
Orl. No more, Madam, but what one woman should doe for an- 10
other in such a case. My Honourable Lord, your Husband would

doe any thing in her behalfe, but shee had rather put her selfe into
your hands, because you (a woman) may doe more with the Duke
your Father.

Infæ. Where lyes this Land?

Orl. Within a stones cast of this place; my Mistris, I think, would
be content to let him enioy it after her decease, if that would serue
his turne, so my Master would yeeld too: but she cannot abide to
heare that the Lord should meddle with it in her life time.

Infæ. Is she then married? why stirres not her Husband in it?

Orl. Her Husband stirres in it vnder hand: but because the other
is a great rich man, my Master is loth to be seene in it too much.

Infæ. Let her in writing draw the cause at large:
And I will moue the Duke.

Orl. 'Tis set downe, Madam, here in blacke and white already:
worke it so, Madam, that she may keepe her owne without distur-
bance, grieuance, molestation, or medling of any other; and she
bestowes this purse of gold on your Ladyship.

Infæ. Old man, Ile pleade for her, but take no fees:
Giue Lawyers them, I swim not in that flood,
Ile touch no gold, till I haue done her good.

Orl. I would all Proctors Clearkes were of your minde, I should
law more amongst them then I doe then; here, Madam, is the
suruey, not onely of the Mannor it selfe, but of the Grange house,
with euery Medow pasture, Plough-land, Cony-borough, Fish-
pond, hedge, ditch, and bush that stands in it.

Infæ. My Husbands name, and hand and seale at armes
To a Loue-letter? Where hadst thou this writing?

Orl. From the foresaid party, Madam, that would keepe the foresaid Land, out of the foresaid Lords fingers.

Infæ. My Lord turnd Ranger now?

Orl. Y'are a good Huntresse, Lady, you ha found your Game
already; your Lord would faine be a Ranger, but my Mistris
requests you to let him runne a course in your owne Parke, if
you'll not doo't for loue, then doo't for money; she has no white
money, but there's gold, or else she praies you to ring him by this
token, and so you shall be sure his nose will not be rooting other
mens pastures.

Infæ. This very purse was wouen with mine owne hands,
This Diamond on that very night, when he 50
Vntyed my Virgin girdle, gaue I him:
And must a common Harlot share in mine?
Old man, to quit thy paines, take thou the gold.
Orl. Not I, Madam, old Seruingmen want no money.
Infæ. *Cupid* himselfe was sure his Secretary,
These lines are euen the Arrowes Loue let flies,
The very Incke dropt out of *Venus* eyes.
Orl. I doe not thinke, Madam, but hee fetcht off some Poet or
other for those lines, for they are parlous Hawkes to flie at wenches.
Infæ. Here's honied poyson, to me he ne'r thus writ, 60
But Lust can set a double edge on wit.
Orl. Nay, that's true, Madam, a wench will whet any thing, if it be
not too dull.
Infæ. Oathes, promises, preferments, Iewels, gold,
What snares should breake, if all these cannot hold?
What creature is thy Mistris?
Orl. One of those creatures that are contrary to man; a woman.
Infæ. What manner of woman?
Orl. A little tiny woman, lower then your Ladiship by head and
shoulders, but as mad a wench as euer vnlaced a petticote: these 70
things should I indeed haue deliuered to my Lord your Husband.
Infæ. They are deliuered better: Why should she
Send backe these things?
Orl. Ware, ware, there's knauery.
Infæ. Strumpets like cheating gamesters will not win
At first: these are but baites to draw him in.
How might I learne his hunting houres?
Orl. The Irish Footman can tell you all his hunting houres, the
Parke he hunts in, the Doe he would strike, that Irish Shackatory
beates the bush for him, and knowes all; he brought that Letter, 80
and that Ring; he is the Carrier.
Infæ. Knowest thou what other gifts haue past betweene them?
Orl. Little Saint *Patricke* knowes all.
Infæ. Him Ile examine presently.

*69 by head] *stet* Q

Orl. Not whilest I am here, sweet Madam.
Infæ. Be gon then, and what lyes in me command.

Enter Bryan. *Exit* Orlando.

Infæ. Come hither sirra, how much cost those Satins,
And cloth of Siluer, which my husband sent
By you to a low Gentlewoman yonder?
Bryan. Faat Sattins? faat Siluers, faat low Gentlefolkes? dow pratest dow knowest not what, yfaat la.
Infæ. She there, to whom you carried letters.
Bryan. By dis hand and bod dow saist true, if I did so, oh how? I know not a letter a de Booke yfaat la.
Infæ. Did your Lord neuer send you with a Ring, sir, Set with a Diamond?
Bryan. Neuer, sa crees sa me, neuer; he may runne at a towsand rings yfaat, and I neuer hold his stirrop, till he leape into de saddle. By Saint *Patricke*, Madam, I neuer touch my Lords Diamond, nor euer had to doe, yfaat la, with any of his precious stones.

Enter Hipollito.

Infæ. Are you so close, you Bawd, you pandring slaue?
Hip. How now? why *Infælice*? what's your quarrell?
Infæ. Out of my sight, base varlet, get thee gone.
Hip. Away you rogue.
Bryan. *Slawne loot*, fare de well, fare de well. *Ah marragh frofat boddah breen.* *Exit.*
Hip. What, growne a fighter? prethee what's the matter?
Infæ. If you'll needs know, it was about the clocke:
How workes the day, my Lord, (pray) by your watch?
Hip. Lest you cuffe me, Ile tell you presently:
I am neere two.
Infæ. How, two? I am scarce at one.
Hip. One of vs then goes false.
Infæ. Then sure 'tis you,
Mine goes by heauens Diall, (the Sunne) and it goes true.
Hip. I thinke (indeed) mine runnes somewhat too fast.
Infæ. Set it to mine (at one) then.

Hip.   One? 'tis past:
'Tis past one by the Sunne.
Infæ.   Faith then belike,
Neither your clocke nor mine does truely strike,
And since it is vncertaine which goes true,
Better be false at one, then false at two.
Hip.   Y'are very pleasant, Madam.
Infæ.   Yet not merry.   120
Hip.   Why *Infælice*, what should make you sad?
Infæ.   Nothing my Lord, but my false watch, pray tell me,
You see, my clocke, or yours is out of frame,
Must we vpon the Workeman lay the blame,
Or on our selues that keepe them?
Hip.   Faith on both.
He may by knauery spoile them, we by sloth,
But why talke you all riddle thus? I read
Strange Comments in those margines of your lookes:
Your cheekes of late are (like bad printed Bookes)   130
So dimly charactred, I scarce can spell,
One line of loue in them. Sure all's not well.
Infæ.   All is not well indeed, my dearest Lord,
Locke vp thy gates of hearing, that no sound
Of what I speake may enter.
Hip.   What meanes this?
Infæ.   Or if my owne tongue must my selfe betray,
Count it a dreame, or turne thine eyes away,
And thinke me not thy wife.   *She kneeles.*
Hip.   Why doe you kneele?
Infæ.   Earth is sinnes cushion: when the sicke soule feeles
Her selfe growing poore, then she turnes begger, cryes
And kneeles for helpe; *Hipollito* (for husband   140
I dare not call thee) I haue stolne that Iewell
Of my chaste honour (which was onely thine)
And giuen it to a slaue.
Hip.   Hah?
Infæ.   On thy pillow

125 our] D3; your Q

Adultery and lust haue slept, thy Groome
Hath climbed the vnlawfull tree, and pluckt the sweets,
A villaine hath vsurped a husbands sheetes.
Hip. S'death, who, (a Cuckold) who?
Infœ.   This Irish Footman.
Hip. Worse then damnation, a wild Kerne, a Frogge,
A Dog: whom Ile scarce spurne. Longed you for Shamrocke?
Were it my fathers father (heart) Ile kill him,   150
Although I take him on his death-bed gasping
'Twixt heauen and hell; a shag-haired Cur? Bold Strumpet,
Why hangest thou on me? thinkst Ile be a Bawde
To a Whore, because she's Noble?
Infœ.   I beg but this,
Set not my shame out to the worlds broad eye,
Yet let thy vengeance (like my fault) soare hye,
So it be in darkned clowdes.
Hip.   Darkned! my hornes
Cannot be darkned, nor shall my reuenge.
A Harlot to my slaue? the act is base,
Common, but foule, so shall not thy disgrace: 160
Could not I feed your appetite? oh women
You were created Angels, pure and faire;
But since the first fell, tempting Deuils you are,
You should be mens blisse, but you proue their rods:
Were there no Women, men might liue like gods.
You ha beene too much downe already, rise,
Get from my sight, and henceforth shun my bed,
Ile with no Strumpets breath be poysoned.
As for your Irish *Lubrican,* that spirit
Whom by prepostrous charmes thy lust hath raised   170
In a wrong Circle, him Ile damne more blacke
Then any Tyrants soule.
Infœ.   *Hipollito?*
Hip. Tell me, didst thou baite hookes to draw him to thee,
Or did he bewitch thee?

        160 not] D3 (*see line* 185); *om.* Q
        173 hookes] Dyce; Hawkes Q

Infæ.   The slaue did woo me.
Hip.   Two wooes in that Skreech-owles language?
Oh who would trust your corcke-heeld sex? I thinke
To sate your lust, you would loue a Horse, a Beare,
A croaking Toade, so your hot itching veines
Might haue their bound, then the wild Irish Dart
Was throwne. Come, how? the manner of this fight.   180
Infæ.   'Twas thus, he gaue me this battery first. Oh I
Mistake, beleeue me, all this in beaten gold:
Yet I held out, but at length by this was charm'd.
What? change your Diamond wench, the act is base,
Common, but foule, so shall not your disgrace:
Could not I feed your appetite? Oh Men,
You were created Angels, pure and faire,
But since the first fell, worse then Deuils you are.
You should our shields be, but you proue our rods.
Were there no Men, Women might liue like gods.   190
Guilty my Lord?
Hip.   Yes, guilty my good Lady.
Infæ.   Nay, you may laugh, but henceforth shun my bed,
With no whores leauings Ile be poysoned.   *Exit.*
Hip.   O're-reach'd so finely? 'Tis the very Diamond
And Letter which I sent: this villany
Some Spider closely weaues, whose poysond bulke
I must let forth. Who's there without?
Seru.   My Lord calls. —   *Within.*
Hip.   Send me the Footman.
Seru.   Call the Footman to my Lord. *Bryan, Bryan.*   200

                Enter Bryan.

Hip.   It can be no man else, that Irish Iudas,
Bred in a Country where no venom prospers
But in the Nations blood, hath thus betraid me.
Slaue, get you from your seruice.
Bryan.   Faat meanest thou by this now?

        175 Two wooes] *i.e.* Tu-whoos *as the basis for the pun*
        183 by] om. Q   *184 Diamond wench] stet* Q

Hip. Question me not, nor tempt my fury, villaine,
  Couldst thou turne all the Mountaines in the land,
  To hills of gold, and giue me; here thou stayest not.
Bryan. I faat, I care not.
Hip. Prate not, but get thee gone, I shall send else. 210
Bryan. I, doe predy, I had rather haue thee make a scabbard of my
  guts, and let out all de Irish puddings in my poore belly, den to be
  a false knaue to de I faat, I will neuer see dyne own sweet face more.
  A mawhid deer a gra, fare de well, fare de well, I wil goe steale
  Cowes agen in *Ireland*. *Exit.*
Hip. He's damn'd that rais'd this whirlewind, which hath blowne
  Into her eyes this iealousie: yet Ile on,
  Ile on, stood armed Deuils staring in my face,
  To be pursued in flight, quickens the race,
  Shall my blood streames by a wiues lust be bard? 220
  Fond woman, no: Iron growes by strokes more hard,
  Lawlesse desires are seas scorning all bounds,
  Or sulphure which being ram'd vp, more confounds,
  Strugling with mad men, madnes nothing tames,
  Winds wrastling with great fires, incense the flames.
  Exit.

[ACT III, Scene ii]

Enter Matheo, Bellafront, *and* Orlando.

Bell. How now, what ayles your Master?
Orl. Has taken a yonger brothers purge, forsooth, and that
  workes with him.
Bell. Where is his Cloake and Rapier?
Orl. He has giuen vp his Cloake, and his Rapier is bound to the
  Peace: If you looke a little higher, you may see that another hath
  entred into hatband for him too. Sixe and foure haue put him into
  this sweat.
Bell. Where's all his money?

208 and giue] Dyce; and to giue Q

III. ii]   THE HONEST WHORE, PART 2

Orl. 'Tis put ouer by exchange: his doublet was going to be 10
translated, but for me: if any man would ha lent but halfe a ducket
on his beard, the haire of it had stuft a paire of breeches by this
time; I had but one poore penny, and that I was glad to niggle out,
and buy a holly-wand to grace him thorow the streete. As hap
was, his bootes were on, and them I dustied, to make people thinke
he had beene riding, and I had runne by him.
Bell. Oh me, how does my sweet *Matheo*?
Math. Oh Rogue, of what deuilish stuffe are these Dice made off?
of the parings of the Deuils cornes of his toes, that they runne thus
damnably. 20
Bell. I prethee vex not.
Math. If any handy-crafts man was euer suffred to keep shop in
hell, it will be a Dice-maker; he's able to vndoe more soules then
the Deuill; I plaid with mine owne Dice, yet lost. Ha you any
money?
Bell. Las I ha none.
Math. Must haue money, must haue some, must haue a Cloake,
and Rapier, and things: will you goe set your limetwigs, and get
me some birds, some money?
Bell. What limetwigs should I set? 30
Math. You will not then? Must haue cash and pictures: doe ye
heare, (frailty) shall I walke in a *Plimouth* Cloake, (that's to say)
like a rogue, in my hose and doublet, and a crabtree cudgell in my
hand, and you swimme in your Sattins? must haue money, come.
Orl. Is't bed-time, Master, that you vndo my Mistris?
Bell. Vndoe me? Yes, yes, at these riflings I
Haue beene too often.
Math. Helpe to flea, *Pacheco*.
Orl. Fleaing call you it?
Math. Ile pawne you by'th Lord, to your very eye-browes. 40
Bell. With all my heart, since heauen will haue me poore,
As good be drown'd at sea, as drown'd at shore.
Orl. Why heare you, sir? yfaith doe not make away her Gowne.
Math. Oh it's Summer, it's Summer: your onely fashion for a
woman now, is to be light, to be light.

15 them] Dyce *query*; then Q

173

Orl. Why, pray sir, employ some of that money you haue of mine.
Math. Thine? Ile starue first, Ile beg first; when I touch a penny of that, let these fingers ends rot.
Orl. So they may, for that's past touching. I saw my twenty pounds flye hie.   [*Aside.*] 50
Math. Knowest thou neuer a damn'd Broker about the Citty?
Orl. Damn'd Broker? yes, fiue hundred.
Math. The Gowne stood me in aboue twenty Duckets, borrow ten of it, cannot liue without siluer.
Orl. Ile make what I can of it, sir, Ile be your Broker,
But not your damb'd broker: Oh thou scuruy knaue,
What makes a wife turne whore, but such a slaue?   *Exit.*
Math. How now little chicke, what aylest, weeping for a handfull of Taylors shreds? pox on them, are there not silkes enow at Mercers?   60
Bell. I care not for gay feathers, I.
Math. What doest care for then? why doest grieue?
Bell. Why doe I grieue? A thousand sorrowes strike
At one poore heart, and yet it liues. *Matheo,*
Thou art a Gamester, prethee throw at all,
Set all vpon one cast, we kneele and pray,
And struggle for life, yet must be cast away.
Meet misery quickly then, split all, sell all,
And when thou hast sold all, spend it, but I beseech thee
Build not thy mind on me to coyne thee more,   70
To get it wouldst thou haue me play the whore?
Math. 'Twas your profession before I married you.
Bell. Vmh? it was indeed: if all men should be branded
For sinnes long since laid vp, who could be saued?
The Quarter day's at hand, how will you doe
To pay the Rent, *Matheo*?
Math. Why? doe as all of your occupation doe against Quarter daies; breake vp house, remoue, shift your lodgings, pox a your Quarters.

77 your] our Q

174

Enter Lodouico.

Lod. Where's this Gallant?
Math. Signior *Lodouico*? how does my little Mirror of Knighthood? this is kindly done yfaith: welcome by my troth.
Lod. And how doest, frolicke? Saue you faire Lady. Thou lookest smug and brauely, Noble *Mat.*
Math. Drinke and feed, laugh and lie warme.
Lod. Is this thy wife?
Math. A poore Gentlewoman, sir, whom I make vse of a nights.
Lod. Pay custome to your lips, sweet Lady.
Math. Borrow some shells of him, some wine, sweet heart.
Lod. Ile send for't then yfaith.
Math. You send for't? Some wine I prethee.
Bell. I ha no money.   [*Aside, to him.*]
Math. S'blood, nor I: What wine loue you *Signior*?
Lod. Here, or Ile not stay, I protest; trouble the Gentlewoman too much?   *Exit* Bellafront.
And what newes flies abroad, *Matheo*?
Math. Troth, none. Oh *Signior*, we ha beene merry in our daies.
Lod. And no doubt shall agen. The Diuine powers
Neuer shoot Darts at mortall men, to kill them.
Math. You say true.
Lod. Why should we grieue at want? Say the world made thee
Her Minnion, that thy head lay in her lap,
And that she danc't thee on her wanton knee,
She could but giue thee a whole world: that's all,
And that all's nothing; the worlds greatest part
Cannot fill vp one corner of thy heart.
Say, the three corners were all filld, alas!
Of what art thou possest: a thinne blowne glasse,
Such as by Boyes is puft into the aire.
Were twenty Kingdomes thine, thou'dst liue in care:
Thou could'st not sleepe the better, nor liue longer,
Nor merrier be, nor healthfuller, nor stronger.

*99 mortall men] men | Mortall Q

If then thou want'st, thus make that want thy pleasure,
No man wants all things, nor has all in measure.
Math. I am the most wretched fellow: sure some left-handed Priest christned me, I am so vnlucky: I am neuer out of one puddle or another, still falling.

Enter Bellafront, *and* Orlando.

Math. Fill out wine to my little finger.
With my heart yfaith.
Lod. Thankes, good *Matheo*. 120
To your owne sweet selfe.
Orl. All the Brokers hearts, sir, are made of flint, I can with all my knocking, strike but sixe sparkes of fire out of them, here's sixe duckets, if youle take them.
Math. Giue me them: an euill conscience gnaw them all, moths and plagues hang vpon their lowsie wardrobs.
Lod. Is this your man, *Matheo*? An old Seruingman.
Orl. You may giue me t'other halfe too, sir: that's the Begger.
Lod. What hast there, gold?
Math. A sort of Rascalls are in my debt, (God knowes what) and 130
they feed me with bits, with crummes, a pox choke them.
Lod. A word, *Matheo*: be not angry with me,
Beleeue it that I know the touch of time,
And can part copper (tho it be gilded o're)
From the true gold: the sailes which thou doest spread,
Would show well, if they were not borrowed.
The sound of thy low fortunes drew me hither,
I giue my selfe vnto thee, prethee vse me,
I will bestow on you a suite of Sattin,
And all things else to fit a Gentleman, 140
Because I loue you.
Math. Thankes, good Noble Knight.
Lod. Call on me when you please, till then farewell. *Exit.*
Math. Hast angled? hast cut vp this fresh Salmon?
Bell. Wudst haue me be so base?
Math. It's base to steale, it's base to be a whore:

*127 An old Seruingman.] stet Q

176

Thou't be more base, Ile make thee keepe a doore.   *Exit.*
Orl.   I hope he will not sneake away with all the money, will he?
Bell.   Thou seest he does.
Orl.   Nay then it's well I set my braines vpon an vpright Last; tho 150
my wits be old, yet they are like a witherd pippin, wholsome.
Looke you, Mistris, I told him I had but sixe duckets of the (Knaue)
Broker, but I had eight, and kept these two for you.
Bell.   Thou shouldst haue giuen him all.
Orl.   What, to flie hie?
Bell.   Like waues, my misery driues on misery.   *Exit.*
Orl.   Sell his wiues cloathes from her backe? does any Poulterers
wife pull chickins aliue?   He Riots all abroad, wants all at home;
he Dices, whores, swaggers, sweares, cheates, borrowes, pawnes:
Ile giue him hooke and line, a little more for all this.   160
Yet sure i'th end he'll delude all my hopes,
And shew me a French tricke danc'd on the ropes.
                                                                         Exit.

[ACT III, Scene iii]

Enter at one doore Lodouico *and* Carolo; *at another* Bots,
and Mistris Horsleach; Candido *and his wife*
appeare in the Shop.

Lod.   Hist, hist, Lieutenant *Bots*, how do'st, man?
Caro.   Whither are you ambling, Madam *Horsleach*?
Hors.   About worldly profit, sir: how doe your Worships?
Bots.   We want tooles, Gentlemen, to furnish the trade: they
weare out day and night, they weare out till no mettle bee left in
their backe; wee heare of two or three new Wenches are come vp
with a Carrier, and your old Goshawke here is flying at them.
Lod.   And faith, what flesh haue you at home?
Hors.   Ordinary Dishes, by my troth, sweet men, there's few good
i'th Cittie; I am as well furnisht as any, and tho I say it, as well 10
custom'd.

150 well~A~] ~ . Q

Bots. We haue meates of all sorts of dressing; we haue stew'd meat for your Frenchmen, pretty light picking meat for your Italian, and that which is rotten roasted, for *Don Spaniardo.*
Lod. A pox on't.
Bots. We haue Poulterers ware for your sweet bloods, as Doue, Chickin, Ducke, Teale, Woodcocke, and so forth: and Butchers meat for the Cittizen: yet Muttons fall very bad this yeere.
Lod. Stay, is not that my patient Linnen Draper yonder, and my fine yong smug Mistris, his wife?
Caro. Sirra Grannam, Ile giue thee for thy fee twenty crownes, if thou canst but procure me the wearing of yon veluet cap.
Hors. You'd weare another thing besides the cap. Y'are a Wag.
Bots. Twenty crownes? we'll share, and Ile be your pully to draw her on.
Lod. Doo't presently; we'll ha some sport.
Hors. Wheele you about, sweet men: doe you see, Ile cheapen wares of the man, whilest *Bots* is doing with his wife.
Lod. Too't: if we come into the shop to doe you grace, wee'll call you Madam.
Bots. Pox a your old face, giue it the badge of all scuruy faces, a Masque.
Cand. What is't you lacke, Gentlewoman? Cambricke or Lawnes, or fine Hollands? Pray draw neere, I can sell you a penny-worth.
Bots. Some Cambricke for my old Lady.
Cand. Cambricke? you shall, the purest thred in *Millan.*
Lod. & Caro. Saue you, Signior Candido.
Lod. How does my Noble Master? how my faire Mistris?
Cand. My Worshipfull good Seruant, —
View it well, for 'tis both fine and euen.
Caro. Cry you mercy, Madam, tho mask'd, I thought it should be you by your man. Pray' *Signior*, shew her the best, for she commonly deales for good ware.
Cand. Then this shall fit her, this is for your Ladiship.
Bots. A word, I pray, there is a waiting Gentlewoman of my Ladies: her name is *Ruyna*, saies she's your Kinswoman, and that you should be one of her Aunts.
Wife. One of her Aunts? troth sir, I know her not.

Bots. If it please you to bestow the poore labour of your legs at any time, I will be your conuoy thither? 50
Wife. I am a Snaile, sir, seldome leaue my house, if't please her to visit me, she shall be welcome.
Bots. Doe you heare? the naked truth is: my Lady hath a yong Knight, her sonne, who loues you, y'are made, if you lay hold vpont: this Iewell he sends you.
Wife. Sir, I returne his loue and Iewell with scorne; let goe my hand, or I shall call my husband. You are an arrant Knaue. *Exit.*
Lod. What, will she doe?
Bots. Doe? they shall all doe if *Bots* sets vpon them once, she was as if she had profest the trade, squeamish at first, at last I shewed 60 her this Iewell, said, a Knight sent it her.
Lod. Is't gold, and right stones?
Bots. Copper, Copper, I goe a fishing with these baites. She nibbled, but wud not swallow the hooke, because the Cunger-head her husband was by: but shee bids the Gentleman name any afternoone, and she'll meet him at her Garden house, which I know.
Lod. Is this no lie now?
Bots. Dam me if —
Lod. Oh prethee stay there.
Bots. The twenty crownes, sir. 70
Lod. Before he has his worke done? but on my Knightly word, he shall pay't thee.

Enter Astolpho, Beraldo, Fontinell, *and the Irish Footman.*

Asto. I thought thou hadst beene gone into thine owne Country.
Bryan. No faat la, I cannot goe dis foure or tree dayes.
Ber. Looke thee, yonders the shop, and that's the man himselfe.
Font. Thou shalt but cheapen, and doe as we told thee, to put a iest vpon him, to abuse his patience.
Bryan. I faat, I doubt my pate shall be knocked: but sa crees sa me, for your shakes, I will runne to any Linnen Draper in hell, come preddy. 80
Omn. Saue you Gallants.
Lod. & Caro. Oh, well met!

63 She nibbled...] Dyce; *Lod.* Shee... Q

Cand. You'll giue no more you say? I cannot take it.
Hors. Truly Ile giue no more.
Cand. It must not fetch it. What wud you haue, sweet Gentlemen?
Asto. Nay, here's the Customer.   *Exeunt* Bots *and* Horsleach.
Lod. The Garden-house you say? wee'll boult out your roguery.
Cand. I will but lay these parcels by — My men
Are all at Customehouse vnloding Wares,
If Cambricke you wud deale in, there's the best, 90
All *Millan* cannot sample it.
Lod. Doe you heare? One, two, three. S'foot, there came in four
Gallants, sure your wife is slipt vp, and the fourth man I hold my
life, is grafting your Warden tree.
Cand. Ha, ha, ha: you Gentlemen are full of Iest.
If she be vp, she's gone some wares to show,
I haue aboue as good wares as below.
Lod. Haue you so? nay then —
Cand. Now Gentlemen, is't Cambricks?
Bryan. I predee now let me haue de best wares. 100
Cand. What's that he saies, pray' Gentlemen?
Lod. Mary he saies we are like to haue the best wars.
Cand. The best wars? all are bad, yet wars doe good,
And like to Surgeons, let sicke Kingdomes blood.
Bry. Faat a Deuill pratest tow so, a pox on dee, I preddee let me
see some Hollen, to make Linnen shirts, for feare my body be
lowsie.
Cand. Indeed I vnderstand no word he speakes.
Caro. Mary, he saies, that at the siege in *Holland* there was much
bawdry vsed among the Souldiers, tho they were lowsie. 110
Cand. It may be so, that's likely, true indeed,
In euery garden, sir, does grow that weed.
Bryan. Pox on de gardens, and de weedes, and de fooles cap dere,
and de cloutes; heare? doest make a Hobby-horse of me.
Omn. Oh fie, he has torne the Cambricke.
Cand. 'Tis no matter.
Asto. It frets me to the soule.

> 102, 103 (*twice*) wars] D3; wares Q
> 115 the] D²; de Q

Cand. So doest not me.
My Customers doe oft for remnants call,
These are two remnants now, no losse at all.   120
But let me tell you, were my Seruants here,
It would ha cost more. — Thanke you Gentlemen,
I vse you well, pray know my shop agen.   *Exit.*
Omn. Ha, ha, ha; come, come, let's goe, let's goe.
                                                Exeunt.

[ACT IV, SCENE i]

Enter Matheo (*braue*) *and* Bellafront.

Math. How am I suited, *Front*? am I not gallant, ha?
Bell. Yes, sir, you are suited well.
Math. Exceeding passing well, and to the time.
Bell. The Taylor has plaid his part with you.
Math. And I haue plaid a Gentlemans part with my Taylor, for I owe him for the making of it.
Bell. And why did you so, sir?
Math. To keepe the fashion; It's your onely fashion now of your best ranke of Gallants, to make their Taylors waite for their money, neither were it wisedome indeed to pay them vpon the first edition 10 of a new suite: for commonly the suite is owing for, when the lynings are worne out, and there's no reason then, that the Taylor should be paid before the Mercer.
Bell. Is this the suite the Knight bestowed vpon you?
Math. This is the suite, and I need not shame to weare it, for better men then I would be glad to haue suites bestowed on them. It's a generous fellow, — but — pox on him — we whose Pericranions are the very Limbecks and Stillitories of good wit, and flie hie, must driue liquor out of stale gaping Oysters. Shallow Knight, poore Squire *Tinacheo*: Ile make a wild Cataine of forty 20 such: hang him, he's an Asse, he's alwaies sober.
Bell. This is your fault to wound your friends still.
Math. No faith, *Front*, *Lodouico* is a noble Slauonian: it's more rare to see him in a womans company, then for a Spaniard to goe

into *England*, and to challenge the English Fencers there. — One knockes, — See — [*Exit* Bellafront.] *La, fa, sol, la, fa, la,* rustle in Silkes and Satins: there's musique in this, and a Taffety Petticoate, it makes both flie hie, — *Catzo.*

Enter Bellafront, *after her* Orlando *like himselfe, with foure men after him.*

Bell. *Matheo?* 'tis my Father.
Math. Ha, Father? It's no matter, hee findes no tatterd Prodigals 30 here.
Orl. Is not the doore good enough to hold your blue Coates? away, Knaues. Weare not your cloathes thred-bare at knees for me; beg Heauens blessing, (not mine.) Oh cry your Worship mercy, sir, was somewhat bold to talke to this Gentlewoman, your wife here.
Math. A poore Gentlewoman, sir.
Orl. Stand not, sir, bare to me; I ha read oft
That Serpents who creepe low, belch ranker poison
Than winged Dragons doe, that flie aloft. 40
Math. If it offend you, sir? 'tis for my pleasure.
Orl. Your pleasure be't, sir; vmh, is this your Palace?
Bell. Yes, and our Kingdome, for 'tis our content.
Orl. It's a very poore Kingdome then; what, are all your Subiects gone a Sheepe-shearing? not a Maid? not a Man? not so much as a Cat? you keepe a good house belike, iust like one of your profession, euery roome with bare walls, and a halfe-headed bed to vault vpon (as all your bawdy-houses are.) Pray who are your Vpholsters? Oh, the Spiders, I see, they bestow hangings vpon you.
Math. Bawdy-house? Zounds sir — 50
Bell. Oh sweet *Matheo*, peace. Vpon my knees
I doe beseech you, sir, not to arraigne me
For sinnes, which heauen, I hope, long since hath pardoned.
Those flames (like lightning flashes) are so spent,
The heate no more remaines, then where ships went,
Or where birds cut the aire, the print remaines.
Math. Pox on him, kneele to a Dog?

28 makes] D²; make Q   40 Than] D²; That Q

Bell.   She that's a Whore,
Liues gallant, fares well, is not (like me) poore,
I ha now as small acquaintance with that sinne,   60
As if I had neuer knowne it; that, neuer bin.
Orl.   No acquaintance with it? what maintaines thee then? how doest liue then? has thy husband any Lands? any Rents comming in, any Stocke going, any Ploughs iogging, any Ships sailing? hast thou any Wares to turne, so much as to get a single penny by? Yes, thou hast Ware to sell,
Knaues are thy Chapmen, and thy Shop is Hell.
Math.   Doe you heare, sir?
Orl.   So sir, I do heare, sir, more of you then you dreame I do.
Math.   You flie a little too hie, sir.   70
Orl.   Why, sir, too hie?
Math.   I ha suffred your tongue, like a bard Cater trea, to runne all this while, and ha not stopt it.
Orl.   Well, sir, you talke like a Gamester.
Math.   If you come to bark at her, because shee's a poore rogue; look you, here's a fine path, sir, and there, theres the doore.
Bell.   Matheo?
Math.   Your blue Coates stay for you, sir.
I loue a good honest roaring Boy, and so —
Orl.   That's the Deuill.   80
Math.   Sir, sir, Ile ha no *Ioues* in my house to thunder Auaunt: she shall liue and be maintained, when you, like a keg of musty Sturgeon, shall stinke. Where? in your Coffin. How? be a musty fellow, and lowsie.
Orl.   I know she shall be maintained, but how? she like a Queane, thou like a Knaue; she like a Whore, thou like a Thiefe.
Math.   Theife? Zounds Thiefe?
Bel.   Good dearest *Mat.* — Father.
Math.   Pox on you both, Ile not be braued: New Sattin scornes to be put downe with bare bawdy Veluet. Thiefe?   90
Orl.   I Thiefe, th'art a Murtherer, a Cheater, Whoremonger, a Pot-hunter, a Borrower, a Begger —
Bell.   Deare Father.

76 theres] Dyce; there Q

Math. An old Asse, a Dog, a Churle, a Chuffe, an Vsurer, a Villaine, a Moth, a mangy Mule, with an old veluet foot-cloth on his backe, sir.
Bell. Oh me!
Orl. Varlet, for this Ile hang thee.
Math. Ha, ha, alas.
Orl. Thou keepest a man of mine here, vnder my nose. 100
Math. Vnder thy beard.
Orl. As arrant a smell-smocke, for an old Mutton-munger, as thy selfe.
Mat. No, as your selfe.
Orl. As arrant a purse-taker as euer cride, Stand, yet a good fellow, I confesse, and valiant, but he'll bring thee to'th Gallowes; you both haue robd of late two poore Country Pedlers.
Math. How's this? how's this? doest thou flie hie? rob Pedlers? beare witnes *Front*, rob Pedlers? my man and I a Thiefe?
Bell. Oh, sir, no more. 110
Orl. I Knaue, two Pedlers, hue and cry is vp, Warrants are out, and I shall see thee climbe a Ladder.
Math. And come downe againe as well as a Bricklayer, or a Tyler. How the vengeance knowes he this? If I be hanged, Ile tell the people I married old *Friscabaldoes* Daughter, Ile frisco you, and your old carkas.
Orl. Tell what thou canst; if I stay here longer, I shall bee hang'd too, for being in thy company; therefore, as I found you, I leaue you.
Math. Kneele, and get money of him. 120
Orl. A Knaue and a Queane, a Thiefe and a Strumpet, a couple of Beggers, a brace of Baggages.
Math. Hang vpon him. I, I, sir, fare you well; we are so: follow close — we are Beggers — in Sattin — to him.
Bell. Is this your comfort, when so many yeeres
You ha left me frozen to death?
Orl. Freeze still, starue still.
Bell. Yes, so I shall: I must: I must and will.
If as you say I'm poore, relieue me then,
Let me not sell my body to base men. 130

You call me Strumpet, Heauen knowes I am none:
Your cruelty may driue me to be one:
Let not that sinne be yours, let not the shame
Of common Whore liue longer then my name.
That cunning Bawd (Necessity) night and day
Plots to vndoe me; driue that Hag away,
Lest being at lowest ebbe, as now I am,
I sinke for euer.
Orl. Lowest ebbe, what ebbe?
Bell. So poore, that (tho to tell it be my shame) 140
I am not worth a dish to hold my meate;
I am yet poorer, I want bread to eate.
Orl. It's not seene by your cheekes.
Math. I thinke she has read an Homely to tickle to the old rogue.
Orl. Want bread? there's Sattin: bake that.
Math. S'blood, make Pasties of my cloathes?
Orl. A faire new Cloake, stew that; an excellent gilt Rapier.
Math. Will you eat that, sir?
Orl. I could feast ten good fellowes with those Hangers.
Math. The pox you shall. 150
Orl. I shall not (till thou beggest,) thinke thou art poore;
And when thou beggest, Ile feed thee at my doore,
As I feed Dogs, (with bones) till then beg, borrow,
Pawne, steale, and hang, turne Bawde. When th'art no Whore,
                              [*Aside.*]
My heart-strings sure would crack, were they strained more.
                              Exit.
Math. This is your Father, your damn'd — confusion light vpon all the generation of you; he can come bragging hither with foure white Herrings (at's taile) in blue Coates without roes in their bellies, but I may starue ere he giue me so much as a cob.
Bell. What tell you me of this? alas. 160
Math. Goe trot after your Dad, doe you capitulate, Ile pawne not for you, Ile not steale to be hanged for such an hypocriticall close common Harlot: away, you Dog — Braue yfaith! Vds foot, Giue me some meate.

*154 When th'art no Whore,] *stet* Q

Bell. Yes, Sir. *Exit.*
Math. Goodman slaue, my man too, is gallop'd to the Deuill athe t'other side: *Pacheco*, Ile checo you. Is this your Dads day? *England* (they say) is the onely hell for Horses, and onely Paradise for Women: pray get you to that Paradise, because y'are called an *Honest Whore*; there they liue none but honest whores with a pox: 170 Mary here in our Citty, all your sex are but foot-cloth Nags: the Master no sooner lights, but the man leapes into the saddle.

Enter Bellafront.

Bell. Will you sit downe I pray, sir?
Math. I could teare (by'th Lord) his flesh, and eate his midriffe in salt, as I eate this: — must I choake — my Father *Friscabaldo*, I shall make a pittifull Hog-louse of you *Orlando*, if you fall once into my fingers — Here's the sauorest meat: I ha got a stomacke with chafing. What Rogue should tell him of those two Pedlers? A plague choake him, and gnaw him to the bare bones: come fill.
Bell. Thou sweatest with very anger, good sweet, vex not, 180 'Las, 'tis no fault of mine.
Math. Where didst buy this Mutton? I neuer felt better ribbes.
Bell. A neighbour sent it me.

Enter Orlando.

Math. Hah, neighbour? foh, my mouth stinkes, you whore, doe you beg victuals for me? Is this Sattin doublet to bee bumbasted with broken meat? *Takes vp the stoole.*
Orl. What will you doe, sir?
Math. Beat out the braines of a beggerly —
Orl. Beat out an Asses head of your owne; away, Mistris.
Exit Bellafront.
Zownds, doe but touch one haire of her, and Ile so quilt your cap 190 with old Iron, that your coxcombe shall ake the worse these seuen yeeres for't: Does she looke like a roasted Rabbet, that you must haue the head for the braines?
Math. Ha, ha: Goe out of my doores, you Rogue, away foure markes, trudge.

171 your] D3 *query*; our Q

Orl. Foure markes? no, sir, my twenty pound that you ha made flie hie, and I am gone.
Math. Must I be fed with chippings? y'are best get a clap-dish, and say y'are Proctor to some Spittle-house. Where hast thou beene, *Pacheco*? come hither my little Turky-cocke.
Orl. I cannot abide, sir, to see a woman wrong'd, not I.
Math. Sirra, here was my Father-in-law to day.
Orl. Pish, then y'are full of Crownes.
Math. Hang him, he would ha thrust crownes vpon me, to haue falne in againe, but I scorne cast-cloathes, or any mans gold.
Orl. But mine: how did he brooke that (sir?)
Math. Oh: swore like a dozen of drunken Tinkers; at last growing foule in words, he and foure of his men drew vpon me, sir.
Orl. In your house? wud I had bin by.
Math. I made no more adoe, but fell to my old locke, and so thrashed my blue Coates, and old crabtree-face my father-in-law, and then walkt like a Lion in my grate.
Orl. Oh Noble Master!
Math. Sirra, he could tell me of the robbing the two Pedlers, and that warrants are out for vs both.
Orl. Good sir, I like not those crackers.
Math. Crackhalter, wut set thy foot to mine?
Orl. How, sir? at drinking.
Math. We'll pull that old Crow my Father: rob thy Master. I know the house, thou the seruants: the purchase is rich, the plot to get it easie, the Dog will not part from a bone.
Orl. Pluck't out of his throat then: Ile snarle for one, if this can bite.
Math. Say no more, say no more, old cole, meet me anon at the signe of the Shipwracke.
Orl. Yes, sir.
Math. And dost heare, man? — the Shipwracke.   *Exit.*
Orl. Th'art at the Shipwracke now, and like a swimmer
Bold (but vnexpert) with those waues doest play,
Whose dalliance (whorelike) is to cast thee away.

Enter Hipollito *and* Bellafront.

And here's another Vessell, (better fraught,
But as ill man'd) her sinking will be wraught,
If rescue come not: like a Man of warre
Ile therefore brauely out: somewhat Ile doe,
And either saue them both, or perish too.   *Exit.*
Hip.   It is my fate to be bewitched by those eyes.
Bell.   Fate? your folly.
Why should my face thus mad you? 'las, those colours
Are wound vp long agoe, which beauty spred,
The flowres that once grew here, are withered.   240
You turn'd my blacke soule white, made it looke new,
And should I sinne, it ne'r should be with you.
Hip.   Your hand, Ile offer you faire play: When first
We met i'th Lists together, you remember
You were a common Rebell; with one parlee
I won you to come in.
Bell.   You did.
Hip.   Ile try
If now I can beate downe this Chastity
With the same Ordnance; will you yeeld this Fort,
If with the power of Argument now (as then)
I get of you the conquest: as before   250
I turnd you honest, now to turne you whore,
By force of strong perswasion?
Bell.   If you can,
I yeeld.
Hip.   The allarm's strucke vp: I'm your man.
Bell.   A woman giues defiance.
Hip.   Sit.
Bell.   Beginne:
'Tis a braue battaile to encounter sinne.
Hip.   You men that are to fight in the same warre,
To which I'm prest, and pleade at the same barre,
To winne a woman, if you wud haue me speed,
Send all your wishes.

Bell.   No doubt y'are heard, proceede.
Hip.   To be a Harlot, that you stand vpon,
The very name's a charme to make you one.
Harlot was a Dame of so diuine
And rauishing touch, that she was Concubine
To an English King: her sweet bewitching eye
Did the Kings heart-strings in such loue-knots tye,
That euen the coyest was proud when she could heare
Men say, Behold; another Harlot there;
And after her all women that were faire
Were Harlots call'd, as to this day some are:
Besides her dalliance, she so well does mix,
That she's in Latine call'd the *Meretrix*.
Thus for the name; for the profession, this,
Who liues in bondage, liues lac'd, the chiefe blisse
This world below can yeeld, is liberty:
And who (than whores) with looser wings dare flie?
As *Iunoes* proud bird spreads the fairest taile,
So does a Strumpet hoist the loftiest saile.
She's no mans slaue; (men are her slaues) her eye
Moues not on wheeles screwd vp with Iealowsie.
She (Horst, or Coacht) does merry iourneys make,
Free as the Sunne in his gilt Zodiake:
As brauely does she shine, as fast she's driuen,
But staies not long in any house of Heauen,
But shifts from Signe, to Signe: her amorous prizes
More rich being when she's downe, then when she rizes.
In briefe, Gentlemen haunt them, Soldiers fight for them,
Few men but know them, few or none abhorre them:
Thus (for sport sake) speake I, as to a woman,
Whom (as the worst ground) I would turne to common:
But you I would enclose for mine owne bed.
Bell.   So should a husband be dishonoured.
Hip.   Dishonoured? not a whit: to fall to one
(Besides your husband) is to fall to none,
For one no number is.

        262 Harlot] *i.e.* [H]arlotta

Bell.   Faith, should you take
One in your bed, would you that reckoning make?
'Tis time you sound retreate.
Hip.   Say, haue I wonne,
Is the day ours?
Bell.   The battaile's but halfe done,
None but your selfe haue yet sounded alarmes,
Let vs strike too, else you dishonour armes.
Hip. If you can win the day, the glorie's yours.   300
Bell. To proue a woman should not be a whore,
When she was made, she had one man, and no more,
Yet she was tied to lawes then, for (euen than)
'Tis said, she was not made for men, but man.
Anon, t'increase earths brood, the law was varied,
Men should take many wiues: and tho they married
According to that Act, yet 'tis not knowne,
But that those wiues were onely tied to one.
New Parliaments were since: for now one woman
Is shared betweene three hundred, nay she's common;   310
Common? as spotted Leopards, whom for sport
Men hunt, to get the flesh, but care not for't.
So spread they Nets of gold, and tune their Calls,
To inchaunt silly women to take falls:
Swearing they are Angels, (which that they may win)
They'll hire the Deuill to come with false Dice in.
Oh Sirens suttle tunes! your selues you flatter,
And our weake sex betray; so men loue water,
It serues to wash their hands, but (being once foule)
The water downe is powred, cast out of doores,   320
And euen of such base vse doe men make whores.
A Harlot (like a Hen) more sweetnes reapes,
To picke men one by one vp, then in heapes:
Yet all feeds but confounding. Say you should taste me,
I serue but for the time, and when the day
Of warre is done, am casheerd out of pay:
If like lame Soldiers I could beg, that's all,
And there's lusts Rendez-vous, an Hospitall.

Who then would be a mans slaue, a mans woman?
She's halfe staru'd the first day that feeds in Common. 330
Hip. You should not feed so, but with me alone.
Bell. If I drinke poison by stealth, is't not all one?
Is't not ranke poison still? with you alone!
Nay say you spide a Curtezan, whose soft side
To touch, you'd sell your birth-right, for one kisse
Be rack'd, she's won, y'are sated: what followes this?
Oh, then you curse that Bawd that toald you in,
(The Night) you curse your lust, you loath the sin,
You loath her very sight, and ere the day
Arise, you rise glad when y'are stolne away. 340
Euen then when you are drunke with all her sweets,
There's no true pleasure in a Strumpets sheetes.
Women, whom Lust so prostitutes to sale,
Like Dancers vpon ropes; once seene, are stale.
Hip. If all the threds of Harlots lyues are spun,
So coorse as you would make them, tell me why
You so long loued the trade?
Bell.   If all the threds
Of Harlots lyues be fine as you would make them,
Why doe not you perswade your wife turne whore,
And all Dames else to fall before that sin? 350
Like an ill husband (tho I knew the same,
To be my vndoing) followed I that game.
Oh when the worke of Lust had earn'd my bread,
To taste it, how I trembled, lest each bit,
Ere it went downe, should choake me (chewing it?)
My bed seem'd like a Cabin hung in Hell,
The Bawde Hells Porter, and the lickorish wine
The Pander fetch'd, was like an easie Fine,
For which, me thought I leas'd away my soule,
And oftentimes (euen in my quaffing bowle) 360
Thus said I to my selfe, I am a whore,
And haue drunke downe thus much confusion more.
Hip. It is a common rule, and 'tis most true,
Two of one trade neuer loue; no more doe you.

Why are you sharpe 'gainst that you once profest?
Bell. Why doate you on that, which you did once detest?
I cannot (seeing she's wouen of such bad stuffe)
Set colours on a Harlot base enough.
Nothing did make me, when I loued them best,
To loath them more then this: when in the street 370
A faire yong modest Damsell I did meet,
She seem'd to all a Doue (when I pass'd by)
And I (to all) a Rauen: euery eye
That followed her, went with a bashfull glance:
At me, each bold and ieering countenance
Darted forth scorne: to her (as if she had bin
Some Tower vnvanquished) would they vaile,
'Gainst me swolne Rumor hoisted euery saile.
She (crown'd with reuerend praises) passed by them,
I (tho with face maskt) could not scape the hem, 380
For (as if Heauen had set strange markes on Whores,
Because they should be pointing stocks to man)
Dress vp in ciuilest shape a Curtizan,
Let her walke Saint-like, notelesse, and vnknowne,
Yet she's betraid by some tricke of her owne.
Were Harlots therefore wise, they'd be sold deare:
For men account them good but for one yeere:
And then like Almanackes (whose dates are gone)
They are throwne by, and no more lookt vpon.
Who'le therefore backward fall, who will lanch forth 390
In Seas so foule, for ventures no more worth?
Lusts voiage hath (if not this course) this crosse,
Buy ne'r so cheape, your Ware comes home with losse.
What, shall I sound retreat? the battaile's done:
Let the world iudge which of vs two haue won.
Hip. I!
Bell.   You? nay then as cowards doe in fight,
What by blowes cannot, shall be saued by flight.   *Exit.*
Hip.   Flie to earths fixed Center: to the Caues

383 Dress] Drest Q

Of euerlasting horror, Ile pursue thee,
(Tho loaden with sinnes) euen to Hells brazen doores. 400
Thus wisest men turne fooles, doting on whores.
Exit.

[ACT IV, Scene ii]

Enter the Duke, Lodouico, *and* Orlando [*as* Pacheco]: *after them* Infælice, Carolo, Astolfo, Beraldo, Fontinell.

Orl. I beseech your Grace (tho your eye be so piercing) as vnder a poore blue Coate, to cull out an honest Father from an old Seruingman: yet good my Lord discouer not the plot to any, but onely this Gentleman that is now to be an Actor in our ensuing Comedy.
Duke. Thou hast thy wish, *Orlando,* passe vnknowne,
Sforsa shall onely goe along with thee,
To see that Warrant serued vpon thy Sonne.
Lod. To attach him vpon fellony, for two Pedlers: is't not so?
Orl. Right, my Noble Knight: those Pedlers were two Knaues of 10
mine; he fleec'd the men before, and now he purposes to flea the Master. He will rob me, his teeth water to be nibbling at my gold, but this shal hang him by'th gills, till I pull him on shore.
Duke. Away: ply you the businesse.
Orl. Thankes to your Grace: but my good Lord, for my Daughter—
Duke. You know what I haue said.
Orl. And remember what I haue sworne: She's more honest, on my soule, then one of the Turkes Wenches, watcht by a hundred Eunuches.
Lod. So she had need, for the Turkes make them whores. 20
Orl. He's a Turke that makes any woman a Whore, hee's no true Christian I'm sure. I commit your Grace.
Duke. Infælice.
Infæ. Here, sir.
Lod. Signior Friscabaldo.
Orl. Frisking agen, *Pacheco?*
Lod. Vds so, *Pacheco?* wee'll haue some sport with this Warrant:

'tis to apprehend all suspected persons in the house: Besides, there's one *Bots* a Pander, and one Madam *Horsleach* a Bawde, that haue abus'd my friend, those two Coneyes will we ferret into the pursenet.

Orl. Let me alone for dabbing them o'th necke: come, come.
Lod. Doe ye heare, Gallants? meet me anon at *Matheos*.
Omn. Enough. *Exeunt* Lodouico *and* Orlando.
Duke. Th'old Fellow sings that note thou didst before,
Onely his tunes are, that she is no Whore,
But that she sent his Letters and his gifts,
Out of a Noble Triumph o're his Lust,
To shew she trampled his Assaults in dust.
Infæ. 'Tis a good honest seruant, that old man.
Duke. I doubt no lesse.
Infæ. And it may be my husband,
Because when once this woman was vnmaskt,
He leueld all her thoughts, and made them fit:
Now he'd marre all agen, to try his wit.
Duke. It may be so too, for to turne a Harlot
Honest, it must be by strong Antidots,
'Tis rare, as to see Panthers change their spots.
And when she's once a Starre (fixed) and shines bright,
Tho 'twere impiety then to dim her light,
Because we see such Tapers seldome burne,
Yet 'tis the pride and glory of some men,
To change her to a blazing Starre agen,
And it may be, *Hipollito* does no more.
It cannot be, but y'are acquainted all
With that same madnesse of our Sonne-in-law,
That dotes so on a Curtizan.
Omn. Yes, my Lord.
Caro. All the City thinkes he's a Whoremonger.
Asto. Yet I warrant, he'll sweare, no man markes him.
Ber. 'Tis like so, for when a man goes a wenching, tis as if he had a strong stincking breath, euery one smells him out, yet he feeles it not, tho it be rancker then the sweat of sixteene Bearewarders.

60 tis] is Q

Duke. I doubt then you haue all those stinking breaths,
You might be all smelt out.
Carr. Troth my Lord, I thinke we are all as you ha bin in your
youth when you went a Maying, we all loue to heare the Cuckoo
sing vpon other mens Trees.
Duke. It's well that you confesse: but Girle, thy bed
Shall not be parted with a Curtizan —
'Tis strange, 70
No frowne of mine, no frowne of the poore Lady,
(My abused child, his wife) no care of fame,
Of Honor, Heauen or Hell, no not that name
Of Common Strumpet, can affright, or woo
Him to abandon her; the Harlot does vndoe him,
She has bewitched him, robd him of his shape,
Turnd him into a beast, his reason's lost,
You see he lookes wild, does he not?
Caro. I ha noted
New Moones in's face, my Lord, all full of change.
Duke. He's no more like vnto *Hipollito*, 80
Then dead men are to liuing — neuer sleepes,
Or if he doe, it's dreames; and in those dreames
His armes worke, — and then cries — Sweet — what's her name,
What's the drabs name?
Asto. In troth, my Lord, I know not,
I know no drabs, not I.
Duke. Oh, *Bellafront*!
And catching her fast, cries, My *Bellafront*.
Caro. A drench that's able to kill a Horse, cannot kill this disease
of Smock-smelling, my Lord, if it haue once eaten deepe.
Duke. Ile try all Phisicke, and this Med'cine first:
I haue directed Warrants strong and peremptory 90
(To purge our Citty *Millan*, and to cure
The outward parts, the Suburbes) for the attaching
Of all those women, who (like gold) want waight,
Citties (like Ships) should haue no idle fraight.
Caro. No, my Lord, and light wenches are no idle fraight,

68 that] Spencer (*i.e.* yᵗ); yet Q

But what's your Graces reach in this?
Duke. This (*Carolo.*) If she whom my Son doates on,
Be in that Muster-booke enrold, he'll shame
Euer t'approach one of such noted name.
Caro. But say she be not?
Duke. Yet on Harlots heads
New Lawes shall fall so heauy, and such blowes
Shall giue to those that haunt them, that *Hipollito*
(If not for feare of Law) for loue to her,
If he loue truely, shall her bed forbeare.
Caro. Attach all the light heeles i'th Citty, and clap em vp? why, my Lord? you diue into a Well vnsearchable: all the Whores within the walls, and without the walls? I would not be he should meddle with them for ten such Dukedomes; the Army that you speake on, is able to fill all the prisons within this Citty, and to leaue not a drinking roome in any Tauerne besides.
Duke. Those onely shall be caught that are of note.
Harlots in each street flow:
The fish being thus i'th net, our selfe will sit,
And with eye most seuere dispose of it. —
Come, Girle.
Caro. Araigne the poore Whore.
Asto. Ile not misse that Sessions.
Font. Nor I.
Ber. Nor I, tho I hold vp my hand there my selfe.

Exeunt.

[ACT IV, Scene iii]

Enter Matheo, Orlando [*as* Pacheco], *and* Lodouico.

Math. Let who will come (my Noble Shauileir) I can but play the kind Hoast, and bid vm welcome.
Lod. We'll trouble your house (*Matheo*) but as Dutchmen doe in Tauernes (drinke, be merry, and be gone.)

98 Muster-booke] Dyce; Master-booke Q

Orl. Indeed if you be right Dutchmen, if you fall to drinking, you must be gone. [*Aside.*]
Math. The worst is, my wife is not at home; but we'll flie hie (my generous Knight) for all that: there's no Musike when a woman is in the consort.
Orl. No, for she's like a paire of Virginals, alwaies with Iackes at her taile. [*Aside.*]

Enter Astolfo, Carolo, Beraldo, Fontinell.

Lod. See, the Couy is sprung.
Omn. Saue you Gallants.
Math. Happily encounterd, sweet bloods.
Lod. Gentlemen, you all know *Signior Candido*, the Linnen Draper, he that's more patient then a browne Baker, vpon the day when he heates his Ouen, and has forty Scolds about him.
Omn. Yes, we know him all, what of him?
Lod. Wud it not be a good fit of mirth, to make a piece of English cloth of him, and to stretch him on the Tainters, till the threds of his owne naturall humor cracke, by making him drinke healths, Tobacco, dance, sing bawdy songs, or to run any bias according as we thinke good to cast him?
Caro. 'Twere a Morris dance worth the seeing.
Asto. But the old Fox is so crafty, we shall hardly hunt him out of his den.
Math. To that traine I ha giuen fire already; and the hook to draw him hither, is to see certaine pieces of Lawne, which I told him I haue to sell, and indeed haue such: fetch them downe, Pacheco.
Orl. Yes, sir, I'm your Water-spanniell, and will fetch any thing: but Ile fetch one dish of meat anon, shall turne your stomacke, and that's a Constable. *Exit.*

Enter Bots *vshering Mistris* Horsleach.

Omn. How now? how now?
Caro. What Gally-foist is this?
Lod. Peace, two dishes of stew'd prunes, a Bawde and a Pander.

25 him] D3; *om.* Q

My worthy Lieutenant *Bots*; why, now I see th'art a man of thy word, welcome; welcome Mistris *Horsleach*: Pray Gentlemen, salute this reuerend Matron.

Hors. Thankes to all your Worships.   40

Lod. I bade a Drawer send in wine too: did none come along with thee (Grannam) but the Lieutenant?

Hors. None came along with me but *Bots*, if it like your Worship.

Bots. Who the pox should come along with you but *Bots*?

Enter two Vintners.

Omn. Oh braue! march faire.

Lod. Are you come? that's well.

Math. Here's Ordnance able to sacke a Citty.

Lod. Come, repeat, read this Inuentory.

1. *Vint.* *Imprimis*, a pottle of Greeke wine, a pottle of Peter sa meene, a pottle of Charnico, and a pottle of Liattica.   50

Lod. Y'are paid?

2. *Vint.* Yes Sir.   *Exeunt Vintners.*

Math. So shall some of vs be anon, I feare.

Bots. Here's a hot day towards: but zounds, this is the life out of which a Soldier sucks sweetnesse, when this Artillery goes off roundly, some must drop to the ground: Cannon, Demy-cannon, Saker, and Basalisk.

Lod. Giue fire, Lieutenant.

Bots. So, so: Must I venture first vpon the breach? to you all, Gallants: *Bots* sets vpon you all.   60

Omn. Its hard (*Bots*) if we pepper not you, as well as you pepper vs.

Enter Candido.

Lod. My noble Linnen Draper! Some wine: Welcome old Lad.

Math. Y'are welcome, *Signior*.

Cand. These Lawnes, sir?

Math. Presently, my man is gone for them: we ha rigged a Fleet, you see here, to saile about the world.

Cand. A dangerous Voyage, sailing in such Ships.

Bots. There's no casting ouer boord yet.

50 Liattica] Dyce (Leatica); Ziattica Q

Lod. Because you are an old Lady, I will haue you be acquainted with this graue Cittizen, pray bestow your lips vpon him, and bid him welcome.

Hors. Any Cittizen shall be most welcome to me: — I haue vsed to buy ware at your shop.

Cand. It may be so, good Madam.

Hors. Your Prentices know my dealings well; I trust your good wife be in good case: if it please you, beare her a token from my lips, by word of mouth.

Cand. I pray no more forsooth, 'tis very well, indeed I loue no sweet meats: — Sh'as a breath stinkes worse then fifty Polecats. Sir, a word, is she a Lady?

Lod. A woman of a good house, and an ancient, shee's a Bawde.

Cand. A Bawde? Sir, Ile steale hence, and see your Lawnes some other time.

Math. Steale out of such company? *Pacheco?* my man is but gone for em: Lieutenant *Bots*, drinke to this worthy old fellow, and teach him to flie hie.

Omn. Swagger: and make him doo't on his knees.

Cand. How, *Bots?* now blesse me, what doe I with *Bots?* no wine in sooth, no wine, good Master *Bots.*

Bots. Gray-beard, Goats pizzle: 'tis a health, haue this in your guts, or this, there: I will sing a bawdy song, sir, because your vergis face is melancholly, to make liquor goe downe glib: will you fall on your maribones, and pledge this health, 'tis to my Mistris, a whore?

Cand. Here's Ratsbane vpon Ratsbane: Master *Bots*, I pray, sir, pardon me: you are a Soldier, presse me not to this seruice, I am old, and shoot not in such pot-gunnes.

Bots. Cap, Ile teach you.

Cand. To drinke healths, is to drinke sicknesse: Gentlemen, pray rescue me.

Bots. Zounds, who dare?

Omn. We shall ha stabbing then?

Cand. I ha reckonings to cast vp, good Master *Bots.*

Bots. This will make you cast em vp better.

Lod. Why does your hand shake so?

Cand. The palsie, *Signiors*, danceth in my blood.
Bots. Pipe with a pox, sir, then, or Ile make your blood dance —
Cand. Hold, hold, good Master *Bots*, I drinke.   [*On his knees.*]
Omn. To whom?
Cand. To the old Countesse there.
Hors. To me, old Boy? this is he that neuer drunke wine: once agen too't.
Cand. With much adoe the poison is got downe,
Tho I can scarce get vp; neuer before
Dranke I a whores health, nor will neuer more.

Enter Orlando *with Lawnes.*

Math. Hast bin at Gallowes?
Orl. Yes, sir, for I make account to suffer to day.
Math. Looke, *Signior*: here's the Commodity.
Cand. Your price?
Math. Thus.
Cand. No: too deare: thus.
Math. No: O fie, you must flie higher: yet take em home, trifles shall not make vs quarrell, we'll agree, you shall haue them, and a penniworth, Ile fetch money at your shop.
Cand. Be it so, good *Signior*, send me going.
Math. Going? a deepe bowle of wine for *Signior Candido*.
Orl. He wud be going.
Cand. Ile rather stay, then goe so: stop your Bowle.

Enter Constable and Bilmen.

Lod. How now?
Bots. Is't Shroue-tuesday, that these Ghosts walke.
Math. What's your businesse, Sir?
Const. From the Duke: you are the man wee looke for, *Signior*, I haue Warrant here from the Duke, to apprehend you vpon fellony for robbing two Pedlers: I charge you i'th Dukes name goe quickly.
Math. Is the winde turn'd? well: this is that old Wolfe, my Father-in-law: seeke out your Mistris, Sirra.

Orl. Yes, Sir: as shafts by piecing are made strong,
So shall thy life be straightned by this wrong. *Exit.*
Omn. In troth we are sorry.
Math. Braue men must bee crost, pish, it's but Fortunes Dice
rouing against me: Come, sir, pray vse me like a Gentleman, let
me not be carried through the streets like a Pageant.
Const. If these Gentlemen please, you shall goe along with them.
Omn. Bee't so: come.
Const. What are you, sir?
Bots. I, sir? sometimes a figure, sometimes a cipher, as the State
has occasion to cast vp her accounts: I'm a Soldier.
Const. Your name is *Bots*, is't not?
Bots. Bots is my name, *Bots* is knowne to this Company.
Const. I know you are, Sir: what's she?
Bots. A Gentlewoman, my Mother.
Const. Take em both along.
Bots. Me? Sirrr.
Billmen. Aye Sirrr.
Const. If he swagger, raise the street.
Bots. Gentlemen, Gentlemen, whither will you drag vs?
Lod. To the Garden house. *Bots*, are we euen with you?
Const. To Bridewell with em.
Bots. You will answer this. *Exeunt.*
Const. Better then a challenge, I haue warrant for my worke, sir.
Lod. Wee'll goe before. *Exeunt.*
Const. Pray doe.
Who, *Signior Candido?* a Cittizen of your degree
Consorted thus, and reuelling in such a house?
Cand. Why, sir? what house I pray?
Const. Lewd, and defamed.
Cand. Is't so? thankes, sir: I'm gone.
Const. What haue you there?
Cand. Lawnes which I bought, sir, of the Gentleman
That keepes the house.
Const. And I haue warrant here,
To search for such stolne Ware: these Lawnes are stolne.

*155 Aye] Rhys; And Q

Cand. Indeed!
Const. So he's the Thiefe, you the Receiuer:
I'm sorry for this chance, I must commit you.
Cand. Me, sir, for what?
Const. These Goods are found vpon you,
And you must answer't.
Cand. Must I so?
Const. Most certaine.
Cand. Ile send for Bayle.
Const. I dare not: yet because
You are a Cittizen of worth, you shall not
Be made a pointing stocke, but without Guard
Passe onely with my selfe.
Cand. To Bridewell too?
Const. No remedy.
Cand. Yes, patience: being not mad,
They had mee once to Bedlam, now I'm drawne 180
To Bridewell, louing no Whores.
Const. You will buy Lawne? —
Exeunt

[ACT V, Scene i]

Enter at one doore Hipollito; *at another*, Lodouico,
Astolfo, Carolo, Beraldo, Fontinell.

Lod. Yonder's the Lord *Hipollito*, by any meanes leaue him and me
together: Now will I turne him to a Madman.
Omn. Saue you, my Lord. *Exeunt.*
Lod. I ha strange newes to tell you.
Hip. What are they?
Lod. Your Mare's i'th pound.
Hip. How's this?
Lod. Your Nightingale is in a Limebush.
Hip. Ha?
Lod. Your Puritanicall *Honest Whore* sits in a blue gowne. 10
Hip. Blue Gowne!

v. i, v. ii]   THE HONEST WHORE, PART 2

Lod.   She'll chalke out your way to her now: she beats chalke.
Hip.   Where, who dares?
Lod.   Doe you know the Bricke-house of Castigation, by the
Riuer side that runnes by *Millan*: the Schoole where they pro-
nounce no letter well but O?
Hip.   I know it not.
Lod.   Any man that has borne Office of Constable, or any woman
that has falne from a Horse-load to a Cart-load, or like an old
Hen that has had none but rotten egges in her nest, can direct you   20
to her: there you shall see your Puncke amongst her back-friends,
there you may haue her at your will, for there she beates Chalke,
or grindes in the Mill, with a whip deedle, deedle, deedle, deedle:
ah little monkey.
Hip.   What Rogue durst serue that Warrant, knowing I loued her?
Lod.   Some Worshipfull Rascall, I lay my life.
Hip.   Ile beat the Lodgings downe about their eares
That are her Keepers.
Lod.   So you may bring an old house ouer her head.
Hip.   Ile to her —   30
Ile to her, stood armed Fiends to guard the doores.   *Exit.*
Lod.   Oh me! what Monsters are men made by whores?
If this false fire doe kindle him, there's one Faggot more to the
bonfire, now to my Bridewell Birds, what Song will they sing?
                                                           Exit.

[ACT V, SCENE ii]

Enter Duke, Carolo, Astolfo, Beraldo, Fontinell,
three or foure Masters of Bridewell: Infælice.

Duke.   Your Bridewell? that the name? for beauty, strength,
Capacity and forme of ancient building,
(Besides the Riuers neighbourhood) few houses
Wherein we keepe our Court can better it.
1. *Master.*   Hither from forraigne Courts haue Princes come,
And with our Duke did Acts of State Commence,
Here that great Cardinall had first audience,

(The graue *Campayne*,) that Duke dead, his Sonne
(That famous Prince) gaue free possession
Of this his Palace, to the Cittizens,
To be the poore mans ware-house: and endowed it
With Lands to'th valew of seuen hundred marke,
With all the bedding and the furniture, once proper
(As the Lands then were) to an Hospitall
Belonging to a Duke of *Sauoy*. Thus
Fortune can tosse the World, a Princes Court
Is thus a prison now.
  Duke.   'Tis Fortunes sport:
These changes common are: the Wheele of Fate
Turnes Kingdomes vp, till they fall desolate.
But how are these seuen hundred Markes by'th yeere
Imployde in this your Worke-house?
  1. *Master.*   Warre and Peace
Feed both vpon those Lands: when the Iron doores
Of warres burst open, from this House are sent
Men furnisht in all Martiall Complement.
The Moone hath thorow her Bow scarce drawn to'th head,
(Like to twelue siluer Arrowes) all the Moneths,
Since sixteen hundred Soldiers went aboord:
Here Prouidence and Charity play such parts,
The House is like a very Schoole of Arts,
For when our Soldiers (like Ships driuen from Sea,
With ribs all broken, and with tatterd sides,)
Cast anchor here agen, their ragged backes
How often doe we couer? that (like men)
They may be sent to their owne Homes agen.
All here are but one swarme of Bees, and striue
To bring with wearied thighs honey to the Hiue.
The sturdy Begger, and the lazy Lowne,
Gets here hard hands, or lac'd Correction.
The Vagabond growes stay'd, and learnes to 'bey,
The Drone is beaten well, and sent away.
As other prisons are, (some for the Thiefe,
Some, by which vndone Credit gets reliefe

v. ii] THE HONEST WHORE, PART 2

 From bridled Debtors; others for the poore)
 So this is for the Bawd, the Rogue, and Whore.
Caro. An excellent Teeme of Horse.
1. *Master.*   Nor is it seene,
 That the whip drawes blood here, to coole the Spleene
 Of any rugged Bencher: nor does offence
 Feele smart, on spitefull, or rash euidence:
 But pregnant testimony forth must stand,
 Ere Iustice leaue them in the Beadles hand,   50
 As Iron, on the Anuill are they laid,
 Not to take blowes alone, but to be made
 And fashioned to some Charitable vse.
Duke. Thus wholsom'st Lawes spring from the worst abuse.

   Enter Orlando [*as* Pacheco] *before* Bellafront.

Bell. Let mercy touch your heart-strings (gracious Lord)
 That it may sound like musike in the eare
 Of a man desperate, (being i'th hands of Law.)
Duke. His name?
Bell.   *Matheo.*
Duke.   For a robbery?
 Where is he?
Bell.   In this House.
Duke.   Fetch you him hither —
   Exit Bellafront *and one of the Masters of Bridewell.*
 Is this the Party?   60
Orl. This is the Hen, my Lord, that the Cocke (with the Lordly
 combe) your Sonne-in-law would crow ouer, and tread.
Duke. Are your two Seruants ready?
Orl. My two Pedlers are pack'd together, my good Lord.
Duke. 'Tis well: this day in Iudgement shall be spent,
 Vice (like a wound launc'd) mends by punishment.
Infæ. Let me be gone, my Lord, or stand vnseene;
 'Tis rare when a Iudge strikes, and that none dye,
 And 'tis vnfit then, women should be by.
1. *Master.* Wee'll place you, Lady, in some priuat roome.   70

   48 on] D3; or Q   59 he?] Dyce; she? Q

205

Infæ. Pray doe so. *Exit.*
Orl. Thus nice Dames sweare, it is vnfit their eyes
Should view men caru'd vp for Anatomies,
Yet they'll see all, so they may stand vnseene,
Many women sure will sinne behind a Skreene.

Enter Lodouico.

Lod. Your Sonne (the Lord *Hipollito*) is entred.
Duke. Tell him we wish his presence. A word *Sforsa*:
On what wings flew he hither?
Lod. These, — I told him his Larke whom he loued, was a
Bridewell Bird, he's mad that this Cage should hold her, and is come
to let her out.
Duke. 'Tis excellent: away, goe call him hither.
Exit Lodouico.

Enter one of the Gouernours of the House, Bellafront *after him with*
Matheo, *after him the Constable. Enter at another doore,* Lodouico
and Hipollito: Orlando *steps forth and brings in two Pedlers.*

Duke. You are to vs a stranger (worthy Lord)
'Tis strange to see you here.
Hip.   It is most fit,
That where the Sunne goes, *Attomyes* follow it.
Duke. *Attomyes* neither shape, nor honour beare:
Be you your selfe, a Sunne-beame to shine cleare.
Is this the Gentleman?
Stand forth and heare your accusation.
Math. Ile heare none: I flie hie in that: rather then Kites shall
seize vpon me, and picke out mine eyes to my face, Ile strike my
tallons thorow mine owne heart first, and spit my blood in theirs:
I am here for shriuing those two fooles of their sinfull packe: when
those Iack-dawes haue cawde ouer me, then must I cry guilty, or
not guilty; the Law has worke enough already, and therefore Ile
put no worke of mine into his hands, the Hangman shall ha't first,
I did pluck those Ganders, did rob them.
Duke. 'Tis well done to confesse.
Math. Confesse and be hanged, and then I flie hie, is't not so? that

for that? a gallowes is the worst rub that a good Bowler can meet *100*
with: I stumbled against such a post, else this night I had plaid the
part of a true Sonne in these daies, vndone my Father-in-law, with
him wud I ha run at leape-frogge, and come ouer his gold, tho I
had broke his necke for't: but the poore Salmon Trout is now in
the Net.
Hip. And now the Law must teach you to flie hie.
Math. Right, my Lord, and then may you flie low; no more
words, a Mouse, Mum, you are stop'd.
Bell. Be good to my poore husband, deare my Lords.
Math. Asse, why shouldst thou pray them to be good to me, *110*
when no man here is good to one another?
Duke. Did any hand worke in this theft but yours?
Math. O, yes, my Lord, yes: — the Hangman has neuer one
Sonne at a birth, his Children alwaies come by couples: Tho I
cannot giue the old dog, my Father, a bone to gnaw, the Daughter
shall bee sure of a Choke-peare. — Yes, my Lord, there was one
more that fiddled my fine Pedlers, and that was my wife.
Bell. Alas, I?
Orl. O euerlasting, supernaturall superlatiue Villaine!
Omn. Your wife, *Matheo*?
Hip. Sure it cannot be. *120*
Math. Oh, Sir, you loue no quarters of Mutton that hang vp, you
loue none but whole Mutton; she set the robbery, I perform'd it;
she spur'd me on, I gallop'd away.
Orl. My Lords.
Bell. My Lords, (fellow giue me speach) if my poore life
May ransome thine, I yeeld it to the Law,
Thou hurt'st thy soule (yet wipest off no offence)
By casting blots vpon my Innocence:
Let not these spare me, but tell truth: no, see
Who slips his necke out of the misery, *130*
Tho not out of the mischiefe: let thy Seruant
That shared in this base Act, accuse me here,
Why should my Husband perish, he goe cleare?
Orl. A good Child, hang thine owne Father.

100 that?] ~ ⟨Q   *129 no] *stet* Q   134 good] D²; god Q

Duke. Old fellow, was thy hand in too?
Orl. My hand was in the Pye, my Lord, I confesse it: my Mistris I see, will bring me to the Gallowes, and so leaue me; but Ile not leaue her so: I had rather hang in a womans company, then in a mans; because if we should go to hell together, I should scarce be letten in, for all the Deuils are afraid to haue any women come amongst them, as I am true Thiefe, she neither consented to this fellony, nor knew of it.
Duke. What fury prompts thee on to kill thy wife?
Math. It's my humor, Sir, 'tis a foolish Bag-pipe that I make my selfe merry with: why should I eate hempe-seed at the Hangmans thirteene-pence halfe-penny Ordinary, and haue this whore laugh at me as I swing, as I totter?
Duke. Is she a Whore?
Math. A sixe-penny Mutton Pasty, for any to cut vp.
Orl. Ah, Toad, Toad, Toad.
Math. A Barbers Citterne for euery Seruingman to play vpon, that Lord, your Sonne, knowes it.
Hip. I, sir, am I her Bawd then?
Math. No, sir, but she's your Whore then.
Orl. Yea Spider, doest catch at great Flies?
Hip. My Whore?
Math. I cannot talke, sir, and tell of your Rems, and your rees, and your whirligigs, and deuices: but, my Lord, I found em like Sparrowes in one nest, billing together, and bulling of me, I tooke em in bed, was ready to kill him, was vp to stab her —
Hip. Cloze thy ranke Iawes: pardon me, I am vexed,
Thou art a Villaine, a malicious Deuill,
Deepe as the place where thou art lost, thou lyest,
Since I am thus far got into this storme,
Ile thorow, and thou shalt see Ile thorow vntoucht,
When thou shalt perish in it.

Enter Infælice.

Infæ.   'Tis my cue
To enter now: roome, let my Prize be plaid,
I ha lurk'd in Cloudes, yet heard what all haue said,

v. ii]   THE HONEST WHORE, PART 2

What Iury more can proue, she has wrong'd my bed,
Then her owne husband, she must be punished;   170
I challenge Law, my Lord, Letters, and Gold,
And Iewels from my Lord that woman tooke.
Hip. Against that blacke-mouthed Deuill, against Letters, and
            Gold,
And against a iealous Wife I doe vphold,
Thus farre her reputation, I could sooner
Shake the *Appenine*, and crumble Rockes to dust,
Then (tho *Ioues* showre rayned downe) tempt her to lust.
Bell. What shall I say?

Hee discouers himselfe.

Orl. Say thou art not a Whore, and that's more then fifteene
women (amongst fiue hundred) dare sweare without lying: this 180
shalt thou say, no let mee say't for thee; thy Husband's a Knaue,
this Lord's an honest Man; thou art no Puncke, this Lady's
a right Lady. *Pacheco* is a Thiefe as his Master is, but old *Orlando*
is as true a man as thy Father is: I ha seene you flie hie, sir, and
I ha seene you flie low, sir, and to keepe you from the Gallowes,
sir, a blue Coat haue I worne, and a Thiefe did I turne, mine owne
men are the Pedlers, my twenty pound did flie hie, sir, your wiues
Gowne did flie low, sir: whither flie you now, sir? you ha scap'd
the Gallowes, to the Deuill you flie next, sir. Am I right, my
Liege?   190
Duke. Your Father has the true Phisicion plaid.
Math. And I am now his Patient.
Hip.   And be so still,
'Tis a good signe when our cheekes blush at ill.
Const. The Linnen Draper (*Signior Candido*)
He whom the Citty tearmes the Patient man,
Is likewise here for buying of those Lawnes
The Pedlers lost.
Infæ.   Alas good *Candido*.   *Exit Constable.*
Duke. Fetch him: and when these payments vp are cast,
Weigh out your light Gold, but let's haue them last.

Enter Candido, *and Constable.*

Duke. In Bridewell, *Candido?*
Cand. Yes, my good Lord. 200
Duke. What make you here?
Cand. My Lord, what make you here?
Duke. I'm here to saue right, and to driue wrong hence.
Cand. And I to beare wrong here with patience.
Duke. You ha bought stolne Goods.
Cand. So they doe say, my Lord,
Yet bought I them vpon a Gentlemans word,
And I imagine now, as I thought then,
That there be Theeues, but no Theeues Gentlemen.
Hip. Your Credit's crack'd being here.
Cand. No more then Gold
Being crack'd which does his estimation hold.
I was in Bedlam once, but was I mad? 210
They made me pledge Whores healths, but am I bad,
Because I'm with bad people?
Duke. Well, stand by,
If you take wrong, wee'll cure the iniurry.

Enter Constable, after him Bots, *after him two Beadles,
one with Hempe, the other with a Beetle.*

Duke. Stay, stay, what's he? a prisoner?
Const. Yes, my Lord.
Hip. He seemes a Soldier?
Bots. I am what I seeme, Sir, one of Fortunes Bastards, a Soldier, and a Gentleman, and am brought in here with Master Constables band of Bilmen, because they face mee downe that I liue (like those that keepe Bowling-alleyes) by the sinnes of the people, in being a Squire of the body. 220
Hip. Oh, an Apple-squire.
Bots. Yes, sir, that degree of scuruy Squiers, and that I am maintained by the best part that is commonly in a woman, by the worst players of those parts, but I am knowne to all this company.

206 imagine] D²; magine Q   213 S.D. *him* Bots] *them* Bots Q

v. ii]   THE HONEST WHORE, PART 2

Lod.   My Lord, 'tis true, we all know him, 'tis Lieutenant *Bots.*
Duke.   *Bots,* and where ha you serued, *Bots?*
Bots.   In most of your hottest Seruices in the Low-countries: at the *Groyne* I was wounded in this thigh, and halted vpon't, but 'tis now sound. In *Cleueland* I mist but little, hauing the bridge of my nose broken downe with two great stones, as I was scaling a Fort: 230 I ha beene tryed, Sir, too, in *Gelderland,* and scap'd hardly there from being blown vp at a Breach: I was fired, and lay i'th Surgeons hands for't, till the fall of the leafe following.
Hip.   All this may be, and yet you no Soldier.
Bots.   No Soldier, sir? I hope these are Seruices that your proudest Commanders doe venture vpon, and neuer come off sometimes.
Duke.   Well, sir, because you say you are a Soldier, Ile vse you like a Gentleman: make roome there, Plant him amongst you, we shall haue anon Strange Hawkes flie here before vs: if none light   240 On you, you shall with freedome take your flight: But if you proue a Bird of baser wing, Wee'll vse you like such Birds, here you shall sing.
Bots.   I wish to be tried at no other weapon.
Duke.   Why is he furnisht with those inplyments?
1. *Master.*   The Pander is more dangerous to a State, Then is the common Thiefe, and tho our lawes Lie heauier on the Thiefe, yet that the Pander May know the Hangmans ruffe should fit him too, Therefore he's set to beat Hempe.
Duke.   This does sauour   250 Of Iustice, basest Slaues to basest labour. Now pray, set open Hell, and let vs see The Shee-Deuils that are here.
Infæ.   Me thinkes this place Should make euen *Lais* honest.
1. *Master.*   Some it turnes good, But (as some men whose hands are once in blood, Doe in a pride spill more) so, some going hence, Are (by being here) lost in more impudence: Let it not to them (when they come) appeare,

That any one does as their Iudge sit here:
But that as Gentlemen you come to see,   260
And then perhaps their tongues will walke more free.
Duke. Let them be marshall'd in: be couerd, all
Fellowes now, to make the Sceane more Comicall.
Caro. Will not you be smelt out, *Bots*.
Bots. No, your brauest whores haue the worst noses.

> *Enter two of the Masters: a Constable after them, then
> Dorathea Target,* braue, *after her two Beadles, th'one
> with a wheele, the other with a blue Gowne.*

Lod. Are not you a Bride, forsooth?
Dor. Say yee?
Caro. He wud know if these be not your Bridemen.
Dor. Vuh, yes, sir: and looke yee, doe you see the Bride-laces that
I giue at my wedding, will serue to tye Rosemary to both your   270
Coffins when you come from hanging — Scab?
Orl. Fie, Puncke, fie, fie, fie.
Dor. Out you stale stinking head of Garlicke, foh, at my heeles.
Orl. My head's clouen.
Hip. O, let the Gentlewoman alone, she's going to shrift.
Asto. Nay to doe penance.
Caro. I, I, goe Puncke, goe to the Crosse and be whipt.
Dor. Mary mew, mary muffe, mary hang you goodman Dog:
whipt? doe yee take me for a base Spittle whore? in troth Gentle-
men, you weare the cloathes of Gentlemen, but you carry not the   280
mindes of Gentlemen, to abuse a Gentlewoman of my fashion.
Lod. Fashion? pox a your fashions, art not a whore?
Dor. Goodman Slaue.
Duke. O fie, abuse her not, let vs two talke,
What mought I call your name, pray?
Dor. I'm not ashamed of my name, Sir, my name is Mistris *Doll
Target*, a Westerne Gentlewoman.
Lod. Her Target against any Pike in *Millan*.
Duke. Why is this wheele borne after her?
1. *Master.* She must spinne.   290
Dor. A coorse thred it shall be, as all threds are.

Asto. If you spin, then you'll earne money here too?
Dor. I had rather get halfe a Crowne abroad, then ten Crownes here.
Orl. Abroad? I thinke so.
Infœ. Doest thou not weepe now thou art here?
Dor. Say yee? weepe? yes forsooth, as you did when you lost your Maidenhead: doe you not heare how I weepe? *Sings.*
Lod. Farewell *Doll.*
Dor. Farewell Dog. *Exit.* [*with* 2. *Master and beadles*]. 300
Duke. Past shame: past penitence, why is that blue Gowne?
1. *Master.* Being stript out of her wanton loose attire,
That Garment she puts on, base to the eye,
Onely to cloath her in humility.
Duke. Are all the rest like this?
1. *Master.* No, my good Lord.
You see, this Drab swells with a wanton reyne,
The next that enters has a different straine.
Duke. Variety is good, let's see the rest. *Exit Master.*
Bots. Your Grace sees I'm sound yet, and no Bullets hit me.
Duke. Come off so, and 'tis well. 310
Omn. Here's the second Messe.

Enter the two Masters, after them the Constable, after him Penelope Whore-hound, *like a Cittizens wife, after her two Beadles, one with a blue Gowne, another with Chalke and a Mallet.*

Pen. I ha worne many a costly Gowne, but I was neuer thus guarded with blue Coats, and Beadles, and Constables, and —
Caro. Alas faire Mistris, spoyle not thus your eyes.
Pen. Oh sweet sir, I feare the spoyling of other places about me that are dearer then my eyes; if you be Gentlemen, if you be men, or euer came of a woman, pitty my case, stand to me, sticke to me, good sir, you are an old man.
Orl. Hang not on me, I prethee, old Trees beare no such fruit.
Pen. Will you bayle me, Gentlemen? 320
Lod. Bayle thee, art in for debt?
Pen. No God is my Iudge, sir, I am in for no debts, I payd my

322 God] D²; — Q

Taylor for this Gowne, the last fiue shillings a weeke that was
behind, yesterday.
Duke. What is your name, I pray?
Pen. *Penelope Whore-hound*, I come of the *Whore-hounds*. How
does Lieutenant *Bots*.
Omn. A ha *Bots*.
Bots. A very honest woman, as I'm a Soldier, a pox *Bots* ye.
Pen. I was neuer in this pickle before, and yet if I goe amongst 330
Cittizens wiues, they ieere at me: if I goe among the Loose-bodied
Gownes, they cry a pox on me, because I goe ciuilly attyred, and
sweare their trade was a good trade, till such as I am tooke it out
of their hands: good Lieutenant *Bots*, speake to these Captaines to
bayle me.
1. *Master.* Begging for bayle still? you are a trim gossip, goe giue
her the blue Gowne, set her to her chare, worke Huswife, for your
bread, away.
Pen. Out you Dog, a pox on you all, women are borne to curse
thee, but I shall liue to see twenty such flat-caps shaking Dice for 340
a penny-worth of Pippins: out, you blue-eyed Rogue. *Exit.*
Omn. Ha, ha, ha.
Duke. Euen now she wept, and praid, now does she curse?
1. *Master.* Seeing me: if still she had staid, this had beene worse.
Hip. Was she euer here before?
1. *Master.* Fiue times at least,
And thus if men come to her, haue her eyes
Wrung, and wept out her bayle.
Omn. *Bots*, you know her?
Bots. Is there any Gentleman here, that knowes not a Whore, and
is he a haire the worse for that? 350
Duke. Is she a City-dame, she's so attyred?
1. *Master.* No, my good Lord, that's onely but the vaile
To her loose body, I haue seene her here
In gayer Masking Suits, as seuerall Sawces
Giue one Dish seuerall Tastes, so change of Habits
In Whores is a bewitching Art: to day
She's all in colours to besot Gallants,
Then in modest blacke, to catch the Cittizen,

v. ii] THE HONEST WHORE, PART 2

And this from their Examinations drawne.
Now shall you see a Monster both in shape 360
And nature quite from these, that sheds no teare,
Nor yet is nice, 'tis a plaine ramping Beare,
Many such Whales are cast vpon this Shore.
Omn. Let's see her.
1. *Master.*   Then behold a swaggering Whore.   *Exit.*
Orl. Keep your grownd, *Bots.*
Bots. I doe but trauerse to spy aduantage how to arme my selfe.

Enter the two Masters first, after them the Constable, after them a Beadle beating a Bason, then Catyryna Bountinall, *with Mistris* Horsleach, *after them another Beadle with a blue head guarded with yellow.*

Cat. Sirra, when I cry hold your hands, hold, you Rogue-Catcher, hold: Bawd, are the French Chilblaines in your heeles, that you can come no faster? are not you (Bawd) a Whores Ancient, and must not I follow my Colours? 370
Hors. O Mistris *Katherine*, you doe me wrong to accuse mee here as you doe, before the right Worshipfull: I am knowne for a motherly honest woman, and no Bawd.
Cat. Mary foh, honest? burnt at fourteene, seuen times whipt, sixe times carted, nine times duck'd, search'd by some hundred and fifty Constables, and yet you are honest? Honest Mistris *Horsleach*, is this World, a World to keepe Bawds and Whores honest? How many times hast thou giuen Gentlemen a quart of wine in a gallon pot? how many twelue-penny Fees, nay two shillings Fees, nay, when any Embassadours ha beene here, how many halfe crowne 380 Fees hast thou taken? how many Carriers hast thou bribed for Country Wenches? how often haue I rinst your lungs in *Aqua vitæ*, and yet you are honest?
Duke. And what were you the whilest?
Cat. Mary hang you, Master Slaue, who made you an examiner?
Lod. Well said, belike this Deuill spares no man.
Cat. What art thou prethee?
Bots. Nay what art thou prethee?
Cat. A Whore, art thou a Thiefe?

215

Bots. A Thiefe, no, I defie the calling, I am a Soldier, haue borne Armes in the Field, beene in many a hot Skyrmish, yet come off sound.
Cat. Sound with a pox to yee, yee abominable Rogue! you a Soldier? you in Skirmishes? where? amongst pottle pots in a Bawdy-house? Looke, looke here, you Madam Wormeaten, doe not you know him?
Hors. Lieutenant *Bots*, where haue yee beene this many a day?
Bots. Old Bawd, doe not discredit me, seeme not to know me.
Hors. Not to know yee, Master *Bots*? as long as I haue breath, I cannot forget thy sweet face.
Duke. Why, doe you know him? he saies he is a Soldier.
Cat. He a Soldier? a Pander, a Dog that will licke vp sixe pence: doe yee heare, you Master Swines snout, how long is't since you held the doore for me, and cried too't agen, no body comes, yee Rogue you?
Omn. Ha, ha, ha, y'are smelt out agen, *Bots*.
Bots. Pox ruyne her nose for't, and I be not reuenged for this — vm yee Bitch.
Lod. Dee yee heare yee, Madam? why does your Ladiship swagger thus? y'are very braue, me thinkes.
Cat. Not at your cost, Master Cods-head. Is any man here bleare-eyed to see me braue?
Asto. Yes, I am, because good Cloathes vpon a Whores backe is like faire painting vpon a rotten wall.
Cat. Mary muffe Master Whoremaster, you come vpon me with sentences.
Ber. By this light has small sence for't.
Lod. O fie, fie, doe not vex her. And yet me thinkes a creature of more scuruy conditions should not know what a good Petticoate were.
Cat. Mary come out, y'are so busie about my Petticoate, you'll creepe vp to my placket, and yee cood but attaine the honour, but and the outsides offend your Rogueships, looke o'the lining, 'tis Silke.
Duke. Is't Silke 'tis lined with then?
Cat. Silke? I Silke, Master Slaue, you wud bee glad to wipe your

v. ii]   THE HONEST WHORE, PART 2

nose with the skirt on't: this 'tis to come among a company of
Cods-heads that know not how to vse a Gentlewoman.
Duke. Tell her the Duke is here.
1. *Master.* Be modest, *Kate*, the Duke is here. 430
Cat. If the Deuill were here, I care not: set forward, yee Rogues,
and giue attendance according to your places, let Bawds and Whores
be sad, for Ile sing and the Deuill were a dying. *Exeunt.*
Duke. Why before her does the Bason ring?
1. *Master.* It is an emblem of their reuelling,
The whips we vse lets forth their wanton blood,
Making them calme, and more to calme their pride,
In stead of Coaches they in Carts doe ride.
Will your Grace see more of this bad Ware?
Duke. No, shut vp shop, wee'll now breake vp the faire, 440
Yet ere we part — you, sir, that take vpon yee
The name of Soldier, that true name of worth,
Which, action not vaine boasting best sets forth,
To let you know how farre a Soldiers name
Stands from your title, and to let you see,
Soldiers must not be wrong'd where Princes be:
This bee your sentence.
Omn. Defend your selfe, *Bots.*
Duke. First, all the priuat sufferance that the house
Inflicts vpon Offenders, you (as the basest) 450
Shall vndergoe it double, after which
You shall bee whipt, sir, round about the Citty,
Then banisht from the Land.
Bots. Beseech your Grace.
Duke. Away with him, see it done, Panders and Whores
Are Citty-plagues, which being kept aliue,
Nothing that lookes like goodnes ere can thriue.
Now good *Orlando*, what say you to your bad Sonne-in-law?
Orl. Mary this, my Lord, he is my Sonne-in-law, and in law will
I be his Father: for if law can pepper him, he shall be so parboild, 460
that he shall stinke no more i'th nose of the Common-wealth.
Bell. Be yet more kinde and mercifull, good Father.
Orl. Doest thou beg for him, thou precious mans meat, thou? has

217

he not beaten thee, kickt thee, trod on thee, and doest thou fawne
on him like his Spanniell? has hee not pawnd thee to thy Petticoate,
sold thee to thy smock, made yee leape at a crust, yet woodst haue
me saue him?

Bell. Oh yes, good sir, women shall learne of me,
To loue their husbands in greatest misery,
Then shew him pitty, or you wracke my selfe. 470

Orl. Haue yee eaten Pigeons that y'are so kinde-hearted to your
Mate? Nay, y'are a couple of wilde Beares, Ile haue yee both
baited at one stake: but as for this Knaue, the Gallowes is thy due,
and the Gallowes thou shalt haue, Ile haue iustice of the Duke, the
Law shall haue thy life, what, doest thou hold him? let goe his
hand: if thou doest not forsake him, a Fathers euerlasting blessing
fall vpon both your heads: away, goe, kisse out of my sight, play
thou the Whore no more, nor thou the Thiefe agen,
My house shall be thine,
My meate shall be thine, 480
And so shall my wine,
But my money shall bee mine,
And yet when I die,
(So thou doest not flie hie)
Take all, yet good *Matheo,* mend.
Thus for ioy weepes *Orlando,* and doth end.

Duke. Then heare, *Matheo*: all your woes are stayed
By your good Father-in-law: all your Ills
Are cleare purged from you by his working pills.
Come *Signior Candido*, these greene yong wits 490
(We see by Circumstance) this plot hath laid,
Still to prouoke thy patience, which they finde
A wall of Brasse, no Armour's like the minde;
Thou hast taught the Citty patience, now our Court
Shall be thy Spheare, where from thy good report,
Rumours this truth vnto the world shal sing,
A Patient man's a Patterne for a King.

Exeunt.

FINIS.

TEXTUAL NOTES

I.i

124 *Iacomo*]   Spencer's transposition of *Old* at the start of two lines of verse best emends the original difficulty of having Matheo kill an old man who was son to a still living father of the same name. But since in the quarto the passage in question is set as prose, we must suppose that though the manuscript was correctly lined, the compositor mistook or ignored the fact in his typesetting. For a similar example, see II.i.37–38.

I.ii

85 there]   With this emendation of Q *here*, the sense is: Even though she has been dead for a long time, she is still with me *here* [in my heart], and our present separation is not permanent since she has travelled *there* [to heaven] ahead of me but I shall join her soon.

I.iii

S.D. 1. *Guest wearing a long hat*,]   This is a paraphrase for what in the manuscript was probably *Long.* or *Long-hat*. See line 78 for the speech-prefix *Long.* and the confusion of this character with Lodovico again in the speech-prefix at line 15 where editors have usually substituted *Candido*.

II.i

14 hang? Tosse]   The meaning of this phrase is obscure. Rhys, followed by Neilson, emended to *hang toff*; and Spencer to *hang't off*. These seem to be somewhat desperate expedients scarcely more satisfactory than the original. In the circumstances we cannot know whether *Tosse* is a verb or a noun. However, its capitalization may lead to the suspicion that the only corruption is the lack of some punctuation mark after *hang*, and that *Tosse* is supposed to be a kind of exclamation standing by itself. If so, O.E.D. produces two possible meanings, even three. *Toss* as verb or noun can signify a quick upward or backward movement of the head, lifting or jerking the head. Thus one tosses one's head to show unconcern, and Matheo may thus be dismissing his late plight, with a grisly double meaning. One may also *toss off* a drink with energetic action, or dispose of some object in an off-hand manner. Once again, it is possible for *Tosse* to be an exclamation showing lack of concern. Finally, through *tossing a coin*, the general idea of a gamble may associate itself with the word. Of these, the first may seem more plausible, although double meanings may well inhere. Whatever the precise situation, it would seem that Matheo, after indicating

that he intends to fly high, expresses his opinion of his close escape from hanging by a word intended to show his contempt. The only other possibility that might occur would be *Tosse* as a cant name for the hangman, whom Matheo is inviting to hang himself, but this is not recorded.

98 I drinke....] The three italic *I*'s may be for emphasis (Rhys, Neilson, and Spencer so reproduce them), but the odds are they represent instead a depletion of the roman sorts in the printer's case. However, if so, distribution would need to be assumed immediately, at the foot of the page (foot of C3ᵛ, line 100), for roman sorts reappear invariably in the next page.

III.i

69 by head] The line is not tightly set and in some copies the word *by* ending the line is spread. Just possibly an *a* may have dropped out at the end after *by*.

183 by this] All editors beginning with Dyce emend Q *this* to *thus*, reading *at length thus was charm'd*. Such an alteration of Q *at length this was charm'd* is plausible enough. But Infelice accompanies her words by showing Hippolito the three gifts. The first, the letter, is *this battery*; the second, the purse of gold, is *all this*; hence it is almost inevitable that the third, the diamond, should be *this* also, and one must add the necessary *by*.

184 Diamond wench] This Q reading should not be emended, as with various editors, to make *wench* a verb. *Diamond wench* means *the girl to whom you give diamonds*, and *change* is *exchange*. Thus, rather vulgarly, Infelice is accusing Hippolito of having exchanged her for Bellafront. For a similar phrase, *diamond courtier*, see *Westward Ho*, V.iv.203.

III.ii

99 mortall men] Q lines 'And...agen. | The...men | Mortall...them.' If, as likely, this lineation was suggested to the compositor by the accidental rhyme of *agen* and *men*, the inversion was doubtless his, as well, to make all neat.

127 An old Seruingman.] Dyce's assignment of this phrase to Matheo was followed by Rhys and Neilson but rejected by Spencer. The justification for altering Q would be in part the suspicion that the end of Lodovico's question with Matheo's name made the compositor overlook the speech-prefix for Matheo; and in part Orlando's following remark presumably addressed to Matheo as *you*. But we cannot be sure that Orlando did not address Lodovico, instead, although we can be sure that the use of *sir* prevents Orlando's line from being an aside. The emendation is tempting but not obligatory.

IV.i

54 When th'art no Whore,] All editors have followed Dyce in attaching this clause to Orlando's previous words, the presumed sense being, 'turn bawd after you have been forced by old age to abandon your profession of whore'. But to retain the Q modification, as here, is to give Orlando another aside to inform the audience of his belief in Bellafront's virtue despite his words addressed to her. The meaning, I take it, is: 'When you are no whore, and I have been forced to abuse you as one, if I continued to do so my heart strings would crack.'

IV.iii

155 Aye] This emendation of Q *And* is speculative but perhaps a shade better than supplying *you* after *And*.

V.ii

129 no,] Spencer emends to *now*. However, Bellafront's *no* seems to refer to Matheo's silence and thereby his refusal to tell truth as she has begged.

PRESS-VARIANTS IN Q (1630)

[The following copies are collated: BM¹ (British Museum 644.b.21[2]), BM² (British Museum C.12.f.4[3]), Bodl¹ (Bodleian Library Mal. 235[4]), Bodl² (Bodleian Mal. 788[2]), Bodl³ (Bodleian Mal. 192[6], *wants* L2–4), Dyce (Victoria and Albert Museum), Worc (Worcester College, Oxford), CSmH (Henry E. Huntington Library), CtY (Yale University), DFo¹ (Folger Shakespeare Library cs 47), DFo² (Folger cs 224), DLC (Library of Congress), ICN (Newberry Library), ICU (University of Chicago), MH (Harvard University), NN (New York Public Library), TxU (University of Texas).]

Sheet B (*inner forme*)

Corrected: BM¹⁻², Bodl¹,³, Dyce, Worc, CSmH, CtY, DFo¹⁻², DLC, ICN, ICU, MH, NN, TxU.
Uncorrected: Bodl².

Sig. B2.
I.ii.45 writ there,] writ, there

Sig. B3ᵛ.
I.ii.135 nor] no,

Sheet C (*inner forme*)

Corrected: BM¹⁻², Bodl¹,³, Dyce, Worc, CtY, DFo¹⁻², DLC, ICN, ICU, MH, NN, TxU.
Uncorrected: Bodl², CSmH.

Sig. C2.
I.iii.121 ſharpen] ſharp en

Sig. C4.
II.i.103 broke?] broake?

Sheet G (*outer forme*)

Corrected: BM¹⁻², Bodl²⁻³, Worc, CSmH, DFo¹⁻², DLC, ICN, ICU, MH, NN, TxU.
Uncorrected: Bodl¹, Dyce, CtY.

Sig. G1.
IV.i.58 that's a] that 'a

Sheet H (*inner forme*)

Corrected: BM[1-2], Bodl[1-3], Dyce, Worc, CSmH, CtY, DFo[1-2], DLC, ICN, MH, NN, TxU.
Uncorrected: ICU.

Sig. H3ᵛ.
  IV.ii.98 -booke enrold] -book eenrold
Sig. H4.
  IV.iii.1 Shauileir] Sheuileir

EMENDATIONS OF ACCIDENTALS

I.i

11 *Ber.*] *Bercaldo.*
24 S.D. Anthonio₍ₐ₎] ~ ,
33 *Ber.*] *Bert.*
36 Costermongers] Coster-|mongers
61, 66 *Font.*] *Fron.*
67 *Ber.*] *Berc.*
69 *Font.*] *Fron.*
70 *Ber.*] *Bert.*
76 about] abont
80 *Font.*] *Fro.*
81, 83 *Ber.*] *Bert.*
84 Table-booke] Table-|booke
94 Husband.] ~ ,
104 away,] ~ ₍ₐ₎
105–110 I doe...and come.] *prose in* Q

117–118 I'm sorry...*Mathæo.*] *one line in* Q
123–130 What was he...writes he here.] *prose in* Q
124 Florentine] *Florentine*
129 yes,] ~ ₍ₐ₎
148–151 I come...Court?] *prose in* Q
159 To] to
163–165 I am bold...leaues.] *prose in* Q
170–172 Not one...Character.] *prose in* Q
182 Is the Coach...sorrell.] Q *lines* gone? | Saddle
187 wut] wit

I.ii

S.D. Beraldo] Bercaldo
7 *Ber.*] *Berc.*
14 againe] aine *in* CSmH *letters dropped out*
25 S.D. Orlando] Orlaudo
46–47 I eate...voice.] Q *lines* I eate...Snakes. | My...cry | Hem...voice.
51 it.] ~ ,
67–78 After...ha?] Q *lines* After ...drawne: | For...couetous, | Am...debt, | Sit...side, | Nor ...feete. | Wenching...wrong, | No...fee; | I...home. | I...sheete: | But...me. | I... Age. | I...so? | If...eyes, | May...ha?
77 eyes.] ~ ,
80–82 I haue...Iocundare?] Q *lines* I...little, | Haue...things; I ...Iocundare?

84 She's...from me,] Q *lines* She's ...Countries, | Yet...from me, | Here....
91 pruinde] prumde
93 downe.] ~ ,
119 That...heart,] Q *lines* of | Ice
126 man:] ~ ,
127 showne:] ~ ,
139 Gally-pot] Gally-|pot
141–142 I almost...her?] *prose in* Q
145–146 her wrongs] Q *begins new line with* Her
152 she's —] ~ .
162–165 'Tis foolery...choke her.] Q *lines* 'Tis...her! | Were... Beere, | I...nailes | To... haire, | Vnlesse...her.
185 Giue] Gine
203–205 My beard...euen like] *prose with lines above in* Q

[1.iii, III. i]   EMENDATIONS OF ACCIDENTALS

I.iii

3 Me...sight.] Q *lines* Me thinkes | It's
48–49 That...it.] Q *lines* a Company, | And
79 Since...bare,] Q *lines* that | Shall

82–87 Oh, peace...these else.] *prose in* Q
97–98 I pray...well.] *prose in* Q
122 sir?] ~ .

II.i

1–2 Oh...welcome.] *prose in* Q
22–23 Thou...sound.] *prose in* Q
26–27 Nay...swagger.] *prose in* Q
51–52 But...poore,] Q *lines* But ...his | Fortunes...poore,
83 world,] ~ ⋏
83 out,] ~ ⋏
87 more —] ~ .
103 broake] Q(u); broke Q(c)
110 is —] ~ ;
126–127 Or...first.] Q *lines* Bacon, | Hee'll
140 Gods so] Godsso
156 Harke ⋏ you,] ~ , ~ ⋏

162–164 Ile take...it.] *prose in* Q
170–171 Drinke...this.] *prose in* Q
187 varlet's] varlot's
189–191 Fellow...him.] *prose in* Q
195–196 Would thou...hye,] Q *lines* Would...shalt | Please...hye,
195 please ⋏ me,] ~ , ~ ⋏
219 Stone-cutter] Stone-|cutter
247 If not, by this.] Q *runs-on with line* 246
255 Mutton-|munger] Muttonmunger
256 Sheepe-|biter] Sheepe-biter

II.ii

4 *Signior*] Signior
5 Yes,...drunke:] ~ : ... ~ ,
16–18 Were I...doo't.] *prose in* Q
22–23 Say...bud.] *prose in* Q
34–37 Well...cleane.] *prose in* Q
52–53 I hope...ready.] *prose in* Q

56 oath —] ~ ⋏
58 not —] ~ .
62 fast then,] ~ , ~ ⋏
69 Sirrah] sirrah
128 You ha...friends.] *run on as prose in* Q

III.i

35 Plough-land] Plough-|land
35 Fish-|pond] Fish-pond
38 To] to
40 Land,] *clear comma in* MH *only*
72–73 They...things?] *prose in* Q
87–89 Come...yonder?] *prose in* Q
95–96 Did...Diamond?] *prose in* Q
105 *Slawne loot*] *roman in* Q
108–111 If...two.] *prose in* Q
138–144 Earth...Groome] *prose in* Q

141 stolne] flolne
148–154 Worse...Noble?] *prose in* Q
149 Shamrocke] Shamocke
164 rods:] ~ .
165 gods.] ~ :
173–180 Tell me...fight.] *prose in* Q
187 Angels] Augels
202–203 prospers ⋏ ... blood,] ~ , ... ~ ⋏

BCD II 225 15

III.ii

36–37 Vndoe...often.] Q *lines* Vndoe...riflings | I...often.
58–60 How now...Mercers?] Q *lines* How...weeping | For...Mercers?
81 Knight-|hood] Knight-hood
98–99 And...them.] Q *lines* And ...agen. | The...men | Mortall...them.
101–106 Why...heart] Q *lines* Why ...want? | Say...that | Thy ...thee | On...whole | World ...worlds | Greatest...heart.
108 possest: ...glasse,] ~ , ... :
115 left-handed] left-|handed
128 You...Begger.] Q *lines* You ...sir: | That's the Begger.
143 Call...farewell.] Q *lines* Call ...please, | Till then farewell.

III.iii

39–40 My...euen.] *prose in* Q
39 Seruant, —] ~ , ∧
45 Gentlewoman] Gentlewomon
61 Knight] Kuight
89 Custome-|house] Custome-house

IV.i

66–67 Yes...Hell.] *prose in* Q run-on with above
72 trea] tra
91 Whoremonger] Whore-|monger
95 foot-cloth] foot-|cloth
153–155 As...more.] Q *lines* As... beg, | Borrow...Bawde. | When...sure | Would...more.
181 'Las] 'las
194–195 away ∧ ...markes,] ~ , ... ~ ∧
198 clap-dish] clap-|dish
200 Turky-cocke] Turky-|cocke
216 Good∧] ~ ,
231 And] *Orl.* And
283–284 Heauen, ...Signe:] ~ : ... ~ ,
300 If...yours.] Q *lines* day, | The
318 betray; ...water,] ~ , ... ~ ;
335 birth-right, ...kisse∧]
~ ∧ ... ~ ,
374 glance:] ~ ∧
383 Curtizan,] ~ .

IV.ii

15 Daughter —] ~ .
50 burne,] ~ .
70 'Tis strange,] Q *runs-on with line* 69
78–79 I ha...change.] Q *lines* I... Moones | In's...change.
83–84 His...name?] Q *lines* His ...her | Name...name?
91–92 (To...attaching] Q *lines* (To...outward | Parts...attaching
101–102 New...*Hipollito*] Q *lines* New...shall | Giue...*Hipollito*
111 note.] ~ ,
115 Come, Girle.] Q *runs-on with line* 114 [come]
119 Nor...selfe.] Q *lines* Nor I, | Tho...selfe.

226

[IV. iii, V. ii] EMENDATIONS OF ACCIDENTALS

IV.iii

10–11 No...taile.] Q *lines*
    Virginals, | Alwaies
106 *Signiors*] Signiors

164–165 Who...house?] *prose in* Q
168–181 Lawnes which...louing no
    Whores.] *prose in* Q

V.i

33–34 If...sing?] Q *lines* If...Faggot | More...Birds, | What...sing?

V.ii

40 away.] ~ ₐ
58–59 For...he?] *prose in* Q
73 Should] Sould
77 *Sforsa*] *Storsa*
79 These, —...Larke ₐ] ~ ,
    ₐ ... ~ —
88–89 Is...accusation.] *one line in* Q
103 leape-frogge] leape-|frogge
126 May] may
160 him,] ~ ₐ
171–172 I...tooke.] Q *lines* I... Iewels | From...tooke.
192–193 And be...ill.] *one line in* Q
197 *Exit*ₐ] ~ .
240–241 Strange...flight:] Q *lines* Strange...you, | You...flight:
245 Why ₐ] ~ ,
245 inplyments] in plyments
262–263 couerd, all Fellowes now,] ~ ₐ ~ , ~ , ~ ₐ
269 Bride-laces] Bride-|laces

286 *Dor.*] *Cor.*
339 borne] berne
345–347 Fiue...bayle.] *prose in* Q
356–360 In Whores...shape] Q *lines* In...in | Colours...blacke, | To...Examinations | Drawne...shape
359 drawne.] ~ ,
367 -Catcher] -*Catcher*
383 *vitæ*] *uitæ*
411 -head.] ~ ,
413–414 Yes...wall.] Q *lines* Yes, I am, | Because...backe | Is...wall.
418–420 O...were.] Q *lines* O... her. | And...conditions | Should...were.
421 Mary come out,] *separate line in* Q
479–485 My house...mend.] *prose in* Q

227 15-2

THE MAGNIFICENT, Entertainment:

Giuen to King *Iames*, Queene *Anne* his wife, and *Henry Frederick* the Prince, vpon the day of his Maiesties Trvumphant Passage (from the Tower) through his Honourable Citie (and Chamber) of *London*, being the 15. of March. 1603.

As well by the English as by the Strangers: VVith the speeches and Songes, deliuered in the seuerall Pageants.

Mart. *Templa Deis, mores populis dedit, otia ferro, Astra suis, Cælo sydera, serta Ioui.*

Tho. Dekker.

Imprinted at London by T. C. for Tho. Man the yonger. 1604.

TEXTUAL INTRODUCTION

THE MAGNIFICENT ENTERTAINMENT (Greg, *Bibliography*, no. 202[a]) was entered in the Stationers' Register by Thomas Man the younger on 2 April 1604, the title corresponding to that on the printed title-page down to the date 15 March 1603. If the entry were made from the already printed quarto, as likely, and not from a manuscript title, its date would closely approximate to that of publication. Since Dekker clearly is working up his descriptions after the event, the interval of slightly over a fortnight might be about right for the manuscript to be written and hurriedly set in type. In spite of the prior entry by Edward Blount on 19 March of Jonson's part of the *Entertainment*, Man seems to have had control over the entire account, for on 14 May the Court of the Company decided to end a controversy between the two stationers by ordering Blount to sell to Man at the rate of six shillings per ream the four hundred copies remaining of his Jonson stock.

As Sir Walter Greg has pointed out,[1] the quarto first edition of the *Entertainment*, according to the imprint printed for Man by T[homas] C[reede], was in fact manufactured at five different printing-houses, the division of the sheets being A–B, C–D, E, F–H, I. The first section A–B was printed by Creede, sheets F–H by Humphrey Lownes, and sheet I by Edward Allde. The printers of sheets C–D and E have not been identified. Division of a book into so many short sections is somewhat rare for a relatively brief pamphlet like the *Entertainment*, but doubtless it was so ordered for maximum speed in producing a coronation souvenir.

A second edition, *The Whole Magnificent Entertainment*, was also printed in 1604, by Edward Allde for Thomas Man (Greg, no. 202[b]). This edition, in part impressed from standing type of

---

[1] The earliest discussions of the printing of this edition and its relation to the second edition, *The Whole Magnificent Entertainment*, are summarized and corrected in Greg's *Bibliography*. Further investigation was made in my 'Notes on Standing Type in Elizabethan Printing', *Papers of the Bibliographical Society of America*, XL (1946), 218–222. For the present edition I have resurveyed the problem once more and have been able to add a few revised details in fact and interpretation.

the first, differs from the earlier edition in two respects: (1) English translations are added to the Latin speeches, for the Oration delivered by Mulcaster's scholar the English substituting for the Latin text; (2) some parts of the general text contain altered readings. This *Whole Entertainment* redivided the printing among four houses: Allde printed A–B and I; the same printer as in the first edition produced C–D; the original printer of sheet E reprinted this and added to his stint sheet F from Lownes's original section; Lownes produced the two sheets G–H.

Since the facts of this reprinting have a distinct textual importance, they must be listed in some detail. For Q2 (*Whole Entertainment*) Allde reset Q1's sheets A–B, condensing by two pages so that in Q2 gathering A is a half-sheet instead of a full sheet with a preliminary blank leaf. To this work he added the reimpression of the final sheet I, both formes from standing type with the exception of some lines which had apparently been disturbed in the process of tying up the type or in its reimposition. Thus the bottom five lines on I2^v are reset (lines 1550–1554, | thought...do I |), and the top eight lines on I3 (lines 1554–1561, | heere...though |). It is also clear that the first two lines on I4 have been disturbed (lines 1665–1666, | Caruers...appoyn-|) and reset in the right half of the lines.[1] The top ten lines of I3^v (lines 1579–1586) have pied very badly but have not been reset. On I4 the note 'To the Reader' and the errata list have been dropped and a large ornament substituted. That Allde had actually been the printer of sheet I in Q1 is shown by his impression of the same sheet from standing type in Q2, and also by the fact that in resetting A–B in Q2 he made the same use of medial *j* found in Q1 only in sheet I.

On the evidence of his use of standing type, the unknown printer of C–D in Q1 was presumably the same in Q2. He impressed the inner forme of sheet C from standing type but reset the outer forme. Since the first of the added English translations appears in sheet D, the typography is compressed to make room and the page for page

[1] In my opinion the type was truly disturbed by pieing, and thus the alteration of Q1 spelling *Harrison* to *Harison* was compositorial and not a change marked in copy. However, it is of interest that in the *Arches of Triumph* Harrison's name though spelled with double *r* in the engraved title is *Harison* in those engravings which do not give merely his initials.

correspondence of the two quartos is broken. The fifteen lines of standing type of the Latin *Italians Speech* on sig. D1 of Q1 is broken in two, and the first seven lines placed at the foot of C4ᵛ in Q2, this representing the only standing type in the outer forme of Q2's sheet C. The inner forme of gathering D from Q1 was kept standing but appears partly in the inner and partly in the outer forme of Q2. The reset portions in Q2 sheet D represent the outer forme of Q1 except for the fifteen lines of Latin from D1 thriftily left standing. The reimposition of type standing from inner D was accompanied by a trifling accident. What had been lines 13–14 on sig. D4 of Q1 (lines 565–566, | being...*Pyramides*; |) were reset, doubtless when they were pied in reimposition, as the top two lines of D4 in Q2. A few minor resettings of a line or two in length were made to save space by incorporating brief carry-overs in a single line. Thus from D1ᵛ of Q1, lines 464–465 (| wise... inscripti-|on) are condensed into a single line by resetting in D2 of Q2. Similarly, what are four lines on D4 of Q1 (lines 560–563, | presence...these: |) are condensed to three in Q2.[1] Sheet D of Q2 ends by resetting on sig. D4ᵛ the text of sig. E1 and the first six lines of E1ᵛ from Q1 (lines 595–618), this being necessitated by the expansion caused by the two English translations. Sheet E in Q1 had been set by a different printer from that of C–D in Q1 and Q2, and hence its standing type was not available.

In Q2 the printer of sheet E in Q1 reimpresses this sheet and takes over the responsibility for F from Lownes. Both inner and outer formes of E are preserved standing, save for the type from Q1 sig. E1 to line 6 of E1ᵛ brought over into Q2 sheet D (the first line of Q2 sig. E1 beginning with line 7 of Q1 sig. E1ᵛ). Page for page coincidence of the two editions is restored with sig. E4 (line 773, | ter shapes). Sheet F, inner and outer formes, is reset in Q2 since the Lownes standing type was not used by the different printer in Q2.

In the Lownes section of Q2, comprising sheets G and H, the

[1] Although in a technical sense made in standing type, spelling variants in such resettings are not adopted in the present text or recorded in the apparatus since they are unauthoritative and result from mechanical causes. Moreover, the nonsense words formed in Q2 at the top of sig. I3ᵛ (lines 1579–1586) by the pieing of the type have not been listed.

inner forme of sheet G was left standing but the outer forme was reset except for seven lines of Latin from sig. G3 (lines 1126–1134). Both formes of H were impressed from standing type; but the substitution of the English translation for the Latin of the Oration on sigs. H1^v–2^v and its introductory two lines gave Lownes his proper stint of resetting.

The evidence for the whole quarto shows an invariable distribution in Q1 only of the outer forme when any distribution of type is undertaken, but an attempt to salvage the difficult-to-set Latin from a forme scheduled for distribution. Moreover, whenever a gathering in Q2 is printed by a press different from that in Q1, the type is completely reset. Finally, about one-half of the book is left in standing type. When, as with Allde in sheets A–B or the printer of E–F, a printing-house has considerable resetting in its share, both formes of a sheet may be left standing as compensation. Otherwise, the pattern points to deliberate distribution and resetting of about a half of the book in its second edition.[1] The inescapable inference follows that this pattern is not accidental but that Man from the start had planned a second edition and had worked out the appropriate orders to his printers with the intent to circumvent the rule limiting the number of impressions which could be taken from a given typesetting. Although strictly speaking this procedure violated the make-work regulations of the Stationers' Company,

---

[1] The evidence is surveyed in more detail in *P.B.S.A.*, *op. cit.*, pp. 220–222. The reassignment in Q2 appears to be due to a more imperative reason than the desire merely to even the stints of the various printers, especially of those two who had been given only one sheet in Q1. If we may believe that Allde and the printer of sheet E would balk at printing a single sheet without resetting, or that the law might be satisfied if a sufficient portion of each printer's work was reset, the rearrangement becomes clear. The printer of E was given F to reset (F being taken away from Lownes, who retained G–H and reset approximately half of these two sheets), and Allde was presented with A–B. Since no standing type from Q1 was used for A–B in Q2, it is obvious that Creede had no connexion with the second edition. For the other printers, either the additional English translations requiring new composition satisfied the requirements, or else they reset the outer forme of each sheet. In Q2 no one printer's section was entirely impressed from standing type. Such an assignment of work averaging one-half resetting cannot have occurred fortuitously. It was planned, at least in general, from the start of Q1, and was carried through with considerable success. The one odd feature is the dropping of Creede and the consequent expansion of Allde's share.

TEXTUAL INTRODUCTION

Man seems on this occasion—as later with *The Honest Whore*—to have satisfied the compositors and to have escaped censure.

The following table gives the distribution of reset and of standing type by line number of the present text, the pages indicated being those of Q1. For visual clarity, an asterisk denotes standing lines, and hence the absence of an asterisk means that the lines are reset in Q2.

    1–229   A–B
    230–254   C1
*255–292   C1^v–2
    293–340   C2^v–3
*341–390 [...kingdoms,] C3^v–4
    390–408   C4^v
*409–419   D1 top
    420–436   translation not in Q1
    437–445   D1 foot
*446–490 [...handes:] D1^v–2 (except 464–465)
    490–533 [vpon...] D2^v–3
*534–577   D3^v–4 (except 560–563)
    578–594   D4^v
    595–618   E1–1^v (top)
*619–816   E1^v (line 7)–4^v
    817–1025 [...side) in] F1–4^v
    1025–1049 [that...of an] G1
*1049–1093 [Arbor...] G1^v–2
    1094–1125   G2^v–3 (line 6)
*1126–1134   G3 (lines 7–15)
    1135–1147 [...which] G3 (remainder)
*1147–1198 [colour...] G3^v–4
    1199–1220   G4^v
*1221–1234   H1
    1235–1276   H1^v–2^v (omitted in Q2)
    1277–1336   (English for Latin)
*1337–1444   H3–4^v
*1445–1620   I1–4^v (except 1550–1558, 1565–1566)

When in the light of this breakdown, we come to examine the variants between Q1 and Q2 both in standing and in reset type, one very interesting conclusion is reached. Only in the Lownes sheets G–H of Q2 are alterations at all frequent, and only in this section, apparently, is it possible that Q2 variants originated with Dekker.

Sheets A–B and I, Allde's section. In the standing type of sheet I only three variants appear: on I 3 ᵛ the extra 'summa' is removed (1588) and a letter is correctly turned (1596); on I 4 a full stop is added (or brought up to ink). In reset A–B two possible good variants are found, *about* for *aboue* (192), and *Banners* for *Bannerets* (195). That the first variant is almost certainly in error seems to be shown by the description in the Harrison *Arches*, which places the arch, as in Q 1, *above* the Conduit in Fleetstreet.[1] The second variant may have been created by the reduction of a relatively unfamiliar to a more common word. In these reset sheets errors at lines 124 and 216 are not corrected, and (though it is not evidence) a substantive error is followed at line 198. There is no positive evidence in favour of authorial correction or revision in these sheets; and indeed Q 2 was reset utilizing a copy of Q 1 with uncorrected inner B.

Sheets C–D, unknown printer same as in Q 1. The standing type of inner C is not altered in any way. In the resetting of outer C the only substantive change is the necessary substitution of *erected* for *directed* at line 340, a correction not beyond the capabilities of a compositor. In sheet D two alterations (lines 486, 487) are made in the capitalization within standing type; but both—while useful and even desirable—are not necessarily authorial.

Sheets E–F, printer unknown. In the reset portion of Q 1 sheet E brought over to D 4 ᵛ in Q 2, a correction is made in the Latin at line 618. For the rest, the Latin is corrected in standing type at lines 630, 632, 659, 660 and 661 on E 1 ᵛ and E 2. Perhaps the change in the Latin at reset line 618 on D 4 ᵛ, therefore, was made by the same agent marking copy. In sheet F, which resets a Q 1 Lownes sheet, only one substantive change appears, at line 927, and on the evidence this is probably not right. Two sidenotes are added, but there is nothing in these sheets to enforce the view that the author was responsible for any changes.

Sheets G–H, Lownes section. With these two sheets there is at once a marked change. In the standing type of inner G alterations are made in the accidentals on G I ᵛ at lines 1054 and 1063, with a substantive variant at line 1055; G 2 has a substantive correction in

---

[1] It is significant that though the *Arches* is based on Q 2, it agrees here with Q 1 against Q 2.

line 1074; in G3ᵛ nine alterations appear in the accidentals, and in G4 in an accidental at line 1177 and in the addition of a necessary direction at line 1198. In the reset outer forme, the accidentals variants are difficult to identify as due to copy; but a necessary substantive change, not wholly obvious, appears at line 1027, and the architectural descriptions are altered at lines 1041, 1047 and 1048. No substantive changes occur in reset G2ᵛ and G3, but in G3 one correction is made at line 1127 in the brief standing-type section. On G4ᵛ a substantive alteration with no difficulty about it is made at line 1210; but curiously the erratum at line 1205 is wrongly corrected.

Sheet H has much the same story. In the standing type, useful changes in the accidentals were made at lines 1232, 1340, 1362, 1372, 1373, 1397, 1398, 1421, 1427, 1429 and 1444. Substantive alteration occurs at lines 1395, 1402 (in Latin), and 1404. The first and third correct serious Q1 errors but ones which were obviously wrong readings.

When the two sheets are combined, therefore, we see that for the architectural details on G1, and possibly for at least two substantive variants in sheet H, some source outside the printing house was almost certainly responsible. That this agent must have been Dekker is not wholly demonstrable, however. Possibly some interested builder like Harrison communicated to Lownes the revised measurements. But whether such a person would know that a second edition was contemplated is perhaps doubtful, and whether he would bother is just as dubious. If this agent was a builder, and if he was responsible for the change of *foote* to *feete* in the standing type at line 1055, he was guilty of not knowing his business, for he attempted to correct one error with another (see the text note to this line). A less experienced author might be held responsible, perhaps. The variants in the accidentals are all well-advised but give no definite sign of authorial revision, except possibly the precision of the hyphens added to compound words at lines 1152 and 1164, and the addition of round brackets, which Dekker rather favoured, at lines 1168–1169, may point in his direction. There need be no great difficulty with the failure to alter correctly the erratum direction at line 1205 if we suppose that Dekker—if he were a reviser in these sheets—left that to the printer, who misinterpreted the instructions.[1]

The working hypothesis that Dekker was responsible for the Q2 variants in sheets G–H offers certain difficulties which need consideration. First, if Dekker made these corrections, the large number in these two sheets as compared with the very few elsewhere would almost necessarily enforce the belief that he did not take a copy of Q1 and mark it throughout to correct the text for Q2. And in fact it would need to be argued on the evidence that authorial correction was confined exclusively to sheets G–H. Nevertheless, if we may attach significance to the one correction in the Latin when a few lines were reset on D4^v, the remainder being standing type on E1, and associate this change with the alterations made in the standing type of the same speech (D and E being impressed by different printers), some agent other than the individual printers would seem to have marked a copy of Q1, or provided a list of errors in the Latin, possibly throughout the volume. Whether or not the agent were Dekker, it is reasonable to suppose that this person was the one who made the English translations and took occasion to indicate errors in the Latin as in that process he encountered them. We have no evidence, indeed, on which to assign these English translations to Dekker. He could not have written the Latin for any of the speeches, since all were independent entertainments, and the fact that as chief contriver of the city's entertainments he was the natural person to describe them in the published account does not require him to have acted as translator in the second edition. If the translator were not Dekker, we may reasonably suppose that his task was confined to the translation and its offshoot of suggesting corrections in the Latin. Given the lack of substantive alteration in the English text of sheets A–B, F, I, and very likely also C (at least with any authority), we should have difficulty in assigning to this same source the alterations in G–H. On the other hand, if Dekker were the translator, we may perhaps find it difficult to account for his lack of interest in altering his English text any-

---

[1] Interestingly enough, the editor of the 1795 Somers volume, though unacquainted with Q2, independently arrived at the same wrong reading through a similar misinterpretation of the errata instructions.

where but in sheets G–H. It may appear, then, to be most logical to conjecture that—if Dekker were the corrector of G–H—a publisher's agent was brought in to make the translations for Q2.[1]

However, the possibility must be considered that since the major alterations are confined only to the two sheets which Lownes printed in Q2, this printer was the chief agent in the alterations within these sheets. On the evidence that sheet F, which was Lownes's in Q1 but given to another printer in Q2, does not contain alterations in Q2 similar to those in G–H, there can be little question of a marked copy of Q1 being provided. Yet it is difficult to imagine the precise circumstances in which Dekker would be able to make considerable alterations in the copy for sheets held by one printer but not for others. Special errors in G–H cannot be advanced as an excuse, for Lownes's original sheet F in Q1 was just as faulty; and indeed from the fact that several errors were unaltered in gathering F when it was reset for Q2 it is clear that no effort was made to include it in the area of correction. It is suspicious, therefore, that substantial alteration was made only in sheets printed by Lownes in the second edition, and one cannot escape the question whether they may not have been the printer's responsibility after all.

The changes in the architectural details at lines 1041, 1047 and 1048 require outside authority, however; and if we may lean full weight on the error made in altering line 1055, the authority was very likely being transmitted at second-hand. That is, whereas the three above-mentioned changes must have been provided for the corrector by some outside source, it would seem that at line 1055 he made the change himself without fully understanding the nature of the original error. (We cannot ignore, of course, the possibility that in this isolated case the printer was responsible; but one would

[1] That this may be the more reasonable view could be argued from the fact that many of the Q1 Latin errors corrected in Q2 do not seem to be compositor's variants. Since Dekker presumably copied these Latin speeches from various sources, the errors were either copied by him without correction or else originated in his copying. On the other hand, he must have been producing the manuscript for Q1 in a hurry; and the labour of translation would certainly expose errors he may have passed over thoughtlessly in copying. In the outer forme of sheet H in Q1 a proof-reading change is made in the Latin in the same forme as English variants which there is some reason to ascribe to Dekker, but there is reason to believe that this alteration was incorrect.

believe ordinarily that the change at line 1055 was part of the other revision.) If the reasons seem valid for ruling out here the agent who had been concerned with the Latin, we are left with the clear choice between Dekker and the printer, the latter accepting some outside information about the details of the arch. Yet whether an agent who was not Dekker could make the further changes is perhaps open to question. The alterations in the accidentals would seem to go far beyond a printer's concern or that of an ordinary corrector. Possibly some outside source, or else the printer, could solve the misreading *Eronie* at line 1395 (although the solution evaded Dyce and Bullen); but the correction of *parts* at line 1404 to *praters* might seem to require first-hand information. All in all, so far as one can reconstruct probabilities, I incline to the simpler view that Dekker was the corrector of sheets G–H for Q2 but very likely of no other part.[1]

Why his attentions were confined to G–H is by no means clear; but I take it that there is a connexion between this fact and the fact that Lownes was the only printing house that we have evidence Dekker visited during the printing of Q1. That he visited Lownes's shop seems to be reasonably certain from the fact that the errata list is confined to errors in the Lownes sheets, a situation that would not obtain if Dekker had read over all the sheets in some central place before sheet I (with its errata list) was printed. It would appear that Dekker must have been present in Lownes's printing-house to make the notes for the errata list. Whether there were special relations between Dekker and Lownes we do not know. All that is evident is that Dekker confined his errata list to Lownes's sheets, that he must have visited the shop late in the course of printing Q1 in order to see these sheets, that while there he *may* have made certain press-corrections in Q1 sheet H, and finally that the alterations in the Q2 Lownes section differ markedly in number and in kind from those in other sheets. If the final statement in this series is in fact intimately related to the others, as I suggest, it follows that Dekker would have gone to Lownes's shop just before Lownes put the type

[1] The retention in Q2 of errors in sheet F as serious as those altered in G–H does not promote the hypothesis that Dekker supplied a second errata list for the whole edition which was utilized in Q2.

for sheets G–H of Q2 on the press and there made the alterations that we can identify in the standing type,[1] as well as others that—for the substantives—we can assume are his in the reset pages.

This being the working theory on which the present text is based, it follows that alterations only between lines 1025 and 1444 (sigs. G1–H4ᵛ) can be considered as authorial and of specific authority. When in this edition alterations from Q2 are adopted elsewhere, it is only because they seem advisable or else are necessary corrections, not because of any belief on my part that they are authorial.

Two further matters need attention before consideration of the textual problem is closed. So far as can be determined by collation of the listed copies of Q1, only the inner formes of sheets B and I, the outer forme of C, and the inner and outer formes of sheet H, were press-corrected. The two substantive corrections in inner B (lines 198, 216) demanded excellent proof-reading and perhaps consultation of the manuscript, even though by mischance the correction of line 216 was incomplete. If all the alterations came from one source here, as is likely, the case for Dekker is not demonstrable. Moreover, if we take it that there is a significance in the fact that here (line 109) and in *The Honest Whore*, Part I (V.ii.79), the spelling *fraighted* for *frighted* is found to be altered in the Q1 *Entertainment* in proof, and in *The Honest Whore* by resetting in Q2, it might follow that *fraighted* is a Dekker spelling changed by a conservative proof-reader to a more conventional form. Hence there appears to be some evidence against Dekker's connexion with the proof-correction of inner B; certainly there is nothing that positively requires his hand.

The case for sheet H is more complex and involves us once more in Dekker's hypothetical relations with Lownes. The running-titles show that sheet H was printed with only one skeleton-forme, the same both for inner and outer, and therefore necessarily on only one press. In theory this method of presswork offers opportunities for alterations to be discovered in both formes; and in Q1 the inner forme exists in three states representing two successive rounds of press-correction, but the outer forme in no less than four states (see

[1] One cannot be positive that they were not made during the process of printing, but multiple collation of Q2 has not revealed any press-variants.

the listing of Press-Variants in the apparatus, pp. 305–6), requiring the forme to be unlocked three separate times. In the inner forme only the Latin was affected, and—significantly—on sig. H4 two serious errors in the English were left untouched (*Eronie* and *parts*, lines 1395 and 1404), which do not appear in the errata list. There is some reason to believe, then, that Dekker never saw this forme. Since the second round of correction was concerned with a different page from the first, it is just possible that the proof-reader sent back his alterations to the press as he finished reading only part of the forme and hence that the corrections to H4 mark the completion only of the original process of proofing.[1]

The case is rather different for the outer forme of sheet H, since here the first round affected three pages together, then after a considerable interval alterations were made in two of the same pages, and finally after a brief interval one of the pages was corrected for the third time. In the first round of correction the same sort of alterations were made in the Latin on H2^v as had appeared in the inner forme. The simultaneous alteration of *beeing* to *being* on H3 is interesting. The spelling with the double *ee* in the participle is not found in Q1 in any of the sheets set by other printers, but it occurs four times in Lownes's sheet F as well as the two times here. (That we do not find it in sheet G may perhaps imply some proof-reading in that sheet not revealed by collation; and in fact the earliest state of outer H is confined, among the copies collated, to only two examples.) Whether the spelling *beeing* was a Dekker characteristic form normalized by a proof-reader, or else a compositor's aberrant spelling, is not certain. Dekker favoured the double *ee* in his addition to *Sir Thomas More* but unfortunately a participle does not appear there. Sporadic *beeing* spellings are found in his printed texts, as in *Westward Hoe*, however, and there is no apparent bar to the theory that in Lownes's sheets the compositor had truly reproduced his manuscript only to be checked

---

[1] That the interval between the two stages of correction was relatively brief is indicated by the fact that in the copies collated only two examples appeared containing the first stage alone. That proof was sometimes read and marked on copy in stages for a forme is demonstrated in Shakespeare's First Folio by Charlton Hinman, 'Mark III: New Light on the Proof-Reading for the First Folio of Shakspere', *Studies in Bibliography*, III (1950), 150–152. Outer K of 1 *Honest Whore* is somewhat similar.

by the proof-reader. If this hypothesis is correct, it removes all responsibility from Dekker for the first round of alterations. Since in the final round of correction only the Latin on H2^v was affected, if Dekker were to have anything to do with proof-reading this sheet we must suppose that he had the press stopped to correct the two errors in the English of H3. If so, perhaps the renewal of correction in the Latin (an unusual circumstance) can be assigned to him, although the whole question is very speculative.[1]

In short, what we have in the outer forme is the correction of two errors in the English text, one as obviously an error as the two left uncorrected in the inner forme but the other scarcely a noticeable corruption, sandwiched between correction to the Latin like that of the inner forme but which included an alteration to the accidentals not likely to have been authorial. When we relate this evidence to the facts provided by the errata list and by the alterations made in Q2, it may not seem too far-fetched to suppose that Dekker was responsible for the second (but less likely the third) round of the proof-correction of the outer forme. While in the shop he presumably made notes for an errata list of errors in sheets F and G already printed off. That he missed the two serious and obvious errors in the inner forme of H can be explained if we conjecture that the outer forme of the sheet was first on the press. Since the method of printing with only one skeleton-forme precluded pulling proofs of the alternate forme to that being read at the moment, it is probable that Dekker left the house before the inner forme was placed on the

---

[1] If Dekker stopped the press to alter the readings in lines 1347 and 1353 in H3 (and the second requires either the author, or else the proof-reader's reference to copy despite a superficially satisfactory meaning), the faulty alteration of a full stop to a comma in the Latin of line 1266 may have been his, but could have been the printer's. No great perspicuity is involved, since the comma after *honestamentum* in line 1267 suggested parallel structure for *adscribere*. The third stage of correction, involving the Latin in H2^v is more puzzling, since these represent errors previously overlooked by the proof-reader for the printing house. But whether Dekker or the proof-reader caught these can only be guessed at. It would appear that very soon after the press was stopped for the second round of correction, sig. H2^v was read through with more care, and, despite the corrections made on the two previous occasions, two more errors were found. Since the first stage is almost certainly due to the proof-reader (see the spelling variants on sig. H3), perhaps it was he who completed the proof-correction on H2^v. On the other hand, Dekker *could* have turned his attention more scrupulously to H2^v after his initial quick glance-through.

press and hence never saw it. This conjecture, in turn, assists the major hypothesis that he made up his errata list for the faulty sheets F and G in Lownes's shop, and not when these sheets were collected together with the rest. For if he had read sheet H at his leisure after it was completely printed, it is most probable that the two important errors in sig. H 4 of the inner forme would have been listed in the errata along with the errors of sheets F and G. The hypothesis seems to hold together, and is offered here with as much confidence as one can place in what can be only an articulated series of conjectures.[1] If the first part as relates to Q 1 be accepted, then it may perhaps follow that the evidence against Dekker's having submitted a marked copy of Q 1 to serve as the basis of the alterations in Q 2, especially when the lack of correction in sheet F is duly weighed, may serve to establish, conjecturally, the authority only of the alterations in Lownes's Q 2 sheets G–H (lines 1025–1444). In my own view, this thereupon excludes Dekker as the author of the English translations of the Latin and hence of the corrections made in the Latin in Q 2.[2]

The textual procedure for dealing with this situation is quite clear. The copy-text on which the present edition is based is Q 1, *The Magnificent Entertainment*, representing that printed edition nearest in descent to Dekker's holograph manuscript, a document

---

[1] Some additional evidence may be offered for what its interpretation is worth. The suggestion was made above that the fact that there are only two copies of inner H in its intermediate state of correction, combined with the fact that the next stage concerned a previously uncorrected page, might be taken as indicating only a sectionally performed single proof-reading operation. On the other hand, the circumstances of the proof-reading of outer H are unusual and opposed at every point to the conditions of inner H. In the outer forme, although correction was initially made at a correspondingly early stage, a considerable number of copies was thereupon printed before the press was again stopped for further correction in the very same pages. Although such double press-correction is not unknown in Elizabethan dramatic printing, it is unusual; and when viewed in connexion with the other evidence suggesting authorial interference in outer H, it is tempting to believe that the length of time elapsing before the proof was read again corresponded with the appearance of Dekker in Lownes's shop.

[2] That is, if one agrees in associating the list of corrections in the Latin, which appears to have been given to two printers, if not three, with the act of translation, it would seem to be incredible that Dekker should confine himself only to this list except in sheets G–H, the more especially since the Q 2 alterations in G–H do not seem to be associated exclusively with the printer but to depend, at least in part, on some outside agent.

which there is every reason to suppose stands directly behind the printed version. Within this printing, of the known alterations in press I take it that only the second round of correction to the outer forme of sheet H stems from the author, although I do not exclude the possibility that the final corrections which took place shortly after were his also. The authorial press-alterations must be accepted without question. For the rest, since they appear to emanate from the printing-house proof-reader I adopt them as my judgement dictates, not as authoritative in any sense, but only in so far as I consider them to be necessary or at least advisable. When in my opinion they are rationalizations and sophistications, I reject them without hesitation.

A second authority is available in Q2, *The Whole Magnificent Entertainment*, a mixed text which contains some variants appearing both in standing and in reset type. In my opinion, some agent was employed by the publisher to translate the Latin, and in the course of this work he listed some (though not all) of the errors in the Latin requiring correction. I have serious doubts whether this agent was Dekker, and though I include the English translations they are enclosed within brackets. Except for sheets G–H, I take it that all alterations in standing type within Q2 come either from this agent or from the printing-houses.[1] Hence I treat these variants according to the criteria applied to the non-authoritative press-variants in Q1. On the other hand, since I take it that the variants in the standing type in sheets G–H are Dekker's own markings, I adopt them without question. Variants in reset type in all sheets other than G–H have, of course, less authority than variants introduced in standing type, but all are considered on their merits. The substantive variants in the reset type in sheet G have higher authority than those in other sheets although less than those in standing type in G–H. On the evidence of the standing type in G–H, it is reasonable to assume that some of the accidentals variants

[1] Given the number of copies of Q1 which have been collated, it is unlikely that any of the apparent alterations in standing type in Q2 are instead the corrected state of the Q1 press-variant type, the collated copies of Q1 representing the uncorrected state. Some of the errors in the reset Q2 formes may perhaps have come about from the use of an unidentified uncorrected state of a Q1 forme, but speculation in this particular case is idle.

in reset type in G represent Dekker's alterations; but the impossibility of distinguishing these from compositor's variants has led me to follow the copy-text Q1 in this matter.

Three other early documents claim attention. The first is the edition of the *Entertainment* printed in Edinburgh in 1604 by Thomas Finlason (Greg, no. 202[c]). This edition used Q1 as its copy and, except for inner I, followed the corrected states of the formes in so far as they have been identified. No fresh authority appears, and indeed the printer did not even make the corrections called for by the Q1 errata. The few alterations adopted in this present text from the Edinburgh quarto, therefore, have no authority and are taken from this source only as a matter of convenience. The Edinburgh printing, listed here as Q3, very likely followed in point of time on the issue of Q2, since one would expect Q1 to have been run off and supplemented by Q2 before a copy of Q1 could reach Edinburgh and be reset in its entirety. However, there is no actual evidence about the temporal relations of Q2 and Q3, and fortunately the point is of no importance for textual purposes.

Entered before Dekker's description of the entertainments, and therefore presumably earlier issued, was *Ben Jonson, his Part of King James his Royall and Magnificent Entertainment*, printed by V[alentine] S[immes] for Edward Blount, 1604 (Greg. no. 200). Although he reprints Middleton's speech with proper credit (lines 1409-1468), Dekker does not mention Jonson by name, and a slight airiness may perhaps be detected in his very brief summaries of the substance of Jonson's elaborately written speeches. The Jonson *Part* concerns three of the entertainments: the first arch (Dekker, lines 214-263), the seventh arch (Dekker, lines 1498-1533), and the Pageant in the Strand (Dekker, lines 1558-1574). The descriptions provide many details wanting in Dekker and print the speeches which he merely mentions. There is nothing, however, to assist in fixing the Dekker text.[1]

---

[1] Nevertheless, an interesting point develops. On sig. D4, commenting on the Strand Pageant, Jonson distinguishes it from his accounts of the two other entertainments as one to which he had to adapt his speeches: 'To which body (being framd before) we were to apt our soule.' This implies what Dekker has seemed to suggest in lines 139-159, that the framing of the allegory for each arch was the work of the poets involved, so that the themes as well as the literary clothes of each entertainment

TEXTUAL INTRODUCTION

Of more importance for the Dekker text is the third document, the Harrison *Arches of Triumph* (Greg, no. 208). This work, mentioned by Dekker in lines 222–229 as in preparation, has a dedication by Harrison subscribed 16 June 1604, a date perhaps coinciding roughly with that of publication. The volume consists of engravings of the seven arches constructed in the City, with letterpress descriptions on the opposite pages. Since the text is replete with architectural details, the descriptions are very likely Harrison's own; nevertheless it is noticeable that he is thoroughly familiar with Dekker's *Entertainment* and that he borrows freely from its phraseology. When space is available, the speeches (or parts of speeches) are reprinted. The Jonson speeches at the first and seventh arches appear without substantive variation, and in such a conservative manner as regards spelling, punctuation, and capitalization as to make it evident that a printed Jonson *Part* served as copy.

The remaining speeches came from Dekker's *Entertainment*, and from the fact that the English translations are the same as those in *The Whole Entertainment* it is clear that Q2 had been published before the text of the *Arches* was made up and that it served ultimately as copy for the *Arches*. However, there seems to be a curious difference between the reprints of the Jonson and the Dekker portions. The separate collation of the *Arches* text, given here in the textual apparatus, shows that some literary revisions were made in the Dekker text beyond the authority of a compositor. There are three varieties: (1) cutting for reasons of space; (2) indifferent changes from carelessness or, commonly, for improvement of usage; (3) literary alterations, as in the changes at lines 1424, 1432 and 1442. Although the change of *moude* to *moue* (line 1424), and of *vertue* to *Vertues* (line 1432), might well have been a minor

were their inventions. If this is so, we may infer on the evidence that where Dekker is full in description and reproduces without comment the speeches and songs, the work is his. The exception is presumably the two arches of the Italians and Belgians, which are stated to have been of their own construction, and the Latin speeches associated with these arches, as well as other Latin which Dekker could not have been asked to write, such as the address from the steps of the Mercers' school. It would seem, then, that Dekker was responsible for the entertainments concerned with the fourth, fifth, and sixth arches. From the fact that John Webster joined Dekker in writing commendatory odes to Harrison's *Arches*, one might expect Webster to have had a share in the exercises; but if so the fact is not mentioned by Dekker.

improvement drawn from the context by any indifferent agency, the alteration at line 1442 of *figurde all in* to *which here figure* seems definitely on another plane, even though it is designed to overcome a difficulty, real or fancied, in the text. It is perhaps significant that these are the only alterations in the text of any moment,[1] that they appear in a cluster, and finally that they are all from sig. H4^v of Lownes's portion of Q1–2, a page which did not receive press-correction in Q1 (so far as is known) although presumably read over by Dekker who made corrections elsewhere in the forme. Collation of a number of copies fails to reveal any press-variants here (or elsewhere) in Q2.

The clustering of these variants in this particular place is interesting, but even more interesting is the fact that there appears to be a difference in the reproduction of the Jonson and the Dekker portions within the *Arches*. Although the Jonson lines are printed verbatim, there are a number of conscious alterations in Dekker's. It is also of importance that whereas the typesetting of the *Arches* conservatively reproduces that of Jonson's *Part*, the relationship of the Dekker section in the *Arches* to Q2, though obvious, is not nearly so exact. Since if the copy were similar it is difficult to envisage why a compositor would treat Jonson differently from Dekker, we are bound to draw certain inferences from the evidence. Although it is certain that the Jonson copy for the *Arches* was his printed quarto, for Dekker two alternatives must be seriously considered: (1) the copy was a manuscript independent of Q2 except in so far as it may have had some intimate connexion with the manuscript behind Q1 and also the Q2 additions, in other words a manuscript furnished by Dekker; or (2) a manuscript copy was made of the pertinent parts of Q2 required for the *Arches*, and during the process of copying, or subsequently, editorial as well as scribal variants were formed.

The first alternative has little to recommend it. Although Dekker was sufficiently interested in the *Arches* to contribute an Ode to assist the designer with whom he must have worked closely, there was no need for him to furnish an independent manuscript when the

[1] To exclude the necessary but simple corrections made by *Arches* at lines 822 and 866; and also the use of more formal pronouns in addressing the king.

matter was readily available in print. In addition to this, if the hypothesis that the English translations are not Dekker's be accepted, the case for the manuscript loses force. However, one prefers physical evidence to speculation about probabilities, and this is fortunately present. It is perhaps only a matter of opinion, but at least in my view the similarities in punctuation and capitalization, and occasionally in spelling, are too marked between Q2 and *Arches* to justify a theory that they go back radially through different transcriptions to a common original. Yet at the same time the dissimilarities in these same accidentals when compared with the relatively faithful reproduction of the Jonson text are seemingly too marked to allow the printed Q2 text to have served as actual copy for *Arches*. Nevertheless, we cannot doubt that Q2 itself somehow lies behind the *Arches* material. A significant piece of mechanical evidence demonstrates this beyond question. In Q1 the last word on sig. F4ᵛ is *in* (line 1025), the text between F4ᵛ and G1 reading, 'begging...(since I dare not...lackey by your royall side) in | that yet these my greene Followers and my selfe may bee ioyfull fore-runners of your expected approch'. This word *in* is syntactically neither smooth nor necessary, but its omission in reset Q2 is almost certainly due not to literary but only to mechanical reasons; i.e. it was overlooked at the end of the page, or could not conveniently be included in a properly justified line. (Sheet F makes no substantive 'improvements' in reset Q2.) Thus when the *Arches* text also omits this *in*, we have good evidence that it does so because it is copying Q2. However, the accidentals differences being too great (in comparison with the Jonson material) for Q2 to have served as the immediate copy, it seems necessary to posit a transcript made from Q2 to serve as printer's copy for the *Arches*. At first sight such a transcript may seem rather odd, but only this hypothesis will fit all the evidence; and it is not impossible that— owing to the need for condensation—it seemed more convenient for Harrison to make a manuscript copy from Q2 of the material he wanted, regardless of how he had treated Jonson's *Part*, reproduced *in extenso*.[1]

[1] On sig. E1 of *Arches* in the English version of the Dutchmen's oration the *Arches* text reads dubiously, 'he who through the loynes of so many Kingdomes',

The working hypothesis that a transcript was made from Q2 does not completely settle the question of the authority of the significant *Arches* variants, however, for such a transcript might have originated with the author. Yet, when we consider how the *Arches* is put together and the way in which space had to be carefully estimated between the Harrison descriptions of the arches and the reprints of the speeches from the entertainments, it may seem most probable that Dekker had nothing to do with such edited transcriptions, and that these must be assigned to the *Arches* compiler. In connexion with the literary value of the alterations in *Arches*, one can say that whereas an easy correction is made at line 822, and a more dubious but probably necessary one at line 866, the change of tense from *moude* to *moue* (line 1424) is perhaps the result of a misunderstanding (the Elements have stopped their movement by the time the speech is made, and therefore the preterite in Q is accurate). In line 1432 the case for altering *vertue* to *Vertues* is less clear. It is possible that in Q 1–2 the singular derived by contamination from the singular in the line immediately above, and that in line 1431 James's *virtus* is referred to but in line 1432 his four virtues which were represented in the arch (lines 1374–1377 and 1443–1444). Although this may seem to be the 'harder' and even the more attractive reading, yet to hold it one is forced with some strain to interpret the singular *glorious object* as pertaining to the appearance of James himself (for which there is no justification) or back to *Vertue* of line 1431, even though the natural referent is certainly *vertue* in line 1432. In this context the change at line 1432 in the *Arches* line reveals itself as a feeble attempt to escape a fancied difficulty. In 1442 the four allegorical characters do not *figure* James but instead are *figurde all in* him, as in the original; that is, they are portrayed more accurately in his mind, actions, and words

whereas the Q2 text is, 'hee who through the loynes of so many Grand-fathers, hath brought thee to so many Kingdomes'. This does not seem to be a condensation in *Arches* but instead an error caused by eyeskip. However, the evidence is ambiguous, since such a skip could have been made by scribe copying from Q2, by compositor copying from a scribal transcript, or by compositor copying Q2. Since in Q2 'Kingdomes' comes in the line below immediately beneath the start of 'many', it is possible that the eyeskip occurred in the process of transcribing Q2, and therefore by the scribe, according to the working hypothesis adopted here.

than they are by the personifications on the arch. This appears to be the heart of the compliment, destroyed by the *Arches* change. When we consider, finally, that this change comes in Middleton's lines and is therefore unlikely to be authorial, a literal-minded editor and not any authoritative source would seem to be responsible here as elsewhere in the *Arches* text; and hence the critical evidence joins with the 'bibliographical' to deny authority to the Dekker text in its *Arches* form. As a result, only Q1 appears to be a substantive text throughout; and only sheets G–H in Q2 are substantive. For the rest, whenever alterations are drawn from other sources the emendations cannot be authoritative in the same sense.

Because of the problems involved, and because the estimate of Q2's general lack of authority is only a working hypothesis, special treatment has been necessary in the apparatus. In the footnotes to the text, elsewhere confined to substantive editorial alterations in the copy-text, for this *Entertainment* I have indicated as well all variants whether accidental or substantive in the standing type of Q2 and all substantive variants not mere misprints in the reset type. By this treatment any reader who differs in his estimate of Q2's authority will have readily available the maximum amount of textual information. To avoid excessive duplication, the accidentals variants in Q2 standing type are listed only in the footnotes and are not repeated in the appendix Emendations of Accidentals (p. 307) drawn from reset portions of Q2 as well as other sources. The Historical Collation does not differ in principle from that adopted for other plays: only substantive variants recorded in the footnotes are collated there as well as rejected substantive variants from Q3 and those accidentals variants which for one reason or another may be thought of as semi-substantive. (See the Textual Introduction in Vol. I for fuller details.)

For the reader's convenience, in the footnotes I add (*s*) to the siglum of a variant recorded in Q2 standing type, and (*r*) in Q2 reset type. But I have not followed this practice in the various appendix listings, since I have provided earlier in this introduction the line numbers of standing and of reset type. A separate collation is given for the *Arches*.

For uniformity I have modified Allde's use of medial *j* in sheet I

THE MAGNIFICENT ENTERTAINMENT

of the Q1 copy-text and have printed it as *i* to conform to the usage in the other gatherings.

Except for the Pearson reprint of 1873, the whole text of the *Entertainment* has been reprinted only three times, each from Q1: first in 1795, *A Collection of... Tracts...from the Somers-Collections,* ed. R. Edwards; then in a reprint in *Somers Tracts,* vol. III, of 1810; and finally in vol. I of *The Progresses of King James the First* (1828), ed. J. Nichols, a freely modernized version. The Middleton lines, with some introductory text, have been edited by Dyce in *Works of Thomas Middleton* (1840), vol. V, this being reprinted by A. H. Bullen in his edition of Middleton (1886), vol. VII. These editions have been collated.

The present text is based on a collation of the sixteen copies of Q1 at the British Museum (C.34.c.23 and Ashley 612), Bodleian (Mal. 602[1]), the Dyce Collection in the Victoria and Albert Museum, the Boston Public Library, the William A. Clark Library, Folger Shakespeare Library, Harvard University, Henry E. Huntington Library, Library of Congress, University of Illinois, Newberry Library, New York Public Library, Pierpont Morgan Library, University of Texas, and Yale University. Press-variants appearing in the inner forme of sheet B, outer C, and the inner and outer formes of H have been recorded. Copies of Q2 at the Bodleian (Gough. Lond. 122[3] and Douce D 206), Folger Shakespeare Library (Q1 title-leaf substituted), Elizabethan Club of Yale University, and Henry E. Huntington Library have been collated with each other without disclosing any press-variation. Q3 has been collated against the copy-text from the British Museum copy (C.33.d.15), as also the pertinent sections of Harrison's *Arches of Triumph* from the British Museum copy.

[The Magnificent Entertainment Given to King James]

A DEVICE

(proiected downe, but till now not publisht,) that should haue serued at his Maiesties first accesse to the Citie.

The sorrow and amazement, that like an earthquake began to shake the distempered body of this Iland (by reason of our late Soueraigns departure,) being wisely and miraculously preuented, and the feared wounds of a ciuill sword, (as *Alexanders* fury was with Musicke) being stopt from bursting forth, by the sound of Trompets that proclaimed King *Iames*: All mens eyes were presently turnd to the North, standing euen stone-stil in their Circles, like the poynts of so many Geometricall needles, through a fixed and Adamantine desire to behold this fortie-fiue yeares wonder now brought forth by *Tyme*: their tongues neglecting all language else, saue that which spake zealous prayers, and vnceasable wishes, for his most speedy and longd-for arriuall. Insomuch that the Night was thought vnworthy to be crownd with sleepe, and the day not fit to be lookt vpon by the Sunne, which brought not some fresh tydings of his Maiesties more neare and neerer approach.

At the length *Expectation* (who is euer waking) and that so long was great, grew neare the time of her deliuery, *Rumor* comming all in a sweate to play the Midwife, whose first comfortable words were, that this *Treasure* of a Kingdome (a Man-Ruler) hid so many yeares from vs, was now brought to light, and at hand.

Martiall. *Et populi vox erat vna, Venit.*

And that he was to be conducted through some vtter part of this his Citie, to his royall Castle the *Tower*, that in the age of a man (till this very minute) had not bene acquainted nor borne the name of a

Kings Court. Which Entrance of his (in this maner) being fam'de abroad, Because his louing Subiects the Citizens would giue a taste of their dutie and affection: The *Deuice* following was suddeinly made vp, as the first seruice, to a more royall and serious ensuing Entertainment; And this (as it was then purposed) should haue bene performed about the Barres beyond Bishops-gate.

The Deuice.

Saint *George*, Saint *Andrew*, (the Patrons of both Kingdomes) hauing a long time lookt vpon each other, with countenances rather of meere strangers, then of such neare Neighbours, vpon the present aspect of his Maiesties approach toward *London*, were (in his sight) to issue from two seuerall places on horsebacke, and in compleate Armour, their Brestes and Caparisons suited with the Armes of *England* and *Scotland*, (as they are now quartered) to testifie their leagued Combination, and newe sworne Brother-hood. These two armed Knights, encountring one another on the way, were to ride hand in hand, till they met his Maiestie. But the strangenesse of this newly-begotten amitie, flying ouer the earth, It calles vp the *Genius* of the Cittie, who (not so much mazde, as wondring at the Noueltie) Intersepts their Passage.

And most aptly (in our Iudgement) might this *Domesticum Numen* (the *Genius* of the place) lay iust clayme to this preheminence of first bestowing Salutations and welcomes on his Maiestie, *Genius* being held (*Inter fictos Deos*), to be God of Hospitalitie and Pleasure: and none but such a one was meet to receiue so excellent and princely a Guest.

Or if not worthy, for those two former respects: Yet being *Deus Generationis*, and hauing a power aswell ouer Countries, hearbs and trees, as ouer men, and the Cittie hauing now put on a *Regeneration*, or new birth; the induction of such a Person, might (without a Warrant from the court of *Critists*) passe very currant.

To make a false florish here with the borrowed weapons of all the old Maisters of the noble Science of Poesie, and to keepe a tyrannicall coyle, in Anatomizing *Genius*, from head to foote, (only to shew how nimbly we can carue vp the whole messe of the Poets) were to play the Executioner, and to lay our Cities houshold God on the rack, to make him confesse, how many paire of Latin sheets, we haue shaken and cut into shreds to make him a garment. Such feates of Actiuitie are stale, and common among Schollers, (before whome it is protested we come not now (in a Pageant) to Play a Maisters prize) For *Nunc ego ventosæ Plebis suffragia venor.*

The multitude is now to be our Audience, whose heads would miserably runne a wooll-gathering, if we doo but offer to breake them with hard words. But suppose (by the way) contrary to the opinion of all the Doctors) that our *Genius* (in regarde the place is *Feminine*, and the person it selfe, drawne *Figura Humana, sed Ambiguo sexu*) should at this time be thrust into womans apparell. It is no Schisme: be it so: our *Genius* is then a Female; Antique, and reuerend both in yeares and habit: a Chaplet of mingled flowres, (Inter-wouen with branches of the Plane Tree) crowning her Temples: her haire long and white: her Vesture a loose roabe, Changeable and powdred with Starres: And being (on horsebacke likewise) thus furnished, this was the tune of her voyce.

Genius Locj.

Stay: wee coniure you, by that Potent Name,
Of which each Letter's (now) a triple charme:
Stay; and deliuer vs, of whence you are,
And why you beare (alone) th'ostent of Warre,
When all hands else reare *Oliue*-boughs and *Palme*:
And *Halcyonean* dayes assure all's calme.
When euery tongue speakes Musick: when each Pen
(Dul'd and dyde blacke in Galle) is white agen,
And dipt in *Nectar*, which by *Delphick*-fire
Being heated, melts into an *Orphean*-quire.
When *Troyes* proud buildings shew like *Fairie*-bowers,
And Streets (like Gardens) are perfum'd with Flowers:
And Windowes glazde onely with wondring eyes;
(In a *Kings* looke such admiration lyes!)
And when soft-handed *Peace*, so sweetly thriues,
That *Bees* in *Souldiers* Helmets build their Hiues:
When *Ioy* a tip-toe stands on *Fortunes* Wheele,
In silken Robes: How dare you shine in Steele?

Saint George.

Ladie, What are you that so question vs?

Genius.

I am the places *Genius*, whence now springs
A *Vine*, whose yongest Braunch shall produce Kings:
This little world of men; this precious Stone,
That sets out *Europe*: this (the glasse alone,)
Where the neat Sunne each Morne himselfe attires, 100
And gildes it with his repercussiue fires.
This Iewell of the Land; *Englands* right Eye:
Altar of *Loue*; and Spheare of Maiestie:
Greene *Neptunes* Minion, bou't whose Virgin-waste,
Isis is like a Cristall girdle cast.
Of this are we the *Genius*; here haue I,
Slept (by the fauour of a Deity)
Fortie-foure Summers and as many Springs,
Not fraighted with the threats of forraine Kings.
But held vp in that gowned State I haue, 110
By twice Twelue-Fathers politique and graue:
Who with a sheathed Sword, and silken Law,
Do keepe (within weake Walles) Millions in awe.

I charge you therefore say, for what you come?
What are you?
Both.   Knights at Armes.
S. Geo.   *Saint George.*
S. And.   *Saint Andrew.*
     For *Scotlands* honour I.
S. Geo.   For *Englands* I.
     Both sworne into a League of Vnitie.

Genius.

I clap my hands for Ioy, and seate you both
Next to my heart: In leaues of purest golde,

109 fraighted] Q1(u); frighted Q1(c)

This most auspicious loue shall be enrold. 120
Be ioynde to vs: And as to earth we bowe,
So, to those royall feet, bend your steelde brow.
In name of all these *Senators*, (on whom
Vertue builds more, then those of Antique *Rome*)
Shouting a cheerefull welcome: Since no clyme,
Nor Age that has gon or'e the head of Time,
Did e're cast vp such Ioyes nor the like Summe
(But here) shall stand in the world yeares to come,
Dread *King*, our hearts make good, what words do want,
To bid thee boldly enter *Troynouant*. 130

Rerum certa salus, Terrarum gloria Cæsar!   Mart.
   Sospite quo, magnos credimus esse Deos:
Dilexere priùs pueri, Iuvenesque senesque,   Idem.
   At nunc Infantes te quoque Cæsar *amant.*

This should haue beene the first Offring of the Citties Loue: But his Maiestie not making his *Entrance* (according to expectation) It was (not vtterly throwne from the Alter) but layd by.

Mart. *Iam Crescunt media Pægmata celsa via.*

By this time Imagine, that *Poets* (who drawe speaking Pictures) and *Painters* (who make dumbe Poesie) had their heads and hands 140 full; the one for natiue and sweet Inuention: the other for liuely Illustration of what the former should deuise: Both of them emulously contending (but not striuing) with the proprest and brightest Colours of Wit and Art, to set out the beautie of the great *Triumphant-day*.

For more exact and formall managing of which Businesse, a Select number both of Aldermen and Commoners (like so many Romane *Ædiles*) were (*Communi Consilio*) chosen forth, to whose discretion, the *Charge, Contriuings, Proiects*, and all other *Dependences*, owing to so troublesome a worke, was intirely, and 150 Iudicially committed.

Many dayes were thriftily consumed, to molde the bodies of these

124 those] Nichols; these Q 1–2(r)–3

Tryumphes comely, and to the honour of the Place: and at last, the stuffe whereof to frame them, was beaten out. The Soule that should giue life, and a tongue to this *Entertainment*, being to breathe out of Writers Pens. The Limmes of it to lye at the hard-handed mercy of Mychanitiens.

In a moment therefore of Time, are Carpenters, Ioyners, Caruers, and other Artificers sweating at their Chizzells.

Vir. *Accingunt Omnes operi.*

Not a finger but had an Office: He was held vnworthy euer after to *sucke the Honey-dew of Peace*, that (*against his comming, by whom our Peace weares a triple Wreathe*) would offer to play the Droane. The Streets are surueyed; heigthes, breadths, and distances taken, as it were to make *Fortifications*, for the *Solemnities*. Seauen pieces of ground, (like so many fieldes for a battaile) are plotted foorth, vppon which these Arches of Tryumph must shew themselues in their glorie: aloft, in the ende doe they aduance their proude foreheads.

Virg: — *Circum pueri, Innuptæque Puellæ,
Sacra Canunt, funemque manu contingere gaudent.*

Euen children (might they haue bin suffred) would gladly haue spent their little strength, about the *Engines*, that mounted vp the Frames: Such a fire of loue and ioy, was kindled in euery brest.

The day (for whose sake, these wonders of Wood, clymde thus into the clowdes) is now come; being so earely vp by reason of Artificiall Lights, which wakened it, that the Sunne ouer-slept himselfe, and rose not in many houres after, yet bringing with it into the very bosome of the Cittie, a world of people. The Streets seemde to bee paued with men: Stalles in stead of rich wares were set out with children, open Casements fild vp with women.

All Glasse windowes taken downe, but in their places, sparkeled so many eyes, that had it not bene the day, the light which reflected from them, was sufficient to haue made one: hee that should haue compared the emptie and vntroden walkes of *London*, which were to be seen in that late mortally-destroying Deluge, with the thronged streetes now, might haue belieued, that vpon this day, began a new *Creation,* and that the Citie was the onely Workhouse wherein sundry Nations were made.

A goodly and ciuil order was obserued, in Martialling all the Companies according to their degrees: The first beginning at the vpper end of Saint *Marks* Lane, and the last reaching aboue the Conduit in *Fleetstreete*: their Seats, being double-railde: vpon the vpper part wheron they leaned, the Streamers, Ensignes, and Bannerets, of each particular Company decently fixed: And directly against them, (euen quite through the body of the Citie, so hie as to Temple-Barre) a single Raile (in faire distance from the other) was likewise erected to put off the multitude. Amongst whose tongues (which in such Consorts neuer lye still,) tho there were no Musicke, yet as the Poet sayes:

Mart. *Vox diuersa sonat, populorum est vox tamen vna.*

Nothing that they speake could bee made any thing, yet all that was spoken, sounded to this purpose, that still his Maiestie was comming. They haue their longings: And behold, A farre off they spie him, richly mounted on a white Iennet, vnder a rich Canopy, sustained by eight Barons of the *Cinqueports*; the Tower seruing that morning but for his with-drawing Chamber, wherein hee made him ready: and from thence stept presently into his Citie of *London,* which for the time might worthily borrow the name of his *Court Royall*: His passage alongst that Court, offering it selfe (for more State) through seuen Gates, of which the first was erected at *Fanchurch.*

Thus presenting it selfe.

It was an vpright Flat-square, (for it contained fiftie foote in the perpendiculer, and fiftie foote in the Ground-lyne) the vpper roofe thereof (on distinct *Grices*) bore vp the true moddells of all the notable Houses, Turrets, and Steeples, within the Citie. The Gate vnder which his Maiestie did passe, was 12. foote wide, and 18.

Fanchurch.

192 aboue] Q1; about Q2(r)   195 Bannerets] Q1; Banners Q2(r)
198 whose] Q1(c); whom, Q1(u)–Q2(r)
202 speake] Q1]; *i.e.,* spake *as in* Q2(r)
216 on] one Q1–2(r)–3
216 Grices] Q1(c); Gate Q1(u)–2(r)

foote hie: A Posterne likewise (at one side of it) being foure foote wide, and 8. foote in heigth: On either side of the Gate, stood a great French Terme, of stone, aduanced vpon wodden Pedestalls; two half Pilasters of Rustick, standing ouer their heads. I could shoote more Arrowes at this marke, and teach you without the Carpenters Rule how to measure all the proportions belonging to this *Fabrick*. But an excellent hand being at this instant curiously describing all the seuen, and bestowing on them their faire prospectiue limmes, your eye shall hereafter rather be delighted in beholding those Pictures, than now be wearied in looking vpon mine.

The Personages (as well Mutes as Speakers) in this Pageant, were these: *viz*.

1   The highest Person was *The Brittayne Monarchy*.
2   At her feet, sate *Diuine Wisdome*.
3   Beneath her, stood *The Genius of the City*, A man.
4   At his right hand was placed a Personage, figuring, *The Counsell of the City*.
5   Vnder all these lay a person representing *Thamesis* the *Riuer*.

Sixe other persons (being daughters to *Genius*) were aduaunced aboue him, on a spreading *Ascent*, of which the first was,

1   *Gladnesse*.
2   The second, *Veneration*.
3   The third, *Promptitude*.
4   The fourth, *Vigilance*.
5   The fift, *Louing affection*.
6   The sixth, *Vnanimity*.

Of all which personages, *Genius* and *Thamesis* were the only Speakers: *Thamesis* being presented by one of the children of her Maiesties Reuels: *Genius* by Master *Allin* (seruant to the young Prince) his gratulatory speach (which was deliuered with excellent Action, and a well tun'de audible voyce) being to this effect: That *London* may be prowd to behold this day, and therefore in

226–227 prospectiue] i.e. *perspective*

THE MAGNIFICENT ENTERTAINMENT

name of the Lord *Maior* and *Aldermen*, the *Councell, Commoners* and *Multitude,* the heartiest Welcome is tendered to his Maiesty, that euer was bestowed on any King, &c.

Which Banquet being taken away with sound of Musicke, there, ready for the purpose, his Maiestie made his entrance into this his Court Royall: vnder this first Gate, vpon the Battlements of the worke, in great Capitalls was inscribed, thus: *The Wayts and Haultboyes of London.*

LONDINIVM.

And vnder that, in a smaller (but not different) *Caracter,* was written,
CAMERA REGIA:
The Kings Chamber.

Too short a time (in their opinions that were glewed there together so many houres, to behold him) did his Maiestie dwell vpon this first place: yet too long it seemed to other happy Spirits, that higher vp in these *Eliȝian* fields awaited for his presence: he sets on therefore (like the Sunne in his Zodiaque) bountifully dispersing his beames amongst particular Nations: the brightnesse and warmth of which, was now spent first vpon the *Italians,* and next vpon the *Belgians*: The space of ground, on which their *magnificent Arches* were builded, being not vnworthy to beare the name of the great Hall to this our Court Royal: wherein was to be heard and seene the sundry languages and habits of Strangers, which vnder Princes Roofes render excellent harmony.

In a paire of Scales doe I weigh these two Nations, and finde them (neither in hearty loue to his Maiestie, in aduancement of the Cities honor, nor in forwardnesse to glorifie these *Triumphes*) to differ one graine.

To dispute which haue done best, were to doubt that one had done well. Call their inuentions therefore *Twynnes*: or if they themselues doe not like that name, (for happily they are emulous of one glory) yet thus may we speake of them.

— *Facies non omnibus vna,*   Ouid.
Nec diuersa tamen,Qualem decet esse sororum.

Because, whosoeuer (*fixis oculis*) beholds their proportions,

Expleri mentem nequit, ardescitque tuendo. Virg.

Gracious street. The street, vpon whose breast, this *Italian* Iewell was worne, was neuer worthy of that name which it carries, till this houre: For here did the Kings eye meete a second Obiect, that inticed him by tarrying to giue honor to the place. And thus did the queintnesse of the *Engine* seeme to discouer it selfe before him.

The Italians Pageant.

The building tooke vp the whole bredth of the Street, of which, the lower part was a Square, garnished with foure great Columnes: In the midst of which Square, was cut out a fayre and spacious high Gate, arched, being twenty seuen foot in the perpendicular lyne, and eyghteene at the ground lyne: ouer the Gate, in golden Caracters, these verses (in a long square) were inscribed:

> *Tu Regere Imperio populos Iacobe memento,*
> *Hæ tibi erunt Artes, Pacique imponere morem,*
> *Parcere Subiectis, et debellare superbos.*

And directly aboue this, was aduanc'd the Armes of the Kingdome, the Supporters fairely cut out to the life: ouer the Lyon (some prety distance from it) was written,

IACOBO REGI MAGN.

And aboue the head of the *Vnicorne*, at the like distance, this,

HENRICI VII. ABNEP.

In a large Square erected aboue all these, King *Henry* the seuenth was royally seated in his Imperiall Robes, to whome King *Iames* (mounted on horsebacke) approches, and receyues a Scepter, ouer both their heads these words being written,

HIC VIR, HIC EST.

Betweene two of the *Columnes*, (on the right hand) was fixed vp a square table, wherein, in liuely and excellent colours, was lim'd

304 out] Q1; *om.* Q2(r)

a woman, figuring *Peace*, her head securely leaning on her left hand, her body modestly bestowed (to the length) vpon the earth: In her other hand, was held an *Oliue* branch, the *Ensigne* of Peace, her word was out of *Virgil*, being thus,

— *Deus nobis hæc otia fecit.*

Beneath that peece, was another square Table, reaching almost to the Bases of the two *Columnes*: In which, two (seeming) Sea personages, were drawne to the life, both of them lying, or rather leaning on the bosome of the earth, naked; the one a woman, her backe onely seene; the other a man, his hand stretching and fastning it selfe vpon her shoulder: the word that this dead body spake, was this,

I Decus, I Nostrum.

Vpon the left-hand side of the Gate, betweene the other two *Columnes*, were also two square Tables: In the one of which were two persons portrayed to the life, naked, and wilde in lookes, the word,

Expectate solo Trinobanti.

And ouer that, in another square, carying the same proportion, stoode a woman vpright, holding in her hand a Shield, beneath whom was inscribed in golden *Caracters*,

— *Spes ô fidissima rerum.*

And this was the shape and front of the first great *Square*, whose top being flat, was garnished with *Pilasters*, and vpon the roofe was erected a great *Pedestall*, on which stood a Person carued out to the life, (a woman) her left hand leaning on a sword, with the poynt downeward, and her right hand reaching foorth a Diadem, which shee seemde by bowing of her knee and head, to bestow vpon his Maiestie.

On the foure corners of this vpper part, stoode foure naked portraytures (in great) with artificiall Trumpets in their hands.

In the Arch of the Gate, was drawne (at one side) a companie of

339 roofe] roote Q1–2(r)–3
340 erected] Q2(r); directed Q1

Palme trees, young, and as it were but newly springing, ouer whose branches, two naked winged Angels, flying, held foorth a Scroll, which seem'd to speake thus,

Spes altera.

On the contrarie side, was a Vine, spreading it selfe into many branches, and winding about *Oliue,* and *Palme* trees: two naked winged Angels hanging likewise in the Ayre ouer them, and holding a Scrol betweene them, fild with this inscription,

Vxor tua, sicut vitis abundans,
Et filii tui, sicut palmites Oliuarum.

If your imaginations (after the beholding of these obiects) will suppose, that his Maiestie is now gone to the other side of this *Italian Trophee;* doe but cast your eyes backe, and there you shall finde iust the same proportions, which the fore-part, or Brest of our Arch carrieth, with equall number of *Columnes,* Pedestals, Pilasters, Lim'd peeces, and Carued Statues. Ouer the Gate, this *Distichon* presents it selfe.

Nonne tuo Imperio satis est Iacobe potiri?
Imperium in Musas, Aemule quæris? Habes.

Vnder which verses, a wreathe of *Lawrell* seem'd to be ready to be let fall on his Maiesties head, as hee went vnder it, being held betweene two naked Antique women, their bodies stretching (at the full length) to compasse ouer the Arch of the Gate. And aboue those verses, in a faire Azure table, this inscription was aduanc'd in golden *Capitals*:

EXPECTATIONI ORBIS TERRARVM,
REGIB. GENITO NVMEROSISS.
REGVM GENITORI FAELICISS.
REGI MARTIGENARVM AVGVSTISS.
REGI MVSARVM GLORIOSISS.

Itali statuerunt lætitiæ & cultus
Signum.

On the right hand of this backe-part, betweene two of the 380
Columnes was a square table, in which was drawne a Woman,
crown'd with beautifull and fresh flowres, a *Caducæus* in her hand:
All the notes of a plenteous and liuely Spring being caried about her.
The soule that gaue life to this speaking picture, was:

— *Omnis feret omnia Tellus.*

Aboue this peece, in another square, was portrayed a *Tryton,* his
Trumpet at his mouth, seeming to vtter thus much,

Dum Cælum stellas.

Vpon the left hand of this back-part, in most excellent colours,
Antikely attir'd, stood the four kingdoms, *England, Scotland, France* 390
and *Ireland,* holding hands together; this being the language of
them all,

Concordes stabili Fatorum Numine.

The middle great Square, that was aduaunced ouer the *Freeze* of
the Gate, held *Apollo,* with all his Ensignes and properties belonging
vnto him, as a *Sphere, Bookes,* a *Caducæus,* an *Octoedron,* with other
Geometricall Bodies, and a Harpe in his left hand: his right hand with
a golden Wand in it, poynting to the battel of *Lepanto* fought by
the *Turks,* (of which his Maiestie hath written a *Poem*) and to doe him
Honour, *Apollo* himselfe doth here seeme to take vpon him to 400
describe: his word,

Fortunate Puer.

These were the Mutes, and properties that helpt to furnish out
this great *Italian Theater*: vpon whose Stage, the sound of no voice
was appointed to be heard, but of one, (and that, in the presence
of the *Italians* themselues) who in two little opposite galleries vnder
and within the Arch of the gate, very richly and neately hung,
deliuered thus much Latine to his Maiestie:

The Italians speach.

Salue, Rex magne, salue. Salutem Maiestati tuæ Itali, fœlicissimum 410
Aduentum læti, fœlices sub Te futuri, precamur. Ecce hîc Omnes,

383–384 her. The] her, the Q 1–2(s)–3

Exigui munere, pauculi Numero: Sed magni erga Maiestatem tuam animi, multi obsequij. At nec Atlas, qui Cœlum sustinet, nec ipsa Cœli conuexa, altitudinem attingant meritorum Regis optimi; Hoc est, eius, quem de Teipso expressisti doctissimo (Deus!) et admirabili penicillo: Beatissimos populos, vbi et Philosophus regnat, et Rex Philosophatur. Salue, Rex nobilissime, salue, viue, Rex potentissime, fœliciter. Regna, Rex sapientissime, fœliciter, Itali optamus omnes, Itali clamamus omnes: Omnes, omnes.

[The Italians speech in English. 420

All hayle, mighty Monarch! We (the Italians) ful of ioy to behold your most happy presence, and full of hopes to enioy a felicity vnder your Royall wing, do wish and pray for the health of your Maiestie. Behold, here we are all: meane in merite: few in number; but towardes your Soueraigne Selfe, in our loues, great: in our duties, more. For neither *Atlas*, who beares vp heauen; no, nor the arched Roofe it selfe of heauen, can by many many degrees reach to the top, and glorious height of a good and vertuous Kings deseruings. And such a one is he, whom (good God!) most liuely, most wisely and in wonderfull colours, you did then pensill downe in your own 430 person, when you said, that those people were blest, where a Philosopher rules, and where the Ruler playes the Philosopher. All haile, thou Royallest of Kings: liue, thou mightiest of Princes, in all happinesse: Reigne, thou wisest of Monarchs, in all prosperity: These are the wishes of vs *Italians*: the hearty wishes of vs all: Thus wee cry all, all, euen all.]

Hauing hoysted vp our Sailes, and taken leaue of this *Italian* shore, let our next place of casting anker, be vpon the Land of the 17. Prouinces; where the *Belgians*, (attired in the costly habits of their own natiue Countrey, without the fantasticke mixtures of other 440 Nations) but more richly furnished with loue, stand ready to receyue his Maiestie: who (according to their expectation) does most gratiously make himselfe and his Royall traine their Princely ghests. The house which these *Strangers* haue builded to entertain him in, is thus contriu'de.

420–436 The Italians speech....] Q2 *only*

The Pageant of the Dutch-men, by the Royall Exchange.

The Foundation of this, was (as it were by *Fate*) layd neere vnto a royall place; for it was a royall and magnificent labour: It was bounded in with the houses on both sides the street, so prowdly (as all the rest also did) did this extend her body in bredth. The passage of State, was a Gate, large, ascending eighteene foot high, aptly proportion'd to the other lymmes, and twelue foot wyde, arched; two lesser Posternes were for common feet, cut out and open'd on the sides of the other.

Within a small *Freeze*, (and kissing the very forhead of the Gate) the *Aedifice* spake thus,

Vnicus à Fato surgo non Degener Hæres.

Whil'st lifting vp your eye to an vpper larger *Freeze*, you may there be enriched with these golden Capitalls,

IACOBO, ANGL. SCOT. FRANC. HIBERN.
REGI OPT. PRINC. MAX. BELGAE ded.

But bestowing your sight vpon a large Azure Table, lyned quite through with Caracters of gold, likewise you may for your paynes receiue this inscription,

ORBIS RESTITVTOR. PACIS FVND. RELIG.
    PROPVG. D. IAC. P. F. REGI. P. P.
D. ANNAE REGIAE CONIVG. SOR. FIL.
    NEPTI, ET D. HENRICO. I. FIL. PRINC.
    IVVENT.
IN PVBL. VRBIS ET ORBIS LAETITIA,
    SECVLIQVE FAELICITAT. XVII. BELGIAE
    PROV. MERCATORES BENIGNE REGIA
    HAC IN VRBE EXCEPTI, ET
S. M. VESTRAE OB ANTIQ. SOCIALE FOEDVS,
    ET D. ELIZ. BENEFICENT. DEVOTI.
FAVSTA OMNIA ET FOELICIA AD IMPERII
    AETERNITAT. PRECANTVR.

Aboue which (being the heart of the *Trophee*) was a spacious square roome, left open, Silke Curtaines drawne before it, which (vpon the approch of his Maiestie) being put by, 17. yong *Damsels*, (all of them sumptuously adorned, after their countrey fashion,) sate as it were in so many Chaires of State, and figuring in their persons, the 17. *Prouinces* of *Belgia*, of which euery one caried in a Scutchion (excellently pencilde) the Armes and Coate of one.

Aboue the vpper edge of this large square Roome, and ouer the first Battlement, in another Front, aduanc'd for the purpose, a square Table was fastened vpright, in which was drawne the liuely picture of the *King*, in his Imperial Robes; a Crowne on his head, the Sword and Scepter in his handes: vpon his left side stood a woman, her face fixed vpon his, a burning hart in her right hand, her left hanging by, a *Heron* standing close vnto her: vpon his other side stood vpright (with her countenance directed likewise vpon him) another woman, winged, and in a *Freeze* beneath them, which tooke vp the full length of this Square: this inscription set out it selfe in golden wordes:

— *Vtroque Satellite Tutus*.

Suffer your eyes to be wearied no longer with gazing vp so high at those *Sun-beams*, but turne them aside to looke below through the little *Posternes*: whose State sweld quickly vp to a greatnes, by reason of two *Columnes*, that supported them on either side. In a Table, ouer the right-hand *Portall*, was in perfect colours, drawne a Serpent, pursude by a Lion: betweene them, Adders and Snakes, chasing one another, the Lion scornfully casting his head backe, to behold the violence of a blacke storme, that heauen powred downe, to ouertake them: the sound that came from all this, was thus:

— *Sequitur grauis Ira feroces*.

The opposite body to this (on the other side, and directly ouer the other *Portall*, whose pompe did in like maner leane vpon, and vphold it selfe by two mayne *Columnes*) was a square peece, in which were to be seene, Sheepe browzing, Lambes nibbling, Byrds flying in the Ayre, with other arguments of a serene and vntroubled season, whose happinesse was proclaymed in this maner,

— *Venit alma Cicuribus Aura*.

486 square] Q2(s); Square Q1   487 Front] Q2(s); front Q1

Directly aboue this, in a square Table, were portrayed two *Kings*, reuerently and antiquely attyrde, who seem'd to walke vpon these golden lines,

> *Nascitur in nostro Regum par Nobile Rege*
> *Alter Iesiades, Alter Amoniades.*

From whome, leade but your eye, in a straight line, to the other side, (ouer the contrary Posterne) and there in a second vpper Picture, you may meete with two other *Kings*, not fully so antique, but as rich in their Ornaments; both of them, out of golden letters, composing these wordes,

> *Lucius ante alios, Edwardus, & inde* IACOBVS
> *Sextus, & hic sanxit, sextus & ille fidem.*

And these were the *Nerues*, by which this great *Triumphall* Body was knit together, in the inferiour parts of it, vpon the shoulders whereof, (which were garnished with rowes of *Pilasters*, that supported Lions rampant, bearing vp Banners) there stood another lesser Square, the head of which wore a Coronet of *Pilasters* also; and aboue them, vpon a *Pedestal*, curiously closed in betweene the tayles of two Dolphins, was aduanced a Woman, holding in one hand, a golden Warder, and poynting with the fore-finger of the other hand vp to heauen. She figur'd *Diuine Prouidence*, for so at her feete was written, *Prouida Mens Cœli.*

Somewhat beneath which, was to bee seene an Imperiall Crowne, two Scepters being fastened (crosse-wise) vnto it, and deliuering this speach, — *Sceptra hæc concredidit vni.*

At the elbowes of this vpper Square, stood vpon the foure corners of a great *Pedestall*, foure *Pyramides*, hollow, and so neately contriu'de, that in the night time (for anger that the Sunne would no longer looke vpon these earthly beauties) they gaue light to themselues, and the whole place about them: the windowes, from whence these artificiall beames were throwne, being cut out in such a fashion, that (as *Ouid*, describing the Palace of the Sunne, sayes)

> *Clara micante Auro, Flammasque imitante Pyropo,*

So did they shine afarre off, like Crysolites, and sparkled like Carbuncles: Betweene those two *Pyramides* that were lifted vp on the right hand, stood *Fortitude*; her Piller resting it selfe vpon this golden line,

Perfero curarum pondus, Discrimina temno.

Betweene the two *Pyramides* on the other side, *Iustice* challenged her place, being knowne both by her habit and by her voyce, that spake thus,

Auspice me Dextra solium Regale perennat.

Wee haue held his Maiestie too long from entring this third Gate of his *Court Royall*; It is now hie time, that those eyes, which on the other side ake with rolling vp and downe for his gladsome presence, should inioy that happinesse. Beholde, hee is in an instance passed thorough; The Obiects that there offer themselues before him, being these:

Our *Belgick Statue* of Triumph, weares on her backe, as much riches, as she caried vpon her brest, being altogether as glorious in *Columnes*; standing on Tip-toe, on as loftie and as proude *Pyramides*; her walkes encompa'st with as strong and as neate *Pilasters*: the colours of her garments are as bright, her adornements as many: For,

In the square Field, next and lowest, ouer one of the Portals, were the Dutch Countrey people, toyling at their Husbandrie; women carding of their Hemp, the men beating it, such excellent Art being exprest in their faces, their stoopings, bendings, sweatings, &c. that nothing is wanting in them but life (which no colours can giue) to make them bee thought more than the workes of Paynters.

Lift vp your eyes a little aboue them, and beholde their *Exchange*; the countenaunces of the Marchants there being so liuely, that bargaines seeme to come from their lippes.

But in stead of other speach, this is onely to bee had,

PIO INVICTO,
R. IACOBO,
QVOD FEL. EIVS AVSPICIIS VNIVERSVM
BRIT. IMPERIVM PACAT, MARE TVTVM
PORTVS APERIT.

566 proude] Q1; prowd Q2(s?)

Ouer the other Portall, in a square (proportion'd, to the bignes of those other) men, women and children (in Dutch habits) are busie at other workes: the men Weauing, the women Spinning, the children at their Hand-loomes, &c. Aboue whose heads, you may with little labour, walke into the *Mart*, where as well the *Froe*, as the *Burger*, are buying and selling, the praise of whose industrie (being worthy of it) stands publisht in gold, thus,   590

QVOD MVTVIS COMMERCIIS, ET ARTIFICVM,
NAVTARVMQVE SOLERTIA CRESCAT,
DESIDIA EXVLAT, MVTVAQVE
AMICITIA CONSERVETVR.

Iust in the midst of these foure Squares, and directly ouer the Gate, in a large Table, whose feete are fastned to the *Freeʒe*, is their fishing and shipping liuely and sweetely set downe: The *Skipper* (euen though he be hard tugging at his Net) loudly singing this:

> *Quod Celebret hoc Emporium prudenti industria suos,*
> *Quouis Terrarum Negotiatores emittat, exteros*   600
> *Humaniter admittat, foris famam, domi diuitias augeat.*

Let vs now clime vp to the vpper battlementes; where, at the right hand *Time* standes: at the left (in a direct line) his daughter *Trueth*; vnder her foote is written,
                          Sincera.
And vnder his,
                          Durant.
                  Sincera Durant.

In the midst of these two, three other persons are rancked to- geather, *Art*, *Sedulitie*, and *Labour*: beneath whom, in a Freeze 610 rouing along the whole breadth of that Square, you may find these wordes in gold,
           Artes, Perfecit, Sedulitate, Labor.

As on the foreside, so on this, and equall in heigth to that of *Diuine Prouidence*, is the figure of a Woman aduaunced: beneath

*599 *Celebret*] *Celeb:* Q 1–2 (r)–3

whom, is an imperiall Crowne, with branches of Oliue, fixed (crosse-wise) vnto it, and giues you this word,

Sine Cæde et Sanguine.

And thus haue we bestowed vpon you, all the dead Cullours of this Picture, (wherein notwithstanding, was left so much life) as can come from Art. The speaking instrument, was a Boy, attyred all in white Silke, a wreath of Lawrell about his temples: from his voyce came this sound.

Sermo ad Regem.

Quæ tot Sceptra tenes forti, Rex maxime, dextra,
  Prouida Mens summi Numinis illa dedit.
Aspice ridentem per gaudia Plebis Olympum,
  Reddentem et plausus ad sua verba suos,
Tantus honos paucis, primi post secula mundi
  Obtigit, et paucis tantum onus incubuit,
Nam Regere imperijs populum fœlicibus vnum,
  Ardua res, magnis res tamen apta viris.
At non vnanimes nutu compescere gentes,
  Non hominis pensum, sed labor ille Dei,
Ille ideò ingentes qui temperat orbis habenas,
  Adiungit longas ad tua fræna manus.
Et menti de mente sua prælucet, et Artem
  Regnandi, regnum qui dedit ille, docet.
Crescentes varijs Cumulat virtutibus annos,
  Quas inter pietas, culmina summa tenet.
Hac proauos reddis patriæ, qui barbara Gentis
  Flexêre inducto Numine corda feræ.
Hac animos tractas rigidos, subigisque rebelles,
  Et leue persuades quod trahis ipse iugum,
Illi fida comes terram indignata profanam,
  Aut nunc te tanto Rege reuersa Themis.

618 *et*] Q2(r); *at* Q1 630 *onus*] Q2(s); *vnus* Q1
632 *Ardua res*] Q2(s); *Arduares* Q1
634 *hominis*] *homines* Q1–2(s)–3
635 *temperat*] Q3; *temperet* Q1–2(s) 638 *ille*] *illa* Q1–2(s)–3

Assidet et robusta soror, ingentibus ausis
Pro populo carum tradere prompta caput.
Quin et Regis amor, musæ et dilectus Apollo,
Regali gaudent subdere plectra manu. 650
Aurea et vbertas solerti nata labore,
Exhibet aggestas Ruris et vrbis opes.
Sunt hæc dona Poli, certa quæ prodita fama
Miratum vt veniat, venit vterque polus.
Venimus et Belgæ, patrijs Gens exul ab oris
Quos fouit tenero mater Eliza sinu.
Matri sacratum, Patri duplicamus amorem,
Poscimus et simili posse fauore frui.
Sic diù Panthaici tibi proferat alitis æuum,
Sceptra per Innumeros qui tibi tradit Auos. 660
Sic Regina tui pars altera, et altera proles,
Spes populi longum det, capiatque decus.

[*Which Verses vtter thus much in English Prose.*]

Great KING, those so many Scepters, which euen fill thy right hand, are all thine owne, onely by the prouidence of Heauen: Behold Heauen it selfe laughes to see how thy Subiects smile, and thunders out loude plaudities, to heare their *Aues*. This honor of Soueraigntie, being at the beginning of the world, bestowed but vpon few; vpon the heads of few, were the cares of a Crowne set: for to sway onely but one Empire (happily) as it is a labour, hard; so 670 none can vndergoe the waight, but such as are mightie: But, (with a becke as it were) to controule many Nations, (and those of different dispositions too) ô! the Arme of man can neuer doe that, but the finger of GOD. God therefore (that guides the Chariot of the world) holds the Raynes of thy Kingdome in his owne hand: It is hee, whose beames, lend a light to thine: It is hee, that teaches thee the Art of *Ruling*; because none but hee, made thee a *King*. And therefore, as thou grow'st in yeeres, thou waxest old in *Vertues*: of

647 *Assidet*] *Assidat* Q1-2(s)-3   656 *Quos fouit*] Q3; *Quosfouit* Q1-2(s)
659 *diù Panthaici*] Q2(s) [*Diù*]; *Deum Panthaeci* Q1
660 *Innumeros*] Q2(s); *Iunumeros* Q1
661 *tui*] Q2(s); *tua* Q1   665–704 *Which Verses....*] Q2 *only*
675 *holds*] *hold* Q2

all thy Vertues, *Religion* sitting highest. And most worthy; for by *Religion*, the heartes of barbarous Nations are made soft: By *Religion*, Rebellion has a yoake cast about her necke, and is brought to beleeue, that those Lawes, to which thou submittest euen thy royall selfe, are most easie. With *Religion*, *Iustice* keepes companie; who once fled from this prophane Worlde: but hearing the name of *KING IAMES*, shee is againe returned. By her side, sits her Sister *Fortitude*; whose life is ready (in Heroicke actions) to be lauishly spent, for the safetie of thy people. Besides, to make these Vertues full, *Apollo*, and the *Muses*, resigne, the one his Golden *Lyre*; the other their *Lawrell*, to thy Royall handes: whilst *Plentie* (daughter to *Industrie*) layes the blessinges both of Countrey and Cittie, in heapes at thy feete. These are the giftes of Heauen: the fame of them spreading it selfe so farre, that (to wonder at them) both the *Poles* seeme to come togither. Wee (the *Belgians*) likewise come, to that intent: a Nation banisht from our owne Cradles; yet nourcde and brought vp in the tender boosome of Princely Mother, *ELIZA*. The *Loue*, which wee once dedicated to her (as a Mother) doubly doe wee vow it to you, our Soueraigne, and Father; intreating wee may be sheltred vnder your winges now, as then vnder hers: our Prayers being, that hee who through the loynes of so many Grand-fathers, hath brought thee to so many Kingdomes, may likewise multiply thy yeeres, and lengthen them out to the age of a *Phœnix*: And that thy *Queene*, (who is one part of thy selfe) with thy *Progeny*, (who are the second hopes of thy people) may both giue to, and receaue from thy Kingdome, Immortall glory.]

Whilst the tongues of the *Strangers* were imployed in extolling the gracious Aspect of the *King*, and his Princely behauiour towardes them, his Maiestie (by the quicknes of *Time*, and the earnestnesse of expectation, whose eyes ran a thousand wayes to finde him) had won more ground, and was gotten so far as to Saint *Mildreds* Church in the *Poulterie*: close to the side of which, a Scaffold was erected; where (at the Cities cost) to delight the Queene with her owne country Musicke, nine Trumpets, and a Kettle Drum, did very sprightly and actiuely sound the *Danish march*: Whose cunning and quicke stops, by that time they had tóucht the last Ladyes eare in the traine, behold, the *King* was aduaunced vp so hie as to *Cheapeside*: into which place (if *Loue* himselfe had entered, and seene so many gallant Gentlemen, so many Ladyes, and beautifull creatures, in whose eyes glaunces (mixt with modest lookes) seemde to daunce courtly Measures in their motion) he could not haue chosen, to haue giuen the Roome any other name, then, *The Presence Chamber*.

720

The stately entraunce into which, was a faire Gate in height 18. foote. In breadth 12. The thicknesse of the passage vnder it, being 24. Two Posternes stoode wide open on the two sides, either of them being 4. foote wide, and 8. foote high. The two Portals that ietted out before these Posternes, had their sides open foure seuerall wayes, and serued as Pedestalles (of Rusticke) to support two *Pyramides*, which stoode vpon foure great Balles, and foure great Lions: the Pedestalles, Balles, and *Pyramides*, deuowring in their full vpright heigth, from the ground line to the top, iust 60. foote. But burying this Mechanicke Body in scilence, let vs now take note in what fashion it stood attyred. Thus then it went appareled.

Soper lane.

730

The Deuice at Soper-lane end.

Within a large Compartiment, mounted aboue the forehead of the Gate, ouer the Freeze, in Capitalles was inscribed this Title:

NOVA FÆLIX ARABIA.

Vnder that shape of *Arabia*, this Iland being figured: which two names of *New*, and *Happie*, the Countrey could by no merit in it selfe, challenge to be her due, but onely by meanes of that secret influence accompanying his Maiestie wheresoeuer hee goes, and working such effectes.

740

The most worthy personage aduaunced in this place, was *Arabia Britannica*, a Woman, attyred all in White, a rich Mantle of Greene cast about her, an imperiall Crowne on her head, and a Scepter in one hand, a Mound in the other; vpon which she sadly leaned: a rich Veyle (vnder the Crowne) shadowing her eyes, by reason that her countenaunce (which till his Maiesties approach, could by no worldly obiect be drawne to looke vp) was pensiuely deiected: her ornamentes were markes of *Chastetie* and *Youth*: the Crowne, Mound, and Scepter, badges of Soueraigntie.

Directly vnder her in a Cant by her selfe, *Fame* stood vpright: A Woman in a Watchet Roabe, thickly set with open Eyes, and Tongues, a payre of large golden Winges at her backe, a Trumpet in her hand, a Mantle of sundry cullours trauersing her body: all these Ensignes desplaying but the propertie of her swiftnesse, and aptnesse to disperse Rumors.

In a Descent beneath her, being a spatious Concaue roome, were exalted fiue Mounts, swelling vp with different ascensions: vpon which sate the fiue *Sences*, drooping: *Viz̄.*

1	*Auditus,*	Hearing.
2	*Visus,*	Sight.
3	*Tactus,*	Feeling.
4	*Olfactus,*	Smelling.
5	*Gustus,*	Taste.

Appareled in Roabes of distinct cullours, proper to their natures; and holding Scutchions in their handes: vpon which were drawne Herogliphicall bodyes, to expresse their qualities.

Some prettie distaunce from them (and as it were in the midst before them) an artificiall Lauer or Fount was erected, called the *Fount of Arete* (*Vertue.*) Sundry Pipes (like veines) branching from the body of it: the water receiuing libertie but from one place, and that very slowly.

At the foote of this Fount, two personages (in greater shapes then the rest) lay sleeping: vpon their brestes stucke their names, *Detractio, Obliuio*: The one holdes an open Cuppe; about whose brim, a wreath of curled Snakes were winding, intimating that whatsoeuer his lippes toucht, was poysoned: the other helde a blacke Cuppe couerd, in token of an enuious desire to drowne the worth and memorie of Noble persons.

Vpon an Ascent, on the right hand of these, stood the three *Charites* or *Graces*, hand in hand, attyred like three Sisters.

770 *Arete*] Q2(s); *Arate* Q1

Aglaia, ⎫   ⎧ Brightnesse, or Maiestie.
Thalia, ⎬ Figuring ⎨ Youthfulnes, or florishing.
Euphrosine, ⎭   ⎩ Chearfulnes, or gladnes.

They were all three Virgins: their countenaunces laboring to smother an innated sweetnes and chearefulnes, that appareled their cheekes; yet hardly to be hid: their Garmentes were long Roabes of sundry coloures, hanging loose: the one had a Chaplet of sundry Flowers on her head, clusterd heere and there with the Fruites of the earth. The seconde, a Garland of eares of Corne. The third, a wreath of Vine-branches, mixt with Grapes and Oliues.

Their haire hung downe ouer their shoulders loose, and of a bright cullour, for that *Epithite* is properly bestowed vpon them, by *Homer* in his Himne to *Apollo.*

PVLCHRICOMÆ CHARITES.

The Bright Hayrde Graces.

They helde in their handes pensild Shieldes: vpon the first, was drawne a Rose: on the second, three Dyce: on the third, a branch of Mirtle.

Figuring ⎨ *Pleasantnesse.*
         ⎨ *Accord.*
         ⎩ *Florishing.*

In a direct line against them, stoode the three *Howres*, to whom in this place we giue the names of *Loue, Iustice,* and *Peace*: they were attyred in loose Roabes of light cullours, paynted with Flowers: for so *Ouid* apparrels them.

Conueniunt pictis incinctæ vestibus Horæ.

Winges at their feete, expressing their swiftnesse, because they are Lackies to the Sunne: *Iungere equos Tytan velocibus imperat Horis.* Ouid.

Each of them helde two Goblets; the one full of Flowers (as Ensigne of the *Spring,*) the other full of rypened Figges, the Cognisance of *Summer.*

789 clusterd] Q2(s); clustard Q1

Vpon the approch of his Maiestie (sad and solemne Musicke hauing beaten the Ayre all the time of his absence, and now ceasing,) *Fame* speakes.

Fama.

Turne into Ice mine eye-balls, whilst the sound
Flying through this brazen trump, may back rebound
To stop *Fames* hundred tongues, leauing them mute,
As in an vntoucht Bell, or stringlesse Lute,   820
For *Vertues* Fount, which late ran deepe and cleare,
Dries, and melts all her body to a teare.
You *Graces*! and you *Houres* that each day runne
On the quicke errands of the golden Sunne,
O say! to *Vertues* Fount what has befell,
That thus her veines shrinke vp.

Charites Horæ.
                         Wee cannot tell.

Euphrosine.

Behold the fiue-folde guard of *Sence* which keepes
The sacred streame, sit drooping: neere them sleepe
Two horred Monsters: *Fame*! summon each *Sence*,
To tell the cause of this strange accidence.   830

Heereupon *Fame* sounding her Trumpet; *Arabia Britannica*, lookes cheerefully vp, the *Senses* are startled: *Detraction* and *Obliuion* throw off their iron slumber, busily bestowing all their powers to fill their cups at the Fount with their olde malitious intention to sucke it drie; But a strange and heauenly musicke suddainly striking through their eares, which causing a wildnes and quicke motion in their lookes, drew them to light vpon the glorious presence of the *King*, they were suddainly thereby daunted and sunke downe; The Fount in the same moment of *Tyme*, flowing fresh and aboundantly through seuerall pipes, with Milke, Wine,   840
and Balme, whilst a person (figuring *Circumspection*) that had watcht day and night, to giue note to the world of this blessed *Tyme*, which hee foresawe would happen, steps forth on a mounted Stage

822 Dries] *Arches*; Drie Q 1–2(r)–3

278

extended 30. foote in length from the maine building, to deliuer to his Maiestie the interpretation of this dumbe Mysterie.

This Presenter was a Boy, one of the Choristers, belonging to *Paules*.

His Speech.

Great Monarch of the West, whose glorious Stem,
Doth now support a triple Diadem,　　　　　　　　850
Weying more than that of thy grand Grandsire *Brute*,
Thou that maist make a King thy substitute,
And doest besides the Red-rose and the white,
With the rich flower of *France* thy garland dight,
Wearing aboue Kings now, or those of olde,
A double Crowne of Lawrell and of gold,
O let my voyce passe through thy royall eare,
And whisper thus much, that we figure here,
A new *Arabia*, in whose spiced nest
A *Phœnix* liu'd and died in the Sunnes brest,　　　860
Her losse, made Sight, in teares to drowne her eyes,
The Eare grew deafe, Taste like a sick-man lyes,
Finding no rellish: euery other *Sence*,
Forgat his office, worth and excellence,
Whereby this Fount of *Vertue* gan to freeze,
Threatned to be drunke vp by two enemies,
Snakie *Detraction*, and *Obliuion*,
But at thy glorious presence, both are gone,
Thou being that sacred *Phœnix*, that doest rise,
From th'ashes of the first: Beames from thine eyes　　870
So vertually shining, that they bring,
To *Englands* new *Arabia*, a new Spring:
For ioy whereof, *Nimphes*, *Sences*, *Houres*, and *Fame*,
Eccho loud Hymnes to his imperiall name.

At the shutting vp of this Speech, his Maiestie (being readie to goe on,) did most graciouslie feede the eyes of beholders with his presence, till a Song was spent: which to a loude and excellent Musicke (composed of Violins and an other rare Artificiall Instru-

866 vp] *Arches*; *om*. Q 1–2 (r)–3

ment,) wherein besides sundrie seuerall sounds effus'd (all at one time) were also sensibly distinguisht the chirpings of birds, was by two Boyes (Choristers of *Paules*) deliuered in sweete and rauishing voyces.

Cant.

Troynouant is now no more a Citie:
    O great pittie! is't not pittie?
And yet her Towers on tiptoe stand,
Like Pageants built on Fairie land,
    And her Marble armes,
    Like to Magicke charmes,
Binde thousands fast vnto her,
That for her wealth and beauty daily wooe her,
    yet for all this, is't not pittie?
Troynouant is now no more a Cittie.

2

Troynouant is now a Sommer Arbour,
    or the nest wherein doth harbour,
The Eagle, of all birds that flie,
The Soueraigne, for his piercing eie,
    If you wisely marke,
    Tis besides a Parke,
Where runnes (being newly borne)
With the fierce Lyon, the faire Vnicorne,
    or else it is a wedding Hall,
Where foure great Kingdomes holde a Festiuall.

3

Troynouant is now a Bridall Chamber,
    whose roofe is gold, floore is of Amber,
By vertue of that holy light,
That burnes in *Hymens* hand, more bright,
    Than the siluer Moone,
    Or the Torch of Noone,
Harke what the Ecchoes say!

> *Brittaine* till now nere kept a Holiday:
> for *Ioue* dwels heere: And tis no pittie,
> If *Troynouant* be now no more a Cittie.

Nor let the scrue of any wresting comment vpon these words,

> *Troynouant is now no more a Citie.*

Enforce the Authors inuention away from his owne cleare, straight, and harmelesse meaning: all the scope of this fiction stretching onely to this point, that *London* (to doo honour to this day, wherein springs vp all her happines) beeing rauished with vnutterable ioyes, makes no account (for the present) of her ancient title, to be called a Citie, (because that during these tryumphes, shee puts off her formall habite of Trade and Commerce, treading euen Thrift it selfe vnder foote,) but now becomes a Reueller and a Courtier. So that, albeit in the end of the first Stanza tis said,

> *Yet for all this, is't not pittie,*
> *Troynouant is now no more a Cittie.*

By a figure called *Castigatio* or the mender, heere followes presently a reproofe; wherein tytles of Sommer Arbor; The Eagles nest, a wedding Hall, &c. are throwne vpon her, the least of them being at this time by vertue of Poeticall Heraldrie, but especiallie in regard of the State that now vpholds her, thought to be names of more honour, than that of her owne. And this short Apologie, doth our verse make for it selfe, in regard that some, (to whose setled iudgement and authoritie the censure of these Deuises was referred,) brought (though not bitterly) the life of those lines into question: But appealing with *Machætas* to *Phillip*, now these reasons haue awakend him: let vs followe King *Iames*, who hauing passed vnder this our third gate, is by this time, graciously receauing a gratulatorie Oration from the mouth of Sir *Henry Mountague*, *Recorder* of the Citie, a square lowe gallorie, set round about with pilasters, beeing for that purpose erected some 4. foote from the ground, and ioyned

---

916–917 cleare, straight,] Q1 *errata*; cleare strength Q1 *text*
921 that during] Q1 *errata*; aluring Q1 *text*; during Q2(r)
927 heere] Q1; there Q2(r)

THE MAGNIFICENT ENTERTAINMENT

to the front of the Crosse in *Cheape*; where likewise stood all the Aldermen, the Chamberlaine, Town-clarke, and Counsell of the Citie.

The Recorders Speech

High Imperiall Maiestie, it is not yet a yeere in dayes since with acclamation of the People, Citizens, and Nobles, auspitiouslie heere at this Crosse was proclaimed your true succession to the Crowne. If then it was ioyous with Hats, hands, and hearts, lift vp to heauen to crie *King Iames*, what is it now to see King *Iames*? Come therefore O worthiest of Kings as a glorious Bridegroome through your Royall chamber: But to come neerer, *Adest quem querimus*. Twentie and more are the Soueraignes wee haue serued since our conquest, but Conquerour of hearts it is you and your Posteritie, that we haue vowed to loue and wish to serue whilst *London* is a Citie. In pledge whereof my Lord Maior, the Aldermen, and Commons of this Citie, wishing a golden Reigne vnto you, present your Greatnes with a little cup of gold.

3. Cuppes of Golde giuen by the Cittie.

At the end of the Oration three Cups of gold were giuen (in the name of the Lord Maior, and the whole Body of the Citie,) to his Maiestie, the young Prince, and the Queene.

All which but aboue all (being gifts of greater value) the loyall hearts of the Citizens, beeing louingly receaued; his Grace was (at least it was appointed he should haue beene) met on his way neere to the Crosse, by *Syluanus* drest vp in greene Iuie, a Cornet in his hand, being attended on by foure other *Syluans* in Iuie likewise, their bowes and quiuers hanging on their shoulders, and winde Instruments in their hands.

Vpon sight of his Maiestie, they make a stand, *Syluanus* breaking forth into this abrupt passion of ioy.

Syluanus.

The Pageant at the litle Conduit.

Stay *Syluans*, and let the loudest voyce of Musicke proclayme it (euen as high as Heauen) that hee is come.

954 Conquerour] Q1; Conquerours Q2(r)
959–961 3. Cuppes...Cittie.] Q2(r); om. Q1
971–972 The Pageant...Conduit.] Q2(r); om. Q1

282

Alter Apollo redit, Nouus En, iam regnat Apollo.

Which acclamation of his was borne vp into the ayre, and there mingled with the breath of their musicall Instruments: whose sound beeing vanished to nothing, Thus goes our Speaker on.

Syluanus.

Most happie Prince, pardon me, that being meane in habite, and wilde in apparance, (for my richest liuorie is but leaues, and my stateliest dwelling but in the woodes,) thus rudely with piping *Syluanes*, I presume to intercept your royall passage. These are my walkes: yet stand I heere, not to cut off your way, but to giue it a full and a bounteous welcome, beeing a Messenger sent from the Lady *Eirene* my Mistresse, to deliuer an errand to the best of all these Worthies, your royall selfe. Many Kingdomes hath the Lady sought out to abide in, but from them all, hath shee beene most churlishly banished: not that her beautie did deserue such vnkindnes, but that (like the eye of Heauen) hers were too bright, and there were no Eagles breeding in those nests, that could truly beholde them.

At last heere she ariued, *Destinie* subscribing to this Warrant, that none but this Land should be her Inheritance. In contempt of which happines, *Enuie* shootes his impoisoned stings at her heart, but his Adders (being charmed) turne their daungerous heads vpon his owne bosome. Those that dwell far off, pine away with vexing to see her prosper, because all the acquaintance which they haue of her, is this, that they know there is such a goodly Creature as *Eirene*, in the world, yet her face they know not: whilst all those that heere sleepe vnder the warmth of her wings, adore her by the sacred and Cœlestiall name of *Peace*, for number being (as her blessings are) infinite.

Her daughter *Euporia* (well knowne by the name of *Plentie*) is at this present with her, (being indeede neuer from her side) vnder yonder Arbour they sit, which after the daughters name is called, *Hortus Euporiæ* (*Plenties Bower:*) Chast are they both, and both maydens in memorie of a Virgine, to whom they were nurse children: for whose sake (because they were bound to her for their life,) mee, haue they charged to lay at your imperiall feete, (being your hereditarie due) the tribute of their loue: And with it thus to say.

That they haue languished many heauie moneths for your presence, which to them would haue beene, (and proud they are that it shall be so now,) of the same operation and influence, that the Sunne is to the spring, and the spring to the earth: hearing therefore what trebble preferment you haue bestowed vpon this day, wherein besides the beames of a glorious Sunne, two other cleare and gracious starres shine cheerefullie on these her homely buildings: Into which (because no dutie should bee wanting) shee hath giuen leaue euen to Strangers, to bee Sharers in her happines, by suffering them to bid you likewise welcome. By mee (once hers, now your vassaile,) shee entreates, and with a knee sinking lower than the ground on which you tread, doo I humbly execute her pleasure, that ere you passe further, you would deigne to walke into yonder Garden: the *Hesperides* liue not there but the *Muses*, and the *Muses* no longer than vnder your protection. Thus farre am I sent to conduct you thither, prostrately begging this grace, (since I dare not, as beeing vnwoorthie, lackey by your royall side) in that yet these my greene Followers and my selfe may bee ioyfull fore-runners of your expected approch, away *Syluans*.

And being (in this their returne) come neare to the Arbor, they gaue a signe with a short florish from all their Cornets, that his Maiestie was at hand: whose princely eye whilest it was delighting it selfe with the quaint obiect before it, a sweete pleasure likewise courted his eare in the shape of Musicke, sent from the voyces of nine Boyes (all of them Queristers of *Paules*) who in that place presenting the nine *Muses* sang the dittie following to their Viols and other Instruments.

But, least leaping too bluntly into the midst of our Garden at first, we deface the beautie of it, let vs send you round about it, and suruey the Walles, Allies, and quarters of it as they lye in order.

This being the fashion of it.

The passages through it were two gates, arched and grated Arbor-wise, their heigth being 18. foote, their breadth 12.: from the

1027 *Syluans*] Q2(r); *Syluanus* Q1   1041 18. ... 12.] Q2(r); 16. ... 10. Q1

roofe, and so on the sides, downe to the ground, Cowcumbers, Pompions, Grapes, and all other fruits growing in the land, hanging artificially in clusters: Betweene the two gates, a payre of stayres were mounted with some 20. assents: at the bottome of them (on two pillers) were fixed two Satiers carued out in wood; the sides of both the gates, being strengthened with foure great French termes standing vpon pedestals, taking vp in their full height 25. foote.

The vpper part also caried the proportion, of an Arbor, being closde with their round tops, the midst whereof was exalted aboue the other two, *Fortune* standing on the top of it. The garnishments for the whole Bower, being Apples, Peares, Cheries, Grapes, Roses, Lillies, and all other both fruits and flowers most artificially molded to the life. The whole frame of this Somer banqueting house, stood (at the ground line) vpon 44. foote; the *Perpendicular* stretching it selfe to 45. Wee might (that day) haue called it, *The Musicke roome*, by reason of the chaunge of tunes, that danced round about it; for in one place were heard a noyse of cornets, in a second, a consort, the third, (which sate in sight) a set of Viols, to which the *Muses* sang.

The principall persons aduancde in this Bower, were, *Eirene* (*Peace*) and *Euporia* (*Plenty*) who sate together.

Eirene.

Peace: Was richly attired, her vpper garment of carnation, hanging loose, a Robe of White vnder it, powdred with Starres, and girt to her: her haire of a bright colour, long, and hanging at her back, but inter-wouen with white ribbands, and Iewels: her browes were encompast with a wreath compounded of the Oliue, the Lawrell, and the Date tree: In one hand shee held a *Caducæus*, (or *Mercuries* rod, the god of eloquence:) In the other, ripe eares of corne gilded: on her lap sate a Doue: All these being ensignes, and furnitures of *Peace*.

1047 termes] Q2(r); frames Q1 1048 25.] Q2(r); 20. Q1
1054 Somer] Q2(s); somer Q1 *1055 44.] 4. Q1–2(s)–3
1055 foote] Q1; feete Q2(s) 1063 *Eirene*] Q2(s); *Eierene* Q1

Euporia.

Plenty: Her daughter sate on the left hand, in changable colours, a rich mantle of Gold trauersing her bodie: her haire large and loosely spreading ouer her shoulders: on her head a crowne of Poppy and Mustard seede; the antique badges of *Fertilitie* and *Abundance*. In her right hand a *Cornucopia*, filde with flowers, fruits, &c.

Chrusos.

Directly vnder these, sate *Chrusos*, a person figuring Gold, his dressing, a tinsell Robe of the colour of Gold.

Argurion.

And close by him, *Argurion*, Siluer, all in white tinsell; both of them crownde, and both their hands supporting a Globe, betweene them, in token that they commaunded ouer the world.

Pomona.

Pomona, the goddesse of garden fruits; sate at the one side of Gold and Siluer; attirde in greene, a wreath of frutages circling her temples: her armes naked: her haire beautifull, and long.

Ceres.

On the other side sate *Ceres*, crowned with ripened eares of Wheate, in a loose straw-coloured roabe.

In two large descents (a little belowe them) were placde at one end,

| The nine Muses. | { Clio. Euterpe. Thalia. Melpomene. Terpsicore. Erato. Polymnia. Vrania. Calliope. } | With musicall instrumentes in their hands, to which they sung all the day. |

1074 on] Q2(s); of Q1

The 7 liberall Artes.
{ *Grammer.*
Logique.
Rhetorique.
Musicke.
Arithmeticke.
Geometry.
Astrology. }
At the other end.

Holding shieldes in their hands, expressing their seuerall offices.

Vpon the verie vpper edge of a faire large Freeze, running quite along the full breadth of the Arbor, and iust at their feete were planted rankes of artificiall Artichocks and roses.

To describe what apparrell these *Arts*, and *Muses* wore, were a hard labour, and when it were done, all were but idle. Few Taylors know how to cut out their garments: they haue no Wardrob at all, not a Mercer, nor Merchant, though they can all write and read verie excellently well, will suffer them to bee great in their bookes. But (as in other countries) so in this of ours, they goe attirde in such thin clothes, that the winde euerie minute is readie to blowe through them: happy was it for them, that they tooke vp their lodging in a summer arbour, and that they had so much musicke to comfort them, their ioies (of which they do not euerie daie tast,) being notwithstanding now infinitelie multiplied, in this, that where before they might haue cryed out till they grew horse, and non would heare them, now they sing,

Aderitque vocatus Apollo.

A *Chorus* in full voices answering it thus.

Ergo alacris Syluas, et cætera rura voluptas
Panaque pastoresque tenet, Driadasque puellas,
Nec Lupus insidias pecori, nec retia Ceruis
Vlla dolum meditantur, amat bonus otia Daphnis;
Ipsi lætitia voces ad sidera iactant
Intonsi montes: ipsæ iam carmina Rupes,
Ipsa sonant Arbusta, Deus, Deus ille!

Syluanus (as you may perceiue by his office before) was but sent of an errand: there was another of a higher calling, a Trauailer, and

1127 A] Q2(s); *om.* Q1

THE MAGNIFICENT ENTERTAINMENT

one that had gon ouer much grownd, appointed to speake to his Maiesty, his name *Vertumnus*, the maister Gardner, and husband to *Pomona*: To tell you what cloathes hee had on his backe were to doo him wrong, for hee had (to say truth) but one suite: homelie it was, yet meete and fit for a Gardener: In steade of a hat, his browes were bound about with flowers, out of whose thicke heapes, here and there peeped a queene apple, a cherie, or a peare, this boon-grace hee made of purpose to keepe his face from heate, (because he desired to looke louelie) yet the sunne found him out, and by casting a continuall eye at him, whilst the old man was dressing his arbours, his cheekes grew tawnie, which colour for the better grace, he himselfe interpreted, blushing. A white head he had, and Sunne-burnt hands: in the one he held a weeding hooke, in the other a grafting knife: and this was the tenor of his speech. That he was bound to giue thanks to heauen, In that the arbour and trees which growing in that fruitfull *Cynthian* garden, began to droop and hang-downe their greene heades, and to vncurle their crisped forlocks, as fearing, and in some sort, feeling the sharpenesse of Autumnian malice, are now on the sudden by the diuine influence apparelled with a fresh and more liuely verdure than euer they were before. The nine *Muses* that could expect no better entertainement than sad banishment, hauing now louely and amiable faces: *Arts* that were threatned to be trod vnder foot by Barbarisme, now (euen at sight of his Maiestie, who is the *Delian* Patron both of the *Muses* and *Arts*) being likewise aduanced to most high preferment whilst the very rurall and Syluane troopes dancd for ioy: the Lady therfore of the place *Eirene*, (his mistris) in name of the Prætor, Consuls and Senators of the City, who carefully pruine this garden, (weeding-out al hurtful and idle branches that hinder the growth of the good,) and who are indeede, *Ergatai Pistoi*, faithfull Laborers in this peice of ground, Shee doth

    1148 interpreted,] Q2(s); ~ ˌ Q1
    1148 Sunne-burnt] Q2(s); sunne-burnt Q1
    1152 fruitfull] Q1; fruitful Q2(s) [*for justification*]
    1152 hang-downe] Q2(s); hang downe Q1
    1153 fearing,] Q2(s); ~ ˌ Q1
    1155 diuine] Q2(s); deuine Q1
    1159 Maiestie,] Q2(s); ~ ˌ Q1
    1164 weeding-out] Q2(s); weeding out Q1

THE MAGNIFICENT ENTERTAINMENT

in al their names, (and he in behalfe of his Lady) offer them selues, this Arbor, the bowers and walkes, yea her children (gold and siluer) with the louing and loyall harts of all those the Sons of peace, standing about him, to be disposde after his royal pleasure. And so wishing his happie Arriual, at a more glorious bower, to which he is now going, yet welcoming him to this, and praying his Maiesty not to forget this poore Arbor of his Lady, Musicke is commanded to cary all their praiers for his happie reigne, with the loud *Amen* of all his Subiects, as hie as heauen.

Cant.

Shine *Titan* shine.
Let thy sharpe raies be hurld
Not on this vnder world,
For now tis none of thine.

These first four lines were sung by one alone, the single lines following, by a *Chorus* in full voices.

Chor. No, no, tis none of thine.

2

But in that spheare,
Where what thine armes infolde,
Turnes all to burnisht gold,
Spend thy guilt arrowes there,
Chor. Doe, doe, shoote onelie there.

3

Earth needes thee not:
Her childbed daies are done,
And Shee another Sunne,
Faire as thy selfe has got.
Chor. A new new Sunne is got.

1168–1169 (gold...siluer)] Q2(s); ∧ ~ ... ~ , Q1
1177 *Titan*] Q2(s); Titan Q1

4

O this is Hee!
Whose new beames make our Spring,
Men glad and birdes to Sing,
Hymnes of praise, ioy, and glee.
Chor. Sing, Sing, O this is hee!

5

That in the North
First rizing: shonne (so far)
Bright as the morning Starre,
At his gaie comming forth.
Chor. See, see, he now comes forth.

6

How soone ioies varie?
Had still hee staide! O then
Happie both place and men,
But here hee list not tarrie.
Chor. O griefe! hee list not tarrie.

7

No, no, his beames,
Must equally deuide,
Their heate to Orbes beside,
Like nourishing siluer streames.
Chor. Ioies slide awaie like streames.

8

Yet in this lies
Sweete hope: how far soeuer,
Hee bides, no cloudes can seuer,
His glorie from our eyes.
Chor. Drie, drie, your weeping eies.

1194 Hee] Q1 *errata*; had Q1 *text*   1198 *Chor.*] Q2(s); *om.* Q1
*1205 Had still hee staide!] Q1 *errata*; Here staide had still! Q1 *text*; Heere staide hee still! Q2(r)
1208 hee] Q1 *errata*; had Q1 *text*   1207 hee] Q1 *errata*; had Q1 *text*
   1210 equally] Q2(r); equall Q1

9

And make heauen ring,
His welcomes showted loudelie,   1220
For Heauen it selfe lookes proudly,
That earth has such a King.
Chor. Earth has not such a King.

His Maiestie dwelt here a reasonable long time, giuing both good allowance to the song and Musick, and liberally bestowing his eye on the workemanship of the place: from whence at the length departing, his next entrance was, as it were, into the closet or rather the priuy chamber to this our Court royall: through the windowes of which he might behold the Cathedrall Temple of Saint *Paule*: vpon whose lower batlements an Antheme was sung, by the 1230 Quiristers of the Church to the musicke of loud instruments: which being finisht, a latine Oration was *Viua voce* deliuered to his Grace, by one of maister *Mulcasters* Schollers, at the dore of the free-schole fownded by the Mercers.

Oratio habita, et ad Regem, et coram
Rege præ schola Paulina.

Breuis ero, ne ingratus sim, Rex serenissime, licet, et plané, et plenè putem Regem tam prudentem, in tam profusa suorum lætitia, ita se hodie patientia contra tædium armauisse, ne vllius tœdij ipsum posset tœdere. Ædificium hoc magno sumptu suo extructum Dominus 1240 *Iohannes Collettus Ecclesiæ Paulinæ Decanus, sub Henrico septimo, maiestatis tuæ prudentissimo abauo, erudiendæ pueritiæ consecrauit, vt huius scholæ infantia tuo in Regnum Anglicanum iure coetanea existat. Tanta magnificentia conditum parique magnificentia dotatum fidelissimæ Mercerorum huius vrbis primariæ semper, hodie etiam Prætoriæ societati tuendum testamento moriens commendauit. Quæ societas, et de mortui fundatoris spe, et nostræ educationis studio fidem*

        1232 Grace] Q2(s); grace Q1
        1235–1276 Oratio....] *om.* Q2
        1245 *primariæ*] primaria Q1(c); *prima via* Q1(u)
        1247 *de mortui*] Q1(u); *demortui* Q1(c)
        1247 *spe*] Q1(u); *spei* Q1(c)

suam sanctissimè exoluit. Hic nos cum multis alijs erudimur, qui communi nomine totius pueritiæ Anglicanæ, a Domino Rege, licet sponte sua ad omnia optima satis incitato, humillimé tamen contendimus, vt quemadmodum sua ætatis ratione in omni re adultioribus prospicit, ita in summæ spei Principis Henrici gratiam tenerioribus, parique cum ipso ætate pueris, in scholarum cura velit etiam consulere. Virgæ enim obsequium, sceptri obedientiam et parit, et præit, inquit preceptor meus. Quique metu didicit iuuenis parere puerque, grandibus imperiis officiosus erit. Habent scholæ Anglicanæ multa, in quibus Regiam maiestatis correctionem efflagitant, ne inde in Academias implumes euolent vnde in Rempublicam implumiores etiam è prima nuditate emittuntur. Quod malum à Preceptore nostro accepimus: qui annos iam quatuor supra quinquaginta publice, priuatimque erudiendæ pueritiæ præfuit, et hæc scholarum errata, cum aliquo etiam dolore suo, et passim, et sparsim deprehendit. Nostra hæc schola fundatorem Collettum hominem tam pium; tutores Merceros homines tam fidos consequuta, quam esset fœlix, si placeret, Domino etiam Regi, quod Regibus Angliæ, ad summam apud suos charitatem sæpissimè profuit, huic Mercerorum principi societati, fratrem se, et conciuem adscribere. Quantum huic vrbi ornamentum, quantum societati honestamentum, Quantum scholæ nostræ emolumentum? Quantus etiam Regi ipsi honos inde accederet, mauult, qui hoc vult alias inter alia per otium Regi suo apperire, quam hodie cum tædio et præter aream eidem explicare. Omnipotens Deus Iesus Christus et cum eo, ac per eum noster, et Pater, et Deus serenissimum Regem Iacobum, honoratissimam Reginam Annam, nobilissimum Principem Henricum, reliquamque Regiæ stirpis ad omnia summa natam sobolem diu nobis ita incolumes tueatur, vt cum huius vitæ secundissimum curriculum confeceritis, beatissimam vitæ cælestis æternitatem consequamini. Dixi.

    1252 *summæ*] Q1(c); *summa* Q1(u)
    1266 *adscribere.*] Q1(u); ~ , Q1(c)
    1268 *scholæ*] Q1(c); *schola* Q1(u)
    1273 *reliquamque*] Q1(c); *relinquamque* Q1(u)
    1274 *summa*] Q1(c); *summam* Q1(u)

THE MAGNIFICENT ENTERTAINMENT

[THE ORATION DELIVERED
at Paules Schoole by one of Maister
Mulcasters Schollers.

Most Gratious Souereigne, my Speech shall not be long, for feare it appeare loathsome: yet doo I fully and freely beleeue, that a King (so crowned with wisedome as your selfe) hath (this day) put on such strong Armor of patience to beare-off tediousnesse, in this so maine and vniuersall meeting of Ioy in his Subiects, that the extension and stretching out of any part of time, can by no meanes seeme irksome vnto him. This building receiued her foundation from the liberall purse of *Iohn Collet*, (Dean of *Paules* Church, vnder *Henry* the 7. great Graund-father to your Maiesty:) and was by him consecrated to learning for the erudition of youth; to the intent that the infancy of this Schoole may now, by your right to the kingdome of England, grow vp to a ful and ripe age. Which work of his, so magnificent for the building, so commendable for the endowments, he by last will and Testament bequeathed, to the faithful Society and Brotherhood of the Mercers, alwaies the cheifest, and now this yeere, by reason of a Lord Maior, (who is a member amongst them) more than the chiefest of the Companies of this City. Which Society haue most religiously performed al rites both due to the hopes of our deceased Fownder, and to the Ornaments of our education. Within these wals, we, with many other sucke the milke of learning: and in the general name of all the youth in *England*, most humbly intreate of our Lord the king (who of himselfe, wee know, is forwarde inough to aduance all goodnesse) that, as by reason of his manlie yeares, his cheifest care is spent about looking to, and gouerning men, so (notwithstanding) in fauour of that his Royal Sonne *Henry* (Prince of vnspeakeable hopes,) he would a little suffer his eie to descend and behold our Schoole, and therein to prouide that those who are but greene in yeeres, and of equall age with that his Princelie issue, may likewise receiue a vertuous education. For the obedience which is giuen to the rod, brings along with it obedience to the Scepter, nay (as our Maister tels vs) it goes euen before it.

1277–1336 THE ORATION....] Q2 *only*

293

THE MAGNIFICENT ENTERTAINMENT

Quique metu didicit, iuuenis parere, puerque,
Grandibus Imperijs officiosus erit.

Our Schooles of *England*, are in many lims deformed whose crookednesse require the hand of a King, to set them straight: least out of these young nests, those that are there bred, flying without their fethers into Vniuersities, shold afterward light vpon the branches of the common wealth, more naked, than at first, by reason they were not perfectly fledgd. Which euil hath bin discouered by the obseruation of our Teacher: who now by the space of more than 50.4. yeeres (both publiquelie and priuatelie) hath instructed youth, and with no little griefe of his own hath both here and abroad sifted out these grosse vices, that are mingled amongst Schooles. O how happy therfore should this our Nursery of learning be, if (after hauing first met with *Collet* a fownder so religious, and secondly the Mercers our patrons men so faithfull, and vertuous,) our Lord the King would now at last also be pleased (considering many Kings of *England* by doing so haue won wonderfull loue from their subiects) to suffer his Royall name to be rolled amongst the Citizens of *London*, by vouchsafing to be free of that worthie, and chiefest Society of Mercers! What glorie should thereby rize vp to the City? what dignity to that Society? to this our Schoole what infinite benefite? what honour besides our Souereigne himselfe might acquire, he that makes this wish now, wisheth rather, (in fitter place, and at fitter howers) to discouer to his Prince, than now cleane beyond his aime, to ouershoote himselfe by tediousnesse. The Almighty, &c.]

Our next Arch of triumph, was erected aboue the Conduit in Fleetstreete, into which (as into the long and beauteous gallery of the Citie) his Maiestie beeing entered; a farre off (as if it had beene some swelling Promontory, or rather some inchanted Castle guarded by tenne thousand harmelesse spirits) did his eye encounter another Towre of Pleasure.

1311 didicit] dedicit Q2
1339 beeing] Q1(u); being Q1(c)
1340 Promontory] Q2(s); Promentory Q1

THE MAGNIFICENT ENTERTAINMENT

Presenting it selfe.

Fourescore and ten foote in height, and fiftie in breadth; the gate twentie foote in the perpendicular line, and fourteene in the groundline: The two Posternes were answerable to these that are set downe before: ouer the posternes riz vp in proportionable measures, two turrets, with battlementes on the tops: The middest of the building was laid open to the world, and great reason it should be so, for the Globe of the world, was there seene to mooue, being fild 1350 with all the degrees, and states that are in the land: and these were the mechanicall and dead limmes of this carued bodie. As touching those that had the vse of motion in it, and for a neede durst haue spoken, but that there was no stuffe fit for their mouthes.

The principall and worthiest was *Astræa,* (*Iustice*) sitting aloft, as being newly descended from heauen, gloriously attirde; all her garments beeing thickely strewed with starres: a crowne of starres on her head: a Siluer veile couering her eyes. Hauing tolde you that her name was *Iustice,* I hope you will not put mee to describe what properties she held in her hands, sithence euery painted cloath can 1360 informe you.

Directly vnder her, in a Cant by her selfe, was *Arete* (Vertue) inthronde, her garments white, her head crowned, and vnder her *Fortuna*: her foote treading on the Globe, that moude beneath her: Intimating, that his Maiesties fortune, was aboue the world, but his vertues aboue his fortune.

Inuidia.

Enuy, vnhandsomely attirde all in blacke, her haire of the same colour, filletted about with snakes, stood in a darke and obscure place by her selfe, neere vnto *Vertue,* but making shew of a fearful- 1370 nesse to approach her and the light: yet still and anon, casting her

1347 posternes riz vp] Q1(c); posternes. *Viz.* Vp Q1(u)
1353 neede] Q1(c); minde Q1(u)
1357 beeing] Q1(u); being Q1(c)
1362 *Arete*] Dyce; *Arate* Q1–2(s)–3
1362 Vertue] Q2(s); vertue Q1

eyes, sometimes to the one side beneath, where on seuerall Grieces sate the foure Cardinall vertues:

Viz. {
Iustitia.
Fortitudo.
Temperantia.
Prudentia.
} In habiliments, fitting to their natures.

And sometimes throwing a distorted and repining countenance to the other opposite seate, on which, his Maiesties foure kingdomes were aduanced.

Viz. {
England.
Scotland.
France.
Ireland.
}

All of them, in rich Robes and Mantles; crownes on their heads, and Scepters with pensild scutchions in their hands, lined with the coats of the particuler kingdomes: for very madnesse, that she beheld these glorious obiects, she stood feeding on the heads of Adders.

The foure Elements in proper shapes, (artificially and aptly expressing their qualities) vpon the approch of his Maiestie, went round in a proportionable and euen circle, touching that cantle of the Globe, (which was open) to the full view of his Maiestie, which being done, they bestowed themselues in such comely order, and stood so, as if the Engine had beene held vp on the tops of their fingers.

Vpon distinct Ascensions, (neatly raisde within the hollow wombe of the Globe) were placed all the States of the land, from the Nobleman to the Ploughman, among whom there was not one word to bee heard, for you must imagine as *Virgil* saith:

Ægl. 4. *Magnus ab integro seclorum nascitur ordo.*
Iam redit et *virgo redeunt Saturnia regna.   * Astræ

1372 Grieces] Q2(s); Greeces Q1   1373 Cardinall] Q2(s); cardinall Q1
1395 Engine] Q2(s); Eronie Q1   1397 Vpon] Q2(s); vpon Q1
1398 States] Q2(s); states Q1   1402 et] Q2(s); at Q1
1402 Astræa.] Q2(s); *in* Q1 *placed without asterisk to left of line* 1402 *in same type as* Ægl. 4

That it was now the golden world, in which there were few praters.

All the tongues that went in this place, was the tongue of *Zeale*, whose personage was put on by *W. Bourne*, one of the seruants to the young Prince.

And thus went his speach.

> The populous Globe of this our English Ile,
> Seemde to mooue backward, at the funerall pile,   1410
> Of her dead female Maiestie. All States
> From Nobles downe to spirits of meaner Fates,
> Mooude opposite to Nature and to Peace,
> As if these men had bin Th'Antipodes,
> But see, the vertue of a Regall eye,
> Th'attractiue wonder of mans Maiestie,
> Our Globe is drawne in a right line agen,
> And now appeare new faces, and new men.
> The Elements, Earth, Water, Ayre, and Fire,
> (Which euer clipt a naturall desire,   1420
> To combat each with other,) being at first,
> Created enemies to fight their worst,
> See at the peacefull presence of their King,
> How quietly they moude, without their sting:
> Earth not deuouring, Fire not defacing,
> Water not drowning, and the Ayre not chasing:
> But propping the queint Fabrick that heere stands,
> Without the violence of their wrathfull hands.
>   Mirror of times, lo where thy *Fortune* sits,
> Aboue the world, and all our humaine wits,   1430
> But thy hye Vertue aboue that: what pen,
> Or Art, or braine can reach thy vertue then?
> At whose immortall brightnes and true light,
> *Enuies* infectious eyes haue lost their sight,

    1404 praters] Q2(s); parts Q1
    1421 other,)...first,] Q2(s); ~,... ~,) Q1
    1427 propping] Q2(s); proping Q1
    1429 *Fortune*] Q2(s); *Fotune* Q1

Her snakes (not daring to shoot-forth their stings
Gainst such a glorious obiect) downe she flings
Their forkes of Venome into her owne mawe,
Whilst her ranke teeth the glittering poisons chawe,
For tis the property of *Enuies* blood,
To dry away at euery kingdomes good,   1440
Especially when shee had eyes to view,
These foure maine vertues figurde all in you,
Iustice in causes, *Fortitude* gainst foes,
Temp'rance in spleene, and *Prudence* in all those,
And then so rich an Empyre, whose fayre brest,
Contaynes foure Kingdomes by your entrance blest,
By *Brute* diuided, but by you alone,
All are againe vnited and made *One*,
Whose fruitfull glories shine so far and euen,
They touch not onely earth, but they kisse heauen,   1450
From whence *Astræa* is descended hither,
Who with our last Queenes Spirit, fled vp thither,
Fore-knowing on the earth, she could not rest,
Till you had lockt her in your rightfull brest.
And therefore all Estates, whose proper Arts,
Liue by the breath of Maiestie, had harts
Burning in holy Zeales immaculate fires,
With quenchles Ardors, and vnstaind desires,
To see what they now see, your powerful Grace,
Reflecting ioyes on euery subiects face: 1460
These paynted flames and yellow burning Stripes,
Vpon this roab, being but as showes and types,
Of that great Zeale. And therefore in the name
Of this glad Citie, whither no Prince euer came,
More lou'd, more long'd for, lowely I intreate,
You'ld be to her as gracious as y'are great:
So with reuerberate shoutes our Globe shall ring,
The Musicks close being thus: God saue our King.

1444 *Temp'rance*] Q2(s); *Temprance* Q1

If there be any glorie to be won by writing these lynes, I do freelie bestow it (as his due) on *Thomas Middleton*, in whose braine they were begotten, though they were deliuered heere: *Quæ nos non fecimus ipsi, vix ea nostra voco.*

But hauing peiced vp our wings now againe with our owne feathers; suffer vs a while to be pruning them, and to lay them smooth, whilst this song, which went foorth at the sound of Hault-boyes, and other lowde instruments, flyes along with the trayne.

Cant.

Where are all these Honors owing?
Why are seas of people flowing?
   Tell mee, tell me *Rumor*,
   Though it be thy Humor
   More often to be lying,
Than from thy breath to haue trueth flying:
   Yet alter, now, that fashion,
   And without the streame of passion,
   Let thy voyce swim smooth and cleare,
When words want gilding, then they are most deere.

Behold where *Ioue* and all the States,
Of Heau'n, through Heau'ns seauen siluer gates,
   All in glory riding
   (Backs of Clowds bestriding)
   The milky waie do couer,
Which starry Path being measur'd ouer,
   The Deities conuent,
   In *Ioues* high Court of Parliament.
Rumor thou doest loose thine aymes,
This is not *Ioue*, but One, as great, King IAMES.

And now take we our flight vp to Temple-bar, (the other ende of this our Gallery) where by this time, his Maiestie is vpon the poynt of giuing a gratious and Princely Fare-well to the Lord Maior, and

1469 these] Q1; thes Q2(s) [*type dropped out*]
1493 Which] With Q1–2(s)–3

the Citie. But that his eye meeting a seauenth beautifull obiect, is inuited by that, to delay awhile his (lamented) departure.

The Building being set out thus.

The Front or Surface of it was proportioned in euery respect like a Temple, being dedicated to *Ianus*, as by this inscription ouer the *Ianus* head may appeare.

*Iano Quadrifronti
Sacrum.*

The height of the whole Aedifice, from the grownd line to the top, was 57. foote, the full bredth of it 18. foote: the thicknes of the Passage 12.

The personages that were in this Temple, are these.

1. The principall person, *Peace*.
2. By her stood, *Wealth*.
3. Beneath the feet of *Peace*, lay *Mars* (War) groueling.
4. And vpon her right hand (but with some little descent) was seated *Quiet*, the first hand-maid of *Peace*.
5. Shee had lying at her feete, *Tumult*.
6. On the other side was the seconde hand-mayd, *Libertie*, at whose feete lay a Catte.
7. This person trod vpon *Seruitude*.
8. The third handmaid was *Safety*.
9. Beneath her was *Danger*.
10. The fourth attendant was *Fælicitie*:
11. At her feete, *Vnhappines*.

Within the Temple was an Altar, to which, vpon the approch of the King, a *Flamin* appeares, and to him, the former *Genius* of the Citie.

The effect of whose speech was, that whereas the *Flamin* came to performe rites there, in hônour of one *Anna* a goddesse of the

1507 *Quadrifronti*] *Quadri fronti* Q 1-2; *Quadri-fronti* Q 3

Romaines, the *Genius* vowes, that none shall doe Sacrifice there, but himselfe, the offring that he makes being, the Heart of the Citie, &c.

And thus haue wee (lowely and aloofe) followed our Soueraigne through the seauen Triumphal gates of this his Court Royall, which name, as *London* receiued at the rysing of the *Sunne*; so now at his going from her (euen in a moment) She lost that honour: And being (like an Actor on a Stage) stript out of her borrowed Maiestie, she resignes her former shape and title of Citie; nor is it quite lost, considering it went along with him, to whom it is due. For such Vertue is begotten in Princes, that their verie presence hath power to turne a Village to a Citie, and to make a Citie appeare great as a Kingdome. Behold how glorious a Flower, Happinesse is, but how fading. The Minutes (that lackey at the heeles of *Time*) run not faster away then do our ioyes. What tongue could haue exprest the raptures on which the soule of the Citie was carried beyond it selfe, for the space of manie houres? What wealth could haue allurde her to haue closde her eies, at the comming of her King, and yet See, her Bridegrome is but stept from her, and in a Minute (nay in shorter time, then a thought can be borne) is she made a Widdow. All her consolation being now, to repeate ouer by roate those Honors, which lately she had perfectly by hart: And to tell of those ioyes, which but euen now, shee reallie behelde; yet thus of her absent, beloued, do I heare her gladly and heartily speaking.

> *In freta dum Fluvii Current: dum montibus vmbræ,*
> Virg. *Lustrabunt Conuexa, Polus dum sidera pascit,*
> *Semper Honos, Nomenque tuum, Laudesque manebunt.*

The Pageant in the Strond.

The Citie of *Westminster* and Dutchy of *Lancaster,* perceiuing what preparation their neighbor citie made to entertain her Soueraigne; though in greatnes they could not match her, yet in greatnes of Loue and Duetie, they gaue testimonie, that both were equall. And in token they were so, hands and hearts went together: and in the Strond, erected vp a Monument of their affection.

The Inuention was a Rayne-bowe, the Moone, Sunne, and the seauen Starres, called the *Pleiades,* being aduaunced betweene two

Pyramides: *Electra* (one of those seauen hanging in the aire, in figure of a Comet) was the speaker, her words carrying this effect.

That as his Maiestie had left the Citie of *London*, happy, by deliuering it from the noyse of tumult: so he would crowne this place with the like ioyes; which being done, shee reckons vp a number of blessings, that will follow vpon it.

The worke of this was thought vpon, begun and made perfect in twelue daies.

As touching those fiue which the Citie builded, the *Arbor* in Cheap-side, and the Temple of *Ianus*, at Temple-bar, were both of them begun and finisht in sixe weekes. The rest were taken in hande, first in March last, after his Maiestie was proclaymed, vpon which, at that time, they wrought till a Moneth after Saint *Iames* his day following, and then gaue ouer by reason of the sicknes: At this second setting vpon them, six weekes more were spent.

The Citie elected sixteene Comitties, to whom the Mannaging of the whole busines was absolutely referred: of which number, foure were Aldermen, the other graue Commoners.

There were also Committies appoynted as Ouerseers, and Serueyors of the workes.

Artificum Operariumque in hoc tam
celebri apparatu, summa.

The Citie imployed in the Framing, building, and setting vp of their fiue *Arches*, these officers and worke-men.

A Clarke that attended on the Committies.
Two officers that gaue Summons for their meetings. &c.
A clarke of the Workes.
Two master-Carpenters.
Painters.
Of which number, those that gaue the maine direction, and vndertooke for the whole busines, were only these seauen.

1588 summa.] Q2(s); *in line below* Q1 *adds a second* summa *omitted by* Q2
1596 number] Q2(s); nnmber Q1

{ William Friselfield.
George Mosse.
Iohn Knight.
Paul Isacson.
Samuell Goodrick.
Richard Wood.
George Heron. }

  Caruers.   24

Ouer whom, *Stephen Harrison* Ioyner was appoynted chiefe; who was the sole Inuentor of the Architecture, and from whom all directions, for so much as belonged to Caruing, Ioyning, Molding, and all other worke in those fiue Pageants of the Citie (Paynting excepted) were set downe.

Ioyners.	80
Carpenters.	60
Turners.	6
Laborers to them.	6
Sawyers.	12
Laborers during all the time, and for the day of the Triumph.	70

Besides these, there were other Artificers, As:
Plommers, Smythes, Molders.

To the Reader.

Reader, you must vnderstand, that a regard, being had that his Maiestie should not be wearied with teadious speeches: A great part of those which are in this Booke set downe, were left vnspoken: So that thou doest here receiue them as they should haue bene deliuered, not as they were. Some errours wander vp and downe in these sheetes, vnder the Printers warrant: which notwithstanding may by thy Authoritie be brought in, and receiue their due Correction. [5 errata.] Other faults pardon, these I thinke are the grosest.

FINIS.

1611 Ioyners.] Q2(s); ~ ₐ Q1 1621–1629 To the Reader....] Q1; *om.* Q2

TEXTUAL NOTES

599 *Celebret*] The Qq abbreviation *Celebr:* cannot be conventionally expanded into any sensible form. A verb is required by the construction in the same mood as *emittat*. Nichols expanded to *celebrum*.

1055 44.] Q1 reads: 'The whole frame of this Somer banqueting house, stood (at the ground line) vpon 4. foote; the *Perpendicular* stretching it selfe to 45.' With the usual omission of all measurements, and the substitution of a dash, the *Arches of Triumph* repeats the crucial phrase, 'stood... vpon — foote'. All other arches have had their width and height provided, though not in such terms, and with the use of 'foot'; but the phrase 'stood vpon' has been literally applied at lines 541–542: 'At the elbowes of this vpper Square, stood vpon the foure corners of a great *Pedestall*, foure *Pyramides*....' If this clear usage were applied to the '4. foote' of line 1055, the only way in which that could make sense would be to suppose that Dekker was stating the arch, with its central gate and posterns, had four contacts with the ground. The use of the conventional 'ground line' and the immediate provision in parallel of the vertical height, however, lead to the view that what is intended is in fact the horizontal measurement. When the proportions of the arch are worked out according to the scale of the *Arches* engraving, one sees that the width is 44 feet. Thus it would seem that we have in Q1 a simple misprint of '4.' for '44.', which has been misunderstood and sophisticated in Q2 by changing 'foote' to 'feete'.

1205 Had still hee staide!] The Q1 text reads, 'Here staide had still!', and the errata list demands, 'For, *Here stayd*, Had still. But here *Had* list not tary. Read for euery *Had*, hee.' This was misinterpreted by the Q2 compositor, who altered to 'Heere staide hee still!'

PRESS-VARIANTS IN Q1 (1604)

[Copies collated: BM¹ (British Museum C.34.c.23), BM² (Ashley 612), Bodl (Bodleian Mal. 602[1]), Dyce (Victoria and Albert), CLUC (W. A. Clark), CSmH (Huntington), CtY (Yale), DFo (Folger), DLC (Congress), ICN (Newberry), IU (Illinois), MB (Boston Public), MH (Harvard), NN (New York Public), NNP (Morgan), TxU (Texas).]

SHEET B (*inner forme*)

Corrected: BM¹, Bodl, CSmH, DLC, MH, NN, TxU.
Uncorrected: BM², Dyce, CLUC, CtY, DFo, ICN, IU, MB, NNP.

Sig. B1ᵛ.
  109 *frighted*] *fraighted*

Sig. B2.
  127 *Ioyes,*] *Ioyes*
  128 *world,*] *world*
  133 *Dilexere*] *Delexere*

Sig. B3ᵛ.
  198 whose] whom,

Sig. B4.
  216 *Grices*] Gate

SHEET C (*outer forme*)

Corrected: IU, NNP.
Uncorrected: BM¹⁻², Bodl, Dyce, CLUC, CSmH, CtY, DFo, DLC, ICN, MB, MH, NN, TxU.

Sig. C3.
  339 *Pilafters*] *Pelafters*
  340 *Pedeftall*] *Padeftall*

SHEET H (*outer forme*)

1st stage corrected: BM¹, Dyce, CLUC, DFo, ICN, MB, MH, NN, TxU.
Uncorrected: BM², NNP.

Sig. H1.
  1233 one of] one

Sig. H2ᵛ.
  1268 *fcholae*] *fchola*
  1273 *Annam,*] *Annam*
  1273 *ftirpis*] *ftripis*

Sig. H3.
1339 being] beeing
1349 building] bnilding
1357 being] beeing
      2nd stage corrected: CtY
Sig. H2ᵛ.
1266 *aſcribere,*] *aſcribere.*
Sig. H3.
1347 poſternes riz vp] poſternes. *Viz.* Vp
1353 neede] minde
     3rd stage corrected: Bodl, CSmH, DLC, IU
Sig. H2ᵛ.
1273 *reliquamque*] *relinquamque*
1274 *ſumma*] *ſummam*

SHEET H (*inner forme*)

  1st stage corrected: DFo, NN.
  Uncorrected: BM¹⁻², Dyce, ICN, MB, MH, NNP.
Sig. H1ᵛ.
1245 *primaria*] *prima via*
1247 *demortui*] *de mortui*
1247 *ſpei*] *ſpe*
Sig. H2.
1252 *ſummae*] *ſumma*
  2nd stage corrected: Bodl, CLUC, CSmH, CtY, DLC, IU, TxU.
Sig. H4.
1402 *virgo] virgo
1402 Aſtræa [*right margin*]] *left margin*
1402 Saturnia] Satarnia

EMENDATIONS OF ACCIDENTALS

32 a long] along Q 1–3
34 Maiesties] *Maiesties* Q 1–3
40, 46, 136 Maiestie] *Maiestie* Q 1–3
71 Female; Antique,] ~, ~ ; Q 1–3
73 (Inter-wouen...Tree)] ₍ ~ ... ~ (Q 1–3
85 *Delphick*-fire] hyphen doubtful
115 *Andrew.*] Q 2; ~ ₍ Q 1
116 *Englands* I.] Q 3; ~ ~ ₍ Q 1–2
127 Ioyes₍] Q 1 (u); ~ , Q 1 (c)
128 world₍] Q 1 (u); ~ , Q 1 (c)
168 fore-|heads] fore-heads Q 1
188 Workhouse] Work-|house Q 1
210 (for] ₍ ~ Q 1–3 [Q 2 (offering]
315 square] Square Q 1–3
337 ó] Q 3; ô Q 1–2
341 life,] Q 1 cw; ~ ₍ Q 1 text
566 *Columnes*;] ~ , Q 1–3
612 gold,] ~ . Q 1, 3; ~ : Q 2
617 word,] ~ . Q 1, 3; ~ : Q 2
642 *Numine*₍] ~ , Q 1–3
709 Saint] *S.* Q 1–3
763 *Olfactus,* Smelling.] Q 3; ~ . ~ ₍ Q 1–2
823 *Houres*] Q 2; houres Q 1
832 *Sences*] Q 2; sences Q 1
861 Sight] sight Q 1–3
862 Taste like] Q 3; Tastelike Q 1–2
878–9 Instrument,)] ~ , ₍ Q 1–3
890 Binde] binde Q 1–3
909 Or] Q 2; or Q 1
923 foote,)] Q 2; ~ , ₍ Q 1
929 Hall] Q 2; Hãll Q 1
935 (though...bitterly)] Q 2; ₍ ~ ... ~ ₍ Q 1
950 *King*] Q 2; King Q 1
980 *Syluanes,*] Q 2; ~ . Q 1
994 acquaintance] Q 2; acquaintauce Q 1

1000 *Plentie*)] Q 2; ~ , Q 1
1018 hers,] Q 2; ~ ₍ Q 1
1041 12.:] ~ . ₍ Q 1–3
1067 inter-wouen] inter-|wouen Q 1
1069 *Caducæus*] *Caducæns* Q 1–3
1073 *Euporia*] Q 3; *Euporie* Q 1–2
1077 *Abundance.*] ~ , Q 1–3
1101 *Vrania*] *Vranio* Q 1–3
1107 *Arithmeticke.*] Q 2; ~ ₍ Q 1
1125 sing,] ~ . Q 1–3
1175 Subiects,] ~ ₍ Q 1–3
1239 *tædium*] *taedium*
1240 *Ædificium*] Q 3; *Ædificium* Q 1–2
1251 *ratione*₍] ~ , Q 1–3
1252 *summæ*] *summae* Q 1 (c) *summa* Q 1 (u)
1254 *præit,*] ~ ₍ Q 1–3
1268 *scholæ*] *scholae* Q 1 (c); *schola* Q 1 (u)
1275 *confeceritis*] Q 3; *coufeceritis* Q 1
1276 *consequamini*] Q 3; *cousequamini* Q 1
1320 priuatelie)] ~ ₍ Q 2
1325 vertuous,)] ~ , ₍ Q 2
1336 Almighty,] ~ . Q 2
1345 ground-|line] ground-line Q 1
1411 States] states Q 1–3
1426 Waternot] Q 3; Waternot Q 1–2
1446 blest,] ~ ₍ Q 1–3
1470 *Thomas*] Tho. Q 1–3
1484 now,] ~ ₍ Q 1–3
1487 deere.] Q 3; ~ ₍ Q 1–2
1516 3.] Q 3; ~ , Q 1–2
1520 *Libertie,*] ~ ₍ Q 1–3
1524 *Danger.*] Q 3; ~ , Q 1–2
1525 10.] Q 3; ~ ₍ Q 1–2
1525 was₍] Q 3; ~ , Q 1–2
1526 11.] Q 3; ~ ₍ Q 1–2
1585 Ouerseers] Ouer-|seers Q 1
1596 vnder-|tooke] vndertooke Q 1

HISTORICAL COLLATION OF EARLY EDITIONS

31 *George,*] *George,* & Q2
32 a long] along Q1–3
32 countenances] countenance Q2
36 Brestes₍ₐ₎] Breste: Q3
47 *Inter fictos*] *Interfictos* Q3
64 For] *om.* Q2
65 would] will Q3
84 is] in Q2
90 lyes!] ~ . Q2
104 bou't] 'bout Q2
133 *Dilexere*] *Delexere* Q1(u)–2
166 plotted] blotted Q3
177 wakened] weakned Q3
192 aboue] about Q2
195 Bannerets] Banners Q2
198 whose₍ₐ₎] whom, Q1(u)–2
202 speake] spake Q2
216 on] one Q1–3
216 *Grices*] *Gate* Q1(u)–2
260 vnder] after Q3
288 *Gracious street.*] *om.* Q3
304 out] *om.* Q2
320 *otia fecit*] *otiafecit* Q3
325 his] her Q2
339 roofe] roote Q1–3
340 erected] directed Q1, 3
409 speach.] speach in Latine. Q2
420–36 The Italians....] *om.* Q1, 3
491 in her] *om.* her Q3
496 *Vtroque*] *Viroque* Q3
502 pursude] sude Q3
581–83 QVOD...] Q2 *sets inscription in small italic lowercase to save space*
618 *et*] *at* Q1, 3
630 *onus*] *vnus* Q1, 3
632 *Ardua res*] *Arduares* Q1
634 *hominis*] *homines* Q1–3
635 *temperat*] *temperet* Q1–2
638 *ille*] *illa* Q1–3
656 *Quos fouit*] *Quosfouit* Q1–2
659 *diù Panthaici*] *Deum Panthaeci* Q1; *Diù Panthaici* Q2; *Deus Panthaeci* Q3
660 *Innumeros*] *Iunumeros* Q1, 3
661 *tui*] *tua* Q1, 3
663–704 Which Verses....] *om.* Q1, 3
675 holds] hold Q2
722 *Soper lane.*] *om.* Q3
770 *Arete*] *Arate* Q1, 3
822 Dries] Drie Q1–3
829 *Fame*] *Fama* Q3
866 vp] *om.* Q1–3
885, 892 is't] it's Q3
916–917 cleare, straight] cleare strength Q1 (*text*), 3
921 that during] aluring Q1 (*text*), 3; during Q2
924 tis] it is Q3
927 heere] there Q2
954 Conquerour] Conquerours Q2
959–960 3. Cuppes....] *om.* Q1, 3
972–973 The Pageant....] *om.* Q1, 3
1025 in] *om.* Q2
1027 *Syluans*] *Syluanus* Q1, 3
1029 Cornets] Comets Q2
1034 the dittie] *om.* the Q3
1041 18....12.] 16....10. Q1, 3
1047 termes] frames Q1, 3
1048 25.] 20. Q1, 3
1055 44.] 4. Q1–3
1055 foote] feete Q2
1069 *Caducæus*] *Caducæns* Q1–3
1074 on] of Q1, 3

HISTORICAL COLLATION OF EARLY EDITIONS

1127 A] *om.* Q1, 3
1194 Hee] had Q1 *(text)*, 3
1198 *Chor.*] *om.* Q1, 3
1205 Had still hee staide] Here staide had still Q1 *(text)*, 3; Heere staide hee still Q2
1207, 1208 hee] had Q1 *(text)*, 3
1210 equally] equall Q1, 3
1235–1276 Oratio....] *om.* Q2
1244 *dotatum*] *dodatum* Q3
1245 *primariæ*] *prima via* Q1(u); *primaria* Q1(c)–3
1247 *de mortui*] *demortui* Q1(c)–Q2
1247 *spe*] *spei* Q1(c)–2; *om.* Q3
1256 *Regiam*] *Regiæ* Q3
1277–1336 THE ORATION....] *om.* Q1, 3
1311 *didicit*] *dedicit* Q2, *om.* Q1, 3
1362 *Arete*] *Arate* Q1–3
1395 Engine] Eronie Q1, 3
1398–1399 Nobleman...Ploughman] Noblemen...Ploughmen Q3
1402 *et*] *at* Q1, 3
1404 praters] parts Q1, 3
1431 thy] by Q3
1439 property] properties Q3
1470 *Thomas*] Tho. Q1–2; *T.* Q3
1475 of] of the Q3
1493 Which] With Q1–3
1500 and Princely] *om.* Q3
1531 there] *om.* Q3
1532 shall] should Q3
1548 closde] close Q3
1555 *In freta*] *Infreta* Q2
1555 *vmbræ*] *vnbræ* Q2
1556 *pascit*] *pascet* Q3
1588 summa.] summa. | summa. Q1
1621–1629 To the Reader....] *om.* Q2–3

Substantive Variants in Harrison's *Arches of Triumph* (1604)

417 *Rex nobilissime, salue,*] *om.*
422 your] thy
423 your...your] thy...thy
425 your] thy
430 you did] thou didst
430 your] thine
431 you said, that] thou saydst
436 Thus wee cry all,] *om.*
666 how] *om.*
667 thunders] thunder
676 teaches] teacheth
687 lauishly] *om.*
692 of them] then
697 you] thee
698 your] thy
698 then] *om.*
700 Grand-fathers...so many] *om.*
820 in] is
822 Dries] Drie Q1–3; Dries *Arches*
866 vp] *om.* Q1–3; vp *Arches*
869 doest] doth
981 heere, not] not heere
983–996 to deliuer...whilst all] *om.*
996 heere] *om.*
998–999 for number...infinite] *om.*
1011 so now] now so
1025 in] *om.*
1424 moude] moue
1432 vertue] Vertues
1442 figurde all in] which here figure

309

VVEST-VVARD
HOE.

As it hath beene diuers times Acted
by the Children of Paules.

Written by Tho: Decker, and
Iohn Webster.

Printed at London, and to be sold by Iohn Hodgets
dwelling in Paules Churchyard.
1 6 0 7

TEXTUAL INTRODUCTION

WESTWARD HO (Greg, *Bibliography*, no. 257) was entered in the Stationers' Register by Henry Rockett on 2 March 1605 as 'A comodie called westward Hoe presented by the Children of Paules', with the additional notation 'provided yt he get further aucthoritie before yt be printed'. This entry was subsequently crossed out, and 'Vacat' added in the margin. The provisional nature of the entry very likely indicates either that the proprietors had got wind of Rockett's publication plans and had protested, or else that the warden suspected the company would object vigorously to publication. In either case, the manuscript brought to be registered could not have come from the theatre. The further authority required seems to mean only that something more than the warden's hand was necessary in view of the evidence that the copy had not been released by the Children's company. It is unlikely that anything in the play itself was thought to call for approval by an official censor.[1] Hence unless the entry is all we have left of a 'bad quarto' nipped in the bud (and there is no reason to suppose so), Dekker himself was the natural person to have sold the manuscript to Rockett.

The view that the provisional entry resulted from the warden's doubts as to the company's approval is furthered by the vacating of the entry, and also by the fact that on the break-up of the Children's company in 1607, *Westward Ho* was one of the various Children's plays which were immediately placed in print. Since Rockett had failed to establish a copyright, the field was clear; and when the first and only quarto appeared in 1607, without second entry, the seller was listed in the imprint as John Hodgetts. Sir Walter Greg

---

[1] The possibility exists, of course, that the incident of the Earl could have been suspected as reflecting on some prominent nobleman. If Chambers (*Elizabethan Stage*, III, 254–255) is right that the trouble over *Eastward Ho* arose from its publication, and not from its acting, the provisional entry could have resulted from a distrust of plays emanating from the Children. But the entry for *Westward Ho* may have preceded the production of *Eastward Ho*; and since the play was harmless Rockett should not have been forced to cancel his entry if this were the reason. The theatrical company's authorization seems to have been the desideratum.

notices the title-page device as William Jaggard's and speculates that Jaggard may have been the actual publisher.

The dissolution of the Children's company did not release the actual play-book for printing but instead only gave the opportunity for what was very likely the original 'foul papers' manuscript to be sent to press. We cannot know whether Rockett had earlier sold his rights in the manuscript, such as they were and amounting only to physical possession, or whether when his copyright was refused he returned the manuscript to Dekker, who in 1607 made a second transaction. All that is evident is that the printed quarto was set from 'foul papers', presumably without transcriptional link. The chief evidence rests on the confusion surrounding Mistress Tenterhook's Christian name, in combination with a high diversity of forms in the speech-prefixes for certain characters.

For example, in I.ii the stage-direction reads, '*Enter Master Tenterhooke, his Wife,...*', the speech-heading for Mistress Tenterhook is *Moll*, and she is various times addressed as *Moll* by her husband and by Monopoly. Again, in III.i her speech-prefix is *Mist. Tent.*, but she is twice addressed as *Moll* in spite of the fact that in the intervening scene, II.iii, she has been *Clare* in stage-direction and speech-prefixes. After III.i she is consistently addressed as *Clare* and is so named in stage-directions and speech-headings. Mistress Justiniano, who in the stage-direction in I.i is *Marchants Wife*, with the speech-prefix *Ma. Wife*, becomes *Mistress Justiniano* in stage-directions and speech-headings beginning with II.ii; and in IV.ii and V.iv is called *Moll* by her husband. It seems evident that the early assignment of *Moll* to Clare Tenterhook is an unrevised error.

The names of the other wives are not confused, but their speech-headings vary. In I.ii Mistress Honeysuckle is *Hony.*, but she is named *Judith* in the stage-direction in II.i and is *Iud.* in the speech-prefixes, as also in II.iii, V.i, V.iv, though *Mist. Hony.* in III.iv. The same sequence is followed for Mistress Wafer, who is *Wafer* in speech-headings in I.ii and *Mistress Wafer* in the stage-direction, *Mist. Waf.* in III.iii and III.iv, but *Mab.* in II.iii, V.i, and V.iv. Justiniano, though disguised as Parenthesis, is given the speech-prefix *Iust.* in II.i, III.iii, IV.i, but *Par.* in II.iii, IV.ii, and V.iv.

We are justified in assuming that these irregularities faithfully reflect the manuscript copy, especially in view of the fact that when a change in compositors was made at the beginning of sig. H1, the very end of V.i, the new workman continued in V.iv the same speech-prefixes found earlier in V.i. Such diverse prefixes are customarily normalized in prompt copy, and it is possible that an alert book-keeper would correct the anomaly of speech-headings and address by which Mistress Tenterhook was first given the name later assigned to Mistress Justiniano.

The pattern of the running-titles indicates the probability that the quarto was printed on two presses and thus was typeset by two compositors. The skeleton-forme which imposed the outer forme of sheet B was used again for inner C, inner E, and outer G. A second skeleton, which had imposed outer A, was employed for inner B, inner and outer D, and inner G. A third skeleton, first appearing in outer C, also imposed outer E and inner and outer F. For sheet H a fourth skeleton-forme was constructed, which printed both formes; and for half-sheet I a fifth skeleton appears. The pattern of the skeleton-formes would fit presswork in which one press perfected for the other, the working press perhaps perfecting its own sheets, as in sheets D and F, if the other press were transferred to other printing. Slight changes in the printer's measure point to more than one compositor in sheets A–G.

Unquestionably a different compositor and press entered to set and print sheet H and half-sheet I. The measure is narrower, and the contraction for 'them', which has invariably been *'em*, becomes with one exception *'hem*. Such a change in compositors and the entrance of another press toward the end of a book is often the result of an attempt to speed completion of the work; but if this were the case with *Westward Ho* some very expert casting-off of copy was managed, for the new compositor started sig. H1 recto with the second word of a sentence, 'I | ha not beene...' (V.i.246–247). One would suppose that in marking-off copy the first word 'I' would have been included with the rest of the sentence. Although this 'I' is set rather close at the foot of sig. G4^v, there is no sign on this page, or earlier, of condensation or of spacing-out; hence it is more plausible to take it that the entrance of a different compositor on sig. H1 corresponded with the resumption of printing after an interruption than it is to assume that a third press (not known to be owned by Jaggard) was introduced to speed the later sheets.

There are various carelessnesses in the printing, and some misreading of copy, but on the whole—considering that the copy was almost certainly Dekker's 'foul papers', with whatever small part that Webster contributed—the typesetting was reasonably correct. Two formes, outer A and inner E, were extensively corrected in press, and outer F much less so. The remaining formes in which variants have been observed, inner D, outer E, and outer I have only one or two press-alterations apiece, and these may perhaps represent a second round of proof-reading, not the original.[1] Whatever the case for the other formes, there can be little question that the corrector of outer forme A was not the author but instead the printing-house reader. One would suspect this from the normalization of the eccentric spelling 'Coucouldes' to 'Cuckoldes' on sig. A3 recto (I.i.89), but demonstration comes in the next line with the alteration of 'wist' to 'means'. The passage read in the uncorrected state, 'Many are honest, either because they haue not wist, or because they haue not opportunity to be dishonest....' Unable to degarble 'wist', the corrector guessed at 'means', which in his view made tolerable sense even though it destroys the point of the continuation, '...and this Italian Your Husbands Countryman, holdes it impossible any of their Ladies should be excellent witty, and not make the vttermost vse of their beauty...'.

There is some possibility that inner forme E containing a larger number of substantive alterations, including the alteration of the error 'induce' on sig. E1ᵛ (III.iii.12) to 'in dure' with the characteristic Dekker division, was authoritatively overseen; but proofreader's reference to copy may explain the variants as well. For the other formes the evidence is quite negative. No errors are corrected which could not have been caught by an alert printing-house reader. Possibly not all the formes were read in press, although the copies collated cannot be assumed to exhaust all possible variants; yet

[1] Since outer E is the alternate forme to heavily corrected inner E, in the normal printing process it should have been proof-read before machining. But the use of two presses could have changed this procedure.

TEXTUAL INTRODUCTION

where there is evidence for correction we see a rather better than average care for picking up compositorial errors as well as for imposing 'printing-house style' on the pointing. Perhaps owing to the nature of the copy, a few of the compositorial misreadings were serious. The nature of the copy may possibly also be to blame for the fact that much of the verse is mislined on the rare occasions when it appears. I do not follow Sir Walter Greg in the theory that the final song represents that sung by Birdlime in V.iii. I take it, instead, that the plea for applause makes this an exit or epilogue song; hence the direction *Exeunt* after the final prose text may represent either the compositor's intervention or else a legitimate direction to clear the stage before the re-entry of the singers.

Except for the Pearson reprint of 1873, the play has been edited previously only by the Rev. Alexander Dyce in *The Works of John Webster* (1st ed. 1830), for which I have used the 1859 revised edition; and by William Hazlitt, *The Dramatic Works of John Webster* (1st ed. 1857). Except for accidentals, emendations adopted from these editors are recorded. A photographic facsimile of a British Museum copy (C.12.f.3[4]) was issued in 1914 by J. S. Farmer for Tudor Facsimile Texts.

The present text is based on a collation of the following seventeen copies, substantially all those which have been recorded: British Museum copy 1 (644.b.26), copy 2 (C.12.f.3[4]), and copy 3 (Ashley 614); Bodleian copy 1 (Mal. 235[5]), and copy 2 (Mal. 186[5]; Dyce Collection in Victoria and Albert Museum; Eton College; Worcester College, Oxford (imperfect: wanting A1–B1); Boston Public Library; Chapin Library of Williams College; University of Chicago (imperfect: wanting A1); Folger Shakespeare Library; Henry E. Huntington Library; Harvard University; New York Public Library; University of Texas; and Yale University.

[PERSONS

EARL
JUSTINIANO, an Italian Merchant
HONEYSUCKLE ⎫
TENTERHOOK ⎬ Citizens
WAFER ⎭
SIR GOSLING GLOW-WORM
FRANK MONOPOLY, nephew to the Earl
LINSTOCK
CAPTAIN WHIRLPOOL
AMBUSH, a sergeant
CLUTCH, his yeoman
BONIFACE, prentice to Honeysuckle
PHILIP, servant to Tenterhook
Boy, prentice to Wafer
HANS, a drawer
Chamberlain
Tailor
Scrivener
Servants to the Earl
Fiddlers

MISTRESS JUSTINIANO
MISTRESS JUDITH HONEYSUCKLE
MISTRESS CLARE TENTERHOOK
MISTRESS MABEL WAFER
BIRDLIME, a bawd
LUCE, a whore
CHRISTIAN, servant to Birdlime]

West-ward Hoe

SCÆNE LONDON,

ACTUS PRIMUS, SCÆNA PRIMA.

Enter Mistris Birdlime *and Taylour.*

Bird. Stay Taylour, This is the House, pray thee looke the gowne be not rufled: as for the Iewels and Pretious Stones, I know where to finde them ready presently. Shee that must weare this gowne if she wil receiue it, is Maister *Iustinianos* wife (the *Italian* Marchant): my good old Lord and Maister, that hath beene a Tylter this twenty yeere, hath sent it. Mum Taylor, you are a kinde of Bawd. Taylor, if this Gentlewomans Husband should chaunce to bee in the way now, you shall tell him that I keepe a Hot-house in Gunpowder Ally (neere crouched Fryers) and that I haue brought home his wiues foule Linnen, and to colour my knauery the better, I haue heere three or foure kindes of complexion, which I will make shewe of to sell vnto her: the young Gentlewoman hath a good Citty wit, I can tell you, shee hath red in the Italian Courtyer, that it is a speciall ornament to gentlewomen to haue skill in painting.

Tay. Is my Lord acquainted with her?

Bird. O, I.

Tay. Faith Mistris *Birdlime* I doe not commend my Lordes choyce so well: now me thinkes he were better to set vp a Dairy, and to keepe halfe a score of lusty wholesome honest Countrey Wenches.

Bird. Honest Countrey Wenches, in what hundred shall a man find two of that simple vertue?

Tay. Or to loue some Lady, there were equality and coherence.

Bird. Taylor, you talk like an asse, I tel thee ther is equality inough betweene a Lady and a Citty dame, if their haire be but of a colour: name you any one thing that your cittizens wife coms short of to your Lady. They haue as pure Linnen, as choyce painting, loue greene Geese in spring, Mallard and Teale in the fall, and Woodcocke

in winter. Your Cittizens wife learnes nothing but fopperies of
your Ladie, but your Lady or Iustice-a-peace Madam, carries high
wit from the Citty, namely, to receiue all and pay all: to awe their
Husbands, to check their Husbands, to controule their husbands;
nay, they haue a tricke ont to be sick for a new gowne, or a Car-
canet, or a Diamond, or so: and I wis this is better wit, then to
learne how to weare a Scotch Farthingale: nay more.

Enter Prentise.

Heere comes one of the seruants: you remember Taylor that I am
deafe: obserue that.
Tay. I thou art in that like one of our young Gulles, that will not
vnderstand any wrong is done him, because hee dares not answer it.
Bird. By your leaue Batcheller: is the gentlewoman your Mistris
stirring?
Prent. Yes she is moouing.
Bird. What sayes he?
Tay. Shee is vp.
Bird. Wheres the Gentleman your Maister, pray you?
Prent. Wher many women desire to haue their husbands, abroad.
Bird. I am very thicke of hearing.
Prent. Why abroad? you smell of the Bawd.
Bird. I pray you tell her heres an olde Gentlewoman would speake
with her.
Prent. So. [*Exit.*]
Tay. What, will you be deafe to the gentlewoman when shee
comes to?
Bird. O no, shees acquainted well inough with my knauery.

Enter [*Mistress* Iustiniano] *the Marchants Wife.*

She comes.
How do you sweet Ladie?
Mist. Iust. Lady?
Bird. By Gods me I hope to call you Lady eare you dye, what
mistris do you sleepe well on nights.

34 wis] Q(c); wist Q(u)   53 to] *i.e.,* too
57 *Mist. Iust.*] Q *speech prefixes in this scene are forms of* Ma. Wife

320

Mist. Iust. Sleepe, I as quietly as a Clyent hauing great businesse with Lawyers.

Bird. Come, I am come to you about the old suit: my good Lord and maister hath sent you a veluet gowne heare: doe you like the colour? three pile, a pretty fantasticall trimming, I would God you would say it by my troth. I dreamt last night, you lookt so prettily, so sweetly, me thought so like the wisest Lady of them al, in a veluet gowne.

Mist. Iust. Whats the forepart?

Bird. A very pretty stuffe, I know not the name of your forepart, but tis of a haire colour.

Mist. Iust. That it was my hard fortune, beeing so well brought vp, hauing so great a portion to my marriage, to match so vnluckily? Why my husband and his whole credit is not worth my apparell, well, I shall vndergoe a strange report in leauing my husband.

Bird. Tush, if you respect your credit, neuer thinke of that, for beauty couets rich apparell, choyce dyet, excellent Physicke, no German Clock nor Mathematicall Ingin whatsoeuer requires so much reparation as a womans face, and what meanes hath your Husband to allow sweet Docter *Glister-pipe*, his pention. I haue heard that you haue threescore Smocks, that cost three poundes a Smocke, will these smockes euer hold out with your husband? no, your linnen and your apparell must turne ouer a new leafe I can tell you.

Tay. O admirable Bawd? O excellent *Birdlime*?

Bird. I haue heard he loued you before you were married intyrely, what of that? I haue euer found it most true in myne owne experyence, that they which are most violent dotards before their marryage are most voluntary Coucouldes after. Many are honest, either because they haue not wit, or because they haue not opportunity to be dishonest, and this Italian your Husbands Countryman, holdes it impossible any of their Ladies should be excellent witty, and not make the vttermost vse of their beauty, will you be a foole then?

*78 nor] Q(c); no Q(u)   83 leafe] Q(c); lease Q(u)
*90 wit] Dyce; wist Q(u); means Q(c)

Mist. Iust. Thou do'st perswade me to Ill, very well.
Bird. You are nice and peeuish, how long will you holde out thinke you? not so long as *Ostend*.

Enter Iustiniano *the Marchant.*

Passion of me, your husband? Remember that I am deafe, and that I come to sell you complexion: truely Mistris I will deale very reasonably with you.
Iust. What are you? Say ye?
Bird. I forsooth.
Iust. What my most happy wife?
Mist. Iust. Why your Iealiousie?
Iust. Iealiousie: in faith I do not feare to loose
That I haue lost already: What are you?
Bird. Please your good worship I am a poor Gentlewoman, that cast away my selfe vppon an vnthrifty Captaine, that liues now in *Ireland*, I am faine to picke out a poore liuing with selling complexion, to keepe the frailty (as they say) honest.
Iust. Whats he? complexion to? you are a bawd.
Bird. I thanke your good worship for it.
Iust. Do not I know these tricks,
That which thou makest a colour for thy sinne,
Hath beene thy first vndoing? painting, painting.
Bird. I haue of all sorts forsooth? Heere is the burned powder of a Hogs Iaw-bone, to be laide with the Oyle of white Poppy, an excellent *Fucus* to kill Morphew, weede out Freckles, and a most excellent ground-worke for painting; Heere is *Ginimony* likewise burnt, and puluerized, to be mingled with the iuyce of Lymmons, sublimate Mercury, and two spoonefuls of the flowers of Brimstone, a most excellent receite to cure the flushing in the face.
Iust. Doe you heare, if you haue any businesse to dispatch with that deafe goodnesse there, pray you take leaue: opportunity, that which most of you long for (though you neuer bee with Child) opportunity? Ile find some idle businesse in the mean time, I wil, I will in truth, you shall not neede feare me, or you may speake French, most of your kinds can vnderstand French: god buy you.
Being certaine thou art false: sleepe, sleepe my braine,

For doubt was onely that, which fed my paine. *Exit* Iustiniano.
Mist. Iust. You see what a hel I liue in, I am resolu'd to leaue him.
Bird. O the most fortunat Gentlewoman, that will be so wise, and so, so prouident, the *Caroche* shall come.
Mist. Iust. At what houre?
Bird. Iust when women and vintners are a cuniuring: at midnight. O the entertainment my Lord will make you, sweet Wines, lusty dyet, perfumed linnen, soft beds, O most fortunat Gentlewoman. [*Exeunt* Birdlime *and* Taylor.]

Enter Iustiniano.

Iust. Haue you done? haue you dispatch? tis well, and in troth what was the motion?
Mist. Iust. Motion, what motion?
Iust. Motion, why like the motion in law, that staies for a day of hearing, yours for a night of hearing. Come lets not haue Aprill in your eyes I pray you, it shewes a wanton month followes your weeping? Loue a woman for her teares? Let a man loue Oisters for their water, for women though they shoulde weepe licour enough to serue a Dyer, or a Brewer, yet they may bee as stale as Wenches, that trauaile euery second tyde betweene Graues ende, and Billingsgate.
Mist. Iust. This madnesse shewes very well.
Iust. Why looke you, I am wonderous merry, can any man discerne by my face, that I am a Cuckold? I haue known many suspected for men of this misfortune; when they haue walkt thorow the streetes, weare their hats ore their eye-browes, like pollitick penthouses, which commonly make the shop of a Mercer, or a Linnen Draper, as dark as a roome in Bedlam. His cloak shrouding his face, as if he were a Neopolitan that had lost his beard in Aprill, and if he walk through the street, or any other narrow road (as tis rare to meete a Cuckold) hee duckes at the penthouses, like an Antient that dares not flourish at the oath taking of the *Pretor*, for feare of the signe-posts? Wife, wife, do I any of these? Come what newes from his Lordship? has not his Lordships vertue once gone against the haire, and coueted corners.
Mist. Iust. Sir, by my soule I will be plaine with you.

Iust. Except the forehead deere wife, except the forehead.

Mist. Iust. The Gentleman you spake of hath often solicited my loue, and hath receiued from me most chast denials.

Iust. I, I, prouoking resistance, tis as if you come to buy wares in the Citty, bid mony fort, your Mercer, or Gold-smith sayes, truely I cannot take it, lets his customer passe his stall; next, nay perhaps two, or three, but if he finde he is not prone to returne of himselfe, hee cals him backe, and backe, and takes his mony: so you my deere wife, (O the pollicy of women, and Tradsmen: theile bite at any thing.)

Mist. Iust. What would you haue me do? all your plate and most part of your Iewels are at pawne, besides I heare you haue made ouer all your estate to men in the Towne heer? What would you haue me do? would you haue mee turne common sinner, or sell my apparell to my wastcoat and become a Landresse?

Iust. No Landresse deere wife, though your credit would goe farre with Gentlemen for taking vp of Linnen: no Landresse?

Mist. Iust. Come, come, I will speake as my misfortune prompts me, Iealiousie hath vndone many a Cittizen, it hath vndone you, and me. You married me from the seruice of an honorable Lady, and you knew what matches I mought haue had, what woulde you haue me to do? I would I had neuer seene your eies, your eies.

Iust. Very good, very good.

Mist. Iust. Your prodigality, your diceing, your riding abroad, your consorting your selfe with Noble men, your building a summer house hath vndone vs, hath vndoone vs? What would you haue me doe?

Iust. Any thing: I haue sold my House, and the wares int? I am going for *Stoad* next tide, what will you do now wife?

Mist. Iust. Haue you indeed?

Iust. I by this light als one, I haue done as some Cittizens at thirty, and most heires at three and twenty, made all away, why doe you not aske me now what you shall do?

Mist. Iust. I haue no counsell in your voiage, neither shall you haue any in mine.

Iust. To his Lordship: wil you not wife?

Mist. Iust. Euen whether my misfortune leades me.

Iust. Goe, no longer will I make my care thy prison.

Mist. Iust. O my fate; well sir, you shall answere for this sinne which you force mee to; fare you well, let not the world condemne me, if I seeke for mine owne maintenance.

Iust. So, so.

Mist. Iust. Do not send me any letters; do not seeke any reconcilement. By this light Ile receiue none, if you will send mee my apparell so, if not choose, I hope we shall neare meete more.

Exit Marchants Wife.

Iust. So, farewell the acquaintance of all the mad Deuils that haunt Iealiousie, why should a man bee such an asse to play the antick for his wiues appetite? Immagine that I, or any other great man haue on a veluet Night-cap, and put case that this night-cap be to little for my eares or forehead, can any man tell mee where my Night-cap wringes me, except I be such an asse to proclaime it? Well, I do play the foole with my misfortune very handsomly. I am glad that I am certaine of my wiues dishonesty; for a secret strumpet, is like mines prepard to ruine goodly buildings. Farewel my care, I haue told my wife I am going for *Stoad*; thats not my course, for I resolue to take some shape vpon me, and to liue disguised heere in the Citty; they say for one Cuckolde to knowe that his friend is in the like head-ake, and to giue him counsell, is as if there were two partners, the one to bee arrested, the other to baile him: my estate is made ouer to my friends, that doe verily beleeue, I meane to leaue *England*. Haue amongst you Citty dames? You that are indeede the fittest, and most proper persons for a Comedy, nor let the world lay any imputation vpon my disguise, for Court, Citty, and Countrey, are meerely as maskes one to the other, enuied of some, laught at of others, and so to my comicall businesse.

Exit Iustiniano

[ACT I, Scene ii]

Enter Maister Tenterhooke, *his Wife,* Maister *Monopoly, a Scriuener and a Casheire* [Philip *a seruant*].

Tent. Clare.
Mist. Tent. What would hart?
Tent. Wheres my *Casheire*, are the summes right? Are the bonds seald?
Seru. Yea sir.
Tent. Will you haue the bags seald?
Mono. O no sir, I must disburs instantly: we that be Courtyers haue more places to send money to, then the diuell hath to send his spirits: theres a great deale of light gold.
Tent. O sir, twill away in play, and you will stay till to morrow you shall haue it all in new soueraignes.   10
Mono. No, in-troth tis no matter, twill a way in play, let me see the bond? let me see when this mony is to bee paid? the tenth of August. The first day that I must tender this mony, is the first of Dog-daies.
Scriu. I feare twill be hot staying for you in *London* then. [*Aside.*]
Tent. Scriuener, take home the bond with you. [*Exit Scriuener.*] Will you stay to dinner sir? Haue you any Partridge *Clare*?
Mist. Tent. No in-troth hart, but an excellent pickeld Goose, a new seruice: pray you stay.   20
Mono. Sooth I cannot: by this light I am so infinitly, so vnboundably beholding to you?
Tent. Well *Signior*, Ile leaue you; My cloake there?
Mist. Tent. When will you come home hart?
Tent. Introth selfe I know not, a friend of yours and mine hath broke.
Mist. Tent. Who sir?
Tent. Maister *Iustiniano* the Italian.
Mist. Tent. Broke sir.

*1 Clare] Moll Q
2 Mist. Tent.] Q speech prefixes in this scene are forms of Moll.
18, 36, 43 Clare] Moll Q

Tent. Yea sooth, I was offred forty yesterday vpon the Exchange, to assure a hundred.
Mist. Tent. By my troth I am sorry.
Tent. And his wife is gone to the party.
Mist. Tent. Gone to the party? O wicked creature?
Tent. Farewell good maister *Monopoly*, I pre-thee visit mee often.
                                                    Exit Tenterhooke.
Mono. Little *Clare*, send away the fellow?
Mist. Tent. *Phillip, Phillip.*
Seru. Heere forsooth.
Mist. Tent. Go into Bucklers-bury and fetch me two ounces of preserued *Melounes*, looke there be no Tobacco taken in the shoppe when he weighes it.
Seru. I forsooth.
Mono. What doe you eate preserued Melounes for *Clare*?
Mist. Tent. Introth for the shaking of the hart, I haue heere sometime such a shaking, and downwards such a kind of earth-quake (as it were.)
Mono. Doe you heare, let your man carry home my mony to the ordinary, and lay it in my Chamber, but let him not tell my host that it is mony: I owe him but forty pound, and the Rogue is hasty, he will follow me when he thinks I haue mony, and pry into me as Crowes perch vpon Carion, and when he hath found it out, prey upon me as Heraldes do vpon Funerals.   [*Exit Seruant.*].
Mist. Tent. Come, come, you owe much mony in Towne: when you haue forfeited your bond, I shall neare see you more?
Mono. You are a Monky, Ile pay him for's day: Ile see you to morrow to.
Mist. Tent. By my troth I loue you very honestly, you were neuer the gentleman offred any vnciuility to me, which is strange me-thinks in one that comes from beyond Seas, would I had giuen a Thousand pound I could not loue thee so.
Mono. Do you heare, you shall faine some scuruy dysease or other, and go to the *Bath* next spring,

        Enter Mistris Honisuckle, *and Mistris* Wafer.

Ile meete you there.

Mist. Hony. By your leaue sweet mistris *Tenterhooke*.
Mist. Tent. O, how dost partner?
Mono. Gentlewomen I stayed for a most happy wind, and now the breath from your sweet, sweet lips, should set me going: good mistris *Honisuckle*; good mistris *Wafer*, good mistris *Tenterhooke*, I will pray for you, that neither riuallshippe in loues, purenesse of painting, or riding out of town, not acquainting each other with-it, be a cause your sweet beautyes do fall out, and raile one vpon another.
Mist. Waf. Raile sir, we do not vse to raile.
Mono. Why mistris, railing is your mother tongue as well as lying.
Mist. Hony. But, do you thinke we can fall out?
Mono. In troth beauties (as one spake seriously) that there was no inheritance in the amity of Princes, so thinke I of Women, too often interviewes amongst women, as amongst Princes, breeds enuy oft to others fortune, there is only in the amity of women an estate for will, and euery puny knowes that is no certaine inheritance.
Mist. Waf. You are merry sir.
Mono. So may I leaue you most fortunat gentlewoman. *Exit.*
Mist. Tent. Loue shoots heare.
Mist. Waf. *Tenterhooke*, what Gentleman is that gon out, is he a man?
Mist. Hony. O God and an excellent Trumpetter, He came lately from the vniuersity, and loues Citty dames only for their victuals, he hath an excellent trick to keepe Lobsters and Crabs sweet in summer, and cals it a deuise to prolong the dayes of shelfish, for which I do suspect he hath beene Clarke to some Noblemans kitchen. I haue heard he neuer loues any Wench, tell shee bee as stale as Frenchmen eate their wilde foule, I shall anger her.
Mist. Tent. How stale good Mistris nimble-wit? [*Aside.*]
Mist. Hony. Why as stale as a Country Ostes, an Exchange Sempster, or a Court Landresse.
Mist. Tent. He is your cousin, how your tongue runs?
Mist. Hony. Talke and make a noise, no matter to what purpose,

64 *Mist. Hony.*] Q *speech prefixes in this scene are forms of* Hony.
73 *Mist. Waf.*] Q *speech prefixes in this scene are forms of* Wafer.

I haue learn'd that with going to puritan Lectures. I was yesterday
at a banquet, wil you discharge my ruffes of some wafers, and how
doth thy husband *Wafer?*

Mist. Waf. Faith very well.

Mist. Hony. He is iust like a Torchbearer to Maskers, he wears
good cloathes, and is rankt in good company, but he doth nothing:
thou art faine to take al, and pay all.

Mist. Tent. The more happy she, would I could make such an
asse of my husband to. I heare say he breeds thy childe in his teeth
euerie yeare.

Mist. Waf. In faith he doth.

Mist. Hony. By my troth tis pitty but the foole shoulde haue the
other two paines incident to the head.

Mist. Waf. What are they?

Mist. Hony. Why the head-ake and horn-ake.
I heard say that he would haue had thee nurst thy Childe thy selfe to.

Mist. Waf. That he would truely.

Mist. Hony. Why theres the policy of husbands to keepe their
Wiues in. I doe assure you if a Woman of any markeable face in
the Worlde giue her Childe sucke, looke how many wrinckles be in
the Nipple of her breast, so many will bee in her foreheade by that
time twelue moneth: but sirra, we are come to acquaint thee with
an excellent secret: we two learne to write.

Mist. Tent. To write?

Mist. Hony. Yes beleeue it, and wee haue the finest Schoole
maister, a kind of Precision, and yet an honest knaue to: by my
troth if thou beest a good wench let him teach thee, thou mayst
send him of any arrant, and trust him with any secret; nay, to see
how demurely he will beare himselfe before our husbands, and how
iocond when their backes are turn'd.

Mist. Tent. For Gods loue let me see him.

Mist. Waf. To morrow weele send him to thee: til then sweet
Tenterhook we leaue thee, wishing thou maist haue the fortune to
change thy name often.

Mist. Tent. How? change my name?

Mist. Waf. I, for theeues and widdowes loue to shift many names,
and make sweet vse of it to.

Mist. Tent. O you are a wag indeed. Good *Wafer* remember my school master. Farewel good *Honysuckle*.
Mist. Hony. Farewel *Tenterhooke*.
Exeunt.

ACTUS SECUNDUS, Scæna Prima.

Enter Boniface *a prentice brushing his Maisters cloake and Cappe, singing.*

Enter Master Honisuckle *in his night-cap trussing himselfe.*

Hony. *Boniface*, make an ende of my cloake and Cap.
Bon. I haue dispatch em Sir: both of them lye flat at your mercie.
Hony. Fore-god me thinkes my ioynts are nimbler euery Morning since I came ouer then they were before. In *France* when I rise, I was so stiffe, and so starke, I would ha sworne my Legs had beene wodden pegs: a Constable new chosen kept not such a peripateticall gate: But now I'me as Lymber as an Antiant that has flourisht in the raine, and as Actiue as a *Norfolk* tumbler.
Bon. You may see, what change of pasture is able to doe.
Hony. It makes fat Calues in *Rumny* Marsh, and leane knaues in *London*: therefore *Boniface* keepe your ground: Gods my pitty, my forehead has more cromples, then the back part of a counsellors gowne, when another rides vppon his necke at the barre: *Boniface* take my helmet: giue your mistris my night-cap. Are my Antlers swolne so big, that my biggen pinches my browes. So, request her to make my head-piece a little wyder.
Bon. How much wider sir.
Hony. I can allow her almost an ynch: go, tell her so, very neere an inch.
Bon. If she bee a right Cittizens wife, now her Husband has giuen her an inch, sheele take an ell, or a yard at least. *Exit.*

Enter Signior Iustiniano *the Merchant, like a wryting Mecanicall Pedant.*

Hony. Maister *Parenthesis! Salue, Salue Domine.*
Iust. Salue tu quoque: Iubeo te saluere plurimum.

Hon. No more *Plurimums* if you loue me, lattin whole-meates are now minc'd, and serude in for English Gallimafries: Let vs therefore cut out our vplandish Neates tongues, and talke like regenerate Brittains.

Iust. Your worship is welcome to *England*: I powrd out Orisons for your arriuall.

Hony. Thanks good maister *Parenthesis*: and *Que nouelles*: what 30 newes flutters abroad? doe Iack-dawes dung the top of *Paules* Steeple still.

Iust. The more is the pitty, if any dawes do come into the temple, as I feare they do.

Hony. They say Charing-crosse is falne downe, since I went to *Rochell*: but thats no such wonder, twas old, and stood awry (as most part of the world can tel.) And tho it lack vnder-propping, yet (like great fellowes at a wrastling) when their heeles are once flying vppe, no man will saue em; downe they fall, and there let them lye, tho they were bigger then the Guard: Charing-crosse 40 was olde, and olde thinges must shrinke aswell as new Northern cloth.

Iust. Your worship is in the right way verily: they must so, but a number of better things between Westminster bridge and temple barre both of a worshipfull, and honorable erection, are falne to decay, and haue suffred putrifaction, since Charing fell, that were not of halfe so long standing as the poore wry-neckt Monument.

Hony. Whose within there? One of you call vp your mistris! tell her heeres her wryting Schoolemaster. I had not thought master *Parenthesis* you had bin such an early stirrer. 50

Iust. Sir, your vulgar and foure-peny-pen-men, that like your *London* Sempsters keepe open shop, and sell learning by retaile, may keepe their beds, and lie at their pleasure: But we that edifie in priuate, and traffick by whole sale, must be vp with the lark, because like Country Atturnies, wee are to shuffle vp many matters in a fore-noone. Certes maister *Honisuckle*, I would sing *Laus Deo*, so I may but please al those that come vnder my fingers: for it is my duty and function, *Perdy*, to be feruent in my vocation.

Hony. Your hand: I am glad our Citty has so good, so necessary, and so laborious a member in it: we lacke painfull and expert pen- 60 men amongst vs. Maister *Parenthesis* you teach many of our Merchants sir, do you not?

Iust. Both Wiues, Maides, and Daughters: and I thanke God, the very worst of them lye by very good mens sides: I picke out a poore liuing amongst em, and I am thankefull for it.

Hony. Trust me I am not sorry: how long haue you exercizd this quality?

Iust. Come Michaell-tide next, this thirteene yeare.

Hony. And how does my wife profit vnder you sir? hope you to do any good vpon her.

Iust. Maister *Honisuckle* I am in great hope shee shall fructify: I will do my best for my part: I can do no more then another man can.

Hony. Pray sir ply her, for she is capable of any thing.

Iust. So far as my poore tallent can stretch, It shall not be hidden from her.

Hony. Does she hold her pen well yet?

Iust. She leanes somewhat too hard vppon her pen yet sir, but practise and animaduersion will breake her from that.

Hony. Then she grubs her pen.

Iust. Its but my paines to mend the neb agen.

Hony. And where abouts is shee now maister *Parenthesis*? Shee was talking of you this morning, and commending you in her bed, and told me she was past her letters.

Iust. Truely sir she tooke her letters very suddenly: and is now in her Minoms.

Hony. I would she were in her Crotchets too maister *Parenthesis*: ha-ha, I must talke merily sir.

Iust. Sir so long as your mirth bee voyde of all Squirrility, tis not vnfit for your calling: I trust ere few daies bee at an end to haue her fal to her ioyning: for she has her letters *ad vnguem*: her A. her great B. and her great C. very right: D. and E. dilicate: hir double F. of a good length, but that it straddels a little to wyde: at the G. very cunning.

Hony. Her H. is full like mine: a goodly big H.

Iust. But her double LL. is wel: her O. of a reasonable Size: at her

70 any] Dyce; any any Q

p. and q. neither Marchantes Daughter, Aldermans Wife, young countrey Gentlewoman, nor Courtiers Mistris, can match her.
Hony. And how her v.
Iust. You sir, She fetches vp you best of al: her single you she can fashion two or three waies: but her double you, is as I would wish it.
Hony. And faith who takes it faster; my wife, or mistris *Tenterhook?*
Iust. Oh! Your wife by ods: sheele take more in one hower, then I can fasten either vpon mistris *Tenterhooke*, or mistris *Wafer*, or Mistris *Flapdragon* (the Brewers wife) in three.

Enter Iudyth, Honysuckle *his wife.*

Hony. Do not thy cheekes burne sweete chuckaby, for wee are talking of thee.
Mist. Hony. No goodnesse I warrant: you haue few Cittizens speake well of their wiues behind their backs: but to their faces theile cog worse and be more suppliant, then Clyents that sue in *forma paper*: how does my master? troth I am a very trewant: haue you your *Ruler* about you maister? for look you, I go cleane awry.
Iust. A small fault: most of my schollers do so: looke you sir, do not you thinke your wife will mend: marke her dashes, and her strokes, and her breakings, and her bendings?
Hony. She knowes what I haue promist her if shee doe mende: nay by my fay *Iude*, this is well, if you would not flie out thus, but keepe your line.
Mist. Hony. I shal in time when my hand is in: haue you a new pen for mee Maister, for by my truly, my old one is stark naught, and wil cast no inck: whether are you going lamb?
Hony. To the Custome-house: to the Change, to my Ware-house, to diuers places.
Mist. Hony. Good *Cole* tarry not past eleuen, for you turne my stomak then from my dinner.
Hony. I wil make more hast home, then a Stipendary Swizzer does after hees paid, fare you well Maister *Parenthesis*.

110 *Mist. Hony.*] Q *speech prefixes in this scene are forms of* Iud.

Mist. Hony. I am so troubled with the rheume too: Mouse whats good fort?

Hony. How often haue I tolde you, you must get a patch. I must hence. *Exit.*

Mist. Hony. I thinke when als done, I must follow his counsell, and take a patch, I had had one long ere this, but for disfiguring my face: yet I haue noted that a masticke patch vpon some womens Temples, hath bin the very rheuwme of beauty.

Iust. Is he departed? Is old *Nestor* marcht into *Troy*?

Mist. Hony. Yes you mad Greeke: the Gentlemans gone.

Iust. Why then clap vp coppy-bookes: downe with pens, hang vp inckhornes, and nowe my sweete *Honisuckle*, see what golden-winged Bee from *Hybla*, flies humming, with *Crura thymo plena*, which he wil empty in the Hiue of your bosome.

Mist. Hony. From whom.

Iust. At the skirte of that sheete in blacke worke is wrought hys name, breake not vp the wildfoule, till anon, and then feed vpon him in priuate: theres other irons i'th fire: more sackes are comming to the Mill. O you sweet temptations of the sonnes of *Adam*, I commende you, extol you, magnifie you: Were I a Poet by *Hipocrene* I sweare, (which was a certaine Well where all the Muses watred) and by *Pernassus* eke I sweare, I would rime you to death with praises, for that you can bee content to lye with olde men all night for their mony, and walk to your gardens with yong men i'th day time for your pleasure: Oh you delicat damnations: you do but as I wud do: were I the proprest, sweetest, plumpest, Cherry-cheekt, Corrall-lipt woman in a kingdome, I would not daunce after one mans pipe.

Mist. Hony. And why?

Iust. Especially after an old mans.

Mist. Hony. And why, pray!

Iust. Especially after an old Cittizens.

Mist. Hony. Still, and why.

Iust. Marry because the Suburbes, and those without the bars, haue more priuiledge then they within the freedome: what need one

135 had had] haue had Q
136 haue] had Q

woman doate vpon one Man? Or one man be mad like *Orlando* for one woman.

Mist. Hony. Troth tis true, considering how much flesh is in euery Shambles.

Iust. Why should I long to eate of Bakers bread onely, when theres so much Sifting, and bolting, and grynding in euery corner of the City; men and women are borne, and come running into the world faster then Coaches doe into Cheap-side vppon *Symon* and *Iudes* day: and are eaten vp by Death faster, then Mutton and porridge in a terme time. Who would pin their hearts to any Sleeue: this world is like a Mynt, we are no sooner cast into the fire, taken out agen, hamerd, stampt, and made Currant, but presently wee are changde: the new Mony (like a new Drab) is catcht at by Dutch, Spanish, Welch, French, Scotch, and English: but the old crackt King *Harry* groates are shoueld vp, feele bruzing, and battring, clipping, and melting, they smoake fort.

Mist. Hony. The worlds an Arrant naughty-pack I see, and is a very scuruy world.

Iust. Scuruy? worse then the conscience of a Broome-man, that carryes out new ware, and brings home old shoes: a naughty-packe? Why theres no Minute, no thought of time passes, but some villany or other is a brewing: why, euen now, now, at holding vp of this finger, and before the turning downe of this, some are murdring, some lying with their maides, some picking of pockets, some cutting purses, some cheating, some weying out bribes. In this Citty some wiues are Cuckolding some Husbands. In yonder Village some farmers are now—now grynding the Iaw-bones of the poore: therefore sweete Scholler, sugred Mistris *Honisuckle*, take Summer before you, and lay hold of it? why, euen now must you and I hatch an egge of iniquity.

Mist. Hony. Troth maister I thinke thou wilt proue a very knaue.

Iust. Its the fault of many that fight vnder this band.

Mist. Hony. I shall loue a Puritans face the worse whilest I liue for that Coppy of thy countenance.

Iust. We are all wethercocks, and must follow the winde of the present: from the byas.

Mist. Hony. Change a bowle then.

Iust. I will so; and now for a good cast: theres the Knight, sir *Goslin Glo-worme.*
Mist. Hony. Hees a Knight made out of waxe.
Iust. He tooke vp Silkes vppon his bond I confesse: nay more, hees a knight in print: but let his knight-hood be of what stamp it will, from him come I, to intreate you, and Mistris *Wafer,* and mistris *Tenterhook,* being both my schollers, and your honest pew fellowes, to meet him this afternoon at the Rhenish-wine-house ith Stillyard. Captaine *Whirlepoole* will be there, young *Lynstock* the 210 Alder-mans Son and Heire, there too: will you steale forth, and tast of a Dutch Bun, and a Keg of Sturgeon?
Mist. Hony. What excuse shall I coyne now?
Iust. Fewh! excuses: You must to the pawne to buy Lawne: to Saint Martins for Lace; to the Garden: to the Glasse-house; to your Gossips: to the Powlters: else take out an old ruffe, and go to your Sempsters: excuses? Why, they are more ripe then medlers at Christmas.
Mist. Hony. Ile come. The hower.
Iust. Two: the way — through *Paules*: euery wench take a piller, 220 there clap on your Maskes: your men will bee behind you, and before your prayers be halfe don, be before you, and man you out at seuerall doores. Youle be there?
Mist. Hony. If I breath. *Exit.*
Iust. Farewell. So: now must I goe set the tother Wenches the selfe same Coppy. A rare Scholemaister, for all kind of handes, I. Oh: What strange curses are powred downe with one blessing? Do all tread on the heele? Haue all the art
To hood-winke wise men thus? And (like those builders
Of *Babels* Tower) to speake vnknowne tongues, 230
Of all (saue by their husbands) vnderstood:
Well, if (as Iuy bout the Elme does twine)
All wiues loue clipping, theres no fault in mine.
But if the world lay speechles, euen the dead
Would rise, and thus cry out from yawning graues,
Women make men, or Fooles, or Beasts, or Slaues.

Exit.

214 Fewh!] Dyce (*cf.* II.ii.209); Few ˄ Q   225 *Iust.*] Dyce; *Iud.* Q

[ACT II,] Scæna 2.

Enter Earle and Mistris Birdlime.

Earl. Her answer! talke in musick: Wil she come?
Bird. Oh my sides ake in my loines, in my bones? I ha more need of a posset of sacke, and lie in my bed and sweate, than to talke in musick: no honest woman would run hurrying vp and down thus and vndoe her selfe for a man of honour, without reason? I am so lame, euery foot that I set to the ground went to my hart. I thoght I had bin at Mum-chance my bones ratled so with iaunting? had it not bin for a friend in a corner, I had kickt vp my heeles.
Takes Aqua-vitæ.
Earl. Minister comfort to me, Wil she come.
Bird. All the Castles of comfort that I can put you into is this, that the iealous wittal her husband, came (like a mad Oxe) belowing in whilst I was ther. Oh I ha lost my sweet breth with trotting.
Earl. Death to my hart? her husband? What saith he?
Bird. The freeze-Ierkin Rascal out with his purse, and cal'd me plaine Bawd to my face.
Earl. Affliction to me, then thou spak'st not to her?
Bird. I spake to her, as Clients do to Lawiers without money (to no purpose) but Ile speak with him, and hamper him to, if euer he fall into my clutches: Ile make the yellow-hammer her husband knowe, (for all hees an Italian) that theres a difference betweene a cogging Baud and an honest motherly gentlewoman. Now, what cold whetstones ly ouer your stomacher? wil you haue some of my *Aqua*? Why my Lord.
Earl. Thou hast kild me with thy words.
Bird. I see bashful louers, and young bullockes are knockt down at a blow: Come, come, drinke this draught of Cynamon water, and plucke vp your spirits: vp with em, vp with em. Do you hear, the whiting mop has nibled.
Earl. Ha?
Bird. Oh? I thought I should fetch you: you can *Ha* at that: Ile make you Hem anon. As I'me a sinner I think youl find the sweetest,

sweetest bedfellow of her. Oh! she lookes so sugredly, so simpringly, so gingerly, so amarously, so amiably. Such a redde lippe, such a White foreheade, such a blacke eie, such a full cheeke, and such a goodly little nose, nowe shees in that French gowne, Scotch fals, Scotch bum, and Italian head-tire you sent her, and is such an intycing shee-witch, carrying the charmes of your Iewels about her. Oh!

Earl. Did she receiue them? speake: Here is golden keyes
T'vnlock thy lips. Did she vouchsafe to take them? 40

Bird. Did she vouchsafe to take them, thers a question: you shall find she did vouchsafe: The troath is my Lord, I gotte her to my house, there she put off her own cloths my Lord and put on yours my Lord, prouided her a Coach, Searcht the middle Ile in *Pawles*, and with three Elizabeth twelue-pences prest three knaues my Lord, hirde three Liueries in Long-lane, to man her: for al which so God mend me, I'me to paie this night before Sun-set.

Earl. This showre shall fil them al: raine in their laps,
What golden drops thou wilt.

Bird. Alas my Lord, I do but receiue it with one hand, to pay it 50 away with another, I'me but your Baily.

Earl. Where is she?

Bird. In the greene veluet Chamber; the poore sinneful creature pants like a pigeon vnder the hands of a Hawke, therefore vse her like a woman my Lord: vse her honestly my Lorde, for alas shees but a Nouice, and a verie greene thinge.

Earl. Farewel: Ile in vnto her.

Bird. Fie vpont, that were not for your honor: you know gentlewomen vse to come to Lords chambers, and not Lordes to the Gentlewomens; Ide not haue her thinke you are such a Rank- 60 ryder: walke you heere: Ile becken, you shal see ile fetch her with a wet finger?

Earl. Do so.

Bird. Hyst? why sweet heart, mistris *Iustiniano*, why prettie soule tread softlie, and come into this roome: here be rushes, you neede not feare the creaking of your corke shooes.

39 Here is] Heres is Q (*cf.* IV.i.192)

Enter Mistris Iustiniano.

So, wel saide, theres his honour. I haue busines my Lord, very now the marks are set vp. Ile get me twelue score off, and giue Ayme. *Exit.*
Earl. Y'are welcome: Sweet y'are welcome. Blesse my hand 70
With the soft touch of yours: Can you be Cruell
To one so Prostrate to you? Euen my Hart,
My Happines, and State lie at your feet:
My Hopes me flattered that the field was woon,
That you had yeilded, (tho you Conquer me)
And that all Marble scales that bard your eies
From throwing light on mine, were quite tane off,
By the Cunning Womans hand, that Workes for me,
Why therefore do you wound me now with frownes?
Why do you flie me? Do not exercise 80
The Art of woman on me? I'me already
Your Captiue: Sweet! Are these your hate, or feares.
Mist. Iust. I wonder lust can hang at such white haires.
Earl. You giue my loue ill names, It is not lust:
Lawlesse desires wel tempred may seem Iust.
A thousand mornings with the early Sunne,
Mine eies haue from your windowes watcht to steale
Brightnes from those. As oft vpon the daies
That Consecrated to deuotion are,
Within the Holy Temple haue I stood 90
Disguis'd, waiting your presence: and when your hands
Went vp towards heauen to draw some blessing down,
Mine (as if all my Nerues by yours did moue,)
Beg'd in dum Signes some pitty for my Loue,
And thus being feasted onely with your sight,
I went more pleased then sickmen with fresh health,
Rich men with Honour, Beggers do with wealth.
Mist. Iust. Part now so pleas'd, for now you more Inioy me.
Earl. O you do wish me Phisicke to destroy me.
Mist. Iust. I haue already leapt beyond the bounds 100

*87 from] *stet* Q

Of modesty, in piecing out my wings
With borrowed feathers: but you sent a Sorceres
So perfect in her trade, that did so liuely
Breath forth your passionate Accents, and could drawe
A Louer languishing so piercingly,
That her charmes wrought vppon me, and in pitty
Of your sick hart which she did Countefet,
(Oh shees a subtle Beldam!) see I cloth'd
My limbes (thus Player-like) in Rich Attyres,
Not fitting mine estate, and am come forth,   110
But why I know not?
Earl.   Will you Loue me?
Mist. Iust.   Yes,
If you can cleare me of a debt thats due
But to one Man, Ile pay my hart to thee.
Earl.   Whose that?
Mist. Iust.   My Husband.
Earl.   Vmh.
Mist. Iust.   The sums so great
I know a kingdome cannot answer it,
And therefore I beseech you good my Lord,
To take this gilding off, which is your owne,
And henceforth cease to throw out golden hookes
To choake mine honor: tho my husbands poore,
Ile rather beg for him, then be your Whore.   120
Earl.   Gainst beauty you plot treason, if you suffer
Tears to do violence to so faire a Cheeke.
That face was nere made to looke pale with want.
Dwell heere and bee the Soueraigne of my fortunes.
Thus shall you go attir'd.
Mist. Iust.   Till lust be tir'd.
I must take leaue my Lord.
Earl.   Sweet Creature stay,
My Cofers shall be yours, my Seruants yours,
My selfe wil be your seruant, and I sweare
By that which I houlde deare in you, your beauty
(And which Ile not prophane) you shall liue heere   130

340

As free from base wrong, as you are from blackenesse,
So you will deigne, but let mee inioy your sight,
Answere mee will you.
Mist. Iust.   I will thinke vpont.
Earl. Vnlesse you shall perceiue, that al my thoughts,
And al my actions bee to you deuoted,
And that I very iustly earne your loue,
Let me not tast it.
Mist. Iust.   I wil thinke vpon it.
Earl. But when you find my merits of full weight,
Wil you accept their worth?
Mist. Iust.   Ile thinke vpont.
Ide speake with the old woman.
Earl.   She shall come,   140
Ioyes that are borne vnlookt for, are borne dumb. *Exit.*
Mist. Iust. Pouerty, thou bane of Chastity,
Poison of beauty, Broker of Mayden-heades,
I see when Force, nor Wit can scale the hold,
Wealth must. Sheele nere be won, that defies golde.
But liues there such a creature: Oh tis rare,
To finde a woman chast, thats poore and faire.

            Enter Birdlime.

Bird. Now lamb! has not his Honor dealt like an honest Nobleman
with you. I can tel you, you shal not find him a Templer, nor one
of these cogging Cattern pear-coloured-beards, that by their good 150
wils would haue no pretty woman scape them.
Mist. Iust. Thou art a very bawd: thou art a Diuel
Cast in a reuerend shape; thou stale damnation!
Why hast thou me intist from mine owne Paradice,
To steale fruit in a barren wildernes.
Bird. Bawde and diuel, and stale damnation! Wil womens tounges
(like Bakers legs) neuer go straight.
Mist. Iust. Had thy *Circæan* Magick me transformd
Into that sensuall shape for which thou Coniurst,
And that I were turn'd common Venturer,   160
I could not loue this old man.

Bird. This old man, vmh: this old man? doe his hoarye haires sticke in your stomacke? yet methinkes his siluer haires shoulde mooue you, they may serue to make you Bodkins: Does his age grieue you? foole? Is not old wine wholesommest, olde Pippines toothsommest, old wood burne brightest, old Linnen wash whitest, old souldiors Sweet-hart are surest, and olde Louers are soundest. I ha tried both.

Mist. Iust. So wil not I.

Bird. Youd haue some yong perfum'd beardles Gallant board you, that spits al his braines out ats tongues end, wud you not? 170

Mist. Iust. No, none at al, not anie.

Bird. None at al? what doe you make there then? why are you a burden to the worlds conscience, and an eie-sore to wel giuen men, I dare pawne my gowne and al the beddes in my house, and al the gettings in Michaelmas terme next to a Tauerne token, that thou shalt neuer be an innocent.

Mist. Iust. Who are so?

Bird. Fools? why then are you so precize: your husbands down the wind, and wil you like a haglers Arrow, be down the weather, Strike whilst the iron is hot. A woman when there be roses in her cheekes, Cherries on her lippes, Ciuet in her breath, Iuory in her teeth, Lyllyes in her hand, and Lickorish in her heart, why shees like a play. If new, very good company, very good company, but if stale, like old *Ieronimo*: goe by, go by. Therefore as I said before, strike. Besides: you must thinke that the commodity of beauty was not made to lye dead vpon any young womans hands: if your husband haue giuen vp his Cloake, let another take measure of you in his Ierkin: for as the Cobler, in the night time walks with his Lanthorne, the Merchant, and the Lawyer with his Link, and the Courtier with his Torch: So euery lip has his Lettice to himselfe: the Lob has his Lasse, the Collier his Dowdy, the Westerne-man his Pug, the Seruing-man his Punke, the student his Nun in white Fryers, the Puritan his Sister, and the Lord his Lady: which worshipfull vocation may fall vppon you, if youle but strike whilest the Iron is hot. 180 190

*170 Gallant] Dyce; Gallants Q

Mist. Iust. Witch: thus I breake thy Spels: Were I kept braue, On a Kings cost, I am but a Kings slaue. *Exit.*

Bird. I see, that as Frenchmen loue to be bold, Flemings to be drunke, Welchmen to be cald *Brittons*, and Irishmen to be Costermongers, so Cocknyes, (especially Shee-Cocknies) loue not *Aqua-vite* when tis good for them.

Enter Monopoly.

Mono. Saw you my vncle?

Bird. I saw him euen now going the way of all flesh (thats to say) towardes the Kitchin: heeres a letter to your worship from the party.

Mono. What party?

Bird. The *Tenterhook* your wanton.

Mono. From her? Fewh? pray thee stretch me no more vppon your *Tenterhook*: pox on her? Are there no Pottecaries ith Town to send her Phisick-bils to, but me: Shees not troubled with the greene sicknesse still, Is she?

Bird. The yellow Iaundis, as the Doctor tels me: troth shees as good a peat: she is falne away so, that shees nothing but bare skin and bone: for the Turtle so mournes for you.

Mono. In blacke?

Bird. In black? you shall find both black and blew if you look vnder her eyes.

Mono. Well: sing ouer her ditty when I'me in tune.

Bird. Nay, but will you send her a Box of *Mithridatum* and Dragon water, I meane some restoratiue words. Good Maister *Monopoly*, you know how welcome yare to the Citty, and will you master *Monopoly*, keepe out of the Citty; I know you cannot, would you saw how the poor gentlewoman lies.

Mono. Why how lies she?

Bird. Troth as the way lies ouer Gads-hill, very dangerous: you would pitty a womans case if you saw her: write to her some treatise of pacification.

Mono. Ile write to her to morrow.

Bird. To morrow; sheele not sleepe then but tumble, and if she might haue it to night, it would better please her.

Mono. Perhaps Ile doot to night, farewell.
Bird. If you doot to night, it would better please her then to morrow.
Mono. Gods so, dost heare, I'me to sup this night at the Lyon in Shoredich with certen gallants: canst thou not draw forth some dilicate face, that I ha not seene, and bring it thither, wut thou?
Bird. All the painters in *London* shal not fit for colour as I can; but we shall haue some swaggering?
Mono. All as ciuill (by this light) as Lawyers.
Bird. But I tell you, shees not so common as Lawyers, that I meane to betray to your Table: for as I'me a Sinner, shees a Knights Cozen; a *Yorkshire* gentlwoman, and only speakes a little broad, but of very good carriage.
Mono. Nay thats no matter, we can speake as broad as she? but wut bring her?
Bird. You shall call her Cozen, do you see: two men shall waite vpon her, and Ile come in by chance: but shall not the party bee there?
Mono. Which party?
Bird. The writer of that simple hand.
Mon. Not for as many Angels as there be letters in her Paper: Speake not of mee to her, nor our meeting if you loue mee: wut come?
Bird. Mum, Ile come.
Mono. Farewell.
Bird. Good Maister *Monopoly*, I hope to see you one day a man of great credite.
Mono. If I be, Ile build Chimnies with Tobacco but Ile smoake some: and be sure *Birdlime* Ile sticke wooll vpon thy back.
Bird. Thankes sir, I know you wil, for all the kinred of the *Monopolies* are held to be great Fleecers.

Exeunt.

[ACT II, Scene iii]

Enter sir Gozlin: Lynstocke, Whirlepoole, *and the three Cittizens wiues maskt*, Iudyth [Honysuckle], Mabell [Wafer], *and* Clare [Tenterhook].

Goz. So, draw those Curtaines, and lets see the pictures vnder em.
Lyn. Welcome to the Stilliard faire Ladies.
All 3. Thankes good maister *Lynstocke*.
Whirl. Hans: some wine *Hans*.
         Enter Hans *with cloth and Buns*.
Hans. Yaw, yaw, you sall hebben it mester:
Old vine, or new vine?
Goz. Speake women.
Mist. Hony. New wine good sir *Gozlin*: wine in the must, good Dutchman, for must is best for vs women.
Hans. New vine? vell: two pots of new vine.   *Exit* Hans. 10
Mist. Hony. An honest Butterbox: for if it be old, theres none of it coms into my belly.
Mist. Waf. Why *Tenterhooke* pray thee lets dance friskin, and be mery.
Lyn. Thou art so troubled with *Monopolies*, they so hang at thy heart stringes.
Mist. Tent. Pox a my hart then.   *Enter* Hans *with Wine*.
Mist. Hony. I and mine too, if any Courtier of them all set vp his gallowes there: wench vse him as thou dost thy pantables, scorne to let him kisse thy heele, for he feedes thee with nothing but 20 Court holy bread, good words, and cares not for thee: sir *Gozlin*, will you tast a Dutch whatch you callum.
Mist. Waf. Heere maister *Lynstocke*, halfe mine is yours. *Bun, Bun, Bun, Bun.*   *Enter* [Iustiniano *as*] Parenthesis.
Iust. Which roome? where are they? wo ho, ho, ho, so ho boies.
Goz. Sfoot whose that? lock our roome.

  11 *Mist. Hony.*] Q *speech prefixes in this scene are forms of* Iud.
  13 *Mist. Waf.*] Q *speech prefixes in this scene are forms of* Mab.
  17 *Mist. Tent.*] Q *speech prefixes in this scene are forms of* Cla.
  25 *Iust.*] Q *speech prefixes in this scene are forms of* Par.

Iust. Not till I am in: and then lock out the diuell tho he come in the shape of a puritan.
All 3. Scholemaister, welcome? well-come in troth?
Iust. Who would not bee scratcht with the bryers and brambles to haue such burs sticking on his breeches: Saue you gentlemen: O noble Knight.
Goz. More wine *Hans*.
Iust. Am not I (gentlemen) a Ferret of the right haire, that can make three Conies bolt at a clap into your pursenets? ha? little do their three husbands dreame what coppies I am setting their wiues now? wert not a rare Iest if they should come sneaking vppon vs like a horrible noise of Fidlers.
Mist. Hony. Troth Ide not care: let em come: Ide tell em, weede ha none of their dull Musicke.
Mist. Waf. Heere mistris *Tenterhooke*.
Mist. Tent. Thanks good mistris *Wafer*.
Iust. Whose there? Peepers: Intelligencers: Euesdroppers.
Omn. Vds foot, throw a pot ats head?
Iust. Oh Lord? O Gentlemen, Knight, Ladies, that may bee, Cittizens wiues that are, shift for your selues, for a paire of your husbands heads are knocking together with *Hans* his, and inquiring for you.
Omn. Keepe the doore lockt.
Mist. Hony. Oh I, do, do: and let sir *Gozlin* (because he has bin in the low Countries) swear gotz Sacrament, and driue e'm away with broken Dutch.
Iust. Heres a wench has simple Sparkes in her: shees my pupile Gallants: Good-god? I see a man is not sure that his wife is in the Chamber, tho his owne fingers hung on the Padlocke: Trap-doores, false Drabs, and Spring-lockes, may cozen a Couy of Constables. How the silly Husbands might heere ha beene guld with Flemish mony: Come: drinke vp *Rhene*, *Thames* and *Mæander* dry, Theres Nobody.
Mist. Hony. Ah thou vngodly maister.
Iust. I did but make a false fire, to try your vallor, because you cryed let em come. By this glasse of womans wine, I would not ha seene their Spirits walke heere, to bee dubd deputy of a Ward, I,

they would ha Chronicled me for a Foxe in a Lambes skin: But come: Is this merry Midsomer night agreed vpon? when shal it be? where shall it be?

Lyn. Why faith to morrow at night.
Whirl. Weele take a Coach and ride to *Ham*, or so.
Mist. Tent. O fie vpont: a Coach? I cannot abide to be iolted.
Mist. Waf. Yet most of your Cittizens wiues loue iolting? 70
Goz. What say you to *Black-wall*, or *Lime-house*?
Mist. Hony. Euery roome there smels to much of Tar.
Lyn. Lets to mine host *Dogbolts* at *Brainford* then, there you are out of eyes, out of eares, priuate roomes, sweet Lynnen, winking attendance, and what cheere you will?
Omn. Content, to *Brainford*?
Mist. Waf. I, I, lets go by water, for sir *Gozlin* I haue heard you say you loue to go by water.
Mist. Hony. But wenches, with what pullies shall wee slide with some clenly excuse, out of our husbandes suspition, being gone 80 West-ward for smelts all night.
Iust. Thats the blocke now we all stumble at: Winde vp that string well, and all the consorts in tune.
Mist. Hony. Why then goodman scraper tis wound vp, I haue it. Sirra *Wafer*, thy childes at nurse, if you that are the men could prouide some wise asse that could keepe his countenance —
Iust. Nay if he be an Asse he will keepe his countenance.
Mist. Hony. I, but I meane, one that could set out his tale with audacity, and say that the child were sick, and neare stagger at it: That last should serue all our feete. 90
Whirl. But where will that wise Asse be found now?
Iust. I see I'me borne still to draw Dun out ath mire for you: that wise beast will I be. Ile bee that Asse that shall grone vnder the burden of that abhominable lye. Heauen pardon me, and pray God the infant be not punisht fort. Let me see: Ile breake out in some filthy shape like a Thrasher, or a Thatcher, or a Sowgelder, or something: and speak dreamingly, and swear how the child pukes, and eates nothing (as perhaps it does not) and lies at the mercy of God, (as all children and old-folkes doe) and then scholler *Wafer*, play you your part. 100

347

Mist. Waf. Feare not me, for a veny or two?
Iust. Where will you meet ith morning?
Goz. At some Tauerne neare the water-side, thats priuate.
Iust. The Grey-hound, the Greyhound in Black-fryers, an excellent *Randeuous*.
Lyn. Content, the Greyhound by eight?
Iust. And then you may whip forth two first, and two next, on a sudden, and take Boate at Bridewell Dock most priuately.
Omn. Beet so: a good place?
Iust. Ile go make ready my rusticall properties: let me see scholler hie you home, for your child shall bee sicke within this halfe howre.
                                                                Exit.
                    Enter Birdlime.

Mist. Hony. Tis the vprightest dealing man? Gods my pitty, whose yonder?
Bird. I'me bold to presse my selfe vnder the Cullors of your company, hearing that Gentlewoman was in the roome: A word mistris?
Mist. Tent. How now, what saies he?
                                    [*Talks apart with* Birdlime.]
Goz. Zounds whats she? a Bawd, bith Lord Ist not?
Mist. Waf. No indeed sir *Gozlin*, shees a very honest woman, and a Mid-wife.
Mist. Tent. At the Lyon in Shoredich? And would he not read it? nor write to me? Ile poyson his Supper?
Bird. But no words that I bewrayd him.
Mist. Tent. Gentlemen I must be gone. I cannot stay in faith: pardon me: Ile meete to morrow: come Nurse, cannot tarry by this element.
Goz. Mother, you: Grannam drinke ere you goe.
Bird. I am going to a womans labour, indeede sir, cannot stay.
                                                                Exeunt.
Mist. Waf. I hold my life the blacke-beard her husband whissels for her.

118 whats] Dyce; what Q
129 *Mist. Waf.*] Dyce; *Amb.* Q (*misprint for* Mab(?), *or signifying two unidentified characters, who would be the two remaining women,* Mistress Wafer *and* Honeysuckle)

Mist. Hony. A reckoning: Breake one, breake all.
Goz. Here *Hans*, draw not, Ile draw for all as Ime true knight.
Mist. Hony. Let him: amongst women this does stand for law, The worthiest man (tho he be foole) must draw.

Exeunt.

ACTUS TERTIUS Scæna Prima.

Enter maister Tenterhooke *and his wife.*

Tent. What booke is that sweet hart?
Mist. Tent. Why the booke of bonds that are due to you.
Tent. Come, what doe you with it? Why do you trouble your selfe to take care about my businesse?
Mist. Tent. Why sir, doth not that which concerns you, concerne me. You told me *Monopoly* had discharged his bond, I finde by the booke of accounts heere, that it is not canceld. Eare I would suffer such a cheating companion to laugh at me, Ide see him hanged I. Good sweete hart as euer you loued me, as euer my bedde was pleasing to you, arrest the knaue, we were neuer beholding to him for a pin, but for eating vp our victuals. Good Mouse enter an action against him.
Tent. In troth loue I may do the gentleman much discredit, and besides it may be other actions may fall very heauy vpon him.
Mist. Tent. Hang him, to see the dishonesty of the knaue.
Tent. O wife, good words: A Courtier, A gentleman.
Mist. Tent. Why, may not a Gentleman be a knaue, that were strange infaith: but as I was a saying, to see the dishonesty of him, that would neuer come since he receiued the mony to visit vs you know. Maister *Tenterhook* he hath hung long vpon you. Maister *Tenterhooke* as I am vertuous you shall arrest him.
Tent. Why, I know not when he will come to Towne.
Mist. Tent. Hees in town: this night he sups at the Lyon in Shoaredich, good husband enter your action, and make hast to the Lyon presently, theres an honest fellow (Sergeant *Ambush*) will doe it in a trice, he neuer salutes a man in Curtesie, but he catches him as if he would arrest him. Good hart let Seriant *Ambush* ly in waite for him.

Tent. Well at thy entreaty I will doe it. Giue me my Cloake there,
[*Calls to seruant within.*]
buy a linck and meet me at the Counter in Woodstreete; busse me Clare.

Mist. Tent. Why now you loue me. Ile goe to bed sweet hart.

Tent. Do not sleep till I come *Clare*.   *Exit* Tenterhook.

Mist. Tent. No lamb, baa sheep, if a woman will be free in this intricate laborinth of a husband, let her marry a man of a melancholy complexion, she shal not be much troubled with him. By my sooth my Husband hath a hand as dry as his braines, and a breath as stronge as six common gardens. Wel my husband is gon to arrest *Monopoly*. I haue dealt with a Sargeant priuatly, to intreate him, pretending that he is my Aunts Son, by this meanes shal I see my young gallant that in this has plaid his part. When they owe mony in the Citty once, they deale with their Lawyers by atturny, follow the Court though the Court do them not the grace to allow them their dyet. O the wit of a woman when she is put to the pinch.

Exit Mistris Tenterhook.

[ACT III, Scene ii]

Enter maister Tenterhooke, *Sergeant* Ambush,
and yeoman Clutch.

Tent. Come Sergeant *Ambush*, come yeoman *Clutch*, yons the Tauerne, the Gentleman will come out presently: thou art resolute?

Amb. Who I, I carry fire and sword that fight for me, hear, and heare. I know most of the knaues about *London*, and most of the Theeues to, I thanke God, and good intelligence.

Tent. I wonder thou dost not turne Broker then.

Amb. Pew; I haue bin a Broker already; for I was first a Puritan, then a Banquerout, then a Broker, then a Fencer, and then Sergeant, were not these Trades woulde make a man honest? peace the doore opes, wheele about yeoman *Clutch*.

31, 33 *Clare*] *Moll* Q (*see note to* I.ii.1)

350

Enter Whirlpoole, Linstocke, *and* Monopoly *vnbrast.*

Mono. And eare I come to sup in this Tauerne again. Theres no more attendance then in a Iaile, and there had bin a Punk or two in the company then we should not haue bin rid of the drawers: now were I in an excellent humor to go to a valting house, I wold break downe all their Glass-windowes, hew in peeces all their ioyne stooles, tear silke petticotes, ruffle their Periwigges, and spoyle their Painting, O the Gods what I could do: I could vndergo fifteene bawds by this darknes, or if I could meete one of these Varlets that wear Pannier-ally on their baks (Sergeants) I would make them scud so fast from me, that they should think it a shorter way betweene this and Ludgate, then a condemned Cutpurse thinkes it between Newgate and Tyburne.

Lyn. You are for no action to night.

Whirl. No Ile to bed.

Mono. Am not I drunke now: *Implentur veteris bacchi, pinguisque Tobacco.*

Whirl. Faith we are all heated.

Mono. Captaine *Whirlepoole* when wilt come to Court and dine with me?

Whirl. One of these daies *Franke,* but Ile get mee two Gaunlets for feare I lose my fingers in the dishes, their bee excellent shauers I heare in the most of your vnder offices? I protest I haue often come thether, sat downe, drawne my knife, and eare I could say grace all the meate hath bin gone. I haue risen, and departed thence as hungry, as euer came Countrey Atturny from Westminster? Good night honest *Franke,* doe not swagger with the watch *Franke.* *Exeunt* [Whirlpoole, Lynstocke].

Tent. So now they are gone you may take him.

Amb. Sir I arrest you?

Mono. Arrest me, at whose suite you varlets?

Clutch. At maister *Tenterhookes.*

Mono. Why you varlets dare you arrest one of the Court.

Amb. Come will you be quiet sir?

20 wear] Dyce; were Q
26 *pinguisque*] Dyce; *pinquisq̃* Q

Mono. Pray thee good yeoman call the gentlemen back againe. Theres a Gentleman hath carried a hundred pound of mine home with him to his lodging, becaus I dare not carry it ouer the fields, Ile discharge it presently.

Amb. Thats a trick sir, you would procure a reskue.

Mono. Catchpole do you see, I will haue the haire of your head 50 and beard shaued off for this, and eare I catch you at *Grayes Inne* by this light law.

Amb. Come will you march.

Mono. Are you Sergeants Christians? Sirra thou lookest like a good pittyfull rascall, and thou art a tall man to it seemes, thou hast backt many a man in thy time I warrant.

Amb. I haue had many a man by the backe sir.

Mono. Welsaide in-troth, I loue your quality, las tis needfull euery man should come by his own: but as God mend me gentlemen I haue not one crosse about me, onely you two. Might not you let 60 a Gentleman passe out of your handes, and say you saw him not? Is there not such a kinde of mercy in you now and then my Maisters, as I liue, if you come to my lodging to morrowe morning, Ile giue you fiue brace of Angelles? good yeoman perswade your graduat heere: I know some of you to be honest faithfull Drunkards, respect a poore Gentleman in my case.

Tent. Come, it wil not serue your turne, Officers looke to him, vpon your perril.

Mono. Do you heare sir, you see I am in the hands of a couple of Rauens here, as you are a Gentleman lend me forty shillings, let 70 me not liue if I do not pay you the forfeiture of the whole bond, and neuer plead Conscience.

Tent. Not a penny, not a penny: God night sir.

Exit Tenterhook.

Mono. Well, a man ought not to swear by anie thing in the hands of Sergeants but by siluer, and because my pocket is no lawful Iustice to Minister any such oath vnto me, I will patiently incounter the Counter. Which is the dearest warde in Prison Sergeant! the knights ward?

Amb. No sir, the Maisters side.

61 Gentleman] Dyce; Gentlemen Q

Mono. Well the knight is aboue the maister though his Table be 80 worse furnisht: Ile go thether.
Amb. Come sir, I must vse you kindly: the Gentlemans Wife that hath arrested you —
Mono. I what of her.
Amb. She saies you are her Antes sonne.
Mono. I, I am?
Amb. She takes on so pittifully for your Arresting, twas much against her wil (good Gentlewoman) that this affliction lighted vpon you.
Mono. She hath reason, if she respect her poore kindred. 90
Amb. You shall not go to prison.
Mono. Honest Sergeant, Conscionable Officer, did I forget my selfe euen now, a vice that sticks to me alwaies when I am drunke to abuse my best friends: where didst buy this buffe? Let me not liue but Ile giue thee a good suite of durance, Wilt thou take my bond Sergeant? Wheres a Scriuener, a Scriuener good Yeoman? you shal haue my sword and hangers to paie him.
Amb. Not so Sir: but you shall be prisoner in my house: I do not thinke but that your Cosin will visit you there i'th morning, and take order for you. 100
Mono. Well said; wast not a most treacherous part to arrest a man in the night, and when he is almost drunk, when he hath not his wits about him to remember which of his friends is in the Subsedy: Come did I abuse you, I recant, you are as necessary in a city as Tumblers in *Norfolke*, Sumners in *Lancashire*, or Rake-hels in an Armie.

Exeunt.

[ACT III, SCENE iii]

Enter [Iustiniano *as*] Parenthesis *like a Colliar, and a Boy.*

Iust. Buy any small Coale, buy any smal Coale.
Boy. Collier, Collier?
Iust. What saist boy.

*86 I, I am] I, am Q

Boy. Ware the Pillory.

Iust. O boy the pillory assures many a man that he is no cukold, for how impossible weare it a man should thrust his head through so small a Loope-hole if his foreheade were brauncht boy?

Boy. Collier: how came the goose to be put vpon you, ha?

Iust. Ile tell thee, the Tearme lying at *Winchester* in *Henry* the Thirds daies, and many French Women comming out of the Isle of *Wight* thither (as it hath alwaies beene seene) though the Isle of *Wight* could not of long time neither in dure Foxes nor Lawyers, yet it could brook the more dreadful Cockatrice, there were many Punkes in the Towne (as you know our Tearme is their Tearme) your Farmers that would spend but three pence on his ordinarie, woulde lauish halfe a Crowne on his Leachery: and many men (Calues as they were) would ride in a Farmers foule bootes before breakefast, the commonst sinner had more fluttering about her, then a fresh punke hath when she comes to a Towne of Garrison, or to a vniuersity. Captains, Schollers, Seruingmen, Iurors, Clarks, Townesmen, and the Blacke-guarde vsed all to one Ordinarye, and most of them were cald to a pittifull reckoning, for before two returnes of Michaelmas, Surgeons were full of busines, the cure of most secresie grew as common as Lice in *Ireland*, or as scabbes in *France*. One of my Tribe a Collier carried in his Cart forty maim'd souldiors to *Salsbury*, looking as pittifully as Dutchmen first made drunke, then carried to bee-heading. Euery one that mette him cried, ware the Goose Collier, and from that day to this, thers a record to be seene at *Croiden*, howe that pittifull waftage which in deede was vertue in the Collier, that all that time would carry no Coales, laid this Imputation on all the posterity.

Boy. You are ful of tricks Colliar.

Iust. Boy where dwels maister *Wafer*?

Boy. Why heare! what wouldst? I am one of his Iuvinals?

Iust. Hath he not a child at nursse at *More-clacke*?

Boy. Yes, dost thou dwel there?

Iust. That I do, the Child is wonderous sicke: I was wild to acquaint thy maister and Mistris with it.

Boy. Ile vp and tel them presently. [*Exit.*]

23 cure] care Q

Iust. So, if al should faile me, I could turne Collier. O the villany of this age, how ful of secresie and silence (contrary to the opinion of the world) haue I euer found most women. I haue sat a whol afternoone many times by my wife, and lookt vpon her eies, and felt if her pulses haue beat, when I haue nam'd a suspected loue, yet all this while haue not drawne from her the least scruple of confession. I haue laine awake a thousand nights, thinking she wold haue reuealed somewhat in her dreames, and when she has begunne to speake any thing in her sleepe, I haue iog'd her, and cried I sweete heart. But when wil your loue come, or what did hee say to thee ouer the stall? Or what did he do to thee in the Garden-chamber? Or when wil he send to thee any letters, or when wilt thou send to him any mony, what an idle coxcombe iealousie wil make a man.

Enter Wafer *and his wife* [*with Boy*].

Well, this is my comfort that heere comes a creature of the same head-peece.
Mist. Waf. O my sweet Child, wheres the Collier?
Iust. Here forsooth.
Mist. Waf. Run into Bucklers burry for two ounces of Draggon water, some Spermacæty and Treakle. What is it sicke of Coliar? a burning Feauer?
Iust. Faith mistris I do not know the infirmity of it: wil you buy any smal Coale, say you?
Waf. Prethee go in and empty them, come be not so impatient.
Mist. Waf. I, I, I, if you had groand fort as I haue done you wold haue bin more natural. Take my riding hat, and my kirtle there: Ile away presently?
Waf. You wil not go to night, I am sure.
Mist. Waf. As I liue but I wil.
Waf. Faith sweet hart I haue great busines to night, stay til to morrow and Ile go with you.
Mist. Waf. No sir I wil not hinder your busines. I see how little you respect the fruits of your owne bodie. I shal find some bodye to beare me company.
Waf. Wel, I wil deferre my busines for once, and go with thee.

Mist. Waf. By this light but you shal not, you shal not hit me i'th teeth that I was your hindrance, wil you to Bucklers burry sir?

[*Exit Boy.*]

Waf. Come you are a foole, leaue your weeping.

Mist. Waf. You shal not go with me as I liue.   *Exit* Wafer.

Iust. Puple.

Mist. Waf. Excellent maister.

Iust. Admirable Mistris, howe happie be our Englishwomen that are not troubled with Iealous husbands; why your Italians in general are so Sun-burnt with these Dog-daies, that your great Lady there thinkes her husband loues her not if hee bee not Iealious: what confirmes the liberty of our women more in *England*, then the Italian Prouerbe, which saies if there were a bridge ouer the narrow Seas, all the women in *Italy* would shew their husbands a Million of light paire of heeles, and flie ouer into *England*.

Mist. Waf. The time of our meeting? Come?

Iust. Seauen.

Mist. Waf. The place.

Iust. In Blacke Friers, there take Water, keepe a loofe from the shore, on with your Masks, vp with your sails, and *West-ward Hoe*.

Mist. Waf. So.   *Exit Mistris* Wafer.

Iust. O the quick apprehension of women, the'ile groape out a mans meaning presently, wel, it rests now that I discouer my selfe in my true shape to these Gentlewomens husbands: for though I haue plaid the foole a little to beguile the memory of mine owne misfortune, I woulde not play the knaue, though I be taken for a Banquerout, but indeed as in other things, so in that, the worlde is much deceiued in me, for I haue yet three thousand pounds in the hands of a sufficient friend, and all my debts discharged. I haue receiued here a letter from my wife, directed to *Stode*, wherein shee most repentantly intreateth my return, with protestation to gyue me assured tryall of her honesty. I cannot tell what to thinke of it, but I will put it to the test, there is a great strife betweene beautie, and Chastity, and that which pleaseth many is neuer free from temptation: as for Iealousie, it makes many Cuckoldes, many fooles,

78 *Exit* Wafer.] Q *places after line* 77.

III. iii, III. iv]   WESTWARD HO

and many banquerouts: It may haue abused me and not my wifes honesty: Ile try it: but first to my secure and doting Companions. 110

Exit.

[ACT III, SCENE iv]

Enter Monopoly *and Mistris* Tenterhooke.

Mono. I beseech you Mistris *Tenterhooke,* Before God Ile be sicke if you will not be merry.

Mist. Tent. You are a sweet Beagle.

Mono. Come, because I kept from Towne a little, let mee not liue if I did not heare the sicknes was in Towne very hot: In troth thy hair is of an excellent colour since I saw it. O those bright tresses like to threds of gold.

Mist. Tent. Lye, and ashes, suffer much in the city for that comparison.

Mono. Heres an honest Gentleman wil be here by and by, was 10 borne at *Foolham*: his name is *Gosling Gloo-worme.*

Mist. Tent. I know him, what is he?

Mono. He is a Knight: what aild your husband to be so hasty to arrest me.

Mist. Tent. Shal I speak truly? shal I speak not like a woman.

Mono. Why not like a woman.

Mist. Tent. Because womens tongues are like to clocks, if they go too fast they neuer goe true, t'was I that got my husband to arrest thee, I haue.

Mono. I am beholding to you. 20

Mist. Tent. For sooth I coulde not come to the speech of you, I thinke you may be spoken with all now.

Mono. I thanke you, I hope youl baile me Cosin?

Mist. Tent. And yet why should I speak with you, I protest I loue my husband.

Mono. Tush let not any young woman loue a man in yeares too well.

Mist. Tent. Why?

110 Companions] Dyce; Companion Q
*12 know him] *stet* Q

Mono. Because heele dye before he can requite it.
Mist. Tent. I haue acquainted *Wafer* and *Honysuckle* with it, and they allow my wit for't extreamly. O honest Sergeant.

Enter Ambush.

Amb. Welcome good mistris *Tenterhooke.*
Mist. Tent. Sergeant I must needs haue my Cosin go alittle Way out of Town with me, and to secure thee, here are two Diamonds, they are worth two hundred pound, keepe them til I returne him.
Amb. Well tis good securitie.
Mist. Tent. Do not come in my husbandes sight in the meane time.

Enter Whirlepoole, Gozling Glo-worme, Linstocke,
Mistris Honnysuckle, *and* Mistris Wafer.

Amb. Welcom Gallants.
Whirl. How now *Monopoly* Arrested?
Mono. O my little *Honysuckle* art come to visit a Prisoner?
Mist. Hony. Yes faith as Gentlemen visit Marchants, to fare wel, or as Poets young quaint Reuellers, to laugh at them. Sirrha if I were some foolish Iustice, if I woulde not beg thy wit neuer trust me. [*To Mist.* Tent.]
Mist. Tent. Why I pray you?
Mist. Hony. Because it hath bin conceald al this while, but come shal we to boat, we are furnisht for attendants as Ladies are, We haue our fooles, and our Vshers.
Sir Goz. I thanke you Madame, I shall meete your wit in the close one day.
Mist. Waf. Sirra, thou knowest my husband keeps a Kennell of hounds?
Mist. Hony. Yes.
Whirl. Doth thy husband loue venery?
Mist. Waf. Venery?
Whirl. I, hunting, and venery are words of one signification.
Mist. Waf. Your two husbands and hee haue made a match to go find a Hare about Bushy Causy.

*30 *Mist. Tent.*] Dyce; *Mono.* Q
37 S.D. Gozling Glo-worme] Dyce; Glo-worme, Gozling, Q
57 husbands] Dyce; husband, Q
58 Bushy Causy] Dyce; Busty Causy Q

Mist. Tent. Theile keepe an excellent house till we come home againe.

Mist. Hony. O excellent, a Spanish dinner, a Pilcher, and a Dutch supper, butter and Onions.

Lyn. O thou art a mad wench.

Mist. Tent. Sergeant carry this ell of Cambrick to mistris *Birdlime*, tel her but that it is a rough tide, and that she feares the water, she should haue gone with vs.

Sir Goz. O thou hast an excellent wit.

Whirl. To Boat hay?

Mist. Hony. Sir *Gozlin*? I doe take it your legs are married.

Sir Goz. Why mistris?

Mist. Hony. They looke so thin vpon it.

Sir Goz. Euer since I measurd with your husband, I haue shrunk in the calfe.

Most. Hony. And yet you haue a sweet tooth in your head.

Sir Goz. O well dealt for the Calues head, you may talke what you will of legs, and rising in the small, and swelling beneath the garter. But tis certain when lank thighes brought long stockings out of fashion, the Courtiers Legge, and his slender tilting staffe grew both of a bignesse. Come for *Brainford*.

Exeunt.

ACTUS QUARTUS, SCÆNA PRIMA.

Enter Mistris Birdlime *and* Luce.

Bird. Good morrow mistris *Luce*: how did you take your rest to night? how doth your good worship like your lodging? what will you haue to breakfast?

Luce. A poxe of the Knight that was here last night, he promist to haue sent me some wilde foule; hee was drunk Ile be stewed else.

Bird. Why do not you think he will send them?

Luce. Hang them: tis no more in fashion for them to keepe their promises, then tis for men to pay their debtes. He will lie faster then a Dog trots: what a filthy knocking was at doore last night; some puny Inn-a-court-men, Ile hold my contribution.

Bird. Yes in troth were they, ciuill gentlemen without beards, but to say the truth, I did take exceptions at their knocking: took them a side and said to them: Gentlemen this is not well, that you should come in this habit, Cloakes and Rapiers, Boots and Spurs, I protest to you, those that be your Ancientes in the house would haue come to my house in their Caps and Gownes, ciuilly, and modestly. I promise you they might haue bin taken for Cittizens, but that they talke more liker fooles. Who knocks there? vp into your Chamber. [*Exit* Luce.] *Enter master* Honisuckle.
Who are you, some man of credit? that you come in mufled thus. 20
Hony.   Whose aboue?
Bird.   Let me see your face first. O maister *Honisuckle*, why the old party: the old party.
Hony.   Pew I will not go vp to her: no body else?
Bird.   As I liue will you giue me some Sacke? wheres *Opportunity*.
                                                            Enter Christian.
Hony.   What dost call her?
Bird.   Her name is *Christian*, but mistris *Luce* cannot abide that name, and so she cals her *Oppertunity*.
Hony.   Very good, good.
Bird.   Ist a shilling, bring the rest in *Aqua vite*. [*Exit* Christian.] 30
Come shals go to Noddy.
Hony.   I and thou wilt for halfe an hower.
Bird.   Heere are the Cardes? deale, God send mee Duces and Aces with a Court Card, and I shall get by it.
Hony.   That can make thee nothing.
Bird.   Yes if I haue a coate Card turne vp.
Hony.   I shew foure games?
Bird.   By my troth I must shew all and little enough to, sixe games: play your single game, I shall double with you anone.
Pray you lend me some siluer to count my games? 40
How now is it good Sack?   *Enter* Christian.
Chri.   Theres a gentleman at doore would speake with you.
Hony.   Gods so, I will not be seene by any means.

                    Enter Tenterhook.

Bird.   Into that closet then? What another mufler?

Tent. How dost thou mistris *Birdlime*?
Bird. Master *Tenterhooke* the party is aboue in the dining Chamber.
Tent. Aboue.
Bird. All alone? [*Exit* Tenterhook.]
Hony. Is he gone vp? who wast I pray thee?
Bird. By this sacke I will not tel you! say that you were a contry Gentleman, or a Cittizen that hath a young wife, or an Inne of Chauncery Man, should I tell you? Pardon me; this Sacke tastes of Horse-flesh, I warrant you the leg of a dead horse hangs in the But of Sacke to keepe it quicke?
Hony. I beseech thee good Mistris *Birdlime* tel me who it was.
Bird. O God sir we are sworne to secrecy as wel as Surgeons. Come drinke to me, and lets to our game.

Tenterhooke *and* Luce *aboue.*

Tent. Who am I?
Luce. You, pray you vnblind me, Captaine *Whirlpoole*, no, maister *Lynstock*: pray vnblind me, you are not sir *Gozling Glo-worme*, for he weares no Ringes of his fingers! Maister *Freeze-leather*, O you are *George* the drawer at the Miter, pray you vnblinde mee, Captaine *Puckfoist*, Maister *Counterpane* the Lawier, what the diuel meane you, beshrew your heart you haue a very dry hand, are you not mine host *Dog-bolt* of *Brainford*, Mistris *Birdlyme*, maister *Honysuckle*, Maister *Wafer*.
Tent. What the last of al your Clients.
Luce. O how dost thou good Cosin.
Tent. I you haue many Cosins.
Luce. Faith I can name many that I do not know, and suppose I did know them what then? I will suffer one to keepe me in diet, another in apparrel; another in Phisick; another to pay my house rent. I am iust of the Nature of *Alcumy*; I wil suffer euery plodding foole to spend monie vpon me, marrie none but some worthie friend to inioy my more retir'd and vse-full faithfulnes.
Tent. Your loue, your loue.
Luce. O I, tis the curse that is laid vppon our quallitie, what wee gleane from others we lauish vpon some trothlesse welfac'd younger Brother, that Loues vs onely for maintainance.

Tent. Hast a good tearme *Luce?*
Luce. A pox on the Tearme, and now I thinke ont, saies a gentleman last night let the pox be in the Towne seauen yeare, Westminster neuer breeds Cob-webs, and yet tis as catching as the plagu, though not al so general. there be a thousand bragging Iackes in *London,* that wil protest they can wrest comfort from me when (I sweare) not one of them know wheather my palme be moiste or not: In troth I loue thee: You promist me seuen Elles of Cambrick.

Wafer knocks and enters [below.]

Bird. Whose that knocks?
Hony. What, more Sacks to the Myl, Ile to my old retirement.
[Exit.]
Bird. How doth your good worship, Passion of my hart, what shift shall I make. How hath your good worship done, a long time?
Waf. Very well Godamercy.
Bird. Your good worship I thinke be riding out of towne.
Waf. Yes beleeue me, I loue to be once a weeke a horsebacke, for methinks nothing sets a man out, better than a Horse.
Bird. Tis certen, nothing sets a woman out better than a man.
Waf. What, is mistris *Luce* aboue?
Bird. Yes truely.
Waf. Not any company with her.
Bird. Company? Shall I say to your good worship and not lie, she hath had no company (let me see how long it was since your Worship was heare) you went to a Butchers feast at Cuckoldshauen the next day after Saint *Lukes* day. Not this fortnight, in good truth.
Waf. Alasse, good soule.
Bird. And why was it? Go to, go to, I thinke you know better than I. The wench asketh euery day when will Master *Wafer* be heere: And if Knightes aske for her, shee cries out at stayre-hed, As you loue my life let em not come vp, Ile do my selfe vyolence if they enter: Haue not you promist hir somwhat?
Waf. Faith, I thinke she loues me.
Bird. Loues: Wel, wud you knew what I know, then you wud say

88 *Bird.*] om. Q

somwhat. In good faith shees very poore, all her gowns are at pawne: she owes me fiue pound for her dyet, besides forty shillings I lent her to redeem two halfe silke Kirtles from the Brokers, And do you thinke she needed be in debt thus, if shee thought not of Some-body.

Waf. Good honest Wench.

Bird. Nay in troth, shees now entring into bond for fiue poundes more, the Scriuener is but new gon vp to take her bond.

Waf. Come, let her not enter into bond, Ile lend her fiue pound, ile pay the rest of her debts, Call downe the Scriuener?

Bird. I pray you when he comes downe, stand mufled, and Ile tell him you are her brother.

Waf. If a man haue a good honest wench, that liues wholy to his vse, let him not see hir want. *Exit* Birdlime *and enter aboue.*

Bird. O, mistris *Luce,* mistris *Luce,* you are the most vnfortunate Gentlewoman that euer breathde: your young wild brother came newly out of the Countrey, he calles me Bawd, sweares I keepe a Bawdy house, saies his sister is turned whore, and that he wil kill, and slay any man that he finds in her company.

Tent. What conuayance wil you make with me mistris *Birdlime.*

Luce. O God let him not come vp, tis the swaggringst wilde-oats.

Bird. I haue pacified him somwhat, for I told him, that you were a Scriuener come to take a band of her, now as you go foorth say she might haue had so much mony if she had pleased, and say, she is an honest Gentlewoman and al wil be wel.

Tent. Inough, farewel good *Luce.*

Bird. Come change your voice, and muffle you.

[*Exeunt* Birdlime, Tenterhooke *aboue.*]

Luce. What trick should this be, I haue neuer a brother, Ile hold my life some franker customer is come, that shee slides him off so smoothly.

Enter [*below*] Tenterhooke *and* Birdlime.

Tent. The Gentlewoman is an honest Gentlewoman as any is in *London,* and should haue had thrice as much money vpon her single bond for the good report I heare of her.

Waf. No sir, hir friends can furnish her with mony.

Tent. By this light I should know that voice, *Wafer*, od'sfoote are you the Gentlewomans Brother?
Waf. Are you turnd a Scriuener *Tenterhooke*?
Bird. I am spoild.
Waf. Tricks of mistris *Birdlyme* by this light.

Enter Honysuckle.

Hony. Hoick Couert, hoick couert, why Gentlemen is this your hunting?
Tent. A Consort, what make you here *Honysuckle*?
Hony. Nay what make you two heare, O excellent mistris *Birdlime* thou hast more trickes in thee then a Punke hath Vnckles, cosins, Brothers, Sons or Fathers: an infinit Company.
Bird. If I did it not to make your good worships merry, neuer beleeue me, I wil drinke to your worship a glasse of Sack.

Enter Iustiniano.

Iust. God saue you.
Hony. & Waf. Maister *Iustiniano* welcome from *Stoad*.
Iust. Why Gentlemen I neuer came there.
Tent. Neuer there! where haue you bin then?
Iust. Mary your daily guest I thanke you.
Omn. Ours.
Iust. I yours.
I was the pedant that learnt your wiues to write, I was the Colliar that brought you newes your childe was sicke, but the truth is, for ought I knowe, the Childe is in health, and your wiues are gone to make merry at *Brainford*.
Waf. By my troth good wenches, they little dreame where we are now.
Iust. You little dreame what gallants are with them.
Tent. Gallants with them! Ide laugh at that.
Iust. Foure Gallants by this light, Maister *Monopoly* is one of them.
Tent. *Monopoly*? Ide laugh at that in faith.
Iust. Would you laugh at that! why do ye laugh at it then, they are ther by this time, I cannot stay to giue you more particular intelligence: I haue receiued a letter from my wife heare, if you will cal me at *Putney*, Ile beare you company.

149 you] Dyce; your Q

IV. i] WESTWARD HO

Tent. Od'sfoot what a Rogue is Sergeant *Ambush*, Ile vndo him by this light.
Iust. I met Sergeant *Ambush*, and wild him come to this house to you presently, so Gentlemen I leaue you! Bawd I haue nothing to say to you now; do not thinke to much in so dangerous a matter for in womens matters tis more dangerous to stand long deliberating, then before a battaile. *Exit* Iustiniano.
Waf. This fellowes pouerty hath made him an arrant knaue.
Bird. Will your worship drinke any *Aquavitæ*?
Tent. Apox on your *Aquavitæ*. *Monopoly*, that my wife vrged me 190 to arrest gon to *Brainford*. *Enter* Ambush.
Here comes the varlet.
Amb. I am come sir to know your pleasure.
Tent. What hath *Monopoly* paid the mony yet?
Amb. No sir, but he sent for mony.
Tent. You haue not caried him to the counter, he is at your house stil?
Amb. O Lord I sir as melancholike &c.
Tent. You lie like an arrant varlet, by this candle I laugh at the iest.
Bird. And yet hees ready to cry. 200
Tent. Hees gone with my wife to *Brainford*, and there bee any Law in *England* Ile tickle ye for this.
Amb. Do your worst, for I haue good security and I care not, besides it was his cosin your wiues pleasure that he should goe along with her.
Tent. Hoy day, her cosin, wel sir, your security.
Amb. Why sir two Diamonds here.
Tent. O my hart: my wiues two Diamonds,
Wel, youle go along and iustifie this. *Enter* Luce.
Amb. That I wil sir. 210
Luce. Who am I? [*Covers his eyes.*]
Tent. What the Murrion care I who you are, hold off your Fingers, or Ile cut them with this Diamond.
Luce. Ile see em ifaith,
So, Ile keepe these Diamonds tell I haue my silke gowne, and six els of Cambricke.

192 Here] Dyce; Heres Q(c); heres Q(u)

365

Tent. By this light you shal not.
Luce. No, what do you think you haue Fops in hand, sue me for them.
Waf. & Hony. As you respect your credit lets go. [*Exeunt.*] 220
Tent. Good *Luce* as you loue me let me haue them, it stands vpon my Credit, thou shalt haue any thing, take my pursse.
Luce. I will not be crost in my humour sir.
Tent. You are a dam'd filthy punke, what an vnfortunate Rogue was I, that euer I came into this house.
Bird. Do not spurne any body in my house you were best.
Tent. Well, well. [*Exit.*]
Bird. Excellent *Luce*, the getting of these two Diamondes maie chaunce to saue the Gentlewomens credit; thou heardst all.
Luce. O I, and by my troath pittye them, what a filthy Knaue was 230 that betraied them.
Bird. One that put me into pittifull feare, master *Iustiniano* here hath laied lurking like a sheep-biter, and in my knowledge hath drawne these gentlewomen to this misfortune: but Ile downe to Queene-hiue, and the Watermen which were wont to carrie you to Lambeth *Marsh*, shall carry mee thither: It may bee I may come before them; I thinke I shal pray more, what for feare of the water, and for my good successe then I did this twelvemonth.

[*Exeunt.*]

[ACT IV,] SCÆNA 2.

Enter the Earle and three Seruingmen.

Earl. Haue you perfum'd this Chamber?
Omn.   Yes my Lord.
Earl. The banquet?
Omn.   It stands ready.
Earl.   Go, let musicke
Charme with her excellent voice an awfull scilence
Through al this building, that her sphæry soule
May (on the wings of Ayre) in thousand formes
Inuisibly flie, yet be inioy'd. Away.

IV. ii]   WESTWARD HO

1. *Seru.* Does my Lorde meane to Coniure that hee drawes this strange Characters.
2. *Seru.* He does: but we shal see neither the Spirit that rises, nor the Circle it rises in.
3. *Seru.* Twould make our haire stand vp an end if wee shoulde, come fooles come, meddle not with his matters, Lords may do any thing.   *Exeunt.*

Earl. This night shal my desires be amply Crownd,
And al those powers, that tast of man in vs,
Shall now aspire that point of happines,
Beyond which, sensuall eies neuer looke, (sweet pleasure!)
Delicious pleasure? Earths Supreamest good,
The spring of blood, tho it dry vp our blood.
Rob me of that, (tho to be drunke with pleasure,
As ranke excesse euen in best things is bad;
Turnes man into a beast) yet that being gone,
A horse and this (the goodliest shape) al one.
We feed: weare rich attires: and striue to cleaue
The stars with Marble Towers, fight battailes: Spend
Our blood to buy vs names: and in Iron hold
Will we eate roots, to imprison fugitiue gold:
But to do thus, what Spell can vs excite,
This the strong Magick of our appetite:
To feast which richly, life it selfe vndoes,
Whoo'd not die thus? to see, and then to choose?
Why euen those that starue in Voluntary wants,
And to aduance the mind, keepe the flesh poore,
The world Inioying them, they not the world,
Wud they do this, but that they are proud to sucke
A sweetnes from such sowrenes; let em so,
The torrent of my appetite shall flow
With happier streame. A woman! Oh, the Spirit
And extract of Creation! This, this night,
The Sun shal enuy. What cold checks our blood?
Her bodie is the Chariot of my soule,
Her eies my bodies light, which if I want,
Life wants, or if possesse, I vndo her;

Turne her into a diuel, whom I adore,
By scorching her with the hot steeme of lust.
Tis but a minutes pleasure: and the sinne
Scarce acted is repented. Shun it than:
O he that can Abstaine, is more than man!
Tush. Resolu'st thou to do ill: be not precize,
Who writes of *Vertue* best, are slaues to vize, *Musick.* 50
The musicke sounds allarum to my blood,
Whats bad I follow, yet I see whats good.

Whilst the song is heard, the Earle drawes a Curten, and sets forth a Banquet: he then Exit, and Enters presently with Iustiniano *attird like his wife maskt: leads him to the table, places him in a chaire, and in dumbe signes, Courts him, til the song be done.*

Earl. Fayre! be not doubly maskt: with that and night,
Beautie (like gold) being vs'd becomes more bright.
Iust. Wil it please your Lordship to sit, I shal receiue smal pleasure if I see your Lordship stand.
Earl. Witch, hag, what art thou proud damnation?
Iust. A Marchants wife.
Earl. Fury who raizd thee vp, what com'st thou for!
Iust. For a banquet. 60
Earl. I am abus'd, deluded: Speake what art thou?
Vds death speake, or ile kil thee, in that habit
I lookt to find an Angel, but thy face,
Shewes th'art a Diuel.
Iust. My face is as God made it my Lord: I am no diuel vnlesse women be diuels, but men find em not so, for they daily hunte for them.
Earl. What art thou that dost cozen me thus?
Iust. A Marchants wife I say: *Iustinianos* wife. Shee, whome that long burding piece of yours, I meane that Wicked mother *Bird-* 70 *lyme* caught for your honor. Why my Lord, has your Lordshippe forgot how ye courted me last morning.
Earl. The diuel I did.

52 S.D. Iustiniano] Parenthesis Q
55 *Iust.*] Q *speech prefixes in this scene are forms of* Par.

Iust. Kist me last morning.
Earl. *Succubus*, not thee.
Iust. Gaue me this Iewel last morning.
Earl. Not to thee *Harpy*.
Iust. To me vpon mine honestie, swore you would build me a lodging by the *Thames* side with a watergate to it: or els take mee a lodging in Cole-harbor.
Earl. I swore so.
Iust. Or keep me in a Laborinth as *Harry* kept *Rosamond* wher the Minotaure my husband should not enter.
Earl. I sware so, but gipsie not to thee?
Iust. To me vppon my honour, hard was the siege, which you laid to the Christal wals of my chastity, but I held out you know: but because I cannot bee too stony harted, I yeelded my Lord, by this token my Lord (which token lies at my heart like lead) but by this token my Lord, that this night you should commit that sinne which we al know with me.
Earl. Thee?
Iust. Do I looke vgly, that you put thee vppon me: did I giue you my hand to horne my head, thats to say my husband, and is it com to thee: is my face a filthyer face, now it is yours, then when it was his: nor haue I two faces vnder one hoode. I confesse I haue laid mine eyes in brine, and that may chaunge the coppy. But my Lord I know what I am.
Earl. A Sorceresse, thou shalt witch mine eares no more, If thou canst pray, doot quickly for thou diest.
Iust. I can praie but I wil not die, thou liest:
My Lord there drops your Ladie; And now know,
Thou vnseasonable Lecher, I am her husband
Whom thou wouldst make whore, read: she speakes there thus,
Vnlesse I came to her, her hand should free   [*Shewes letter.*]
Her Chastitie from blemish, proud I was
Of her braue mind, I came, and seeing what slauerie
Pouertie, and the frailtie of her Sex
Had, and was like to make her Subiect to,
I begd that she would die, my suite was granted,

*95 nor] Q(u); or Q(c)

I poison'd her, thy lust there strikes her dead, 110
Hornes feard, plague worse, than sticking on the head.

[*Draws a curtain and discovers Mistris* Iustiniano *as though dead.*]

Earl. Oh God thou hast vndone thy selfe and me,
None liue to match this peece, thou art to bloudie,
Yet for her sake, whom Ile embalme with teares,
This Act with her I bury, and to quit
Thy losse of such a Iewel, thou shalt share
My liuing with me, Come imbrace.
Iust. My Lord.
Earl. Villaine, dambd mercilesse slaue, Ile torture thee
To euery ynch of flesh: what ho: helpe, whose there?
Enter Seruingmen.
Come hither: heres a murderer, bind him. How now, 120
What noise is this. *Enter the* 1. *Seruingman.*
1. *Seru.* My Lord there are three Cittizens face mee downe, that heres one maister *Parenthesis* a schoolemaister with your Lordship and desire he may be forth-comming to em.
Iust. That borrowed name is mine. Shift for your selues:
Away, shift for your selues; fly, I am taken.
Earl. Why should they flye thou Skreech-owle.
Iust. I wil tel thee,
Those three are partners with me in the murder,
We foure commixt the poison, shift for your selues.
Earl. Stops mouth, and drag him backe: intreat em enter. 130

Enter the three Cittizens [Tenterhook,
Honysuckle, Wafer].

O what a conflict feele I in my bloud,
I would I were lesse great to be more good:
Y'are welcome, wherefore came you! guard the dores;
When I behold that obiect, al my sences
Reuolt from reason, he that offers flight,
Drops downe a Coarse.
Al. 3. A Coarse?

120 S.D. 1. *Seruingman*] Dyce; 1. *Seruingmen* Q

370

1. *Seru.* I a coarse, do you scorn to be worms meat more then she?
Iust. See Gentlemen, the Italian that does scorne,
  Beneath the Moone, no basenes like the horne,
  Has powr'd through all the veines of yon chast bosome,
  Strong poison to preserue it from that plague,
  This fleshly Lord: he doted on my wife,
  He would haue wrought on her and plaid on me.
  But to pare off these brims, I cut off her,
  And guld him with this lie, that you had hands
  Dipt in her blood with mine, but this I did,
  That his staind age and name might not be hid.
  My Act (tho vild) the world shall crowne as iust,
  I shall dye cleere, when he liues soyld with lust:
  But come: rise *Moll*. Awake sweete *Moll*, th'ast played
  The woman rarely, counterfetted well.
1. *Seru.* Sure sh'as nine liues.
Iust. See, *Lucrece* is not slaine,
  Her eyes which lust cald Suns, haue their first beames,
  And all these frightments are but idle dreames:
  Yet (afore *Ioue*) she had her knife prepard
  To let hir bloud forth ere it should run blacke?
  Do not these open cuts now, coole your back?
  Methinkes they should: when *Vice* sees with broad eyes
  Her vgly forme, she does hirselfe despise.
Earl. Mirror of dames, I looke vpon thee now,
  As men long blind, (hauing recouered sight)
  Amazd: scarce able are to endure the light:
  Mine owne shame strikes me dumb: henceforth the booke
  Ile read shall be thy mind, and not thy looke.
Hony. I would either wee were at *Braineford* to see our wiues, or our wiues heere to see this Pageant.
Tent. So would I, I stand vpon thornes.
Earl. The iewels which I gaue you: weare: your fortunes,
  Ile raise on golden Pillars: fare you well,

158 hir] Dyce (her); his Q (cf. l. 161(u))
160 sees] Q(c); *om.* Q(u)
161 hirselfe] Q(c); himselfe Q(u)

Lust in old age like burnt straw, does euen choake
   The kindlers, and consumes, in stincking Smoake. *Exit.*
Iust. You may follow your Lord by the smoake, Badgers.
1. *Seru.* If fortune had fauord him, wee might haue followed you
   by the hornes. *[Exeunt.]*
Iust. Fortune fauors fooles, your Lords a wise Lord: So: how
   now? Ha? This that makes me fat now, ist not Rats-bane to you
   Gentlemen, as pap was to *Nestor*, but I know the inuisible sins of
   your wiues hang at your eye-lides, and that makes you so heauy
   headed.
Tent. If I do take em napping I know what Ile do.
Hony. Ile nap some of them.
Tent. That villaine *Monopoly*, and that sir *Gozlin* treads em all.
Waf. Wud I might come to that treading.
Iust. Ha ha, so wud I: come *Moll*: the booke of the siedge of
   Ostend, writ by one that dropt in the action, will neuer sell so well,
   as a report of the siedge between this *Graue*, this wicked elder and
   thy selfe, an impression of you two, wold away in a May-morning:
   was it euer heard that such tyrings, were brought away from a
   Lord by any wench but thee *Moll*, without paying, vnlesse the
   wench connycatcht him? go thy waies: if all the great Turks
   Concubins were but like thee, the ten-penny-infidell should neuer
   neede keep so many geldings to ney ouer em: come shal this
   Westerne voyage hold my harts?
All 3. Yes, yes.
Iust. Yes, yes: Sfoot you speake as if you had no harts, and look
   as if you were going westward indeede: to see how plaine dealing
   women can pull downe men: *Moll* youle helpe vs to catch Smelts
   too?
Mist. Iust. If you be pleasd.
Iust. Neuer better since I wore a Smock.
Hony. I feare our oares haue giuen vs the bag.
Waf. Good, Ide laugh at that.
Iust. If they haue, would whores might giue them the Bottle:

178 This] Q(u); This is Q(c)	178 makes] Q(c); make Q(u)
186 so wud] Dyce; sownd Q	192 thy] Dyce; thy thy Q
204 laugh] Dyce; laught	*205 whores] wheres Q

come march whilst the women double their files: Married men see, theres comfort: the Moones vp: fore *Don Phœbus*, I doubt we shall haue a Frost this night, her hornes are so sharp: doe you not feele it bite.

Tent. I do, Ime sure. 210

Iust. But weele sit vppon one anothers skirts ith Boate, and lye close in straw, like the hoary Courtier. Set on
To *Brainford* now: where if you meete fraile wiues,
Nere sweare gainst hornes, invaine dame Nature striues.
Exeunt.

ACTUS QUINTUS, Scæna Prima.

Enter Monopoly, Whirlepoole, Lynstock, *and the wiues,*
Iudyth [Honysuckle], Mabell [Wafer], *and*
Clare [Tenterhooke], *their Hats off.*

Mono. Why Chamberlin? will not these Fidlers be drawn forth? are they not in tune yet? Or are the Rogues a fraid ath Statute, and dare not trauell so far without a passe-port?
Whirl. What Chamberlin?
Lyn. Wheres mine host? what Chamberlin. *Enter Chamberlin.*
Cham. Anon sir, heere sir, at hand sir.
Mono. Wheres this noise? what a lowsie Townes this? Has *Brainford* no musick int.
Cham. They are but rozining sir, and theile scrape themselues into your company presently. 10
Mono. Plague a their Cats guts, and their scraping: dost not see women here, and can we thinkst thou be without a noise then?
Cham. The troth is sir, one of the poore instruments caught a sore mischance last night: his most base bridge fell downe, and belike they are making a gathering for the reparations of that.
Whirl. When they come, lets haue em with apox.
Cham. Well sir, you shall sir.

S.D. *the*] Hazlitt; *their* Q

Mono. Stay Chamberlin: wheres our knight sir *Gozlin?* wheres sir *Gozlin.*

Cham. Troth sir, my master, and sir *Gozlin* are guzling: they are dabling together fathom deepe: the Knight hath drunke so much Helth to the Gentleman yonder, on his knees, that hee has almost lost the vse of his legs.

Mist. Hony. O for loue, let none of em enter our roome, fie.

Mist. Waf. I wud not haue em cast vp their accounts here, for more then they meane to be drunke this tweluemonth.

Mist. Tent. Good Chamberlin keepe them and their Helthes out of our company.

Cham. I warrant you, their Helthes shall not hurt you.   *Exit.*

Mono. I, well said: they're none of our giuing: let em keep their owne quarter: Nay I told you the man would soake him if hee were ten Knights: if he were a Knight of Gold theyd fetch him ouer.

Mist. Tent. Out vpon him?

Whirl. Theres a Liefetennant and a Captaine amongst em too.

Mono. Nay, then looke to haue some body lie on the earth fort: Its ordinary for your Liefetennant to be drunke with your Captaine, and your Capten to cast with your Knight.

Mist. Tent. Did you neuer hear how sir *Fabian Scarcrow* (euen such another) tooke me vp one night before my husband being in wine.

Mist. Waf. No indeede, how was it?

Mist. Tent. But I thinke I tooke him downe with a witnesse.

Mist. Hony. How? Good *Tenterhooke.*

Mist. Tent. Nay Ile haue all your eares take part of it.

Omn. Come, on then.

Mist. Tent. He vsd to freequent me and my Husband diuerse times; And at last comes he out one morning to my husband, and sayes, maister *Tenterhooke* saies he, I must trouble you to lend mee two hundred pound about a commodity which I am to deale in, and what was that commodity but his knighthood.

Omn. So.

---

20 *Cham.*] Dyce; Q *omits speech prefix and runs on with* Mist. Tent.'s *speech above.*
24 *Mist. Hony.*] Q *speech prefixes in this scene are forms of* Iud.
25 *Mist. Waf.*] Q *speech prefixes in this scene are forms of* Mab.
27 *Mist. Tent.*] Q *speech prefixes in this scene are forms of* Cla.

Mist. Tent. Why you shall Maister *Scarcrow* saies my good man: So within a little while after, Maister *Fabian* was created Knight.
Mono. Created a Knight! thats no good heraldry: you must say dubd.
Mist. Tent. And why not Created pray.
Omn. I wel done, put him downe ats owne weapon.
Mist. Tent. Not Created, why al things haue their being by creation.
Lyn. Yes by my faith ist. 60
Mist. Tent. But to returne to my tale.
Whirl. I mary: marke now.
Mist. Tent. When he had climb'd vp this costly ladder of preferment, he disburses the mony backe agen very honorably: comes home, and was by my husbande inuited to supper: There supt with vs besides, another Gentleman incident to the Court, one that hadde bespoke me of my husband to help me into the banqueting house and see the reuelling: a young Gentlewoman, and that wagge (our schoolemaister) maister *Parenthesis*, for I remember he said grace, methinks I see him yet, how he turn'd vp the white a'th eie, 70 when he came to the last Gaspe, and that he was almost past Grace.
Mist. Waf. Nay he can doot.
Mist. Tent. All supper time, my New-minted knight, made Wine the waggon to his meat, for it ran downe his throat so fast, that before my Chamber-maid had taken halfe vp, he was not scarce able to stand.
Mono. A generall fault at Cittizens tables.
Mist. Tent. And I thinking to play vpon him, askt him, Sir *Fabian Scarcrow* quoth I, what pretty Gentlewoman wil you raise 80 vp now to stal her your Lady? but he like a foul-mouthd man, swore zounds Ile stal neuer a punke in *England*. A Lady, theres too many already: O fie Sir *Fabian* (quoth I) will you cal her that shall bee your wife such an odious name! and then he sets out a throat and swore agen (like a stinking breathd knight as he was) that women were like horses.
Mist. Hony. & Mist. Waf. O filthy knaue.

68 Gentlewoman] Dyce (*cf. lines* 89, 91); Gentleman Q   83 too] Dyce; two Q

375

Mist. Tent.   Theyde break ouer any hedge to change their pasture, tho it were worse: Fie man fie, (saies the Gentlewoman.)
Mono.   Very good.
Mist. Tent.   And he bristling vp his beard to raile at her too, I cut hym ouer the thumbs thus: why sir *Fabian Scarcrow* did I incense my husband to lend you so much mony vpon your bare worde, and doe you backbite my friends, and me to our faces! I thought you had had more perseuerance; if you bore a Knightly and a degenerous mind you would scorne it: you had wont to be more deformable amongst women: Fie, that youle be so humorsome: here was Nobodie so egregious towardes you sir *Fabian*! and thus in good sadnes, I gaue him the best wordes I coulde picke out to make him ashamd of his doings.
Whirl.   And how tooke he this Correction.
Mist. Tent.   Verie heauily: for he slept presentlie vpont: and in the morning was the sorriest Knight, and I warrant is so to this daie, that liues by bread in *England*.
Mono.   To see what wine and women can do, the one makes a man not to haue a word to throw at a Dogge, the other makes a man to eat his owne words, tho they were neuer so filthy.
Whirl.   I see these Fiddlers cannot build vp their bridge, that some Musicke may come ouer vs.
Lyn.   No faith they are drunke too, what shals do therefore.
Mono.   Sit vp at Cards al night?
Mist. Waf.   Thats Seruingmans fashion.
Whirl.   Drinke burnt wine and Egs then?
Mist. Hony.   Thats an exercise for your sub-burbe wenches.
Mist. Tent.   No no, lets act vpon our posset and so march to bed, for I begin to wax light with hauing my Natural sleepe puld out a mine eies.
Omn.   Agreed: beet so, the sacke posset and to bed.
Mono.   What Chamberlain? I must take a pipe of Tobacco.
3. Women.   Not here, not here, not heare.
Mist. Waf.   Ile rather loue a man that takes a purse, then him that takes Tobacco.
Mist. Tent.   By my little finger Ile breake al your pipes, and burne

88 any] Q(c); an Q(u)   116 a] Q(c); *om.* Q(u)

the Case, and the box too, and you drawe out your stinking smoake afore me.

Mono. Prethee good mistris *Tenterhooke*, Ile ha done in a trice.

Mist. Tent. Do you long to haue me swoune?

Mono. Ile vse but halfe a pipe introth.

Mist. Tent. Do you long to see me lie at your feet!

Mono. Smell toot: tis perfum'd.

Mist. Tent. Oh God? Oh God? you anger me: you stir my bloud: you moue me: you make me spoile a good face with frowning at you: this was euer your fashion, so to smoake my Husband when you come home, that I could not abide him in mine eye: hee was a moate in it me thought a month after: pray spawle in another roome: fie, fie, fie.

Mono. Well, well, come, weele for once feed hir humor.

Mist. Hony. Get two roomes off at least if you loue vs.

Mist. Waf. Three, three, maister *Lynstocke* three.

Lyn. Sfoote weele dance to *Norwich*, and take it there, if youle stay till we returne agen? Heeres a stir, youle ill abide a fiery face, that cannot endure a smoaky nose.

Mono. Come lets satisfie our appetite.

Whirl. And that wil be hard for vs, but weele do our best.

Exeunt.

Mist. Tent. So: are they departed? What string may wee three thinke that these three gallants harp vppon, by bringing vs to this sinfull towne of *Brainford*? ha?

Mist. Hony. I know what string they would harpe vppon, if they could put vs into the right tune.

Mist. Waf. I know what one of em buz'd in mine eare, till like a Theefe in a Candle, he made mine eares burne, but I swore to say nothing.

Mist. Tent. I know as verily they hope, and brag one to another, that this night theile row westward in our husbands whirries, as wee hope to bee rowd to *London* to morrowe morning in a paire of oares. But wenches lets bee wise, and make Rookes of them that I warrant are now setting pursenets to conycatch vs.

127 *Mist. Tent.*] Dyce; *Mono.* Q

Both. Content.

Mist. Tent. They shall know that Cittizens wiues haue wit enough to out strip twenty such guls; tho we are merry, lets not be mad: be as wanton as new married wiues, as fantasticke and light headed to the eye, as fether-makers, but as pure about the heart, as if we dwelt amongst em in Black Fryers.

Mist. Waf. Weele eate and drinke with em.

Mist. Tent. Oh yes: eate with em as hungerly as souldiers: drinke as if we were Froes: talke as freely as Iestors, but doe as little as misers, who (like dry Nurses) haue great breastes but giue no milke. It were better we should laugh at theis popin-Iayes, then liue in feare of their prating tongues: tho we lye all night out of the Citty, they shall not find country wenches of vs: but since we ha brought em thus far into a fooles Paradice, leaue em int: the Iest shal be a stock to maintain vs and our pewfellowes in laughing at christnings, cryings out, and vpsittings this twelue month: how say you wenches, haue I set the Sadle on the right horse.

Both. O twill be excellent.

Mist. Waf. But how shall we shift em off?

Mist. Tent. Not as ill debters do their Creditors (with good wordes) but as Lawyers do their Clyents when their ouerthrown, by some new knauish tricke: and thus it shall bee: one of vs must dissemble to be suddenly very sick.

Mist. Hony. Ile be she.

Mist. Tent. Nay, tho we can all dissemble well, yet Ile be she: for men are so iealous, or rather enuious of one anothers happinesse (Especially in this out of towne gossipings) that he who shall misse his hen, if hee be a right Cocke indeede, will watch the other from treading.

Mist. Waf. Thats certaine, I know that by my selfe.

Mist. Tent. And like *Esops* Dog, vnlesse himselfe might eate hay, wil lie in the manger and starue: but heele hinder the horse from eating any: besides it will be as good as a Welch hooke for you to keepe out the other at the Staues end: for you may boldly stand vppon this point, that vnlesse euery mans heeles may bee tript vp, you scorne to play at football.

*168 theis] their Q

Mist. Hony. Thats certaine: peace I heare them spitting after their Tobacco.

Mist. Tent. A chaire, a chaire, one of you keepe as great a coyle and calling, and as if you ran for a midwife: tho'ther holde my head: whylst I cut my lace.

Mist. Waf. Passion of me? maister *Monopoly*, maister *Linstocke* and you be men, help to daw mistris *Tenterhooke*: O quickly, quickly, shees sicke and taken with an Agony.

Enter as she cryes Monopolie, Whirlepoole, *and* Lynstocke.

Omn. Sick? How? how now? whats the matter?

Mono. Sweete *Clare* call vp thy spirits.

Mist. Tent. O maister *Monopoly*, my spirits will not come at my calling, I am terrible and Ill: Sure, sure, I'me struck with some wicked planet, for it hit my very hart: Oh I feele my selfe worse and worse.

Mono. Some burnt Sack for her good wenches: or possit drink, poxe a this Rogue Chamberlin, one of you call him: how her pulses beate: a draught of Cynamon water now for her, were better than two Tankerdes out of the *Thames*: how now? Ha.

Mist. Tent. Ill, ill, ill, ill, ill.

Mono. I'me accurst to spend mony in this Towne of iniquity: theres no good thing euer comes out of it: and it stands vppon such musty ground, by reason of the Riuer, that I cannot see how a tender woman can do well int. Sfoot? Sick now? cast down now tis come to the push.

Mist. Tent. My mind misgiues me that als not sound at *London*.

Whirl. Poxe on em that be not sounde, what need that touch you?

Mist. Tent. I feare youle neuer carry me thither.

Omn. Puh, puh, say not so.

Mist. Tent. Pray let my cloathes be vtterly vndone, and then lay mee in my bed.

Lyn. Walke vp and downe a little.

Mist. Tent. O maister *Lynstock*, tis no walking will serue my turne: haue me to bed good sweete Mistris *Honisuckle*, I doubt that olde Hag *Gillian* of *Braineford* has bewitcht me.

Mono. Looke to her good wenches.

Mist. Waf. I so we will, and to you too: this was excellent.
Exeunt.
Whirl. This is strange.
Lyn. Villanous spitefull luck: no matter, tother two hold byas.
Whirl. Peace, marke how hees nipt: nothing greeues mee so much as that poore *Pyramus* here must haue a wall this night betweene him and his *Thisbe*.
Mono. No remedy trusty *Troylus*: and it greeues me as much, that youle want your false *Cressida* to night, for heeres no sir *Pandarous* to vsher you into your Chamber.
Lyn. Ile somon a parlee to one of the Wenches, and see how all goes.
Mono. No whispring with the common enimy by this Iron: he sees the Diuell that sees how all goes amongst the women to night: Nay Sfoot? If I stand piping till you dance, damne me.
Lyn. Why youle let me call to em but at the key-hole.
Mono. Puh, good maister *Lynstocke*, Ile not stand by whilst you giue Fire at your Key-holes? Ile hold no Trencher till an other feedes: no stirrup till another gets vp: be no doore-keeper. I ha not beene so often at Court, but I know what the back-side of the Hangings are made of. Ile trust none vnder a peece of Tapistry, *viz.* a Couerlet.
Whirl. What will you say if the Wenches do this to gull vs?
Mono. No matter, Ile not be doubly guld, by them and by you: goe, will you take the lease of the next chamber and doe as I do.
Both. And whats that?
Mono. Any villanie in your company, but nothing out on't; will you sit vp, or lie by'te.
Whirl. Nay lie sure, for lying is most in fashion.
Mono. Troth then; Ile haue you before mee.
Both. It shall be youres.
Mono. Yours ifaith: Ile play *Ianus* with two faces and looke a squinte both wayes for one night.
Lyn. Well Sir, you shall be our dore-keeper.
Mono. Since we must swim, lets leape into one flood, Weele either be all naught, or els all good.
Exeunt.

231 tother] Q(u); th,other Q(c)

[ACT V, Scene ii]

Enter a noyse of Fidlers, following the Chamberlyn.

Cham. Come, come, come, follow mee, follow mee. I warrant you ha lost more by not falling into a sound last night, than euer you got at one Iob since it pleas'd to make you a noise: I can tell you, gold is no money with 'hem: follow me and fum, as you goe; you shall put something into their eares, whilst I prouide to put something into their bellies. Followe close and fum —
Exeunt.

[ACT V, Scene iii]

Enter Sir Gozlin *and* Bird-lime *puld along by him.*

Goʒ. What kin art thou to Long-*Meg* of Westminster? th'art like her.
Bird. Some-what a like Sir at a blush, nothing a kin Sir, sauing in height of minde, and that she was a goodly Woman.
Goʒ. Mary *Anbree*, do not you know me? had not I a sight of this sweete Phisnomy at Rhenish-wine house ha! last day ith Stilliard ha! whither art bound Galley-foist? whether art bound? whence com'st thou female yeoman a-the gard?
Bird. From *London* Sir.
Goʒ. Dost come to keepe the dore *Ascapart.*
Bird. My reparations hether is to speake with the Gentlewoman here that drunke with your worshippe at the Dutch-house of meeting.
Goʒ. Drunke with mee, you lie, not drunke with me: but 'faith what wou'dst with the Women? they are a bed: art not a mid-wife? one of hem told mee thou wert a night woman.

Musick within: the Fidlers.

Bird. I ha brought some women a bed, in my time Sir.
Goʒ. I and some yong-men too, ha'st not *Pandora*? howe now! where's this noyse.

Bird. Ile commit your worship.
Goz. To the Stockes? art a Iustice? shalt not commit mee: dance first 'faith, why scrapers, appeare vnder the wenches Comicall Window, byth' Lord! Vds Daggers? cannot sinne be set a shore once in a raigne vpon your Country quarters, but it must haue fidling? what set of Villaines are you, you perpetuall Ragamuffins? [*Enter Fidlers.*]
Fid. The Towne Consort Sir.
Goz. Consort with a pox? cannot the shaking of the sheets be danc'd without your Town piping? nay then let al hel rore.
[*Draws sword.*]
Fid. I beseech you Sir, put vp yours, and wee'le put vp ours.
Goz. Play you louzie *Hungarians*: see, looke the Maipole is set vp, weele dance about it: keepe this circle *Maquerelle*.
Bird. I am no Mackrell, and ile keepe no Circles.
Goz. Play, life of *Pharao* play, the Bawde shall teach mee a Scotch Iigge.
Bird. Bawd! I defie thee and thy Iigges whatsoeuer thou art: were I in place where, Ide make thee proue thy wordes.
Goz. I wud proue 'hem Mother best be trust: why doe not I know you Granam? and that Suger-loafe? ha! doe I not *Magæra*.
Bird. I am none of your Megges, do not nick-name me so: I will not be nickt.
Goz. You will not: you will not: how many of my name (of the *Glowormes*) haue paid for your furr'd Gownes, thou Womans broker.
Bird. No Sir, I scorne to bee beholding to any Glo-worme that liues vppon Earth for my furre: I can keepe my selfe warme without Glowormes.
Goz. Canst sing Wood-pecker? come sing and wake 'hem.
Bird. Wud you should well know it, I am no singing Woman.
Goz. Howle then! sfoote sing, or howle, or Ile break your Estrich Egshell there.
Bird. My Egge hurts not you, what doe you meane to florish so.
Goz. Sing Madge, Madge, sing Owlet.

*22–23 Comicall Window] *stet* Q

Bird. How can I sing with such a sowre face — I am haunted with a caugh and cannot sing.
Goz. One of your Instruments Mowntibankes, come, here clutch: clutch.
Bird. Alas Sir, I'me an olde woman, and knowe not how to clutch an instrument.
Goz. Looke marke too and fro as I rub it: make a noyse: its no 60 matter: any hunts vp, to waken vice.
Bird. I shall neuer rub it in tune.
Goz. Will you scrape?
Bird. So you will let me go into the parties, I will sawe, and make a noyse.
Goz. Doe then: shatt into the parties, and part 'hem: shat my leane *Læna*.
Bird. If I must needes play the Foole in my olde dayes, let mee haue the biggest instrument, because I can hold that best: I shall cough like a broken winded horse, if I gape once to sing once. 70
Goz. No matter, cough out thy Lungs.
Bird. No Sir, tho Ime olde, and worme-eaten Ime not so rotten —
Coughes.

A SONG.

Will your worship be ridde of me now.
Goz. Faine, as rich-mens heyres would bee of their gowtye dads: thats the hot-house, where your parties are sweatinge: amble: goe, tell the Hee parties I haue sent 'hem a Maste to their shippe.
Bird. Yes forsooth Ile do your errand. *Exit.*
Goz. Halfe musty still by thundring *Ioue*: with what wedge of villanie might I cleaue out an howre or two? Fidlers, come: strike vp, march before mee, the Chamberlaine shall put a Crowne for 80 you into his bill of *Items*: you shall sing bawdie songs vnder euery window ith Towne: vp will the Clownes start, downe come the Wenches, wee'le set the Men a fighting, the Women a scolding, the Dogs a barking, you shall go on fidling, and I follow dancing *Lantæra*: curry your instruments: play and away.
Exeunt.

85 S.D. *Exeunt.*] Dyce; *Exit.* Q

[ACT V, Scene iv]

Enter Tenter-hooke, Hony-suckle, Wafer, Iustiniano, *and his wife, with* Ambush *and* Chamberlayn.

Hony. Serieant *Ambush*, as th'art an honest fellow, scowte in some back roome, till the watch-word be giuen for sallying forth.
Amb. Duns the Mouse. *Exit.*
Tent. — A little low-woman saist thou, — in a Veluet-cappe — and one of 'hem in a Beauer? brother *Honny-suckle*, and brother *Wafer*, hearke — they are they.
Waf. But art sure theyr husbands are a bed with 'hem?
Cham. I thinke so Sir, I know not, I left 'hem together in one roome: and what diuision fell amongst 'hem, the fates can descouer, not I.
Tent. Leaue vs good Chamberlaine, wee are some of their friends: leaue vs good Chamberlaine: be merry a little: leaue vs honest Chamberlaine — *Exit* [*Chamberlain*].
Wee are abuzd, wee are bought and sold in *Brainford* Market; neuer did the sicknesse of one belyed nurse-child, sticke so cold to the heartes of three Fathers: neuer were three innocent Cittizens so horribly, so abhominably wrung vnder the withers.
Both. What shall wee do? how shall we helpe our selues?
Hony. How shall we pull this thorne out off our foote before it rancle?
Tent. Yes, yes, yes, well enough; one of vs stay here to watch: doe you see: to watch: haue an eye, haue an eare. I and my brother *Wafer*, and Maister *Iustiniano*, will set the towne in an insurrection, bring hither the Constable, and his Bill-men, breake open vpon 'hem, take 'hem in their wickednesse, and put 'hem to their purgation.
Both. Agreed.
Iust. Ha, ha, purgation.
Tent. Wee'le haue 'hem before some Countrey Iustice of *Coram*

S.D. Iustiniano] Dyce; Parenthesis Q
15 belyed] *i.e.*, be-lied (*cf.* V.iv.259)
28 *Iust.*] Q *speech prefixes in this scene are forms of* Par.

v. iv] WESTWARD HO

(for we scorne to be bound to the Peace) and this Iustice shall
draw his Sword in our defence, if we finde 'hem to be Malefactors
wee'le ticle 'hem.
Hony. Agreed: doe not stay, but doo't: come.
Iust. Are you mad? do you know what you doe? whether will you runne?
All 3. To set the Towne in an vprore.
Iust. An vprore! will you make the Townes-men think, that Londoners neuer come hither but vpon Saint *Thomases* night? Say you should rattle vp the Constable: thrash all the Countrey together, hedge in the house with Flayles, Pike-staues, and Pitch-forkes, take your wiues napping, these Westerne Smelts nibling, and that like so many *Vulcans*, euery Smith should discouer his *Venus* dancing with *Mars*, in a net? wud this plaster cure the head-ake.
Tent. I, it wood.
Both. Nay it shud.
Iust. *Nego Nego*, no no, it shall bee prou'd vnto you, your heads would ake worse: when women are proclaymed to bee light, they striue to be more light, for who dare disproue a Proclamation.
Tent. I but when light Wiues make heauy husbands, let these husbands play mad *Hamlet*, and crie reuenge; come, and weele do so.
Mist. Iust. Pray stay, be not so heady at my intreaty.
Iust. My wife intreats you, and I intreat you to haue mercy on your selues, though you haue none ouer the women. Ile tell you a tale: this last Christmas a Cittizen and his wife (as it might be one of you) were inuited to the Reuells one night at one of the Innes a Court: the husband (hauing businesse) trusts his wife thither to take vp a roome for him before: shee did so: but before shee went; doubts a rising, what blockes her husband would stumble at, to hinder his entrance, It was consulted vpon, by what token, by what trick, by what banner, or brooch he should bee knowne to bee hee when hee wrapt at the Gate.
All 3. Very good.
Iust. The croud he was told would be greate, their clamors

*33 stay] say Q
46 Both.] Dyce (*Hony. & Waf.*); *All 3.* Q
36 in] Dyce; an Q
64 greate] greater Q

greater, and able to droune the throats of a shoule of fishwiues: he himselfe therefore deuises an excellent watch-word, and the signe at which he would hang out himselfe, should be a horne: he would wind his horne, and that should giue 'hem warning that he was come.

All 3. So.

Iust. The torchmen and whifflers had an *Item* to receaiue him: he comes, ringes out his horne with an allarum, enters with a showte, all the house rises (thinking some sowgelder prest in) his wife blusht, the company Iested, the simple man like a begger going to the stocks laught, as not being sencible of his own disgrace, and hereupon the punyes set downe this decre that no man shall hereafter come to laugh at their reuells (if his wife be entred before him) vnles he cary his horne about him.

Waf. Ile not trouble them.

Iust. So if you trompet a broad and preach at the market crosse, your wiues shame, tis your owne shame.

All 3. What shall we doe then!

Iust. Take my councell, Ile aske no fee fort: bar our host: banish mine hostes, beate a way the Chamberlin, let the ostlers walke, enter you the chambers peaceably, locke the dores gingerly, looke vpon your wiues wofully, but vpon the euill-doers, most wickedly.

Tent. What shall wee reap by this.

Iust. An excellent haruest, this, you shall heare the poore mouse-trapt-guilty-gentlemen call for mercy; your wiues you shall see kneeling at your feet, and weeping, and wringing, and blushing, and cursing *Brainford* and crying *pardona moy, pardona moy, pardona moy*, whilst you haue the choise to stand either as Iudges to condemne 'hem, beadles to torment 'hem, or confessors to absolue 'hem: And what a glory will it be for you three to kisse your wiues like forgetfull husbands, to exhort and forgiue the young men like pittifull fathers; then to call for oares, then to cry hay for *London*, then to make a Supper, then to drowne all in Sacke and Suger, then to goe to bed, and then to rise and open

81 your wiues] Dyce; you wiues Q
83 our] out Q
94 absolue] Dyce; absolued Q

v. iv]   WESTWARD HO

shop, where you may aske any man what he lacks with your cap off, and none shall perceiue whether the brims wring you.   100
Tent. Weele raise no townes.
Hony. No, no, lets knock first.
Waf. I thats best, Ile somon a parle. —   *Knocks.*
Mist. Tent. Whose there? haue you stock-fish in hand that you beat so hard: who are you?   [*Within.*]
Tent. Thats my wife; let *Iustiniano* speak, for al they know our Tongues.
Mist. Tent. What a murren aile these colts, to keepe such a kicking. *Monopoly?*
Iust. Yes.   110
Mist. Tent. Is Master *Lynstock* vp too, and the Captaine.
Iust. Both are in the field: will you open your dore?
Mist. Tent. O you are proper Gamsters to bring false dice with you from *London* to cheat your selues. Ist possible that three shallowe women should gul three such Gallants.
Tent. What meanes this.
Mist. Tent. Haue we defied you vpon the wals all night to open our gates to you ith morning. Our honest husbands they (silly men) lie praying in their beds now, that the water vnder vs may not be rough, the tilt that couers vs may not be rent, and the 120 strawe about our feete may keepe our pritty legs warme. I warrant they walk vpon Queen-hiue (as *Leander* did for *Hero*) to watch for our landing, and should we wrong such kind hearts? wud we might euer be trobled with the tooth-ach then.
Tent. This thing that makes fooles of vs thus, is my wife.
Knockes.
Mist. Waf. I, I knock your bellies full, we hugg one another a bed and lie laughing till we tickle againe to remember how wee sent you a Bat-fowling.
Waf. An Almond Parrat: that's my *Mabs* voice, I know by the sound.   130
Iust. Sfoote you ha spoild halfe already, and youle spoile al, if

104 *Mist. Tent.*] Q speech prefixes in this scene are forms of Cla.
106 speak,] Dyce; ~ ₐ Q
126 *Mist. Waf.*] Q speech prefixes in this scene are forms of Mab.

you dam not vp your mouths; villanie! nothing but villany, Ime afraid they haue smelt your breaths at the key hole, and now they set you to catch Flounders, whilst in the meane time, the concupiscentious Malefactors make 'em ready and take *London* napping.

All 3.   Ile not be guld so.

Tent.   Shew your selues to be men, and breake open dores.

Iust.   Breake open doores, and shew your selues to be beasts: if you break open dores, your wiues may lay flat burglary to your charge. 140

Hony.   Lay a pudding; burglarie.

Iust.   Will you then turne *Coridons* because you are among clowns? shal it be said you haue no braines being in *Brainford*.

All 3.   Maister *Iustiniano* we will enter and set vpon 'em.

Iust.   Well do so: but enter not so that all the countrey may crie shame of your doings: knocke 'hem downe, burst open *Erebus*, and bring an old house ouer your heads if you do.

Waf.   No matter, weele beare it of with head and shoulders.

Knocks. [*Mist.* Wafer *looks out.*]

Mist. Waf.   You cannot enter indeed la, gods my pittikin our three husbands somon a parlee: let that long old woman either 150 creepe vnder the bed or else stand vpright behind the painted cloth.   *Exit.*

Waf.   Doe you heare: you *Mabel?*

Mist. Waf.   Lets neuer hide our heads now, for we are descouered.

Hony.   But all this while, my *Hony-suckle* appeares not.

Iust.   Why then two of them haue pitcht their tents there and yours lies in Ambuscado with your enemy there.

Hony.   Stand vpon your gard there, whilst I batter here.

Knock [*at the other door*].

Mono.   Who's there?

Iust.   Hold, Ile speake in a small voice like one of the women; 160 here's a friend: are you vp? rize, rize; stir, stirre.

Mono.   Vds foote, what Weasell are you? are you going to catch Quailes, that you bring your pipes with you. Ile see what troubled Ghost it is that cannot sleepe.   *Lookes out.*

144 *All* 3.] Dyce; om. Q   144 *Iustiniano*] Parenthesis Q
148 of] *i.e.* off

388

Tent. O Maister *Monopoly* God saue you.
Mono. Amen, for the last time I sawe you, the Diuell was at mine elbow in Buffe, what! three mery men, and three mery men, and three merry men be we too.
Hony. How do's my wife Maister *Monopoly*.
Mono. Who? my ouerthwart neighbour: passing well: this is 170 kindly don: Sir *Goȝlin* is not far from you: wee'le ioyne our Armies presently, here be rare fields to walk in — Captaine rize, Captain *Lynstock* bestir your stumps, for the *Philestins* are vpon vs.
Exit.
Tent. This *Monopoly* is an arrant knaue, a cogging knaue, for all hees a Courtier, if *Monopoly* bee sufferd to ride vp and downe with other mens wiues, hee'le vn-do both Citty and Countrey.

Enter the three wiues.

Iust. *Mol*, maske thy selfe, they shall not know thee.
All 3. Women. How now sweet hearts, what make you here.
Waf. Not that which you make here.
Tent. Mary you make Bulls of your husbands. 180
Mist. Tent. Buzzards do we not? out you yellow infirmities: do al flowers shew in your eyes like Columbines.
Waf. Wife what saies the Collier? is not thy Soule blacker then his coales? how does the child? howe does my flesh and bloud wife?
Mist. Waf. Your flesh and bloud is very well recouered now mouse —
Waf. I know tis: the Collier has a sack-full of newes to empty.
Tent. *Clare* Where be your two ringes with Diamonds?
Mist. Tent. At hand sir, here with a wet finger. 190
Tent. I dreamt you had lost 'hem — what a prophane varlet is this shoulder clapper, to lye thus vpon my wife and her ringes.

Enter Monopoly, Whyrlpoole *and* Lynstock.

All 3. Saue you gentlemen.
Tent. Hony. Waf. And you and our wiues from you.
Mono. Your wiues haue saude themselues for one.

178 *Women.*] om. Q

Tent. Maister *Monopoly*, tho I meet you in hie *Germany*, I hope you can vnderstand broken English, haue you dischargd your debt.

Mono. Yes Sir; with a duble charge, your *Harpy* that set his ten commandements vpon my backe had two Dyamondes to saue him harmles.

Tent. Of you Sir.

Mono. Me Sir, do you think there be no dyamond courtiers.

Enter Ambush.

Tent. Sargent *Ambush* issue forth, *Monopoly* Ile cut off your conuoy maist, Sargant *Ambush*, I charge you as you hope to receaue comfort from the smell of *Mace* speake not like a Sargent, but deale honestly, of whome had you the dyamondes.

Amb. Of your wife Sir if Ime an honest man.

Mist. Tent. Of me you peuter-buttoned rascall.

Mono. Sirra you that liue by nothing but the carion of poultry.

Mist. Tent. Schoole Maister harke heither.

[*Whispers to* Iustiniano.]

Mono. Where are my Iems and pretious stones that were my bale.

Amb. Forth comming Sir tho your mony is not, your crediter has 'hem.

Iust. Excellent, peace; why Maister *Tenterhooke*, if the dyamondes be of the reported value, Ile paie your mony, receaue 'em, keepe 'hem till Maister *Monopoly* be fatter ith purse: for Maister *Monopoly* I know you wil not be long empty Master *Monopoly*.

Mist. Tent. Let him haue 'hem good *Tenterhooke*, where are they.

Tent. At home, I lockt 'hem vp. —

Enter Birdlime.

Bird. No indeed for-sooth, I lockt 'hem vp, and thos are they your wife has, and those are they your husband (like a bad liuer as he is) would haue giuen to a neice of mine, (that lies in my house to take phisick) to haue committed fleshly treason with her.

Tent. I at your house — you old —

Bird. You perdy, and that honest batchiler, neuer call me old for the matter.   [*Points to* Honysuckle.]

Mist. Hony. Motherly woman hees my husband and no Batchelers buttons are at his doublett.

Bird. Las, I speake Innocently and that leane gentleman set in his staffe there: But as Ime a sinner, both I and the yong woman had an eye to the mayne chance, and tho they brought more a bout 'hem than capten *Candishis* voiage came to, they should not, nor could not (vnles I had bin a naughty woman) haue entred the straytes.

All 3. Women. Haue we smelt you out foxes.

Mist. Tent. Doe you come after vs with hue and cry when you are the theeues your Selues.

Mist. Hony. Murder I see cannot be hid, but if this old *Sybill* of yours speake oracles, for my part, Ile be like an Almanacke that threatens nothing but foulewether.

Tent. That bawd has bin dambd fiue hundred times, and is her word to be taken.

Iust. To be dambd once is enough, for any one of her coate.

Bird. Why Sir, what is my coat that you sitt thus vpon my Scirts.

Iust. Thy Coat is an ancient Coat, one of the seauen deadly sinnes. put thy coat first to making; but do you heare, you mother of Iniquity, you that can loose and find your eares when you list, go, saile with the rest of your baudie-traffikers to the place of sixe-penny Sinfulnesse the subvrbes.

Bird. I scorne the Sinfulnesse of any subvrbes in Christendom: tis wel knowne I haue vp-rizers and downe-lyers within the Citty, night by night, like a prophane fellow as thou art.

Iust. Right, I know thou hast, Ile tell you Gentle-folkes, theres more resort to this Fortune-teller, then of forlorne wiues married to old husbands, and of Greene-sicknesse Wenches that can get no husbands to the house of a wise-Woman. Shee has tricks to keepe a vaulting house vnder the Lawes nose.

Bird. Thou dost the Lawes nose wrong to bely mee so.

Iust. For either a cunning woman has a Chamber in her house or a Phisition, or a picture maker, or an Attorney, because all these are good Clokes for the raine. And then if the female party that's

---

228 *Mist. Hony.*] Q *speech prefixes in this scene are forms of* Iud.
236 *Women.*] om. Q

cliented aboue-Staires, be yong, Shees a Squires daughter of lowe
degree, that lies there for phisicke, or comes vp to be placed with
a Countesse: if of middle age, shees a Widow, and has sutes at the
terme or so.

Mist. Hony. O fie vpon her, burne the witch, out of our company.

Mist. Tent. Lets hem her out off *Brainford*, if shee get not the
faster to *London*.

Mist. Waf. O no, for Gods sake, rather hem her out off *London* 270
and let her keepe in *Brainford* still.

Bird. No you cannot hem me out of *London*; had I known this
your rings should ha bin poxt ere I wud ha toucht 'hem: I will take
a paire of Oares, and leaue you.   *Exit*.

Iust. Let that ruine of intemperance bee rakt vp in dust and ashes,
and now tell me, if you had raysed the Towne, had not the tiles
tumbled vpon your heads: for you see your Wiues are chast, these
Gentlemen ciuill, all is but a merriment, all but a May-game; she
has her Diamonds, you shall haue your money, the child is
recouered, the false Collier discouered, they came to *Brainford* to 280
be merry, you were caught in Bird-lime; and therefore set the
Hares-head against the Goose-giblets, put all instruments in tune,
and euery husband play musicke vpon the lips of his Wife whilst
I begin first.

Omn. Come wenches bee't so.

Mist. Tent. Mistris *Iustiniano* ist you were asham'd all this while
of shewing your face, is she your wife Schoolemaister.

Iust. Looke you, your Schoole-maister has bin in *France*, and lost
his hayre, no more *Parenthesis* now, but *Iustiniano*, I will now play
the Merchant with you. Looke not strange at her, nor at mee, the 290
story of vs both, shall bee as good, as an olde wiues tale, to cut off
our way to *London*.

Enter Chamberlain.

How now?

Cham. Alas Sir, the Knight yonder Sir *Goȝlin* has almost his
throat cut by Powlterers and Townes-men and rascalls, and all the
Noise that went with him poore fellowes haue their Fidle-cases
puld ouer their eares.

Omn. Is Sir *Goȝlin* hurt?

Cham. Not much hurt Sir, but he bleedes like a Pig, for his crowne's crackt.
Mist. Hony. Then has he beene twise cut ith head since we landed, once with a Pottle-pot: and now with old iron.
Iust. Gentlemen hasten to his rescue some, whilst others call for Oares.
Omn. Away then to *London.*
Iust. Farewell *Brainford.*
Gold that buyes health, can neuer be ill spent,
Nor howres laid out in harmelesse meryment.

Finis Actus Quintus.

SONG.

Oares, Oares, Oares, Oares:
   To London hay, to London hay:
Hoist vp sayles and lets away,
For the safest bay
For vs to land is London shores.
Oares, Oares, Oares, Oares:
Quickly shall wee get to Land,
If you, if you, if you,
Lend vs but halfe a hand.
O lend vs halfe a hand.

                                   Exeunt.

FINIS.

308 Q *provides* '*Exeunt.*' *after* 'meryment'.

TEXTUAL NOTES

I.i

78 nor] This is the reading of the corrected state for uncorrected *no*. It is a natural correction, and the odds are it is right. Yet since the proof-alterations in this forme are not authorial, one should notice that *no* would make sense if a necessary comma before it had been inadvertently omitted. On the other hand, if *no Mathematicall Ingin whatsoeuer* were to be parenthetical, we should expect a closing comma in addition to a prefixed comma; but both are wanting. The absence of one comma could be explained, but to explain the lack of the second as a double error is more difficult than to accept *no* as a misprint correctly altered to *nor*.

90 wit] Uncorrected Q reads *wist*, but corrected alters to *means*. Dyce, whose notes show he had compared several copies and seen both states, emends to *wit*, pointing to *witty* in line 93 as justification. Hazlitt follows Dyce. Although the original error could be explained most simply as transposition from MS *wits*, the singular form is the more natural. It seems clear that the proof-reader was not able to ungarble the error, and therefore substituted *means* (possibly with line 79 in mind), even though this was tautological before *or opportunity*.

I.ii

1 Clare] Q reads *Moll*, and throughout this scene the Q speech prefixes are forms of *Moll*, altered in the present edition to *Mist. Tent*. The same error appears in III.i.31, 33. But Mistress Justiniano is several times called *Moll* by her husband, and Mistress Tenterhook is later invariably addressed as *Clare*.

II.ii

87 from] The phrase *from your windowes* has given difficulty, and Dyce, though not Hazlitt, emended to *'fore*. It is quite possible that the corruption does indeed lie in *from*, and that the *from* in the next line *Brightnes from those* has caused memorial confusion in the typesetting and displaced some other word like *'fore*. But *those* is not entirely free from suspicion. The general intent of the lines may be glossed from *The Magnificent Entertainment*, lines 182–184: 'All Glasse windowes taken downe, but in their places, sparkeled so many eyes, that had it not bene the day, the light which reflected from them, was sufficient to haue made one.' At best the sense of the lines in *Westward Ho* is given in contorted language, and hence the quarto reading may be defended. As in the *Entertainment*, it would seem

that the brightness of the lady's eyes is supposed to be brighter than the reflection of the sun on her glass windows, the analogy being made when she leans from her windows in the early morning and thus substitutes for the sun's glitter. Hence the Earl may be referring to his watching to steal brightness from her eyes as they look through (and thus *from*) her windows when she arises. Her eyes looking through the windows make them brighter than the reflections of the rising sun from the glass. Or, more simply, he has watched to steal brightness from those (her eyes) looking out from her windows.

170 Gallant] The Dyce-Hazlitt emendation of the singular for Q *Gallants* may well be sophistication; on the other hand, the Q reading is just as likely to be compositor's memorial corruption stemming from the preceding *some*, in view of the subsequent use of the singular *his*.

III.iii

86 I, I am] Q *I, am* may represent only an intrusive comma in a statement that could be interpreted either as an affirmative or else a surprised question. The odds are, however, that the punctuation marks a skipped repetition *I, I am* (Aye, I am), representing Monopoly's quick seizing on the point of the plot.

III.iv

12 know him] Dyce emends to *know him not*, which superficially accords with Mistress Tenterhook's next question but not with the fact that she had been with Sir Gosling at the Steelyard. Just possibly this is the result of collaborative confusion and an original *not* has been removed in revision without sufficient consequential alteration. On the other hand, there is nothing to suggest that Dekker did not have a hand in both scenes. *What is he?* doubtless means that she knows him slightly but not enough to know his true qualities. The phrase is sometimes used as a leading question from one familiar with the person but willing to be amused by an answering analysis or 'character', though here we have only the single contemptuous *He is a Knight* from Monopoly.

30 *Mist. Tent.* Q, which is here printing speeches continuously, assigns this speech to Monopoly by the prefix *Mono*. There is no temptation to run these words on with Monopoly's immediately preceding speech in view of Ambush's answer to what should be her and not Monopoly's greeting. Moreover, the subject of the *it* with which the other women have been acquainted is not the joke Monopoly has just told but instead her device to tether Monopoly by having her husband arrest him. This is clearly shown by line 43 when she is congratulated on the wit of her device. Dyce's assignment of the speech, therefore, is certainly correct. For a similar prefix error, see V.i.127.

IV.ii

95 nor]   Just as at line 106 when the corrector of this forme mistook *slauerie* for the first element of a series, so here he seems to have misunderstood the meaning when he substituted *or* for original *nor*. The next sentence shows that *nor* is right and that it involves a play on words with *two faces* as hypocrisy.

205 whores]   Q *wheres* makes no sense whatever, and the Dyce-Hazlitt emendation *theirs* is little better. The difficulty of distinguishing *o* and *e* in Secretary hand suggests the present reading although some guesswork is involved in the interpretation. Their oars (*i.e.* watermen) have *given them the bag*, that is, have slipped away. To *give the bottle*, therefore, must involve some pun or allusion to the previous phrase. I suggest that *bottle* here means a bottle or truss of hay, and that this involves the cry *hay* as in 'To Boat hay?' (III.iv.68) and 'then to call for oares, then to cry hay for London' (V.iv.97). The connexion of *whores* with hay, I suggest, is a reference to Bridewell Dock (see III.iii.108); and the whole complex pun may, finally, have been started by connecting *bag* with the bag of the bee from Queen-hive, where boats were also taken (IV.i.235; V.iv.122). The similarity of sound in *oars* and *whores* completes the obscure joke. Possibly there is a glancing reference, as well, to various conventional indecencies which grew up about searching for a needle in a bottle of hay.

V.i

168 theis]   Q reads *their popin-Iayes*, but since popinjay-parrot is the allusion, it is likely that the compositor has suffered memorial corruption here from the subsequent *their prating tongues*. The nearest *O.E.D.* definition that would make any sense at all is the use of popinjay as 'a mark set up to shoot at', but even here the sense is better with *these* than with *their*.

V.iii

22–23 Comicall Window]   The meaning of this is unknown, unless some theatrical allusion is intended.

V.iv

33 stay]   Dyce and Hazlitt reprint Q *say*, which makes dubious idiom. For some question of the *stay-say* confusion, though in reverse, see *Shoemakers' Holiday*, V.i.1.

PRESS-VARIANTS IN Q (1607)

[Copies collated: BM[1] (British Museum, 644.b.26), BM[2] (C.12.f.3[4]), BM[3] (Ashley 614); Bodl[1] (Bodleian, Mal. 235[5]), Bodl[2] (Mal. 186[5]); Dyce (Victoria and Albert Museum); Eton (Eton College); Worc (Worcester College, Oxford, wants A1–B1); CSmH (Henry E. Huntington Library); CtY (Yale University); DFo (Folger Shakespeare Library); ICU (University of Chicago); MB (Boston Public Library); MH (Harvard University); MWiW–C (Chapin Collection of Williams College); NN (New York Public Library); TxU (University of Texas).]

SHEET A (*outer forme*)

Corrected: Bodl[1], Dyce, Eton, CSmH, CtY, MB, MH, MWiW–C, TxU.
Uncorrected: BM[1–3], Bodl[2], DFo, ICU, NN.

Sig. A2[v].
  I.i.34 wis] wift
  54 S.D. *Enter*] *Eneer*

Sig. A3.
  r-t *WEST-*] *WAST-*
  I.i.77 rich apparell] tich appatell
  77 Phyficke.] Phyficke,
  77 No] no
  78 nor] no
  78 Ingin] Ingin:
  78 whatfoeuer,] whatfoeuer
  78 face:] face,
  83 leafe] leafe
  84 *Birdlime*] *Birdline*
  89 Cuckolds] Coucouldes
  90 means] wift

SHEET C (*outer forme*)

Corrected: BM[1–3], Bodl[1–2], Eton, CSmH, CtY, DFo, ICU, MB, MH, MWiW–C, NN, TxU.
Uncorrected: Dyce, Worc.

Sig. C1.
  II.i.134 als] all
Sig. C4[v].
  II.ii.158 tranfformd] tranfford

Sheet D (*inner forme*)

Corrected: BM¹⁻³, Bodl², Dyce, Worc, CSmH, CtY, DFo, MB, MH, NN, TxU.
Uncorrected: Bodl¹, Eton, ICU, MWiW–C.

Sig. D2.
II.iii.17 S.D. Enter] Eeter

Sig. D4.
III.i.34 baa] be a

Sheet E (*outer forme*)

Corrected: BM¹⁻³, Bodl¹, Worc, CSmH, CtY, DFo, MB, MWiW–C, NN.
Uncorrected: Bodl², Dyce, Eton, ICU, MH, TxU.

Sig. E3.
III.iv.17 clocks] clacks

Sig. E4ᵛ.
IV.i.64 the] ths

Sheet E (*inner forme*)

Corrected: BM¹⁻³, Bodl¹⁻², Dyce, Worc, CSmH, CtY, DFo, ICU, MB, MH, MWiW–C, NN, TxU.
Uncorrected: Eton.

Sig. E1ᵛ.
III.iii.S.D. *Colliar,*] *Colliar*
    12 in dure] induce
    16 men] man
    20 Captains] Captaine
    27 made] mad

Sig. E2.
III.iii.40 Collier.] Collier,
    59 Sperma cæty] Spermacity

Sig. E4.
IV.i.46 Mafter] Miftris

PRESS-VARIANTS IN Q (1607)

SHEET F (*outer forme*)

Corrected: BM¹⁻³, Bodl¹⁻², Dyce, Eton, CSmH, CtY, DFo, ICU, MB, MH, MWiW–C, NN, TxU.
Uncorrected: Worc.

Sig. F1.
   IV.i.94 loue] lone
      127 O, mift.] O, miftris
      127 vnfortunate] fortunate

Sig. F3.
   IV.ii.40 blood?] blood,

Sig. F4ᵛ.
   IV.ii.141 yon] your

SHEET F (*inner forme*)

Corrected: BM¹⁻³, Bodl¹⁻², Dyce, Eton, CSmH, CtY, DFo, ICU, MB, MH, MWiW–C, NN, TxU.
Uncorrected: Worc.

Sig. F1ᵛ.
   IV.i.133 swaggringft wild-oats] swaggring wilde-oats
      137 Gentlewoman] Gentlewomen
      138 Inough,] Inough
      139 *Bird.*] *Btrd.*

Sig. F2.
   IV.i.169 Child] Childe
      169 your] our
      182 light] lighr
      192 Heres] heres

Sig. F3ᵛ.
   IV.ii.62 thee:] thee,
      69 *Iuftinianos*] *Iuftianos*
      69 She] Shee

Sig. F4.
   IV.ii.80 Cole-harbor] Cold-harbor
      84 *Gipfie*] gipfie
      95 or] nor
      106 flauerie,] flauerie

Sheet G (*outer forme*)

Corrected: BM¹⁻³, Bodl¹⁻², Dyce, Eton, CSmH, CtY, DFo, ICU, MB, MH, MWiW–C, NN, TxU.
Uncorrected: Worc.

Sig. G1.
    IV.ii.160 fees] *om.*
           161 hirſelfe] himſelfe
           178 ha] Ha
           178 is] *om.*
           178 makes] make

Sig. G2ᵛ.
    V.i.88 any] an

Sig. G3.
    V.i.109 Muſicke] Mnſicke
         116 ſleep] ſleepe
         116 out a mine] out mine
         120 here.] heare.

Sig. G4ᵛ.
    V.i.216 now] now,
         231 ſpiteful] ſpitefull
         231 th,other two] tothertwo
         236 *Pandarus*] *Pandarous*

Sheet I (*outer forme*)

Corrected: BM¹⁻³, Bodl¹⁻², Eton, DFo, ICU, MWiW–C, NN, TxU.
Uncorrected: Dyce, Worc, CSmH, CtY, MB, MH.

Sig. I2ᵛ.
    V.iv.303 to] fo

EMENDATIONS OF ACCIDENTALS

I.i

4 Marchant):] ~)_∧
57 Lady?] ~ .
77 Physicke, no] Q(u); Physicke. No Q(c)
78 whatsoeuer_∧] Q(u); ~ , Q(c)
79 face,] Q(u); ~ : Q(c)
88 experyence] experyencc

89 Coucouldes] Q(u); Cuckoldes Q(c)
106 That] that
130 For] for
135 cuniuring:] ~ _∧
189 your building] yout...
215 be such] besuch
224 to my] to. My

I.ii

8 places] placcs
28 Italian] *Italian*
37 *Phillip,*] *Phill.*
45 earth-|quake] earth-quake

70 with-it] with-|it
90 shel-|fish] shel-fish
91 Noble-|mans] Noblemans
97 cousin] consin

II.i

S.D. *Cappe, singing.*] *Cappe. singing*_∧
27 Brittains] *Brittains*
35, 40, 46 Charing-crosse] Charing-crosse
56 fore-noone] for-enoone
60 pen-|men] pen-|men
92 right:] ~ _∧
96 her_∧ double] ~ : ~
124 Ware-house] Ware-|house

145 *Iust.*] *Iufl.*
183 Broome-man] Broome-|man
191 Iaw-bones] Iaw-|bones
203 *Goslin*] *Gosl n*
211 too:] ~ ,
212 Sturgeon?] ~ .
226 of handes] ofhandes
228–231 Do all...vnderstood:] *prose in* Q
230 tongues,] ~ .

II.ii

8 corner,] ~ .
8 I had...heeles.] *separate line in* Q *below* S.D. Takes Aqua-vitæ.
15 Bawd to] Bawdt o
44 Lord,] L.
48–49 This...wilt.] *prose in* Q
56 verie] yerie (*some copies have tail of* y *broken off*)
60 Rank-|ryder] Rank-ryder

70 Y'are] Y are
85 Iust.] ~ _∧
86–92 A thousand...down,] *prose in* Q
100–111 I haue already...know not?] *prose in* Q
109 Player-like)] ~ _∧
112–113 If...thee.] *lined in* Q: If... Man, | Ile...thee.

121–124 Gainst...fortunes.] *prose in* Q
125–126 Till...Lord] *prose in* Q
128–136 My selfe...earne your loue.] *prose in* Q
138 weight] wcight
139 Wil] wil
139 worth?] ~ .
144–145 I see...defies golde.] *prose in* Q

146 rare,] ~ .
147+S.D. *Enter*...] S.D. *after line* 146 *in* Q
150 Cattern] *very doubtfully, a hyphen may follow in* Q
160 Venturer] Veuturer
174 and] aud
184 new,] ~ ˄
222 Monopoly,] Q *cw*; ~ ˄ Q *text*
226 Gads-hill] *Gads-hill*

II.iii

1 So,] ~ ˄
25 so˄] ~ ,
29 well-come] well-|come
55 Trap-|doores] Trap-doores
81 West-ward] West-|ward

86 countenance —] ~ .
106 Content,] ~ ˄
119 indeed˄...*Goʒlin*,] ~ , ... ~ ˄
134 the] The

III.i

17 Why,] ~ ˄
20 Maister] *Maister* [twice]

37 Husband] Husbaud

III.ii

3 resolute?] ~ .
13 or] ot
34 downe, drawne˄] ~ ˄ ~ ,

42 *Clutch*.] *Clouch*
82 kindly:] ~ ˄
83 you —] ~ .

III.iii

12 Lawyers,] ~ .
47–48 begunne to] begunneto
50–51 Garden-|chamber] Garden-chamber

59 Spermacæty] Sperma cæty Q(c); Spermacity Q(u)
77 foole,] ~ ˄
77 your] ycur
108 temptation] tem-|tation

III.iv

65 *Birdlime*,] *Bird.*

IV.i

11 but] bnt
84 in˄] ~ .
120 her] ber
128 Gentlewoman] Q *cw*; gentle-woman Q *text*

133 wilde-oats] Q(u); wild-oats Q(c)
169 Childe] Q(u); Child Q(c)
189 Will] will
197 stil?] ~ .

[IV. ii, V. iv] EMENDATIONS OF ACCIDENTALS

IV.ii

31 choose?] ~ ₍ₐ₎
49 precize,] ~ ₍ₐ₎
52 S.D. heard, the] heard. The
62 thee,] Q(u); ~ : Q(c)
65 face] faee
69 Shee] Q(u); She Q(c)
84 gipsie] Q(u); *Gipsie* Q(c)
100 wil] wll

106 slauerie₍ₐ₎] Q(u); ~ , Q(c)
137 A] a
178 Ha] Q(u); ha Q(c)
213–215 Set on...striues.] *prose in Q, although white space precedes and succeeds* Set on, *and to* Brainford *begins a separate line*

V.i

65 inuited] invited
116 sleepe] Q(u); sleep Q(c)
120 heare] Q(u); here Q(c)
124–5 smoake afore] smokea-|fore
167 misers, who] misers. Who
175 *Both.*] *Boath.*
200 mistris] *mistris*

204 come at] comet a (*some copies only;* Worcester College *correct*)
231 spitefull] Q(u); spiteful Q(c)
236 *Pandarous*] Q(u); *Pandarus* Q(c)
254 ont;] ~ ₍ₐ₎
258 *Both.*] *Booth.*

V.iii

6 house₍ₐ₎ ha!] ~ ! ~ ₍ₐ₎
8 yeoman a-the gard] yeoman-a the gard
25 Raga-|muffins] Ragamuffins

31 Maipole] Mai-|pole
71 matter,] ~ ₍ₐ₎
80 vp,] ~ .
83 fighting,] ~ ₍ₐ₎

V.iv

S.D. *wife.*] ~ ₍ₐ₎
5 'hem] 'him
9 descouer,] ~ ₍ₐ₎
16 neuer] never
24 Bill-men] Bill-|men
33 doo't:] ~ ₍ₐ₎
38 Londoners] *Londoners*
40 Pitch-|forkes] Pitch-forkes
51 *Hamlet*, ...revenge;] ~ ; ... ~ ,
61 trick,] ~ ,,
66 an excellent] anexcellent
76 here-|after] hereafter
82 *All* 3.] *All.*
90 kneeling] kneelig
103 best,] ~ ₍ₐ₎
106 Thats] thats

108–109 kicking. *Monopoly?*] ~ ? ~ .
132 mouths;] ~ ₍ₐ₎
153 *Mabel?*] ~ :
199 Yes] yes
200 commandements] commande-mets
202 Of] of
215 Excellent, peace;] ~ ; ~ ,
216 mony,] ~ ₍ₐ₎
230 Las] las
249 sixe-|penny] sixe-penny
251 Christendom:] ~ ₍ₐ₎
267 witch,] ~ ₍ₐ₎
273 ere] er-
279 money,] ~ '
312 For] for

NORTH-VVARD
HOE.

Sundry times Acted *by the Children of* Paules.

By Thomas Decker, and
Iohn Webster.

Imprinted at London by G. Eld.
1607.

TEXTUAL INTRODUCTION

NORTHWARD HO (Greg, *Bibliography*, no. 250) was entered by George Eld in the Stationers' Register on 6 August 1607: 'Entred for his copie vnder thandes of S^r. Geo Bucke k^t and the Wardens a booke Called. Northward Ho.' Since Eld's edition, the first and only quarto, is dated 1607, we may assume that publication followed shortly after the entry. John Webster's share in the writing does not seem to have been extensive.

Like that of *Westward Ho*, the copy for *Northward Ho* seems to have been released for printing as a consequence of the dissolution of its owners the Children. But whether, as seems likely with its companion play, the copy was foul papers is less certain. The stage-directions in *Northward Ho* are more succinct and less descriptive, and in this respect differ from those in *Westward Ho*; nor are there present the widely variant forms of speech-prefixes. In Act V Mistress Mayberry, who has been *Wife.*, becomes *Mist. May.*, and in III.ii.133 Leapfrog, who has been *Frog.*, is given the prefix *Leap.* This last is venial and without value as evidence, and the first could well have escaped the normalizing attentions of a scribe or book-keeper. At II.i.104 appears what could be either a prompt-book or author's specification of a property: *A watch*. On the other hand, various of the stage-directions are faulty. At II.ii.34 the quarto does not indicate the entrance of Greenshield and Featherstone, nor at II.ii.154 is the exit of Kate and Featherstone provided. In the same scene, II.ii.101, the necessary withdrawal of Bellamont 'aloof' is not specified, nor is Mayberry's withdrawal at V.i.49. Greenshield's entrance at III.ii.45 is not listed. In IV.iii about line 56 the Musician is not brought off the stage. The opening of I.ii brings on Philip 'arrested' but the direction does not specify the two sergeants who arrested him, one of whom, at least, has a speaking part. The crux at II.ii.175 may signify no more than the accidental omission of a line in the printing, but it could also represent the effects of incomplete revision. The entrance of the Fiddlers about V.i.57 is not specified. In IV.iii.41 the direction *Enter the Phisition* could be a relic of authorial revision or else of prompt-book alteration reducing the cast of characters. The first is perhaps the more likely because of the references to him in the text as *Musition*, connecting him with Italy, followed by the later scene in which he talks Italian with Bellamont. Some incomplete reworking seems to be present here, as manifested by the Physician-Musician's mute entrance and abrupt exit (unmarked), as if his 'humour' were taciturnity, whereas the reverse later proves true. All in all, though the evidence is perhaps not of the clearest, it would seem that the copy was probably author's papers, perhaps with preliminary prompt markings and some cuts.

The presswork was not always of the best, and as a consequence some of the punctuation marks ink indistinctly in various copies, requiring a reconstruction by collation. On the evidence of the running-titles, which identify the skeleton-formes, a temporary suspension of printing took place after sheet B (end of line at II.i.25). When printing was resumed with sheet C, new skeletons were constructed; moreover, the evidence that C 1, 3 is missigned D 1, 3, and that D 1, 3 is missigned E 1, 3 suggests the use of two presses, one perfecting for the other.

The quarto offers a superficially clean text. A few deep-rooted difficulties appear to refer back to the manuscript; but some isolated corruptions are doubtless the work of the compositor(s). Collation has disclosed only one press-corrected forme, that of inner E.

Except for the Pearson reprint of 1873, the play has been edited previously only by Dyce in *The Works of John Webster* (1st edition 1830), for which I have used the revised edition of 1859; and by William Hazlitt, *The Dramatic Works of John Webster* (1st edition 1857). Emendations from these editors have been recorded. A photographic facsimile of a British Museum copy (C.12.f.3[5]) was issued in 1914 for Tudor Facsimile Texts.

The present text is based on a collation of the following eighteen copies, substantially all those that have been recorded: British Museum copy 1 (644.b.25), copy 2 (C.12.f.3[5]), copy 3 (Ashley 613); Bodleian copy 1 (Mal. 219[6]), copy 2 (Mal. 235[6]); Dyce Collection in the Victoria and Albert Museum; Eton College; King's College, Cambridge; Worcester College, Oxford; Henry E.

TEXTUAL INTRODUCTION

Huntington Library; Folger Shakespeare Library; Library of Congress; Boston Public Library (containing two E gatherings); Harvard University; New York Public Library; Library of Carl Pforzheimer; the University of Texas; and Yale University.

In the quarto the speeches of Hans van Belch are printed in black-letter. These have been put into roman in the present text without further comment.

[PERSONS

MAYBERRY
BELLAMONT
PHILIP BELLAMONT, his son
LUKE GREENSHIELD
FEATHERSTONE
LEVERPOOL
CHARTLEY
JACK HORNET
HANS VAN BELCH
ALLUM
CAPTAIN JENKINS
LEAPFROG
SQUIRREL
PRENTICE
FULL-MOON
CHAMBERLAIN
TAILOR
DRAWER

MISTRESS MABEL MAYBERRY
KATE GREENSHIELD
DOLL
HOSTESS

Servants, Fiddlers, Sergeants. Bedlamites: Musician, Bawd]

North-ward Hoe

ACTVS PRIMVS. [Scene i]

Enter Luke Greene-shield *with* Fetherstone *booted.*

Feth. Art sure old *Maybery* Innes here to night?
Green. Tis certaine: the honest knaue Chamberleine that hath bin my Informer, my baud, euer since I knew *Ware* assures me of it, and more, being a Londoner though altogether vnacquainted, I haue requested his company at supper.
Feth. Excellent occasion: how wee shall carry our selues in this busines is onely to be thought vpon.
Green. Be that my vndertaking: if I do not take a full reuenge of his wiues puritanicall coynesse.
Feth. Suppose it she should be chast?
Green. O hang her: this art of seeming honest makes many of our young sonnes and heires in the Citty, looke so like our prentises,— Chamberlaine.
Chamb. Heare Sir.

Enter Chamberlaine.

Green. This honest knaue is call'd *Innocence*, ist not a good name for a Chamberlaine? he dwelt at *Dunstable* not long since, and hath brought me and the two Butchers Daughters there to interuiew twenty times and not so little I protest: how chance you left *Dunstable* Sirra?
Chamb. Faith Sir the towne droopt euer since the peace in *Ireland*, your captaines were wont to take their leaues of their *London* Polecats, (their wenches I meane Sir) at *Dunstable*: the next morning when they had broke their fast togeather the wenches brought them to *Hockly 'ith hole,* and so the one for *London*, the other for *Westchester*, your onely rode now Sir is *Yorke, Yorke* Sir.
Green. True, but yet it comes scant of the Prophesy; *Lincolne* was, *London* is, and *Yorke* shall-be.
Chamb. Yes Sir, tis fullfild, *Yorke* shalbe, that is, it shalbe *Yorke*

still, surely it was the meaning of the prophet: will you haue some
Cray-fish, and a Spitchcocke. 30

Enter Maybery *with* Bellamont.

Feth. And a fat Trout.
Chamb. You shall Sir; the Londoners you wot of—
Green. Most kindly welcome—I beseech you hold our bouldnesse excused Sir.
Bell. Sir it is the health of Trauailers, to inioy good company: will you walke.
Feth. Whether Trauaile you I beseech you.
May. To *London* Sir: we came from *Sturbridge.*
Bell. I tel you Gentlemen I haue obseru'd very much with being at *Sturbridge*; it hath afforded me mirth beyond the length of fiue 40 lattin Comedies; here should you meete a *Nor-folk* yeoman ful-but; with his head able to ouer-turne you; and his pretty wife that followed him, ready to excuse the ignorant hardnesse of her husbands forhead; in the goose market number of freshmen, stuck here and there, with a graduate: like cloues with great heads in a gammon of bacon: here two gentlemen making a mariage betweene their heires ouer a wool-pack; there a Ministers wife that could speake false lattine very lispingly; here two in one corner of a shop: Londoners selling their wares, and other Gentlemen courting their wiues; where they take vp petticoates you shold 50 finde schollers and towns-mens wiues crouding togither while their husbands weare in another market busie amongst the Oxen; twas like a campe for in other Countries so many Punks do not follow an army. I could make an excellent discription of it in a Comedy: but whether are you trauailyng Gentlemen?
Feth. Faith Sir we purposed a dangerous voiage, but vpon better consideration we alterd our course.
May. May we without offence pertake the ground of it.
Green. Tis altogither triuial in-sooth: but to passe away the time till supper, Ile deliuer it to you, with protestation before hand, 60 I seeke not to publish euery gentle-womans dishonor, only by the passage of my discource to haue you censure the state of our quarrel.

Bell. Forth Sir.
Green. Frequenting the company of many marchants wiues in the Citty, my heart by chance leapt into mine eye to affect the fairest but with al the falsest creature that euer affection stoopt to.
May. Of what ranck was she I beseech you.
Feth. Vpon your promise of secresie.
Bell. You shall close it vp like treasure of your owne, and your selfe shall keepe the key of it.
Green. She was and by report still is wife to a most graue and well reputed Cittizen.
May. And entertaind your loue.
Green. As Meddowes do Aprill: the violence as it seemed of her affection—but alas it proued her dissembling, would at my comming and departing be-dew her eyes with loue dropps; O she could the art of woman most feelingly.
Bell. Most feelingly.
May. I should not haue lik'd that feelingly had she beene my wife, giue vs some sack heare and in faith—we are all friends; and in priuate—what was her husbands name,—Ile giue you a carouse by and by.
Green. O you shall pardon mee his name, it seemes you are a Cittizen, it would bee discourse inough for you vpon the exchange this fort-night should I tell his name.
Bell. Your modesty in this wiues commendation; on sir.
Green. In the passage of our loues, (amongst other fauours of greater valew) she bestowed vpon me this ringe which she protested was her husbands gift.
May. The poesie, the poesie—O my heart, that ring good infaith?
Green. Not many nights comming to her and being familiar with her —
May. Kissing and so forth.
Green. I Sir.
May. And talking to her feelingly.
Green. Pox on't, I lay with her.
May. Good infaith, you are of a good complexion.

*87 commendation] *stet* Q

Green. Lying with her as I say: and rising some-what early from her in the morning, I lost this ring in her bed.
May. In my wiues bed.
Feth. How do you Sir.
May. Nothing: lettes haue a fire chamberlaine; I thinke my bootes haue taken water I haue such a shudering: ith' bed you say?
Green. Right Sir, in Mistris *Maiberies* sheetes.
May. Was her name *Maybery.*
Green. Beshrew my tongue for blabbing, I presume vpon your secresy.
May. O God Sir, but where did you find your loosing?
Green. Where I found her falsnesse: with this Gentleman; who by his owne confession pertaking the like inioyment; found this ring the same morning on her pillowe, and sham'd not in my sight to weare it.
May. What did shee talke feelingly to him too; I warrant her husband was forth a Towne all this while, and he poore man trauaild with hard Egges in's pocket, to saue the charge of a baite, whilst she was at home with her Plouers, Turkey, Chickens; do you know that *Maibery.*
Feth. No more then by name.
May. Hee's a wondrous honest man; lets be merry; will not your mistresse?—gentlemen, you are tenants in common I take it.
Feth. & Green. Yes.
May. Will not your Mistresse make much of her husband when he comes home, as if no such legerdemaine had bin acted.
Green. Yes she hath reason for't, for in some countries, where men and women haue good trauailing stomackes, they begin with porredge; then they fall to Capon or so-forth: but if Capon come short of filling their bellies, to their porridge againe, 'tis their onely course, so for our women in *England.*
May. This wit taking of long iourneys: kindred that comes in ore the hatch, and sailing to Westminster makes a number of Cuckolds.
Bell. Fie what an idle quarrell is this, was this her ring?
Green. Her ring Sir.
May. A pretty idle toy, would you would take mony for't.

*131 wit] *stet* Q

Feth. & Green. Mony sir.
May. The more I looke on't, the more I like it.
Bell. Troth 'tis of no great valew, and considering the losse, and finding of this ring made breach into your friendship, Gentlemen, with this trifle purchase his loue, I can tell you he keepes a good Table. 140
Green. What my Mistris gift?
Feth. Faith you are a merry old Gentleman; Ile giue you my part in't.
Green. Troth and mine, with your promise to conceale it from her husband.
May. Doth he know of it yet?
Green. No Sir.
May. He shall neuer then I protest: looke you this ring doth fitte me passing well. 150
Feth. I am glad we haue fitted you.
May. This walking is wholesome, I was a cold euen now, now I sweat for't.
Feth. Shalls walke into the Garden *Luke.* Gentlemen weele downe and hasten supper.
May. Looke you, we must be better acquainted that's all.
Green. Most willingly; Excellent, hee's heat to the proofe, lets with-draw, and giue him leaue to raue a little.

Exeunt Greenshield *and* Fetherstone.

May. Chamberlaine, giue vs a cleane Towell.

Enter Chamberlaine.

Bell. How now man? 160
May. I am foolish old *Maybery*, and yet I can be wise *Maybery* too; Ile to *London* presently, begon Sir.

[*Exit Chamberlaine.*]

Bell. How, how?
May. Nay, nay, Gods pretious you doe mistake mee Maister *Bellamont*; I am not distempered, for to know a mans wife is a whore, is to be resolu'd of it, and to be resolued of it, is to make no question of it, and when a case is out of question; what was I saying?

415

Bell. Why looke you, what a distraction are you falne into?
May. If a man be deuorst, doe you see, deuorst *forma Iuris*, 170 whether may he haue an action or no, gainst those that make hornes at him?
Bell. O madnesse! that the frailty of a woman should make a wise man thus idle! yet I protest, to my vnderstanding this report seemes as farre from truth, as you from patience.
May. Then am I a foole, yet I can bee wise and I list too: what sayes my wedding ring?
Bell. Indeed that breeds some suspition: for the rest most grose and open, for two men, both to loue your wife, both to inioy her bed, and to meete you as if by miracle, and not knowing you, vpon 180 no occasion in the world, to thrust vpon you a discourse of a quarrell, with circumstance so dishonest, that not any Gentleman but of the countrie, blushing would haue publisht. I and to name you: doe you know them?
May. Faith now I remember, I haue seene them walke muffled by my shop.
Bell. Like enough; pray God they doe not borrow mony of vs twixt *Ware* and *London*: come striue to blow ouer these clowdes.
May. Not a clowd, you shall haue cleane Moone-shine, they haue good smooth lookes the fellowes. 190
Bell. As Iet, they will take vp I warrant you, where they may bee trusted; will you be merry?
May. Wonderous merry; lets haue some Sack to drowne this Cuckold, downe with him: wonderous merry: one word and no more; I am but a foolish tradesman, and yet Ile be a wise tradesman.
Exeunt.

[ACT I, Scene ii]

Enter Doll *lead betweene* Leuer-poole, *and* Chartley, *after them* Philip *arrested [by two Sergeants].*

Phil. Arrest me? at whose sute? *Tom Chartley, Dick Leuer-poole,* stay, Ime arrested.
Omn. Arrested?

I. ii] NORTHWARD HO

1. Ser.   Gentlemen breake not the head of the peace; its to no purpose, for hee's in the lawes clutches, you see hee's fangd.
Doll.   Vds life, doe you stand with your naked weapons in your hand, and doe nothing with em? put one of em into my fingers, Ile tickle the pimple-nosed varlets.
Phil.   Hold *Doll*, thrust not a weapon vpon a mad woman, Officers step back into the Tauerne, you might ha tane mee ith streete, and 10 not ith' Tauerne entrie, you Cannibals.
2. Ser.   Wee did it for your credit Sir.
Chart.   How much is the debt? Drawer, some wine.

Enter Drawer.

1. Ser.   Foure score pound: can you send for Baile Sir? or what will you doe? wee cannot stay.
Doll.   You cannot, you pasty-footed Rascalls, you will stay one day in hell.
Phil.   Foure score pounds drawes deepe; farewell *Doll*, come Serieants, Ile step to mine Vncle not farre off, here-by in Pudding lane, and he shall baile mee: if not, *Chartly* you shall finde me 20 playing at Span-counter, and so farewell. Send mee some Tobacco.
1. Ser.   Haue an eye to his hands.
2. Ser.   Haue an eye to his legges.   *Exeunt.*
Doll.   Ime as melancholy now?
Chart.   Villanous spitefull luck, Ile hold my life some of these sawsie Drawers betrayd him.
Draw.   Wee sir! no by Gad Sir, wee scorne to haue a *Iudas* in our company.
Leuer.   No, no, hee was dogd in, this is the end of all dycing.
Doll.   This is the end of all whores, to fall into the hands of knaues. 30 Drawer, tye my shoe pry thee: the new knot as thou seest this: *Philip* is a good honest Gentleman, I loue him because heele spend, but when I saw him on his Fathers Hobby, and a brace of Punkes following him in a coach, I told him hee would run out, hast done boy?
Draw.   Yes forsooth: by my troth you haue a dainty legge.
Doll.   How now good-man rogue.

12 2. *Ser.*] Dyce. *Ser.* Q   *16 pasty-footed] *stet* Q

BCD II   417   27

Draw. Nay sweete Mistresse *Doll.*

Doll. *Doll!* you reprobate! out you Bawd for seauen yeares by the custome of the Citty.

Draw. Good Mistris *Dorothy*; the pox take mee, if I toucht your legge but to a good intent.

Doll. Prate you: the rotten toothd rascall, will for sixe pence fetch any whore to his maisters customers: and is euery one that swims in a Taffatie gowne Lettis for your lippes? vds life, this is rare, that Gentlewomen and Drawers, must suck at one Spiggot: Doe you laugh you vnseasonable puck-fist? doe you grin?

Chart. Away Drawer: hold pry thee good rogue, holde my sweete *Doll*, a pox a this swaggering. [*Exit Drawer.*]

Doll. Pox a your gutts, your kidneys; mew: hang yee, rooke: I'me as melancholy now as Fleet-streete in a long vacation.

Leuer. Melancholy? come weele ha some muld Sack.

Doll. When begins the terme?

Chart. Why? hast any suites to be tryed at Westminster?

Doll. My Sutes you base ruffian haue beene tryed at Westminster already: so soone as euer the terme begins, Ile change my lodging, it stands out a the way; Ile lye about Charing-crosse, for if there be any stirrings, there we shall haue 'em: or if some Dutch-man would come from the States! oh! these Flemmings pay soundly for what they take.

Leuer. If thou't haue a lodging West-ward *Doll*, Ile fitte thee.

Doll. At Tyburne will you not? a lodging of your prouiding? to bee cal'd a Lieutenants, or a Captaines wench! oh! I scorne to bee one of your Low-country commodities, I; is this body made to bee mainteined with Prouant and dead pay? no: the Mercer must bee paide, and Sattin gownes must bee tane vp.

Chart. And gallon pots must be tumbled downe.

Doll. Stay: I haue had a plot a breeding in my braines—
Are all the Quest-houses broken vp?

Leuer. Yes, long since: what then?

Doll. What then? mary then is the wind come about, and for those poore wenches that before Christmasse fled West-ward with bag and baggage, come now sailing alongst the lee shore with a Northerly winde, and we that had warrants to lie without the

liberties, come now dropping into the freedome by Owle-light sneakingly.
Chart. But *Doll*, whats the plot thou spakst off?
Doll. Mary this: Gentlemen, and Tobacco-stinckers, and such like, are still buzzing where sweete meates are (like Flyes) but they make any flesh stinke that they blow vpon: I will leaue those fellowes therefore in the hands of their Landresses: Siluer is the Kings stampe, man Gods stampe, and a woman is mans stampe, wee are not currant till wee passe from one man to another.
Both. Very good.
Doll. I will therefore take a faire house in the Citty: no matter tho it be a Tauerne that has blowne vp his Maister: it shall be in trade still, for I know diuerse Tauernes ith Towne, that haue but a Wall betweene them and a hotte-house. It shall then bee giuen out, that I'me a Gentlewoman of such a birth, such a wealth, haue had such a breeding, and so foorth, and of such a carriage, and such quallities, and so forth: to set it off the better, old *Iack Hornet* shall take vppon him to bee my Father.
Leuer. Excellent, with a chaine about his neck and so forth.
Doll. For that, Saint *Martins* and wee will talke: I know we shall haue Gudgions bite presently: if they doe boyes, you shall liue like Knights fellowes; as occasion serues, you shall weare liueries and waite, but when Gulls are my winde-falls, you shall be Gentlemen, and keepe them company: seeke out *Iack Hornet* incontinently.
Leuer. Wee will; come *Chartly*, weele playe our partes I warrant.
Doll. Doe so:—
The world's a stage, from which strange shapes we borrow:
To day we are honest, and ranke knaues to morrow.
Exeunt.

[ACT I, SCENE iii]

Enter Maybery, Bellamont, *and a Prentice.*

May. Where is your Mistris, villaine? when went she abroad?
Prent. Abroad Sir, why assoone as she was vp Sir.
May. Vp Sir, downe Sir, so sir: Maister *Bellamont*, I will tell you a strange secret in Nature, this boy is my wiues bawd.

Bell. O fie sir, fie, the boy he doe's not looke like a Bawde, he has no double chin.

Prent. No sir, nor my breath does not stinke, I smell not of Garlick or *Aqua-vitæ*: I vse not to bee drunke with Sack and Sugar: I sweare not God dam me, if I know where the party is, when 'tis a lye and I doe know: I was neuer Carted (but in haruest) neuer whipt but at Schoole: neuer had the Grincoms: neuer sold one Maiden-head ten seuerall times, first to an Englishman, then to a Welshman, then to a Dutchman, then to a pockie Frenchman, I hope Sir I am no Bawd then.

May. Thou art a *Baboune,* and holdst me with trickes, whilst my Wife grafts, grafts, away, trudge, run, search her out by land, and by water.

Prent. Well Sir, the land Ile ferret, and after that Ile search her by water, for it may be shees gone to *Brainford*. *Exit.*

May. Inquire at one of mine Aunts.

Bell. One of your Aunts, are you mad?

May. Yea, as many of the twelue companies are, troubled, troubled.

Bell. Ile chide you: goe too, Ile chide you soundly.

May. Oh maister *Bellamont*!

Bell. Oh Maister *Maybery*! before your Seruant to daunce a Lancashire Horne-pipe: it shewes worse to mee, then dancing does to a deafe man that sees not the fiddles: Sfoot you talke like a Player.

May. If a Player talke like a mad-man, or a foole, or an Asse, and knowes not what hee talkes, then Ime one: you are a Poet Maister *Bellamont*, I will bestow a piece of Plate vpon you to bring my wife vpon the Stage, wud not her humor please Gentlemen.

Bell. I thinke it would: yours wud make Gentlemen as fatt as fooles: I wud giue two peeces of Plate, to haue you stand by me, when I were to write a iealous mans part: Iealous men are eyther knaues or Coxcombes, bee you neither: you weare yellow hose without cause.

May. With-out cause, when my Mare beares double: without cause?

Bell. And without wit.

May. When two Virginall Iacks skip vp, as the key of my instrument goes downe!
Bell. They are two wicked elders.
May. When my wiues ring does smoake for't.
Bell. Your wiues ring may deceiue you.
May. O Maister *Bellamont*! had it not beene my wife had made me a Cuckold, it should neuer haue greeued mee.
Bell. You wrong her vpon my soule.
May. No, she wrongs me vpon her body.   50

Enter a Seruingman.

Bell. Now blew-bottle? what flutter you for, Sea-pye?
Seru. Not to catch fish Sir, my young Maister, your sonne maister *Philip* is taken prisoner.
Bell. By the *Dunkirks*.
Seru. Worse: by Catch-polls: hee's encountred.
Bell. Shall I neuer see that prodigall come home.
Seru. Yes Sir, if youle fetch him out, you may kill a Calfe for him.
Bell. For how much lyes he?
Seru. The debt is foure score pound, marry he chargde mee to tell you it was foure score and ten, so that he lies onely for the odde   60 ten pound.
Bell. His childs part shal now be paid, this mony shalbe his last, and this vexation the last of mine: if you had such a sonne maister *Maiberie.*
May. To such a wife, twere an excellent couple.
Bell. Release him, and release me of much sorrow, I will buy a Sonne no more: goe redeeme him.   [*Exit Seruant.*]

Enter Prentice and Maiberies *wife.*

Prent. Here's the party Sir.
May. Hence, and lock fast the dores, now is my prize.
Prent. If she beate you not at your owne weapon, wud her   70 Buckler were cleft in two peeces.   *Exit.*
Bell. I will not haue you handle her too roughly.
May. No, I will like a Iustice of peace, grow to the point: are not you a whore: neuer start: thou art a Cloth-worker, and hast turnd me.

Wife. How Sir, into what Sir, haue I turn'd you?
May. Into a Ciuill Suite: into a sober beast: a Land-rat, a Cuckold: thou art a common bedfellow, art not? art not?
Wife. Sir this Language, to me is strange, I vnderstand it not.
May. O! you studie the french now.
Wife. Good Sir, lend me patience.
May. I made a sallade of that herbe: doest see these flesh-hookes, I could teare out those false eyes, those Cats eyes, that can see in the night: punck I could.
Bell. Heare her answer for her selfe.
Wife. Good Maister *Bellamont*,
Let him not do me violence: deere Sir,
Should any but your selfe shoote out these names,
I would put off all female modesty,
To be reueng'd on him.
May. Know'st thou this ring? there has bin old running at the ring since I went.
Wife. Yes Sir, this ring is mine, he was a villayne,
That stole it from my hand: he was a villayne:
That put it into yours.
May.   They were no villaynes,
When they stood stoutly for me: tooke your part:
And stead of collours fought vnder my sheetes.
Wife. I know not what you meane.
May. They lay with the: I meane plaine dealing.
Wife. With me! if euer I had thought vncleane,
In detestation of your nuptiall pillow:
Let *Sulpher* drop from Heauen, and naile my body
Dead to this earth: that slaue, that damned fury
(Whose whips are in your tongue to torture me)
Casting an eye vnlawfull on my cheeke,
Haunted your thre-shold daily, and threw forth
All tempting baytes which lust and credulous youth,
Apply to our fraile sex: but those being weake
The second seige he layd was in sweete wordes.
May. And then the breach was made.

99 the] *i.e.* thee

Bell.   Nay, nay, heare all.   110
Wife.   At last he takes me sitting at your dore,
Seizes my palme, and by the charme of othes
(Back to restore it straight) he won my hand,
To crowne his finger with that hoope of gold.
I did demand it, but he mad with rage
And with desires vnbrideled, fled and vow'd,
That ring should mee vndo: and now belike
His spells haue wrought on you. But I beseech you,
To dare him to my face, and in meane time
Deny me bed-roome, driue me from your board,   120
Disgrace me in the habit of your slaue,
Lodge me in some discomfortable vault
Where neither Sun nor Moone may touch my sight,
Till of this slander I my soule acquite.
Bell.   Guiltlesse vpon my soule.
May.   Troth so thinke I.
I now draw in your bow, as I before
Suppos'd they drew in mine: my streame of ielozy,
Ebs back againe, and I that like a horse
Ran blind-fold in a Mill (all in one circle)
Yet thought I had gon fore-right, now spy my error: 130
Villaines you haue abus'd me, and I vow
Sharp vengeance on your heads: driue in your teares,
I take your word ya're honest, which good men,
Very good men will scarce do to their wiues.
I will bring home these serpents, and allow them
The heate of mine owne bosome: wife I charge you
Set out your hauiours towards them in such collours,
As if you had bin their whore, Ile haue it so,
Ile candy o're my words, and sleeke my brow,
Intreate 'em that they would not point at me,   140
Nor mock my hornes, with this Arme Ile embrace 'em
And with this—go too.
Wife.   Oh we shall haue murder—
You kill my heart.
May.   No: I will shed no bloud,

423

But I will be reueng'd, they that do wrong
Teach others way to right: Ile fetch my blow
Faire and a far off, and as Fencers vse
Tho at the foote I strike, the head Ile bruize.

Enter Philip *and seruant.*

Bell. Ile ioyne with you: lets walke: oh! heres my Sonne.
Welcome a shore Sir: from whence come you pray.
Phil. From the house of praier and fasting—the Counter.
Bell. Art not thou asham'd, to bee seene come out of a prison.
Phil. No Gods my Iudge, but I was asham'd to goe into prison.
Bell. I am told sir, that you spend your credit and your coine vpon a light woman.
Phil. I ha seene light gold sir, passe away amongst Mercers.
Bell. And that you haue layd thirty or fortie pounds vpon her back in taffaty gownes, and silke petticoates.
Phil. None but Taylors will say so, I nere lay'd any thing vpon her backe: I confesse I tooke vp a petticoate and a raiz'd fore-part for her, but who has to do with that?
May. Mary that has euery body Maister *Philip.*
Bell. Leaue her company, or leaue me, for shee's a woman of an ill name.
Phil. Her name is *Dorothy* sir, I hope thats no il name.
Bell. What is she? what wilt thou do with her?
Phil. Sbloud sir what does he with her?
Bell. Doest meane to marry her? of what birth is shee? what are her commings in, what does she liue vpon?
Phil. Rents sir, Rents, shee liues vpon her Rents, and I can haue her.
Bell. You can.
Phil. Nay father, if destiny dogge mee I must haue her: you haue often tould mee the nine Muses are all women, and you deale with them, may not I the better bee allowed one than you so many? looke you Sir, the Northerne man loues white-meates, the Southerly man Sallades, the Essex man a Calfe, the Kentishman a Wag-taile, the Lancashire man an Egg-pie, the Welshman Leekes and Cheese,

175 Southerly] Southery Q

and your Londoners rawe Mutton, so Father god-boy, I was borne in *London*.

Bell. Stay, looke you Sir, as hee that liues vpon Sallades without Mutton, feedes like an Oxe, (for hee eates grasse you knowe) yet rizes as hungry as an Asse, and as hee that makes a dinner of leekes will haue leane cheekes, so, thou foolish Londoner, if nothing but raw mutton can diet thee, looke to liue like a foole and a slaue, and to die like a begger and a knaue, come Maister *Maiberie*, farewell boy.

Phil. Farewell father Snot—Sir if I haue her, Ile spend more in mustard and vineger in a yeare, then both you in beefe.

Both. More saucy knaue thou.

Exeunt.

ACTUS 2. SCENA I.

Enter Hornet, Doll, Leuerpoole *and* Chartly *like seruingmen.*

Horn. Am I like a fidlers base violl (new set vp,) in a good case boies? ist neate, is it terse! am I hansome? ha!

Omn. Admirable, excellent.

Doll. An vnder sheriffe cannot couer a knaue more cunningly.

Leuer. Sfoot if he should come before a Church-warden, he wud make him peu-fellow with a Lords steward at least.

Horn. If I had but a staffe in my hand, fooles wud thinke I were one of *Simon* and *Iudes* gentlemen vshers, and that my apparell were hir'd: they say three Taylors go to the making vp of a man, but Ime sure I had foure Taylors and a halfe went to the making of me thus: this Suite tho' it ha bin canuast well, yet tis no law-suite, for twas dispatcht sooner than a posset on a wedding night.

Doll. Why I tel thee *Iack Hornet,* if the Diuel and all the Brokers in long lane had rifled their wardrob, they wud ha beene dambd before they had fitted thee thus.

Horn. Punck, I shall bee a simple father for you: how does my chaine show now I walke.

Doll. If thou wert hung in chaines, thou couldst not show better.

Chart. But how sit our blew-coates on our backes.

Doll. As they do vpon banckrout retainers backes at Saint *Georges* feast in *London*: but at Westminster, It makes 'em scorne the badge of their occupation: there the bragging velure-caniond hobbi-horses, praunce vp and downe as if some a the Tilters had ridden 'em.

Horn. Nay Sfoot, if they be banckrouts, tis like some haue ridden 'em: and there-vpon the Cittizens Prouerbe rises, when hee sayes; he trusts to a broken staffe.

Doll. *Hornet*, now you play my Father, take heed you be not out of your part, and shame your adopted Daughter.

Horn. I will looke grauely *Doll*, (doe you see boyes) like the fore-man of a Iury: and speake wisely like a Lattin Schoole-maister, and be surly and dogged, and proud like the Keeper of a prison.

Leuer. You must lie horribly, when you talke of your lands.

Horn. No shop-keeper shall out lye mee, nay, no Fencer: when I hem boyes, you shall duck: when I cough and spit gobbets *Doll*—

Doll. The pox shall be in your lungs *Hornet*.

Horn. No *Doll*, these with their high shoes shall tread me out.

Doll. All the lessons that I ha prickt out for 'em, is when the Wether-cock of my body turnes towards them, to stand bare.

Horn. And not to be sawcie as Seruing-men are.

Chart. Come, come, we are no such creatures as you take vs for.

Doll. If we haue but good draughts in my peeter-boate, fresh Salmon you sweete villaines shall be no meate with vs.

Horn. Sfoot nothing mooues my choller, but that my chaine is Copper: but tis no matter, better men than old *Iack Hornet* haue rode vp Holburne, with as bad a thing about their neckes as this: your right whiffler indeed hangs himselfe in Saint *Martins*, and not in Cheape-side.

Doll. Peace, some-body rings: run both, whilst he has the rope in's hand, if it be a prize, hale him, if a man a war, blow him vp, or hang him out at the maine yeards end. [*Exeunt.*]

Horn. But what ghosts (hold vp my fine Girle) what ghosts haunts thy house?

Doll. Oh! why diuerse: I haue a Clothiers Factor or two; a Grocer that would faine Pepper me, a Welsh Captaine that laies hard seege, a Dutch Marchant, that would spend al that he's able to make ith'

II. i] NORTHWARD HO

low countries, but to take measure of my Holland sheetes when
I lye in 'em: I heare trampling: 'tis my Flemish Hoy.

  Enter Leuerpoole, Chartly, *and* Hans van Belch.

Hans. Dar is vor you, and vor you: een, twea, drie, vier, and viue 60
skilling, drinks Skellum vpsie freese: nempt, dats v drinck gelt.
Leuer. Till our crownes crack agen Maister *Hans van Belch.*
Hans. How ist met you, how ist vro? vrolick?
Doll. Ick vare well God danke you: Nay Ime an apt scholler and
can take.
Hans. Datt is good, dott is good: Ick can neet stay long: for Ick
heb en skip come now vpon de vater: O mine schoonen vro, wee
sall dance lanteera, teera, and sing Ick drincks to you min here,
van:—wat man is dat vro.
Horn. Nay pray sir on. 70
Hans. Wat honds foot is dat *Dorrothy.*
Doll. Tis my father.
Hans. Gotts Sacrament! your vader! why seyghen you niet so to
me! mine heart tis mine all great desire, to call you mine vader ta
for Ick loue dis schonen vro your dochterkin.
Horn. Sir you are welcome in the way of honesty.
Hans. Ick bedanck you: Ick heb so ghe founden vader.
Horn. Whats your name I pray.
Hans. Min nom bin *Hans van Belch.*
Horn. *Hans Van Belch!* 80
Hans. Yau, yau, tis so, tis so, de dronken man is alteet remember
me.
Horn. Doe you play the marchant, sonne *Belch.*
Hans. Yau vader: Ick heb de skip swim now vpon de vater: if
you endouty, goe vp in de little Skip dat goe so, and bee puld vp
to Wapping, Ick sal beare you on my backe, and hang you about
min neck into min groet Skip.
Horn. He Sayes *Doll,* he would haue thee to Wapping and hang
thee.
Doll. No Father I vnderstand him, but maister *Hans,* I would not 90

  *65 take] *stet* Q   67 schoonen] Dyce; schoomen Q
   68 drincks] Hazlitt; brincks Q   79 Min] Hazlitt; Mun Q

be seene hanging about any mans neck, to be counted his Iewell, for any gold.

Horn. Is your father liuing Maister *Hans.*

Hans. Yau, yau, min vader heb schonen husen in *Ausburgh*: groet mine heare is mine vaders broder, mine vader heb land, and bin full of fee, dat is beasts, cattell.

Chart. He's lowzy be-like.

Hans. Min vader bin de groetest fooker in all *Ausbourgh*.

Doll. The greatest what?

Leuer. Fooker he saies.

Doll. Out vpon him.

Hans. Yaw yaw, fooker is en groet min here, hees en elderman vane Citty, gots sacrament, wat is de clock? Ick niet stay. *A watch.*

Horn. Call his watch before you, if you can.

Doll. Her's a pretty thing: do these wheeles spin vp the houres! whats a clock.

Hans. Acht: yaw tis acht.

Doll. We can heare neither clock, nor Iack going, wee dwell in such a place that I feare I shall neuer finde the way to Church, because the bells hang so farre; Such a watch as this, would make me go downe with the Lamb, and be vp with the Larke.

Hans. Seghen you so, dor it to.

Doll. O fie: I doe but iest, for in trueth I could neuer abide a watch.

Hans. Gotts sacrament, Ick niet heb it any more.

Exeunt Leuer-poole *and* Chartly.

Doll. An other peale! good father lanch out this hollander.

Horn. Come Maister *Belch*, I will bring you to the water-side, perhaps to Wapping, and there ile leaue you.

Hans. Ick bedanck you vader. *Exeunt.*

Doll. They say Whores and bawdes go by clocks, but what a Manasses is this to buy twelue houres so deerely, and then bee begd out of 'em so easily? heele be out at heeles shortly sure for he's out about the clockes already: O foolish young man how doest thou spend thy time?

103 niet] met Q   120 *Exeunt.*] Dyce; *Exit.* Q

Enter Leuer-poole *first, then* Allom *and* Chartly.

Leuer. Your grocer.
Doll. Nay Sfoot, then ile change my tune: I may curse such leaden-heeld rascalls; out of my sight: a knife, a knife I say: O Maister *Allom*, if you loue a woman, draw out your knife and vndo me, vndo me. 130
Allom. Sweete mistris *Dorothy*, what should you do with a knife, its ill medling with edge tooles, what's the matter Maisters! knife God blesse vs.
Leuer. Sfoot what tricks at noddy are these.
Doll. Oh I shal burst, if I cut not my lace: I'me so vext! my father hee's ridde to Court one way about a matter of a thousand pound weight; and one of his men (like a roague as he is) is rid another way for rents, I lookt to haue had him vp yesterday, and vp to day, and yet hee showes not his head; sure he's run away, or robd and run thorough; and here was a scriuener but euen now, to put my 140 father in minde of a bond, that wilbe forfit this night if the mony be not payd Maister *Allom*. Such crosse fortune!
Allom. How much is the bond?
Chart. O rare little villaine.
Doll. My father could take vp, vpon the barenesse of his word fiue hundred pound: and fiue too.
Allom. What is the debt?
Doll. But hee scornes to bee—and I scorne to bee—
Allom. Pree thee sweete Mistris *Dorothy* vex not, how much is it?
Doll. Alas Maister *Allom*, tis but poore fifty pound. 150
Allom. If that bee all, you shall vpon your worde take vp so much with me: another time ile run as far in your bookes.
Doll. Sir, I know not how to repay this kindnesse: but when my father—
Allom. Tush, tush, tis not worth the talking: Iust fifty pound? when is it to be payd.
Doll. Betweene one and two.
Leuer. That's wee thre.

*127 curse] Dyce; cause Q
136 Court one way] Dyce; Court: one was Q

Allom. Let one of your men goe along, and Ile send your fifty pound!

Doll. You so bind mee sir,—goe sirra: Maister *Allom*, I ha some quinces brought from our house ith Country to preserue, when shall we haue any good Suger come ouer? the warres in *Barbary* make Suger at such an excessiue rate; you pay sweetely now I warrant sir, do you not.

Allom. You shal haue a whole chest of Sugar if you please.

Doll. Nay by my faith foure or fiue loues wil-be enough, and Ile pay you at my first child Maister *Allom*.

Allom. Content ifaith, your man shall bring all vnder one, ile borrow a kisse of you at parting.

Enter Captaine Iynkins.

Doll. You shall sir, I borrow more of you.

Exeunt Allom *and* Leuer-poole.

Chart. Saue you Captaine.

Doll. Welcome good captaine *Iynkins*.

Capt. What is hee a Barber Surgeon, that drest your lippes so.

Doll. A Barber! hee's my Taylor; I bidde him measure how hie, hee would make the standing coller of my new Taffatie Gowne before, and hee as Tailors wilbe sawcie and lickerish, laid mee ore the lippes.

Capt. Vds bloud ile laie him crosse vpon his coxcomb next daie.

Doll. You know tis not for a Gentlewoman to stand with a knaue, for a small matter, and so I wud not striue with him, onelie to be rid of him.

Capt. If I take Maister prick-louse ramping so hie againe, by this Iron (which is none a gods Angell) Ile make him know how to kisse your blind cheekes sooner: mistris *Dorothy Hornet*, I wud not haue you bee a hornet, to licke at Cowsherds, but to sting such shreds of rascallity: will you sing a Tailor shall haue mee my ioy?

Doll. Captaine, ile bee lead by you in any thing! a Taylor! foh.

Capt. Of what stature or sise haue you a stomach to haue your husband now?

Doll. Of the meanest stature Captaine, not a size longer than your selfe, nor shorter.

175 my] Dyce; may Q

Capt. By god, tis wel said; all your best Captaine in the Low-countries are as taller as I: but why of my pitch Mistris *Dol?*
Doll. Because your smallest Arrowes flie farthest; ah you little hard-fauord villaine, but sweete villaine, I loue thee beecause thou't draw a my side, hang the roague that will not fight for a woman.
Capt. Vds blould, and hange him for vrse than a roague that will slash and cut for an oman, if she be a whore.
Doll. Pree the good Captaine *Iynkins*, teach mee to speake some welch, mee thinkes a Welchmans tongue is the neatest tongue!—
Capt. As any tongue in the vrld, vnlesse *Cra ma crees*, that's vrse.
Doll. How do you say, I loue you with all my heart.
Capt. Mi cara whee, en hellon.
Doll. Mi cara whee, en hel-hound.
Capt. Hel-hound, o mondu, my cara whee, en hellon.
Doll. O, my cara whee en hellon.
Capt. Oh! and you went to wryting schoole twenty score yeare in *Wales*, by Sesu, you cannot haue better vttrance, for welch.
Doll. Come tit mee, come tat mee, come throw a kisse at me, how is that?
Capt. By gad I kanow not, what your tit mees, and tat mees are, but *mee uatha*—Sbloud I know what kisses be, aswel as I know a Welch hooke, if you will goe downe with *Shrop-sheere* cariers, you shal haue Welch enough in your pellies forty weekes.
Doll. Say Captaine that I should follow your collours into your Country how should I fare there?
Capt. Fare? by Sesu, O there is the most abominable seere! and wider siluer pots to drinck in, and softer peds to lie vpon and do our necessary pusines, and fairer houses, and parkes, and holes for Conies, and more money, besides tosted Sees and butter-milke in *Northwales* diggon: besides, harpes, and Welch Freeze, and Goates, and Cow-heeles, and Metheglin, ouh, it may be set in the Kernicles, wil you march thither?
Doll. Not with your *Shrop-sheire* cariers, Captaine.
Capt. Will you go with Captaine *Ienkin* and see his Couzen *Maddoc* vpon *Ienkin* there, and ile run hedlongs by and by, and barter away money for a new Coach to iolt you in.

228 barter] batter Q (*see* IV.i.248)

Doll. Bestow your Coach vpon me, and two young white Mares, and you shall see how Ile ride.

Capt. Will you? by all the leekes that are worne on Saint *Dauies* daie I will buy not only a Coach, with foure wheeles, but also a white Mare and a stone horse too, because they shal traw you, very lustily, as if the diuill were in their arses.

How now, more Tailors— [*Offers to*] *Exit. Meetes* Phillip.

Phil. How sir; Taylors.

Doll. O good Captaine, tis my Couzen.

        Enter Leuerpoole *at another dore.*

Capt. Is he, I will Couzen you then sir too, one day.

Phil. I hope sir then to Couzen you too.

Capt. By gad I hobe so, fare-well *Sidanien*.   *Exit.*

Leuer. Her's both money, and suger.

Doll. O sweete villaine, set it vp.

        [*Leuerpoole*] *Exit, and Enter presently.*

Phil. Sfoot, what tame suaggerer was this I met *Doll*.

Doll. A Captaine, a Captaine: but hast scap't the *Dunkerks* honest *Philip*? *Philip* ryalls are not more welcome: did thy father pay the shot?

Phil. He pai'd that shot, and then shot pistolets into my pockets: harke wench: chinck chink, makes the punck wanton and the Baud to winck.   *Capers.*

Chart. O rare musick.

Leuer. Heauenly consort, better than old *Moones*.

Phil. But why? why *Dol*, goe these two like Beadells in blew? ha?

Doll. Theres a morrall in that: flea off your skins, you pretious Caniballs: O that the welch Captaine were here againe, and a drum with him, I could march now, ran, tan, tan, tara, ran, tan, tan, sirra *Philip* has thy father any plate in's house.

Phil. Enough to set vp a Gold-smithes shop.

Doll. Canst not borrow some of it? wee shall haue guests to morrow or next day, and I wud serue the hungry rag-a-muffins in plate, tho twere none of mine owne.

Phil. I shall hardly borrow it of him but I could get one of mine Aunts, to beate the bush for mee, and she might get the bird.
Doll. Why pree the, let me bee one of thine Aunts, and doe it for me then. As Ime vertuous and a Gentlewoman ile restore.
Phil. Say no more, tis don.
Doll. What manner of man is thy father? Sfoot ide faine see the witty Monky because thou sayst he's a Poet: ile tell thee, what ile do: *Leuer-poole* or *Chartly*, shall like my Gentleman vsher goe to him, and say such a Lady sends for him, about a sonnet or an epitaph for her child that died at nurse, or for some deuice about a maske or so; if he comes you shall stand in a corner, and see in what State ile beare my selfe: he does not know me, nor my lodging?
Phil. No, no.
Doll. Ist a match Sirs? shalls be mery with him and his muse.
Omn. Agreed, any scaffold to execute knauery vpon.
Doll. Ile send then my vant-currer presently: in the meane time, marche after the Captaine, scoundrels, come hold me vp:
Looke how *Sabrina* sunck ith' riuer *Seuerne*,
So will we foure be drunke ith' ship-wrack Tauerne.

Exeunt.

[ACT II, SCENE ii]

Enter Bellamont, Maybery, *and Mistresse* Maybery.

May. Come Wife, our two gallants will be here presently: I haue promist them the best of entertainment, with protestation neuer to reueale to thee their slander: I will haue thee beare thy selfe, as if thou madest a feast vpon *Simon* and *Iudes* day, to country Gentle-women, that came to see the Pageant, bid them extreamly welcome, though thou wish their throats cut; 'tis in fashion.
Wife. O God I shall neuer indure them.
Bell. Indure them, you are a foole: make it your case, as it may be many womens of the Freedome; that you had a friend in priuate, whom your husband should lay to his bosome: and he in requitall

*263 and she might get the bird] stet Q

should lay his wife to his bosome: what treads of the toe, salutations by winckes, discourse by bitings of the lip, amorous glances, sweete stolne kisses when your husbands backs turn'd, would passe betweene them, beare your selfe to *Greeneshield*, as if you did loue him for affecting you so intirely, not taking any notice of his iourney: theile put more tricks vpon you: you told me *Greeneshield* meanes to bring his Sister to your house, to haue her boord here.

May. Right, shee's some crackt demy-culuerin, that hath miscaried in seruice: no matter though it be some charge to me for a time, I care not.

Wife. Lord was there euer such a husband?

May. Why, wouldst thou haue me suffer their tongues to run at large, in Ordinaries and Cock-pits; though the Knaues doe lye, I tell you Maister *Bellamont*, lyes that come from sterne lookes, and Sattin out-sides, and guilt Rapiers also, will be put vp and goe for currant.

Bell. Right sir, 'tis a small sparke, giues fire to a beautifull womans discredit.

May. I will therefore vse them like informing knaues, in this kinde, make vp their mouthes with siluer, and after bee reueng'd vpon them: I was in doubt I should haue growne fat of late: and it were not for law suites: and feare of our wiues: we rich men should grow out of all compasse: they come, my worthy friends welcome: looke my wiues colour rises already.

[*Enter* Greenshield *and* Fetherstone.]

Green. You haue not made her acquainted with the discouery.

May. O by no meanes: yee see Gentlemen the affection of an old man; I would faine make all whole agen. Wife giue entertainment to our new acquaintance, your lips wife, any woman may lend her lips without her husbands priuity, tis alowable.

Wife. You are very welcome; I thinke it be neere dinner time Gentlemen: Ile will the maide to couer, and returne presently.

Exit.

Bell. Gods pretious why doth she leaue them?

May. O I know her stomack: shee is but retirde into another chamber, to ease her heart with crying a little: it hath euer bin her humor, she hath done it fiue or six times in a day, when Courtiers haue beene heare, if any thing hath bin out of order, and yet euery returne laught and bin as merry: and how is it Gentlemen, you are well acquainted with this roome, are you not?

Green. I had a dellicate banquet once on that table.

May. In good time: but you are better acquainted with my bed chamber.

Bell. Were the cloath of gold Cushins set forth at your entertainement?

Feth. Yes Sir.

May. And the cloath of Tissew Valance.

Feth. They are very rich ones.

May. God refuse me, they are lying Rascals, I haue no such furniture.

Green. I protest it was the strangest, and yet with-all the happiest fortune that wee should meete you two at *Ware*, that euer redeemed such desolate actions: I would not wrong you agen for a million of *Londons*.

May. No, do you want any money? or if you be in debt, I am a hundreth pound ith' Subsidie, command mee.

Feth. Alas good Gentleman; did you euer read of the like pacience in any of your ancient Romans?

Bell. You see what a sweet face in a Veluet cap can do, your cittizens wiues are like Partriges, the hens are better then the cocks.

Feth. I beleeue it in troth Sir, you did oberue how the Gentlewoman could not containe her selfe, when she saw vs enter.

Bell. Right.

Feth. For thus much I must speake in allowance of her modestie, when I had her most priuate she would blush extreamely.

Bell. I, I warrant you, and aske you if you would haue such a great sinne lie vpon your conscience, as to lie with another mans wife.

Feth. Introth she would.

Bell. And tell you there were maides inough in *London*, if a man were so vitiously giuen, whose Portions would help them to husbands though gentlemen gaue the first onset.

Feth. You are a merry ould gentleman infaith Sir: much like to this was her langwage.
Bell. And yet clipe you with as voluntary a bosome; as if she had fallen in loue with you at some Innes a court reuels; and inuited you by letter to her lodging.
Feth. Your knowledge Sir, is perfect without any information.
May. Ile goe see what my wife is doing gentlemen, when my wife enters shew her this ring; and twill quit all suspition.
                    Exit [Maybery. Bellamont *walks aloof*].
Feth. Dost heare *Luke Greenshield* wil thy wife be here presently?
Green. I left my boy to waight vpon her, by this light, I thinke God prouides; for if this cittisen had not out of his ouerplus of kindnes proferd her, her diet and lodging vnder the name of my sister, I could not haue told what shift to haue made; for the greatest part of my mony is reuolted; weele make more vse of him: the whoreson rich Inkeeper of *Doncaster* her father shewed himselfe a ranke ostler: to send her vp at this time a yeare; and by the carier to, twas but a iades trike of him.
Feth. But haue you instructed her to call you brother.
Green. Yes and shele do it, I left her at Bosomes Inne, sheele be here, presently.

    Enter Maybery [*after him Mistress* Maybery *and* Kate].

May. Maister *Greenesheild* your sister is come; my wife is entertaining her, by the masse I haue bin vpon her lips already, Lady you are welcome, looke you maister *Greeneshield*, because your sister is newly come out of the fresh aire, and that to be pent vp in a narrow lodging here ith' cittle may offend her health she shall lodge at a garden house of mine in More feilds where if it please you and my worthy friend heare to beare her company your seuerall lodgings and Ioint commons (to the poore ability of a cittizen) shalbe prouided.
Feth. O God Sir.
May. Nay no complement, your loues comand it: shalls to dinner Gentlemen, come maister *Bellamont*, Ile be the Gentleman vsher to this faire Lady.   [*Exeunt* Maybery *and* Bellamont.]

    90 *Green.*] Dyce; *May.* Q

Green. Here is your ring Mistris; a thousand times,—and would haue willingly lost my best of maintenance that I might haue found you halfe so tractable.

Wife. Sir I am still my selfe, I know not by what means you haue grown vpon my husband, he is much deceaued in you I take it: will you go in to dinner—O God that I might haue my wil of him and it were not for my husband ide scratch out his eyes presently. 120

Exeunt [Mistris Maybery *and* Greenshield].

Feth. Welcome to *London* bonny mistris *Kate*, thy husband little dreams of the familiarity that hath past betwene thee and I *Kate*.

Kate. Noe matter if hee did: he ran away from me like a base slaue as he was, out of *Yorke-shire*, and pretended he would goe the Iland voiage, since I neere heard of him till within this fortnight: can the world condemne me for entertayning a friend, that am vsed so like an Infidel?

Feth. I think not, but if your husband knew of this he'd be deuorst.

Kate. Hee were an asse then; no, wisemen should deale by their 130 wiues as the sale of ordinance passeth in *England*, if it breake the first discharge the workman is at the losse of it, if the second the Marchant, and the workman ioyntly, if the third the Marchant, so in our case, if a woman proue false the first yeare, turne her vpon her fathers neck, if the second, turne her home to her father but allow her a portion, but if she hould pure mettaile two yeare and flie to seueral peeces, in the third, repaire the ruines of her honesty at your charges, for the best peece of ordinance, may bee crackt in the casting, and for women to haue cracks and flaues, alas they are borne to them, now I haue held out foure yeare, doth my husband 140 do any things about *London*, doth he swagger?

Feth. O as tame as a fray in Fleetestreete, when their are nobody to part them.

Kate. I euer thought so, we haue notable valiant fellowes about *Doncaster*, theile give the lie and the stab both in an instant.

Feth. You like such kind of man-hood best *Kate*.

Kate. Yes introth for I think any woman that loues her friend, had rather haue him stand by it then lie by it, but I pray thee tel me, why must I be quarterd at this Citizens garden house, say you.

Feth. The discourse of that wil set thy bloud on fire to be reuengd on thy husbands forhead peece.

Enter Bellamont and Mistris Maybery.

Wife. Wil you go in to dinner sir?
Kate. Wil you lead the way forsoth?
Wife. No sweete forsothe weele follow you.
[*Exeunt* Kate *and* Featherstone.]
O Maister *Bellamont*: as euer you tooke pitty vpon the simplicity of a poore abused gentlewoman: wil you tell me one thing.
Bell. Any thing sweet Mistris *Mayberrie*.
Wife. I but will you doe it faithfully?
Bell. As I respect your acquaintance I shall doe it.
Wife. Tell me then I beseech you, doe not you thinke this minx is some naughty packe whome my husband hath fallen in loue with, and meanes to keepe vnder my nose at his garden house.
Bell. No vpon my life is she not.
Wife. O I cannot beleeue it, I know by her eies she is not honest, why should my husband proffer them such kindnes? that haue abused him and me; so intollerable: and will not suffer me to speake; theres the hell ont, not suffer me to speake.
Bell. Fie fie, he doth that like a vserer, that will vse a man with all kindnes, that he may be carelesse of paying his mony, vpon his day, and after-wards take the extremitie of the forfature; your iealousie is Idle: say this were true, it lies in the bosome of a sweete wife to draw her husband from any loose imperfection, from wenching, from Iealosie, from couitousnes, from crabbednes, which is the old mans common disease, by her politicke yealding. She maye doe it from crabednes, for example I haue knowne as tough blades as any are in *England* broke vpon a fetherbed,— come to diner.
Wife. Ile be ruled by you Sir, for you are very like mine vncle.
Bell. Suspition workes more mischiefe, growes more strong,
To seuer chast beds then aparant wrong. *Exeunt.*

151 S.D. *Mistris*] Dyce; *Maist.* Q   *166 so] fo Q   *175 She] Dyce; *Bell.* She Q
180 wrong] Dyce; wrongs Q   180 S.D. *Exeunt.*] *Exit.* Q

ACTVS 3. SCÆNA i.

Enter Doll, Chartly, Leuerpoole *and* Phillip.

Phil. Come my little Punke with thy two Compositors to this vnlawfull printing house, thy pounders, my old poeticall dad wilbe here presently; take vp thy State in this chayre, and beare thy selfe as if thou wert talking to thy pottecary after the receipt of a purgation: looke scuruily vpon him: sometimes be merrie and stand vppon thy pantoffles like a new elected scauinger.

Doll. And by and by melancholicke like a Tilter that hath broake his staues foule before his Mistrisse.

Phil. Right, for hee takes thee to bee a woman of a great count: harke vpon my life hee's come. 10

Doll. See who knocks: thou shalt see mee make a foole of a Poet, that hath made fiue hundred fooles.

[*Exit* Leuerpoole *and enter again.*
Phillip *and* Chartly *stand aloof.*]

Leuer. Please your new Lady-ship hee's come.

Doll. Is hee? I should for the more state let him walke some two houres in an vtter roome: if I did owe him money, 'twere not much out of fashion; but come enter him: Stay, when we are in priuate conference send in my Tayler.

Enter Bellamont *brought in by* Leuerpoole.

Leuer. Looke you my Ladie's a sleepe, sheele wake presently.

Bell. I come not to teach a Starling sir, God-boy-you.

Leuer. Nay in trueth Sir, if my Lady should but dreame you had 20 beene heare.

Doll. Who's that keepes such a prating?

Leuer. 'Tis I Madam.

Doll. Ile haue you preferd to be a Cryer: you haue an exlent throate for't: pox a the Poet is he not come yet?

Leuer. Hee's here Madam.

---

*2 printing] painting Q
2 pounders, my] Dyce; pounders a my Q

Doll. Crie you mercy: I ha curst my Monkey for shrewd turnes a hundred times, and yet I loue it neuer the worse I protest.
Bell. Tis not in fashion deere Lady to call the breaking out of a Gentlewomans lips, scabs, but the heate of the Liuer.
Doll. So sir: if you haue a sweete breath, and doe not smell of swetty linnen, you may draw neerer, neerer.
Bell. I am no friend to Garlick Madam.
Doll. You write the sweeter verse a great deale sir, I haue heard much good of your wit maister Poet: you do many deuises for Cittizens wiues: I care not greatly because I haue a Citty Laundresse already, if I get a Citty Poet too: I haue such a deuise for you, and this it is. *Enter Tayler.* O welcome Tayler: do but waite till I dispatch my Tayler, and Ile discouer my deuice to you.
Bell. Ile take my leaue of your Ladiship.
Doll. No: I pray thee stay: I must haue you sweate for my deuice Maister Poet.
Phil. He sweats already beleeue it.
Doll. A cup of wine there: what fashion will make a woman haue the best bodie Taylor.
Tay. A short dutch wast with a round cathern-wheele fardingale: a close sleeue with a cartoose collour and a pickadell.
Doll. And what meate will make a woman haue a fine wit Maister Poet.
Bell. Fowle madam is the most light, delicate, and witty feeding.
Doll. Fowle sayst thou: I know them that feede of it euery meale, and yet are as arrant fooles as any are in a kingdome of my credit: hast thou don Taylor? [*Exit Taylor*] now to discouer my deuice sir: Ile drinck to you sir.
Phil. Gods pretious, wee nere thought of her deuice before, pray god it be any thing tollerable.
Doll. Ile haue you make twelue poesies for a dozen of cheese trenchers.
Phil. O horrible!
Bell. In welch madam?
Doll. Why in welch sir.
Bell. Because you will haue them seru'd in with your cheese Ladie.

47 collour] *i.e.* collar

Doll. I will bestow them indeede vpon a welch Captaine: one that loues cheese better than venson, for if you should but get three or four Cheshire cheeses and set them a running down Hiegate-hill, he would make more hast after them than after the best kennell of hounds in *England*; what think you of my deuice?
Bell. Fore-god a very strange deuice and a cunning one.
Phil. Now he begins to eye the goblet.
Bell. You should be a kin to the *Bellamonts*, you giue the same Armes madam.
Doll. Faith I paid sweetely for the cup, as it may be you and some other Gentlemen haue don for their Armes.
Bell. Ha, the same waight: the same fashion: I had three nest of them giuen mee, by a Nobleman at the christing of my sonne *Philip*.
Phil. Your sonne is come to full age sir: and hath tane possession of the gift of his God-father.   [*Comes forward with* Chartly.]
Bell. Ha, thou wilt not kill mee.
Phil. No sir, ile kill no Poet least his ghost write satires against me.
Bell. Whats she?
Phil. A good common welthes woman, shee was borne for her Country, and has borne her Country.
Bell. Heart of vertue? what make I here?
Phil. This was the party you rail'd on: I keepe no worse company than your selfe father, you were wont to say venery is like vsery that it may be allowed tho it be not lawfull.
Bell. Wherefore come I hither.
Doll. To make a deuice for cheese-trenchers.
Phil. Ile tell you why I sent for you, for nothing but to shew you that your grauity may bee drawne in: white haires may fall into the company of drabs aswell as red beardes into the society of knaues: would not this woman deceiue a whole camp ith Low-countries, and make one Commander beleeue she only kept her cabbin for him, and yet quarter twenty more in't.

73 Gentlemen] Dyce; Gentleman Q
83 A good common welthes woman, shee was borne] *in* Q *concludes* Bellamont's *speech in line* 82. Philip's *speech begins in* Q 'For her Country'.

Doll. Pree the Poet what doest thou think of me.
Bell. I thinke thou art a most admirable, braue, beautifull Whore.
Doll. Nay sir, I was told you would raile: but what doe you thinke of my deuice sir: nay, but you are not to depart yet Maister Poet: wut sup with me? Ile cashiere all my yong barnicles, and weele talke ouer a peice of mutton and a partridge, wisely.
Bell. Sup with thee that art a common vndertaker? thou that doest promise nothing but watchet eyes, bumbast calues and false perywigs.
Doll. Pree the comb thy beard with a comb of black leade, it may be I shall affect thee.
Bell. O thy vnlucky starre! I must take my leaue of your worshippe: I cannot fit your deuice at this instant: I must desire to borrow a nest of goblets of you: O villanie! I wud some honest Butcher would begge all the queanes and knaues ith Citty and cary them into some other Country, they'd sell better than Beefes and Calues: what a vertuous Citty would this bee then! mary I thinke there would bee a few people left int, vds foot, guld with Cheesetrenchers and yokt in entertainment with a Taylor? good, good.
Exit.

Phil. How doest *Doll?*
Doll. Scuruie, very scuruie.
Leuer. Where shalls suppe wench?
Doll. Ile suppe in my bedde: gette you home to your lodging and come when I send for you, ô filthy roague that I am.
Phil. How! how, mistris *Dorothy?*
Doll. Saint *Antonies* fire light in your Spanish slops: vds life, ile make you know a difference, betweene my mirth and melancholy, you panderly roague.
Omn. We obserue your Ladiship.
Phil. The puncks in her humer—pax. *Exeunt.*
Doll. Ile humor you and you pox mee: vds life haue I lien with a Spaniard of late, that I haue learnt to mingle such water with my Malago? O ther's some scuruie thing or other breeding; how many seuerall loues of Plaiers, of Vaulters, of Lieutenants haue I entertain'd besides a runner a the ropes, and now to let bloud when

*108 thy] *stet* Q   126 *Exeunt.*] Dyce; *Exit.* Q

the signe is at the heart? should I send him a letter with some Iewel in't, he would requite it as lawiers do, that returne a woodcock pie to their clients, when they send them a Bason and a Eure, I will instantly go and make my selfe drunke, till I haue lost my memory, loue a scoffing Poet?

Exit.

[ACT III, SCENE ii]

Enter Lep-frog *and* Squirill.

Frog. Now *Squirill* wilt thou make vs acquainted with the iest thou promist to tell vs of?

Squir. I will discouer it, not as a *Darby-shere* woman discouers her great teeth, in laughter: but softly as a gentleman courts a wench behind an Arras: and this it is, yong *Greenesheild*, thy Maister, with *Greenesheilds* sister lie in my maisters garden-house here in Morefields.

Frog. Right, what of this?

Squir. Mary sir if the Gentlewoman be not his wife, he commits incest, for Ime sure he lies with her euery night.

Frog. All this I know, but to the rest.

Squir. I will tell thee, the most pollitick trick of a woman, that ere made a mans face looke witherd and pale like the tree in Cuckolds Hauen in a great snow: and this it is, my mistris makes her husband belieue that shee walkes in her sleepe a nights, and to confirme this beleefe in him, sondry times shee hath rizen out of her bed, vnlockt all the dores, gon from Chamber to Chamber, opend her chests, touz'd among her linnen, and when he hath wakte and mist her, comming to question why she coniur'd thus at midnight, he hath found her fast a sleepe, mary it was Cats sleepe, for you shall heare what prey she watcht for.

Frog. Good; forth.

Squir. I ouer-heard her last night talking with thy Maister, and she promist him that assoone as her husband was a sleepe, she would walke according to her custome, and come to his Chamber, marry

136 loue] Dyce; liue Q   3 woman] Dyce; women Q
*5, thy Maister,] ∧ ~ ~ ∧ Q

shee would do it so puritannically, so secretly I meane, that no body should heare of it.
Frog. Ist possible?
Squir. Take but that corner and stand close, and thine eyes shall witnesse it.
Frog. O intollerable witte, what hold can any man take of a womans honesty.
Squir. Hold? no more hold then of a Bull noynted with Sope, and baited with a shoale of Fidlers in *Staffordshire*: stand close I heare her comming.

Enter Kate.

Kate. What a filthy knaue was the shoo-maker, that made my slippers, what a creaking they keepe: O Lord, if there be any power that can make a womans husband sleepe soundly at a pinch, as I haue often read in foolish Poetrie that there is, now, now, and it be thy will, let him dreame some fine dreame or other, that hee's made a Knight, or a Noble-man, or some-what whilst I go and take but two kisses, but two kisses from sweete *Fetherstone*. *Exit.*
Squir. Sfoot hee may well dreame hees made a Knight: for Ile be hangd if she do not dub him.

[*Enter* Greenshield.]

Green. Was there euer any walking spirit, like to my wife? what reason should there bee in nature for this; I will question some Phisition: nor heare neither: vdslife, I would laugh if she were in Maister *Fetherstones* Chamber, shee would fright him, Maister *Fetherstone*, Maister *Fetherstone*.
Within Feth. Ha, how now who cals?
Green. Did you leaue your doore open last night?
Feth. I know not, I thinke my boy did.
Green. Gods light shee's there then, will you know the iest, my wife hath her old tricks, Ile hold my life, my wife's in your chamber, rise out of your bed, and see and you can feele her.
Squir. He will feele her I warrant you?
Green. Haue you her sir?

III. ii]　　　　　　　NORTHWARD HO

Feth. Not yet sir, shee's here sir.
Green. So I said euen now to my selfe before God la: take her vp 60
in your armes, and bring her hether softly, for feare of waking her:

Enter Fetherstone *and* Kate *in his armes.*

I neuer knew the like of this before God la, alas poore *Kate*, looke before God; shees a sleepe with her eyes open: prittie little roague, Ile wake her, and make her ashamd of it.
Feth. O youle make her sicker then.
Green. I warrant you; would all women thought no more hurt then thou doost now, sweet villaine, *Kate, Kate.*
Kate. I longd for the merry thought of a phesant.
Green. She talkes in her sleepe.
Kate. And the foule-gutted Tripe-wife had got it, and eate halfe 70 of it: and my colour went and came, and my stomach wambled, till I was ready to sound: but a Mid-wife perceiued it, and markt which way my eyes went; and helpt mee to it, but Lord how I pickt it, 'twas the sweetest meate me thought.
Squir. O pollitick Mistrisse.
Green. Why *Kate, Kate?*
Kate. Ha, ha, ha, I beshrew your hart, Lord where am I?
Green. I pray thee be not frighted.
Kate. O I am sick, I am sick, I am sick, O how my flesh trembles: oh some of the *Angelica* water, I shal haue the Mother presently. 80
Green. Hold downe her stomach good maister *Fetherstone*, while I fetch some. *Exit.*
Feth. Well dissembled *Kate.*
Kate. Pish, I am like some of your Ladies that can be sick when they haue no stomack to lie with their husbands.
Feth. What mischiuous fortune is this: weel haue a iourney to *Ware Kate*, to redeeme this misfortune.
Kate. Well, Cheaters do not win all wayes: that woman that will entertaine a friend, must as well prouide a Closet or Back-doore for him, as a Fether-bed. 90
Feth. By my troth I pitty thy husband.

61 S.D. *Enter* Fetherstone....] Dyce; Q *places after line* 59
91 By] Dyce; Be Q

445

Kate. Pitty him, no man dares call him Cuckold; for he weares Sattin: pitty him, he that will pull downe a mans signe, and set vp hornes, there's law for him.
Feth. Be sick againe, your husband comes.

Enter Greeneshield *with a broken shin.*

Green. I haue the worst luck; I thinke I get more bumps and shrewd turnes ith' darke, how do's she maister *Fetherstone*.
Feth. Very ill sir, shees troubled with the moother extreamly, I held downe her belly euen now, and I might feele it rise.
Kate. O lay me in my bed, I beseech you.
Green. I will finde a remedy for this walking, if all the Docters in towne can sell it; a thousand pound to a penny she spoile not her face, or breake her neck, or catch a cold that shee may nere claw off againe, how doost wench?
Kate. A little recouerd; alas I haue so troubled that Gentleman.
Feth. None ith' world *Kate*, may I do you any farther seruice.
Kate. And I were where I would be in your bed: pray pardon me, wast you Maister *Fetherstone*, hem, I should be well then. [*Aside.*]
Squir. Marke how she wrings him by the fingers.
Kate. Good night, pray you giue the Gentleman thankes for patience.
Green. Good night Sir.
Feth. You haue a shrewd blow, you were best haue it searcht.
Green. A scratch, a scratch. *Exeunt.*
Feth. Let me see what excuse should I frame, to get this wench forth a towne with me: Ile perswade her husband to take Phisick, and presently haue a letter framed, from his father in law, to be deliuerd that morning, for his wife to come and receiue some small parcell of money in *Enfield chase*, at a Keepers that is her Vncle, then sir he not beeing in case to trauell, will intreate me to accompany his wife, weele lye at *Ware* all night, and the next morning to *London*, Ile goe strike a Tinder, and frame a Letter presently.
Exit.
Squir. And Ile take the paines to discouer all this to my maister

*108 wast] *i.e.* was't *or* was it   114 *Exeunt.*] Dyce; *Exit* Q

old *Maybery*, there hath gone a report a good while, my Maister hath vsed them kindly, because they haue beene ouer familiar with his wife, but I see which way *Fetherstone* lookes. Sfoote ther's neare a Gentleman of them all shall gull a Citizen, and thinke to go scot-free: though your commons shrinke for this be but secret, and my Maister shall intertaine thee, make thee insteed of handling false Dice, finger nothing but gold and siluer wagge, an old Seruing-man turnes to a young beggar, whereas a young Prentise may turne to an old Alderman, wilt be secret?

Frog. O God sir, as secret as rushes in an old Ladyes Chamber.
Exeunt.

ACTVS 4. SCÆNA i.

Enter Bellamont *in his Night-cap, with leaues in his hand, his man after him with lights, Standish and Paper.*

Bell. Sirra, Ile speake with none.
Seru. Not a plaier?
Bell. No tho a Sharer ball,
Ile speake with none, altho it be the mouth
Of the big company, Ile speake with none,—away.
[*Exit Seruant.*]
Why should not I bee an excellent statesman? I can in the wryting of a tragedy, make *Cæsar* speake better than euer his ambition could: when I write of *Pompey* I haue *Pompeies* soule within me, and when I personate a worthy Poet, I am then truly my selfe, a poore vnpreferd scholler.

Enter his Man hastily.

Seru. Here's a swaggering fellow sir, that speakes not like a man of gods making, sweares he must speake with you and wil speake with you.
Bell. Not of gods making? what is he? a Cuckold?
Seru. He's a Gentleman sir, by his clothes.
Bell. Enter him and his clothes: [*Exit Seruant*] clothes sometimes

133 *Frog.*] Leap. Q   133 *Exeunt.*] Dyce; Exit. Q

are better Gentlemen than their Maisters. *Enter the Captaine* [Jenkins] *and the Seruant.* Is this he? Seeke you me sir.

[*Exit Seruant.*]

Capt. I seeke sir, (god plesse you) for a Sentillman, that talkes besides to himselfe when he's alone, as if hee were in Bed-lam, and he's a Poet.

Bell. So sir, it may bee you seeke mee, for Ime sometimes out a my wits.

Capt. You are a Poet sir, are you.

Bell. Ime haunted with a Fury Sir.

Capt. Pray Maister Poet shute off this little pot-gun, and I wil coniure your Fury: tis well lug you sir, my desires are to haue some amiable and amorous sonnet or madrigall composed by your Fury, see you.

Bell. Are you a louer sir of the nine Muses.

Capt. Ow, by gad out a cry.

Bell. Y'are then a scholler sir.

Capt. I ha pickt vp my cromes in Sesus colledge in Oxford one day a gad while agoe.

Bell. Y'are welcome, y'are very welcome, Ile borrow your Iudgement: looke you sir, Ime writyng a Tragedy, the Tragedy of young *Astianax.*

Capt. Styanax Tragedy! is he liuing can you tell? was not *Stianax* a *Mon-mouth* man?

Bell. O no sir, you mistake, he was a Troyane, great *Hectors* Son.

Capt. Hector was grannam to *Cadwallader,* when shee was great with child, god vdge me, there was one young *Styanan* of *Monmouth* sheire was a madder greeke as any is in al *England.*

Bell. This was not he assure yee: looke you sir, I will haue this Tragedy presented in the French Court, by French Gallants.

Capt. By god your Frenchmen will doe a Tragedy enterlude, poggy well.

Bell. It shalbe sir at the marriages of the Duke of *Orleans,* and *Chatilion* the admiral of *France,* the stage—

Capt. Vds bloud, does *Orleans* marry with the Admirall of *France* now.

27 lug] lay Q (*see* IV.ii.22)   32 *Bell.*] Dyce; *Cap.* Q

Bell. O sir no, they are two seuerall marriages. As I was saying the stage hung all with black veluet, and while tis acted, my self wil stand behind the Duke of *Biron*, or some other cheefe minion or so,—who shall, I they shall take some occasion about the musick of the fourth Act, to step to the French King, and say, *Sire, voyla, il et votre treshumble seruiteur, le plu sage, è diuine espirit, monsieur Bellamont*, all in French thus poynting at me, or yon is the learned old English Gentleman Maister *Bellamont*, a very worthie man, to bee one of your priuy Chamber, or Poet Lawreat.

Capt. But are you sure Duke *Pepper-noone* wil giue you such good vrdes, behind your back to your face.

Bell. Oh I, I, I man, he's the onely courtier that I know there: but what do you thinke that I may come to by this.

Capt. God vdge mee, all *France* may hap die in your debt for this.

Bell. I am now wryting the description of his death.

Capt. Did he die in his ped.

Bell. You shall heare: suspition is the Mynion of great hearts, no: I will not begin there: Imagine a great man were to be executed about the seuenth houre in a gloomy morning.

Capt. As it might bee *Sampson* or so, or great *Golias* that was kild by my Countriman.

Bell. Right sir, thus I expresse it in yong *Astianax*.
Now the wilde people greedy of their griefes,
Longing to see, that which their thoughts abhord,
Preuented day, and rod on their owne roofes.

Capt. Could the little horse that ambled on the top of *Paules*, cary all the people; els how could they ride on the roofes!

Bell. O sir, tis a figure in Poetry, marke how tis followed,
Rod on their owne roofes,
Making all Neighboring houses tilde with men; tilde with men! ist not good.

Capt. By Sesu, and it were tilde all with naked Imen twere better.

Bell. You shall heare no more; pick your eares, they are fowle sir, what are you sir pray?

Capt. A Captaine sir, and a follower of god *Mars*.

*54 *Biron*] stet Q

Bell. Mars, *Bachus*, and I loue *Apollo!* a Captaine! then I pardon you sir, and Captaine what wud you presse me for?

Capt. For a witty ditty, to a Sentill-oman, that I am falne in with all, ouer head and eares in affections, and naturall desires.

Bell. An Acrostick were good vpon her name me thinkes.

Capt. Crosse sticks: I wud not be too crosse Maister Poet; yet if it bee best to bring her name in question, her name is mistris *Dorothy Hornet*.

Bell. The very consumption that wasts my Sonne, and the Ayme that hung lately vpon mee: doe you loue this Mistris *Dorothy*?

Capt. Loue her! there is no Captaines wife in *England*, can haue more loue put vpon her, and yet Ime sure Captaines wiues, haue their pellies full of good mens loues.

Bell. And does she loue you? has there past any great matter betweene you?

Capt. As great a matter, as a whole coach, and a horse and his wife are gon too and fro betweene vs.

Bell. Is shee — ifayth Captaine, bee valiant and tell trueth, is she honest?

Capt. Honest? god vdge me, shee's as honest, as a Punck, that cannot abide fornication, and lechery.

Bell. Looke you Captaine, Ile shew you why I aske, I hope you thinke my wenching daies are past, yet Sir, here's a letter that her father brought me from her, and inforc'd mee to take this very day.

Enter a Seruant and Whispers

Capt. Tis for some loue-song to send to me, I hold my life.

Bell. This falls out pat, my man tells mee, the party is at my dore, shall she come in Captaine?

Capt. O I, I, put her in, put her in I pray now.   *Exit Seruant.*

Bell. The letter saies here, that she's exceeding sick, and intreates me to visit her: Captaine, lie you in ambush behind the hangings, and perhaps you shall heare the peece of a Commedy: she comes, she comes, make your selfe away.

Capt. Does the Poet play *Torkin* and cast my *Lucræsies* water too

88 you sir] Dyce; your sir Q

in hugger muggers? if he do, *Styanax* Tragedy was neuer so horrible bloudy-minded, as his Commedy shalbe,—*Tawsone* Captaine *Ienkins*.

Enter Doll.

Doll. Now Maister Poet, I sent for you.
Bell. And I came once at your Ladiships call.
Doll. My Ladiship and your Lordship lie both in one manner; you haue coniur'd vp a sweete spirit in mee haue you not Rimer?
Bell. Why *Medea*! what spirit! wud I were a young man for thy sake.
Doll. So wud I, for then thou couldst doe mee no hurt; now thou doest.
Bell. If I were a yonker, it would be no Imodesty in me to bee seene in thy company; but to haue snow in the lap of Iune; vile! vile: yet come; garlick has a white head, and a greene stalke, then why should not I? lets bee merry: what saies the diuill to al the world, for Ime sure thou art carnally possest with him.
Doll. Thou hast a filthy foot, a very filthy cariers foote.
Bell. A filthy shooe, but a fine foote, I stand not vpon my foote I.
Capt. What stands he vpon then? with a pox god blesse vs?
Doll. A legge and a Calfe! I haue had better of a butcher fortie times for carrying! a body not worth begging by a Barber-surgeon.
Bell. Very good, you draw me and quarter me, fates keepe me from hanging.
Doll. And which most turnes vp a womans stomach, thou art an old hoary man: thou hast gon ouer the bridge of many years, and now art ready to drop into a graue: what doe I see then in that withered face of thine?
Bell. Wrinkles: grauity.
Doll. Wretchednes: griefe: old fellow thou hast be witch me; I can neither eate for thee, nor sleepe for thee, nor lie quietly in my bed for thee.
Capt. Vdsblood! I did neuer see a white flea before. I will clinge you?
Doll. I was borne sure in the dogdayes Ime so vnluky; I, in whome

121 *Tawsone*] Dyce; *Tawsons* Q
*140 carrying! ... body₍ₐ₎] ~ ₍ₐ₎ ... ~ ! Q

neither a flaxen haire, yellow beard, French doublet, nor Spanish hose, youth nor personage, rich face nor mony cold euer breed a true loue to any, euer to any man, am now besotted, doate, am mad, for the carcas of a man, and as if I were a baud, no ring pleases me but a deaths head.

Capt. Sesu, are Imen so arsy varsy.

Bell. Mad for me? why if the worme of lust were wrigling within mee as it does in others, dost thinke Ide crawle vpon thee; wud I low after thee, that art a common calfe-bearer.

Doll. I confesse it.

Capt. Doe you, are you a towne cowe and confesse you beare calues.

Doll. I confesse, I haue bin an Inne for any guest.

Capt. A pogs a your stable-roome; is your Inne a baudy house now?

Doll. I confesse (for I ha bin taught to hide nothing from my Suergeon and thou art he) I confesse that old stinking Sturgeon (like thy selfe) whom I call father, that *Hornet* neuer sweat for me, Ime none of his making.

Capt. You lie, he makes you a punke *Hornet minor*.

Doll. Hees but a cheater, and I the false die hee playes withall, I power all my poyson out before thee, because heareafter I will be cleane: shun me not, loath me not, mocke me not, plagues confound thee, I hate thee to the pit of hell, yet if thou goest thither, ile follow thee, run, ryde, doe what thou canst, ile run and ride ouer the world after thee.

Capt. Cockatrice: you mistris *Salamanders* that feare no burning, let my mare and my mares horse, and my coach come running home agen, and run to an hospitall, and your Surgeons, and to knaues and panders and to the tiuell and his tame to.

Doll. Fiend art thou raized to torment me.

Bell. Shee loues you Captaine honestly.

Capt. Ile haue any man, oman or cilde by his eares, that saies a common drab can loue a Sentillman honestly, I will sell my Coach for a cart to haue you to puncks hall, Pridewell, I sarge you in *Apollos* name, whom you belong to, see her forth-comming, till

170 Sturgeon] Surgeon Q   178 ryde,] ayde ₐ Q

I come and tiggle her, by and by, Sbloud I was neuer Couzend 19
with a more rascall peece of mutton, since I came out a the Lawer
Countries. *Exit.*
Bell. My dores are open for thee, be gon: woman!
Doll. This goates—peezle of thine—
Bell. Away: I loue no such implements in my house.
Doll. Doest not? am I but an implement? by all the maiden-heads
that are lost in *London* in a yeare (and thats a great oth) for this
trick, other manner of women than my selfe shall come to this
house only to laugh at thee; and if thou wouldst labour thy heart
out, thou shalt not do withal. *Exit.* 200

Enter Seruant.

Bell. Is this my Poeticall fury? how now sir!
Seru. Maister *Maybery* and his wife sir ith next roome.
Bell. What are they doing sir?
Seru. Nothing sir, that I see, but onely wud speake with you.
[*Exit Seruant.*]
Bell. Enter 'em: this house wilbe to hot for mee, if this wench cast
me into these sweates, I must shift my selfe, for pure necessity,
haunted with sprites in my old daies!

Enter Maybery *booted, his Wife with him.*

May. A Commedy, a Canterbury tale smells not halfe so sweete
as the Commedy I haue for thee old Poet: thou shalt write vpon't
Poet. 210
Bell. Nay I will write vpon't ift bee a Commedie, for I haue beene
at a most villanous female Tragedie: come, the plot, the plot.
May. Let your man giue you the bootes presently, the plot lies
in *Ware* my white Poet: Wife thou and I this night, will haue mad
sport in *Ware*, marke me well Wife, in *Ware*.
Wife. At your pleasure sir.
May. Nay it shalbe at your pleasure Wife: looke you sir, looke
you: *Fetherstones* boy (like an honest crack-halter) layd open all
to one of my prentices, (for boies you know like women loue to be
doing.) 220
Bell. Very good: to the plot.

May. *Fetherstone* like a crafty mutton-monger, perswades *Greenshield* to be run through the body.
Bell. Strange! through the body?
May. I man, to take phisick: he does so, hee's put to his purgation; then sir what does me *Fetherstone*, but counterfits a letter from an Inkeeper of *Doncaster*, to fetch *Greenshield* (who is needy you know) to a keepers lodge in *Enfeild-chace*, a certaine Vncle, where *Greenshield* should receiue mony due to him in behalfe of his wife. 230
Bell. His wife! is *Greensheild* married? I haue heard him sweare he was a batchiler.
Wife. So haue I a hundred times.
May. The knaue has more wiues than the Turke, he has a wife almost in euery shire in *England*, this parcel Gentlewoman is that Inkeepers Daughter of *Doncaster*.
Bell. Hath she the entertainement of her fore-fathers? wil she keepe all commers company?
May. She help's to passe away stale Capons, sower wine, and musty prouander: but to the purpose, this traine was layd by the 240 baggage her selfe and *Fetherstone*, who it seemes makes her husband a vnicorne: and to giue fire to't, *Greensheild* like an Arrant wittall intreates his friend, to ride before his wife, and fetch the money, because taking bitter pills, he should proue but a loose fellow if he went, and so durst not go.
Bell. And so the poore Stag is to bee hunted in *Enfeild-chace*?
May. No sir, Maister poet there you misse the plot, *Fetherstone* and my Lady *Greenshield* are rid to barter away their light commodities in *Ware*, *Enfeild-chace* is to cold for 'em.
Bell. In *Ware*! 250
May. In durty *Ware*: I forget my selfe wife, on with your ryding suite, and cry *North-ward hoe*, as the boy at *Powles* saies, let my Prentice get vp before thee, and man thee to *Ware*, lodge in the Inne I told thee, spur cut and away.
Wife. Well sir. *Exit.*
Bell. Stay, stay, whats the bottom of this riddle? why send you her away?

248 barter] batter Q (*see* II.i.228)

May. For a thing my little hoary Poet: looke thee, I smelt out my noble stincker *Greensheild* in his Chamber, and as tho my heart stringes had bin crackt, I wept, and sighd, and thumpd, and thumpd, and rau'd and randed, and raild, and told him how my wife was now growne as common as baibery, and that shee had hierd her Taylor to ride with her to *Ware*, to meete a Gentleman of the Court.

Bell. Good; and how tooke he this drench downe.

May. Like Egs and Muscadine, at a gulp: hee cries out presently, did not I tell you old man, that sheed win any game when she came to bearing? hee railes vpon her, wills me to take her in the Act; to put her to her white sheete, to bee diuorc'd, and for all his guts are not fully scourd by his Pottecary, hee's pulling on his bootes, and will ride along with vs; lets muster as many as wee can.

Bell. It wilbe excellent sport, to see him and his owne wife meete in *Ware*, wilt not? I, I, weele haue a whole Regiment of horse with vs.

May. I stand vpon thornes, tel I shake him bith hornes: come, bootes boy, we must gallop all the way, for the Sin you know is done with turning vp the white of an eye, will you ioyne your forces.

Bell. Like a *Hollander* against a *Dunkirke*.

May. March then, this curse is on all letchers throwne,
They giue hornes and at last, hornes are their owne.

Exeunt.

[ACT IV, Scene ii]

Enter Captaine Ienkins, *and* Allom.

Capt. Set the best of your little diminitiue legges before, and ride post I pray.

Allom. Is it possible that mistris *Doll* should bee so bad?

*262 baibery] *stet* Q
267 any] Dyce; my Q
282 S.D. *Exeunt.*] Dyce; *Exit.* Q

Capt. Possible! Sbloud tis more easie for an oman to be naught, than for a soldier to beg, and thats horrible easie, you know.

Allom. I but to connicatch vs all so grosly.

Capt. Your *Norfolke* tumblers are but zanyes to connicatching punckes.

Allom. Shee gelded my purse of fifty pounds in ready money.

Capt. I will geld all the horses in fiue hundred Sheires, but I will ride ouer her, and her cheaters, and her *Hornets*; Shee made a starke Asse of my Coach-horse, and there is a putter-box, whome shee spred thick vpon her white bread, and eate him vp, I thinke shee has sent the poore fellow to *Gelderland*, but I will marse prauely in and out, and packe agen vpon all the low countries in Christendom, as *Holland* and *Zeland* and *Netherland*, and *Cleueland* too, and I will be drunke and cast with maister *Hans van Belch*, but I will smell him out.

Allom. Doe so and weele draw all our arrowes of reuenge vp to the head but weele hit her for her villany.

Capt. I will traw as petter, and as vrse weapons as arrewes vp to the head, lug you, it shalbe warrants to giue her the whippe deedle.

Allom. But now she knowes shees discouered, sheele take her bells and fly out of our reach.

Capt. Flie with her pells! ownds I know a parish that sal tag downe all the pells and sell em to Capten *Ienkens*, to do him good, and if pells will fly, weele flie too, vnles, the pell-ropes hang vs: will you amble vp and downe to maister Iustice by my side, to haue this rascall *Hornet* in corum, and so, to make her hold her whoars peace.

Allom. Ile amble or trot with you Capten: you told me, she threatened her champions should cut for her, if so, wee may haue the peace of her.

Capt. *O mon du! du guin!* follow your leader, *Ienken* shall cut, and Slice, as worse as they: come I scorne to haue any peace of her, or of any oman, but open warres.

Exeunt.

25 Flie] Dyce; Fle Q
27 pells] pelle Q

[ACT IV, Scene iii]

Enter Bellamont, Maybery, Greensheild, Phillip, Leuarpoole, Chartley: *all booted.*

Bell. What? will these yong Gentlemen helpe vs to catch this fresh Salmon, ha! *Phillip*! are they thy friends.
Phil. Yes Sir.
Bell. We are beholding to you Gentlmen that youle fill our consort: I ha seene your faces me thinkes before; and I cannot informe my selfe where.
Both. May be so Sir.
Bell. Shalls to horse, hears a tickler: heigh: to horse.
May. Come Switts and Spurres! lets mount our Cheualls: merry quoth a.   10
Bell. Gentlemen shall I shoote a fooles bolt out among you all, because weele be sure to be merry.
Omn. What ist?
Bell. For mirth on the high way, will make vs rid ground faster then if theeues were at our tayles, what say yee to this, lets all practise iests one against another, and hee that has the best iest throwne vpon him, and is most gald, betweene our riding foorth and comming in, shall beare the charge of the whole iourney.
Omn. Content ifaith.
Bell. Wee shall fitte one a you with a Cox-combe at *Ware* I 20 beleeue.
May. Peace.
Green. Ist a bargen.
Omn. And hands clapt vpon it.
Bell. Stay, yonders the Dolphin without Bishops-gate, where our horses are at rack and manger, and wee are going past it: come crosse ouer: and what place is this?
May. Bedlam ist not?
Bell. Where the mad-men are, I neuer was amongst them, as you loue me Gentlemen, lets see what Greekes are within.   30

*1 helpe] to helpe Q

Green. Wee shall stay too long.
Bell. Not a whit, *Ware* will stay for our comming I warrant you: come a spurt and away, lets bee mad once in our dayes: this is the doore.

Enter Full-moone.

May. Saue you sir, may we see some a your mad-folkes, doe you keepe em?
Full. Yes.
Bell. Pray bestow your name sir vpon vs.
Full. My name is *Full-moone*.
Bell. You well deserue this office good maister *Full-moone*: and 40 what mad-caps haue you in your house?

Enter the Musition.

Full. Diuerse.
May. Gods so, see, see, whats hee walkes yonder, is he mad.
Full. Thats a Musition, yes hee's besides himselfe.
Bell. A Musition, how fell he mad for Gods sake?
Full. For loue of an Italian Dwarfe.
Bell. Has he beene in *Italy* then?
Full. Yes and speakes they say all manner of languages.

Enter the Bawd.

Omn. Gods so, looke, looke, whats shee.
Bell. The dancing Beare: a pritty well-fauourd little woman. 50
Full. They say, but I know not, that she was a Bawd, and was frighted out of her wittes by fire.
Bell. May we talke with 'em maister *Ful-moone*?
Full. Yes and you will; I must looke about for I haue vnruly tenants. *Exit.*
Bell. What haue you in this paper honest friend?
[*Exit Musition.*]
Green. Is this he has al manner of languages, yet speakes none?
Baud. How doe you Sir *Andrew*, will you send for some aquauite for me, I haue had no drinke neuer since the last great raine that fell. 60

41 S.D. *Musition*] Phisition Q

458

Bell. No thats a lye.

Baud. Nay by gad, then you lie, for all y'are Sir *Andrew*, I was a dapper rogue in *Portingall* voiage, not an inch broad at the heele, and yet thus high, I scornd I can tell you to be druncke with raine water then Sir, In those golden and siluer dayes: I had sweete bitts then Sir *Andrew*: how doe you good brother *Timothy*?

Bell. You haue bin in much trouble since that voiage.

Baud. Neuer in bride-wel I protest, as Ime a virgin: for I could neuer abide that bride-wel I protest, I was once sicke, and I tooke my water in a basket, and cary'd it to a doctors.

Phil. In a basket.

Baud. Yes Sir: you arrant foole there was a vrinall in it.

Phil. I cry you mercy.

Baud. The Doctor told me I was with child, how many Lords, Knights, Gentlemen, Cittizens, and others promist me to be godfathers to that child: twas not Gods will: the prentises made a riot vpon my glasse-windowes the Shroue-tuesday following and I miscaried.

Omn. O doe not weepe.

Baud. I ha cause to weepe: I trust Gintlewomen their diet sometimes a fortnight: lend Gentlemen holland shirts, and they sweat 'em out at tennis: and no restitution, and no restitution. But Ile take a new order, I will haue but six stewd prunes in a dish and some of mother *Walls* cakes: for my best customers are taylors.

Omn. Taylors! ha ha.

Baud. I Taylors: giue me your *London* Prentice; your country Gentlemen are growne too polliticke.

Bell. But what say you to such young Gentlemen as these are.

Baud. Foh, they as soone as they come to their lands get vp to *London*, and like squibs that run vpon lynes, they keepe a Spitting of fire, and cracking till they ha spent all, and when my squib is out, what sayes his punke, foh, he stinckes.

Enter the musition.

Me thought this other night, I saw a pretty sight,
Which pleased me much.
A comely country mayd, not squeamish nor afraid,

To let Gentlemen touch.
I sold her maiden-head once, and I sold her maiden-head twice,
And I sould it last to an Alderman of *Yorke*.
And then I had sold it thrice.

Musi. You sing scuruily.

Baud. Mary muffe, sing thou better, for Ile goe sleepe my old sleepes. *Exit.*

Bell. What are you a doing my friend.

Musi. Pricking, pricking.

Bell. What doe you meane by pricking?

Musi. A Gentleman like quallity.

Bell. This fellow is some what prouder, and sulliner then the other.

May. Oh; so be most of your musitions.

Musi. Are my teeth rotten?

Omn. No Sir.

Musi. Then I am no Comfit-maker, nor Vintner, I doe not get wenches in my drincke: are you a musition?

Bell. Yes.

Musi. Weele be sworne brothers then, looke you sweete roague.

Green. Gods so, now I thinke vpon't, a Iest is crept into my head, steale away, if you loue me. *Exeunt: musition sings.*

Musi. Was euer any marchants band set better I set it: walke Ime a cold, this white sattin is to thin vnles it be cut, for then the Sunne enters: can you speake Italian too, *Sapetè Italiano*.

Bell. *Vn poco*.

Musi. Sblood if it be in you, Ile poake it out of you; *vn poco*, come March, lie heare with me but till the fall of the leafe, and if you haue but *poco Italiano* in you, Ile fill you full of more *poco*. March.

Bell. Come on. *Exeunt.*

Enter Maybery, Greeneshilde, Phillip. Full-moone. Leuerpoole, *and* Chartely.

Green. Good Maister *Mayberie, Philip,* if you be kind Gentlemen vp-hold the iest: your whole voiage is payd for.

*118 better] *stet* Q   122 of] Dyce; if Q

May. Follow it then.
Full. The old Gentleman say you, why he talkt euen now aswell in his wittes as I do my selfe, and lookt as wisely.
Green. No matter how he talkes, but his Pericranion's perisht.
Full. Where is he pray?
Phil. Mary with the Musition, and is madder by this time.
Chart. Hee's an excellent Musition himselfe, you must note that.
May. And hauing met one fit for his own tooth: you see hee skips from vs.
Green. The troth is maister *Full-moone*, diuers traines haue bin laide to bring him hither, without gaping of people, and neuer any tooke effect till now.
Full. How fell he mad?
Green. For a woman, looke you sir: here's a crowne to prouide his supper: hee's a Gentleman of a very good house, you shall bee paid well if you conuert him; to morrow morning, bedding, and a gowne shall be sent in, and wood and coale.
Full. Nay sir, he must ha no fire.
Green. No, why looke what straw you buy for him, shall returne you a whole haruest.
Omn. Let his straw be fresh and sweet we beseech you sir?
Green. Get a couple of your sturdiest fellowes, and bind him I pray, whilst wee slip out of his sight.
Full. Ile hamper him, I warrant Gentlemen. *Exit.*
Omn. Excellent.
May. But how will my noble Poet take it at my hands, to betray him thus.
Omn. Foh, tis but a iest, he comes.

Enter Musition and Bellamont.

Bell. *Perdonate mi, si Io dimando del vostro nome*: oh, whether shrunke you: I haue had such a mad dialogue here.
Omn. Wee ha bin with the other mad folkes.
May. And what sayes he and his prick-song?
Bell. Wee were vp to the eares in *Italian* ifaith.
Omn. In *Italian*; O good maister *Bellamont* lets heare him.

136 own] Dyce; one Q

Enter Full-moone, *and two Keepers.* [*The rest steal away.*]

Bell. How now, Sdeath what do you meane? are you mad?
Full. Away sirra, bind him, hold fast: you want a wench sirra, doe you?
Bell. What wench? will you take mine armes from me, being no Heralds? let goe you Dogs.
Full. Bind him, be quiet: come, come, dogs, fie, and a gentleman.
Bell. Maister *Maibery, Philip,* maister *Maibery,* vds foot.
Full. Ile bring you a wench, are you mad for a wench.
Bell. I hold my life my comrads haue put this fooles cap vpon thy head: to gull me: I smell it now: why doe you heare *Full-moone,* let me loose; for Ime not mad; Ime not mad by Iesu!
Full. Aske the Gentlemen that.
Bell. Bith Lord I'me aswell in my wits, as any man ith' house, and this is a trick put vpon thee by these gallants in pure knauery.
Full. Ile trie that, answer me to this question: loose his armes a little, looke you sir, three Geese nine pence; euery Goose three pence, whats that a Goose, roundly, roundly one with another.
Bell. Sfoot do you bring your Geese for me to cut vp.

Strike him soundly, and kick him.

Enter all.

Omn. Hold, hold, bind him maister *Full-moone.*
Full. Binde him you, hee has payd me all, Ile haue none of his bonds not I, vnlesse I could recouer them better.
Green. Haue I giuen it you maister Poet, did the Lime-bush take.
May. It was his warrant sent thee to Bedlam, old *Iack Bellamont,* and maister *Full-ith'moone,* our warrant discharges him; Poet, weele all ride vpon thee to *Ware,* and back agen I feare to thy cost.
Bell. If you doe, I must beare you, thanke you Maister *Greenshield,* I will not dye in your debt: farewell you mad rascals, to horse come, 'tis well done; 'twas well done, you may laugh, you shall laugh Gentlemen: if the gudgeon had beene swallowed by one of you it had bin vile, but by Gad 'tis nothing, for your best Poets indeed are madde for the most part: farewell good-man *Full-moone.*

Full. Pray Gentlemen if you come by call in. *Exit.*
Bell. Yes, yes, when they are mad, horse your selues now if you be men.
May. Hee gallop must that after women rides,
Get our wiues out of Towne, they take long strides.
Exeunt.

ACTVS 5. SCÆNA i

Enter old Maybery *and* Bellamont.

May. But why haue you brought vs to the wrong Inne? and withall possest *Greenshield* that my wife is not in towne: when my proiect was, that I would haue brought him vp into the chamber, where yong *Fetherstone* and his wife lay: and so all his Artillery should haue recoild into his owne bosome.

Bell. O it will fall out farre better, you shall see my reuenge will haue a more neate and vnexpected conueyance: he hath bin all vp and downe the towne, to enquire for a Londoners wife, none such is to be found: for I haue mewd your wife vp already. Mary he heres of a *Yorke-shire* Gentlewoman at next Inne, and thats all the commodity *Ware* affoords at this instant: now sir, he very pollitickly imagins, that your wife is rode to *Puckridge*, fiue mile further, for saith he in such a towne where Hosts will be familiar, and Tapsters saucie, and Chamberlaines worse then theeues intelligencers, theile neuer put foot out of Stirrop: either at *Pucridge* or *Wades-mill* (saith he) you shall finde them: and because our horses are weary, hee's gone to take vp Post horse: my counsaile is onely this, when he comes in, faine your selfe very melancholie, sweare you will ride no farther. And this is your part of the Comedy: the sequell of the iest shall come like money borrowed of a Courtier, and paid within the day, a thing strange and vnexpected.

Enter Greeneshield.

May. Inough, I ha't.
Bell. He comes.

Green. Come gallants, the post horse are ready, tis but a quarter of an houres riding, weele ferrit them and firke them in-faith.
Bell. Are they growne pollitick? when do you see honesty couet corners, or a gentleman thats no thiefe lie in the Inne of a carrier.
May. Nothing hath vndone my wife, but too much riding.
Bell. She was a pritty piece of a Poet indeed, and in her discourse would as many of your Gold-smiths wiues doe, draw her simily from pretious stones, so wittily, as redder then your Ruby, harder then your Diamond, and so from stone to stone, in lesse time then a man can draw on a straight boote, as if she had beene an excellent Lapidary.
Green. Come will you to horse sir?
May. No let her go to the diuell and she will, Ile not stirre a foote further.
Green. Gods pretious ist come to this: perswade him as you are a Gentleman, there will be ballads made of him, and the burthen thereof will be, if you had rode out fiue mile forward, he had found the fatall house of *Braineford* North-ward, O hone, hone, hone o nonero.
Bell. You are merry sir.
Green. Like your Cittizen, I neuer thinke of my debts, when I am a horseback.
Bell. You imagin you are riding from your creditors.
Green. Good infaith: wil you to horse?
May. Ile ride no further.   [*Walks aside.*]
Green. Then ile discharge the post-maister: was't not a pritty wit of mine maister Poet to haue had him rod into *Puckridge*, with a horne before him, ha wast not?
Bell. Good sooth excellent: I was dull in apprehending it: but come since we must stay, wele be mery: chamberlaine call in the musick, bid the Tapsters and maids come vp and dance, what weel make a night of it, harke you maisters, I haue an exellent iest to make old *Maibery* merry, Sfoote weele haue him merry.
                                     [*Enter Fidlers.*]
Green. Lets make him drunke then, a simple catching wit I.
Bell. Go thy waies, I know a Nobleman would take such a delight in thee.

Green. Why so he would in his foole.

Bell. Before God but hee would make a difference, hee would keepe you in Sattin, but as I was a saying weel haue him merry: his wife is gon to *Puckridge*, tis a wench makes him melancholy, tis a wench must make him mery: we must help him to a wench. When your cittizen comes into his Inne, wet and cold, dropping, either the hostis or one of her maids, warmes his bed, puls on his night-cap, cuts his cornes, puts out the candle, bids him command ought, if he want ought: and so after maister cittiner sleepes as quietly, as if he lay in his owne low-country of *Holland*, his own linnen I meane sir, we must haue a wench for him.

Green. But wher's this wench to be found, here are al the moueable peticotes of the house.

Bell. At the next Inne there lodged to night—

Green. Gods pretious a *Yorkeshire* Gentlewoman; I ha't, Ile angle for her presently, weele haue him merry.

Bell. Procure some Chamberlaine to Pander for you.

Green. No Ile be Pander my selfe, because weele be merry.

Bell. Will you, will you?

Green. But how? be a Pander as I am, a gentleman? that were horrible, Ile thrust my self into the out-side of a Fawlconer in towne here: and now I thinke on't there are a company of country plaiers, that are come to towne here, shall furnish mee with haire and beard: if I do not bring her,—weel be wondrous merry.

Bell. About it: looke you sir, though she beare her far aloofe, and her body out of distance, so her mind be comming 'tis no matter.

Green. Get old *Maibery* merry: that any man should take to heart thus the downe fall of a woman, I thinke when he comes home poore snaile, heele not dare to peepe forth of doores least his hornes vsher him. *Exit.*

Bell. Go thy wayes, there be more in *England* weare large eares and hornes, then Stagges and Asses: excellent, hee rides poste with a halter about his neck.

May. How now, wilt take?

Bell. Beyond expectation: I haue perswaded him the onely way

*80 am,] ~ ∧ Q
84 weel be] Dyce; wilbe Q

to make you merry, is to helpe you to a wench, and the foole is gone to pander his owne wife hether.
May. Why heele know her?
Bell. She hath beene maskt euer since she came into the Inne, for feare of discouery.
May. Then sheele know him.
Bell. For that his owne vnfortunate wit helpt my lasie inuention, for he hath disguisd himselfe like a Fawkner, in Towne heare, hoping in that procuring shape, to doe more good vpon her, then in the out-side of a Gentleman.
May. Young *Fetherstone* will know him?
Bell. Hee's gone into the towne, and will not returne this halfe houre.
May. Excellent if she would come.
Bell. Nay vpon my life sheele come: when she enters remember some of your young bloud, talke as some of your gallant commoners will, Dice and drinke: freely: do not call for Sack, least it betray the coldnesse of your man-hood, but fetch a caper now and then, to make the gold chinke in your pockets: I so.
May. Ha old Poet, lets once stand to it for the credit of *Milke-streete*. Is my wife acquainted with this.
Bell. She's perfect, and will come out vpon her qu, I warrant you.
May. Good wenches infaith: fils some more Sack heare.
Bell. Gods pretious, do not call for Sack by any meanes.
May. Why then giue vs a whole Lordship for life in *Rhenish*, with the reuersion in Sugar.
Bell. Excellent.
May. It were not amisse if we were dancing.
Bell. Out vpon't, I shall neuer do it.

Enter Greensheild *disguised, with mistresse* Greensheild.

Green. Out of mine nostrils tapster, thou smelst like *Guild-hall* two daies after *Simon* and *Iude*, of drinke most horribly, off with thy maske sweete sinner of the North: these maskes are foiles to good faces, and to bad ones they are like new sattin out-sides to lousie linings.
Kate. O by no meanes sir, your Merchant will not open a whole

peece to his best costomer, hee that buies a woman, must take her as she falls: Ile vnmaske my hand, heares the sample.

Green. Goe to then, old Poet I haue tane her vp already as a pinnis bound for the straights, she knowes her burden yonder.

Bell. Lady you are welcome: yon is the old Gentleman and obserue him, he's not one of your fat Citty chuffes: whose great belly argues that the felicity of his life consistes in capon, sack, and sincere honesty, but a leane spare bountiful gallant, one that hath an old wife, and a young performance: whose reward is not the rate of a Captaine newly come out of the Low-countries: or a *Yorkeshiere* Atturny in good contentious practice, some angel, no the proportion of your welthy Cittizen to his wench, is, her Chamber, her diet, her phisick, her apparell, her painting, her monkey, her pandar, her euery thing. Youle say your yong Gentleman, is your onely seruice that lies before you like a Calues head, with his braines some halfe yeard from him, but I assure you, they must not onely haue variety of foolery; but also of wenches: whereas your conscionable gray-beard of *Farrington* within, will keepe himselfe, to the ruines of one cast waighting-woman an age: and perhaps, when he's past all other good workes, to wipe out false waightes, and twenty ith hundred, marry her—

Green. O well bould *Tom* (   ) we haue presedents, for't.

Kate. But I haue a husband sir.

Bell. You haue? if the knaue thy husband bee rich, make him poore, that he may borrow mony of this Merchant, and be layd vp in the Counter, or Ludgate, so it shall bee conscience in your old Gentleman, when he hath seized all thy goods, to take the horne and maintaine thee.

Green. O well bould *Tom* (   ) wee haue presedents for't.

Kate. Well if you be not a Nobleman, you are some great valiant Gentleman, by your bearing: and the fashion of your beard: and do but thus to make the Cittizen merry, because you owe him some money.

Bell. O you are a wag.

      132 falls] Dyce; fales Q   *152 Tom (   )] *stet* Q
      156 your] Dyce; you Q   *158 take the horne] *stet* Q
     *161 bearing] bearth Q

May. You are very welcome.

Green. He is tane, excellent, excellent, ther's one will make him merry: is it any imputation to helpe ones friend to a wench?

Bell. No more then at my Lords intreaty, to helpe my Lady to a pritty waighting woman: if he had giuen you a gelding, or the reuersion of some Monopoly, or a new sute of Sattin to haue done this, happily your Sattin would haue smelt of the Pander: but what's done freely, comes like a present to an old Lady, without any reward, and what is done without any rewarde, comes like wounds to a Souldier, very honourably not-with-standing.

May. This is my breeding Gentlewoman: and whether trauaile you? [*Kisses her.*]

Kate. To *London* sir, as the old tale goes, to seeke my fortune.

May. Shall I be your fortune Lady?

Kate. O pardon me sir, Ile haue some young landed heire to be my Fortune, for they fauour shee fooles more then Cittizens.

May. Are you married?

Kate. Yes, but my husband is in garrison ith' Low-countries, is his Colonels bawd, and his Captaines Iester: he sent me word ouer, that he will thriue: for though his apparell lie ith' Lumbard, he keepes his conscience ith' Muster-booke.

May. Hee may do his countrie good seruice Lady.

Kate. I as many of your Captaines do, that fight as the Geese saued the Capitoll, onely with pratling: well, well, if I were in some Noblemans hands now, may be he would not take a thousand pounds for me.

May. No?

Kate. No sir: and yet may be at yeares end, would giue me a brace of hundreth pounds, to marry me to his Bayly, or the Solicitor of his Law sutes: whose this I beseech you?

Enter mistrisse Maybery *her haire loose, with the Hostice.*

Host. I pray you forsooth be patient.

Bell. Passion of my heart, Mistresse *Maybery.* *Exeunt Fidlers.*

Green. Now will shee put some notable trick, vpon her Cuckoldly husband.

May. Why how now Wife, what meanes this? ha?

Wife. Well, I am very well: ô my vnfortunate parents, would you had buried me quick, when you linkt me to this misery.

May. O wife be patient, I haue more cause to raile wife.

Wife. You haue? proue it, proue it: wheres the Courtier, you should haue tane in my bosome: Ile spit my gall in's face, that can tax me of any dishonor: haue I lost the pleasure of mine eyes, the sweetes of my youth, the wishes of my bloud: and the portion of my friends, to be thus dishonord, to be reputed vild in *London*, whilst my husband prepares common diseases for me at *Ware*, O god O god.

Bell. Prettily wel dissembled.

Host. As I am true hostice you are to blame sir, what are you mistris: Ile know what you are afore you depart mistris, dost thou leaue thy Chamber in an honest Inne, to come and inueagle my costomers, and you had sent for me vp, and kist me and vsde me like an hostice, twold neuer haue greeued mee, but to do it to a stranger. [*To* Maybery.]

Kate. Ile leaue you sir.

May. Stay, why how now sweete gentlewoman, cannot I come forth to breath my selfe, but I must bee haunted, — [*aside*] raile vpon olde *Bellamont*, that he may discouer them, — you remember *Fetherstone, Greensheild.*

Wife. I remember them, I, they are two as coging, dishonorable dambd forsworne beggerly gentlemen, as are in al *London*, and ther's a reuerent old gentleman to, your pander in my conscience.

Bell. Lady, I wil not as the old goddes were wont, sweare by the infernall *Stix*; but by all the mingled wine in the seller beneath, and the smoke of Tobacco that hath fumed ouer the vessailes, I did not procure your husband this banqueting dish of sukket, looke you behold the parenthesis. [*Discovers* Greenshield.]

Host. Nay Ile see your face too. [*Unmasks* Kate.]

Kate. My deare vnkind husband; I protest to thee I haue playd this knauish part only to be witty.

Green. That I might bee presently turned into a matter more sollid then horne, into Marble.

200 *Wife.*] *here and for the rest of the scene* Q *speech-prefix is* Mist. May.
212 mistris...mistris] Dyce; maisters...maisters Q

Bell.   Your husband gentlewoman: why hee neuer was a souldier.
Kate.   I but a Lady got him prickt for a Captaine, I warrant you, he wil answere to the name of Captaine, though hee bee none: like a Lady that wil not think scorne to answere to the name of her first husband; though he weare a Sope-boyler.
Green.   Hange of thou diuill, away.   240
Kate.   No, no, *you fled me tother day,*
When I was with child you ran away,
But since I haue caught you now.
Green.   A pox of your wit and your singing.
Bell.   Nay looke you sir, she must sing because weele be merry, what though you rod not fiue mile forward, you haue found that fatall house at *Brainford* Northward, O hone ho no na ne ro.
Green.   God refuse mee Gentlemen, you may laugh and bee merry: but I am a Cockold and I thinke you knew of it, who lay ith segges with you to night wild-ducke.   250
Kate.   No body with me, as I shall be saued: but Maister *Fetherstone,* came to meete me as far as *Roistone.*
Green.   *Fetherstone.*
May.   See the hawke that first stoopt my phesant, is kild by the Spaniell that first sprang all of our side wife.
Bell.   Twas a pretty wit of you sir, to haue had him rod into *Puckeridge* with a horne before him; ha: wast not?
Green.   Good.
Bell.   Or where a Cittizen keepes his house, you know tis not as a Gentleman keepes his Chamber for debt, but as you sayd euen 260 now very wisely, least his hornes should vsher him.
Green.   Very good, *Fetherstone* he comes.

Enter Fetherstone.

Feth.   *Luke Greeneshield,* Maister *Maybery,* old Poet: *Mol* and *Kate,* most hapily incounterd, vdslife how came you heather, by my life the man lookes pale.
Green.   You are a villaine, and Ile mak't good vpon you, I am no seruingman, to feede vpon your reuersion.
Feth.   Go to the ordinary then.

Bell. This is his ordinary sir and in this she is like a *London* ordinary: her best getting comes by the box.   270
Green. You are a dambd villaine.
Feth. O by no meanes.
Green. No, vdslife, Ile go instantly take a purse, be apprehended and hang'd for't, better then be a Cockold.
Feth. Best first make your confession sirra.
Green. Tis this, thou hast not vsed me like a Gentleman.
Feth. A Gentleman: thou a gentleman: thou art a Taylor.
Bell. Ware peaching.
Feth. No sirra if you will confesse ought, tell how thou hast wronged that vertuous Gentlewoman: how thou laiest at her two 280 yeare together to make her dishonest: how thou wouldest send me thether with letters, how duely thou woudst watch the cittizens wiues vacation, which is twice a day; namely the exchainge time, twelue at noone and six at night, and where she refused thy importunity, and vowed to tell her husband: thou wouldest fall downe vpon thy knees, and intreat her for the loue of Heauen, if not to ease thy violent affection, at least to conceale it, to which her pitty and simple vertue consented, how thou tookest her wedding ring from her, Met these two Gentlemen at *Ware*: fained a quarell, and the rest is apparant. This onely remaines: what wrong the 290 poore Gentlewoman hath since receaued by our intollerable lye; I am most hartely sorry for, and to thy bosome will maintaine all I haue said to bee honest.
May. Victorie wife thou art quit by proclamation.
Bell. Sir you are an honest man, I haue knowne an arrant theefe for peaching made an officer, giue me your hand Sir.
Kate. O ffilthy abhominable husband did you all this?
May. Certainely he is no Captaine: he blushes.
Wife. Speake Sir did you euer know me answere your wishes.
Green. You are honest, very vertuously honest.   300
Wife. I wil then no longer be a loose woman, I haue at my husbands pleasure tane vpon me this habit of iealousie: Ime sorry for you, vertue glories not in the spoyle but in the victory.
Bell. How say you by that goodly Sentence; looke you sir, you

304 goodly] Dyce; goody Q

gallants visit cittizens houses, as the Spaniard first sailed to the *Indies*, you pretend bying of wares or selling of lands: but the end proues tis nothing but for discouery and conquest of their wiues for better maintenance. Why looke you, was he a ware of those broken patience when you met him at *Ware*, and possest him of the downfal of his wife: you are a Cockcold, you haue pandred your own wife to this gentleman, better men haue don it, honest *Tom* ( ), wee haue presidents for't, hie you to *London*: what is more Catholick ith City then for husbands daily for to forgiue, the nightly sins of their bedfellowes: if you like not that course but do intend to be rid of her: rifle her at a Tauerne, where you may swallow downe some fifty wisacres sonnes and heires to old tenements, and common gardens: like so many raw yeolkes with Muskadine to bed-ward.

Kate. O filthy knaue, dost compare a woman of my cariadge to a horse.

Bell. And no disparagment; for a woman to haue a high forhead, a quick eare, a full eye, a wide nostrell, a sleeke skin, a straight back, a round hip, and so forth is most comely.

Kate. But is a great belly comly in a horse sir.

Bell. No Lady.

Kate. And what thinke you of it in a woman I pray you.

Bell. Certainly, I am put downe at my owne weapon; I therefore recant the riflying? no there is a new trade come vp for the cast Gentlewomen, of peeriwig making: let your wife set vp ith Strand, and yet I doubt, whither she may or no, for they say, the women haue got it to be a corporation; if you can you may make good vse of it, for you shall haue as good a comming in by haire (tho it be but a falling commodity) and by other foolish tyring, as any betweene Saint *Clements* and *Charing*.

Feth. Now you haue run your selfe out of breath, here me: I protest the gentlewoman is honest, and since I haue wrong'd her reputation in meeting her thus priuately, Ile maintaine her: wilt thou hang at my purse *Kate*, like a paire of barbary buttons, to open when tis full, and close when tis empty?

Kate. Ile be diuorc'd by this Christian element, and because thou

*309 patience] *stet* Q   314 do] Dyce; to Q

thinkst thou art a Cockold, least I should make thee an infidell, in causing thee to beleeue an vntrueth, Ile make thee a Cockold.
Bell. Excellent wench.
Feth. Come, lets go sweete: the Nag I ride vpon beares double, weele to *London*.
May. Do not bite your thumbes sir.
Kate. Bite his thumbe!
Ile make him do a thing worse than this,
Come loue me where as I lay.
Feth. What *Kate*! 350
Kate. He shall father a child is none of his,
O the cleane contrary way.
Feth. O lusty *Kate*. *Exeunt.*
May. Me thought he sayd euen now, you were a Taylor.
Green. You shall heare more of that hereafter, Ile make *Ware* and him stinck ere he goes, if I bee a Taylor, the roagues naked weapon shall not fright me, Ile beate him and my wife both out ath Towne with a Taylors yard. *Exit.*
May. O Valiant sir *Tristram*; roome there.

Enter Philip, Leuer-poole *and* Chartly.

Phil. Newes father, most strang newes out of the Low-countries, 360 your good Lady and Mistris that set you to worke vpon a dozen of cheese-trenchers is new lighted at the next Inne, and the old venerable Gentleman her father with her.
Bell. Let the gates of our Inne be lockt vp, closer than a Noble-mans gates at dinner time.
Omn. Why sir, why?
Bell. If shee enter here, the house wil be infected: the plague is not halfe so dangerous, as a Shee-hornet: *Philip* this is your shuffling a the cardes, to turne vp her for the bottom carde at *Ware*. 370
Phil. No as Ime vertuous sir, aske the two Gentlemen.
Leuer. No in troth sir; shee told vs, that inquiring at *London* for you or your sonne, your man chalkt out her way to *Ware*.
Bell. I wud *Ware* might choake 'em both, Maister *Maybery*, my

363 Gentleman her father] Hazlitt; Gentlemans father Q

horse and I will take our leaues of you? Ile to Bedlam agen rather than stay her.

May. Shall a woman make thee flie thy country? stay, stand to her tho shee were greater than Pope *Ioane,* what are thy braines coniuring for, my poeticall bay-leafe-eater?

Bell. For a sprite a the buttry, that shall make vs all drinck with mirth if I can raize it: stay, the chicken is not fully hatcht, hit I beseech thee: So; come! wil you be secret Gentlemen and assisting.

Omn. With browne bills, if you thinke good.

Bell. What wil you say, if by some trick we put this little Hornet into *Fetherstones* bosome, and marry 'em togither.

Omn. Fuh, tis impossible.

Bell. Most possible, Ile to my trencher-woman, let me alone for dealing with her: *Fetherstone* Gentlemen shalbe your patient.

Omn. How! how?

Bell. Thus: I will close with this country Pedlar mistrisse *Dorothy* (that trauels vp and downe to exchange Pinnes for Cunny-skins) very louingly, she shall eate of nothing but sweet-meates in my company (good words) whose taste when she likes, as I know shee will, then will I play vpon her with this Artillery, that a very proper man, and a great heyre (naming *Fetherstone*) spyed her from a window, when shee lighted at her Inne, is extreamly falne in loue with her, vowes to make her his wife, if it stand to her good liking, euen in *Ware*; but being (as most of your young Gentlemen are) some-what bashfull, and ashamde to venture vpon a woman—

May. Citty and suburbes can iustifie it: so sir.

Bell. Hee sends mee (being an old friend) to vndermine for him: Ile so whet the wenches stomack, and make her so hungry, that she shall haue an appetite to him, feare it not; *Greenesheild* shall haue a hand in it too, and to bee reuengde of his partner, will I know strike with any weapon.

Leuer. But is *Fetherstone* of any meanes? els you vndoe him and her.

May. Hee has land betweene *Foolham* and *London*, he would haue made it ouer to me: to your charge Poet, giue you the assault vpon her, and send but *Fetherstone* to mee, Ile hang him by the gills.

Bell. Hees not yet horst sure, *Phillip*, go thy wayes, giue fire to him, and send him hither with a powder presently.
Phil. Hees blowne vp already. *Exit.*
Bell. Gentlemen youle stick to the deuise, and looke to your plot?
Omn. Most Poetically: away to your quarter.
Bell. I marche, I will cast my rider gallants: I hope you see who shall pay for our voyage. *Exit.*

Enter Phillip *and* Fetherstone.

May. That must hee that comes here: Maister *Fetherstone*, O Maister *Fetherstone*, you may now make your fortunes weigh ten stone of Fethers more then euer they did: leape but into the Saddle now, that stands empty for you, you are made for euer.
Leuer. An Asse Ile be sworne.
Feth. How for Gods sake? how?
May. I would you had, what I could wish you, I loue you, and because you shall be sure to know where my loue dwels, looke you sir, it hangs out at this signe: you shall pray for *Ware*, when *Ware* is dead and rotten: looke you sir, there is as pretty a little Pinnas, struck saile hereby, and come in lately; shee's my kinsewoman, my fathers youngest Sister, a warde, her portion three thousand; her hopes if her Grannam dye without issue, better.
Feth. Very good sir.
May. Her Gardian goes about to marry her to a Stone-cutter, and rather than sheele be subiect to such a fellow, sheele dye a martyr, will you haue all out? shee's runne away, is here at an Inne ith' towne, what parts so euer you haue plaid with mee, I see good parts in you, and if you now will catch times hayre that's put into your hand, you shall clap her vp presently.
Feth. Is she young? and a pretty wench?
Leuer. Few Cittizens wiues are like her.
Phil. Yong, why I warrant sixteene hath scarce gone ouer her.
Feth. Sfoot, where is she? if I like her personage, aswell as I like that which you say belongs to her personage, Ile stand thrumming of Caps no longer, but board your Pynnis whilst 'tis hotte.
May. Away then with these Gentlemen with a French gallop, and to her: *Phillip* here shall runne for a Priest, and dispatch you.

Feth. Will you gallants goe along: wee may be married in a Chamber for feare of hew and crie after her, and some of the company shall keepe the doore.

May. Assure your soule shee will be followed: away therefore. [*Exeunt* Featherstone, Philip, Leuerpoole, *and* Chartly.] Hees in the *Curtian* gulfe, and swallowed horse and man: hee will haue some body keepe the doore for him, sheele looke to that: I am yonger then I was two nights agoe, for this phisick.—how now?

Enter Captaine, Allom, Hans, *and others booted.*

Capt. God plesse you; is there not an arrant scuruy trab in your company, that is a Sentill-woman borne sir, and can tawg Welch, and Dutch, and any tongue in your head?

May. How so? Drabs in my company: doe I looke like a Drab-driuer?

Capt. The Trab will driue you (if she put you before her) into a pench hole.

Allom. Is not a Gentleman here one Maister *Bellamont* sir of your company.

May. Yes, yes, come you from *London*, heele be here presently.

Capt. Will he? *tawsone*, this oman, hunts at his taile like your little Goates in *Wales* follow their mother, wee haue warrants here from maister Sustice of this shire, to shew no pitty nor mercie to her, her name is *Doll.*

May. Why sir, what has she committed? I thinke such a creature is ith' towne.

Capt. What has she committed: ownds shee has committed more then man-slaughters, for shee has committed her selfe God plesse vs to euerlasting prison: lug you sir, shee is a punke, she shifts her louers (as Captaines and Welsh Gentlemen and such) as she does her Trenchers when she has well fed vpon't, and that there is left nothing but pare bones, shee calls for a cleane one, and scrapes away the first.

Enter Bellamont, *and* Hornet, *with* Doll *betweene them,* Greeneshield, Kate, Mayberies *wife,* Phillip, Leuerpoole, *and* Chartley.

May. Gods so Maister *Fetherstone,* what will you do? here's three come from *London,* to fetch away the Gentlewoman with a warrant.

Feth. All the warrants in *Europe* shall not fetch her now, she's mine sure enough: what haue you to say to her? shee's my wife.

Capt. Ow! Sbloud doe you come so farre to fishe and catch Frogs? your wife is a Tilt-boate, any man or oman may goe in her for money; shee's a Cunny-catcher: where is my mooueable goods cald a Coach, and my two wild peasts, pogs on you wud they had trawne you to the gallowes.

Allom. I must borrow fiftie pound of you Mistris Bride.

Hans. Yaw vro, and you make me de gheck, de groet foole, you heb mine gelt to: war is it?

Doll. Out you base scums, come you to disgrace mee in my wedding shooes?

Feth. Is this your three thousand pound ward, yee tolde mee sir she was your Kinswoman.

May. Right, one of mine Awnts.

Bell. Who payes for the Northren voyage now lads?

Green. Why do you not ride before my Wife to *London* now? the Woodcocks ith' Sprindge.

Kate. O forgiue me deere husband! I will neuer loue a man that is worse than hangd, as he is.

May. Now a man may haue a course in your Parke?

Feth. Hee may sir.

Doll. Neuer I protest, I will bee as true to thee, as *Ware* and *Wades-mill* are one to another.

Feth. Well, it's but my fate: Gentlemen, this is my opinion, it's better to shoote in a Bow that has beene shot in before, and will neuer start, than to draw a faire new one, that for euery Arrow will bee warping: Come wench wee are ioynd, and all the Dogs in *France* shall not part vs: I haue some lands, those Ile turne into money, to pay you, and you, and any: Ile pay all that I can for thee, 510 for Ime sure thou hast paid me.

Omn. God giue you ioy.

May. Come lets be merry, lye you with your owne Wife, to be sure shee shall not walke in her sleepe: a noyse of Musitians Chamberlaine.

This night lets banquet freely: come, weele dare,
Our wiues to combate ith' greate bed in Ware.

Exeunt.

FINIS.

TEXTUAL NOTES

I.i

87 in this wiues commendation] The sense here is obscure, but attempts to emend have not materially clarified the intention. Dyce contented himself with an exclamation mark after Q *commendation*; but Hazlitt emended *in* to *is*. The latter, at least, is scarcely an improvement. I take it that *O.E.D.* 'renown, credit, repute' is meant here; though this sense is customarily attached to the plural, it is not unknown in the singular. Whether the remark is a true exclamation or else a rhetorical suspension, it would appear to be ironic, the true meaning being the reverse: 'Though you have given us in profusion, or immoderately (even immodestly in the present-day sense), the details of this loose woman's adultery, she is so deserving of public exposure that you are behaving now with excessive moderation (or false modesty) in concealing her name to preserve her reputation.' However, *modesty* can mean not only 'moderation' but also 'a sense of shame' (*Hamlet*, II.ii.290), which would also be appropriate here, especially if there is a possible latent meaning in *commendation* of 'having or bearing in trust'. Another play on words is possible. Since Bellamont is fond of satirical thrusts at these young men, he may be saying, in effect: 'You have been so far from moderate in your *commendation*, or approving description, of this wife's amorousness, that it is astonishing to find you so shamefast, or moderate, in her *commendation*, or concern for her reputation, as to stick at revealing her name. However, get on with the account.' It is most unlikely that *wiues* is a verb. Nor is it likely that we have a misprint here and should read *Your* (i.e. *you're*) modest in.... Bellamont's speech is half ironical suspension and half exclamation.

131 wit] Dyce silently emends Q *wit* to *with*, and, changing the colon after *iourneys* to a comma, makes the phrase the first of a series of three: 'This, with taking of long journeys, kindred that' *etc*. At first sight there is something to be said for the series interpretation: (1) the husband being away on long journeys gives his wife undue temptation to console herself; (2) gallants pretend distant relationship as an excuse for familiarity (as by the gulling word 'cousin' [1 *Honest Whore*, I.ii.119–122] with its concomitant play on 'aunt'), and worm their way by this means into a wife's affections; and (3) sailing to Westminster. This last presents some difficulty. Ordinarily, Westminster connotes the law courts, and if this is a true series of equal and independent elements, we might read (3) a husband so occupied with his business and legal affairs that he is excessively away from home in term time may find he has provided opportunity for being

cuckolded. In the series of three as Dyce emends, *This* must refer back to Greenshield's explanation for wives' unfaithfulness, with Mayberry thereupon producing three additional causes. Such a reference, however, in context, may seem rather forced. Moreover, it may necessitate the assumption of double error if the colon after *iourneys* is taken as a strong stop. It is true that Dekker was in the habit of punctuating a series with colons where we should use commas; nevertheless, if the colon after *iourneys* is not an error but an example of this habit, double error still obtains since then the comma after *hatch* should be a colon. Single error can be assumed only by arguing that Q *wit* is not a simple mechanical error of omission but instead a true misreading, and that the compositor punctuated what follows on the basis of his original misunderstanding. This is not an attractive line of argument, for if *wit* is wrong it is almost certainly an inadvertent error. The problem would be somewhat simplified if we were able to proceed on the hypothesis that Q punctuation accurately reflects the syntax intended. According to Q, the general statement is made that long journeys provide opportunity for wives' infidelities, followed by two specific illustrations. *This* need not refer back to Greenshield's reasons but instead look forward to the proposition about to be advanced. We should need to understand the familiar idiom, *This 'tis*. In the first of the two illustrations, *hatch* may mean the lower part of a double door: the 'kindred', therefore, would in a sense force themselves into the house only partly barred against their entrance. Less commonly, it could mean, roughly, a part of the deck of a ship, and the image would then be that of surreptitious boarders from outside. By a play, both meanings could be intended, of course, and there be—if the allusion is in fact nautical—some glance at the cant phrase of 'sailing in another's boat', like 'riding in another's boots', for substituting for the husband in the marital bed. Although the *hatch* as low door is the more common, yet the addition of *sailing to Westminster* may cause one to suspect that a common nautical image binds the two elements together. According to the Q construction, it is much less likely that it is the husband who is thus sailing, but instead the wife and presumably her 'kindred'. If so, the allusion is not to the law courts but rather to the royal court at Westminster; and I should interpret it as referring to the 'kindred' taking the wife to see fashionable life in the form of courtly revels in the banqueting house in Westminster (Whitehall), and thus completing her downfall. All this is what happens when husbands are away on long journeys. If this is the sentence structure and at least approximately the sense, it may be seen that there is no urgent necessity to emend *wit* to *with* (especially when we recall that Dyce's emendation rested on quite different premises). By retaining Q *wit*, the colon after *iourneys* indicates, as frequently, a semi-exclamation, and the general ironic sense is: This is the wisdom (*i.e.* in fact, one's lack of judgement) in taking these long journeys; these journeys permit *etc*. If so, Mayberry's whole speech is very likely an aside. Such an assignment would help to explain Bellamont's hurried intervention, 'Fie what an idle quarrel is this, was this her ring?' as an expedient change of subject to prevent Mayberry from revealing himself in his agitation, the more especially since Bellamont's words are not very appropriate if Mayberry (according to the *This with* sense) is agreeing with Greenshield, and elaborating on Greenshield's reasons for marital infidelity, as part of a dialogue. For *Westminster* as the court, see II. i. 22–24.

I.ii

16 pasty-footed] Although the exact sense of Doll's abuse is not clear, one would hesitate to make the natural orthographic but colourless emendation to *hasty-footed*. We need not assume an error here.

II.i

127 curse] Q *cause* is manifestly corrupt, and though 'course', 'chase', and 'chouse' have been suggested, Dyce's emendation to *curse* seems best to solve the crux. To my mind, the case rests on *leaden-heeld rascalls*, which I see no reason to apply to Allom specifically or to the gulls in general. Moreover, *may* is an odd word if the reading is 'course' or something similar, and there would be double error in the semicolon after *rascalls*, a lighter point than the colon in series. The basic meaning, also, would not jibe, since Doll would be saying, 'It is possible for me to gull such stupid people'; but Doll can gull clever Bellamont and has no such low opinion of her abilities. On the other hand, if Leverpool and Chartley are the rascals (and they provide the necessary plural), it is they who—because they are leaden-heeled—are being ordered out of her sight. (She is scarcely telling Allom to go away when she immediately after begs a knife from him.) It seems proper, therefore, to associate *out of my sight* with her cursing the rascals her servants. She curses them as a part of her pretence because they have not been able, presumably, to bring her good news, or have been slow in trying to find her father or his missing servant. Hence we have the usual series separated by colons (the semicolon likely an internal stop in a single element). Allom enters after *ile change my tune,* and the changed tune begins with *I may curse such leaden-heeld rascalls,* which he is supposed to hear. The words *I may* mean 'I have cause to' or 'I may be permitted to'; and since Allom might be shocked at Doll's violent treatment of the servants in her acute distress, the words serve as an excuse to him for her otherwise unseemly action. And, of course, she never does curse them, but only orders them away in wrath for their supposed dilatory action, a command they have no intention of obeying.

263 and she might get the bird] The proverb is: I beat the bush and another takes the bird. There is no need here to emend *she* to *I* in conformity. Philip is, in fact, playing with the proverb by saying, 'I could get one of

my aunts (*i.e.* mistresses or whores) to beat the bush, and in such a case I am afraid she rather than I would get the bird (secure the plate). We may notice that this lends point to Doll's promise in line 265 to restore.

II.ii

166 so]   Q *fo* appears to be a simple misprint for *so* (fo), rather than the expletive 'foh'. Mistress Mayberry nowhere else indulges in such a strong expression, and the lack of following punctuation does not greatly encourage the reading. *Intollerable* is doubtless 'intolerably' (*i.e.* excessively, or greatly), and the preceding semicolon only a slightly heavy comma for emphasis.

175 She may doe it from crabednes...]   There is obvious difficulty here in the continuity, not to be set right by any simple transposition in line 173 of *crabbednes* and *couitousnes*. Moreover, disruption seems to be indicated even more strongly by Q's repetitious speech-prefix *Bell.* placed before this line 175. It is possible that the crux results from unresolved drafting in the manuscript, and it could be that one of the troubles is the repetition of *crabbednes*. Traditionally, covetousness is assigned as the especial disease of old men, and therefore it is odd to find crabbedness in the climactic position. It may be that Bellamont's original series ended with *crabbednes* and that Dekker thereupon substituted *couetousnes* without clearly deleting the other word. However, this hypothesis does not explain the superfluous speech-prefix beginning a fresh line as if by a new speaker. Hence it is probable that a line or so by Mistress Mayberry querying Bellamont's statement has been lost, and that his continuation *She may doe it* was originally in answer to this question. Even so, there is still the suspicion that the *from crabbednes* of line 173 is a fossil, and I am inclined to believe that it originally ended the series and then was imperfectly deleted when Dekker decided to continue with a separate discourse on crabbedness and its cure in response to the wife's lost question.

III.i

2 printing house, thy pounders]   Once one accepts that Q *painting* is a misreading for *printing*, the meaning of *pounders*, which puzzled Dyce and Hazlitt, presents no difficulty. The word is in apposition to *compositors* and alludes to the assistants at the press who pounded the type with the inkballs to work the thick ink thoroughly onto the metal. Possibly there could be a play on 'pound-keepers', the officials who rounded up stray cattle (Doll's gulls) and impounded them, or on Leverpool and Chartley as the pestles for Doll's mortar. The real difficulty comes in the Q reading *thy pounders a my old poeticall dad*. Since the plan had been to send either Leverpool or Chartley as Doll's gentleman usher to deliver her message to

Bellamont, the subject of *wilbe here presently* cannot be *pounders* but, instead, *dad*. It seems most probable that we have here a compositor's sophistication based on his misreading, *painting*. Not recognizing the printing reference (the dolt), he took *pounders* to be messengers, who pounded on Bellamont's door, and he thus not only neglected the necessary comma after *pounders* but also supplied the rationalizing *a*, meaning 'to' or 'of'.

108 thy vnlucky starre!] There is some temptation to emend *thy* to *my*, as a memorial contamination in Q from *thy* and *thee* in the previous line. However, Q makes sufficient sense if we take it that Bellamont is addressing Doll. We know that she was beautiful and (more doubtfully) a gentlewoman. Bellamont has paid unwilling tribute to her in line 98. Thus it is possible that in *thy vnlucky starre* he is exclaiming on the astrological influences which turned a clever and beautiful woman to a life of debauchery and would lead her to the insolence of her previous remark. Less likely, it might be addressed to Philip, as an allusion to the influences which have put him under Doll's domination. One would scarcely like to argue that Bellamont takes seriously Doll's remark that she might favour him, despite what is to come.

III.ii

5 thy Maister] Q omits commas about this phrase, but they are very necessary, for *thy Maister* is not in apposition to *Greenshield* but instead refers to Featherstone, and thus forms the second element in a series of three. For the identification of Squirrel as Mayberry's apprentice and of Leap-Frog as Featherstone's boy, see IV.i.218–221. Thus there is no clash in line 5 with *thy Maister* of line 23.

108 pray pardon me, wast you Maister *Fetherstone*] Dyce, followed by Hazlitt, takes these words as direct speech, and those before and after as asides. This is surely the intention. Despite the repetition of the polite indefinite *the Gentleman* in line 110, it would seem that Kate pretends at line 108 to recognize Featherstone for the first time. Thus *hem, I should be well then* continues the opening aside, broken only by the words of recognition.

IV.i

54 Biron] Hazlitt suggests, in view of the Captain's *Pepper-noone* in line 61, that we should here read *Epernon*, and he so emends. This conjecture seems very plausible. However, *Biron* cannot be a misprint, as Hazlitt calls it, but—if *Epernon* is right—an author's slip, not of the pen but rather of failure to revise in accord with second thoughts. The difficulty is, we cannot be sure of the direction of the revision, and whether *Biron* has substituted for *Epernon* (leaving *Pepper-noone* as the fossil), or the other way round.

140 for carrying! a body not worth begging] Q *for carrying a body! not worth begging*... is manifestly corrupt in the placement of the exclamation mark. If one chose, one might transpose it after *times*, and read: 'A leg and a calf! I have had better from a butcher forty times! So far as they are of any use, they are good only for carrying a body which even a Barber-surgeon would not be interested in receiving as a gift.' However, there is some strain on the syntax (and the imagination) in such a reading. It seems much more plausible to place the necessary transposition as near as possible to the error, as in the present text, whereupon a perfectly smooth reading results: 'A leg and a calf! I have had better forty times free from a Butcher merely if I would carry the unsaleable meat away from his shop! A shrivelled body not worth begging for dissection by a Barber-surgeon!'

262 baibery] Dyce and Hazlitt emend to *bribery*; but bayberry is a common bush, and there is a glance at the name of Mayberry.

IV.iii

1 helpe] One may toss a coin whether Q *to* before *helpe* is intrusive, or else some such word as *come* has, instead, been omitted inadvertently.

118 better I set it] Idiomatically, *better* equals 'better than', although it is possible, of course, that *than* has been accidentally left out. Dyce chose to place a query after *better*, thus altering the meaning considerably.

V.i

80 as I am, a Gentleman] Dyce and Hazlitt take this phrase to be merely the usual asseveration, 'as I am a gentleman'. But Q's punctuation of the whole speech is slightly against this view, and so is the context. Lines 104–105 seem to make it obvious that what is required is merely the insertion of a comma after *am*. What is horrible is not the pandering itself, but procuration by one dressed like Greenshield as a gentleman.

152 Tom (   )] The parentheses may substitute for an indecent word but more likely represent an indecent movement of the legs imitating the bow-legged walk of a man afflicted with venereal disease. See *Patient Grissil*, III.ii.49 and note.

157–158 to take the horne] For this, the Q reading, *take thee home* is queried. Although *the* is a rare spelling of the pronoun *thee*, in the circumstances we must suppose that it is intended here as the article and that the compositor believed he was following his manuscript in setting *horne*. Although he had sophisticated the text in line 156 by substituting, or misreading, *you* (y^u) for *your* (y^r), corruption is not demonstrable in *take the horne*. There are various possible meanings for *take*, including 'acquiesce, put up with' (*Hamlet*, II.ii.604), closely associated with 'to take on or upon oneself', although this latter ordinarily requires a following *on*. It seems best to follow Q, and to interpret the sense as: 'When the old Gentleman (Mayberry) has cuckolded your husband and then bankrupted him and you, it will be only just if he bears your expenses as his mistress and *takes the horne*, that is, puts himself into the position of being cuckolded by someone else, as was your husband, since it is obvious you are a light woman.' It would be only just for Mayberry to *take over* or *take on* the horn (cuckoldom) from the husband, since he has also taken his goods. It may not be quite over-scrupulous to object that a citizen, especially Mayberry, would scarcely be able to take his mistress *home*, where his wife lived, nor does the word *maintaine* encourage this emendation: see V.i.308.

161 bearing] For Q *bearth* has been queried *breath* and *breadth*, neither of which is satisfactory. It is probable that Q is corrupt. *O.E.D.* offers no satisfactory sense from *berth*, and for *birth* only a rare medieval Scottish use meaning weight and, doubtfully, bulk. Unless the reading were *girth*, it would seem that *bearing* is a plausible guess which may be supported orthographically.

309 those broken patience] If this is corrupt, as seems possible, the correction escapes me. Were *patience* what it seems, the best Elizabethan sense would be, 'Was Mayberry aware that his "indulgence, leave, permission" had been abused' etc. With rather more strain, perhaps, we might take it that it was Greenshield's *patience* at being held at bay by the wife which had broken, resulting in his stealing of the ring. But neither is really satisfactory, and the plural *those* seems to be an added complication. My own feeling is that there is a good chance *those* is correct and that the *ce* ending stands for singular *t* or plural *ts*, as in 'instance' for 'instant' in *The Magnificent Entertainment*, line 561. If so, *patience* could be 'patent(s)', and the allusion would continue the reference to the Spaniards. 'As the Spaniards were given patent(s) only to trade in the Indies but broke these by turning to discovery and conquest under the guise of trade, so you gallants come to merchants' houses pretending business but really intent only on improving your income by seducing their wives and securing money from the infatuated women. You (Greenshield) had patent(s) to come to Mayberry's house on business; but was he aware when you lied to him at Ware that you had broken those patents, like the Spaniards, and had attempted the conquest of his wife?' That in the play Greenshield is not described as frequenting Mayberry's house in his absence on the plea of business may be of small account. Dekker may simply have forgotten, or else he may have imagined that this was the pretence employed to excuse his original visits to the house before he discovered his amorous intentions and 'broke his patents'.

PRESS-VARIANTS IN Q (1607)

[Copies collated: BM[1] (British Museum 644.b.25), BM[2] (C.12.f.3[5]), BM[3] (Ashley 613); Bodl[1] (Bodleian Mal. 219[6]), Bodl[2] (Mal. 235[6]); Dyce (Victoria and Albert Museum); Eton (Eton College); King's (King's College Cambridge); Worc (Worcester College Oxford); CSmH (Huntington); CtY (Yale); DFo (Folger); DLC (Congress); MB (Boston Public, 2 copies of sig. E); MH (Harvard); NN (New York Public); Pforz (Pforzheimer); TxU (University of Texas).]

SHEET E (*inner forme*)

Corrected: BM[1-2], Dyce, Eton, CSmH, CtY, DLC, MB, MH, NN, Pforz.
Uncorrected: BM[3], Bodl[1-2], King's, DFo, MB, TxU.

Sig. E1[v].
   III.ii.66 warrant]   watrant
Sig. E2.
   III.ii.132 fecret?] fecret.
   IV.i.S.D. *SCENA*] *SÆNA*
Sig. E4.
   IV.i.120 muggers] nuggers

EMENDATIONS OF ACCIDENTALS

I.i

1 night?] ~ ,
2 certaine:] ~ ₐ
4 more,] ~ ₐ
4 Londoner] *Londoner*
10 chast?] ~ ,
19 *Dunstable*] dunstable
24 *London,*] ~ ₐ
25 now Sir] nowSir
25 *Yorke,*] ~ ₐ
32 of —] ~ :
38 Sir:] ~ ₐ
40 *Sturbridge*] sturbridge

59 Flemmings] *Flemmings*
65 pay?] Q *text*; ~ : Q *cw*

44 forhead;] ~ ,
44 market] markt
44 freshmen,] ~ ;
92 infaith?] ~ :
94 her —] ~ .
105 say?] ~ ;
110 loosing?] ~ ;
158 S.D. Q *places after line* 156
174 protest, . . . vnderstanding ₐ]
 ~ ₐ . . . ~ ,
183 countrie, blushing ₐ] ~ ₐ ~ ,

I.ii

74 winde,] ~ .
99 *Chartly*] *Charely*

I.iii

12–13 Englishman . . . Welshman
 . . . Dutchman . . . Frenchman]
 italic
39 without] with-|out
51 for,] ~ ₐ
82 flesh-hookes] flesh-|hookes
86 *Bellamont*] *Bellomont*

132 teares,] ~ ₐ
135 serpents, . . . them ₐ] ~ ₐ . . . ~ ,
142–143 Oh . . . heart.] *one line in* Q
146 Fencers] Feneers
150, 152 *Phil.*] *Pil.*
151 not ₐ . . . asham'd,] ~ , . . . ~ ₐ

II.i

21 Westminster] *Westminster*
22 hobbi-|horses] hobbi-horses
30 see] sce
31 Schoole-maister] Schoole-|
 maister
36 *Doll* —] ~ .
49 Cheape-side] *Cheape-side*
56 Welsh Captaine] *Welsh* Gaptaine
57 Dutch] *Dutch*
68 dance] dauce
81 remember] remenber
84 vater:] ~ ₐ

94 *Ausburgh:*] ~ ₐ
98 groetest] grotest
98 *Ausbourgh*] *Ausbrough*
102 elder-|man] elderman
127 *Doll.* Nay] *Dol.e*Nay
146 too] toe
165 warrant ₐ sir,] ~ , ~ ₐ
196 beecause] bee-|cause
214 *Shrop-sheere*] *Shrop-|sheere*
221 butter-milke] butter-|milke
274 lodging?] ~ .

487

II.ii

18 mis-|caried] mis-|caried
32 wiues:] ~ ,
39 priuity,] ~ ˄
57 Rascals] Rascols
66 Romans] *Romans*
69 troth˄ Sir,] ~ , ~ ˄
78 *London*] london
80 husbands] hubsbands
84 inuited] invited
89 *Greenshield*] *Greeshield*
89 presently?] ~ .
94 him:] ~ ,
96 and] and and

111 complement,] ~ ˄
112 *Bellamont*,] ~ ˄
130 *Kate*.] *Rat*.
130 then; no,] ~ , ~ ˄
141 *London*,] ~ ˄
144 *Kate*.] *Ra*.
147, 153 *Kate*.] *Rat*.
161 naughty] noughty
166 suffer] luffer
167 hell ont,] hellont˄
173 couitousnes,] couituousnes˄
179 mischiefe,] ~ ˄

III.i

S.D. Sc*æ*na] S*æ*na
33 *Bell*.] *Pel*.
38 S.D. *Tayler*] *Taylcr*
100 sir: nay,] ~ , ~ :
109 worshippe:] ~ ˄
112 Country,] ~ ˄
119 lodging] odging (*most copies; see line 122*)
122 ile] ille (*all copies except* BM3 *the*

l *of* lodging *dropped down between* l *and* l *of* ile)
128 a] *dropped down in* BM3 *to form* amy *with* my *of line* 128
128 Spaniard] *Spaniard*
129 Malago?] ~ ,
130 Plaiers,] ~ ˄
133 returne] re-|returne
133 wood-|cock] wood-cock

III.ii

6 More-|fields] More-fields
31 man take] mant ake
61 her:] Q *text*; ~ , Q *cw*
67 doost˄ now,] ~ , ~ ˄
71–2 wambled, ...sound:] ~ : ... ~ ,

89 Back-doore] Back-|doore
118 morning, ...wife˄]
 ~ ˄ ... ~ ,
126 Sfoote] sfoote

IV.i

S.D. Sc*æ*na] S*æ*na Q(u); Scena Q(c)
2 plaier?] ~ :
18 Is] is
36 Iudgement:] ~ ˄
40 Troyane,] *Troyane*˄
42 *Mon*-|*mouth*] *Mon-mouth*
45, 56, 58 French] *French*

46 Frenchmen] *Frenchmen*
49 stage —] ~ .
59 English] *English*
69 Imagine] I magine
70 seuenth] 7.
104 shee —] ~ ?
105 honest?] ~ .
110 father˄ ... her,] ~ , ... ~ ˄

EMENDATIONS OF ACCIDENTALS [IV. i, V. i]

112 party$_\wedge$] ~ ,
151 before.] ~ $_\wedge$
159 *Imen*] *I men*
171 (like]$_\wedge$ ~

173 lie,] ~ $_\wedge$
196 maiden-heads] maiden-|heads
246 -*chace?*] ~ $_\wedge$

IV.ii

12 putter-box] putter-|box
15 agen] Q *text*; againe Q *cw*
34 *mon du! du guin*] *mon du! u dguin*

35 peace of] peaceof
36 oman] onam
36 S.D. *Exeunt.*] *Eeunt.*

IV.iii

5 consort:] ~ $_\wedge$
5 ha] ho
11 among] a mong
41 house?] ~ ,
46 Italian] *Italian*
53 *Ful-moone?*] ~ $_\wedge$
57 none?] ~ $_\wedge$
74 Lords,] ~ $_\wedge$

75 god-|fathers] god-fathers
82 But] but
123 March,] ~ $_\wedge$
124 *poco.*] ~ $_\wedge$
139 without] withour
173 Iesu!] ~ :
185 Bedlam] B*edlam*

V.i

9 Mary] mary
19 farther. And] farther, and
47 You] Q *cw*; Vou Q *text*
54 stay, ...mery:] ~ : ... ~ ,
66 When] when
67 either] eirher
68 cornes,] ~ $_\wedge$ (*doubtful in* Q)
85 it:] ~ $_\wedge$
87 that] thar
92 excellent,] ~ $_\wedge$
94 now,] ~ $_\wedge$
115 *Milke-|streete*] *Milke-|streete*
132 hand,] ~ $_\wedge$
138 gallant,] ~ $_\wedge$
154 haue?] ~ ,
174 not-with-standing] not-with-|standing
180 Fortune] Forrune
184 his] is
191 No?] ~ .
203 haue?] ~ ,
219 haunted, —] ~ , $_\wedge$

220 them, —] ~ , $_\wedge$
221 *Fetherstone,*] ~ $_\wedge$
234 sollid] sodllid
238 that] thar
239 first] firsi
241–3 *No, no...*] roman *in* Q
254 stoopt$_\wedge$ ... phesant,] ~ , ... ~ $_\wedge$
257 not?] ~ ;
260 Chamber] Chamher
262 good,] ~ $_\wedge$
263 *Greeneshield,*] ~ $_\wedge$
276 this,] ~ $_\wedge$
290 This] this
290 remaines:] ~ $_\wedge$
298 Captaine:] ~ $_\wedge$
304 Sentence; ...sir,] ~ , ... ~ ;
305 Spaniard] *Spaniard*
308 maintenance. Why] ~ $_\wedge$ why
308 a ware] *i.e.,* aware
310 Cockcold,] ~ $_\wedge$
311 gentleman,] ~ $_\wedge$

321 forhead,] ~ :
329 Gentlewomen] Gentlewemen
329 peeriwig] peeriwip
348–9 *Ile make*...] roman in Q
351–2 *He shall*....] roman in Q
353 *Kate*] Rate
354 sayd_∧...now,] ~ , ... ~ _∧
359 S.D. Philip,] ~ _∧
364 Noble-|mans] Noble-mans

392 Cunny-skins] Cunny-|skins
400 woman —] ~ .
445 French] *French*
454 S.D. Allom,] ~ .
456 Welch] *Welch*
457 Dutch] *Dutch*
458 Drab-|driuer] Drab-driuer
474 Welsh] *Welsh*
477 S.D. *them*,] ~ _∧

THE
WHORE OF
BABYLON.

As it was acted by the Princes
Seruants.

Vexat Censura Columbas.

Written by THOMAS DEKKER.

LONDON
Printed for Nathaniel Butter.
1607.

TEXTUAL INTRODUCTION

THE WHORE OF BABYLON (Greg, *Bibliography*, no. 241) was entered on 20 April 1607 in the Stationers' Register to Nathanael Butter and John Trundell: 'Entred for their copie vnder the handes of Sr Geo. Buck. k^t. and m^r White Warden. A booke called the Whore of Babilon.' The first and only quarto appeared in the same year, printed for Butter, its title-page in red and black.

There can be little doubt that the printer's copy was Dekker's own manuscript. The speculation has been advanced that the play is a revision of *Truth's Supplication to Candlelight*, for which Henslowe, for the Admiral's men, was paying Dekker in January of 1600, and buying a robe for Time in April, although Sir E. K. Chambers (*Elizabethan Stage*, III, 296) cautiously observes, 'I do not feel sure that it would have been allowed to be staged in Elizabeth's lifetime.'

In *Lectori* Dekker alludes to a performance of the play at which he was not present and one at which, seemingly, he feared it was 'made a cripple'. Whether he is referring only to bad acting and possibly to memorial failure on the part of the actors, or, in addition, to their cutting of the text, is not certain, perhaps. At any rate, it would seem that the text represented by the quarto is a revision and expansion of whatever version it was that he originally submitted for the performance(s) referred to in *Lectori*.[1] This is quite clear from the imperfectly resolved writing of III.i. Here it seems evident from the direction at line 130 that Paridel in an earlier

---

[1] The *Lectori* reference is cast in such vague terms that one cannot tell whether Dekker is writing of a public or private performance. The general impression given, however, is that the initial presentation of the play is on his mind, at least the initial presentation in a form approximating the text of the quarto. In II.i.110–111 he seems to be envisaging performance in a public theatre: 'some of them in places as big as this, and before a thousand people, rip vp the bowels of vice...'. But even this interpretation could be disputed as applying instead to performance in a place which differed from the public theatre in which the plays satirized were acted. Moreover, whatever the intention, the place of the performance mentioned in *Lectori* could readily have differed from that which the author expected when he wrote the play; and it must also be kept in mind that the lines in question may be part of a revision subsequent to the performance and made for the reading public. Little weight can be put on them as evidence.

version was present in Babylon with Campeius and Ropus (the latter identified as *Lupus*, subsequently changed); and in the speech-prefixes at lines 133 and 140 he is included in the responses, though only two are provided for in the prefix at line 180. In III.ii, however, the explicit statement is made in line 25 that Paridel has not gone to Babylon. Part, or all, of this latter scene, therefore, must be an addition.[1] Doubtless various other sections of the play represent similar revision (as in the reference to King James in III.i.235–244, provided there is anything to the hypothesis that the present version is based on the 1600 *Truth's Supplication*), and it is possible that the quarto in form and content may differ materially from that acted in the performance(s) mentioned in *Lectori*.

The *Lectori* reference appears to be to a comparatively recent acting, not to a performance seven years before. Hence, if the identification with *Truth's Supplication* is correct (and this is undemonstrable) it would seem that whatever performance Dekker had in mind must have differed, in turn, from the text of the 1600 Admiral's play, for it is scarcely conceivable that anything resembling the political and personal references in the printed play would have been permitted under Elizabeth. However, the identification with the Admiral's play rests only on the similar characters Time and Truth, and is therefore uncertain, for we cannot be sure that Dekker did not take over these allegorical persons from an earlier play and incorporate them in different material in *The Whore of Babylon*. The references post-dating the Admiral's production (such as that to Essex, to James, and perhaps to *The Isle of Dogs*) cannot be cited in favour of a revision of *Truth's Supplication*: these could have been inserted, instead, as part of Dekker's revision for publication of whatever form of the *Babylon* play it was that is referred to in *Lectori*.

[1] On the other hand, it would be possible to argue that Paridel was *added* to the Babylon scene, and the next episode cut, as part of a revision for theatrical performance; and hence that Dekker in giving the full text has provided the cut scene (III.ii) but failed to straighten out the precedent action. This is a plausible point of view and would be aided by regarding the omission of Paridel from the speech-prefix at III.i.180 as an oversight in revision. Yet the difficulty with the names Lupus-Ropus remains. Moreover, if the printer's copy was Dekker's own manuscript (as seems certain), the theory cannot be maintained, for this manuscript—not having a theatrical origin—would not contain theatrical cuts. Foul-papers cut and marked by the book-keeper cannot be postulated here. Such are the disappointments of textual criticism.

With the exception of the 1873 Pearson reprint, the play has not previously been edited. The present text is based on a collation of the following seventeen copies, substantially all those which have been recorded: British Museum copy 1 (C.34.c.29), copy 2 (C.12.f.4[1]), copy 3 (Ashley 613); Bodleian Library copy 1 (Mal. 235[7]), copy 2 (Mal. 162[1]); Dyce Collection in the Victoria and Albert Museum; Eton College; Worcester College Oxford copy 1 (wants L 1), copy 2 (wants A 1–3, L 1); Library of Congress; Folger Shakespeare Library; Harvard University; Henry E. Huntington Library; Newberry Library (wants L 1); New York Public Library; University of Texas; and Yale University. In the three press-variant formes revealed by this collation the alterations appear to be non-authorial.

There is a break between sheets G and H of the quarto. No catchword appears on G 4 ᵛ, and starting with sig. H 1 (IV.ii.72) the headlines change in their typesetting and the printer's measure is slightly wider. Since the entrance of a new compositor comes so late, it is likely that the extra workman was brought in to speed completion of the printing and that copy was cast-off for his stint when the original compositor was still far from the end of his section. It is probable, therefore, that sheets E–G and H–K (and half-sheet L) were simultaneously set and printed on two presses. Otherwise we must posit a sufficient delay in the printing following sheet G to allow for distribution of the skeleton-formes. The missing catchword on G 4 ᵛ, however, rather points to simultaneous printing.

The Worcester College copy 2 has been in considerable part cut and marked up seemingly for production. The hand is unknown and is more likely to be late than early seventeenth century. One may speculate that possibly there was some proposal to take advantage of the uproar accompanying the Popish Plot. Various minor textual revisions are made, chiefly in reference. For example, at I.i.44 *bright Empresse* is deleted and *holy mother* written in as part of the general scheme to change the Empress to the Church or the Pope, as in I.ii.9 the substitution of *priest* for *woman* and of *prelate* for *Queene*. In I.i.46 *Fairie* is deleted and *English* substituted, as elsewhere. In line 63 *Curtizan* becomes *heritic*, in line 78 *Babylon* is changed to *rome*, and in line 81 *Titania* to *Elizabeth*. No attempt is made, however, to straighten out the various tangles in the text or directions.

DRAMMATIS PERSONÆ.

TITANIA the Fairie Queene: vnder whom is figured our late Queene Elizabeth

FIDELI
FLORIMELL
PARTHENOPHIL } Councellors to Titania
ELFIRON

CASTINA
AURA
PHILÆMA } Ladies attendant
AGATHE

CAMPEIUS, a Scholler

PARIDEL, a Doctor

TIME

TRUTH

PLAINE-DEALING

TH'EMPRESSE OF BABYLON: vnder whom is figured *Rome*.

KINGS 3. [1. King, *France*; 2. King, *Holy Roman Empire*; 3. King, *Satyrane* of *Spain*.]

CARDINALS 4. [*Como*, 1. *Cardinal*]

RAGAZZONI } Agents for th'Empresse
CAMPEGGIO

ROPUS a Doctor of Physicke

An ALBANOIS

PALMIO a Iesuite

[GENTLEMAN, sworn to kill *Titania*

GENTLEMAN, cousin to *Paridel*

SAILOR, attendant on 3. King

CONJURER

VOLUNTEER]

MILITES

MINISTRI

15 *Plaine-dealing.*] Q *places after a brace linking* Time *and* Truth *and not as a separate character*

Lectori.

The Generall scope of this Drammaticall Poem, is to set forth (in Tropicall and shadowed collours) the Greatnes, Magnanimity, Constancy, Clemency, and other the incomparable Heroical vertues of our late Queene. And (on the contrary part) the inueterate malice, Treasons, Machinations, Vnderminings, and continual blody stratagems, of that Purple whore of Roome, *to the taking away of our Princes liues, and vtter extirpation of their Kingdomes. Wherein if according to the dignity of the Subiect, I haue not giuen it Lustre, and (to vse the Painters rhethorick) doe so faile in my Depthes and Heightnings, that it is not to the life, let this excuse me; that the Pyramides vpon whose top the glorious Raigne of our deceased Soueraigne was mounted, stands yet so high, and so sharply pointed into the clouds, that the Art of no pen is able to reach it. The streame of her Vertues is so immensurable, that the farther they are waded into, the farther is it to the bottom.*

In sayling vpon which two contrary Seas, you may obserue, on how direct a line I haue steered my course: for of such a scantling are my words set downe, that neither the one party speakes too much, nor the other (in opposition) too little in their owne defence.

And whereas I may, (by some more curious in censure, then sound in iudgement) be Critically taxed, that I falsifie the account of time, and set not down Occurrents, according to their true succession, let such (that are so nice of stomach) know, that I write as a Poet, not as an Historian, and that these two doe not liue vnder one law. How true Fortunes dyall hath gone whose Players (like so many clocks, haue struck my lines, and told the world how I haue spent my houres) I am not certaine, because mine eare stood not within reach of their Larums. But of this my knowledge cannot faile, that in such Consorts, many of the Instruments are for the most part out of tune, And no maruaile; for let the Poet set the note of his Nombers, euen to Apolloes *owne Lyre, the Player will haue his owne Crochets, and sing false notes, in dispite of all the rules of Musick. It fares with these two, as it does with good stuffe and a badde Tayler: It is not mard in the wearing, but in the cutting out. The labours therfore of Writers are as vnhappie as the children of a bewtifull woman, being spoyld by ill nurses, within a month after they come into the world. What a number of throwes doe we endure eare we be deliuered? and yet euen then (tho that heauenly issue of our braine be neuer so faire and so well lymd,) is it made lame by the bad handling of them to whome it is put to learne to goe: if this of mine bee made a cripple by such meanes, yet dispise him not for that* 40 *deformity which stuck not vpon him at his birth; but fell vpon him by mis-fortune, and in recompence of such fauour, you shall (if your Patience can suffer so long) heare now how himselfe can speake.*

PROLOGVE

The Charmes of silence through this Square be throwne,
That an vn-vsde Attention (like a Iewell)
May hang at euery eare, for wee present
Matter aboue the vulgar Argument:
Yet drawne so liuely, that the weakest eye,
(Through those thin vailes we hang betweene your sight,
And this our peice) may reach the mistery:
What in it is most graue, will most delight.
But as in *Lantskip*, Townes and Woods appeare
Small a farre off, yet to the Optick sence,
The mind shewes them as great as those more neere;
So, winged *Time* that long agoe flew hence
You must fetch backe, with all those golden yeares
He stole, and here imagine still hee stands,
Thrusting his siluer locke into your hands.
There hold it but two howres, It shall from Graues
Raize vp the dead: vpon this narrow floore
Swell vp an Ocean, (with an Armed Fleete,)
And lay the Dragon at a Doues soft feete.
These Wonders sit and see, sending as guides
Your Iudgement, not your passions: passion slides,
When Iudgement goes vpright: for tho the Muse
(Thats thus inspir'de) a Nouell path does tread,
Shee's free from foolish boldnes, or base dread.
Loe; scorne she scornes and Enuies ranckling tooth,
For this is all shee does, she wakens *Truth*.

A Dumb shew

He drawes a Curtaine, discouering Truth *in sad abiliments; vncrownd: her haire disheueld, and sleeping on a Rock:* Time *(her father) attired likewise in black, and al his properties (as Sithe, Howreglasse and Wings) of the same Cullor, vsing all meanes to waken* Truth, *but not being able to doe it, he sits by her and mourns. Then enter Friers, Bishops, Cardinals before the Hearse of a Queen, after it Councellors, Pentioners and Ladies, al these last hauing scarfes before their eyes, the other singing in Latin.* Trueth *suddenly awakens, and beholding this sight, shews (with her father) arguments of Ioy, and Exeunt, returning presently:* Time *being shifted into light Cullors, his properties likewise altred into siluer, and* Truth *Crowned, (being cloathed in a robe spotted with Starres) meete the Hearse, and pulling the veiles from the Councellers eyes, they woundring a while, and seeming astonished at her brightnes, at length embrace* Truth *and* Time, *and depart with them: leauing the rest going on.*

This being done, Enter Titania *(the Farie Queene) attended with those Councellors, and other persons fitting her estate:* Time *and* Truth *meete her, presenting a Booke to her, which (kissing it) shee receiues, and shewing it to those about her, they drawe out their swordes, (embracing* Truth,*) vowing to defend her and that booke:* Truth *then and* Time *are sent in, and returne presently, driuing before them those Cardinals, Friers &c. (that came in before) with Images, Croziar staues &c. They gon, certaine graue learned men, that had beene banished, are brought in, and presented to* Titania, *who shewes to them the booke, which they receiue with great signes of gladnesse, and Exeunt Omnes.*

The Whore of Babylon

[ACT I, SCENE i]

Empresse *of* Babylon: *her Canopie supported by four Cardinals: two persons in Pontificall roabes on either hand, the one bearing a sword, the other the keies: before her three Kings crowned, behinde her Friers, &c.*

Empr.   That we, in pompe, in peace, in god-like splendor,
With adoration of all dazeled eies,
Should breath thus long, and grow so full of daies,
Be fruitfull as the Vine, in sonnes and daughters,
(All Emperors, Kings, and Queenes) that (like to Cedars
Vprising from the breast of *Lybanus,*
Or Oliues nurst vp by *Ierusalem*)
Heightened our glories, whilst we held vp them:
That this vast Globe Terrestriall should be cantled,
And almost three parts ours, and that the nations,   10
Who suspiration draw out of this aire,
With vniuersall *Aues*, showtes, and cries,
Should vs acknowledge to be head supreame
To this great body (for a world of yeares:)
Yet now, when we had made our Crowne compleat,
And clos'd it strongly with a triple arch,
And had inrich'd it with those pretious jewels
Few Princes euer see (white haires) euen now
Our greatnesse hangs in ballance, and the stampe
Of our true Soueraignty, clipt, and abas'd.   20
1. *King.*   By whom dread Empresse?
Empr.   Aske these holy Fathers:
Aske those our out-cast sonnes: a throne vsurped
Our chaire is counted, all our titles stolne.
2. *King.*   What blasphemy dare speake so?
Empr.   All our roabes,
Your vestments, (reuerend, yet pontificall:)

501

This sword, these keyes, (that open kingdoms hearts
To let in sweet obedience) All, but borrowed.
3. *King.*   What soule aboue the earth —
Empr.   Our royall signet,
With which, we, (in a mothers holy loue)
Haue sign'd so many pardons, is now counterfeit:
From our mouth flow riuers of blasphemy
And lies; our Babylonian Sinagogues
Are counted Stewes, where Fornications
And all vncleannesse Sodomiticall,
(Whose leprosy touch'd vs neuer) are now daily acted:
Our Image, which (like Romane *Cæsars*) stamp'd
In gold, through the whole earth did currant passe;
Is now blanch'd copper, or but guilded brasse.
3. *King.*   Can yonder roofe, thats naild so fast with starres,
Couer a head so impious, and not cracke?
That Sulphure boyling o're celestiall fires,
May drop in whizing flakes (with skalding vengeance)
On such a horrid sinne!
1. *King.*   No mortall bosome
Is so vnsanctified.
2. *King.*   Who i'st bright Empresse,
That feeds so vlcerous, and so ranke a Spleene?
Empr.   A woman.
Omn.   Woman! who?
Empr.   The Fairie Queene:
Fiue Summers haue scarce drawn their glimmering nights
Through the Moons siluer bowe, since the crownd heads
Of that adored beast, on which we ride,
Were strucke and wounded, but so heal'd againe,
The very scarres were hid. But now, a mortall,
An vnrecouerable blow is taken,
And it must bleed to death.
3. *King.*   Heauen cannot suffer it.
Empr.   Heauen suffers it, and sees it, and giues ayme,
Whilst euen our Empires heart is cleft in sunder:
That strumpet, that inchantresse, (who, in robes

White as is innocence, and with an eye
Able to tempt stearne murther to her bed)
Calles her selfe *Truth*, has stolne faire *Truths* attire,
Her crowne, her sweet songs, counterfets her voyce,　60
And by prestigious tricks in sorcerie,
Ha's raiz'd a base impostor like *Truths* father:
This subtile Curtizan sets vp againe,
Whom we but late banisht, to liue in caues,
In rockes and desart mountaines.
2. *King.*　　　　　　　Feare her not,
Shee's but a shadow.
Empr.　　　　　O t'is a cunning Spider,
And in her nets so wraps the Fairie Queene,
That shee suckes euen her breast: Sh'as writ a booke,
Which shee calles holy Spels.
3. *King.*　　　　　　Weele breake those spels.
Empr. The poles of heauen must first in sunder breake,　70
For from the Fairie shores this Witch hath driuen
All such as are like these (our Sooth-Saiers)
And cal'd false *Seers* home, that of things past,
Sing wonders, and diuine of things to come:
Through whose bewitching tongues runne golden chaines,
To which ten thousand eares so fast are bound,
As spirits are by spells; that all the Tones
Of harmony, that *Babylon* can sound,
Are charmes to Adders, and no more regarded,
Than are by him that's deafe, the sicke mans groanes.　80
Shee, they, *Titania*, and her Fairie Lords,
Yea euen her vassaile elues, in publike scorne
Defame me, call me Whore of *Babylon*.
Omn.　O vnheard of prophanation!
Empr.　Giue out I am common: that for lust, and hire
I prostitute this body: that to Kings
I quaffe full bowles of strong enchanting wines,
To make them dote on me.
Omn.　　　　　　Lets heare no more.
Empr.　And that all Potentates that tread on earth,

With our abhominations should be drunke,
And be by vs vndone.
Omn.   Weele heare no more.
3. King. You haue thrust Furies whips into our hands.
1. King. Say but the word, and weele turne home your wrongs,
In torne and bloody collours.
2. King.   All her bowers,
Shall like burnt offerings purge away (in fire)
Her lands pollution.
Omn.   Let's to armes.
Empr.   Stay: heare me:
Her kingdome weares a girdle wrought of waues,
Set thicke with pretious stones, that are so charm'd,
No rockes are of more force: her Fairies hearts,
Lie in inchanted towers (impregnable)
No engine scales them. Therefore goe you three,
                                 [*To the Kings.*]
Draw all your faces sweetly, let your browes
Be sleekd, your cheekes in dimples, giue out smiles,
Your voyces string with siluer, wooe (like louers)
Sweare you haue hils of pearle: shew her the world,
And say shee shall haue all, so shee will kneele
And doe vs reuerence: but if shee grow nice,
Dissemble, flatter, stoope to licke the dust
Shee goes vpon, and (like to serpents) creepe
Vpon your bellies, in humilitie;
And beg shee would but with vs ioyne a league,
To wed her land to ours: our blessing, goe.
3. King. When mines are to be blowne vp, men dig low.
All three. And so will wee.
Empr.   Prosper: till this sunne set,
The beames that from vs shoot, seeme counterfet.
                                      Exeunt.

       Manent [*the*] *four Cardinals, and certaine Priests.*

1. Card. This physicke cures not me.
2. Card.   Nor me.

3. *Card.*   Nor vs.
1. *Card.*   It is not strong of poyson, to fetch vp
Thats bak't within: my gall is ouerflowne,
My blood growne ranke and fowle: An inflamation
Of rage, and madnes so burnes vp my liuer,
That euen my heart-strings cracke (as in a furnace)
And all my nerues into my eye-balles shrinke,
To shoot those bullets, and my braines at once
Against her soule that ha's halfe dambd vs: falls
Fetcht hie, and neare to heauen, light on no ground,
But in hels bottome, take their first rebound.
2. *Card.*   Such are our falles: we once had mountaine-growth,
With Pines and Cedars.
3. *Card.*   Now with none of both.
1. *Card.*   I could be glad to loose the diuine office
Of my creation, to be turn'd into
A dogge, so I might licke vp but her blood,
That thrusts vs from our vineyards.
Other 3.   So could all.
4. *Card.*   Reuenge were milke to vs.
2. *Card.*   Manna.
1. *Card.*   And it shall.
But how? wee will not (as the head supreame
Ouer all nations, counselleth) licke the dust
The Faierie treads on, nor (like serpents) creepe
Vpon our bellies in humilitie:
This were (with Fencers) basely to giue ground,
When the first bowt may speed: or to sound parly,
Whilst they within, get swords to cut our throats:
No, weele at one blow strike the heart through.
Other 3.   How?
2. *Card.*   By ponyards.
1. *Card.*   No.
3. *Card.*   Poyson.
1. *Card.*   No.
4. *Card.*   Treason.

132, 141, 179 *Other* 3.] *Tres.* Q

1. *Card.*   Neither.
2. *Card.* How (reuerend *Como*) then?
1. *Card.* Thus — let's consult — nay you shal heare.
                                                  [*To priests.*]

You know that all the springs in Fairie land
Ran once to one head: from that head, to vs:
The mountaine and the valley paid vs fruit;
The field her corne, the countrey felt no heat
But from our fires: Plenty still spread our boards,
And Charitie tooke away. We stept not forth
But with a god-like adoration
All knees bowed low vnto vs: why was this?
Why were our gardens *Eden*? why our bowers
Built like to those in *Paradise*? I shall tell you,
It was because the Law most mysticall,
Was not made common: therefore was not vile;
It was because in the great Prophets *Phanes*
And hallowed Temples, we were *Choristers*:
It was because (wise Pylots) we from rockes,
And gulfes infernall, safely set on shore
Mens soules at yonder hauen: or (beeing shipwrackt)
Strong lines forth cast we, suffering none to sinke
To that *Abisse*, which some hold bottomlesse.
But now our very graues
Cannot saue dead mens bones from shame and bruzes:
The monumentall marble Vrnes of bodies
(Laid to rest long agoe) vnrcuerently
Are turned to troughes of water now for jades:
Vast Charnel-houses, where our fathers heads
Slept on the cold hard pillowes of the earth,
Are emptied now, and chang'd to drinking roomes,
Or vaults for baser office.
2. *Card.* What's therefore to be done?
1. *Card.*   This must be done:
This shall be done: They hunted vs like wolues,
Out of their Fairie forrests, whipt vs away
(As vagabonds) mockt vs, and said our fall

Could not be dangerous, because we bore
Our gods vpon our backes: now must we whip them,
But wiselier.
Other 3.   How?
1. Card.   Thus: those that fill our roomes,
Hold Beacons in their eies (blazing with fire
Of a hot-seeming zeale) to watch our entrance,
And to arme all against vs: these we must quench:
They are counted wels of knowledge, poyson these wells:
They are the kingdoms musicke, they the Organs,
Vnto whose sound her Anthems now are sung,
Set them but out of tune, alls out of square,
Pull downe the Church, and none can it repaire,
But *he* that builds it: this is the faggot band
That binds all fast: vndoo't, vndoe the land —
All priests.   Most certaine.
1. Card.   You therefore (the best consort of the soule)
                                                [*To priests.*]
Shepheards (whose flocks are men, lambs, Angels,) you
That hold the roofe of yon Starre-chamber vp,
From dropping downe to grinde the world to dust,
You shall to Fairie land.
All priests.   A joyfull voyage.
1. Card.   Those that sing there the holy Hymnes, as yet
Haue not their voyces cleere, the streame of ceremony
Is scarcely settled, trouble it more: bayte hookes
To take some, some to choake: cast out your net
At first, for all the frie: let vs spread sayles
To draw vnto our shores the Fairie whales.
That *Truth*, whose standard-bearer *Babylon*,
And all we are, is not cleane driuen from thence,
Whither we send you: there shee liues, but liues
A widdow; steps not forth, dares not be seene
During her moneth of mourning: here we write you
How, and with whom to finde her: what shee bids,
That doe: your hire's aboue.

          190, 195, 208, 221   *All priests.*] Card. omn. Q

All priests.   We know it well.
1. *Card.*   And when you see those Fairy fishermen
   Rowe in your streames, when they grow cold in working,   210
   And weary of their owne waters, that the sayles
   (Which stifly beare them vp) flag and hang low,
   And that (like reedes, playing with a paire of winds,)
   They promise facill pliance, then, then shake
   The trees by the root, twi'll make the branches blow,
   And drop their mellowed fruits, euen at your feet,
   Gather them, they are our owne, then is the houre,
   To weane those sonnes of blacke *Apostasi*
   From her, (their stepdame) and to make them take,
   A blessing from our reuerend mothers hands,   220
   Be happie: goe.
All priests.   Wee shall remember you,
   In all our kneelings.
1. *Card.*   Stay: ere you shift Ayre,
   Sprinkle your selues all ore with sacred droppes,
   Take *Periapts*, *Pentacles*, and potent Charmes
   To coniure downe fowle feinds, that will be rayzed
   To vex you, tempt you, and betray your bloud,
   About your necks hang hallowed *Amulets*,
   That may Conserue you from the plagues of Error
   Which will strike at you.
All priests.   Wee obey most holy fathers.
1. *Card.*   And heare you,   230
   If clymbing vp to this haught enterprize
   The foot slip, and (ith' fal) with death you meet —
All priests.   O glorious ladder!
1. *Card.*   A Saints winding sheet.
   Farewell: Mount all the engines of your wit,
   When darts are sent from all parts, some must hit.
                                           Exeunt Priests.
   There is a fellow to whome, because he dare

         215 twi'll] then'le Q (*see* I.ii.285)
         230, 233 *All priests.*] Sacr. Omn. Q
         235 S.D. *Priests.*] Sacr. Q

Not be a slaue to greatnes, nor is molded
Of Court dow (flattering) but (should it thunder)
To his father, doing ill, (would speake ill) our Empresse,
Hath giuen this name, (*Plaine Dealing*): this *Plaine dealing* 240
Haue I shipd hence, and is long since arriued
Vpon the fairy strond: from him I expect,
Intelligence of all Occurrences,
He for the names sake, shall perhaps be welcome,
Into that Harlots Company (whom the fairyes
Thinke honest, and sweare deeply, she is *Truth*.)
That Strumpet by inticement heele bring ouer.
2. *Card.* It came to me in letters (two dayes since)
That this *Plaine dealing* serues the fairy Queene,
And will no more be seene in *Babilon*. 250
1. *Card.* How no more seene in *Babilon*, tis but one lost,
If *Babilon* subscribe to our wise-doome,
Shee shall lodge *Double-Dealing* in his roome.

Exeunt.

[ACT I, Scene ii]

Titania, Fidely, Florimell, Elfiron, *Pentioners.*

Tita. Wee thought the fates would haue closde vp our eyes,
That wee should nere haue seene this day-starre rise:
How many plots were laid to barre vs hence,
(Euen from our Cradle?) but our Innocence,
Your wisedome (fairy Peeres) and aboue all,
That Arme, that cannot let a white soule fall,
Hath held vs vp, and lifted vs thus hie:
Euen when the Arrowes did most thickly flie,
Of that bad woman, (*Babilons* proud Queene)
Who yet (we heare) swels with Inuenomed Spleene. 10
Fid. Whose poyson, shall (like Arrowes shot vpright)
When forth it bursts, to her owne downfall light.
Tita. *Truth* be my witnes (whome we haue imployde,
To purge our Aire that has with plagues destroyed

Great numbers, shutting them in darksome shades)
I seeke no fall of hirs, my Spirit wades,
In Clearer streames; her bloud I would not shed,
To gaine that triple wreath that binds her head,
Tho mine shee would let forth, I know not why,
Only through rancke lust after Souereigntie. 20
 Flor.   Enough it is for me, if with a hand,
(Vnstaind and vn-ambitious) fairy Land
I Crowne with Oliue-branches: all those wounds,
Whose goary mouthes but lately staind our Rounds,

(*a*) *Hen.* 7.   Bleed yet in me: for when great (*a*) *Elfiline*
(Your grandsire) fild this throne, your bowers did shine
With fire-red steele, and not with Fairies eies,
You heard no musicke then, but shriekes and cries,
Then armed Vrchins, and stearne houshold Elues,
Their fatall pointed swords turnd on themselues. 30
But when the royall *Elfiline* sat crowned,
These ciuill woes in their own depth lay drowned.
He to immortall shades beeing gone,

(*b*) *Hen.* 8.   (Fames minion) great King (*b*) *Oberon*,
Titaniaes royall father, liuely springs,
Whose Court was like a campe of none but Kings.
From this great conquering Monarchs glorious stemme,

(*c*) *Edw.* 6.   Three (in direct line) wore his Diadem:
(*d*) *Q. Mar.*
& Q. Eliz.   (*c*) A King first, then a paire of (*d*) Queenes, of whom,
Shee that was held a downe-cast, by Fates doome, 40
Sits now aboue their hopes: her maiden hand,
Shall with a silken thred guide Fairie land.
 Omn.   And may shee guide it —
 Fid.   Euen till stooping time
Cut for her (downe) long yeeres that shee may climbe
(With ease) the highest hill old age goes o're,
Or till her Fairie subiects (that adore
Her birth-day as their beeing) shall complaine,
They are weary of a peacefull, golden raigne.
 Tita.   Which, that they neuer shall, your stately towers

26 (Your] (Our Q

510

Shall keepe their ancient beauty: and your bowers 50
(Which late like prophan'd Temples empty stood,
The tops defac'd by fire, the floores by blood,)
Shall be fill'd full of *Choristers* to sing
Sweet heauenly songs, like birds before the Spring:
The flowers we set, and the fruits by vs sowne,
Shall cheere as well the stranger as our owne.
We may to strange shores once our selues be driuen,
For who can tell vnder what point of heauen
His graue shall open? neither shall our oakes,
Trophies of reuerend Age, fall by our stroaks, 60
Nor shall the brier, or hawthorne (growing vnder)
Feare them, but flie to them, to get from thunder,
And to be safe from forraine wild-fire balles,
Weele build about our waters wooden walles.
Omn. On which weele spend for you our latest liues.

     Enter Parthenophill.

Tita. Fairies I thank you all, Stay who comes here?
Flor. Parthenophill, a Fairie Peere.
Tita. Parthenophill.
Parth.   Bright Empresse, Queene of maides:
To vs your Lords, amidst your Fairie shades
Three Princes (so themselues they style) are come, 70
From whence, they'l vs not learne, and doe intreat
Faire, and a free accesse.
Tita.   What is their businesse?
Parth. The splendor of your glories, which a farre
Shines (as they say, and iustly say) as brightly
As here at hand, hither them drawes, protesting
All faith and seruice to you, and requesting
That they the tribute of their loues may pay,
At your most sacred feet.
Tita.   Allow them entrance.
Parth. They in a Fairie maske, the argument
Of this their dutie, gladly would present. 80
Tita. As best them please.

The Hault-boyes sounding, Titania *in dumbe shew sends her Lords to fetch them in, who enter bare headed, the three Kings queintly attired like Masquers following them, who doing honour to her, intreat to dance with her maides, and doe so: This done they discouer.*

Tita. Your painted cheeks beeing off, your owne discouers,
You are no Fairies.
All three. No: but wounded louers.
Tita. How! louers! what! would you deflower my bed,
And strike off a poore maiden-head?
We know you not: what are you? and from whence?

(*a*) *Spaine.* 3. *King.* The (*a*) land of whom the sunne so enamor'd is,
He lends them his complexion, giues me birth,
The Indian and his gold are both my slaues,
Vpon my sword (as on the Axell tree)   90
A world of kingdomes mooue: and yet I write
Non sufficit. That lustie sonne of *Ioue*
That twelue times shewed himselfe more then a man,
Reard vp two pillars for me, on whose Capitals
I stand (*Colossus*-like) striding ore seas,
And with my head knock at the roofe of Heauen:
Hence come I, this I am, (O most diuine)
All that I am is yours, be you but mine.

(*b*) *France.* 1. *King.* The country (*b*) at whose breast, hundreds of Kings
Haue royally bin fed, is nurce to me: 100
The god of grapes is mine, whose bounteous hand
In clusters deales his gifts to euery land:
My Empire beares for greatnes, pollicy,
State, skill in Arts and Armes, sole soueraigntie
Of this Globe vniuersall. All her Princes
Are warriours borne: whose battels to be told,
Would make the hearers souldiers: t'is a land
Of breath so sweet, and of aspect so faire,
That to behold her, and to conquer her,
(In amorous combats,) great king *Oberon*,   110
Your awefull father, oft ha's thither come,

99 1. *King.*] 2. *King.* Q

Like to a bridegrome, or a Reueller,
And gone agen in goodly triumphs home.
From hence I spring, (fairest and most diuine)
All that this is, is yours, be you but mine.
2. *King.* Be you but mine, and doubly will I treble
Their glories, and their greatnesse: like to thunder
My voyce farre off, shakes kingdomes; whilst mine owne
Stands on Seauen (*a*) hills, whose towers, and pinnacles,   [(*a*) *Rome.*]
And reuerend Monuments, hold in them such worth,   120
And are so sacred, Emperours and Kings
(Like barefoote pilgrims) at her feet doe fall,
Bowing to her trible crowne imperiall.
The language which shee speakes, goes through the world,
To proue that all the world should stoope to her,
And (saue your selfe) they doe; you thinke you leaue
A rich inheritance, if to your sonnes,
Our fluent tongue you leaue, (nor need they more)
Who speake and spend it well, cannot be poore:
On many nations necks, a foot to set,   130
If it be glorious, then may you be great.
1. *King.* We are all pleasd, so please you be the bride,
Of three, we care not which two be deni'd.
2. *King.* For we are brethren, and those sacred breasts
From whence we draw our nourishment, would runne
Nectar to you (sweete as the food of life:)
Our aged mother twentie times an hower,
Would breath her wholesome kisses on your cheeke,
And from her own cup you should drinke that wine
Which none but Princes tast, to make you looke   140
With cheerefull countenance.
3. *King.*   You haue a (*b*) sonne,   (*b*) *The Irish.*
Rebellious, wild, ingratefull, poore, and yet
Apollo from's owne head cuts golden lockes,
To haue them grow on his: his harp is his,
The darts he shoots are his: the winged messenger
That runnes on all the errands of the gods,

116 2. *King.*] 3. *King.* Q

Teaches him swiftnes; hee'l outstrip the windes:
This child of yours is (by adoption)
Our mothers now, her blessing he receiues;
And tho (as men did in the golden Age) 150
He liue ith' open fields, hiding his head
In dampish caues, and woods, (sometimes for feare,)
Yet doe we succour him. This your lost sheep,
We home agen will bring, to your owne fold,
Humbly to graze vpon your Faierie plaines,
Prouided, that you sow them with such seed,
On which your whole land wholesomely may feed.
Tita. We know you now: O what a deale of paines
Would you (as others of this wing haue taken)
To be in Faierie land calld Soueraignes? 160
Thankes for it: rashly nothing must we doe:
When kingdoms marrie, heauen it selfe stands by
To giue the bride: Princes in tying such bands,
Should vse a thousand heads, ten thousand hands:
For that one Acte giues like an enginous wheele
Motion to all, sets all the State a going,
And windes it vp to height, or hurles it down,
The least blast turnes the scale, where lies a crowne:
Weele therefore take aduice. If these thinke fit
We should be yours, you ours, we signe to it: 170
Your counsell Fairie Lords: *Fideli* speake.
Fid. Would you (my royal mistres) haue those christal
Faire, double-leaued doores, where light comes forth
To cheere the world, neuer to open more?
Would you haue all your slumbers turn'd to dreams,
Frightfull and broken? would you see your Lords
(In stead of sitting at your Councell boards)
Locking their graue, white, reuerend heads in steele?
If so, you cannot for all Fairie land
Find men to fit you better.
Tita.   *Florimell,* 180
Breathes there in you *Fidelies* spirit?
Flor.   No Lady.

3. *King.*   No nor in any brest that's sound: true Counceller,
Already you speake musicke: you are strung
With golden chords; Angels guide on your tongue.
Flor.   These potent, politicke, and twin-borne States,
Would to their mitred fortunes tie our fates:
Our Fairie groues are greene, our temples stand
Like goodly watch-towers, wafting passengers
From rockes, t'arriue them in the Holy land:
Peace (here) eats fruits, which her own hand hath sown,   190
Your lambes with lyons play: about your throne,
The Palme, the Lawrell, and the abundant Vine
Grow vp, and with your roses doe entwine.
But if these gripe your Scepter once —
Tita.   What then?
Flor.   Vultures are not more rauenous than these men,
Confusion, tyranie, vproares will shake all,
Tygres, and wolues, and beares, will fil your seat,
In nothing (but in miserie) youle be great:
Those black and poisonous waters that bore down
In their rough torrent, Fairie townes and towers,   200
And drownd our fields in *Marianaes* daies,
Will (in a mercilesse inundation)
Couer all againe: red Seas will flow again:
The Deuill will roare againe: if these you loue,
Be (as the Serpent,) wise then, tho a Doue.
2. *King.*   This hee that speakes in musicke?
Tita.   Are you all,
Of this opinion Lordes?
Omn.   All, all.
All 3. Kings.   Lets hence.
3. *King.*   When close plots faile, vse open violence.
Tita.   Stay: Princes are free-borne, and haue free wils,
Theis are to *vs*, as vallies are to hills,   210
We may, be counceld by them, not controld:
Our wordes our Law.
Elf.   Bright Souereigne.

207 *All 3. Kings.*] *All* 3. Q

Tita. Y'are too bold.
3. *King.* I knew the fort would yeeld.
1. *King.* Attend.
2. *King.* Shees ours.
Tita. You would Combine a League, which these would breake.
1. *King.* A League!
2. *King.* Holy.
3. *King.* Honorable.
Tita. Nay heare me speake,
You court me for my loue, you I imbrace
As maides doe Suiters, with a smiling face
As you doe me: receiue our answere then: —
I cannot loue you: — what! such hardy men
And flie for one repulse? I meane as yet; 220
As yet I'm not at leisure: But I sweare
Euen by my birth-day, by the crowne I weare,
By those sweet waters, which into vs powre
Health, that no sicknes taints, by that blest flower
Vpon whose roseal stalke our peace does grow,
I sweare I will my loue on you bestow,
When one day comes, which now to you Ile name.
1. *King.* The time! O blessed time!
2. *King.* Balme to our sorrow.
3. *King.* Name that most happie houre.
Tita. May be to morrow:
Marke els and iudge whether it may or no: 230
When Lambes of ours, are kild by wolues of yours,
Yet no bloud suckt: when Heauen two Suns endures:
When Soules that rest in vnder-groundes,
Heare Anthems sung, and prayse the soundes:
When drops of water are so spilt,
That they can wash out murders guilt:
When Surgeons long since dead and gone,
Can cure our woundes, being cald vpon:
When from yon towers I heare one cry,
You may kill Princes lawfully: 240
When a Court has no Parasite,

1. ii]   THE WHORE OF BABYLON

When truth speakes false, and falshood right:
When Conscience goes in cloth of gold,
When Offices are giuen, not sold:
When merchants wiues hate costly clothes,
When ther's no lies in tradsmens oathes:
When Farmers by deere yeeres do leeze,
And Lawyers sweare to take no fees:
(And that I hope will neuer, neuer bee)
But then (and not till then) I sweare,   250
Shall your bewitching Charmes sleepe in mine eare.
Away.
      Exeunt Fairies: Manent [*the*] *three Kings.*
1. *King.* Derided to our faces!
2. *King.*   Baffuld!
3. *King.*   Made fooles!
1. *King.* This must not be.
Omn.   It shall not be.
3. *King.*   Reuenge:
Flie to our Empres bosome, there sucke treason,
Sedition, Herezies, confederacies,
The violation of al sacred leagues,
The combination of all leagues vniust,
The dispensation for sacramentall oathes,
And when ye'are swolne with theis, returne againe,
And let their poyson raine downe here in showres: 260
Whole heards of bulls loaden with hallowed curses,
With Interdictions, excommunications,
And with vnbinding Subiects fealties,
And with large pattents to kill Kings and Queens
Driue roaring hither, that vpon their hornes
This Empire may be tost.
2. *King.*   Shee shall bee torne,
Euen ioynt from ioynt: to haue her baited wel,
(If we cannot) wee will vn-kennell hell.
1. *King.* Will not you home with vs?
3. *King.*   No: here Ile lurke,
And in a Doue-like shape rauen vpon Doues: 270

Ile suck allegiance from the common brest,
Poyson the Courtier with ambitious drugs,
Throw bane into the cups where learning drinkes,
Ile be a Saint, a Furie, Angell, Deuill,
Or'e Seas, on this side Seas; Deuils forreners,
With Deuils within hel freedome, Deuils in Vaults,
And with Church Deuil, be it your soules health,
To drinke downe Babylonian Stratagems,
And to forge three-forkt thunderbolts at home,
Whilst I melt Sulphure here: If the sweet bane   280
I lay bee swallowed, oh! a Kingdome bursts,
But if the poysoned hooke be spied, then leuy
Eightie eight Legions, and take open armes,
The *Guidon* shall be mine, Ile beare the Standard.
Omn.   Twi'll be a glorious warre.
1. *King.*   Farewell.
3. *King.*   Bee gon,
Who cleaues a Realmes head, needs more swordes then one.
                                                 Exeunt.

[ACT II, Scene i]

Fideli, Florimell, Parthenophill, Elfiron, [*Footmen.*]

Flor.   These euill Spirits are vext, and tho they vanisht
Like hideous dreames, yet haue they left behind them,
Throbs, and heart-akings, in the generall boosome,
As omynous bodings. Fairy Lackeyes. —
4. *Footmen.*   Here.
Flor.   Flie Sirra through the Ayre and neuer rest
(On paine to be into an vrchin turnd)
Till thou hast fixt vpon the highest gates,
Of our great'st Cities. Ther's a warning peece. Away.
                                              Exit [1].
Fid.   Theis to the Spirits that our waters keepe,
Charge them that none rowst ther, but those whose nets,   10
Are cast out of our Fairy gundolets. Away.   *Exit 2.*

II. i] THE WHORE OF BABYLON

Elf. Theis to the keepers of those royall woods
Where Lyons, Panthers, and the kingly heardes
Feede in one company; that if wild Boares,
Mad Buls, or rauing Beares, breake in for prey,
Hoping to make our groues their wildernes,
Ours may like souldiers bid them battaile. Flie.   *Exit 3.*
Parth. Theis to the Shepheards on our Fairie downs
To warne them not to sleepe, but with sweet Layes
And Iolly pipings driue into fat pastures   20
Their goodly flocks: Wolues are abroad say, Fly.   *Exit 4.*
Fid. Place *Prouidence*, (because she has quick eye:
And is the best at kenning) in our Nauy,
Courage shall wait on her.

         Titania *and her maids* [Aura, Philæma, Agathe,
            Castina] *standing alofe.*

Flor.   No: shees most fit
To goe with vs.
Omn.   Let her in Counsell sit.
Fid. Tis said: and least they breake into our walkes
And kill our fairie deare, or change themselues
Into the shape of Fawnes, being indeed Foxes,
Range all the forrest danger to preuent,
Foresight, beats stormes backe, when most Imminent.   30
Omn. Away then.   *Exeunt.*

        Manent Titania, *and her maides.*

Tita. Wise Pilots? firmest pillers? how it agrees,
When Princes heads sleepe on their counsels knees:
Deepe rooted is a state, and growes vp hie,
When Prouidence, Zeale, and Integritie
Husband it well: Theis fathers twill be said
(One day) make me a grandame of a maid.
Meane time my farewell to such gaudy lures
As here, were thrown vp t'haue me quite ore-thrown,
I charge you maids, entertaine no desires,   40

     24 S.D. Titania *and her maids*...] Q *places in left margin*

So irreligious and vnsanctified:
Oh, they ha snakes sleeky tongues, but hearts more rugged
Then is the Russian Beare: our Fairie bowres
Would turne to Arabian desarts, if such flowers,
(Mortall as killing Hemlocke) here should grow,
Which to preuent, Ile haue you vow.
Aur.   We vowe
By the white balles in bright *Titaniaes* eies,
We their inchantments skorne.
Tita.   It does suffice:
To bind it sure, Strew all your meades with charmes,
Which if they doe no good, shall doe no harme.   50
Aur.   Here comes your new sworne seruant.

                   Enter Plaine dealing.

Tita.   Now Sirra, where haue you bin?
Plain.   Where haue I bin? I haue bin in the brauest prison —
Tita.   What prison? a braue prison? Can there be a braue prison?
Plain.   All your fine men liue and die there, it's the Knights ward, and therefore must needs bee braue: some call it an Ordinarie, but I say tis a prison, for most of our gallants that are serued euery day with woodcockes there, lie there in a manner vpon Execution: they dare not peepe out of doores for feare of Serieants.
Tita.   What are those Serieants?   60
Plain.   Doe not you know (mistresse) what Serieants are? a number of your courtiers are deare in their acquaintance: why they are certaine men-midwiues, that neuer bring people to bed, but when they are sore in labour, that no body els can deliuer them.
Tita.   Are there such places in our kingdome, as Ordinaries, what is the true fashion of them, whats their order?
Plain.   They are out of all true fashion: they keep no order
Tita.   Where about in Fairie land stand they?
Plain.   In your great cittie: and here's the picture of your Ordinarie.
Tita.   When Master Painter please we shall haue it: come Sir.   70
Plain.   Your gallants drink here right worshipfully, eat most impudently, dice most swearingly, sweare most damnably, quarrell most desperatly, and put vp most cowardly. Suppose I were a

young countrey gentleman, and that I were to come in (like an asse) among 'em, new cast into the bonds of sattin.

Tita. What then?

Plain. Mary then doe all the gylt rapiers turne their Tobacco faces in the roome vpon me, and they puffe, they gape on a fresh man like so many stale Oysters at a full tyde: then is there no salt to throw vpon them, and to make them leaue gaping, but this; to cast off his cloake, hauing good cloathes vnderneath, single out some in the roome worse accoustred then himselfe, with him to walke boldly vp and downe strutting, laugh alowd at any thing, talke alowde of nothing, so they make a noise, it is no matter.

Tita. You are growne sirra an obseruer since you came out of *Babylon*.

Plain. Troth mistresse, I left villains and knaues there, and find knaues and fooles here: for your Ordinary is your Isle of Gulles, your ship of fooles, your hospitall of incurable madmen: it is the field where your captaine and braue man is cal'd to the last reckoning, and is ouerthrown horse and foot: it is the onely schoole to make an honest man a knaue: for Intelligencers may heare enough there, to set twenty a begging of lands: it is the strangest Chesse-board in the world.

Tita. Why?

Plain. Because in some games at Chesse, knights are better then pawnes, but here a good pawne is better then a knight.

Tita. Affoard our shores such wonders?

Plain. Wonders? why this one little Cocke-pit, (for none come into it, but those that haue spurs) is able to shew all the follies of your kingdome, in a few Apes of the kingdome.

Tita. Haue we not in our Land Physitions
To purge these red impostumes?

Plain. Troth yes mistresse; but I am *Plaine dealing*, and must speake truth, thou hast many Physitions, some of them sound men, but a number of them more sicke at heart, then a whole parish full of Patients: let them cure themselues first, and then they may better know how to heale others: then haue you other fellowes that take vpon them to be Surgeons, and by letting out the corruption of a State, and they let it out Ile be sworne; for some of them in

places as big as this, and before a thousand people, rip vp the bowels of vice in such a beastly manner, that (like women at an Execution, that can endure to see men quartred aliue) the beholders learne more villany then they knew before: others likewise there be of this consort last named, that are like Beadles bribed, they whip, but draw no blood, and of these I haue made a Rime.
Tita. Let's heare it.
Plain. Those that doe jerke these times, are but like fleas,
They bite the skinne, but leap from the disease.
Tita. Ile haue you Sir (because you haue an eye so sharply pointed) to looke through and through that our great Citie, and like death, to spare the liues of none, whose conscience you find sickly and going.
Plain. If I giue you the copie of the Cities countenance, Ile not flatter the face, as painters do; but shew al the wrinkles of it.
Tita. Doe so, you shall no more to *Babylon*,
But liue with vs, and be our Officer.
Plain. Haue I any kinred in your Court? is there any one of my name an officer? if there bee, part vs; because it will not bee good, to haue two of the *Plain-dealings* in one office, they'l bee beggars if they doe.
Tita. No Sirra, wee'le prouide you shall not want
Whilst vs you serue. Goe learne where *Truth* doth lie.
Plain. Nay, nay, I haue heard of her, she dwelles (they say) at the signe of the Holy Lambe.
Tita. Wee built her vp a lodging at our cost,
To haue her labour in our Vineyards:
For till shee came, no Vines could please our taste,
But of her fining. Set your hand to hers,
Liue with her in one house, fetch from our Court
Maintenance to serue you all: t'will be to her
A comfort to haue you stil by her side,
Shee ha's such prettie and delightfull songs,
That you will count your sorest labour light,
And time well spent only to heare her sing.
Away loose no more minutes.

142 side] sides Q

II. i]   THE WHORE OF BABYLON

Plain.   Not a minute: Ile set more watches then a clockmaker.
                              Exit.
            Elfiron. Paridel.

Titan. Whats yonder man that kneeles?
Elf.   Tis (*a*) *Paridel.*   (*a*) *Doctor*
Titan. Our doctor?   *Parry.*
Pari.   The most wretched in your land.
  The most in soule deiected; the most base,   150
  And most vnseruiceable weede, vnles
  You by your heauenly Influence change his vilenes
  Into a vertuall habit fit for vse.
Tita.   Oh: we remember it; you are condemnd?
Elf.   To Death.
Pari.   Deseruedly.
Tita.   You had your hand
  Not coulored with his bloud.
Elf.   No deerest Lady
  Vpon my vowed Loyalty.
Pari.   The law,
  Hath fastned on me only for attempt,
  It was no actuall nor commenced violence
  That brought death with it, but intent of ill.   160
Tita.   We would not saue them, that delight to kill,
  For so we wound our selues: bloud wrongly spilt
  Who pardons, hath a share in halfe the guilt.
  You strooke our lawes not hard, yet what the edge
  Of Iustice could take from you, mercy giues you
  (Your life.) You haue it signed, rize.
Pari.   May yon Clouds
  Muster themselues in Armies, to confound
  Him that shall wish you dead, hurt, or vncrownd.

            Parthenophill with Campeius.

[*Aside.*]   To run in debt thus basely for a life,
  To spend which, had beene glory! O most vile!   170
  The good I reape from this superfluous grace,

    169 [*Aside.*]] Q *repeats speech-prefix* Par. *for* Paridel

Is but to make my selfe like *Cæsars* horse,
To kneele whilst he gets vp: my backe must beare
Till the chine crack, yet still a seruile feare
Must lay more loades on me, and presse me downe.
When Princes giue life, they so bind men to 'em,
That trusting them with too much, they vndo 'em.
Who then but I, from steps so low would rise?
Great fortunes (earnd thus) are great Slaueries:
Snatcht from the common hangmans hands for this? 180
To haue my mind feele torture! now I see,
When good dayes come, (the Gods so seldome giue them,)
That tho we haue them, yet we scarce beleeue them.
Heart how art thou confinde? and bard of roome,
Thart quicke enough, yet liuest within a tombe.
Tita. His name.
Parth. (a) *Campeius*: Deeply learnd.

(a) Ed. Campion.

Tita. We heare so:
But with it heare (from some whome we haue weied
For iudgement and experience) that he caries,
A soule within him framde of a thousand wheeles:
Yet not one steddy.
Parth. It may be the rumor 190
That thus spreades ouer him, flowes out of hate.
Tita. Belieue vs no: of his, and tothers fate,
The threedes are too vnlike, to haue that wouen.
Camp. To gaine her crowne Ile not kneele thus.
Tita. Besides
The haruest which he seekes is reapde already:
We haue bestowed it.
Parth. Here then dies our sute.
Tita. Now shall you trie with what impatience
That bay tree will endure a little fire,
My Lord, my Lord,
Such swelling spirites hid with humble lookes, 200
Are kingdoms poysons, hung on golden hookes.
Parth. I hope heele proue none such.
Tita. Such men oft proue

Valleyes that let in riuers to confound
The hils aboue them, tho themselues lie drounde.
My Lord, I like not calme and cunning seas
That to haue great ships taken or distrest,
Suffer base gallyes to creepe ore their breast,
Let course harts weare course skins: you know our wil.
Parth. Which (as a doome diuine) I shall fulfill.
Camp. Thrown downe, or raizd?
Parth. All hopes (for this) are gone, 210
Some planet stands in opposition.
Camp. Vmh: So.
                    Exeunt Parthenophill *and* Campeius.
Tita. Now Doctor *Paridell*.
Pari.   An humble suite,
I am growne bold finding so free a giuer,
Where beggers once take almes, they looke for't euer.
Tita. You ha beene sworne our seruant long.
Pari.   Tenne yeares.
Tita. And we should wrong you (since you take vs giuing)
To let you goe with life, that should want liuing,
What is it we can grant you.
Pari. I ha beene by two great Fayries in your land, 220
(Opprest I dare not say) but so beaten downe,
And suncke so low now with my last disgrace,
That all my happy thoughts lie in the dust,
Asham'd to looke vp yet: most humbly therefore
Begge I your gratious leaue that I may vary,
This natiue Aire for Forren.
Tita.   Oh you would trauell,
You may, you haue our leaue: Challenge our hand.
Pari. Stormes are at Sea, when it is calme at land. *Exit.*

                    Fideli. Florimell.

Fid. The Sea-God hath vpon your maiden shoares,
(On Dolphins backes that pittie men distrest) 230
In safetie sett a people that implores,
The Soueraigne mercie flowing from your brest.

Tita. What people are they?
Fid.   Neighbours: tis the nation,
The Nether- With whome our Faries enterchange commerce,
landers   And by negotiation growne so like vs,
That halfe of them are Fayries: th'other halfe
Are hurtfull Spirits, that with sulphurous breath
Blast their corne feilds, deface their temples, cloth
Their townes in mourning, poyson hallowed founts,
And make their goodliest Citties stand (like tombes)   240
Full of dead bodies, or (like pallaces,
From whence the Lords are gone) all desolate.
They haue but seuenteen daughters young and faire,
Vowd to liue vestalls, and not to know the touch
Of any forced or vnreuerend hand.
Yet Lust and Auarice (to get their dowers)
Lay barbarous seidge against their chastitie,
Threaten to rauish them, to make their bodies
The temples of polution, or their bedds,
Graues where their honors shall lie buried.   250
They pray to haue their virgins wait on you,
That you would be their mother, and their nurse,
Their Guardian and their Gouernour; when Princes
Haue their liues giuen 'em, fine and golden threds
Are drawne and spun (for them) by the good fates,
That they may lift vp others in low states.
Tita.   Els let our selfe decline; giue them our presence:
In mysery all nations should be kin,
And lend a brothers hand, vsher them in.
                              Exeunt [Fideli, Florimell].
Stood here my foes (distrest) thus would I grieue them,   260
Not how they ha bin, but how I might relieue them.

Parthenophill.

Parth.   Your good deeds (matchlesse Fayrie) like the Sun,
(Rising but onely in this poynt of heauen)
Spred through the world, So that a Prince (made wretched,

244 not] *om.* Q

By his vnhappy father, that lies slaine
By barbarous swords, and in his goary wounds,
Drownes all the hopes of his posteritie)
Hether, is like an orphan come (from farre)
To get reliefe and remedie gainst those,
That would defeat him of his portion. 270
Tita. Pittie and we had talke before you came,
She hath not taken yet her hand from ours,
Nor shall shee part, vntill those higher powers
Behold that Prince: good workes are theirs, not ou'rs;
Goe: bid him trust his misery in our hands,
Great trees I see do fall, when the shrub stands.
        Exeunt [*Parthenophill, Elfiron*].

  Fideli, Florimell, *the states of the countries*, Parthenophill,
    Elfyron, *the Prince of* Portugal.

    To the States.
  Auxilio tutos dimittam, opibusque Iuuabo.
  Non ignara mali, miseris succurrere disco.
          Exeunt.

[ACT II, SCENE ii]

The third King to his man.

3. *King.* Stands my beard right? the gowne: I must looke graue,
White haires like siluer cloudes a priuiledge haue,
Not to be search'd, or be suspected fowle:
Make away those two turne coates. Suite me next
Like to a Sattin diuell (brauely), flie
Your saylers shape: be here immediatly. *Exit* [*man.*]
So: excellent: a subtile masque: alls fit:
This very cap makes my head swell with wit.
Mongst souldiers, I haue plaid the souldier,
Bin mutinous, raild at the State, cursd peace: 10

  1 S.D. to his man.] *to the King of Portugall.* Q
  6 saylers] sayles Q
  6 S.D. Exit.] *Enter* ‸ Q

They walke with crosse-armes, gaping for a day,
Haue vnder-shorde their eie-lids (like trap windows,)
To keep them open, and with yawning eares,
Lie listning on flocke bolsters, till rebellion
Beat vp her drum: this lards me fat with laughter,
Their swords are drawn halfe way, and all those throats
That are to bleed are mark'd: and all those doores,
Where ciuill Massacres, murders (di'd in graine)
Spoile, riflings, and sweet rauishments shall enter,
Haue tokens stamp'd on them (to make 'em knowne) 20
More dreadfull then the Bils that preach the plague.
From them, with oyl'd hammes (lap'd in seruile blew)
I stole, and fil'd out wine of *Babylon*,
To liue things (made of clods) poore countrey sots,
And drunke they are: whole shires with it do reele,
Poysons run smooth, because men sweetnes feele.
Now to my schoole-men, Learnings fort is strong,
But poorely man'd, and cannot hold out long
When golden bullets batter. — Yonders one —
                              [*Enter* Campeius.]
    Y'are a poore scholler?
Camp.   Yes.
3. King.   What read you?
Camp.   A booke. 30
3. King. So learned, yet so young?
Camp.   Yee may see Sir.
3. King. You feede some discontent?
Camp.   Perhaps I ha cause.
3. King. What troubles you?
Camp.   You trouble me: pray leaue me.
3. King. Put your selfe, and your griefe into my hands.
Camp. Say yee?
3. King. Put your selfe and your grief into my hands.
Camp. Are you a Doctor? your hands Sir, pray why?
3. King. You know me not.
Camp. Do you know your selfe? your busines?
    Are you a scholler?

3. *King.*   Iudge of that by these.
Camp. Oh Sir, I haue seene many heads vnder such wool,
That scarce had braines to line it: if y'are a scholler,
Mee thinks you should know manners, by your leaue Sir.
3. *King.* Pray leaue your name behind you.
Camp.   Name, *Campeius.*
3. *King.* *Campeius*! vmh: *Campeius*? a lucky plannet
Strikes out this houre: *Campeius*! *Babylon*,
His name hath in her tables: on his forehead,
Our Queene hath set her marke: it is a mould
Fit to cast mischeife in: none sooner rent
A Church in two, then Schollers discontent.
I must not loose this Martines nest, — once more
Y'are happely met.
Camp.   This bur stil hang on mee!
And you Sir.
3. *King.* Tell me pray,
Did you neuer tast — I'me bold — did you nee'r tast
Those cleere and redolent fountains that do norish,
In viue and fresh humiditie those plants
That grow on thother side (our opposites)
Those that to vs here, are th'Antipodes,
Cleane against vs in grounds — you feele me — say
Ne're drunke you of that nectar.
Camp.   Neuer.
3. *King.*   Neuer!
I wish you had, I gather from your eyes,
What your disease is, I ha bin your selfe,
This was *Campeius* once (tho not so learn'd)
For I was bred (as you) in Fairy Land,
A Country! well, but tis our country: and so,
Good to breed beggers: Shee starues Arts: fatts fools,
Shee sets vp drinking roomes, and pulls downe schools.
Camp. So Sir.
3. *King.*   No more but so Sir? this discourse
Pallatts not you.
Camp.   Yes.

3. *King.*   Nothing hath passed me
I hope, against my countrey, or the State,
That any can take hold of.
Camp.   If they could,
Tis but mine I, to your no.
3. *King.*   Y'are to sowre:
Vnmellowed: you stand here in the shade,
Out of the warmth of those blest ripening beames, —
Goe to — I grieue that such a blossome —
Camp.   Sir, I know you not: this thing which you haue raiz'd,
Affrights me: schollers of weake temper need
To feare (as they on Sunbankes lie to read)
Adders i'th highest grasse: these leaues but turn'd,
Like willow stickes hard rub'd may kindle fire,
Cities with sparkes as small haue oft beene burn'd.
3. *King.*   Doe you take me for a hangman?
Camp.   I would be loath,
For any harsh tune that my tongue may warble,
To haue the instrument vnstrung.
3. *King.*   You shall not:
Welfare vnto you.
Camp.   And to you. A word Sir:
Bred in this countrey?
3. *King.*   Yes.
Camp.   I am no bird
To breake mine own neast downe: what flight soeuer
Your words make through this ayre (tho it be trobled)
Myne eare Sir, is no reaching Fowling piece,
What passes through it, kills: you may proceed,
Perhaps you would wound that, I wish should bleed.
You haue th'aduantage now,
I put the longest weapon into your hands.
3. *King.*   It shall guard you:
You draw me by this line: let's priuate walke.
Camp.   This paths vnbruz'd: goe on Sir.

              72 any] any you Q
            *91 What passes through it, kills:] *stet* Q

3. *King.*   Sir I loue you.
The Dragons that keep learnings golden tree,
As you now haue, I fought with, conquered them,
Got to the highest bough, eat of the fruit,
And gathered of the seauen-fold leaues of Art,
What I desir'd; and yet for all the Moones
That I haue seene waxe olde, and pine for anger,
I had outwatched them: and for all the candles
I wasted out on long, and frozen nights,
To thaw them into day; I fild my head
With books, but scarce could fil my mouth with bread:
I had the Muses smile, but moneyes frowne,
And neuer could get out of such a gowne.
Camp.   How did you change your starre?
3. *King.*   By changing Aire:
The god of waues washt of my pouertie,
I sought out a new sunne beyond the seas,
Whose beames begat me gold.
Camp.   O me dull asse!
I am nail'd downe by wilfull beggerie,
Yet feele not where it enters: like a horse
My hoofes are par'd to'th quicke (euen til they bleed)
To make me runne from hence, yet this Tortois shell,
(My countrey) lies so heauy on my backe,
Pressing my worth downe, that I slowly creep
Through base and slimie waies.
3. *King.*   Countrey!
Camp.   Shee hangs
Her owne brats at her backe, to teach them begge,
And in her lap sets strangers.
3. *King.*   Yet your countrey.
Camp.   I was not borne to this, not school'd to this,
My parents spent not wealth on me to this,
I will not stay here long.
3. *King.*   Doe not.
Camp.   Beeing hence,
Ile write in gall and poyson gainst my nurce

This Fairie land, for not rewarding merit:
If euer I come backe Ile be a Calthrop
To pricke my countries feet, that tread on me.
3. King. O shee's vnkind, hard-hearted!
Camp. In disputation 130
I dare for latine, hebrew, and the greeke,
Challenge an vniuersitie; yet, (O euill hap!)
Three learned languages cannot set a nap
Vpon this thred-bare gowne: how is Arte curs'd?
Shee ha's the sweetest lymbes, and goes the worst:
Like common Fidlers, drawing down others meate
With lickorish tunes, whilst they on scraps do eate.
3. King. Shake then these seruile fetters off.
Camp. But how?
3. King. Play the mules part, now thou hast suckt a dam
Drie and vnholsome, kicke her sides.
Camp. Her heart — her very heart — 140
Would it were dried to dust, to strew vpon
Th'inuenomed paper vpon which Ile write.
3. King. Know you the Court of *Babylon*?
Camp. I haue read,
How great it is, how glorious, and would venter
A soule to get but thither.
3. King. Get then thither;
You venture none, but saue a soule going thither:
The Queene of *Babylon* rides on a beast,
That carries vp seauen heads.
Camp. Rare.
3. King. Each head crown'd.
Enter his man like a sayler
Camp. O admirable! *with rich attires vnder his arme.*
3. King. Shee with her owne hand
Will fil thee wine out of a golden bowle. 150
There's Angels to conduct thee. Get to sea,
Steal o're, behold, here's one to waft thee hence,
Take leaue of none, tell none, th'art made, farewell.
Camp. Thus to meet heauen, who would not wade through hell?

Exeunt Campeius *and Sayler, manet third King,*
enter Sayler presently.

3. *King.* To flea off this hypocrisie, tis time,
Least worne too long, the Foxes skinne be known:
In our dissembling now we must be braue,
Make me a courtier: come; Asses I see,
In nothing but in trappings, different be
From foote-cloth nags, on which gay fellows ride, 160
Saue that such gallants gallop in more pride.
Away. Stow vnder hatches that light stuffe:
Tis to be worne in *Babylon.* —   *Exit Sayler.*
              At this groue,
And much about this howre, a slaue well moulded,
In profound, learned villany, gaue oath   *Enter Coniurer.*
To meet me: Art thou come! Can thy blacke Arte
This wonder bring to passe?
Con.   See, it is done.
3. *King.* *Titaniaes* picture right.
Con.   This virgin waxe,
Burie I will in slimie putred ground,
Where it may peece-meale rot: As this consumes, 170
So shall shee pine, and (after languor) die.
These pinnes shall sticke like daggers to her heart,
And eating through her breast, turne there to gripings,
Cramp-like Convulsions, shrinking vp her nerues,
As into this they eate.
3. *King.*   Thou art fam'd for euer,
If these thy holy labours well succeed,
Statues of molten brasse shall reare thy name,
The *Babylonian* Empresse shall thee honour.
And (for this) each day shalt thou goe in chaines.
Where wilt thou burie it?
Con.   On this dunghill.
3. *King.*   Good: 180
And bind it down with most effectuall charmes.

533

That whosoeuer with vnhallowed hands,
Shall dare to take it hence, may raue and die.
Con. Leaue me.
3. *King.*   Farewell and prosper: be blinde you skies,
You looke on things vnlawfull with sore eies.   *Exit.*

Dumbe shewe. The Hault-boyes sound, and whilst hee is
burying the picture, Truth *and* Time *enter,* Fideli, Parthenophil,
Elfiron, *and a Guard following aloofe. They discouer the fellow,*
hee is taken, the picture found, hee kneeles for mercy,
but they making signes of refusall, he snatcheth
at some weapon to kill himselfe, is preuented,
and led away.

[ACT III, SCENE i]

The Empres [*of* Babylon], *Cardinals* [, 1. *and* 2. *Kings*] *&c.*

Empr. Who sets those tunes to mocke vs? Stay them.
Omn.   Peace.
1. *King.* Peace there.
1. *Card.*   No more: your musicke must be dombe.
Empr. When those Cælestiall bodies that doe moue,
Within the sacred Spheres of Princes bosomes
Goe out of order, tis as if yon Regiment,
Weare all in vp-roare: heauen should then be vext,
Me thinkes such indignation should resemble,
Dreadfull eclypses, that portend dire plagues
To nations, fall to Empires, death to Kings,
To Citties deuastation, to the world,   10
That vniuersall hot calamitie
Of the last horror. But our royall bloud,
Beates in our veines like seas strugling for bounds,
Aetna burns in vs: bearded Comets shoote
Their vengeance through our eyes: our breath is lightning,
Thunder our voyce; yet, (as the idle Cannon,
Strikes at the Aires Invulnerable brest)

Our darts are phillip'd backe in mockery,
Wanting the poynts to wound.
1. King.   Too neere the heart,
(Most royall Empresse) these distempers sit,
So please you, weele againe assayle her bewtie
In varied shapes, and worke on sutler Charmes,
Again loues poysoned arrowes weele let flie.
Empr. No: proud spirits once denying, still deny.
1. Card. Then be your selfe, (a woman) change those **ouertures**
You made to her of an vnusuall peace,
To an vnusde defiance: giue your reuenge,
A full and swelling saile, as from your greatnes
You tooke, in veyling to her: you haue beene
Too cold in punishment, too soft in chyding,
And like a mother (cause her yeares are greene)
Haue winck't at Errors, hoping time, or councell,
Or her owne guilt (seing how she goes awry,)
Would streigten all. — you find the contrarie.
Empr. What followes?
1. Card.   Sharp chastizment, leaue the Mother
And be the steptdame; wanton her no more
On your Indulgent knee, signe no more pardons
To her Off-fallings and her flyings out:
But let it be a meritorious Act,
Make it a ladder for the soule to climbe,
Lift from the hindges all the gates of heauen;
To make way for him that shall kill her.
Omn.   Good.
1. Card. Giue him an office in yon Starr-chamber,
Or els a Saints place and Canonize him;
So Sanctifie the arme that takes her life,
That sylly soules may go on pilgrimage,
Only to kisse the Instrument (that strikes)
As a most reuerent relique.
Empr.   Be it so.
1. King. In that one word she expires.
Empr.   Her fayrie Lordes

(That play the Pilots nowe, and steere her kingdome 50
In fowlest weather) as white bearded corne
Bowes his proud head before th'imperiall windes,
Shall so ly groueling (heere) when that day comes.
1. *King.* And that it shall come fates themselues prepare.
Empr. True, but old Lyons hardly fall into the snare.
1. *King.* Is not the good and politique *Satyran*
(Our leagued brother, and your vassaile sworne)
Euen now (this very minute) sucking close
Their fairest bosomes? if his traynes take well:
They haue strange workings (down-wards) into hel. 60
Empr. That *Satiran* is this hand: his braines a forge
Still working for vs, he's the trew set clocke
By which we goe, and of our houres doth keepe
The numbred strokes, when we lye bound in sleepe.
1. *Card.* Besides such voluntaries as will serue
Vnder your holy cullors and forsake
The Fairie standard, all such fugitiues
Whose heartes are Babylonized: all the Mutiners,
All the damb'd Crew, that would for gold teare off
The deuills beard: All schollers that doe eate 70
The bread of sorrow, want, and discontent,
Wise *Satyran* takes vp, presses, apparrels
Their backes like Innocent Lambes, their minds like wolues,
Rubs or'e their tongues with poyson, which they spet
Against their owne annointed; their owne Country,
Their very parent. And thus shippes 'em hither,
To make em yours.
Empr.   To vse.
1. *Card.*   Only to imploy them
As Bees: whilst they haue stings, and bring thighs laden
With hony, hiue them, when they are droanes, destroy them.
1. *King.* The earnest which he giues you (adored Empresse,) 80
Are two fit engines for vs.
Empr.   Are they wrought?
2. *King.* They are: and waite in Court your vtmost pleasure,

*81 two] three Q

536

Out of your Cup made wee them drunke with wines,
To sound their hearts, which they with such deuotion
Receiued downe, that euen whilst *Bacchus* swom
From lippe to lippe, in mid'st of taking healths,
They tooke their owne damnation, if their bloud
(As those grapes) stream'd not forth, to effect your good.
Empr.   Let vs behold these fire-workes, that must run
Vpon short lines of life: yet wil *Wee* vse them, 90
Like instruments of musicke, play on them,
A while for pleasure, and then hang them by,
Who Princes can vpbrayd, tis good they die.
For as in building sumptuous pallaces,
We climb by base and slender scaffoldings,
Till wee haue raized the Frame: and that being done,
(To grace the worke) we take the Scaffolds downe,
So must we these: we know they loue vs not,
But Swallow-like when their owne summers past,
Here seeke for heat: or like slight Traualers, 100
(Swolne with vaine-glory, or with lust to see,)
They come to obserue fashions and not mee.
1. *King.*   As Traualers vse them then, till they be gone,
Looke Cheerefully; backs turn'd, no more thought vpon.
Empr.   What are they that fly hither (to our bosome)
But such as hang the wing, such as want neasts;
Such as haue no sound feathers; birds so poore,
They scarce are worth the killing: with the Larke
(The morning's fawlkner) so they may mount hie,
Care not how base and low their risings be? 110
What are they but leane hungry Crowes that tyre
Vpon the mangled quarters of a Realme?
And on the house-tops of Nobilitie
(If there they can but sit) like fatall Rauens,
Or Skrich-Owles croake their fals and hoarsely bode,
Nothing but scaffolds and vnhallowed graues?
1. *King.*   Fitter for vs: yet sit they here like doues.
Empr.   True: like corrupted Churchmen they are doues,
That haue eate carrion: home weele therefore send

These busie-working Spiders to the wals
Of their owne countrey, when their venemous bags
(Which they shall stuffe with scandales, libels, treasons)
Are full and vpon bursting: let them there
Weaue in their politicke loomes nets to catch flies;
To vs they are but Pothecary drugs,
Which we will take as Physicall pils, not food:
Vse them as lancets to let others bloud,
That haue foule bodies, care not whom you wound,
Nor what parts you cut off, to keepe this sound.
Omn. Here come they.

† *Lopes.*   Campeius, *and* †Ropus.

Empr.   Welcome: rise, and rise vp high
In honours and our fauour: you haue thrust
Your armes into our cofers, haue you not?
Both. Yes sacred Empresse.
Camp.   And into our owne,
Haue rayned downe showers of gold.
Empr.   You shall deserue it:
You see what Ocean can replenish you,
Be you but duteous tributarie streames:
But is your temper right? are not the edges
Of your sharpe spirits rebated? are you ours?
Doe not your hearts sinke downe yet? will you on?
Both. Stood death ith' way.
Rop.   Stood hell.
Empr.   Nobly resolu'de:
But listen to vs, and obserue our counsell:
Backe must we send you to the Fairie Land,
Danger goes with you; here's your safetie: listen.
Chuse winds to sayle by; if the wayward seas
Grow stormie, houer, keepe aloofe: if feares,
Shipwracks, and death lie tumbling on the waues,
And will not off, then on: be venturous,

130 S.D. Campeius, *and* †Ropus.] Campeius, Parydell, *and* †Lupus. Q
133, 140 Both.] *All* 3. Q   140 Rop.] *Lup.* Q

Conquests hard got are sweet and glorious.
Being landed, if suspition cast on you
Her narrow eyes, turne your selues then to Moles,   150
Worke vnder ground, and vndermine your countrey,
Tho you cast earth vp but a handfull high,
To make her stumble: if that bloud-hound hunt you,
(That long-ear'd Inquisition) take the thickets,
Climbe vp to Hay-mowes, liue like birds, and eate
The vndeflowred corne: in hollow trees
Take such prouision as the Ant can make:
Flie with the Batt vnder the eeues of night,
And shift your neasts: or like to Ancresses,
Close up your selues in artificiall wals: 160
Or if you walke abroad, be wrapt in clouds,
Haue change of haires, of eie-brows, halt with soldiers,
Be shauen and be old women, take all shapes
To escape taking: But if the ayre be cleere,
Flie to the Court, and vnderneath the wings
Of the Eagle, Faulcon, or some great bird houer,
Oakes and large Beech-trees many beasts doe couer.
He that first sings a Dirge tun'de to the death
Of that my onely foe the Fairie Queene,
Shalbe my loue, and (clad in purple) ride   170
Vpon that scarlet-coloured beast that beares
Seuen Kingdomes on seuen heads.
Camp.   If all the Spels
That wit, or eloquence, or arts can set:
If all the sleights that bookemen vse in schooles
Be powrefull in such happinesse, 'tis mine.
Rop. What physicke can, I dare, onely to grow
(But as I merit shall) vp in your eye.
Empr. Weele erect ladders for you strong and high,
That you shall climbe to starrie dignitie.
Both. We take our leaue dread Empresse.   *Exeunt.*
Empr.   Fare you well: 180
Our benediction goe along with you —
Our malediction and your soules confusion

539

Like shiuer'd towers fall on your luckelesse heads,
And wedge you into earth low as the deepe
Where are the damned, if our world you fire,
Since desperately you'le ride and dare aspire.
1. *King.* But is this all? shall we thus bend our sinews
Onely to emptie quiuers, and to shoot
Whole sheafes of forked arrowes at the Sunne,
Yet neuer hit him?
2. *Card.*   And the marke so faire!   190
1. *Card.* Nay, which is more, suppose that al these torrents
Which from your sea of Greatnesse, you (for your part)
And all those stragling flouds which we haue driuen
With full and stiffe winds to the Fairie Stronds,
Should all breake in at once, and in a deluge
Of Innouation, rough rebellion, factions,
Of massacres, and pale destruction
Swallow the kingdome vp, and that the bloud
Euen of *Titania*'s heart should in deepe crimson
Dye all these waters: what of this? what share   200
Is yours? what land shall you recouer?
1. *King.* All.
1. *Card.* All!
1. *King.* I, all:
Betweene the Transuersaries that doe run
Vpon this crosse staffe, a dull eye may find
In what degree we are, and of what height
Your selfe (our brightest *Ariadne*) is,
Being vnderneath that Tropicke: as those jewels
Of night and day are by alternate course   210
Worne in Heauens fore-head, so when Deaths Winter comes,
And shortens all, those beames of Maiestie,
Which in this oblique and Zodiacall Sphere
Moue with *Titania* now, shall loose their heat,
Where must the next Sun rise but here? from whence
Shall Fairie land get warmth? meerely from hence.
Let but the taper of her life burne out,

    191 1. *Card.*] Q *here and for the rest of the scene gives the prefix* Como.

We haue such torches ready in her land
To catch fire from each other, that the flames
Shall make the frighted people thinke earth burnes, 220
And being dazled with our Copes of Starres,
We shall their temples hallow with such ease,
As 'twere in solemne gay procession.
1. *Card.*   Some lyne sea cards, that know not the seas tast,
Nor scarce the colour: by your charmes I gather
You haue seene Fairie land — but in a Map:
Can tell how't stands: but if you giue't a fall,
You must get bigger bones: for let me whisper
This to your eare; though you bait hookes with gold,
Ten thousand may be nibbling, when none bites, 230
And those you take for Angels, you'le find Sprites.
Say that *Titania* were now drawing short breath,
(As that's the Cone and Button that together
Claspes all our hopes) out of her ashes may
A second †Phœnix rise, of larger wing,   † *King Iames.*
Of stronger talent, of more dreadfull beake,
Who swooping through the ayre, may with his beating
So well commaund the winds, that all those trees
Where sit birds of our hatching (now fled thither)
Will tremble, and (through feare strucke dead) to earth, 240
Throw those that sit and sing there, or in flockes
Driue them from thence, yea and perhaps his talent
May be so bonie and so large of gripe,
That it may shake all *Babilon*.
Empr.   All *Babylon*!
1. *Card.*   Your pardon: but who'le swear
This may not be?
Empr.   How the preuention?
1. *Card.*   Thus; to fell downe their Queen is but one stroake;
Our axe must cleaue the kingdome, that's the Oake.
Empr.   The manner.
1. *Card.*   Easie: whilest our thunderbolts
Are anuiling abroad, call *Satyran* home, 250
He in his fadome metes vast *Argozies*,

541

Huge Galeasses, and such wodden Castles,
As by enchantment on the waters moue:
To his, marry yours and ours; and of them all
Create a braue *Armado*, such a Fleete,
That may breake *Neptunes* backe to carry it:
Such for varietie, number, puissance,
As may fetch all the Fairie Land in turfes,
To make a greene for you to walke vpon
In *Babilon*.
1. *King.*   Inuincible! goe on.   260
1. *Card.*   Now when the volley of those murdring shot
That are to play first on *Titaniaes* breast,
And (yet) leane on their rests, goe off and kill her,
So that the very *Aluerado* giuen,
Sounds the least hope of conquest; then, then shew
Your warlike Pageants dancing on the waues,
Yours is the Land, the Nation are your slaues.
Omn.   Counsell from Heauen!
Empr.   None this shall ouer-whelme:
Braue voyage! Rig out ships, and fetch a Realme.
                                        Exeunt.

[ACT III, Scene ii]

Parydell *and* Palmio.

Palm.   You ariue on a blest shore. The freight you bring
Is good: it will be bought vp of vs all
With our deere blouds: be constant, doe not warpe
In this your zeale to *Babilon*.
Pari.   Graue *Palmio,*
To you I haue vnladen euen my soule,
The wings from home that brought me had sick feathers,
Some you haue puld off: my owne countrey grasse
Was to my feet sharpe needels (stucke vpright)
I tread on downe-beds now.

253 on] of Q

Palm. But are your countreymen
(I meane those that in thought with vs feast richly)
Fed with the course bread of affliction still?
Pari. Still father *Palmio* still, and to relieue them
I dare doe what I told you.
Palm. Noble valour!
Pari. So that I might but read on yonder scrolls,
A warrant writ vnder the seale of Heauen,
To justifie the Act.
Palm. You haue my hand,
And shall haue more. Y'are reconcil'de (Sonne?)
Pari. Yes.
Palm. Who did confesse you?
Pari. Father *Anniball.*
Palm. But did the *Nuntio Campeggio*
Present your letters, and your vowed seruice
At *Babylon.*
Pari. He did: I sued out warrant
For passage safely thither: and from graue *Como*
(One of the capitall Columnes of the state)
This I receiued.
Palm. He sends you here good welcome:
'Tis strong; why went you not?
Pari. I like it not:
There wants a conuoy of some better words,
Which hourely I expect: vpon a Sea
So dangerous, so full of rockes, so narrow,
(Albeit the venture holy and of honour)
I would not gladly sayle, without direction
Of noble Pilots, home I would not come
Basely, but like a glorious voyager.

Enter Ragazzoni.

Palm. Yea, you do well; the *Nuntio Raggazoni*!
Not know him?
Pari. Certes no.

Palm.   Come, you shall meete:
Monsignor, here's a Gentleman desires
To haue your armes about him. —
Rag.   Willingly.
Palm. He vndertakes an action full of merit,
Sans promise or reward, to cure all those
Through Fairie land, that are diseas'd within,
And he will doo't, by letting one veine bloud.   40
Rag. Shootes he at highest?
Palm.   Yes.
Rag.   Draw home, and giue
Your arrowes compasse, that vntill they fall
Full on the head, none see them: you do well:
My hands are yours: good speede. —   *Exit* Ragazoni.

[*Enter*] Campeggio.

Palm.   *Campeggio?*
Now shall you heare some newes.
Campeg.   I doe assure you,
The Mistris of vs all, hath on this paper
Breath'd you a blessing: your deuotion
Is recommended highly, and to nourish
The flames new kindled in you, here's more fewell.
Pari. Licence to go and come, *in verbo imperatricis per omnes* 50
Iurisdictiones Babilonicas absque impedimento.
Good: would it had come sooner.
Campeg.   Why?
Palm.   'Tis generall,
Exceeding absolute and peremptorie.
Pari. It giues me my ful saile: but by deepe vows,
I am to trauell lower, yet if season
Beat me not backe, I will to *Babylon*,
What rubs soe're I meete in letters still,
Ile kisse her sacred hand.
Campeg.   You change not byas.
Pari. Oh good sir, yonder is the goale I run for!

Raggazoni *at one dore, a Gentleman at another.*
Rag. Lend me your speeches both.
Palm.   Yonder comes one   60
Of your owne countrey.
Pari.   Oh I know him Sir.
Palm. Walk in this colledge classe but som few minutes,
Ile send or bring to you a Gentleman,
Next neighbour to your countrey: an *Albanois* —
The man I told you of.
      Exeunt [Palmio, Ragazzoni, Campeggio].
Pari. Thankes Sir.
Gent.   Met happily, I look'd for you.
Pari. Deere countryman the parly we late held
About the land that bred vs, as how order
Was rob'd of ceremonie (the rich robe of order)
How Truth was freckled, spotted, nay made leaprous: 70
How Iustice —
Gent.   Come, no more.
Pari.   Euen now (as then)
You ward blowes off from her, that at all weapons
Strikes at your head: but I repent we drew not
That dialogue out to length, it was so sweet.
Gent. At houres more opportune we shal: but countryman
I heard of late the musicke of my soule,
And you the instrument are made that sounds it:
Tis giuen me, that your selfe hath seal'd to heauen
A bond of your deuotion, to goe forth
As champion of vs all, in that good quarrell,   80
That hath cost many liues.
Pari.   What need we vse
Circumgyrations, and such wheelings? Sir,
Beleeue it, to recouer our sicke Nurse
Ide kill the noblest foster-child she keepes.
Gent. I know what bird you meane, and whom you hate,
But let him stand to fall: no sir, the Deere

Which we all hope you'le strike, is euen the pride
And glory of the Forrest: So, or not?
Pari. My vowes are flowne vp, and it must be done,
So this may be but settled.
Gent. Do you stagger?
Pari. All winds are not yet layd.
Gent. Haue you looked out
For skilfull coasters, that know all the sounds,
The flats, and quicke sands, and can safely land you
Out of all touch of danger?
Pari. I haue met many,
And like a consort they hold seuerall tunes —
Gent. But make they musicke?
Pari. Faith a little jarring:
Sometimes a string or so: yet reuerend *Palmio*,
And *Anniball a Codreto* keepe the streame
In which I swim: the *Nuntio Ragazzoni*
Plies me with wholesome phisicke; so the *Nuntio*,
My honored Friend *Campeggio* makes it cleere,
That it is lawfull.
Gent. Where at stick you then?
Pari. At a small rocke, (a dispensation.)

Raggazzoni, Palmio, Campeggio, *and the* Albonoys.

Gent. You cannot want for hands to helpe you forward:
In such a noble worke your friends are neere;
Deere Countriman, my sword, my state, and honor,
Are for your vse, goe on; and let no heate
Thaw your strong resolution, I shall see you,
Before you take to Sea.
Pari. You shall.
Gent. My dewtie. [*Exit.*]
Palm. This is the worthy Gentleman, to whome
I wish your loue endeer'de: we haue some conference.
[*Palmio's party stand aloof.*]
Pari. Borne Sir in Fairy Land?

Alba. No marry Sir —
An *Albanois*.
Pari. Then for proximitie
Of Countries, let vs enterchange acquaintance,
I wish'd for your embracements, for your name
Is crown'd with titles of integritie,
Iudgement and Learning: let me vpon their *Bases*
Erect a piller, by which *Babylon*,
And all we may be strengthned.
Alba. I pray be apert and plaine.
Pari. Then thus Sir; by the way of Argument
I would a question put, to tast your censure,
Because I doe not soundly relish it.
Alba. Propone it Sir, Ile solue it as I can.
Pari. Suppose that in the field there were an Army,
Commixt of halfe your kinsfolke, friends, and louers,
The other halfe sworne foes, (all countrimen;)
And that the leader of them were your father,
And that this leading father were so partiall,
That to preserue that halfe which loues you not,
Ye would loose that which loues you: and that to take
This Captaines life away, might bring this good,
Of two sides to make one, and saue much bloud:
Would not you doe it.
Alba. Vmh: ya're ful of Ambage:
I answere as my spirits leade me, thus,
I would not doe it.
Pari. Why Sir.
Alba. Because I hold,
Quod non omninò Licet.
Pari. Come, Come, I know (without al commenting)
This text you vnderstand: wey the vtilitie,
That goes with it: the health it giues to thousands;
The sap it spreads through branches which now wither:
The restauration —
Alba. Sir I see to'th bottome,
Of this deepe well you diue in: I doe arme you,

In this strong fight, iust with the selfe same weapons
Which I would weare to guard mee, and those are
My readings and beliefe setled by reading,
And this I find —
Quod non sunt facienda mala, vt veniant bona.
For good; (how great soeuer) must be don,
No ill how small soeuer.
Pari.   Tis no euill,   150
To barre out so great ill, with so great good.
Alba. All good must not be done, but onely that —
Quod benè et legitimè fieri potest: For Sir I know, that *Deus magis amat aduerbia quam nomina. Quia in actionibus magis ei Placent Benè et legitimè quàm bonum. Ita vt nullum bonum Liceat facere, nisi bene et legitime fieri potest. Quod in hoc Casu fieri non potest.*
Pari. Yet (with your fauour) seuerall learned men,
Are cleane from your opinion, and doe hold,
Quòd licet.
Alba. Those learned men perhaps may hold it fit,   160
That to saue many, they to one mans danger,
(Referring all to the depth inscrutable)
May allow of a particular; on no warrant
That they can shew me written, but being stird,
With a humaine compassion to mens liues:
And lesse you reuelation haue diuine,
That bids you do, doe not; Thus you haue mine.
Omn. What so hard at it.
Pari.   We haue done: the time,
Doe's pull me from your sweet societie.
Palm. You will to *Babylon.*
Pari.   I cannot tell;   170
Whether I doe or no, you shall haue notice,
How this great worke goes forward; strengthen mee,
With all your comforts, and commend my seruice
To the most glorious throne: if I get or'e,
There lands blacke vengeance on the Fairy shore.
Omn. If prayers can doe it shall.
                                                  Exeunt.

[ACT III, Scene iii]

Plaine dealing *and* Truth.

Plain. But how shall I know, thou art the right truth?
Truth. Because I am not painted.
Plain. Nay if thou hast no better coulour then that, ther's no trueth in thee, for Im'e sure your fairest wenches are free of the painters.
Truth. Besides I am not gorgious in attire,
But simple, plaine and homely; in mine eyes,
Doues sit, not Sparrowes: on my modest cheekes,
No witching smiles doe dwell: vpon my tongue
No vnchast language lies: my Skins not spotted
With foule disease, as is that common harlot,
That baseborne trueth, that liues in *Babylon.*
Plain. Why? is shee spotted?
Tru. All ouer, with strange vglines, all ouer.
Plain. Then she has got the pox, and lying at my host *Gryncums,* since I left her company: how soeuer it be thou and I will liue honest togither in one house, because my court mistris will haue it so: I haue beene a Trauailer a great while, *Plaine dealing* hath lept from country to country, till he had scarce a paire of soales to carrie him.
Truth. Why? in what Countries haue you beene?
Plain. In more then I had mind to stay in; I haue beene amongst the Turkes too, the Turkes made as much of poore *Plaine dealing,* as those whom we call Christians.
Truth. What man is that great Turke? I neuer saw him.
Plain. Nor euer shalt: why the great Turke is a very little fellow; I haue seene a scuruy little bad paltry Christian, has beene taken for the greatest Turke there.
Truth. Where had you bin, when now you met with me.
Plain. Looking vp and downe for thy selfe: and yet I lie too, now I remember, I was in the citie: our mistresse would needes haue me goe thither, to see fashions: I could make an excellent Taylor for

Ladies and gentlemen, and fooles, for I haue seene more fashions there, then a picture drawer makes skuruy faces, the first two yeares of his trade: its the maddest circle to coniure in, that euer raiz'd spirit.

Truth. Tell me good kinsman, what in the citie saw you?

Plain. What did I see? why Ile tell the cozen; I sawe no more conscience in most of your rich men, then in Tauerne faggots: nor no more sobernes in poore men, then in Tauerne spiggots: I see that citizens fine wiues vndo their husbands (by their pride) within a yeare after they are married; and within halfe a yeare after they be widdowes, knights vndo them: they'le giue a hundred pound to be dubd ladies, and to ride in a coach, when they haue scarce another hundred pound left to keep the horses. But cozen *Truth*, I met in one street a number of men in gowns, with papers in their hands, what are all those?

Truth. Oh! they are the sonnes of Iustice; they are those
That beat the kingdom leuell, keep it smooth
And without rubs: they are the poore mans captaine,
The rich mans souldier, and cal'd Lawiers.

Plain. Lawiers? doest know any of them?

Truth. A few.

Plain. I wondred what they were, I asked one of them if they were going to foot-ball, yes said he, doe you not see those countrey fellowes, we are against them; and who do you thinke shall winne, said I, oh said he, the gownes, the gownes.

Enter Time.

Time. Follow me *Truth*; *Plaine dealing* follow me.   *Exit.*

Plain. He charges like a Constable; come, wee are his watch: follow me? Is our *Time* mad?
O braue mad *Time*.

Exeunt.

38 the] *i.e.* thee

[ACT IV, Scene i]

Dumb shew. A caue suddenly breakes open, and out of it comes Falshood, *(attir'd as* Truth *is) her face spotted, shee stickes vp her banner on the top of the Caue; then with her foot in seuerall places strikes the earth, and vp riseth* Campeius; *a Frier with a boxe: a gentleman with a drawn sword, another with rich gloues in a boxe, another with a bridle.* Time, Truth *with her banner, and* Plain-dealing *enter and stand aloofe beholding all.*

Time. See there's the Caue, where that *Hyena* lurkes,
That counterfets thy voyce, and calles forth men
To their destruction.
Plain. How full of the small poxe shee is, what ayles shee to stamp thus? is the whore mad? how now? Yea do you rise before Doomes day; father *Time*, what conduit-pipes are these, that breake out of the earth thus?
Time. The conduit-heads of treason, which conuey
Conspiracies, scandals, and ciuill discord,
Massacres, poysonings, wrackes of faith and fealtie   10
Through Fairies hearts, to turne them into elues:
See *Truth*, see sonne, the snake slips off his skinne,
A scholler makes a ruffian.
Plain. Now must that ruffian cuffe the scholler, if I were as he.
Time. And see, that shape which earst shew'd reuerend,
And wore, the outward badge of sanctitie,
Is cloath'd in garments of hypocrisie.
Plain. See, see, father, he ha's a iacke in a boxe: whats that?
Time. A wild beast, a mad bull, a bull that roares,
To fright allegiance from true subiects bosoms;   20
That Bull must bellow, at the *Flamins* gate:
His gate, that tends the flockes of all those sheep,
That graze in the fatst pasture of the land,
Beeing all inclos'd: that bull will on his backe
Beare all.
Plain. Whither? whither?

Time. To hell: tis said to heauen
That will but sit him, till with hoofe or horne,
He goare the annointed Fairie.
Plain. Such Bulls haue I seene sent out of *Babylon*, to runne at
people: I should once haue rid vpon one of them, but he that
beg'd my office, broke his necke by the bargaine, and sau'd me a
labour: whats he with the sword, a master of the noble Science?
Truth. A noble villaine: see, he pulls down heauen
With imprecations, if that blade he sheath not,
In our sweet mistresse breast.
Plain. O rogue! what good cloathes hee weares, and yet is a villaine?
Time. I, doe: clap hands vpon't, that poysoned gloue,
Shall strike thee dead to death, with the strong sent
Of thy discouered treason.
Plain. Whats that horse-courser with the bridle?
Time. A slaue, that since he dares not touch her head,
Would worke vpon her hand: — laugh and conspire;
The higher villaines climbe, they fall the higher.
Plain. Stay father, now the Armie comes forward: shee takes downe the flagge, belike their play is done; what will shee beare the collours? thou hast collour enough in thy face already, thou needst no more: did ye euer see a more lowsie band? there's but two rapiers in the whole regiment: now they muster, now they double their files: marke how their hands juggle, and lay about; this is the maine battell: O well florisht Ancient! the day is their's; see, now they sound retrait: whither march they now?

Exeunt [dumb shew].

Time. To death; their falles, thus *Time* and *Truth* proclaime,
They shall like leaues drop from the Tree of shame.
Lets follow them.
Plain. To the gallowes? not I; what doe we know, but this freckled face queane, may be a witch.
Time. Shee is so; shee's that damned sorceresse,
That keepes the inchanted towers of *Babylon*.
This is the *Truth*, that did bewitch thee once.
Plain. Is this speckled toade shee? Shee was then in mine eye, the

goodliest woman that euer wore fore part of Sattin: To see what these female creatures are, when they deale with two or three Nations; how quickly they weare carbuncles and rich stones? now shee is more vgly then a bawd.

Truth. Shee look'd so then; fairenes it selfe doth cloth her
In mens eyes, till they see me, and then they loath her.

Time. Loose no more minutes, come, lets follow them.

Plain. With hue and crie, now I know her: this villanous drab is 70 bawd, now I remember, to the Whore of *Babylon*; and weele neuer leaue her, till shee be carted: her face is full of those red pimples with drinking *Aquauite,* the common drinke of all bawdes: come.

Exeunt.

[ACT IV, SCENE ii]

Titania, Elfiron, Florimel, *a gentleman standing aloofe, and* Ropus.

Tita. What comes this paper for?
Fid. Your hand.
Tita. The cause?
Fid. The Moone that from your beames did borrow light,
Hath from her siluer bow shot pitchy clowds
T'ecclipse your brightnes: heauen tooke your part,
And her surpriz'd; A jurie of bright starres,
Haue her vnworthy found to shine agen:
Your Fairies therefore on their knees intreat,
Shee may be puld out from the firmament,
Where shee was plac'd to glitter.
Tita. Must we then,
Strike those whom we haue lou'd? albeit the children, 10
Whom we haue nourisht at our princely breast,
Set daggers to it, we could be content
To chide, not beat them, (might we vse our will,)
Our hand was made to saue, but not to kill.
Flor. You must not (cause hee's noble) spare his blood.

65 weare] were Q

Tita. We should not, for hee's noble that is good.
Fid. The fall of one, like multitudes on yce,
Makes all the rest, (of footing) be more nyce:
But if by ventring on that glassie floore
Too farre, he sinks, and yet rise with no more harme,
Ten thousand to like danger it doth arme:
All mercy in a Prince, makes vile the state,
All justice makes euen cowards desperate.
Tita. In neither of these seas, spread we our sayles,
But are the impartiall beame between both scales;
Yet if we needs must bow, we would incline
To that where mercy lies, that scale's diuine:
But so to saue were our owne breast to wound,
Nay (which is more) our peoples: for their good,
We must the Surgeon play, and let out blood.
Euery Peeres birth stickes a new starre in heauen,
But falling by *Luciferan* insolence,
With him a Constellation drops from thence.
Giue me his Axe — how soon the blow is giuen?   *Writes.*
Witnesse: so little we in blood delight,
That doing this worke, we wish we could not write.
Let's walke my Lords. *Florimel?*
Flor.   Madame.
Tita.   Stay:
Not one arm'd man amongst vs? you might now
Be all old-beaten souldiers: truth I thanke ye;
If I were now a jewel worth the stealing,
Two theeues might bind you all.
Omn.   With much adoe.
Tita. I marry I commend yon gentleman.
Pray Sir come neere, looke you, hee's well prouided
For all rough wethers: Sir, you may be proud,
That you can giue armes better than these Lords,
I thanke you yet, that if a storme should fall,
We could make you our shelter. A good sword?
This would goe through stich; had I heart to kill

44 may] way Q

IV. ii]   THE WHORE OF BABYLON

    I'de wish no better weapon; but our dayes
    Of quarreling are past; Shall we put vp Sir,   50
    We ha put vp wrongs ere now, but this is right,
    Nay we are not falling yet.   [*Exit Gentleman.*]
Flor.   It did vs good
    To see how your Maiestick presence dawnted
    The silly gentleman.
Tita.   The sillie gentleman!
Fid.   He knew not how to stand, nor what to speak.
Tita.   The silly gentleman? know you him Lords?
    Where is hee?
Flor.   Gotten hence poore wretch with shame.
Tita.   That wretch hath sworne to kill me with that sword.
Omn.   How?
Fid.   The traytor.
Flor.   Locke the Court gates.
Omn.   Guard her person.
                                  Exeunt omnes.
Tita.   You guard it well. Alacke! when louers wooe,   60
    An extreame ioy and feare, them so apall,
    That ouer much loue, shewes no loue at all.
    Zeale sometimes ouer-does her part — It's right —
    When the frais done, Cowards crie whers the Fight.
                                  Pentioners.
            [*Enter*] Florimell.

Flor.   The wolfes in his own snare: O damned slaue!
    I had like to ha made his heart my ponyards graue.
    How got you to this knowledge? — blessed heauen!
Tita.   It came vnto me strangely: from a window,
    Mine eyes tooke marke of him; that he would shoot   70
    Twa's told me, and I tried if he durst doo't.
    Is *Ropus* here, our Doctor?
Rop.   Gratious Lady.
Tita.   You haue a lucky hand since you were ours,
    It quickens our tast well; fill vs of that

        64 Fight] Flight Q   73 *Tita.*] om. Q

You last did minister: a draught, no more,
And giue it fire, euen Doctor how thou wilt.
Rop. I made a new extraction, you shall neuer
Rellish the like.
Tita.   Why, shall that be my last?
Rop. Oh my deere Mistres!
Tita.   Go, go, I dare sware
Thou lou'st my very heart.   *Exit* Ropus.

Enter Parthenophill.

Parth.   This scaly Serpent
Is throwne (as he deserues) vpon the Sword   80
Of Iustice; and to make these tydings twinnes,
I bring this happy newes, *Campeius*,
(A Snake that in my bosome once I warm'd:)
The man for whome —
Tita.   Oh, wee remember him.
Parth. This Owle, that did not loue your sacred light,
Stole or'e the Seas by darknes, and was held
In *Babilon* a bird of noble flight:
They tourn'd him to a Goshawke, fether'd him,
Arm'd him with tallents, and then gaue him bels,
And hither charg'd him fly, he did: and soar'd   90
O're all your goodlyest woods, and thickest groues,
Inticing birdes that had the skill in song,
To learne harsh notes: and those that fail'd in voice,
He taught to pecke the tender blossomes off,
To spoyle the leauy trees, and with sharpe bils
To mangle all the Golden eares of corne.
But now hee's tan'e.
Tita.   Good sheapheards ought not care,
How many foxes fall into the Snare.

Enter Elfyron.

Elf. Your ciuill Doctor, Doctor *Paridell*
Casts Anchor on your shores againe, being freighted   100

556

IV. ii] THE WHORE OF BABYLON

With a good venture, which he saies, your selfe
Must onely haue the sight of.
Tita.   Bring him hither: *Exit* [Elfyron].
Lord *Florimell*, pray call *Fideli* to vs.

     Florimell, Fideli, Ropus.

Tita. Sure 'tis too hot.
Fid.   Oh roague!
Tita.   Set it to coole.
Fid. Hell and damnation, Diuels,
Flor.   What's that?
Fid. The damned'st treason! Dog: you whorsen dog;
O blessed mayd: let not the toad come neere her:
What's this? If't be his brewing, touch it not —
For 'tis a drench to kill the strongest Deuill,
That's Druncke all day with brimstone: come sucke, Weezell, 110
Sucke your owne teat, you — pray, thou art preseru'd.
Tita. From what? From whome?
Fid.   Looke to that Glister-pipe:
One crowne doe's serue thy tourne, but heere's a theefe,
That must haue fifty thousand crownes to steale
Thy life: Here 'tis in blacke and white — thy life,
Sirra thou Vrinall, *Tynoco, Gama,*
Andrada, and *Ibarra,* names of Diuels,
Or names to fetch vp Diuels: thou knowest these Scar-crowes.
Rop. Oh mee! O mercy, mercy! I confesse.
Fid. Well sayd, thou shalt be hang'd then.
Tita.   Haue we for this 120
Heap'd fauours on thee.   *Shee reads the letter.*
Fid. Heape halters on him: call the Guard: out polecat:
            Enter Gard.
He smels, thy conscience stincks, Doctor goe purge
Thy soule, for 'tis diseas'd. Away with *Ropus.*
Omn. Away with him: foh.
Rop.   Here my tale but out.
Fid. Ther's too much out already.
Rop. Oh me accursed! and most miserable. *Exit with Guard.*

Tita. Goodnes of vertue! is my bloud so sweet,
That they would pay so deere for't?
Fid. To sucke Lambes,
What would not Wolues doe, he that this paper writte,
Had neuer meaning we should finger it.
Tita. Our mercy makes them cruell, hunt out these Leopards:
Their own spots will betray them: they build caues
Euen in our parkes: to them, him, and the rest,
Let death be sent, but sent in such a shape,
As may not be too frightfull. Alacke! what glorie
Is it to buffet wretches bound in giues?
The debt is derely paid that's payd with liues.
Oh! leaue vs all.
Enter Elfiron *and* Paridell.

Fid. More Doctors! if this doe
Aswell as tother, best to hang him too. *Exeunt [court]*.

Tytania, Paridell.
Tita. Florimell! Stay, [Florimel *aloofe*.]
But giue vs liberty.
Pari. This is the blessed day for which (through want
Of those bright rayes that sparkle from your eyes)
My frozen soule hath languish'd. Goddesse compleate,
If you, a wretch so meane, will bid to speake,
I shall vnclaspe a booke whose very first line,
(Being not well pointed) is my doome to death:
But if your sacred iudgement (on the Margine,)
Controwle all wresting comments, All your subiects
Will fold me in their bosomes.
Tita. Giue your minde.
Pari. A Pilgrim haue I been on forren shores,
(Your gracious hand allow'd it) in my wandring,
With Monsters I encountred of straunge shape,
Some that suckt poyson vp, and spet it foorth,
Vpon your land: some, that shot forked stinges,
At your most God-like person: all were Gyants,

132 mercy] a mercy Q

    Fighting against the heauen of your blest raigne:
    With these (oh pardon me!) with these I held
    A polliticke league, the lines of all their treasons,
    (Drawne from one damned circle) met in mee,   160
    My heart became the Center, and the point
    Was this — I dare not tell it.
Tita.   Speake?
Pari.   To kill you.
Tita.   How durst you (being our subiect) wade so far?
Pari.   Your eare of mercy. I became a spunge
    To drincke vp all their mischiefe, and lay drown'd
    In their infected waters, (with much loathing,)
    Onely that I before you might wring out
    This their corruption, and my selfe make cleere.
    And now (immortall maid) i'me not vnlike
    A casket wherein papers stuft with danger,
    Haue close beene lockt, but those tane out, the chest   170
    Serues to good vse, so may my loyall brest:
    For from their flintie hearts what sparkes I got,
    Were but to fire themselues.
Tita.   I praise your plotte,
    You make vs now your debter, but a day
    Will come, when we shal pay. My Lord, we want your Arme.
Pari.   Vmh! I feare —
Tita.   Doctor, weele haue (Sir) other Dialogues.
                              Exeunt [Titania *and* Florimell].
Pari.   O shallow foole, thou hast thy selfe vndone,
    Shees hardned and thou melted at one sunne.
                                                Exit.

[ACT IV, SCENE iii]

Enter Como [1. *Cardinall*], *and the three Kings.*

1. *Card.*   Our eyes haue lusted for you, and your presence
    Comes as the light to day, showers to the spring,
    Or health to sicke men.

    1 1. Card.] Q *here and throughout the scene gives the prefix* Como.

3. *King.*   Thankes most reuerend Father.
1. *King.*   Our bloud ranne all to water, yea our soules
Stroue all (at once) t'expire, (when it was blowne
Hither from Faiery land, that all the darts
Which ours heere, and your arme deliuered there,
Fell either short, or lighted vpon yce)
Lest you had lost bloud in the enterprize.
3. *King.*   No, I weare stronger Armour: gamester-like   10
I sawe the dogges brought forth; and set them on,
Till the Diuell parted them; but pluckt off none,
I kept aloofe out of the reach of pawes:
Better to fight with Lions then with lawes.
What drummes are these?
2. *King.*   Musicke of heauen.
1. *Card.*   The dancers
Reuell in steele.
1. *King.*   These march to fill our Fleete.
3. *King.*   From whence weele march with prowd victorious feete,
And walke on Fayeries hearts, their beaten waies
With their owne heades weele paue, whilst ours with bayes,
And oake (the conquering souldiers wreath) we crowne: 20
These hookes, or none, must pull their Cities downe,
Inuasion is the fire: See, See, i'th Ayre
Angels hang beckoning vs to make more haste,
Vengeance deferd growes weake, and runnes to waste.
Whats this? —

       Enter a Herrald before one: sounds once, and staies.

1. *Card.*   Ere we take ship, we must to Court.
Omn.   Away.
3. *King.*   In thunder: tis the souldiers sport.   *Exeunt.*

                The Herrald reades.

Herald.   It is the Imperiall pleasure, decree, peremptory edict, and
    dreadfull command (vpon paine of a curse to be denounced vpon
    him that is disobedient) from her who hath power giuen her to

            3 Father] Fathers Q

make the backes of stubborne Kings her foote-stooles, and Emperours her vassalles: the mother of Nations; the triple-crowned head of the world; the purple-rider of the glorious beast; the most high, most supreame, and most adored Empresse of *Babilon*; that no Captaine Generals of Armies, Generals of Squadrons, Admirals, Colonels, Captaines, or any other Officers of her magnificent, incomparable, formidable, and inuincible *Armada*, which is ordayned to swallow vp the kingdome of *Faiery*, shall presume to set one foote on ship-bord, till her sacred hand hath blessed the enterprize by sealing them all on the forhead, and by bowing their knees before the Beast. Sound, goe on.

Exeunt.

[ACT IV, Scene iv]

Dumb shew: Empresse *on the Beast.* [*Then enter* 1. *Cardinall and the three Kings.*]

Empr. Feeles the base earth our weight? ist common Aire
We suck in and respire? doe seruile clowdes,
(Whose azure winges spread ouer graues and tombes)
Our glorious body circumvolue? dare night
Cast her black-nets into dayes cristall streames,
To draw vp darknesse on our golden beames:
And vs t'ecclipse, why is not *Babilon*
In a contorted chaire made all of starres,
Wound vp by wheeles as high, nay boue the thrones
Supernall, which with *Ioues* owne seate stand euen,
That we might ride heere as the Queene of heauen.
And with a spurne from our controwling foote,
That should like thunder shake th'etheriall floore,
Of life and heauen them both at once bereaue,
That thither vp dare clime without our leaue.
1. *Card.* You doe: you ride there now, this is your Sphere,
Earth is all one with heauen when you are heere.
3. *King.* Yet ther's a hell on earth or if not hell,

Diuels there are or worse then Diuels, that roare
Onely at you.
Empr.   At vs? what dare they roare?
3. King.   Your pardon, and ile tell it.
Empr.   Tell: We feare
No spots, the orbe we shine in is so cleere.
3. King.   Thus then: the Faiery Adders hisse: they call you
The superstitious Harlot: purple whore:
The whore that rides on the rose-coloured beast:
The great whore, that on many waters sitteth,
Which they call many Nations: whilst their Kings,
Are slaues to sate your lust, and that their bloud,
(When with them you haue done) serues as a floud,
For you to drinke or swimme in.
Omn.   O prophane!
Empr.   Goe on: the searching small wounds is no paine.
3. King.   These cowards thus when your back's turnd (that strike)
Follow their blowe and sweare, that where you claime,
Supremacie monarchall ouer Kings,
Tis but your tiranous pride, and not your due.
Empr.   But what your selues giue, what haue we from you?
You say we are your mother, and if so,
Must not sonnes kneele? they pay but what they owe.
3. King.   They say the robes of purple which you weare,
Your scarlet veiles, and mantles are not giuen you
As types of honour and regality,
But dyed so deepe with bloud vpon them spilt,
And that (all or'e) y'are with red murder gilt:
The drinke euen in that golden cup, they sweare
Is wine sophisticated, that does runne
Low on the lees of error, which in taste,
Is sweete and like the neate and holsome iuyce
Of the true grape, but tis ranke poyson downe.
Omn.   Haue we not all it tasted?
Empr.   Nay, vtter all.
Out of their lips you see flowes naught but gall.

20 what_∧] ~ , Q

3. *King.* What can my breath doe more, to blast your cheekes,
And leaue them glowing as red gads of steele?
My tongue's already blistred sounding this,
Yet must I whisper to your sacred eare:
That on your brow (they say) is writ a name
In letters misticall, which they interpret
Confusion, by great *Babylon* they meane
The Citie of *Confusion.*
Empr. View our forhead?
Where are we printed with such Characters?
Point out these markes: Which of you all can lay
A finger on that Moale that markes our face?
3. *King.* They say you can throw mists before our eyes,
To make vs thinke you faire.
Omn. Damnd blasphemies.
1. *Card.* You shall with rods of iron scourge these treasons.
1. *King.* The Mace is in your hand, grinde them to dust.
2. *King.* And let your blowes be sound.
3. *King.* For they are iust.
Empr. Lets heare with what lowde throats our thunder speakes,
Repeate our vengeance o're, which to beare Kings
Must now flie o're the seas with linnen winges.
1. *Card.* Our Galeons, Galeasses, Zabraes, Gallies,
Ships, Pynaces, Patches, huge Caruiles,
For number, rib and belly are so great,
That should they want a Sea neere Faiery land
Of depth to beare them vp, they in their wombs
Might swim with a sea thither: here are breifes
Of your imperiall Armies.
Empr. Reade them lowde:
Thunder ner'e speakes, but the voice crackes a clowde.
1. *Card.* In the first Squadron twelue great Galeons:
Floate like twelue moouing Castles: Zabraes two,
Habilimented gloriously for warre,
With Souldiers, Seamen, shot, and ordinance:
This Squadron stout *Medyna* does command:

68 beare] beate Q

Who of the maine is Captaine Generall.
The second Squadron braue *Ricalde* leades,
Being Admirall to fouretene Galleons.
Flores de Valdes guides the third, the fourth
Followes the silken streamers of the haughty
Pedro de Valdes that tryed warriour.
Oquendo in the fift front cries a Charge.
Bretandona bringes vp the Leuantines   90
With his sixt Squadron: *Gomes de Medyna*
Waftes vp the seauenth like the God of warre,
The eighth obayes *Mendoza*: and the ninth
Fierce *Vgo de Montada*: all these Squadrons,
For vessell, numbred are one hundred thirtie,
The sight of Souldiers, Marriners, and Slaues
Twentie nine thousand, eight hundred thirtie three.
Peeces of brasse for battery these,
Six hundred thirtie: adde to these Gallions
Twentie Caruiles, and Saluees ten: which make   100
The whole *Armada*, eightscore lustie saile.
Add to all these your Generals of Armies,
Your Captaines, Ensigne bearers, (which in role,
Are eightscore and eleauen) the Voluntaries,
With officers and seruants, then the Regiments
That are in pay: to these, all men of orders,
All ministers of iustice: and to these
Supplies of forces that must second vs,
And last that host of starres which from the Moone
Will fall to guide vs on: these totald vp,   110
You shal a hundred thowsand swordes behold
Brandish't at once, whose —   standes
Men will seeme borne with weapons in their handes.
Empr.   Goe: cut the salt fome with your mooned keeles,
And let our Galeons feele euen child-birth panges,
Till their great bellies be deliuered
On the soft Faiery shoares: captiue their Queene,
That we may thus take off her crowne, whilst she

*112 whose—   standes] *stet* Q

Kneeles to these glorious wonders, or be trampled
To death for her contempt: burne, batter, kill,   120
Blow vp, pull downe, ruine all, let not white haires,
Nor red cheekes blunt your wrath, snatch babes from brests,
And when they crie for milke, let them sucke bloud,
Turne all their fieldes to lakes of gellyed goare,
That Sea-men one day sayling by the land
May say, there Faiery kingdome once did stand.
Omn.   They shall.
3. *King.*   Tis done already.
Empr.   To be sure
You all are ours, bow and adore the beast,
On whome we ride.
Omn.   We fall beneath his feete.
Empr.   Be blest, obedience is in sonnes most sweete,   130
O strange, to you he stoopes as you before him,
Humility, he bowes whilst you adore him:
To kindle lustie fires in all your bloud,
A health to all, and as our cup goes rownd,
Draw neere, weele marke you for our chosen flocke,
Who buildes on heartes confirmd, builds on a rocke:
The seale of heauen! who on their foreheads weare it,
We choose for counsaile: on their hands who beare it,
We marke for Action: Heere, a health to all.
Omn.   Braue health! to pledge it, see Kings prostrate fall.   *Kneele.* 140
Empr.   On —
Omn.   On —
3. *King.*   Sing warre thy lowd and loftiest notes.
We winne; our ships meete none but fisher-boates.
                                              Exeunt.

[ACT V, Scene i]

Enter Paridell *and his kinsman.*

Pari.   What if I shewe you a foundation,
Firme as earthes fixed Center? a strong warrant,

141 *Omn.*] *All.* Q

565

To strike the head off, an Iniunction
That bids me doo't: A dispensation
For what I doe: A pardon sign'd, that giues
Indulgence plenarie, and full remission
(For any criminall breach of the highest Law)
After 'tis done: nay more, a voice as cleere
As that of Angels, which proclaimes the act,
Good, honourable, meritorious,
Lawfull, and pyous, what if I shew you this?
Coz. Come, come, you cannot, then let riotous heires
Beg pattents to kill fathers: graunt but this,
Murder may be a faire *Monopoly*,
And Princes stab'd by Acts of parliament:
Who i'st dare that thing meritorious call,
Which feindes themselues count diabolicall?
Pari. Your coldnes makes me wonder: why should you
Ronne vp to'th necke, from drowning to saue her,
That treades vpon your head, your throat; to sincke you?
Coz. Say you should wound me; should I (in reuenge)
Murder my selfe? for what can be the close
But death, dishonour; yea, damnation
To an act so base, nay so impossible.
Pari. Impossible; the parting of the ayre,
Is not more easy: looke vpon the Court,
Through narrowe sights, and shees the fairest marke,
And soonest hit of any: like the Turke
Shee walkes not with a *Ianisarie-Guard*,
Nor (as the Russian) with fowle-big-boand slaues,
Strutting on each side with the slicing Axe,
Like to a payre of hangmen: no, alas:
Her Courts of *Guard* are Ladies, and (sometimes)
Shee's in the garden with as small a trayne,
As is the Sun in heauen: and our Accesse,
May then as easy be as that of Clyents,
To Lawyers out of terme-time.

12 *Coz.*] *Cox.* Q
13 this,] ~ ₐ Q

Coz. Grant all this:
Nay, say the blow were giuen: how would you scape?
Pari. Oh sir, by water. —
Coz. I but —
Pari. Nay, good cozen. —
Coz. You leape as short at safety, as at starres: 40
By water: why the gates will all be lockt,
Wayters you must haue none.
Pari. Heare me.
Coz. Heare me,
You must not haue a man, and if you kill
With powder, ayre betrayes you.
Pari. Powder! no sir,
My dagge shall be my dagger: Good sweete Cozen
Marke but how smooth my pathes are: looke you sir —
Coz. I haue thought vpon a course.
Pari. Nay, nay, heare mine,
You are my marke, suppose you are my marke,
My leuell is thus lowe, but er'e I rise,
My hand's got vp thus hie: the deere being strucke, 50
The heard that stand about so frighted are,
I shall haue leaue to scape, as does a pirate,
Who hauing made a shot through one more strong,
All in that ship runne to make good the breach,
Whilst th'other sailes away. How like you this?
Coz. As I like paper harnesse.
Pari. Ha, well, pawse then:
This bow shall stand vnbent, and not an arrow
Be shot at her vntill we take our ayme
In Saint *Iagoes* parke; a rare, rare Altar!
The fitt'st to sacrifize her bloud vpon: 60
It shall be there: in Saint *Iagoes* parke:
Ha coz! it shall be there: in the meane time,
We may keepe followers (nine or ten a peece)
Without suspition: numbers may worke wonders;
The storme being sudden too: for were the guard

47, 56, 72 *Coz.*] Cox. Q

A hundred strong about her, looke you sir,
All of vs well appoynted — Case of dags
To each man, see you? you shoote there, we heere,
Vnlesse some spirits put the bullets by,
Ther's no escape for her: say the dags faile, 70
Then to our swordes. — Come, ther's no mettle in you.
Coz. No mettle in me? would your warres were honest,
I quickly would finde Armour: what's the goade
So sharpe, that makes you wildely thus to runne
Vpon your certaine ruine?
Pari.   Goad? sharp ponyards,
Why should I spare her bloud?
Coz.   She gaue you yours.
Pari. To ha tan'e it had bin tyrany, her owne lips
Confest I strucke her lawes not hard: I ha spent
My youth, and meanes in seruing her: what reape I?
Wounds (discontents) what giues she me? good words 80
(Sweet meates that rotte the eater:) why, last day
I did but begge of her the maistership
Of *Santa Cataryna,* twas denied me.
Coz. She keepes you to a better.
Pari.   I tush, thats not all:
My bonds are yonder seald; And she must fall.
Coz. Well coz, ile hence.
Pari.   When shall I see you?
Coz.   Hah.
Soone: very soone: sooner than you expect:
Let me but breath, and what I meane to doe,
I shall resolue you.
Pari.   Fare you well.
Coz.   Adue. —
                                          Exeunt.

89 S.D. *Exeunt.*] *Exit.* Q

[ACT V, Scene ii]

Tytania, Elfyron, Parthenophil, Parydel, Florimell.

Flor. Newes; thundring newes sweete Lady: Enuy, Ambition,
Theft sacrilegious, and base treason, lay
Their heads and handes togither, at one pull
To heaue you from your throne: that mannish woman-Diuell,
That lustfull bloudie Queene of *Babylon*,
Hath (as we gather ripe intelligence)
Rigd an Armd fleete, which euen now beates the waues,
Boasting to make their wombes our Cities graues.
Tita. Let it come on: our Generall leades aboue them,
Earth-quakes may kingdomes mooue, but not remooue them. 10

[*Enter*] Fideli.

Fid. He yonder, he that playes the fiend at sea,
The little Captaine that's made all of fire,
Sweares (Flemming-like) by twenty thousand Diuels,
If our tongues walke thus, and our feete stand still,
So many huge ships neere our coasts are come,
An Oyster-boate of ours will scarce finde roome.
He sweares the windes haue got the sailes with childe,
With such big bellies, all the linnen's gone
To finde them linnen, and in *Babylon*,
That ther's not one ragge left.
Tita.   Why swels this fleete? 20
Fid. Thus they giue out, that you sent forth a *Drake*,
Which from their riuers beate their water-fowle,
Tore siluer feathers from their fairest Swannes,
And pluckt the Halcions winges that roue at sea,
And made their wilde-duckes vnder-water diue,
So long, that some neuer came vp aliue.
This Sea-pie *Babylon*, her bug-Beare calles,
For when her bastards cry, let the nurse cry

But this, *the Drake comes*, they hush presently.
For him thei'le cudgell vs: will you ha the troth?
That scarlet-whore is thirstie and no bloud,
But yours, and ours (sweete maide) can doe her good.
Tita.   That drake shal out againe: to counsel Lords.
Fid.   Come, come, short counsell: better get long swordes.
Flor.   Good Lady dread not you, what ere befall —
Fid.   Weel'e die first, yours is the last funeral:
Away, away, away.
Omn.   Posts, posts, cal messengers, posts with al speed.

Exeunt [lords].

Tita.   How? feare?
Why should white bosomes feare a Tyrants Arme?
Tyrants may kill vs, but not doe vs harme.
Are we your prisoners that you garde vs thus?   *Exeunt [guard].*
Stay, And you too, we are alone: when last   *Manet* Paridell.
We entertaynd your speech (as we remember)
Close traines and dangerous you did discouer
To fire which you were praid.
Pari.   I was.
Tita.   And yeelded.
Albeit it were against our life.
Pari.   Most true: —
My reasons —
Tita.   We forget them not: at that time
Here was but one, (true) but one counceller,
Who stood aloofe, heard nothing; and though a bloud
Of courser veines then ours, would haue beene stird
Into a sea tempestuous to boyle vp,
And drowne the Pilate that durst saile so farre,
Yet of our princely grace (tho twas not fitte,
Nor stood with wisdome) did we silence it.
These heaped fauours, notwithstanding (Doctor)
Tis in our eare the hammers lie not still,
But that new clubs of iron are forging now,
To bruise our bones, and that your selfe doe knowe,
The very Anuile where they worke.

Pari.   I —
Tita.   Heare vs,
Because tis thought some of those worser spirits,
And most malignant that at midnight rise
To blast our Faiery circles by the Moone,
Are your Familiars.
Pari.   Madam —
Tita.   Sir anone.
Thee therefore I coniure (if not by faith,
Oathed allegeance, nor thy conscience,
Perhaps this ranckling vlcerateth them)
Yet by thy hopes of blisse, tell, and tell true,
Who i'st must let vs bloud?
Pary.   O vnhappie man;   [*Aside.*]
That thou shouldst breathe thus long: mirrour of women,
I open now my brest euen to the heart,
My very soule pants on my lips: none, none,
I know of none.
Tita.   Well; none: rise and take heede,
They are no common droppes when Princes bleede.
What houre is this? does not my larum strike?
This watch goes false.
Pari.   This watch goes true.   [*Aside.*]
Tita.   All's naught. —
What houre is this?
Pari.   Thy last houre, O heauens, furder
The worke you haue begun: where art thou heart?   [*Aside.*]
Tita.   Oh we see't: Doctor wind vp the wheele, tis downe.
Pari.   Tis downe.
      [*Offers to stab her from behind. She turns, and he kneels.*]
Tita.   How now? what strucke thee downe? thy lookes are wilde:
Why was thine armed hand reard to his height?
What blacke worke art thou doing?
Pari.   Of damnation vpon my selfe.
Tita.   How?
Pari.   Your wordes haue split my heart in thowsand shiuers,
Heere, heere that stickes which I feare will not out.

Better to die than liue suspected. Had not your bright eyes
Turnd backe vpon me, I had long ere this
Layen at your feete a bloudie sacrifice.
Tita. Staind Altars please not vs: why doest thou weepe?
Thou mak'st my good thoughts of thee now declyne,
Who loues not his owne bloud, will ne're spare mine,
Why doest thou weepe?
Pari. When on your face I looke,
Me thinkes I see those Vertues drawne aliue
Which did in *Elfilyne* the seauenth suruiue,
(Your fathers father, and your grandfather,)
And then that you should take me for a serpent
Gnawing the branches of that glorious tree,
The griefe melts euen my soule, O pardon me.
Tita. Contract thy spirits togither, be compos'd;
Take a full man into thee, for beholde
All these blacke clowdes we cleere: looke vp, tis day,
The sunne shines on thee still: weel'e reade: away. —
Pari. O machlesse; im'e all poyson, and yet she
Turnes all to goodnes by wise tempering me.   *Goes off.*
Tita. If thou prou'st copper — well; this makes vs strong
As towers of flint. All traytors are but waues,
That beate at rockes, their owne blowes digge their graues.
                                             Paridell *manet.*
Pari. For not dooing am I damde: how are my spirits
Halde, tortured, and growne wilde? on leaues eternall
Vowes haue I writ so deepe, so bound them vp,
So texted them in characters capitall,
I cannot race them but I blot my name
Out of the booke of sence: mine oath stands filde
On your court-roles. Then keepe it, vp to heauen
Thy ladder's but thus hie: courage, to kill
Ten men I should not freeze thus: yet her murder
Cannot be named bloud-shed, for her Faieries
Are all of faith, and fealty assoyled,
The balme that her annoynted is washt off,
Her crowne is now not hers; vpon the paine

Of a blacke curse, no more must I obey her,
I climbe to heauen by this, climbe then and slay her.
Tita. A tyrants strange, but iust end! — *Reades.*
Ran mad for sleepe, and died. Princes that plunge
Their soules in ranke and godlesse appetites
Must seeke no rest but in the armes of Sprites.
Pari. Nothing to read? that (if my nerues should shrink
And make mine arme reuolt) I might haue colour   130
To vsurp this walke of hers: whats this? see, see
An Angel thrusts this iron into my hand,
My warrant signd from *Babylon* to kill her,
Endorsed, the last will of *Paridell.* — *Reade.*
*Le concede sua Benedictione, plenaria indulgenza,   * The very
Eo remissione di tutti li peccati — tutti li peccati —   wordes of
All, all my sinnes are paid off, paying this,   Cardinal
Tis done, tis done, All you blest powers I charme,   Como his
Now, now, knit all your sinewes to this arme.   letter sent
                                                         to Parry.

As he offers to step to her, he staies sodainly, vpon the approch of
   Fidely, Florimel, Parthenophil, Elfiron, *the Ladies, a Guard, and*
   the Doctors Cozen.

Omn. You ha proou'd your selfe a loyall gentleman.   140
Fid. The hand of Angels guide vs: Shees not heere,
The Queen's kild; treason: Wenches, raise the Court.
Omn. Walke seuerall waies first.
Fid.   Waies; shees murdered: treason.
Tita. Treason; a sword. What traytor dare? who? where?
Flor. A guard: the damned serpent, see, lurkes heere.
Fid. Sure heeres some nest they breed in: paw him fast,
This Woolfe, this Toade (marke, he swelles red with poyson,)
This learned knaue is sworne to murder thee.
Pari. I defie any man that speakes it.
Fid.   Hah: —
Defie this noble, honest gentleman,   150
Defie him, he shal spit it on thy face,
Thy beard scald Doctor.

Pari.   And doest thou betray me?
Saist thou so?
Coz.   And will seale my speech with bloud.
Pari. My no against his yea; My no is as good.
Fid. Better, his yeas goe naked, and your noes
Very well clokd: off, come, truth naked goes,
And heres his naked truth.   — *Shewes his drawn dagger.*
Tita.   Againe.
Pari.   Oh me; —
Now nothing but your mercy me can saue.
Tita. It must not: Princes that would safely liue,
May grieue at traytors falles but not forgiue.   160
Let him be sommond to the barre of shame.
Pari. Tis welcome, a blacke life, ends in blacke fame.   *Exit.*
Omn. Away with him.
Parth.   Now to the busines,
We haue on foote.
Fid.   I, I, looke to the head.
The hangman cures those members.
Tita.   What is done?
Flor. This (sacred Lady:) we with either hand
Haue raisde an Armie both by sea and land.
Your goodly ships beare the most royall freight,
That the world owes (true hearts:) their wombes are ful,
Of noble spirits, each man in his face   170
Shewes a Kings daunting looke, the souldiers stand
So thickly on the decke, so brauely plum'd,
(The Silken streamers wauing or'e their heades)
That (seeing them) you would iudge twere *Pentecost,*
And that the iollie youngsters of your townes,
Had flockt togither in gay multitudes,
For May-games, and for summer merriments,
They looke so cheerely: In such little roome
So many Faieries neuer dwelt at once,
Neuer so many men were borne so soone,   180

       153 *Coz.*] *Cox.* Q
       164 on] one Q

v. ii]   THE WHORE OF BABYLON

   The drum that gaue the call, could not be heard
   For iustling armours: er'e the call was done,
   It was so ringd about with groues of pikes,
   That when they brake on both sides to giue way,
   The beating of the drum was thunders noise,
   Whilst coates of steele clasht so on coates of steele,
   Helmets on helmets that they strucke out fire,
   Which shewd like lightning, or those flames that flie
   From the huge Cyclops-hammer, when they sweate
   To forge *Ioues* thunder: And in such a heate   190
   With quicknes rush they armed forth, captaines swore,
   Harnesse was sure the cloathes they daily wore.
   Men faster came to fight then to a feast.
Fid. Nay, women sued to vs they might be prest.
Parth. Old grandams that on crutches beare vp age,
   Full nimbly buckled Armours on their sonnes,
   And when twas on, she clapt him on his backe,
   And spake thus, runne my boye, fight till th'art dead,
   Thy bloud can neuer be more brauely shed.
Tita. How are the numbers you haue leuied?   200
Fid. What your sea-forces are, this briefe doth speak.
Elf. We haue rais'd double walls to fence your land.
   The one the bodie of a standing Camp,
   Whose tents by this are pitcht in *Beria*,
   On the shores point, to barre the foe from footing.
Tita. Ouer that Camp at *Beria** we create   * *Tilbury.*
   You *Florimell* Lieuetenant Generall.
Elf. The other is to guarde your royall person.
Tita. Whose charge is yours: the sea *Fideli*, yours.
Elf. The standing camp of horsemen and of foote,   210
   These numbers fill.
   Launcers two hundred fifty three. Horsemen seven hundred sixty
      nine. Footemen twenty two thousand.
   The mouing Army, which attends on you,

        198 boye] Q(c); boyes Q(u)
        207 You] Your Q
        212 Launcers] Launces Q

575

Is thus made vp:
Of horsmen and of foote, Launcers four hundred eighty one.
  Light horse-men one thousand four hundred twenty one.
  Footemen thirty four thousand fifty.
Tita. We do not raise our hopes on points of speares.
A handfull is an host, in a good fight,   220
Lambes may beate Lions in a warre not right.
The Generall of all armies be our leader,
Be full of courage Lordes as ya're in yeares.
For this be sure weele not out-liue our peeres.
Fid. Weele al liue, but wil first haue them bi'th eares.
Tita. Goe on, your conduct be the prosperous hand,
Make you the sea good, weele not loose the land.
Your Queene will to the field, It shall be said,
Once souldiers to their Captaine had a Maide.

Exeunt.

[ACT V, SCENE iii]

*Truth and Plaine-dealing leading souldiers with
drum and colours, Time meeting them.*

Time. You sweate well in this haruest.
Plain. Nay, when we come to binde vp the whore of *Babilons*
  Punckes and Pynaces in sheaues, weele sweate worse.
Time. Haue you bestowed the other bandes?
Truth.   I haue.
Time. Incorporate this to you then: tis the mandate
Of your Liefetenant Generall. You fight
In your great Faieries quarrell, and Truthes right,
Stand therefore too't.
Volunteer. I will haue no woundes on my shoulders, I scorn to
  run, or to cry out of warlike kybes in the heele.   10
Time. Goe (thou most God-like maide) and buckle on
The brest-plates fetcht from thine owne Armoury,
Let euery souldier weare one, on each leader
Bestowe a guiding-staffe, and a strong shield

That may as faithfull be to his good sword
As thou art to his heart: head all the speares
With gold of Angell-proofe. Sit like a doue
Vpon the Horsmans helme, and on his face
Fan with thy siluer winges sweete victorie,
Goe, beate thy drum, that men may know thy march, 20
Spread thine owne colours (*Truth*) so let them shine,
Souldiers may sware thei'le follow none but thine.
Away.
Truth. I flie, swift as the winged winges. *Exit.*
Plain. To day is workiday with me for all I haue my best clothes on, what doe you set me to?
Time. Goe thou and sweepe th'abuses from the camp.
Plain. Conscience has left no broomes big enough to doe that cleane.
Time. Then purge the tents of all infectious aires.
Plain. Yonder's one infection new broke out, if it be not stopt 30 from running, will choake vs all.
Time. Name it, ile minister the remedie.
Plain. *Time* may do it, this tis: A Broker and his wife that dropt out of the Hangmans budget but last day, are now eating into the Camp, and are victualers to it: their very Cannes haue hoopes of gold lace now, that hangd Captaines Ierkins all or'e but yesterday: fifteen Liefetenants haue eaten vp their buffe Ierkins with cheese and mustard: Nay this villaine of fourescore ith hundred has set vp three Armourers shops with harnesse caps, and pewter coates, that are linde cleane out with Ale: the Rogue lies euery night vpon as 40 many fethers which grew in souldiers hats, as will vndooe foure hundred Schoolemasters to hire them for their boyes to goe a feasting.
Time. Breede such disorders mongst the souldiers?
Plain. They swarme like lyce: nay his wife tickels it too, for three Muskateeres came but to drinke Tabacco in her cabbin, and she fired their flaskes and tuch-boxes.
Time. Goe ridde the Camp of these, and al like these.
Plain. If any souldier swere ile casheere him too.

36 hangd] bangd Q

Time.   You will scarce leaue two in the Army then.   50
Plain.   What shall I doe with those Pyoners yonder?
Time.   You know the ground, lead them to cast vp trenches.
Away.
Plain.   They are by this time leading one another, for when I left them, I left them all casting, ile now goe see what it comes to.
Exit.

Time.   Ile flie hence to the fleete of *Babylon.*
And from their tacklings and their maine-mast tops,
Time shal shoote vengeance through his bow of steele,
Wedge-like to split their Nauie to the keele.
Ile cut their Princes downe as blades of grasse,   60
As this glasse, so the Babilonian power,
The higher shall runne out to fill the lower.
Exit.

[ACT V, Scene iv]

The Sea fight.

3. *King.*   The sulphurous *Ætna* belcheth on our ships,
Cut Cables, or the whole fleete drownes in fire.
1. *King.*   Holla.
2. *King.*   Of *Babilon.*
1. *King.*   What Hulkes ar these,
That are on fire?
3. *King.*   The Diuels: the sea's on fire,
The Diuel sure takes Tabacco.
1. *King.*   Wher's *Medyna?*
2. *King.*   Close vnder hatches, dares not shew his head.
3. *King.*   Damnation on such liuerd Generals.
Wher's braue *Ricalde?*
2. *King.*   Who?
3. *King.*   Our Admiral:
The Admirall of our Nauy, wise *Ricalde.*
2. *King.*   Our stowte and braue *Ricalde* keepes his bed.   10
3. *King.*   All poxes fire him out; *Pedro de Valdes*

v. iv, v. vi] THE WHORE OF BABYLON

 Hauing about him fifty Canons throates,
 Stretcht wide to barke is boarded, taken.
2. *King.*   Taken?
3. *King.* Without resistance: *Pyementelly* sunke,
 Oquendo burnt, *Moncada* drown'd or slaine.
1. *King.* The ship of all our medicaments is lost.
3. *King.* Dogges eate our medicaments, such are our woundes
 We more shall Sextons neede than Surgeons.
2. *King.* What course is best?
3. *King.*   The best to get the day,
 Is to hoise sayles vp, and away.   20
Omn. Away, away, hoise sailes vp and away.
3. *King.* A world of men and wealth lost in one day.
              Exeunt.

[ACT V, Scene v]

Florimell *followed by Captaines, Marriners and*
Gunners with Linstockes.

Flor. Shoot, shoot, they answer; braue: more Linstocks: shoot:
 This stratagem dropt downe from heauen in fire.
Omn. Board, board, hoyse more sailes vp, they flie, shoot, Shoot.
              Exeunt.

[ACT V, Scene vi]

Titania *in the Camp.*

Tita. We neuer held a royal Court till now:
(Warriours) would it not seeme most glorious,
To haue Embassadors to greete vs thus?
Our chaire of state, a drum: for sumptuous robes
Ruffling about vs, heads cas'd vp in globes
Of bright reflecting steele: for reuellers
(Treading soft measures) marching souldiers.

    13 stretcht] stretch Q

Trust me, I like the martiall life so well,
I could change Courts to campes, in fieldes to dwell.
Tis a braue life: Me thinkes it best becomes   10
A Prince to march thus, betweene guns and drummes.
My fellow souldiers I dare sware youl'e fight,
To the last man, your Captaine being in sight.   *They shoote.*
Volunteer. To the last least mans little finger.   *A peale goes off.*
Fid. What flames through all our bloud your breath inspires.
Tita. For that we come not: no brest heere wants fires.
Twas kindled in their cradles, strength, courage, zeale,
Meete in each bosome like a three-fold floud,
We come with yours to venture our owne bloud.
For you and we are fellowes; thus appeares it,   20
The souldier keeps the crowne on, the prince weares it.
Of all men you we hold the most most deere,
But for a souldier I had not beene heere.
Fid. Doe not their gunnes offend you?
Tita.   How? we are tried,
Wh'im'e borne a souldier by the fathers side.
The Cannon (thunders Zany) playes to vs,
Soft musikes tunes, and more mellodious:
And we more rarely like, because all these,
That now can speake the language of sterne warre,
Could not speake swords, or guns, nay scarce could go,   30
Nay were not borne, but like to new sowne graine
Lay hid i'th mold, when we went to be crown'd,
Tho now th'are tall corne fields, couering the ground.

[Enter] Plaine Dealing.

Plain. Roome, roome, newes, newes, the youngest newes that euer was brought forth amongst men at Armes: a woman (sweete mistris) is brought to bed of a man childe i'th Camp: a boy that lookes as if he would shoote off already: the bed they haue swadled him in, is the peece of an old torne Ancient: his blankets are two souldiers Mandilions: his cradle is the hollow backe-peece of a rustie Armour: his head lies in a Murren thats quilted to keepe him 40

15 our] your Q   28 we] me Q

warme, the first thing that euer he laid hold on, was a truncheon, on
which a Captaine leand to looke vpon him, hee'le bee a warriour I
warrant. A Can of beere is set to his mouth already, yet I doubt
hee'le prooue but a victualer to the Camp: A notable fat double-
chind bulchin.
Tita. A child borne in our Camp! goe giue him fame,
Let him be *Beria* cald, by the Campes name.
Plain. Thats his name then: *Beria*; in steede of a Midwife, a
Captaine shall beare him to the Fount, and if there be any women
to followe it, they shal either traile pikes, or shoote in Caliuers; 50
who would sweate thus to get gossips for an other mans child? but
fathers themselues are guld so sometimes, farewel mistris. *Exit.*

Time, Florimell, *Captaines, Souldiers.*

Tita. With roses vs you crowne, your selfe with palme.
Flor. Had we al woundes, your words are soueraigne balme.
Tita. Are those clowds sperst that stroue to dimme our light?
Flor. And driuen into the gloomie caues of night.
Tita. Our handes be heau'd vp for it.
Time.   Theres good cause,
We'are bownd to doe so by the higher lawes.
Those roaring Whales came with deuouring wombes
To swallow vp your kingdomes: foolish heires;   60
When halfe of them scarce knew where it did stand,
Vnder what *Zenith*, did they share your land.
At dice they plaid for *Faieries*; at each cast
A Knight at least was lost: what doe you set?
This Knight cries one (and names him) no, a Lord
Or none, tis done, he throwes and sweepes the bord,
His hatte is full of Lords vp to the brimme,
The sea threw next at all, wonne all and him,
Would you these Gamesters see now?
Fid.   See now? where?
Thei'le scarce see vs, the last fight cost so deere.   70
Time. Bid you me do it, tis done, *Time* takes such pride,
To waite on you, heele lackie by your side.
Those daies of their Arriuall, battaile, flight,

And ignominious shipwrackes (like lost Arrowes)
Are out of reach: of them the world receaues
But what *Times* booke shewes turning back the leaues,
But if you'le see this *Concubine* of Kinges,
In her maiesticke madnes with her sonnes,
That houre is now but numbring out in sand,
These minutes are not yet run through *Times* hand. 80
For you and for your Faieries sweete delight
Time shall doe this.
Tita. Twil be a glorious sight.
Time. Vnseene you shall both see and heare these wonders,
On the greene Mount of *Trueth*: let the Armie moue,
And meete you in the vale of *Oberon*,
Your captiues are sent thither: quicke as thought
You shall flie hence vpon my actiue winges,
Time at one instant sees all Courts of Kings.

Exeunt [Time, *soldiers &c., manent* Titania *and her Court*]

Time *descending: Enter the* Empresse, *three
Kings, and foure Cardinals.*

Empr. Hence: sting me not: y'are Scorpions to my brest,
Diseases to my bloud: he dies that speakes. 90
3. *King.* Y'are madde.
Ambo. Y'are madde.
4. *Card.* O falles not heauen!
Empr. Be silent:
Be damned for your speech, as y'are for Act:
You are all blacke and close conspirators
In our disgrace.
3. *King.* You lie.
4. *Card.* O horrible!
3. *King.* You Raue yet know not why.
Empr. Thou saist all's lost.
3. *King.* Drownd, burnt, split vpon rockes, cast ouer bord,
Throates cut by Kernes, whose haires like elfe-lockes hang.

91 *Ambo.*] *i.e. the other two Kings* Q

2. *King.*   One of those shamrock-eaters at one breakefast,
Slit fourescore wezand-pipes of ours.
1. *King.*   Of yours,
Oquendo burnt, *Piementelli* Slaine,
Pedro de Valdes tane.
1. *Card.*   Could dwarfes beate Gyants?
3. *King.*   In one day fell fiue hundred. Galleons fifteen
Drownd at the same time, or which was worser taken;
The same day made a thousand prisoners.
Yet not a cherry stone of theirs was sunke.
Not a man slaine nor tane, nor drownd.
Empr.   O damnd!
3. *King.*   Two with two spit-frog Rapiers tooke a Galleon.
1. *Card.*   O pittie her.
3. *King.*   Let her taste al.
Empr.   Fall thunder,
And wedge me into earth, stiffe as I am:
So I may be but deafe, turne me into
A speckled Adder: O you Mountaines fall,
And couer me, that of me, memory
May neuer more be found.
4. *Card.*   O holy mother!
Empr.   Earth, Ile sucke all thy venome to my brest,
It cannot hurt me so as doe my sonnes,
My disobedient, desperate, dampned sonnes,
My heauy curse shall strike you.
1. *Card.*   Oh kneele downe!
Kneele downe and begge a pardon, least her curse —
1. *King.*   I thats the blocke, wee must kneele, or doe worse.
1. *Card.*   Lift vp your sacred head: your children come,
Vpon their knees to take a mothers doome.
Empr.   O *Syrian Panthers*! you spend breath most sweete,
But you are spotted or'e, from head to feete,
This neck ile yoke, — this throate a staires ile make,
By which ile climbe — like stubble thou shalt burne,
In my hot vengeance.

108, 117, 120 1. *Card.*] *Como.* Q

2. *King.*   Vengeance I defie.
I shall fall from thee, since thou makst my brest
Thy scorne, true Kings such basenes will detest.
Electors will I call, and they shall make thee,
But seruant of mine Empire: they shall thrust   130
A ring into thy nostrils.
Empr.   Come let me kisse thy cheeke: I did but iest.
Tita.   Marke: those that most adore her, most are slau'd,
She neuer does grow base, but when shees brau'd.
3. *King.*   You seeme still angry.
Empr.   No, yes: leade the way,
Neuer was day to me thus *Tragicall,*
Great *Babylon* thus lowe did neuer fall.
Tita.   Thankes *Time* for this; lanch forth to *Oberons* vayle.
We are neere shore: your hands to strike our saile.
                                                  Exeunt.

FINIS.

TEXTUAL NOTES

II.ii

1 S.D. *The third King to his man.*] The Q direction reads *The third King to the King of Portugall.* Since this scene appears to be part of a revision (see Textual Introduction), it may be that the original is represented only by this fossil direction. On the other hand, it is perhaps more likely to take it that some statement to the Prince of Portugal, like that to the States, has by mistake been dropped from the close of the preceding scene and thus confused with the opening direction for II.ii. The first lines of II.ii are obviously addressed to the 3. King's man, who next enters at line 148 *like a sayler*, a description which is meaningless unless this servant had already appeared on the stage in his proper shape. The *rich attires* under the man's arm in the direction at line 148 must refer to the order given him in lines 4–5; and at line 155 he helps the 3. King to change to these, as at the opening of the scene he has assisted him in assuming the garments now being discarded at line 151.

6 saylers shape] Q 'flie your sayles shape' is meaningless as it stands. One possibility would be to take *shape* as a verb, and to read 'Flie: your sails shape'; *i.e.* hasten, shape your course away by adjusting your sails, and return immediately. The case is complicated by the fact that to spread one's sails is a favourite Dekker phrase; but 'fly your sails' seems to be of a different order. If we may associate this phrase with the return of the man at line 148 *like a sayler*, it seems reasonable to suppose that the King is here ordering his servant to clothe himself as a sailor, and hence there would be no doubt about who was entering at line 148. *Shape* would then be a noun, in its familiar theatrical meaning of *disguise* or *costume*. And Q *sayles* would be a misprint for *saylers*, as emended in the present text.

6 S.D. *Exit man.*] As a direction Q has only the single word *Enter*, which might refer to the entrance of Campeius (in this text conjecturally placed later) but is suspicious as a misreading since it occurs opposite the line where the servant's exit should be. It would seem unlikely, on the other hand, that the scene opens with the 3. King shouting orders to his man off-stage and that the servant enters at line 6 to dress the King in the gown ordered in line 1. The order for the next change of costume to satin would prove too confusing, and it is evident that the King is being dressed in his scholar's gown as the scene opens.

91 What passes through it, kills:] The syntax is certainly difficult here. The natural referent of *it* is *eare* in line 90; but I do not fancy the resulting meaning: 'My ear is no gun to reach out and shoot down your words when

they are winging through the air: the gun kills only that which is near, *i.e.* which passes through my ear.' On the other hand, if one takes it that *it* is the *Fowling piece* and so moves the comma after *it* to follow *through*, the above meaning would be somewhat clarified. However, if as in the present text we attempt to make sense out of the quarto line as it stands, we must apparently take *it* as referring back to the *ayre* in line 89, and the sense, though contorted, becomes: 'You may say what you choose without danger from me, for my ear is no gun to reach out and to kill what passes through the air.' This would seem to be the simplest and most direct meaning, and the relation of the line 91 *it* to *ayre* would appear to be supported if, as likely, the *it* in line 89 (*tho it be trobled*) is also the air and not the ear.

III.i

81 two] Q reads *three* and in the direction at line 129 brings on *Campeius, Parydell, and Lupus*. The speech-prefixes for lines 133 and 140 provide for responses by the three characters. But in III.ii it is clear that Paridel's scruples have kept him from going to Babylon. Hence, as evidenced by the name *Lupus* for Lopez instead of *Ropus* as found later, it would appear that III.i represents an earlier form of the play with its anomaly overlooked in the revision. See the Textual Introduction.

IV.iv

112 whose — standes] The long dash after *whose* and the following white space before *standes* may perhaps represent a four-syllable word or phrase which was illegible in the manuscript and was overtrustingly left by the compositor for the proof-reader to supply. On the other hand, it is as possible that Dekker himself left the space when the right word did not immediately occur to him, and forgot to go back to insert the necessary noun.

PRESS-VARIANTS IN Q (1607)

[Copies collated: BM¹ (British Museum C.34.c.29), BM² (C.12.f.4[1]), BM³ (Ashley 613), Bodl¹ (Bodleian Mal. 235[7]), Bodl² (Mal. 162[1]), Dyce (Victoria and Albert), Eton (Eton College), Worc¹ (Worcester College Oxford; wants L1), Worc² (wants A1-3, L1), CSmH (Huntington), CtY (Yale), DFo (Folger), DLC (Congress), ICN (Newberry; wants L1), MH (Harvard), NN (New York Public), TxU (Texas).]

SHEET C (*outer forme*)

Corrected: BM¹,³, Bodl¹⁻², Dyce, Eton, Worc¹⁻², CSmH, CtY, DFo, DLC, ICN, MH, NN, TxU.
Uncorrected: BM².

Sig. C4ᵛ.
II.i.8 The'rs] Thei's
10 there] ther
27 kil] kill
27 deare] dear
28 Foxes] foxes
32 pillars] pillers

SHEET D (*inner forme*)

1st stage corrected: Bodl¹.
Uncorrected: Eton, Worc¹⁻², CSmH, CtY, DLC, ICN, MH, NN, TxU.

Sig. D3ᵛ.
II.i.235 negotiation] negotiᵉtion
  2nd stage corrected: BM¹⁻³, Bodl², Dyce, DFo.
Sig. D1ᵛ.
II.i.102 Titan.] Yitan.

SHEET K (*inner forme*)

1st stage corrected: DLC.
Uncorrected: BM³, MH.

Sig. K3ᵛ.
V.vi.12 sweare] sware

587

Sig. K4.
   V.vi.68 won] wone
       2nd stage corrected: BM$^{1-2}$, Bodl$^{1-2}$, Dyce, Eton, Worc$^{1-2}$, CSmH, CtY,
                        DFo, ICN, NN, TxU.
Sig. K1^v.
   V.ii.198 boye] boyes
Sig. K2.
   V.iii.22 sweare] sware

EMENDATIONS OF ACCIDENTALS

Lectori
4 Queene.] ~ ∧
20 curious] curions

I.i
6 Lybanus] Lyhanus
36 Romane] Romane
65–66 Feare...shadow.] one line in Q
80 groanes.] ~ ∧
114 set,] ~ ∧
213 winds,] ~ .
217 them,] ~ ∧
219 her,] ~ .

S.D. Titania,] ~ ∧
4 Innocence,] ~ ∧
6 Arme,] ~)
7 hie:] ~ ,
8 flie,] ~ :
9 Queene)] ~ , ∧
34 Oberon,] ~ ∧
43 it —] ~ ,
51 late∧] ~)
67 Parthenophill] Partbenophill
68 maides:] ~ ∧
69 shades∧] ~ :
80 present] prcsent
81 S.D. headed,] ~ ∧

3 heart-] ~ .
5 through] throug
8 Cities.] ~ ∧
8 Ther's] The'rs Q(c); Thei's Q(u)
10 ther] Q(u); there Q(c)
27 kill] Q(u); kil Q(c)

Prologue
43 and other] aud other

221 happie:] ~ ∧
233 sheet.] ~ ,
234 wit,] ~ ∧
239 father,] ~ .
240 name,] ~ .
240, 249 Plaine dealing] plaine dealing
242 strond] strnod
246 Truth.)] ~ . ∧
248 since) ~ .

I.ii
92 That] that
117 glories,] ~ .
120 reuerend] renerend
182 any] ɐny
194 once —] ~ ,
221 I'm not] I'mnot
252 S.D. Fairies] Faires
255 Herezies,] ~ ∧
256 leagues,] ~ .
276 Vaults,] ~ .
278 Stratagems,] ~ .
283 open] opcn
285 3. King.] 3. Kidg

II.i
32 pillers] Q(u); pillars Q(c)
106 but] bnt
118 but like] butlike or butl ike
157–158 The law...attempt,] one line in Q
164 strooke∧] ~ ,
168 S.D. Parthenophill] Pathenophill

589

179 earnd] eanrd
188 caries,] ~ :
189 wheeles:] ~ '
191 That] that
202 oft proue˰] ~ .
204 drounde.] ~ ,
211 Some] ome
217 you (since] ~ ; ~

228 S.D. Fideli.] ~ ˰
243 daughters] danghters
250 buried.] ~ ,
262 *Parth.*] *Path.*
263 heauen)] ~ ,
276 S.D. Fideli, Florimell,
   ...Parthenophil,]
   ~ ˰ ~ ˰ ... ~ ˰

II.ii

1 gowne:] ~ ˰
5 (brauely),] (~)˰
7 fit:] ~ ,
12 windows,] ~ .
41 wool,] ~ .
48 Queene] Queenc
54–55 Tel...nee'r tast] *one line in* Q
70 Pallatts] Q *cw*; Pallats Q *text*
90 piece,] ~ ˰

100 highest] hig hest
107 fil my] filmy
116 (euen])euen
145–6 Get...thither:] *prose in* Q
148 crown'd] crow'nd
173 turne there] turnethere
173 gripings,] ~ ˰
185 S.D. *fellow*] *follow*

III.i

16 (as]˰ as
38 out:] ~ ,
39 Act,] ~ :
68 Mutiners,] ~ ˰
72 *Satyran*] *Satryan*
72 apparrels˰] ~ ,
73 wolues] woues
76 hither,] ~ .
78 Bees:] ~ ˰

85 *Bacchus*˰] ~ ,
91 instruments] instrnments
176 can, I dare,] ~ ˰ ~ ~ ˰
211 Worne...comes] Q *lines*
   Worne...-head, | So...
212 all,] ~ ˰
245–6 Your...be?] *one line in* Q
246–7 Thus;...stroake] *one line in* Q

III.ii

22 and] aud
60–61 Yonder...countrey.] *one line in* Q
112–113 No...*Albanois.*] *one line in* Q
136–137 Because...*licet.*] *one line in* Q

147–148 And...*bona.*] *one line in* Q
150 euill,] ~ .
152 All...that —] Q *runs-on with following*
159 Are...*licet.*] *one line in* Q

III.iii

14 strange] sttange
18, 23 *Plaine dealing*] plaine dealing

27–28 taken for] takenfor

IV. i, V. ii]   EMENDATIONS OF ACCIDENTALS

IV.i

S.D. *out*] *ont*
S.D. *bridle*.] ~ ,

62–63 eye, the...] Q *lines* eye, |
   The...Sattin: | To....
67 *Truth*.] *Yruth*.

IV.ii

63 sometimes] sometimes-
78–79 Go...heart.] *one line in* Q
84 whome —] ~ —.
88 him,] ~ ₐ
111 pray, thou] pray, | Thou
116 Vrinall] *Vrinall*

123 stincks,] ~ ₐ
126 much out] muchout
129 for't?] ~ ₐ
134 him,] ~ ;
138 liues.] ~ ₐ
144 languish'd.] ~ ₐ

IV.iii

15–16 The dancers...steele.] *one line in* Q

31 triple-|crowned] triple-crowned

IV.iv

14 at] ot
16 now,] ~ ₐ
19–20 Diuils...you.] *one line in* Q
21–22 Tell...cleere.] *one line in* Q

21 feare ₐ] ~ ,
79 two,] ~ .
90 Leuantines] *Leuantines*
141 On — | On —] On: | On:

V.i

13 this,] ~ ₐ
20 head,...throat;] ~ ; ... ~ ,
30 Russian)] ~ ₐ
39 but —] ~ . —
40 *Coz*.] *Crz*.

40 starres:] starre:s
44–46 Powder!...sir —] Q *lines*
   Powder!...dagger: | Good...
   smooth | My...sir,
46 sir —] ~ ,
87 expect:] ~ ,

V.ii

18 gone ₐ] ~ ,
19 linnen,] ~ ₐ
29 presently.] ~ ,
35 befall —] ~ .
36–37 Weel'e...away.] *one line in* Q
39–40 How? ...Arme?] Q *lines*
   How? ...bosomes | Feare...
   Arme?

47–48 Most...reasons —] *one line in* Q
48 reasons —] ~ . —
57 eare ₐ] ~ :
60–61 Heare...spirits,] *one line in* Q
60 I —] ~ .
64 Madam —] ~ .
76–77 All's...this?] *one line in* Q

591

106 Turnes] Tutnes
126 died.] ~ ₐ
149–150 Hah...gentleman,] *one line in Q*

152–153 And...so?] *one line in Q*
157–158 Oh...saue.] *one line in Q*
211–218 These...fifty.] *rough prose in Q*

V.iii

10 run, or] Q *lines* run, | Or
22 sware] Q(u); sweare Q(c)
25 on] | On

26 th'abuses] tha'buses
31 from] | From
53 Away] *run-on with line 52*

V.iv

3–4 What...fire?] *one line in Q*
4–5 The...Tabacco.] *one line in Q*
6 dares] draes

7–9 Damnation...*Ricalde*.] *prose in Q*
9 our] aur

V.vi

12 sware] Q(u); sweare Q(c)
35 amongst] amonst
36 i'th] it'h
44 double-|chind] double-chind
57 Theres] Therers
68 wonne] wone Q(u); won Q(c)
83 wonders,] ~ .
91 O] ô

92 speech, ...Act:] ~ : ... ~ ,
99 yours,] ~ .
102 Galleons] Galleous
103 time, ...taken;] ~ ; ... ~ ,
104 a thousand] 1000.
108 thunder,] ~ .
118 curse —] ~ . —
138 vayle.] ~ ₐ